# *Conflict and Consensus*
## in
### *Modern American History*

# Conflict and Consensus
*in*
## Modern American History

SIXTH EDITION

Edited by

**Allen F. Davis**
Temple University

**Harold D. Woodman**
Purdue University

D.C. HEATH AND COMPANY
Lexington, Massachusetts    Toronto

Acknowledgment is made to the following sources for permission to reproduce material from their collections:

p. 1: The New York Public Library, Astor, Lenox and Tilden Foundations.

p. 47: Courtesy, American Antiquarian Society.

p. 99: Courtesy, American Antiquarian Society.

p. 143: Courtesy of the Library of Congress.

p. 199: Jacob A. Riis Collection, Museum of the City of New York.

p. 297: Courtesy of The New York Historical Society, New York City.

p. 339: Courtesy of the Library of Congress.

p. 393: Walter Sanders, *Life Magazine* © 1948, Time, Inc.

p. 451: Wide World Photos, Inc.

p. 513: Patricia Hollander Gross / Stock, Boston.

Published simultaneously in Canada.

Printed in the United States of America.

International Standard Book Number: 0-669-06750-4

Library of Congress Catalog Card Number: 83-82275

For Gregory and Paul
and
Allan and David

# Preface

We are pleased that the continued success of *Conflict and Consensus in Modern American History* has warranted the publication of this sixth edition. We have retained the basic organization of the earlier editions, as well as the emphasis on the themes of conflict and consensus. We remain convinced that the presentation of conflicting views of particular periods and problems, shown within the context of general interpretations, allows students to deepen their understanding of the historical details and provides them with the means for interpreting the broad sweep of the country's history.

To make the book more useful in the introductory course, we have added new selections that incorporate recent approaches to the theme of conflict and consensus, and we have increased the emphasis on social history and on the history of women and minorities. While retaining a traditional periodization that is compatible with the popular survey texts, we have attempted to integrate, rather than merely add, the new material. Our goal has been to suggest, for example, how events that have been traditionally viewed from the white male perspective take on new meaning when women and blacks are included in the story.

In the third edition we added an introduction that was designed to help the beginning student to understand why historians disagree. We found that readers were often confused rather than enlightened when presented with conflicting interpretations of the same events. Too often they lacked the skills needed to discern the bases of historical disagreements. Because of the favorable response, we have retained (with revisions) this brief introduction to historical methods and philosophy. As a further aid to students we have expanded the chapter introductions, in which we discuss the selections to follow. We have added to these discussions a number of questions and suggestions designed to help the readers understand the arguments and methods the authors use.

In this edition, as in the previous ones, we have avoided presenting only two extreme positions on each problem raised. Such an either/or approach is artificial, and forces students to choose between extremes or to conclude, without adequate evidence, that the truth must be midway between the two extremes. We have, therefore, included at least three selections dealing with the same problem in order to illustrate the subtleties of interpretation.

Our main concern has not been with historiography, although we do direct interested students to relevant historiographical discussions. Beginning students are not especially interested in tracing shifting interpretations, nor should they be at this stage. They should be stimulated to learn *what* happened and *why* it happened by seeing how different historians, viewing the same event, have attempted to answer these questions. We have therefore concentrated not on the evolution of historical writing but on the historical problems themselves. We hope to leave students with a heightened understanding of how various issues in American history are interpreted and at the same time to provide the ammunition for thoughtful and spirited discussions. The brief, annotated bibliographies provided at the end of each chapter are not designed to be exhaustive, but they will help those who might wish to do further reading on a particular interpretation.

*Allen F. Davis*
*Harold D. Woodman*

# Acknowledgments

We wish to thank the various publishers and authors for permission to reprint copyrighted material. This book had its origin in our introductory course in American history at the University of Missouri; our former teaching assistants and students will recognize many of the ideas, as will those with whom we have worked at Temple University and Purdue University. We are grateful for their aid and recognize that in a real sense they have been collaborators. In the preparation of this edition we have received invaluable aid from our students, Robert B. Beeson and Merril D. Smith of Temple University and Earl J. Hess of Purdue University.

We would also like to thank the many teachers and students who have made useful comments on the earlier editions. Their candid evaluations and suggestions have been invaluable. We are especially grateful to Leonora Woodman of Purdue University; Roger D. Launius of Louisiana State University; Robert C. McMath, Jr. of the Georgia Institute of Technology; William E. Pemberton of the University of Wisconsin-La Crosse; Tomas L. Powers of the University of South Carolina-Sumter; Don Hansdorff of the College of Staten Island, City University of New York; Gerald R. Gill of Tufts University; Bennett H. Wall of the University of Georgia; S. J. Adams of Lake Tahoe Community College; Hyman Berman of the University of Minnesota; C. Yuan of Worcester State College; Steven R. Boyd of the University of Texas at San Antonio; John Lankford of the University of Missouri, Columbia; Robert L. Branyan and Lawrence H. Larsen of the University of Missouri, Kansas City; Thomas C. Barrow of Clark University; Franklin Mitchell of the University of Southern California; Lyle Dorsett of the University of Denver; James F. Watts of the City College of the City University of New York; John Burnham of Ohio State University; J. Stanley Lemons of Rhode Island College; William Cutler, Herbert Ershkowitz, Charles Hardy, Robert Miller, and Howard Ohline of Temple University; Richard S. Kirkendall of Iowa State University; Alonzo Hamby of Ohio University; William O. Wagnon, Jr., of Washburn University of Topeka; Alice Kessler-Harris of Hofstra University; Kenneth Wayne Mixon and Henry R. Warnock of Mercer

University; Ross Webb of Winthrop College; Joe P. Dunn of Converse College; Alton Hornsby of Morehouse College; Juliet Walker of the University of Illinois at Urbana-Champaign; Anita Goodstein of the University of the South; and Sharon Alter of William Rainey Harper College.

# Contents

# 4
# *Workers in an Industrial Age*

# 5
# *Migrants to an Urban America*

# 6
# *The Progressive Movement*

# 7
# *The Twenties*

# 8
## *The New Deal*

# 9
## *The United States as a World Power*

# 10
## *Liberalism and the Turbulent 1960s*

# 11
## *America Today and Tomorrow: The 1970s and 1980s*

# Introduction: History and Historians

Most students are usually introduced to the study of history by way of a fat textbook and become quickly immersed in a vast sea of names, dates, events, and statistics. The students' skills are then tested by examinations that require them to show how much of the data they remember; the more they remember, the higher their grades. From this experience a number of conclusions seem obvious: the study of history is the study of "facts" about the past; the more "facts" you know, the better you are as a student of history. The professional historian, whether teacher or textbook writer, is simply one who brings together a very large number of "facts."

Of course, only the most naive of students fail to see that the data of history, the "facts," are presented in an organized manner. Textbooks describe not only what happened, but also why it happened. For example, students learn that Puritans began coming from England to the Massachusetts Bay Colony in the New World in 1630, but they also learn why the Puritans came when they read about the religious persecutions in seventeenth-century England. Similarly, they read of the steady trek of people westward during the nineteenth century; however, at the same time they learn details that explain this movement of people—the availability of fertile lands in the West, the discovery of gold in California, the improvement of roads and other transportation facilities.

But beginning students, even as they come to recognize that their teacher and their textbook are explaining as well as describing events in the past, still have no reason to alter their notion as to what history is all about. They are still working in the realm of "fact." The "fact" of the movement of people into Ohio is explained by the "fact" that fertile land was available there. They may learn more details about the event—how many people went to Ohio, when they arrived, where they settled—and about the explanation—the cost of land in Ohio, the availability of credit, the exhaustion of soils in the eastern states. Or they may be introduced to a fuller explanation when they read that some people came to Ohio to escape their creditors or to seek adventure or to speculate in land. In either case, they are simply learning more "facts." An advanced course in American history in high school differs from the sixth-grade course in American history in that it gives more detail; the older student must remember more "facts."

Students who have been introduced to history in this way may become confused upon discovering in a book like this one that historians often disagree sharply. To be sure, historians present their material in familiar ways; they tell us what happened and why it happened by presenting a mass of historical data. But students soon discover that two or three or more historians dealing with the same event may come to quite different conclusions about it. Sometimes two historians will use two very different sets of "facts" in describing an event, and this leads them to different conclusions. At other times, however, the same "facts" are given different meanings by different historians, and their conclusions therefore differ.

The common-sense reaction to this state of affairs is to conclude that one historian is right while the other is wrong. But common sense will take students no further than this. Presumably, historians who are wrong will have their "facts" wrong. This is seldom the case, however. Students find that all historians argue reasonably—and persuasively. And the "facts"—the names, dates, events, figures—usually turn out to be correct. Moreover, to complicate matters, they often find that contending historians more or less agree on the facts; that is, they use much the same data to come to different conclusions. To state that all are right when they say different things seems irrational; in any case, such an approach is often unacceptable to teachers who expect their students to take a position. The only way out for the baffled students is to choose one point of view for reasons they cannot fully explain. History, which had seemed to be a cut-and-dried matter of memorizing "facts," now becomes a matter of choosing one good interpretation from among many. Historical truth becomes a matter of personal preference, like the choice of one brand-named item over another in a supermarket.

This position is hardly satisfying. And when their teachers inform them that the controversy over historical interpretations is what lends excitement to the study of history, students can only respond that they feel more confusion than excitement. They cannot help but feel that two diametrically opposed points of view about an event cannot both be right; yet they lack the ability to decide between them.

Obviously, there is no easy solution to this problem. Historians do not disagree in order to provide the raw material for "problems" books such as this one; they disagree because each historian views the past from a particular perspective. Once students grasp this, they have taken the first step toward being able to evaluate the work of various historians. But before they can take this first step, students must consider a problem they have more or less taken for granted. They must ask themselves what history really is.

The word *history* has several meanings. In its broadest sense, it denotes the whole of the human past. More restricted is the notion that history is the *recorded* past, that is, that part of human life which has left some sort of record such as folk tales, artifacts, or written documents. Finally, history may be defined as that which historians write about the past.

Of course, the three meanings are related. Historians writing about the past base their accounts on the remains of the past, on the artifacts and documents left by people. Obviously they cannot know everything for the simple reason that not every event, every happening, was fully and completely recorded. And the further back one goes in time, the fewer are the records that remain. In this sense, then, the historian can only approximate history in the first meaning above, that is, history as the entire human past.

But this does not say enough. If historians cannot know everything because not everything was recorded, neither do they use all the records that are available to them. Rather, historians *select* from the total those records they deem most significant. Moreover, to complicate matters a bit more, they also re-create parts of the past for which they have no recorded evidence. Like detectives, they piece together evidence to fill in the gaps in the available records.

Historians are able to select evidence and to create evidence by using some theory or idea of human motivation and behavior. Sometimes this appears to be easy, requiring very little sophistication and subtlety. Thus, for example, historians investigating America's entry into World War I would probably find that the sinking of American merchant ships on the high seas by German submarines was relevant to their discussion. At the same time, they would most likely not use evidence that President Woodrow Wilson was dissatisfied with a new hat he bought during the first months of 1917. The choice as to which fact to use is based on a theory—admittedly, in this case a rather crude theory, but a theory nonetheless. It would go something like this: National leaders contemplating war are more likely to be influenced by belligerent acts against their countries than by their unhappiness with their haberdashers.

The choice, of course, is not always so obvious. But, before pursuing the problem further, it is important to note that a choice must be made. Historians do not just present facts; they present *some* facts and not others. They choose those facts that seem significant and reject others. This is one of the reasons why historians disagree. They have different views or different theories concerning human behavior and therefore find different kinds of information significant.

Perhaps it might appear that it is the subject matter being investigated rather than any theory held by the historian that dictates which facts are significant. But this is not really so. With a little imagination—and poetic license—one could conceive of a psychological explanation for Wilson's actions that would include mounting frustration and anger fed in part, at least, by his strong disappointment with his new hat. In this case the purchase of a new hat would be a relevant fact in explaining Wilson's decision to ask Congress for a declaration of war. If the reader finds this outlandish, it is only because his notion of presidential motivation does not include this kind of personal reaction as an influence in determining matters of state.

If the choices were always as simple as choosing between German submarines and President Wilson's new hat, the problem would be easily resolved. But usually the choices are not so easy to make. Historians investigating United States' entry into World War I will find in addition to German submarine warfare a whole series of other facts that could be relevant to the event under study. For instance, they will find that the British government had a propaganda machine at work in the United States that did its best to win public support for the British cause. They will discover that American bankers had made large loans to the British, loans that would not be repaid in the event of a British defeat. They will read of the interception of the "Zimmerman Note," in which the German foreign secretary ordered the German minister in Mexico, in the event of war, to suggest an alliance between Germany and Mexico whereby Mexico, with German support, could win back territory taken from Mexico by the United States in the Mexican War. They will also find among many American political leaders a deep concern over the balance of power in Europe, a balance that would be destroyed —to America's disadvantage—if the Germans were able to defeat the French and the British and thereby emerge as the sole major power in Europe.

What then are the historians investigating America's entry into World War I to make of these facts? One group could simply conclude that America entered the war for several reasons and then list the facts they have discovered. By doing so, they would be making two important assumptions: (1) those facts they put on their list—in this case, German submarine warfare, British propaganda, American loans, the Zimmerman Note, and concern over the balance of power—are the main reasons, while those they do not list are not important; and (2) those things they put on their list are of equal importance in explaining the U.S. role. But another group of historians might argue that the list is incomplete in that it does not take into account the generally pro-British views of Woodrow Wilson, views that stemmed from the President's background and education. The result will be a disagreement among the historians. Moreover, because the second group raise the question of Wilson's views, they will find a number of relevant facts that the first group would ignore. They will concern themselves with Wilson's education, the influence of his teachers, the books he read, and the books he wrote. In short, although both groups of historians are dealing with the same subject— America's entry into World War I—they will come to different conclusions and use different facts to support their points of view. The facts selected, and those ignored, will depend not on the problem studied but on the points of view of the historians.

Similarly, a third group of historians might maintain that the various items on the list should not be given equal weight, that one of the reasons listed, say bankers' loans, was most important and that the others seemed to be significant only because of the overwhelming power of the bankers to influence American policy. The theory here would be that economic matters are the key to human motivation and that a small number of wealthy bankers have a disproportionate ability to influence government. Again, these historians will disagree with the first two groups, and they will find relevant certain facts that the others overlook—for example, bankers' opinions, the lobbying activities of bankers, financial and political connections between bankers and politicians, and the like.

In the examples given, historians disagree and use different facts or give different emphasis to the same facts because they begin from different premises; in other words, they have different theories of human motivation. But to put the matter in this way is somewhat misleading. It makes it appear that historical scholarship is merely a matter of deduction, as in Euclidean geometry, where conclusions are deduced from a set of given premises termed axioms and postulates. If this were so, historians would have it very easy. They would begin with a premise—for example, human beings are primarily motivated by selfish economic interests—and then they would seek whatever evidence they could find that showed people acting in that manner. They would ignore contrary evidence as unimportant or explain it away as being mere rhetoric designed to hide real motivations. The results of such efforts would be foreordained; the actors and the details might be different, but in the end the explanations would always be the same.

Historians term this approach or method "determinism," and most modern historians reject it. They argue that the premises cannot be merely assumed but must be proved or at least supported by concrete historical information. Nevertheless, historians cannot even begin their investigations without adopting some theory, even if it is expressed vaguely and held tentatively. In the course of their investigations they might alter or refine the original theory or replace it with another. But their final product will always rest upon some kind of theoretical base. Thus, if two historians become convinced by their evidence that different factors motivated the behavior of the people involved in a particular event, they will disagree, presenting different facts and giving different meanings to the same facts.

But there is still another realm of disagreement which, although it often appears similar to that just discussed, in fact stems from something rather different. Historians sometimes disagree because they are not really discussing the same thing. Often they are merely considering different levels of cause and effect. A few examples will illustrate this point.

The simplest level of analysis of cause and effect is to recognize what may be called proximate cause. "I was late for class," you explain, "because I overslept." Or, to use a historical example, "The Civil War began because South Carolina shore batteries under the command of General Beauregard opened fire on the federal garrison at Fort Sumter on April 12, 1861." Neither statement can be faulted on the grounds that it is inaccurate; at the same time, however, neither is sufficient as an explanation of the event being considered. The next question is obvious: Why did you oversleep, or why did relations between one state and the federal government reach the point where differences had to be settled by war? To this you may answer that you were out very late last night at a party, and the historian may respond that the authorities in South Carolina concluded that the election of Abraham Lincoln and his subsequent actions in threatening to supply the federal garrison at Fort Sumter were a clear menace to the well-being of South Carolina.

We have now dug more deeply into the problems, but the answers may still not be sufficient to satisfy us. Again we ask the question why and the answer takes us more deeply into the causes of the events under consideration. As we probe further, of course, the answers become more difficult and more complex. The problems discussed earlier—a theory of motivation and the selection of facts—begin to become increasingly important, and disagreements among historians will begin to emerge. But the potential for another kind of disagreement also arises. The further back or the deeper the historian goes, the more factors there are to be considered and the more tenuous the connection between cause and effect becomes. Historians may disagree about the point at which to begin their analysis, that is, about the location of a point beyond which the causal connection becomes so tenuous as to be meaningless. You might argue that the ultimate cause of your being late to class was the fact that you were born, but obviously this goes back too far to be meaningful. That you were born is, of course, a *necessary* factor—unless that had happened, you could not have been late—but is not a *sufficient* factor; it does not really tell enough to explain your behavior today. Similarly, we could trace the cause of the Civil War back to the discovery of America, but again, this is a necessary but not a sufficient cause.

The point at which causes are both necessary and sufficient is not self-evident. In part, the point is determined by the theoretical stance of historians. If they decide that slavery is the key to understanding the coming of the Civil War, the point will be located somewhere along the continuum of the history of slavery in the United States. But even those historians who agree that slavery is the key to the war will not necessarily agree at what point slavery becomes both necessary and sufficient. The historians who believe that slavery was a constant irritant driving the North and South apart might begin their discussion with the introduction of blacks into Virginia in 1619. They would find relevant the antislavery attitudes of Northerners during the colonial period, the conflict over slavery in the Constitutional Convention, the Missouri Compromise, the militant abolitionist movement of the 1830s, and the Compromise of 1850. But other historians might argue that the slavery issue did not become really significant until it was associated with the settlement of the western lands. They would probably begin their discussion with the Missouri Compromise, and the facts they would find most relevant would be those that illustrated the fear many people had of the expansion of slavery into the new western lands.

Ostensibly, both groups of historians would be discussing the role of slavery in the coming of the Civil War, but actually they would be discussing two different things. For the first group, the expansion of slavery to the West would be only part of a longer and more complex story; for the second group, slavery and the West would be the whole story. Sometimes the same facts would be used by both, with each giving them different weight and significance; at other times one group would find some facts relevant that the other would not.

An important variant of this kind of disagreement among historians may be illustrated by returning to our earlier example of the causes of American entry into World War I. Some historians might set out to discover the effects of British propaganda efforts in molding public and official views toward the war. German submarine warfare, the Zimmerman Note, bankers' loans, and other matters would enter the discussion, but they would all be seen from the perspective of the ways in which the British propaganda machine used them to win American support for the British side.

Historians emphasizing the role of British propaganda would disagree with those emphasizing the influential role of bankers, although both groups of historians would be using many of the same facts to support their points of view. In reality, of course, the disagreement arises at least in part from the fact that the two groups of historians are not really discussing the same things.

The reader should now be in a position to understand something of the sources of disagreement among historians. Historians arrive at different conclusions because they have different notions about human motivation and different ideas about what constitutes necessary and sufficient cause, and because they seek to investigate different aspects of the same problems. All supply their readers with data and information—that is, with "facts"—to support their arguments. And, with rare exceptions, all of the facts presented are accurate.

Clearly, then, historical facts as such have no intrinsic meaning; they take on meaning and significance only when they are organized and presented by historians with a particular point of view. The well-used phrase "let the facts speak for themselves" therefore has no real meaning. The facts do *not* speak for themselves; historians use the facts in a particular way and therefore they, and not the facts, are doing the speaking. In other words, historians give meaning to facts by assessing their significance and by presenting them in a particular manner. In short, they *interpret*. Because different historians use different facts or use the same facts in different ways, their interpretations differ.

Once we understand the sources of differences among historians we are in a better position to evaluate their work. To be sure, our ability to understand why historians disagree will not make it possible to eliminate all disagreement. Only if we could devise a model of unquestioned validity that completely explained human behavior would it be possible for us to end disagreement. Any analysis that began by assuming a different model or explanation would be wrong.*

But we do not have such a complete and foolproof explanatory model. Nor can we expect to find one. Human life is too complicated to be so completely modeled; different problems require different explanatory models or theories. And because historians cannot agree as to which is the best model to employ for any given problem and because they are constantly devising new models, disagreements are destined to remain.

For the readers who have been patient enough to follow the argument to this point, the conclusions stated here may appear somewhat dismal and unrewarding. In convincing them that evaluating a historical interpretation is not like picking an item off a supermarket shelf, have we done more than move them to another store with a different stock on its shelves? If there are many explanatory models to choose from, and if no one of them is complete, foolproof, and guaranteed true, then it would appear that we are simply in another store with different merchandise on display.

Such a conclusion is unwarranted. In the first place, students who are able to understand the premises from which historians begin will be able to comprehend the way historians work and the process by which they fashion interpretation. Moreover, this understanding will enable them to evaluate the work of the historians. For at this stage students are no longer simply memorizing details; nor are they attempting to evaluate a historical essay by trying to discover whether each of the facts presented is true. They can now ask more important questions of the material before them. Are the premises from which historians begin adequate explanations of human behavior? Do the facts they present really flow from their premises and support their conclusions? Are there other data that would tend to undermine their arguments and throw doubt on the adequacy of their premises?

As students attempt to answer these questions, they begin to learn history by thinking and acting like historians. And, as they do, they begin to accumulate knowledge, understanding, and insight in much the same ways that historians do. Historians constantly discover new information: diaries, letters, business records, and family Bibles are always being found in attics, basements, and even in remote corners of large research libraries. Historians also gain new insights from the research of social scientists such as economists, political scientists, sociologists, and psychologists. Investigations by these scholars into such problems as family relationships, the influence of propaganda on behavior, the effects of the money supply on economic change, the relationship

---

* It should be noted in passing that even if we had such a theory, there would be much room for disagreement because we would often lack the required data. Some essential information would be lost through deliberate or accidental destruction. Other information might leave no record. Records of births, deaths, income, and so forth are now required by law, but in earlier days these records were not kept or were kept only sporadically. And telephone and personal conversations might leave no concrete record even though they could have a profound influence on behavior.

between voting patterns and racial and ethnic origin, and the psychological effects of racism all provide insights that may be of value to historians investigating the past. Historians also master and use new techniques. For example, the computer now permits the historian to handle huge masses of data quickly and accurately.

Historians also learn from one another. For example, when one historian discovers the existence of certain political, social, and economic relationships in a given city at a certain time, he or she provides other historians studying other cities, either at the same or different times, with what may be important and enlightening insights. International comparisons of similar events and institutions can also reveal important features that will be invisible or obscure when these events and institutions are viewed from the perspective of a single nation's history. Finally, and perhaps most important, historians are influenced by their own experiences and by the events of their own time. Scholars cannot be entirely objective (nor should they be); they interpret the past through a frame of reference that is influenced by the world in which they live. During World War II, for instance, historians reexamined the causes and consequences of World War I, just as the war in Vietnam provided a new perspective on the Cold War years. The civil rights movement and black radicalism in the 1960s inspired a number of historians to reinterpret the role of abolitionists in the events leading up to the Civil War and to give more attention to race, prejudice, and class conflict in American life. In a similar way the feminist movement is causing a reexamination of the role of women and the family in the American past, while urban violence, the black revolution, and increasing ethnic identity are causing a reassessment of the importance of violence, slavery, and ethnic groups in American history. Their own experiences often help historians to relate the past to the present, but the exact nature of that relationship remains controversial.

At first it may seem frustrating to realize that there is no one easy answer to the problems historians raise and that "truth" is but an elusive yet intriguing goal in a never-ending quest. But when students realize this, they have *begun* their education. At that point, they will find the study of history to be a significant, exhilarating, and useful part of their education. For coming to grips with conflicting interpretations of the past is more than an interesting classroom game; it is part of a larger process of coming to terms with the world around us. Every day we are asked to evaluate articles in newspapers and magazines or reports of events provided by friends or radio commentators. A knowledge of history provides a background for interpreting these accounts; but more than that, the past and the present are so interconnected that one's interpretation of the American Revolution, slavery, the progressive movement, or American foreign policy after World War II are intimately related to one's views toward civil rights and domestic and foreign policy today.

The discussion thus far has emphasized the element of disagreement among historians and has attempted to show beginning students how these disagreements arise and how they should deal with them. But if disagreements arise because historians often start their analyses from different perspectives, it does not follow that there is no agreement at all among historians. On the contrary, groups of historians have tended to assume similar theoretical postures, and the result has been the emergence of "schools" of historical writing. All differences among members of a particular school do not disappear, but their approaches remain similar enough to differentiate them from members of other schools.

Identifying schools and placing historians in them is seldom easy and is always somewhat arbitrary. The reasons are obvious enough: the amount and complexity of works about America's past are so great that it is possible to identify a large number of schools. Moreover, since few historians begin with an explicit ideology or philosophy of history, their work may fit into a number of possible schools. Finally, most good historians do not cling dogmatically to a particular approach. As their research and writing proceeds, as they learn more, or as contemporary events alter their perspectives, their interpretations tend to change.

In organizing this book we have chosen two recurrent and important schools, or interpretive themes, in the writings on American history: conflict and consensus. Admittedly, the choice, in one sense at least, is arbitrary; we could have chosen from a number of other unifying themes. On the other hand, the choice has not been completely arbitrary in that these themes— conflict and consensus—expressed either explicitly or implicitly, may be found in virtually all major interpretations of our country's past. The student who reads the following pages and attempts to evaluate the arguments presented will be faced with two real and meaningful ways to understand the American past and, indeed, to judge the contemporary American scene.

Stripped to its essentials, the task of historians is to deal with change. And nowhere do historians find change more manifest than when they study the United States. Almost in the twinkling of an eye a vast, scarcely populated continent was transformed into a major industrial power of phenomenal complexity. Overnight, virgin forests became fertile farms; Indian trails became roads, highways, and railroads; and empty spaces became bustling cities. Matching this transformation of the physical face of the continent were equally momentous changes in politics, social relations, ideas, and attitudes. For most Americans, constant and rapid change was inevitable if only because it was so obvious. "Ten years in America are like a century in Spain," wrote the German immigrant Francis Leiber soon after his arrival in the United States early in the nineteenth century. "The United States really changes in some respects more within ten years than a country like Spain has within a hundred."

But who could argue that Europe was static and unchanging? True enough, Europe had little in the way of trackless wilderness to be discovered, settled, and transformed; and, true also, Europe was crowded with the remnants of what might appear to be an unchanging past—cathedrals and monuments, aristocratic and royal institutions, and ways of doing things that seemed to have existed time out of mind. But at the same time, Europe periodically exploded into change. Indeed, time after time, Americans saw Europe swept by rebellion and war as one group after another sought, often successfully, to revolutionize European lives and institutions.

Generations of American historians have tried to describe and to explain the vast alterations that have taken place on the North American continent. As they did so, many kept one eye on the changes in European institutions, seeking to compare and to contrast the nature of changes in the Old World with those of the New. But even as they read the historical documents, often in the light of European history and experience, the historians themselves were living through vast and rapid changes taking place around them in the United States.

The writings by American historians have been varied and rich. But from this variety two rather distinct traditions have emerged, each of which has sought to provide an explanation for the course of American history.

One tradition or point of view holds that the key to American history, like that of Europe, is conflict. Historians who adhere to this point of view speak in terms of revolution and class and sectional conflict. They stress the *differences* among Americans—class differences, social differences, political differences. Their emphasis is on fundamental conflicts: democrats versus aristocrats, debtors versus creditors, workers versus businessmen, North versus South, farmers versus railroads, blacks versus whites. Change, they argue, is a function of this never-ending conflict; it arises from the efforts of particular groups and classes to impose their hegemony over American society, or at least to increase their influence over that society.

The other tradition stresses the uniqueness of the American experience by finding a basic consensus in American society. According to this tradition, all Americans of whatever class or station shared what was essentially a common outlook. To be sure, Americans did not all live alike nor did they always agree with one another. But their disagreements, especially when compared with the dissensions that divided European society, were not fundamental. Consensus historians do not ignore class and sectional differences, and they do not deny conflicts between groups such as workers and employers; but they do deny that these conflicts were basic. Americans, they argue, achieved a consensus on fundamentals; if they disagreed, their disagreements were minor differences within an underlying consensus. Change then is the result of a fundamental agreement that change is required and does not arise from a struggle for power.

Although both these themes can be found in the earliest writings on American history, they became dominant interpretive themes only during the twentieth century. The theme of conflict was central to the writings of those Richard Hofstadter has called the "Progressive Historians": Frederick Jackson Turner, Charles A. Beard, and Vernon L. Parrington. Growing up in the midst of the nation's rapid industrialization and living in a time of growing protest against the problems created by that industrialization, these historians saw the past in terms of bitter conflict. Their influence, as the reader of the following pages will discover, was profound.

The theme of consensus was in part a reaction to what was considered to be the overstatements of the conflict school and in part a reaction to the world of the 1950s. At that time, European wars and revolutionary conflicts seemed strangely alien to American society, as did historical interpretations cast in the European mold. Looking at the past, these historians discovered that America had always been different from Europe; Americans had, for the most part, been spared the bitter conflicts that plagued Europe. Like the conflict historians of an earlier generation, the new consensus historians had a great influence on American historical thought.

But the consensus historians were not without their critics. John Higham argued that they were "homogenizing" American history; he accused them of "carrying out a massive grading operation to smooth over America's social convulsions." He and other critics did not simply call for a return to the history of the progressive historians. They argued that the consensus historians had made the American past bland and meaningless, because they ignored real and significant differences that produced sharp conflicts.

There was the danger that the debate would degenerate into nothing more than an argument over the meaning given to the words *conflict* and *consensus.* Indeed, often this was exactly what happened. Usually, however, historians attempted to use insights drawn from the work of their predecessors in the two schools in order to develop new and more meaningful interpretations.

The new work was marked by a number of new techniques and fresh approaches. Quantitative historians, aided by the computer and modern statistical methods and using theories borrowed from economics, sociology, political science, linguistics, anthropology, and psychology, conducted massive investigations of such matters as economic growth patterns, voting behavior, family life, and social mobility. Social historians, using both quantitative and other methods, attempted to write history from the "bottom-up," giving major emphasis to the lives of ordinary people rather than to those at the top. Similarly, they turned their attention to the role and status of women, creating an important dimension of this new history. Social historians also studied local developments in great detail, concerning themselves with small communities, villages, ethnic groups, and local religious and political institutions. The "New Left" historians, although they encompassed a quite diverse group, sought variously to find a radical tradition in American history or to explain the absence of such a tradition.

Although these and other new approaches enriched historical writing and often provided a more subtle and complex story of the nation's past, the themes of conflict and consensus continued to be relevant in the new work. The problems of historical interpretation were not resolved, despite historians' ability to amass more data by using new techniques to mine huge sources of information and by utilizing insights from the social sciences. New methods and techniques could provide new "facts," but the question of which facts to use and what meaning to give them remained.

The lines that divide the conflict from the consensus historians are not so sharp as they once were, and many contemporary historians are drawing from both in their analyses of America's past. Nevertheless, the differences remain and will continue to do so, to the benefit of our persistent search for understanding. In the readings that follow, the reader is introduced to the two traditions of conflict and consensus and their variations through the words of some of their most able exponents.

## SUGGESTIONS FOR FURTHER READING

The literature on the philosophy and practice of history comes from the pens of both philosophers and practicing historians. A few volumes have been written specifically for the beginning student; examples are Walter T. K. Nugent, *Creative History* (Philadelphia, 1967), and Allan J. Lichtman and Valerie French, *Historians and the Living Past* (Arlington Heights, Ill., 1978). More sophisticated but eminently readable are E. H. Carr, *What Is History?* (New York, 1964), Louis Gottschalk, *Understanding History* (New York, 1963), Allan Nevins, *The Gateway to History* (Garden City, N.Y., 1962), and Marc Bloch, *The Historian's Craft* (New York, 1953). An illuminating and superbly written guide to historical research and writing that will show readers how historians work is Jacques Barzun and Henry F. Graff, *The Modern Researcher* (New York, 1970). J. H. Hexter, *Doing History* (Bloomington, Ind., 1971) is an entertaining discussion of the ways in which historians communicate their findings—or fail to do so.

Students interested in the philosophy of history might begin with Hans Meyerhoff, ed., *The Philosophy of History in Our Time* (Garden City, N.Y., 1959), an anthology prefaced by an illuminating introduction. A more difficult collection of readings on the philosophy of history is Patrick Gardiner, ed., *Theories of History* (New York, 1959). The latest scholarship appears in the journal *History and Theory*.

Students wishing to pursue the historiography (that is, the history of historical writing) of the conflict-consensus theme should begin with the progressive historians. Charles A. Beard was a prolific writer, but the best approach to him is through Charles and Mary Beard, *The Rise of American Civilization* (New York, 1927, 1930), a lively and interesting interpretation of the whole course of American history, with an emphasis on class and economic conflict. Beard's *An Economic Interpretation of the Constitution* (New York, 1913, 1935) must be read by any serious student. Vernon Parrington's three-volume *Main Currents in American Thought* (New York, 1927, 1930) complements Beard's work and deals with the relationship of literature and ideas to society and social movements. Frederick Jackson Turner's essays may be found in *The Frontier in American History* (New York, 1920), and *The Significance of Sections in American History* (New York, 1932). There are many discussions of the work and influence of these

---

* Available in paperback edition.

historians; the reader can do no better than to begin with Richard Hofstadter, *The Progressive Historians* (New York, 1968), the work of a perceptive and sensitive critic. This book's great value is enhanced by an outstanding "bibliographical essay" that will lead the student deep into the literature on the subject.

Any serious student of the consensus historians must read and study Louis Hartz, *The Liberal Tradition in America* (New York, 1955) and the key works of Daniel J. Boorstin: *The Genius of American Politics* (Chicago, 1953), *The Americans: The Colonial Experience* (New York, 1958); *The Americans: The Democratic Experience* (New York, 1973); and *The Americans: The National Experience* (New York, 1965). A perceptive discussion of these books as well as of the entire consensus school along with good bibliographical information may be found in the Hofstadter volume cited above. An important and provocative critique of the consensus approach is John Higham, "The Cult of the American Consensus," *Commentary*, 27 (February 1959), pp. 93–100. See also J. Rogers Hollingsworth, "Consensus and Continuity in Recent American Historical Writing," *South Atlantic Quarterly*, 61 (Winter 1962), pp. 40–50, and Gene Wise, "Political 'Reality' in Recent American Scholarship: Progressives versus Symbolists," *American Quarterly*, 22, Part 2 (Summer 1967), pp. 303–28.

A good introduction to the work of the "new left" in much of its variety is Barton J. Bernstein, ed., *Towards a New Past: Dissenting Essays in American History* (New York, 1968). A critical evaluation of the work of this group, which can also serve as an introductory bibliography, is Irwin Unger, "The 'New Left' and American History: Some Recent Trends in United States Historiography," *American Historical Review*, 77 (July 1967), pp. 1237–63. Quantitative history is difficult for the uninitiated, but for those who want a taste of it, a good introduction is William O. Adydelotte, Allan G. Bogue, and Robert William Fogel, eds., *The Dimensions of Quantitative Research in History* (Princeton, N.J., 1972).

In the last decade historians have attempted to blend the themes of conflict and consensus. See John Higham, "Hanging Together: Divergent Unities in American History," *Journal of American History*, 61 (June 1974), pp. 5–28, and Robert H. Wiebe, *The Segmented Society: An Historical Preface to the Meaning of America* (New York, 1975). Nevertheless, many continue to emphasize either conflict or consensus. Samuel P. Huntington, *American Politics: The Promise of Disharmony* (Cambridge, Mass., 1981) finds consensus in the form of a commitment to equality among Americans, but the continued existence of inequalities leads to what he terms a "disharmonic society." Rowland Berthoff, "Peasants and Artisans, Puritans and Republicans: Personal Liberty and Communal Equality in American History," *Journal of American History*, 69 (December 1982), pp. 579–98, finds conflict but concludes that the antagonists were united by a "common ideological ancestry."

A convenient collection of examples of new approaches and methods in recent writing may be found in Felix Gilbert and Stephen R. Graubard, eds., *Historical Studies Today* (New York, 1972). *Reviews in American History*, 10 (December 1982) contains articles surveying the state of scholarship in some twenty subdisciplines in American history. Bernard Sternsher, *Consensus, Conflict and American Historians* (Bloomington, Ind., 1975) examines the theme of this book in great detail.

# Conflict and Consensus

in

## Modern American History

# 1

# *Reconstruction*

The Civil War has had an endless fascination for Americans, who usually see it as a time of great heroism and idealism on the part of both sides in the conflict. But no such rosy aura surrounds the years after the war, the years when an attempt was made to reconstruct the nation and heal the wounds of war. If the Civil War made heroes, Reconstruction produced villains; if the war was marked by tragic idealism, Reconstruction was characterized by venal corruption. Even those historians who find much that was beneficial in Reconstruction conclude that the period ended in dismal failure.

The basic problem facing Northern leaders after the war was how to restore national unity after a bitter and bloody sectional conflict. But there was sharp disagreement as to the best approach. Should the Confederacy be treated as a conquered province, or should the Southern states be welcomed back into the Union as wayward but repentant members of the family? What kind of changes should the ex-Confederate states accept before being allowed to participate once again in the political process?

Even during the war there was disagreement between President Lincoln, who favored treating the seceded states leniently, and some congressional leaders, who argued for harsher peace terms. This executive-legislative battle continued after the assassination of Lincoln, but the mid-term elections of 1866, favorable to the so-called radicals, made it possible for Congress to pass legislation concerning the South over the opposition and vetoes of President Andrew Johnson. Congress quickly passed the Civil Rights Bill, the Freedman's Bureau Bill, and, finally, the Reconstruction Acts of 1867. The Southern states were put under military rule until they approved new constitutions guaranteeing black suffrage, ratified the Fourteenth Amendment, and in other ways satisfied the radical majority in Congress.

As new governments were set up under congressional tutelage in each Southern state, they were declared reconstructed and their representatives and senators admitted to Congress. For the first time, blacks voted and held office, some even serving as their state's senators and representatives in Congress. The Republican-dominated state governments were often marked by corruption and inefficiency, but they also instituted significant and needed reforms in education and welfare. All of them faced sharp and often violent opposition, and one by one they fell from power. None remained when the last troops were removed from the South in 1877.

No period has evoked more impassioned and opinionated historical writing than has Reconstruction. Some historians, seeing the South as victim, have called it a "tragic era," a period during which the defeated South was put to the torture by a vindictive conqueror. Others, sensitive to the position of the black population, have depicted this as a period of betrayal when opportunistic Northerners abandoned the blacks to racist violence and a life of discrimination and fear. One way into the maze of historical writing on Reconstruction is to see it in terms of the Civil War. The following selections

3

show how interpretations of the causes of the Civil War can color the interpretations of its aftermath, Reconstruction.

If we adopt the Beards' analysis that the war was the result of a struggle between industrial and agrarian interests, we could expect that Reconstruction policies would reflect the victory of Northern industrialists. Such is the view presented in the first selection, by William B. Hesseltine. He argues that Reconstruction was simply "the method by which the 'Masters of Capital' sought to secure their victory over the vanquished 'Lords of the Manor.'" The radicals, representatives of Northern industrial capital, wanted political institutions in the South that would support the flow of industrial capital into the region. When these tactics did not achieve their goal, the Republicans abandoned Reconstruction. But they did not abandon their goal; they merely changed tactics from "coercion" to "appeal."

Hesseltine, like the Beards, argues that abolition of slavery was not the main issue in the Civil War, and that therefore protection of the civil rights of freed blacks after the war was not an important issue. The radicals supported civil rights for blacks as a tactic that seemed necessary to reach their main goal, and they abandoned the blacks when their tactics changed. But if slavery is seen as a key issue in the coming of the Civil War, then Reconstruction must be viewed in the context of the end of slavery. The slaves were emancipated as a result of the war. Does it follow from this that emancipation carried with it a promise to open the doors to full equality for the blacks?

In the second selection, James M. McPherson argues that, during the war, emancipation and equality of opportunity became part of Northern war aims. Reconstruction was therefore an effort to accomplish the goals made possible by Northern victory. Emancipation and the guarantee of civil rights for blacks were revolutionary goals, McPherson insists, but for a number of reasons Northerners abandoned the goal of civil rights for blacks. The result was an incomplete revolution, a revolution that achieved only part of its goal.

La Wanda Cox agrees that one of the goals of Reconstruction was to guarantee civil rights for the freed slaves. In the third selection she considers the failure of Reconstruction to achieve this goal in terms of the possible alternatives open to the politicians at the time. She notes that there were other opportunities available and that these were ignored, but she argues also that there were limits to what could be accomplished. To assume that Reconstruction following the Civil War could have achieved the consensus that the Civil Rights movement of the 1960s achieved, she argues, is to ignore the political realities of the time.

Obviously, the Reconstruction era witnessed sharp political and often physical conflict. Less obvious, however, is the source of that conflict. What were the victorious Northerners trying to achieve in the defeated South? Did they succeed? If not, why did they abandon their goals? Did they lack the power? The will? Or did they face problems that really could not be solved in the mid-nineteenth century?

William B. Hesseltine

# Reconstruction: Changing Revolutionary Tactics

By common consent, President Rutherford B. Hayes's withdrawal of the federal troops from the South has been accepted as the end of reconstruction. The President's action, however, was but the outward and visible symbol of an already accomplished revolution in northern sentiment. For a number of years the northern voters had been coming to realize that the effort to force the South into the northern political mold was both costly and futile.

Commentators on the politics of the Reconstruction period have ascribed this reversal of opinion to the rise of new interests among the northern electorate, or have dismissed it with a remark that the people had grown tired of the southern question in politics. Such an interpretation fails to consider that reconstruction itself was an economic as well as a political problem, and that it was not until the political program failed to bring economic results that the control of the South was returned to the southern white man.

Fundamentally, reconstruction was the method by which the "Masters of Capital" sought to secure their victory over the vanquished "Lords of the Manor," and through which they expected to exploit the resources of the southern states. Long before the war was over cotton speculators, acting as the vanguard of an economic army, followed the advancing federal armies and annoyed commanders from the Red River to the Potomac by their persistent efforts to carry on trade with the South. Behind the lines, less

From William B. Hesseltine, "Economic Factors in the Abandonment of Reconstruction," Mississippi Valley Historical Review, XXII (September 1935), pp. 191–220, excluding footnotes. Reprinted by permission of the Organization of American Historians.

mobile entrepreneurs calculated the possibility of carrying the northern economic system into the South at the close of hostilities. In the first months after Appomattox, business men in the North looked for immediate profits from the return of peace and endorsed General Ulysses S. Grant's leniency and President Andrew Johnson's plans for a speedy restoration of the southern states. One of Grant's aides-de-camp found that in the summer of 1865 "all the sober, substantial men" of New York, St. Louis, and Washington were in favor of Johnson's policy. Impressed with the necessity for southern industrial rehabilitation, the New York *Commercial and Financial Chronicle* ingratiatingly assured the South that the northern people contemplated no oppression but would accord the southern states an early readmission to the Union.

Totally ignoring the psychoses of the conquered southerners, northern financial circles seemed to believe that the South would "treat political questions as secondary" until industrial recuperation had been accomplished. This recovery, of course, would be the result of northern capital, in the hands of northern men, flowing into the South. "There can be no way so sure to make the late rebels of the South loyal men and good citizens," declared the New York organ of the financiers, "as to turn their energies to the pursuits of peace, and the accumulation of wealth." When goods from southern factories appeared in the New York markets, they caused this journal to remember that in 1860 there had been 350 woolen mills and 180 cotton mills in the South and that the total value of southern manufactured goods had been over $238,000,000! "Now," proclaimed the hopeful editor, "Northern men, accustomed to business, have gone South and will give a new impetus" to industrial development.

In order to encourage northern men to migrate to the South, commercial newspapers began to advertise the South as the nation's new land of opportunity. The abundance of land, the manufacturing possibilities, the climate, soil, water-power, and timber of the South came in for extensive exposition, and the figures of the South's exports in 1860—over two hundred million dollars—was dangled before the eyes of the northern people. The South was assured that an immigration of new and energetic people would begin as soon as the Johnsonian governments were fully established.

Such roseate dreams of a golden harvest in the South were rudely shattered when the southerners began to take stock of their own position. In the first days after the war planters welcomed ex-officers of the Union armies who came to purchase cotton plantations, but few of these adventurers were successful either in handling negroes or in living harmoniously with their white neighbors. Political differences which engendered social ostracism and even physical violence soon developed, and the northerners returned to their homes none the richer for their experience. Instead of welcoming immigrants and making provisions to receive migrating capitalists, the provisional governments under Johnson's program showed more interest in attempting to solve the economic problems of an agrarian area.

Some efforts, however, were made by several of the states to attract immigrants, and boards of immigration were set up by the Reconstruction governments. But only in Tennessee was there a real enthusiasm for the task. There the East Tennesseans, who had never been a part of the cotton kingdom but had long nursed secret ambitions to become industrialized, controlled the state and made a serious effort to entice northern capital. Newspapers appealed to Tennesseans to advertise their lands, mill and factory sites, and mines in order to attract merchants, manufacturers, and bankers —"the very class of men . . . whose help is needed in developing the wealth of our great State." The legislature generously chartered a number of "immigration" companies in order to assist expected immigrants, and in December, 1867, a State Board of Immigration was established. The board employed an energetic commissioner to advertise the state's resources in the North and in Europe. In radical Missouri there was also a welcome to immigrants, but in other parts of the South a suspicion of the political motives of the migrants caused them to be either ostracized or mistreated.

The attitude of the southerners was not long in being reported to Congress. "Loyal" citizens, Unionists, and northern immigrants appealed to congressmen for protection against the "frightful spirit of lawlessness extant among the late rebels." From Virginia to Texas plaintive letters to congressmen told the story of bad treatment. Already the Radicals in Congress had determined to force Negro suffrage on the South in order to maintain the Republican party in power. Under the added stimulus of the anguished cries of business men both North and South the congressional program of reconstruction was formulated. The Fourteenth Amendment would protect the property of Union men in the South and by disfranchising the leaders of the old agricultural South would enable "loyal" men and Negroes to enact the legislation which would protect the northern capitalist in exploiting the South. When the southern states rejected the amendment, Congress proceeded to carry its program into effect. Only radical Tennessee, whose arms were outstretched in welcome to invading capital, was admitted to representation in Congress.

The passage of the Reconstruction Act of March 2, 1867, renewed the hope of a migration of capital and labor to the South. Union men in Virginia looked forward to the migration of "Northern men with capital and enterprise to develop the resources of our fields and forests." Moreover a political purpose would be served for such people, wrote a citizen of Richmond, "by their social intercourse and votes . . . would do much to neutralize the prejudices and influence of parties inimical to the Government." When General James A. Longstreet renounced his Confederate heresies in favor of southern prosperity, Massachusetts' Ben Butler hastened to welcome him to the radical fold. If all southerners would take Longstreet's views, Butler foresaw that "harmony of feeling, community of interest, unity of action as well as homogeneity of institutions" would follow to produce national well being.

But Longstreet was almost alone in his decision to "accept the results of the war" and the military governments in the South could do little to further the North's exploitation of its southern colony. Men who had gone South for economic reasons took advantage of the changed situation to recoup their losses in politics, and others came from the North solely for the plums of office. But the Union men and northerners in the South continued to find themselves at a disadvantage. The property of loyalists was not safe in the courts, and Ben Butler soon heard appeals from the Unionists to turn the courts over to loyal men. "The Northern man will not come here unless his capital is safe," declared one of Butler's Georgia informants. From Texas it was reported that rebel leaders were growing rich but that there was no hope for Union men. On the advice of the "best financiers" Butler decided to abandon his own extensive investments in the South, although he contemplated, according to one newspaper, a bill which would prevent disfranchised rebels from holding office on railroads or chartered companies.

The New York *Commercial and Financial Chronicle*, a consistent supporter of Johnson's policy, soon found that Congressional Reconstruction was paralyzing business and unnecessarily prolonging southern industrial prostration. If Negro majorities controlled the state legislatures, the paper warned, capital would stay out of the section. Despite this analysis, the Radicals pursued their course and blamed bad conditions on President Johnson. When the Tennessee legislature met in December, 1867, Governor William G. Brownlow, the "Fighting Parson," reported that "men of capital and enterprise" had not come into the state in the expected numbers. This was due to Andrew Johnson's "insane policy" of holding out to "pestilential disloyalists" the hope that they would be restored to power. Butler agreed with this contention and declared that only a new president could insure the property rights of northerners in the South.

During the campaign of 1868 Democratic orators took pains to assert that peace and prosperity could only come through the abandonment of Congressional Reconstruction, but Republicans, saying little of the economic rehabilitation of the South, made much of the southerner's vindictiveness towards the Union men and loyal Negroes of the South. Ku Klux outrages and Democratic murders constituted the main theme of the Republicans, despite the fact that these very stories would serve as a deterrent to capital seeking southern investments. In their belief, interest in manufactures and agriculture would "supersede the excitement of the caucus" and the South would "turn all her energies to . . . developing her immense resources" as soon as the election was over. When friction ceased, business would "spring to its feet . . . manufacture . . . unchain her idle wheels," and "the cotton and rice plantations of the South . . . vie with the cornfields of the West." In the end, the business man of the North voted for the Republicans, not because he was convinced by this reasoning but because the party stood for the payment of the national debt in gold.

Republican success in the election of 1868 was widely interpreted as settling the disorders in the South. "The election of Grant and Colfax means peace," cried Tennessee's Brownlow. "It means that carpetbaggers are not to be molested in Tennessee; that capital, coming to us from abroad, whether of brains or hands, or money, is not to be spurned, prescribed, persecuted, because it comes from north of a given line." According to Horace Greeley, immigrants could now be safely invited into the country, and two-thirds of them would "go to build up the waste places of the South." Greeley also noticed that the election would insure the reconstruction of Virginia where northern capital was waiting for a favorable government before it advanced money for the completion of a railroad from the Ohio to the Chesapeake Bay. Even from ex-Confederates in the South there came echoes of the same conclusion. One Alabamian, who had served in the Confederate army and had voted against Grant, wrote to Butler that his state wanted to "induce men of capital and skill" to come in. "If you are desirous for the welfare of the South, and wish to be personally highly remunerated and at the same time become a public benefactor, you can accomplish these objects better than in any other manner by inducing your men of means and skill to invest their money and skill" in the South. John Letcher, erstwhile war-governor of Virginia, looked forward to a speedy settlement of the political controversies in order that the prosperity of his section might be assured.

President Grant entered office determined to end the conflict in the South. His first action on reconstruction was to submit the constitutions of Virginia, Texas, and Mississippi to a vote without the obnoxious clauses which disfranchised the Confederate leaders. This action was immediately hailed with satisfaction, and northern business men looked to the completion of political reconstruction as the beginning of southern prosperity. In Virginia, the Conservatives of the state rapidly formed a party pledged to the acceptance of the Fifteenth Amendment, to the development of industry, and to the encouragement of immigration. "In short," commented Greeley, "Virginia, having had enough of Civil War and devastation, is about to subordinate political strife to industrial progress and material prosperity, and thus advance to a future of power and wealth undreamed of in her past." On the eve of the Virginia election, General J. D. Imboden, who had served his state from Bull Run to Appomattox, wrote to the *Tribune* that northern men were safe and welcome in Virginia. Millions of white men were needed to develop the state's resources. There was no doubt that Virginia was succumbing to the lure of profits. In May, 1869, General Lee visited Washington on railroad business, and called at the White House to assure Grant that Virginia favored the Fifteenth Amendment and Negro suffrage!

The Virginia elections were the quietest that had taken place in the South since secession, but the resultant Conservative victory struck terror into the ranks of the radical Republican politicians. On economic issues the newly elected governor, Gilbert C. Walker, was in thorough accord with the masters of capital who were backing the Republican party in the North. His party accepted Negro suffrage and stood for the industrialization of the state, yet there was little doubt that the Virginia Conservatives would unite with the northern Democracy in national elections. Faced with this certainty, Republican politicians sought for an excuse to keep the state under military government, while Walker hurried to Washington to lay his case before Grant and to promise that the Conservatives would not recant on their promises to ratify the Fifteenth Amendment.

The dissatisfaction of the politicians with this development was soon revealed. Although the politicians represented the masters of capital who were interested in tariffs, railroads, and the exploitation of the South, they were themselves more interested in the preservation of their party in power. The only member of Grant's cabinet who was a politician was Secretary of the Treasury George S. Boutwell, who immediately declared his unalterable opposition to the Virginia results. Publicly, he counselled caution, taking, according to the disgusted Greeley, "more account of the unity and coherence of the Republican party than of the triumph of its cardinal principle." Intent upon preventing a repetition of this miscarriage Boutwell condemned the Conservative party in Mississippi and persuaded Grant to repudiate his brother-in-law, Louis Dent, whom the Conservatives had nominated for governor. So great was the pressure of the politicians that Grant yielded to their wishes in Texas and threw the weight of the administration's influence into the scales against the Conservative candidate.

Boutwell's attitude foreshadowed the imminent separation between those who would exploit the South for political advantage and those who who sought a field for economic expansion. Moderate Republicans, such as James A. Garfield, deplored the violence that existed in Texas and Mississippi at the same time they commended the peaceful reconstruction of Virginia. Radicals of the Butler stripe, on the other hand, were convinced that Virginia had deceived the Republican party. The victory of the Conservatives in Tennessee in 1869 and the action of the Georgia legislature in expelling its Negro members seemed to them sufficient indication that the South was not yet reconciled to the Union. Butler's own losses in three southern investments had convinced him that capital was not yet safe in the South.

After the election of 1868 Horace Greeley had become the principal exponent of northern infiltration into the South. In much the same manner that he had formerly urged the male youth to seek the West, he now devoted the columns of the powerful New York *Tribune* to urging groups to settle in the South. Southern land which had been worth twenty dollars an acre before the war and would soon be worth that again could be bought for one or two dollars an acre. Advising settlement in colonies, Greeley estimated that three thousand colonists in Florida, five thousand each in Alabama, Louisiana, Arkansas, and Mississippi, and ten thousand each in Virginia, North Carolina, and Texas would make the South Republican and deliver it from "the nightmare which now oppresses . . . politics and industry." Within the South, said Greeley, there was a division between two classes on the issues of reconstruction. The "landholders, merchants and men of property, with all who are inclined to industry and thrift" were opposed by a "decreasing faction of sore-heads and malignants." In issue after issue of his paper, the expansionist editor carried articles by the first class of southerners setting forth the advantages of various sections of the South for immigrants and for capital investments. As the Virginia question arose, Greeley reiterated that the South was begging for immigrants and for northern capital and a *Tribune* correspondent wandered through the South gathering details of the wealth awaiting northern enterprise. North Carolina offered cheap land, docile laborers, ample timber resources, and political peace. In South Carolina there were woolen mills and cotton factories. Tennessee had blast furnaces already established by northern capital and there were rich opportunities for investment in mines of iron, coal, zinc, and copper. The South, editorialized the *Tribune*, had shown a general willingness to come back into the Union on the Greeley platform of "universal amnesty and universal suffrage."

The fundamental issues between the politicians and the business men were clearly brought out in an open letter from Greeley to Butler. Appealing to Butler's practical sense, the editor showed that the Radical program of proscription and disfranchisement had retarded business. In reply, Butler declared that Greeley's course had encouraged the rebels so that they had gained the upper hand in Tennessee and Georgia. In these states, the people had deceived the Republican party. Conditions would have been better if a a half dozen leading rebels had been hung at the end of the war.

In the winter of 1869–70 these divergent views were advanced in the debates over the admission of Virginia and over the treatment to be accorded to recalcitrant Georgia. In the end, Virginia was admitted, although the Radicals had many misgivings. Georgia was remanded to military rule. Not even Greeley could defend the action of the "rebel element" in Georgia and both Moderates and Radicals were agreed that outrages against Republicans in the South should stop. As a means of stopping them, both elements heralded the ratification of the Fifteenth Amendment and supported the "Force Bill" of 1870 which would guarantee the right of suffrage to the Negroes. To the Radicals the martial law in Georgia and the Enforcement Act were means of getting Republican majorities in the South; to the Moderates, the hope of eventual peace carried with it the promise of a prosperous infiltration of northern business in the South. In Greeley's opinion, it was time to "have done with Reconstruction." "The country is . . . sick of it," he added. "So long as any State is held in abeyance, it will be plausibly urged that the Republicans are afraid to trust the People. Let us give every State to herself, and then punish any who violate or defy the guaranties of public and personal rights now firmly imbedded in the Constitution."

Although Moderates and Radicals had agreed on the Fifteenth Amendment and the Enforcement Act there were differences between them on the method to be pursued in the future. Radical politicians of the school of Conkling, Morton, Chandler, and Butler looked to the power of the president to enforce the law, while Greeley and the Moderates continued to appeal to the South's hopes of prosperity as a means of producing peace. The advantages of immigration, the possibility of industrial development, and the potentialities of the South's mineral wealth were constantly kept before the southerners.

Despite Greeley's appeals, the majority of the southern states offered few inducements to northern migrants. The competition of western lands prevented new agricultural groups entering the South, while cases of violence were constantly reported which discouraged those who might have thought of carrying their capital into southern industry. Greeley's Washington correspondent suspected that most of the outrage stories were "manufactured and published in the North to further the personal designs of unscrupulous and ambitious men." Yet a *Tribune* agent in the South in the summer of 1870 found the Ku Klux in undeniable operation. Throughout the congressional campaigns the North was flooded with atrocity stories, and a congressional investigation in the succeeding winter gave ample evidence that the Klan was terrorizing the South. The result of these outrages was the passage of two more acts which would keep the South orderly: the Federal Elections Act of February 28, and the Ku Klux Act of April 20, 1871.

In contemplating the southern scene, Moderates found themselves forced to admit that violence and political murders prevented business recovery and impelled the government to take action. Greeley, however, continued to advise moderation and amnesty as a more suitable means of inducing the southerners to accept a real economic reconstruction. In Congress, Garfield doubted the constitutionality of the "Force Acts" and declared that the legislation was "working on the very edge of the Constitution." Nevertheless, he found that a "kind of party terrorism" forced all Republicans to vote for the measures. To J. D. Cox, Grant's former secretary of the interior, it seemed that Congress was pursuing the wrong course in attempting to conquer the South. "Capital and intelligence must lead," he told Garfield. "Only Butler and W. Philips would make a wilderness and call it peace." The party should organize and appeal to the "thinking and influential native Southerners"—the "intelligent, well-to-do, and controlling class" of southern whites.

Soon after the passage of the Ku Klux Act, Greeley sent correspondents into the South to study conditions. The reporters found that the Klan was overrunning South Carolina, but that the carpetbaggers, who were levying high taxes upon industry and wealth, were giving partial justification for the outrages. Late in May, Greeley himself traveled through the Southwest to speak on the glories of industry at the Texas State Fair. The New Yorker's speeches inspired the editor of the New Orleans *Price Current* to comment that the industrial doctrines of Greeley and Seward had conquered the South. "It is the true duty of the South," declared the New Orleans editor, "to cultivate all those industries the want of which has enslaved her." But Greeley had concluded from his observations that the South would not be prosperous until the carpetbaggers with their taxes and the Ku Klux with its violence had both been driven out. The South, said Greeley, was suffering from "decayed aristocracy and imported rascality."

From the time of his southern trip Greeley was a candidate for the presidency. From what he had seen in the South, however, he changed his earlier ideas that capital would enter the South. The high taxes which the carpetbag and negro governments had imposed was sufficient to prevent the migration of capital, but the editor believed that prosperity might yet come through the efforts of the southerners themselves. There were millions of acres in the South which might be sold to immigrants, and the proceeds devoted to the development of local resources. The primary needs of the South, as Greeley came to see it, were more people, more skill, more energy, and greater thrift. The South did not need more capital than would naturally flow into it if the people should use their available resources. To his earlier program of universal amnesty and universal suffrage, the editor added the proposal that the South should work out its own salvation by encouraging northern immigration and, by driving out carpetbaggers, make a land free from oppressive taxes upon industry.

Opposed to these ideas, which were politically adopted by the Liberal Republicans, the regular Republicans insisted upon the necessity of maintaining control of the politics of the southern states in order to protect migrating capital and people. Social ostracism and personal violence, said President Grant in his message of 1871, prevented "immigration and the flow of much-needed capital into the States lately in rebellion." The South, echoed the New York *Times* in the midst of the campaign, needed local governments which would protect citizens. Only the Republican party could assure solid achievement and national prosperity and "restrain with firmness any resistance to the new order of things." The South had always depended upon outside capital and the war had destroyed whatever accumulation might have existed. "Industry is sluggish, trade creeps from point to point, manufactures are feeble and few," cried the administration journal as it

demanded a continuation of the policy which held out "every encouragement
. . . to Northern and foreign capitalists." As the campaign went on Greeley's
*Tribune* carried more items concerning available southern farm lands and
showed that "had it not been for carpetbag mismanagement, this country
today would be filled with millions of Northern or foreign yeomanry carving
out farms, or working in . . . iron, copper, coal, and marble." At the same
time, Secretary Boutwell went into North Carolina to sing the praises of the
carpetbaggers, and assure the North Carolinians that neither immigrants nor
capital could be safe in Democratic regions. "The business men of the
South," wrote a carpetbagger to the Republican National Committee, "want
stability in business, which the election of Greeley . . . will not insure."

Although other factors combined to prevent Greeley's election, his
southern program had made considerable impression on the voters. The
carpetbaggers had received much unfavorable publicity during the campaign, and the idea that the friction between the races in the South was
caused by dishonest adventurers who drove out industry, was widely spread
over the North. In the next few years the horrors of carpetbaggery were to
be proclaimed by the "liberal" and Democratic press until the masters of
capital were convinced that only the removal of this "swarm of locusts"
would make possible the economic exploitation of the section.

At the close of the election, Greeley sadly turned to advise the southerners to accept the situation, and "set to work to build up their section's
industrial and commercial prosperity." This advice, said the defeated candidate, would sound harsh to men who were unable to pay the enormous
taxes imposed by the carpetbaggers. How little encouragement the South
might receive from the government in such an effort was evident from the
attitude of the administration press. The New York *Times* ridiculed Greeley's
efforts to advise his supporters, and the administration organ in Washington
announced that the South was responsible for any misfortunes which had
come upon it. Acceptance of Republicanism, the paper implied, was the only
hope for the section.

The country had not long to wait for the development of the Republican policy in the South. Following immediately upon the election there
ensued a struggle between two groups of carpetbaggers for the control of
Louisiana. Although President Grant attempted to remain impartial between
the contending factions, the New York *Tribune*, continuing its rôle as the
Bible of the industrialists, lost no opportunity to point out the intimate
connection between Republican policies and the disordered commonwealth.
It spoke feelingly about the "plundered community," showed that its government was founded upon fraud, and declared that the dispute "prostitutes
the business of the State." Louisiana finances were kept before the eye of
the northern people, and the "moneyed interests of the country" were
warned against investments in a state whose governor could sell its railroad

interests without consulting the legislature and which had a debt of twenty-four millions.

At the same time that Louisiana was troubling the political waters other points of the South were contributing testimony to the economic derangements attendant upon carpetbag governments. In Arkansas there were quarrels between factions of the Republican party comparable to those in Louisiana, whilst the debts and taxes of the state were rising. The *Tribune* published a traveller's account of the corruption and the absurdities of the "prostrate State" of South Carolina where a handful of unscrupulous whites controlled the Negro legislature. If anything were needed to impress the lesson it was furnished by the condition in the District of Columbia. At the beginning of reconstruction, Congress had granted the suffrage to the Negroes of the District. Designed as an experiment to show the capacity of the Negro for citizenship, it soon showed the reverse. Under "Boss" Shepherd's direction the Negroes voted for new bond issues and went to the polls to approve the valiant plans which the District governor was making to pull the capital city out of the mud. But the property holders and tax payers of the District, outvoted by the Negroes, ignored the improvements to gaze with horrible forebodings upon the mounting debt. This was sufficiently close to the northern voter and tax payer to clarify his view on the Radical program in the South. Perhaps an underlying fear, which few dared to express, was the danger which was involved in the rising movement of the lower classes throughout the country. The Granger movement in the West was assailing the citadels of private monopoly, and there was a conceivable connection between these elements and the "bottom rails" who had gotten on top in the South. Two years before, one observer had noticed that there were six thousand native adult whites in Georgia "who cannot read or write, and if to them were added the whole bulk of the Negro population, so vast a mass of ignorance would be found that, if combined for any political purpose it would sweep away all opposition the intelligent class might make. Many thoughtful men are apprehensive that the ignorant voters will, in the future, form a party by themselves as dangerous to the interests of society as the communists of France."

Evidence of a growing reaction in the North came simultaneously with these troubles in the South. In May, 1873, Senator Matt Carpenter, long a supporter of the extreme Radical position, visited Louisiana with a congressional committee. To the people of New Orleans the Wisconsin Senator promised a better government and urged that they turn their attention from politics to trade and business. Eugene Hale, a member of Congress from Maine, presiding over his state's Republican convention, announced that he was "tired and sick of some of the carpet-bag governments." Generally, men were coming to the belief that the poverty of the southern states was due to the villainies of the carpetbaggers, and they were coming to perceive that this had a national significance. The "withdrawal of taxes, which the Southern States might pay under favorable circumstances, throws just that additional burden upon the tax-paying property of the North," announced the *Tribune*. Even George F. Hoar came to admit that the character of the carpetbaggers was such that they would not have been tolerated in the North.

With the development of a sentiment of opposition to the carpetbaggers, there came a new hope that a change of policy might throw the South open for migration of capital and for manufacturing. Surveying the situation, it was noticed that only South Carolina and Louisiana were still in 1873 oppressed by excessive taxes, while the other states might welcome northern mills and factories. Virginia, for example, had accepted reconstruction, avoided carpetbaggers, and proceeded forward steadily in industrial development. The lesson was obvious—if the government abandoned its policy of upholding carpetbaggers, prosperity would come to the South. Propositions for moving New England cotton mills to the South were reported and discussed in the press and on the floors of Congress. Even southerners took a new hope from the renewed discussion of capital moving South.

Standing in the way of a change of policy stood the fact that stories of southern outrages had been the stock in trade of the Radicals since 1866 and the politicians had no thought of abandoning so profitable a source of political ammunition. But even the "outrage business" received a death blow in the congressional campaign of 1874. In the midst of the campaign an Alabama congressman published a list of murders and acts of violence which had recently taken place in his state. Long suspicious of such stories, the New York *Tribune* immediately investigated and found no substantial basis for the congressman's charges. Thereafter the accumulating atrocity stories were received dubiously by the northern people. However, the southern carpetbaggers were merely goaded into action by this exposure and a hastily called convention of Republican politicians assembled in Chattanooga to prepare an authentic list of atrocities for the benefit of the northern voter and to convince Congress that further protection should be given at elections. But the convention proved abortive. While a number of the delegates came prepared to contribute atrocity stories and demand more federal interference, a larger number were found to have come to the convention to prevent a "new flood of misrepresentations" which would "frighten men and capital from their neglected fields and factories." This latter class was composed of men who had become identified with the material interests of the South. Delegates from North Carolina were ready to declare that they had not heard of a political assault in their state for more than a year. The convention appointed a committee on "Facts and Statistics" which never reported, and passed general resolutions asserting that violence toward loyal men was common, but the total effect of their meeting was to give the South a clean bill of health. With the "outrage" business played out, the Republicans were deprived of their leading arguments for continuing in power, while the Democrats and the Liberal Republicans insisted that business was injured by the plundering governments of the southern states. Testimony was sedulously gathered by the *Tribune* to show that there were no outrages in Tennessee or Kentucky and that migrating capital was safe in those states.

The eventual victory of those who preferred the economic to the political exploitation of the South was foreshadowed in the election returns. The Democrats won control of Congress, and Republican politicians turned to a new stock taking. "We have got a hard lot from the South," said Postmaster-General Marshall Jewell as he surveyed the carpetbag governments, "and the people will not submit to it any longer, nor do I blame them." To Jewell's mind the carpetbaggers did not have "among them one really first class man." A consul in Germany thought it "too d—d bad that our party should be ruined and have to go to the wall through the careless labors of such cattle" as the Louisiana carpetbaggers. But, said this observer, the people were "tired out with this wornout cry of 'Southern Outrages!!!' Hard times and heavy taxes make them wish the 'nigger' 'everlasting nigger' were in — or Africa. . . . It is amazing the change that has taken place in the last two years in public sentiment." Even Vice-President Wilson concluded that the Republican party would have to change its policy, and noticed, after a trip through the South, that business conditions had improved and a spirit of industry was spreading among the southern whites. Wisconsin's Senator Howe ruefully regarded the wreck of Republican hopes and suddenly remembered that the war was not "fought for the 'nigger'" and the Negro was not "the end and aim of all our effort."

The congressional elections of 1874 marked the abandonment of political reconstruction by the northern voters. The repudiated Radicals continued their course until after they had delivered the presidency to Hayes, but the popular vote in the North was cast in 1876 for Tilden and for a different method of exploiting the South. With the withdrawal of the federal troops from the South, the masters of capital embarked upon a policy of conciliating their former enemies and of slow infiltration into their conquered but stubborn provinces.

A single glimpse at the situation a decade later will suffice to illustrate the new technique which the North came to employ in dealing with the South. In 1885 young William McKinley went to plead with the people of Virginia to send a protectionist to the Senate. "Do you imagine that anybody is coming to Virginia with his money to build a mill, or a factory, or a furnace, and develop your coal and your ore, bring his money down here, when you vote every time against his interests. . . .?" he asked. "If you think so, you might just as well be undeceived now, for they will not come. . . .

Be assured that the Republicans of the North harbor no resentments—only ask for the results of the war. They wish you the highest prosperity and the greatest development." The change from the method of coercion to that of appeal was great, but the hope was still alive that in spite of the abandonment of political reconstruction the South would receive the master of capital with his promises of prosperity.

James M. McPherson

# Reconstruction:
# A Revolution Manqué

More than forty years ago Charles Beard, one of the country's leading historians, described the Civil War era as the Second American Revolution. Beard maintained that Northern victory transferred political and economic power from the old Southern planter aristocracy to the new Northern industrial plutocracy and set in motion the explosive economic growth of the last third of the nineteenth century. Whatever the validity of Beard's argument (it has been challenged by several economic historians), there is no doubt that in the field of race relations the Civil War and Reconstruction did produce revolutionary changes. In a period of less than ten years, four million slaves were emancipated by the force of arms, enfranchised by the national government, and granted equal civil and political rights by the United States Constitution. But this was an aborted revolution; the promise of racial equality was never fully implemented even during Reconstruction; and after 1877, black Americans were gradually repressed into second-class citizenship, from which they are emerging slowly and painfully in our own time. This essay will try to describe the potential revolution of racial equality a century ago and to analyze the reasons for its failure.

Northern war aims evolved through three stages during the Civil War. The earliest and most important war aim, of course, was restoration of the Union. Until late in 1862 this meant the Union "as it was"—with slavery still in it. The North did not go to war to abolish slavery, and it took more

From "The Civil War and Reconstruction: A Revolution of Racial Equality" by James M. McPherson in Seven on Black edited by William G. Shade and Roy C. Herrenkohl (J. B. Lippincott). Copyright © 1969 by William G. Shade and Roy C. Herrenkohl. Reprinted by permission of Harper & Row, Publishers, Inc.

than a year of discussion and agitation to bring the government to a policy of emancipation. Despite his own abhorrence of slavery, Abraham Lincoln was sensitive to the pressures of proslavery conservatives in the North and the need to keep the border slave states in the Union. The election of 1860 had shown that most Northerners, although opposed to the expansion of slavery into new territories, were not in favor of abolishing it where it already existed. The Constitution protected slavery; and Lincoln hoped that he could bring about restoration of the Union constitutionally with a demonstration of federal force and a short war, followed by political negotiations and compromise.

But there were a good many people in the North who wanted to make emancipation a second war aim. These abolitionists (black and white), and Radical Republicans, believed that slavery had caused the war and that Union victory was impossible without elimination of this festering sore. The Radicals, joined by a growing number of moderates, argued with telling effect that emancipation was a military necessity. They pointed out that the 3½ million slaves in the Confederacy constituted more than one-third of its population, raised most of the food and fiber for the South, and did most of the digging, hauling, and construction work for the Confederate army. A blow against slavery would cripple the Southern war effort and attract thousands of freed blacks to the side of the North, where they could work and fight, not only for their own freedom, but for the Union as well.

The military necessity thesis was the most compelling argument for emancipation, but abolitionists also emphasized political and moral considerations. Politically, an antislavery policy would strengthen the Union's diplomatic efforts to keep Great Britain from helping the South, for English public opinion would not tolerate its government's intervention on the side of slavery against freedom. The Radicals also pointed out that even if the Union could be restored by negotiation and compromise, slavery would remain a source of future strife. There could be no internal peace in America, they argued, while four million people were in bondage. Moreover, the North professed to be fighting for the preservation of democratic government; the national anthem declared the Union to be the "land of the free and the home of the brave." But the Northern policy of fighting for the restoration of a slave-holding Union, said the abolitionists, made a mockery of this profession.

By 1862, mainly as a result of developments in the war itself, these arguments began to gain converts. The Confederacy won most of the major battles in the first seventeen months of the war, and a serious danger of British intervention on the side of the South existed in 1862. War weariness and defeatism lowered Northern morale. Lincoln's conservative policy toward slavery alienated the Radical wing of his party. As these pressures built up Lincoln and the Republican Congress took timid and then decisive action against slavery in the second year of the war. Congress passed a series of antislavery and confiscation acts, and in September of 1862 the President issued a preliminary Emancipation Proclamation, stating that all the slaves in states still in rebellion on January 1, 1863, would be freed. The South was still in rebellion on that date, so Lincoln issued his final Emancipation Proclamation. Henceforth, the North officially fought for freedom as well as Union.

Thus the second war aim was proclaimed, to be confirmed by Northern victory and the adoption of the Thirteenth Amendment in 1865. Well before the end of the war, however, Radicals began calling for a third war aim: civil equality for the freedmen. The antislavery ideals of abolitionists and Radical Republicans envisioned not only freedom for black people, but a positive guarantee of equal rights as well. Gradually, fitfully, haltingly, and with doubtful conviction, the North groped toward a commitment to equality as its third war aim; but never was equality so important an objective as Union and emancipation. Many Northerners who supported or accepted emancipation as a military necessity were notably unenthusiastic about this third war aim. It is necessary, not only for a comprehension of the Civil War and Reconstruction but also of the race problem in our own time, to understand the incomplete and halting efforts a century ago to implement equality and the reasons why they failed.

The first step toward equality was the enlistment of black men in the Union army. As Frederick Douglass put it: "Once let the black man get upon his person the brass letters, *U.S.*, let him get an eagle on his button, and a musket on his shoulder and bullets in his pocket, and there is no power on earth which can deny that he has earned the right to citizenship." Undertaken tentatively as an experiment late in 1862, the employment of Negro soldiers proved a success and was prosecuted on a full scale in the last two years of the war. In a sense, this result was a logical outgrowth of emancipation; for one of the purposes of freeing the slaves was to deprive the Confederacy of a vital manpower resource and utilize that resource for the Union, not only by getting black men to dig trenches and haul supplies for the Northern armies (the sort of work slaves did for the South), but by putting them into uniform to fight for Union and freedom.

Despite the initial skepticism of many Northerners, including President Lincoln, black men demonstrated impressive fighting qualities. In a series of battles all over the South in the last two years of war, Negro troopers proved their courage and determination. Thirty-eight black regiments fought in the Union armies that invaded Virginia in 1864, helping to deliver the hammer blows that finally drove Lee's forces to surrender. Negroes were the first soldiers to enter Charleston and Richmond when these important strongholds fell late in the war. By the time the war was over, about 180,000 black men, most of them former slaves, had fought for the Union army, and another 25,000 had served in the navy. More than 37,000 black soldiers lost their lives in the defense of union and freedom. Twenty-one Negroes won Congressional Medals of Honor for their courage on the field of battle. Black troops numbered nearly 10 percent of the total Union forces and constituted an even higher percentage of the Northern armies in the final, decisive year of war. As early as August 1863 General Ulysses S. Grant and President Lincoln declared that the enlistment of black regiments was "the heaviest blow yet dealt to the rebellion." After the war was over, the influential New York *Tribune* said that the use of Negro troops had shortened the war by a year. The performance of black soldiers earned new respect for their race, made emancipation secure, and helped push the North toward a commitment to equality. The contribution of the Negro to the Union war effort created a debt that could be paid only by granting full citizenship to the race.

The drive for equal rights began in the North itself. Before the war, black men did not enjoy first-class citizenship in most Northern states. Several states had "black laws" that barred Negroes from immigration into the state, prohibited testimony by blacks against whites in courts, and otherwise discriminated against people with dark skin. In many parts of the North public accommodations, transportation facilities, hotels, and theaters were off-limits to Negroes. During the war black soldiers were thrown off the horse-drawn streetcars of Washington, Philadelphia, and New York on several occasions. Public schools in most parts of the North were segregated, and in some areas black children were barred from schools altogether. Blacks in Northern cities were frequently threatened by mob violence. In 1862 and 1863 white workingmen, fearful that emancipation would bring a horde of freedmen northward to compete for jobs, killed scores of Negroes in several urban race riots, climaxed by the New York Draft Riots of July 1863.

But the impetus of emancipation and the reputation of black soldiers began to break down racial discrimination in the North. Blacks were admitted to Congressional galleries and to White House receptions for the first time in 1864. A Negro lawyer was granted a license to present cases before the Supreme Court of the United States in 1865, just eight years after Roger B. Taney, as Chief Justice, had declared, in the Dred Scott decision, that black men had no rights that white men were bound to respect. Congress passed a series of laws forbidding discrimination against Negroes in the federal courts, the post office department, and on Washington streetcars. Northern states with "black laws" repealed them during, or shortly after, the war. In the postwar decades many states took even greater steps toward equal rights. Massachusetts passed a public accommodations law in 1865. Several other states followed suit in the 1870s and 1880s. Most Northern states abolished de jure school segregation. This equalitarian legislation was honored more in the breach than in practice, and a great deal of discrimination remained in the North despite the laws, but at least a beginning was made.

The question of Negro suffrage became the major issue of Reconstruction. The right to vote is a basic right of citizenship in a democracy, and the issue of black voters, especially in the South, where Negroes were a majority of the population in three states and a minority of more than 40 percent in three others, generated more conflict, controversy, and dissension than any other single question in the fifteen years after the Civil War. By the end of 1865, most members of the Radical wing of the Republican party were committed to some kind of effort to secure equal voting rights for the freedmen; and by 1867, the moderate majority of the party had also come around to this position.

The prospect of Negro suffrage presented a good many practical difficulties. The four million freedmen were for the most part illiterate, penniless, and totally without political experience. The institution of slavery had crippled the self-reliance, initiative, pride, and manhood of many Negroes. The black people emerging from slavery did not have the social, economic, and educational resources to make themselves the instant equals of their old masters.

Although Radical Republicans were concerned about these problems, most of them suppressed their doubts and emphasized the positive arguments for Negro suffrage as a cornerstone of Reconstruction. The very logic of the Union war effort seemed to require the granting of equal citizenship to the Negro, who had fought not only for his own freedom but for the cause of the North. To have sloughed off these important allies into second-class citizenship would have been a repudiation of the debt that many people thought the Union owed the black man. Moreover, as a practical matter, it became clear that the freedmen would need the ballot to protect their basic civil rights. Republicans feared that if emancipated slaves were left without political power they would be reduced to some form of quasi-slavery or serfdom. The "black codes" passed by most Southern states in the months after the war confirmed this fear. Some of these codes required the arrest of black vagrants (the question of vagrancy to be determined by white sheriffs) and their lease for specified periods of time to white planters, apprenticed black children to white "masters" in certain circumstances, prohibited Negroes in some states from buying or renting land, or in other ways fastened a subordinate legal status upon the freedmen. The black codes presented the Radicals with dramatic evidence of the need for federal protection and political rights for the freedmen.

Many Republicans also feared that if the Southern states were readmitted to the Union without Negro suffrage, they would send Democratic congressmen to Washington and reduce the Republican party once again to to a minority party. Thus the ballot for freedmen became something of a political necessity for the Republicans. But it was not only expediency or partisanship that motivated Republican thinking on this issue. Most Southern Democrats and a sizable proportion of their Northern brethren had been Confederates or Confederate sympathizers. They had fought a bitter war to destroy the Union and preserve slavery, causing 350,000 Northern deaths. Thus it was easy, and not entirely specious, for Northern Republicans (and most Northern voters) to identify the Democratic party with treason and the Republican party with union and freedom. The Northern mood of 1865–69 would not stand for any policy that readmitted the Democratic South to the Union with undiminished political power, thereby "letting the fruits of victory slip from our grasp." In such circumstances, the enfranchisement of the freedmen (who were expected, with good reason, to vote Republican) was patriotic as well as good politics for the Republicans.

There was also a punitive motive for Negro suffrage. Many Northerners, bitter toward "traitors" and "rebels," wanted to destroy the political basis of the Southern "aristocracy" they believed had caused the war and punish the Confederates by temporarily disfranchising them and permanently enfranchising their former slaves, thereby destroying the old political power structure of the South and creating a new Republican coalition of unionist whites and black freedmen.

Thus, for a variety of reasons, including equalitarianism, patriotism, political partisanship, and bitterness, the Radical wing of the Republican party pushed for enfranchisement of the freedmen as the cornerstone of their Reconstruction policy. In some cases this required political courage by Republicans who represented districts where racism was still a potent force. Despite the changes in Northern attitudes toward the Negro caused by the war, latent, and often overt, prejudice was still widespread. Blacks could not vote in most Northern states at the end of the war; many white voters, in spite of their hatred of the South, disliked the prospect of black equality and feared that freedmen's suffrage would be a major step toward equal rights in the North as well as in the South. For this reason, as well as their skepticism about the freedmen's qualifications for the ballot, moderate Republicans (a majority in the party) shied away from Negro suffrage in 1865–66 and tried to find a middle ground between black enfranchisement and readmission of the South with no federal protection at all for the freedmen. Their solution was the Fourteenth Amendment to the Constitution, proposed in 1866, which guaranteed citizenship and civil rights to the freedmen and reduced the representation of Southern states in Congress by the proportion of their adult male citizens who could not vote. Thus the South's political power was reduced, while an inducement was offered for voluntary enfranchisement of the freedmen.

This moderate proposal was sabotaged by President Andrew Johnson and by the short-sighted intransigence of the South. Johnson was a Tennessee Democrat, who remained loyal to the Union during the war and was rewarded with the 1864 vice-presidential nomination of the "Union Party," a wartime coalition of Republicans and War Democrats. After Lincoln's assassination, Johnson gradually gravitated back to his Democratic allegiance, urged the readmission of the Southern states with minimum conditions, and defied the policy of the Republican majority in Congress. With remarkable political ineptitude, Johnson vetoed moderate Congressional legislation, encouraged the Southern states to refuse ratification of the Fourteenth Amendment, alienated the moderate Republicans, and drove them closer to the Radical wing of the party. In the 1866 Congressional elections the Northern voters overwhelmingly repudiated Johnson's policies and gave the Republicans a mandate to push through their Reconstruction program over the President's vetoes.

In the spring of 1867, Congress passed a series of Reconstruction Acts that provided for military administration of the South until new state constitutions could be drawn up instituting universal manhood suffrage. Only after the state governments elected under these constitutions had ratified the Fourteenth Amendment would their representatives be readmitted to Congress. By the end of 1868, eight of the former Confederate states had been restored to the Union under these conditions; in 1869 Congress adopted the Fifteenth Amendment, prohibiting voting discrimination on grounds of race, and required the remaining three Southern states to ratify it before returning to the Union. By 1870, all the ex-Confederate states were under Republican control, with several black officeholders; the Fourteenth and Fifteenth Amendments were in the Constitution; the Union was restored; and the third Northern war aim of equality was achieved.

Or was it? Despite appearances, Radical Reconstruction rested on a weak foundation. During the 1870s the foundation gradually crumbled, and the walls came tumbling down. The framework of the Fourteenth and Fifteenth Amendments remained in the Constitution, to become the basis for the Negro Revolution of the mid-twentieth century; but in the 1870s the nation failed to carry out the promises of equality contained in these amendments.

There were several reasons for this failure. In the first place, most Northern whites were only superficially committed to the equalitarian purposes of Reconstruction, and many were openly hostile. From 1865 to 1869 there was a temporary radicalization of Northern public opinion that made possible the passage of Reconstruction measures enfranchising the freedmen, but this was the result more of war-born anti-Southern sentiment than of genuine pro-Negro feeling. In 1867, when the Reconstruction Acts instituted Negro suffrage in the South, black men could vote in only seven of the twenty Northern states and in none of the four border states. Several times, from 1865 to 1868, Northern voters rejected Negro suffrage amendments to their own state constitutions. Not until the Fifteenth Amendment went into effect in 1870, three years after the Southern freedmen had been enfranchised, did most Negroes in the North have the right to vote. The Northern hostility or indifference to equal rights betokened ill success for an equalitarian Reconstruction policy, which required a strong national commitment if it was to succeed.

A second reason for the failure of Reconstruction was the bitter, sometimes violent, and always well-organized opposition of most Southern whites. Confederate veterans, accustomed to the use of violence to attain political ends, formed such organizations as the Ku Klux Klan, the White League, the Red Shirts, and numerous "rifle clubs" to terrorize Republicans, especially black Republicans, as a means of breaking down and destroying the party in the South. The federal government made several efforts between 1870 and 1874 to enforce equal rights against this Southern counterrevolution. The "Ku Klux Act" of 1871 gave the President sweeping powers to use the armed forces and courts to suppress white terrorist organizations; and this law, when enforced vigorously in 1871–72, was successful in temporarily quelling Southern anti-Republican violence. But a combination of factors after 1873 caused a decline in federal enforcement efforts: Financial depression, which diverted national attention to economic issues; Democratic victory in the Congressional elections of 1874; adverse Supreme Court decisions that stripped enforcement legislation of much of its power; and growing Northern disillusionment with the whole experiment of Reconstruction, which produced diminishing enthusiasm among Republicans for the party's Southern policy. Actually, even with the best of intentions, the federal government could not have completely suppressed the Ku Klux Klan and its sister organizations, since the number of troops in the army was inadequate for the purpose and most of the regiments were on the frontier fighting Indians.

Another dimension of Southern white resistance was the refusal or inability of many property-owning whites (and whites owned most of the property) to pay taxes to the "alien" Republican state governments. During Reconstruction most of the Southern states built public school systems almost from scratch, constructed new charitable and welfare institutions, and undertook ambitious programs of railroad building, aided by state grants and loans. All of this cost money, more money than the South had been accustomed to paying for public and social services, more than property owners were willing or able to pay in taxes, especially when they were opposed, as some of them were, to such innovations as public schools or when they believed that much of the revenue went into the pockets of corrupt officials. The Southern state governments, in some cases, were too weak or unstable to compel payment of taxes, and the resulting deficits were another reason for the collapse of Republican regimes as the 1870s wore on.

A third reason for the failure of Reconstruction was the illiteracy, inexperience, and poverty of the freedmen. It had been illegal to teach slaves (and free blacks, in some states) to read or write. The institution of slavery trained black people to dependence and denied them the opportunity and responsibilities of freedom. It would have been criminal of the North merely to emancipate the slaves, give them equal rights on paper, and then say: "All right, you're on your own—root hog, or die." And to the credit of some Northern people and the federal government, efforts were made to educate and assist the freedmen in their difficult transition from slavery to freedom. In one of the major outpourings of idealism and missionary zeal in American history, freedmen's aid societies in the North sent thousands of teachers to the South to bring literacy to the Negroes. The federal government created the Freedmen's Bureau in 1865. More than a thousand freedmen's schools, supported by Northern philanthropy and aided by the Bureau, were in operation by 1870; and the new public school system of the South was built on the foundation provided by these mission schools. After 1870, the missionary societies concentrated their efforts on secondary schools and colleges to train the teachers, ministers, and leaders of the new black generation. The major institutions of higher learning for Negroes evolved out of these freedmen's schools: Howard, Fisk, and Atlanta Universities; Morehouse, Spelman, and Talladega Colleges; Hampton Institute; Meharry Medical College; and many others. But despite the admirable efforts of the crusade for freedmen's education, 70 percent of Southern blacks were still illiterate in 1880. An effective crash program to educate and train four million freed slaves would have required a far greater commitment of national resources than was undertaken. The mission societies did their best; but after the expiration of the Freedmen's Bureau in 1870, they received no more federal aid. Black Southerners remained at a large educational disadvantage in their relations with white Southerners.

Another facet of the black man's disadvantage was his poverty. Most emancipated slaves owned little more than the clothes on their backs when freedom came. Unless they received some kind of massive economic assistance, it was clear they would remain an economically subordinate class, dependent on whites for employment. Many abolitionists and Radical Republicans believed that there must be an economic reconstruction of the South if civil and political reconstruction were to succeed. The great abolitionist orator, Wendell Phillips, Congressman Thaddeus Stevens, and others urged the adoption of a thorough program of land reform as a basis of Reconstruction. They called for the confiscation of plantations owned by former Confederates, and the redistribution of the land in forty-acre plots to the freedmen. But this proposal threatened the sanctity of private property as a basis of society and was too radical for most Northerners. A small amount of Confederate property was expropriated during the war, and some of these lands found their way to black ownership; but there was no major program of agrarian reform. Most blacks became wage-earners, sharecroppers, or tenant farmers, rather than independent landowning farmers. The South was not reconstructed economically, and consequently political reconstruction rested on an unstable foundation.

Because of educational and economic disadvantages, black people lacked the social and psychological resources to sustain their equal rights in the face of Southern white counterrevolution. This is not to deny that there were effective Negro leaders during Reconstruction. In fact, one of the remarkable things about the era was that this largely uneducated and propertyless people could produce such a group of able leaders. Twenty black men were elected to the national House of Representatives and two to the Senate after the war. Several Negroes served as lieutenant governors, secretaries of state, superintendents of education, and treasurers of Southern states. No black man was elected governor, but one Negro lieutenant-governor, Pinckney B. S. Pinchback, served for a month as acting Governor of Louisiana. Blanche K. Bruce was an outstanding black senator from Mississippi; Robert B. Elliott, of South Carolina, and John R. Lynch, of Mississippi, were talented black congressmen. These men and others provided strong leadership for their race, but they could not overcome the determined white power structure. At least 100,000 black veterans of the Union army lived in the South during Reconstruction. Republican state governors enrolled many of them in state militia regiments to protect the freedmen's rights against terrorism. But there were four or five times as many white veterans of the Confederate army in the South, many of them enrolled in the Ku Klux Klan and similar organizations. These men were better armed and better led than the black militiamen; and in the pitched battles of the violence-wracked years of Reconstruction, the white para-military groups usually prevailed.

One other major reason for the failure of Reconstruction was the instability of the coalition called the Republican Party in the South. This coalition was composed of a small number of Northern whites ("carpetbaggers"), Southern whites ("scalawags"), and the freedmen. Some of the carpetbaggers and scalawags deserved the pejorative connotations of these words, invented by their opponents, but others were honest, sincere men who wanted to make interracial democracy work. Inevitably there was friction among the three components of the Republican coalition. Native white Republicans shared some of the region's dislike for "outsiders," and there were power struggles within the Republican Party that pitted carpetbagger against scalawag. Though blacks provided most of the Republican votes, whites held most of the offices, which produced a growing demand by Negro leaders for greater representation and power in party councils. Many scalawags could not transcend their Southern upbringing and were uncomfortable in a predominantly black party, especially when blacks tried to move into positions of power. Some of the carpetbaggers also had difficulty transcending deeply ingrained racial prejudices. The Southern Democrats, increasingly united and strong under the banner of "home rule and white supremacy," took advantage of racial and other tensions in the Republican Party, and, by a combination of inducements and threats, brought many scalawags over from the "black Republicans" to the "white man's party." The unstable Republican coalition broke into squabbling factions in several Southern states in the 1870s, making it easier for the Democrats, aided by the terrorization of black voters, to gain control of one state after another.

How did the North react to crumbling Republican power in the South? Many Northerners had hoped that with the passage of the Reconstruction Acts and adoption of the Fourteenth and Fifteenth Amendments, the task of restoring the South to the Union and ensuring equal rights would be completed. The North wanted to turn its attention to other issues. As reports of corruption, conflict, and violence filtered up from the South, however, it was clear that Reconstruction was not yet accomplished, and that continuous and vigorous national effort would be required to maintain Negro rights against Southern counterrevolution. But disillusionment and indifference sapped the Northern will. As early as 1870, Horace Greeley's New York *Tribune*, which had been one of the foremost advocates of Radical Reconstruction a few years earlier, declared that it was time to "have done with Reconstruction. The country is sick of it." In the 1870s, *The Nation*, an independent liberal weekly with great influence among Northern intellectuals, became increasingly disenchanted with the results of Negro suffrage. *The Nation* declared that the Republican state governments of South Carolina and Louisiana were "a gang of robbers making war on civilization and morality," and concluded that the average black man "as regards the right performance of a voter's duty is as ignorant as a horse or a sheep." By 1876, *The Nation* had decided that the North should never have attempted "the insane task of making newly-emancipated field hands, led by barbers and barkeepers, fancy they knew as much about government and were as capable of administering it, as the whites."

Many Northern journalists visited the South during the 1870s and wrote feature stories that were increasingly sympathetic to the white viewpoint. James Shepherd Pike, a reporter for the New York *Tribune*, gathered his articles into a book published in 1874 with the title *The Prostrate State: South Carolina Under Negro Government*. This book and others portrayed a South ruled and ruined by "Carpetbag-Negro government." Under the impact of this journalistic barrage, Northern public opinion gradually became indifferent, and even hostile, to the plight of freedmen and Republicans in the South. There was a growing consensus that Reconstruction was a mistake, that the federal government ought to cease its "misguided efforts" to enforce equal rights in the South, and that the Southern people should be left alone to work out the race problem on their own terms. "The whole public are tired of these annual autumnal outbreaks in the South," wrote the United States Attorney General, in refusing a request from the Republican Governor of Mississippi for federal troops to protect Negro voters in 1875. Mississippi was captured by the Democrats in the election, and the Attorney General's remark symbolized Northern indifference to this development.

Widespread reports of Republican corruption, incompetence, and misgovernment were one of the most important factors in turning Northern opinion against Reconstruction. It would be foolish to deny that there was corruption in the South. Like all myths, the myth of greedy, rapacious carpetbaggers, jackal-like scalawags, and incompetent, bribe-taking politicians is based on a modicum of truth. But reality bore only slight relation to the grotesque picture depicted by contemporary journalists and echoed by many historians. Disorder and mistakes inevitably accompany rapid social change such as occurred in the postwar South. The building of railroads, the construction of a public school system, the physical rehabilitation of a region scarred by war, and the democratization of the Southern political system could not have been achieved without a dislocation of values and standards. And the Southern situation should be placed in national perspective. The post-Civil War era was an age of corruption, bribery, and swindling in Northern as well as Southern states and in the federal government itself. All the Southern state governments combined probably did not steal as much from the public treasury as the Tweed Ring in New York City. Even the South Carolina and Louisiana legislatures could scarcely match the brazen bribery that took place in Albany, New York. One contemporary critic charged that the Standard Oil Company could do anything it wanted with the Pennsylvania legislature except refine it.

Despite the propaganda of Southern whites, it was not so much dishonest Republican government that they opposed as it was any Republican government at all, honest or dishonest. The Reconstruction government of Mississippi was clean and honest, yet it, too, was overthrown by terror and intimidation. Why, then, did influential segments of Northern opinion accept the journalistic descriptions of Southern corruption? Primarily because the North, in spite of its superficially pro-Negro attitude of 1865–69, had never really been converted to a genuine belief in racial equality. The Northern radicalism of 1865–69 was produced mainly by war-born hatred for Southern whites and temporary gratitude to black soldiers who had fought for the Union, but as the memories and passions of war faded in the 1870s the underlying racism of the North reasserted itself. Thus the Northern people were willing to believe exaggerated stories of the incompetence and corruption of "Negro-Carpetbag" governments. As the 1876 centennial of American independence approached there was a movement toward sectional reconciliation and a rededication to national unity. This was all very well, but the freedmen became victims of this "clasping of hands across the bloody chasm." The price of reconciliation was "home rule" for the South and a cessation of Northern interference in Southern "domestic affairs."

With the exception of some of the old Radical Republicans and abolitionists still alive in 1876, the North was prepared to retreat from Reconstruction. It was a Presidential election year, and all signs pointed to a Democratic victory. Capitalizing on the economic depression, widespread disgust with the scandals of the Grant administration, and disillusionment with Reconstruction, Democrats hoped to expand their 1874 capture of the House of Representatives into occupation of the White House. The disputed Presidential election of 1876 resulted in one of the most bizarre political crises of American history. Democrat Samuel J. Tilden won a majority of the popular vote, and was only one electoral vote short of victory, with the outcome in the three Southern states still controlled by Republicans—South Carolina, Florida, and Louisiana—in dispute. Two sets of electoral returns were submitted from each state. If Tilden won any of these votes, he was elected; Republican Rutherford B. Hayes needed the electoral votes of all three states to become the nineteenth President. With the Democratic House and Republican Senate deadlocked over the issue, there could be no Congressional counting of electoral votes, as specified by the Constitution. Passions ran high, many feared another civil war, and there was a real danger that no President would be inaugurated on March 4, 1877. Finally, Congress appointed a special commission to canvass the disputed votes. The commission, by a partisan vote, awarded all the electors to Hayes, thereby making him President. Angry Democrats in the House charged fraud and threatened a filibuster to prevent completion of the electoral count. Behind the scenes, however, several Southern Democrats were in consultation with Hayes's lieutenants, and a series of agreements was worked out whereby the Southerners promised to allow a completion of the vote in return for commitments from Hayes to withdraw the last federal troops from South Carolina and Louisiana (where the federal presence was the only power keeping duly elected Republican governments in office), to give political patronage to Southern Democrats, and to use his influence in behalf of appropriations for Southern internal improvements. This "Compromise of 1877" ended the electoral crisis. Hayes took office and promptly withdrew the troops from South Carolina and Louisiana. The Republican governments immediately collapsed and the South became solidly Democratic.

Some Republicans and former abolitionists charged that the compromise was a sellout of the freedmen; in a sense they were right. Hayes's withdrawal of the troops brought an end to meaningful national efforts to enforce the Fourteenth and Fifteenth Amendments in the South until the 1950s. In the three decades after 1877, Southern blacks were gradually disfranchised, Jim-Crowed, and reduced to a degraded second-class citizenship. But Hayes really had had no choice in 1877. Democrats controlled the House and threatened to block appropriations if he tried to use the army in the South; the North had already given up its moral commitment to Reconstruction; and the overthrow of Southern Republican governments was a virtual *fait accompli* by the time Hayes took office.

The Civil War and Reconstruction, therefore, were a revolution manqué. The Union was restored and the slaves freed, but the Negro did not achieve equality. There was a period of bright promise in the late 1860s, but it flickered out in the backlash of the 1870s. A genuine revolution of equality would have required a revolution in institutions and attitudes which did not occur. Despite the enfranchisement of the freedmen, the basic institutional structure of Southern society remained unchanged: The whites retained most of the wealth, property, education, power, and experience. The racial attitudes of both North and South bent just enough to accept (sometimes reluctantly) emancipation, but remained basically opposed to genuine equality. The revolution of racial equality was a failure.

And yet not quite a failure. The Civil War–Reconstruction era produced the system of public schools and private colleges for Negroes that brought literacy to the race and trained future generations of leaders. From the colleges founded by Northern abolitionists and missionaries after the war were graduated, among others, W. E. B. DuBois, Walter White, Thurgood Marshall, Martin Luther King, James Farmer, and Stokely Carmichael. The Fourteenth and Fifteenth Amendments were permanent results of Reconstruction, and in our own time the fusion of educated black leadership and reinvigoration of these Amendments has generated a Second Reconstruction that may produce the racial equality envisaged by the first.

La Wanda Cox

# Reflections on the
# Limits of the Possible

The victory for equal civil and political rights inaugurated by national legislation and the southern state conventions of 1868 was tragically temporary, but
it should not be deprecated. Oppportunities were opened to former slaves and
antebellum free blacks for participation in political power, opportunities they
pursued with vigor. However brief and episodic their role in political decision-
making and their enjoyment of public facilities formerly denied them, free
blacks had defied old taboos and left an imprint upon the institutions of the
South—political, social, and economic—which the resurgence of white supremacy never completely annihilated. Some native white southerners not only
had supported them out of expediency or loyalty to the Union but had come
to accept as valid concepts of racial equity alien to their own past. Yet there
can be no question but that the equality of citizenship embodied in national
and state law during the 1860s lay shattered and apparently unmendable as the
South entered the twentieth century. Most former slaves and their children
still lived in agrarian dependence and poverty, poorly educated, increasingly
disfranchised and segregated, with little protection against a new surge of
white violence.

All accounts of Reconstruction recognize the intensity of white southern
resistance to the new status of blacks imposed by Republicans upon the defeated South. Curiously, in explaining the outcome, generally characterized
by modern historians as the failure of Reconstruction (though with qualification and some dissent), they tend to place major responsibility not upon the
South but upon "the North." By "the North" they usually mean the Republi-

From Lincoln and Black Freedom: A Study in Presidential Leadership by La Wanda Cox
(Copyright © 1981 by the University of South Carolina), quoted by permission of the
University of South Carolina Press.

can party, which held national political power, and sometimes say as much. Their explanation is not free of moral stricture, often patently implicit when not expressly stated. Since the mid-1960s there has seldom been missing from accounts of the "First Reconstruction" the pejorative term "betrayal." Present-day scholars do not indulge in "moral discourse" on black slavery, for as David Donald observed "in the middle of the twentieth century there are some things that do not need to be said." Even less likely is an echo of antebellum aboli-tionist strictures upon slaveholders as "sinners," though there has been lively debate as to whether or not planters harbored a sense of guilt about their peculiar institution. In terms of the moral judgment of history, the vanquished hold an advantage over the victors. Little restraint or understanding has been extended to the latter. Yet few historians would question the statement that those who won the military contest lost the peace. They have not considered the implications. To lose a battle is not to betray a cause; to retreat in the face of a seemingly weak but relentless and resourceful foe is not the equivalent of treachery; to put an end to a bruising fight that has been lost is not without a certain moral justification of its own. In a self-governing nation the will to persevere indefinitely in a just cause, subordinating all else both of interest and conviction, is beyond the realm of reasonable expectation. If Republican politicians and their constituencies of the 1860s and '70s have received little charity, the one professionally acceptable defense of the opprobrium cast upon them is that the political leaders had viable alternatives—viable in the sense that other policies would have changed the outcome, viable also in the sense that such measures could have been perceived and implemented. . . .

\*       \*       \*

If the success of Republicans in reconstructing the South rested upon the precondition of an absence of race prejudice, the limits of the possible were so narrow as to have foreordained failure. Modern scholarship has recog-nized and amply documented the pervasiveness and persistence of racial preju-dice. In some form it contaminated almost all white Americans. Had mid-nineteenth-century America constituted a society utopian in its freedom from "racism," the obstacles to successful reordering of southern society would have been immensely lessened, though European experience suggests that they would not have been completely removed. It does not follow, however, that race prejudice precluded an equality of civil and political rights. Differences in the quality and priority of prejudice, not only between individuals but be-tween the two major parties, provided a significant opening for political action. By the 1860s many northerners who did not find objectionable discrimination against blacks in private and social relationships had come to view as unaccept-able discrimination against blacks in public matters. Most of them were Re-publicans. Prejudices existed among Republicans, but they did not prevent the party from making equal citizenship the law of the land. To explain the break-down of that law by pointing to the racial bias of Republicans is unconvincing unless one assumes that a commitment to civil and political equality can be met only by men who accept and seek to realize the more far-reaching twentieth-century concept of racial equality, a highly questionable premise.

Neither can it be taken for granted that a racism so strong as to reject an equality of basic rights is impervious to change. There is no question but that racial attitudes affect behavior, but it is also recognized that behavior affects racial attitudes, though more slowly. Furthermore, a belief in racial inferiority or an emotional revulsion against accepting one of a different race as an equal does not necessarily result in discriminatory action. That may be held in check by a whole range of countervailing forces—by self-interest or a common goal, by institutions such as law with courts that enforce the law, by a perception of discrimination as unwarranted because it conflicts with other norms of societal behavior. And the experience gained by foregoing discrimination can result in changed views and changed emotional responses. Even when it does not, nondiscriminatory practices may continue. Logically, equality may be indivisible; in practice, it has never been a seamless web.

Failure to enforce black civil and political rights in the South is often attributed to a lack of will on the part of Republican leaders and their constituencies due to their racial views. The explanation may not be susceptible of definite disproof, but it has not been proven and probably cannot be. Many factors entered into the abandonment of the cause of the black man in the South, and Republicans gave up neither quickly or easily. The voting record of regular Republicans in Congress through 1891 remained remarkably consistent and cohesive behind efforts to strengthen federal enforcement of Reconstruction legislation. Democratic party obstruction was equally consistent and created a major roadblock. Republicans enacted a drastic enforcement law in 1870 and another in 1871. For most of the twenty years after the elections of 1870 they did not have the power in Congress to pass additional legislation supportive of black rights but they kept the issue alive. It is true that as early as 1872 some Republicans, notably those who joined the Liberal Republican movement, broke with the policy of national action in support of black rights. But race prejudice was neither a conscious nor a major determinant of their new attitude toward federal intervention in the South. Indeed, the Liberal Republican platform of 1872 tried to reconcile a policy of national retreat with loyalty to the Reconstruction amendments. When Republicans regained control of both houses of Congress in 1890–1891 by only a narrow margin, they passed in the House an enforcement bill to protect black voters but narrowly lost it in the Senate by the perfidy of a few who broke ranks to gain support for silver legislation. On the local front in the northern states, in keeping with party tradition, the Republican record on black rights remained better than that of their opponents.

In 1877 when President Hayes withdrew federal troops and acquiesced to "home rule" for the South, racism was not the key to presidential decision. No critical causal connection has been established between the "betrayal" and race attitudes. There is no doubt but that Hayes' action was related to a general lessening of northern support for intervention in the South. The erosion had been going on for several years, and for that there were a number of reasons. The will to continue the battle was undermined by growing doubt of the wisdom of immediate universal black enfranchisement, increasingly seen as the source of corruption. There was revulsion against the turmoil of disputed elections and the force used to settle them. Many Republicans were discouraged as state after state came under "Redeemer" control, or distracted by the pressure of problems closer at home. There was a general desire in the North for the peace and national reconciliation that Grant had invoked but could not attain as president. Whatever part race prejudice played in weakening Republican support for continuing military intervention, its role was peripheral rather than central. . . .

\*    \*    \*

Race prejudice played a larger role in the obstructionist tactics of northern Democrats than in weakening the will of Republicans. During and after the Civil War, appeal to the race prejudice of their constituencies was a standard procedure in election battles. Yet when it failed to yield decisive political profit, northern Democratic leaders changed tactics. By the mid-1870s they had retreated from public avowals to overturn Reconstruction. By the 1880s in northern states they were wooing black voters by helping to enact local civil rights laws and by giving blacks recognition in patronage appointments. Prejudice had bowed to political advantage. Within little more than a decade, an equal right to the ballot was accepted and institutionalized in both northern parties. Continuing support by northern Democrats in Congress for their southern colleagues in opposing federal enforcement of the right to vote rested upon party advantage in maintaining solidarity with the Democratic South.

Racism linked to southern resistance was more politically formidable. As events developed after Congress repudiated Johnsonian Reconstruction and prescribed its own plan, the appeal to white prejudice was critically important. It enabled Democrats to recapture political ascendancy and to cripple the projected operational arm of congressional policy, the Republican party in the South, as an effective contestant for political power. To attain victory the "Redeemers" mobilized a racism whose many faces were evident about them —conviction that white superiority and black incapacity were nature's law, revulsion against accepting the black man on an equal basis in any capacity as both distasteful and insulting, umbrage at being confronted with violations of the race etiquette to which whites had been conditioned by slavery. Racial hostility was used to organize and to justify terror, intimidation, and fraud, particularly in election contests but also in more mundane activities when freedom led blacks beyond "their place."

Even so, racism alone does not explain southern intransigence. It was strongly reinforced by other factors—by the psychological need of white southerners to avoid "dishonor" in defeat, by fears of economic chaos and race warfare, by shock and outrage at the congressional peace terms of 1867, by a perception of Republican demand for black civil and political equality as punitive. Increased taxation at a time of economic stress helped inflame emotions. The result was resistance, sometimes open and sometimes covert, often violent but also subtle. A guerrilla warfare outmaneuvered and overwhelmed Republican forces in the South and gave way before federal military force only to regroup and strike again. It was a resistance strengthened by a sense of right in safeguarding a social order in which blacks were subordinate to whites. If racism was a crucial element in the failure to establish securely black civil and political rights, it was not because racial prejudice permeated both sections, both parties, and all classes. It was because prejudice in the South was deeply rooted, intrinsic to the social and economic structure, and effectively mobilized for political combat. To induce a change in southern white racial behavior to the extent of accepting the black man as an equal in the courts and at the ballot box and as a free laborer entitled to choose, to move about, to better his condition—that task was not in theory beyond the power of Congress and president but it was an uncertain undertaking that would have tested the political skill of any party and president. Fortuitous circumstances, both political and economic, may well have precluded success. Lincoln's assassination changed the direction of presidential policy, and the downward slide of the postbellum cotton economy of the South reinforced white resistance to change.

A critical question needs to be addressed. Could a greater use of force have brought white southerners to accept civil and political rights for blacks? Neither history nor theory can answer this question with certainty. A number of historians have implied that direct coercion could have effected a fundamental change, that Reconstruction was the nation's great missed opportunity. Few would go so far as Eugene Genovese, who has written that there was no prospect of a better future for blacks unless several thousand leaders of the Lost Cause had been summarily killed. Michael Perman would have had the political and economic power of the southern elite eliminated by means less Draconian and more nearly representative of recent historiographic opinion. He suggests an immediate "edict of the conqueror" enforced by occupying troops to exclude the elite from political power, give suffrage to blacks, confiscate plantations, and divide their lands among the freedmen. Far too good an historian to argue that such an edict had been a practical postwar possibility, he nonetheless believes that had it been possible, it would have worked. William Gillette has taken a more historically realistic approach to the problem. Recognizing that Republicans were not in a position to enforce their Reconstruction program until 1869 when they obtained control of the presidency as well as of Congress, he examines closely the southern record of the Grant years. While he comes to the conclusion that Republicans might have succeeded, or at least achieved a great deal, his analysis of the requirements for success is not reassuring. The skill he sees lacking but needed by Grant might have overtaxed even a Lincoln. According to Gillette, Grant should have been cautious where he was bold, bold where he was timid. He had to be both master politician and resolute soldier. The situation required his effective direction of an expert bureaucracy and an overwhelming military muscle, neither of which was at his disposal. Grant should have overpowered militarily southern white resistance yet come to terms with the fact that "in the long run coercion could not replace a sanctioned consensus." Given the nation's traditional commitment to civilian control and majority rule, "the use of force was self-defeating."

Force *and* consent, how to achieve the one by use of the other, posed a dilemma which by the 1870s strained the bounds of the possible. The outcome would have been only a little less problematic had Reconstruction been formulated in early 1865 and backed by force, i.e., by force alone. Particularly vulnerable is the assumption that by eliminating the power of the landed aristocracy, resistance would have been broken and a new order of equal rights for blacks securely established. There would still have remained for the South as a whole a white majority with prejudices and interests inimical to the advancement of blacks. A stunned acceptance in the despondency of defeat of such peace terms as Perman has outlined would have been no guarantee of their permanent observance by white southerners. Here theory is of some help to speculation. It lends support to Gillette's perception of the need to reconcile the seemingly irreconcilable. Historians have tended to approach the concepts of coercion/consent, or conflict/consensus, as coercion vs. consent or conflict vs. consensus, and not without precedent in political and sociological thought. There exist, however, theoretical analyses that see coercion and consensus as compatible, even complementary. They suggest that the problem, both in theory and practice, is one of interrelationship. Even theorists identified with the view that conflict and coercion are essential to the creation of a new and better social order seldom argue that force alone is sufficient to bring about the change desired. Nor do they overlook the danger that coercion can be self-defeating. The more consensus oriented see force as unable to operate alone over any length of time. The concern to identify "authority," to examine the sources of its "legitimacy," to distinguish authority from "power," to establish the noncoercive forms of power and the nonphysical forms of coercion—these continuing efforts indicate the importance attached to means other than direct force in effecting and maintaining social change. And there is a long tradition of political thought that admonishes caution in trying to force change contrary to traditional convictions lest it provoke deep and bitter reaction. From an approach either through theory or history, it would seem reasonable to conclude that a policy of force *plus* some form and degree of consent—even if the consent, to borrow from P. H. Partridge, were only "a patchwork of divergent and loosely adjusted values, norms, and objectives"— would have had a better chance of success in reordering the South than force alone. Lincoln was capable of a "patchwork" design in implementing policy.

Certainly by the mid-1870s the use of coercion had intensified a deep and bitter reaction. Instead of passive resignation, coercion led to a "negative consensus" that rejected the legitimacy of national authority over the status of blacks, fed resistance, and united white southerners to an unprecedented degree. It is well to be reminded that the coercion used had been considerable. Whatever the formality of consent in the ratification of the Fourteenth Amendment, Congress had left the recalcitrant secession states no effective choice. In the initial enfranchisement of blacks, white southerners were allowed not even the formality of consenting; enfranchisement was mandated by Congress and implemented by military authority and presence. The military also intervened in the reorganization of the South's labor system and in the operation of its local courts. The presence of an occupying army preceded the interim period of military rule set up by Congress in 1867 and did not disappear with the restoration of state authority. Violent resistance to the new order was answered not only by the passage of drastic congressional legislation in 1870 and 1871 but also by the use under these laws of federal armed forces, notably in Mississippi, South Carolina, North Carolina, and Alabama. Troops helped make arrests, guarded prisoners, protected court proceedings, and maintained order at the polls. Over a thousand military arrests were made in three counties of South Carolina in 1871–1872. Federal attorneys obtained 540 criminal convictions in Mississippi in 1872–1873 and 263 in North Carolina in 1873. The district attorney for the northern and middle districts of Alabama obtained indictments of more than 350 persons from two grand juries, one in the fall of 1871 and the other in the spring of 1872. From 1870, when the first enforcement law was passed, through 1874, 3,382 cases under the acts were adjudicated in federal courts in the southern states. In addition, under Grant's direction federal troops in effect decided disputes over who rightfully held elective office in Louisiana, Arkansas, and Mississippi.

The force employed in the 1870s was grossly insufficient for the task at hand. Too often local officials and courts sidestepped justice for blacks without interference. Troops stationed in the South were woefully inadequate in number to contain violent resistance wherever it erupted. Relatively few of the men arrested in South Carolina were brought to trial. In general, indictments were difficult to obtain and even in the federal courts many cases were dismissed. By the end of 1874 little vitality was left in the federal enforcement program. Southern resistance turned increasingly to intimidation and more subtle, less legally vulnerable means than the earlier violence. Democratic power in Congress deprived the executive of resources needed to enforce the laws and prevented legislative action to strengthen them.

Nonetheless, the direct coercion mobilized by the national government in the 1860s and 1870s was substantial, far greater than any similar action in support of desegregation and black voting in the 1950s and '60s. It was large enough to give strong support to the contention that a century ago the amount of force necessary to realize equal civil and political rights in the South was impossible to sustain in a nation whose democratic tradition and constitutional structure limited the use of power, exalted the rule of law, and embodied the concept of government by the consent of the governed. Neither national institutions nor public opinion could be expected to have sustained a military intervention of indefinite length and of sufficient strength to crush all local resistance. And by the mid-1870s, the issue at stake no longer appeared clear-cut, even to northern Republicans. Popular government at the South seemed to have become "nothing but a sham."

Assumptions regarding the potency of national power to effect social change, largely valid for the "Second Reconstruction," may inadvertently have biased historical judgment concerning the earlier period. By the 1950s the capacity for resistance in the South, although still strong, was markedly less than in the post–Civil War decades. Race prejudice remained formidable, but in the wake of Hitler's holocaust and advances in the social sciences, psychology, and biology, prejudice could no longer command arguments of scientific or moral respectability. Despite shocking episodes of violence, white terror never reached the epidemic proportions of the 1860s and '70s. Apparently it was no longer condoned by majority white opinion in the South. Moreover, in the 1950s and '60s not Congress but the judiciary took the initiative in forcing change and remained a vital mechanism for implementing it. The aura of legitimacy created by supportive judicial decisions, lacking in the earlier period, greatly lessened the necessity for direct physical coercion. With a few exceptions, notably at Little Rock in 1957, federal enforcement of court decisions and civil rights legislation proceeded without a show of force. Nor were federal criminal prosecutions numerous. A total of only 323 criminal cases were filed by the newly established civil rights division of the Justice Department from 1958 through mid-1972, only a tenth of the number that had been brought by the attorney general's office in the first five years of the 1870s. Other methods of coercion were available, both more effective and more consonant with the traditional primacy of civil over military authority, of persuasion over force. Civil cases initiated or assisted by the Justice Department far outnumbered criminal ones, and the department was active in negotiating voluntary agreements of compliance and in community counseling. With the great increase in the functions undertaken by the federal government to meet the needs of a mature industrial society, there were at hand powerful monetary and administrative sanctions, and a bureaucracy to use them.

In contrast to the 1870s, during the "Second Reconstruction" votes and time were available to pass a whole array of acts, progressively more comprehensive in scope and more resourceful in their enforcement provisions. What made this achievement possible, according to authorities in the field, was the existence of a national consensus. Although it did not encompass majority white opinion in the South, elsewhere it found support in both major parties, quite unlike the situation in the Civil War era when consensus, on a much more limited program of black rights, existed only within the Republican party. Presidential leadership by the second President Johnson, in contrast to that of the first, was exerted to expand civil rights. In the creation of the national consensus of the 1950s blacks themselves played a key role beyond that open to them a century earlier. Their political influence in the North was considerable because of the numbers who had moved out of the South to fill northern labor needs. The distance from slavery allowed their leaders, South as well as North, to operate with formidable resources, skills, and organization and to present a case that could no longer be evaded by a show of scientific or social justification. They made inescapably visible to white America the injustices piled high during the postemancipation decades.

In short, the "Second Reconstruction" is a false model from which to project in retrospect the limits of the possible a century earlier. As an analogy, however, it suggests the need for far more than direct force to attain success. Its loss of momentum by the 1970s also indicates the difficulty of sustaining a national moral purpose, even with a task recognized as unfinished. In November 1971, the United States Commission on Civil Rights wrote "that the American people have grown somewhat weary, that the national sense of injustice, which was the foundation on which the legislative victories of the 1960s were built, has dimmed." And a few years later other informed analysts agreed. They attributed the fuel for the engine of change during the two previous decades in part to the deceptive clarity of the problems seen through the lens of the New Frontier and the New Society. There had been a naive public faith that new programs of government intervention would quickly bear fruit. Results failed to meet expectations. Advance slowed as injustices were reduced to ones less shockingly visible, as moral issues became clouded by the complexity of problems, as economic conditions turned less favorable, and as conflicts of interest intensified. Analysts concluded that the future was not sanguine. The circumstances of the 1960s had been unusually conducive to change and were not apt to be duplicated. . . .

*   *   *

A fatal weakness of Reconstruction, constitutional historians have argued, arose from the constitutional conservatism of Republican lawmakers, particularly their deference to the traditional federal structure embodied in the Constitution. This led them to preserve the primacy of state responsibility for the rights of citizens, thereby denying to the national government effective power to protect the rights of blacks. It has been contended that Reconstruction required "a major constitutional upheaval," that it "could have been effected only by a revolutionary destruction of the states and the substitution of a unitary constitutional system." Part of the argument is unassailable. The new scholarship has demolished the old stereotype of Republican leaders as constitutional revolutionaries. They had, indeed, been waging a war for constitution as well as for nation with every intent of maintaining both. And the concern of Republicans for state and local government was no superficial adulation of the constitution; it was deeply rooted in their commitment to self-government. Yet unlike Democrats who denounced as unconstitutional any amendment to the constitution that enlarged federal authority at the expense of the states, Republicans did not uphold state rights federalism without qualification. They believed that they had found a way to protect freedmen in their new citizenship status by modifying, rather than destroying, the traditional federal structure. . . .

*       *       *

Similarly circumscribed was any potential role for Lincoln in helping shape economic developments to assure freedmen an escape from poverty and dependence. No explanation for the tragic outcome of the postwar decades for black America has been more generally accepted in modern scholarship than that Reconstruction failed because the national government did not provide land for the freedman. The thesis has been sharply challenged, and the challenge has not been met. The work of historians and economists in exploring afresh the roots of poverty, particularly of black poverty, in the postbellum South afford some relevant perspectives. Between 1974 and 1979 six book-length studies appeared with significant bearing on the problem of black poverty, and others were in progress; conference papers and published articles also reflected the vigor of scholarly interest in the question.

No consensus has developed either as explanation for the continuing dependence and poverty of southern blacks or as an analysis of the potential economic effect of land distribution. However, four of five econometricians who addressed the latter question concluded that grants of land, while desirable and beneficial, would not have solved the predicament of the freedmen and their children. Robert Higgs has written that "historians have no doubt exaggerated the economic impact of such a grant." Gavin Wright holds that "the tenancy systems of the South cannot be assigned primary blame for Southern poverty," that a more equitable distribution of land "would not have produced dramatic improvements in living standards" or "generated sustained progress." In their book, *One Kind of Freedom*, Roger Ransom and Richard Sutch appear to accept what Heman Belz has characterized as the "new orthodoxy" of the historians, but they dramatically qualified that position in a subsequent paper. They argued that confiscation and redistribution would have resulted in little improvement in the postbellum situation, which they characterize as one of economic stagnation and exploitation, unless accompanied by federally funded compensation for landowners thereby providing liquid capital for reinvigorating agriculture and possibly developing manufactures. This retrospective prescription is restrained as compared to the requirements outlined by twentieth-century experts who seek land distribution as an avenue out of rural poverty. They see successful land reform as requiring supplementary government programs providing credit, seed and fertilizer distribution, marketing facilities, rural and feeder transportation, pricing mechanisms affecting both what the farmer buys and what he sells, technical research, and agricultural education.

More than a land program was needed to insure the freedman's economic future. Although areas of land with high fertility prospered, it seems doubtful that income from cotton between the close of the war and the turn of the century, even if equitably distributed, could have sustained much beyond a marginal level of existence for those who worked the cotton fields whether as wage earner, cropper, tenant, or small owner. And the lower South because of its soils and climate, as Julius Rubin has convincingly shown, had no viable alternative to cotton as a commercial crop until the scientific and technological advances of the twentieth century. Nor could nonmarket subsistence farming offer much by way of material reward. The "more" that was needed can be envisaged in retrospect, and was glimpsed by contemporaries, but it is not clear how it could have been achieved. Gavin Wright has concluded that the postbellum South "required either a massive migration away from the region or a massive Southern industrial revolution." Both in the North and the South there was enthusiasm for promoting southern industry, but only the future could reveal how elusive would be that "New South" of ever-renewed expectations. Despite scholarship, new and old, there is no certain explanation of why the South failed to catch up with the North. If historians and economists should agree upon a diagnosis, it is unlikely that they will uncover a remedy that could have been recognized and implemented a century ago. The heritage of slavery most certainly will be part of the diagnosis. It left behind an underdeveloped, overwhelmingly rural economy tied to the world market and bereft of adequate foundations for rapid economic growth. Recovery and growth had to be attempted in a period of initial crop disasters, of disadvantage for primary products in terms of world trade, and by the mid-1870s of prolonged and recurrent economic crises. There were high hopes for southern industrialization in the 1880s, but the effort substantially failed. With opportunity drastically limited in the South and industry expanding in the North, there was yet no great out-migration of blacks until the twentieth century. The reasons for this also are not altogether clear. Neither the restraints placed on southern agricultural labor by law and custom nor the discrimination blacks faced in the North is sufficient explanation. The ways in which European immigrants blocked black advance deserve further study, as does the attitude of blacks themselves both toward leaving the South and toward the unskilled, menial labor which alone might have afforded them large-scale entry into the northern labor market. . . .

*     *     *

There were limits to the possible. Yet the dismal outcome for southern blacks as the nation entered the twentieth century need not have been as unrelieved as it was in fact. More than a land program, the civil and political rights Republicans established in law, had they been secured in practice, could have mitigated the discrimination that worsened their condition and constricted whatever opportunities might otherwise have existed for escape from poverty. Moreover, the extraordinary effort black men made to vote—and to vote independently in the face of white cajolery, intimidation, and economic pressure—strongly suggests that for the emancipated to cast a ballot was to affirm the reality of freedom and the dignity of black manhood.

The priority Republicans gave to civil and political rights in their fight to establish a meaningful new status for ex-slaves has been too readily discounted by historians. Small landholdings could not have protected blacks from intimidation, or even from many forms of economic coercion. They would not have brought economic power. In the face of overwhelming white opposition, they could not have safeguarded the new equality of civil and political status. Where blacks voted freely, on the other hand, there was always the potential for sharing political power and using it as a means to protect and advance their interests. There is considerable evidence that this did happen. Local officials elected by black votes during the years of Republican control upheld blacks against planters, state legislators repealed Black Codes, shifted the burden of taxation from the poor, granted agricultural laborers a first lien on crops, increased expenditures for education. Eric Foner has concluded that at least in some areas Republican Reconstruction resulted in subtle but significant changes that protected black labor and prevented planters from using the state to bolster their position. Harold D. Woodman's study of state laws affecting agriculture confirms the generalization that a legislative priority of the Redeemer governments was passage of measures to give landowners greater control over the labor force. By the end of the century legal bonds had been so tightened that as prosperity returned to cotton culture neither cropper nor renter but only their employer was in a position to profit. In a study of rural Edgefield County, South Carolina, Vernon Burton has found that black voting made possible real gains in economic position and social status between 1867 and 1877. Howard Rabinowitz's examination of the urban South discloses that Republican city governments brought blacks a greater share of elected and appointed offices, more jobs in construction work, in fire and police departments. And beyond immediate gains, black votes meant support for educational facilities through which blacks could acquire the literacy and skills essential for advancement.

Security for black civil and political rights required acceptance by white southerners. An acquiescence induced by a judicious combination of force and consent needed for its perpetuation reinforcement by self-interest. The most effective vehicle of self-interest would have been a Union-Republican party able to command substantial continuing support from native whites. The Republican party that gained temporary dominance through the congressional legislation of 1867 enfranchising blacks failed to meet the test of substantial white support. Despite a strong white following in a few states, its scalawag component from the start was too limited to offset the opposition's attack on it as the party of the black man and the Yankee. And white participation diminished as appeals to race prejudice and sectional animosity intensified.

The potential for a major second party among southern whites existed in the aftermath of Confederate defeat. The Democratic party was in disarray, discredited for having led the South out of the Union and having lost the war. Old Whig loyalties subsumed by the slavery issue had nonetheless endured; southern unionism had survived in varying degrees from wartime adherence to the Union to reluctant support of the Confederacy. Opposition to Jefferson Davis's leadership and willingness to accept northern peace terms had grown as the hope for southern victory diminished. Such sources of Democratic opposition overlapped with the potential for ready recruits to Union-Republicanism from urban dwellers, from men whose origins had been abroad or in the North, from those whose class or intrasectional interests created hostility to the dominant planter leadership of the Democracy. A "New South" of enterprise and industry presented an attractive vision to many a native son. And there were always those who looked to the loaves and the fishes dispensed from Washington.

Had party recruitment and organization, with full presidential support, begun at the end of hostilities and escaped the period of confusion and bitterness that thinned the ranks of the willing during the conflict between Johnson and Congress, the result could have been promising. Greater white support and the accession of black voters by increments might have eased racial tension and lessened deadly factionalism within the party. Lincoln's political skill and Whig background would certainly have served party-building well, as would the perception of presidential policy as one of moderation and reconciliation. The extent to which southern whites did in fact support the Republican party after 1867 despite its image as Radical, alien, and black-dominated, an image that stigmatized and often ostracized them, suggests the potency of a common goal, or a common enmity, in bridging the chasm between the races.

Even under the guidance of a Lincoln, the building of a permanent biracial major party in the South was by no means assured. A broad enduring coalition of disparate elements would face the necessity of reconciling sharply divergent economic interests. Agricultural workers sought maximum autonomy, more than bare necessities, and an opportunity for land ownership while planter-merchants strove to control labor and maximize profit. The burden of increased taxation to meet essential but unaccustomed social services, particularly for blacks, meant an inescapable clash of class and racial interests. Concessions by the more privileged were especially difficult in a South of limited available resources and credit, impoverished by war and enmeshed in inflated costs, crop disasters, and falling cotton prices. By the mid-1870s a nationwide depression intensified regional problems. Efforts to promote a more varied and vigorous economy by state favor, credit, and appropriation became a political liability as the primary effect appeared to be the proliferation of civic corruption and entrepreneurial plunder.

Outside the South a vigorous Republican party and two-party system managed to endure despite the clash of intraparty economic interests. A similar development in the South faced the additional and more intractable conflict inherent in the new black-white relationship. Within the Republican party that took shape after 1867, factionalism often cut between blacks and carpetbaggers, on the one hand, and scalawags on the other; but there was also a considerable amount of accommodation, not all of it from blacks. A study of the voting record of 87 Republicans, 52 of them native whites, who served in the North Carolina House of Representatives in the 1868 to 1870 session shows scalawags trailing carpetbaggers and blacks in voting on issues of Negro rights and support for public schools, yet compiling a positive overall record, a score of 61.2 and 55.9 respectively. On the few desegregation questions that came to a roll call, however, only a small minority of native whites voted favorably. In Mississippi when the black-carpetbagger faction gained control, they quietly ignored the platform calling for school integration even though black legislators were sufficiently numerous and powerful to have pressed the issue. Black office-holding was a similar matter where fair treatment held danger, and black leaders often showed restraint. Such issues were explosive. They not only threatened the unity of the party but undermined its ability to attract white votes or minimize opposition demagoguery and violence. A Lincolnian approach to building an interracial party would have diminished the racial hazard, but could hardly have eliminated it.

The years of political Reconstruction, to borrow an apt phrase from Thomas B. Alexander's study of Tennessee, offered no "narrowly missed opportunities to leap a century forward in reform." Not even a Lincoln could have wrought such a miracle. To have secured something less, yet something substantially more than blacks had gained by the end of the nineteenth century, did not lie beyond the limits of the possible given a president who at war's end would have joined party in an effort to realize "as nearly as we can" the fullness of freedom for blacks.

## SUGGESTIONS FOR FURTHER READING

Claude G. Bowers, *The Tragic Era: The Revolution After Lincoln* (Boston, 1929) argues that during Reconstruction "The Southern people literally were put to the torture" by a "brutal, hypocritical, and corrupt" leadership in the North. E. Merton Coulter perpetuates these views in his more recent *The South During Reconstruction* (Baton Rouge, 1947). But the best introduction to the anti-radical position is the older and very influential William A. Dunning, *Reconstruction, Political and Economic* (New York, 1907).

Howard K. Beale, *The Critical Year: A Study of Andrew Johnson and Reconstruction* (Baton Rouge, 1947) stresses the connection between Radical Republicans and the industrial business interests of the North. W. E. B. DuBois, *Black Reconstruction* (New York, 1935) is a direct answer to the position taken by William A. Dunning and his many students. His stress is on the accomplishments of the Republican Reconstruction governments in the South. The emphasis, however, is on class, not racial, conflict.

* Available in paperback edition.

DuBois should be considered the first of those historians who have been termed "revisionists," that is, those who have sought to revise the uniformly negative picture of Reconstruction as painted by Dunning and his followers. But it took a quarter-century before the new interpretation suggested by DuBois became accepted. Among the many important revisionist interpretations are the following: John Hope Franklin, *Reconstruction After the Civil War* (Chicago, 1961); Kenneth M. Stampp, *The Era of Reconstruction* (New York, 1965); James M. McPherson, *The Struggle for Equality: Abolitionists and the Negro in the Civil War and Reconstruction* (Princeton, N.J., 1964); Willie Lee Rose, *Rehearsal for Reconstruction: The Port Royal Experiment* (Indianapolis, 1964); Leon Litwak, *Been in the Storm So Long: The Aftermath of Slavery* (New York, 1979).

C. Vann Woodward's monumental and influential study, *Origins of the New South* (Baton Rouge, La., 1951), deals with the post-Reconstruction years in the South but offers important insights into the meaning of Reconstruction. Woodward argues that the Civil War marked a fundamental turning point in southern history. More recent studies have stressed what may be termed economic and social reconstruction, emphasizing the effects of emancipation and the postwar settlement on the life and labor of the southern landlords, the yeomen, and the freed slaves. Some of these tend to support, others to revise Woodward's interpretation. See, Jonathan M. Wiener, *Social Origins of the New South* (Baton Rouge, La., 1978); Gavin Wright, *The Political Economy of the Cotton South* (New York, 1978), Chapter VI; Jay R. Mandle, *The Roots of Black Poverty* (Durham, N.C., 1978); Roger L. Ransom and Richard Sutch, *One Kind of Freedom* (Cambridge, England, 1977); Robert Higgs, *Competition and Coercion* (Cambridge, England, 1977).

The literature on Reconstruction is enormous and varied. Students who desire to follow changing interpretations or to find books and articles relating to any aspect of the period might look into the following surveys of the historical literature: Bernard A. Weisberger, "The Dark and Bloody Ground of Reconstruction Historiography," *Journal of Southern History*, 25 (November 1959), 427–447; Richard O. Curry, "The Civil War and Reconstruction, 1861–1877: A Critical Overview of Recent Trends and Interpretations," *Civil War History*, 20 (September 1974), 215–228; and Eric Foner, "Reconstruction Revisited," *Reviews in American History*, 10 (November 1982), 82–100.

2

# *Business in an Industrial Age*

Most historians and economists agree that America's industrial revolution—or, to use W. W. Rostow's striking phrase, "the take-off into sustained growth"—began in the early nineteenth century. But it was the massive industrial expansion in the late nineteenth century that transformed the United States into the world's leading industrial power. Older industries such as textiles and meat packing expanded, and new industries such as oil, electricity, steel, and automobile manufacturing began and grew into giants by the early decades of the twentieth century. Industrialism became more pervasive, spreading from the Northeast to the Midwest and beyond. Heavy industry became more important as measured by the value of its products, and large-scale production dominated American industries.

The results were profound. Industry's voracious appetite for raw materials stimulated the growth of mining, the drilling of oil, the output of farms, and the exploitation of timber and other natural resources. Large-scale production required heavy capital expenditures that fostered the expansion of banking and security markets. Giant firms required skilled leadership and a disciplined and efficient working class. And, finally, the distribution of goods necessitated the expansion of facilities for transportation, warehousing, wholesaling, and retailing.

As the output of goods and services soared, many Americans celebrated their nation's growing industrial might. But others began to point to serious problems. Smaller firms found it increasingly difficult to compete with the larger, richer, and more highly mechanized firms. Thousands of small businesses went bankrupt or were absorbed into the larger firms. In industry after industry, monopoly or oligopoly (control by a very few firms) seemed to be replacing competition. A relatively few men, the leaders of the new industrial empires, seemed to be dominating American life by controlling output, prices, wages, and working conditions; because of their wealth, they were exerting undemocratic influence on politics.

Critics complained of corruption and venality in public and private life and traced the cause to the materialism of the business classes. "Society, in these states, is canker'd, crude, superstitious, and rotten," charged Walt Whitman in his "Democratic Vistas." He decried the "depravity of the business classes" and the "corruption, bribery, falsehood, maladministration" in government on all levels. In 1873 Mark Twain and Charles D. Warner published a long and rambling novel in which they described corruption and decay behind the glittering facade of progress, a novel aptly entitled The Gilded Age.

For such critics, the period was one of conflict. Rapacious business leaders, often termed "robber barons," supported by a corrupt government, enriched themselves at the expense of less fortunate businessmen and of the public at large. The results were high prices, shoddy merchandise, poor service, and the rule of a business elite that ignored the well-being of the people.

Others deny that this is an accurate portrayal of the age of industrial expansion. They call the business leaders "industrial statesmen," energetic leaders who were innovators, organizers, and risk takers with the foresight, the talent, and the courage necessary to industrialize the nation. They invested their money and their talents in the organization of modern enterprise, always seeking new methods to expand production, to lower costs, and to make more goods and services available to the people. Although these men were motivated by a desire for wealth and power, the net result of their efforts was substantial progress for the entire nation. In a word, then, there was no basic conflict between the aims and methods of the business community and the needs and desires of the entire nation.

These differing views are illustrated in the selections that follow. Readers should note that the answers provided differ in part, at least, because the historians pose different questions. Is the question to be raised one of morality, that is, the ethical behavior of the industrialists? Or is the problem an assessment of efficiency and organization? Is it possible to condemn the industrialists as robber barons while commending them for being innovators and leaders? Do critics accept the value of industrial expansion but condemn the ways in which it occurred? Or do critics question the benefits of industrialism?

In the first selection, Alan Trachtenberg describes the ambivalent response to the growing mechanization of production in the late nineteenth century. The machine seemed to represent progress, but at the same time it appeared menacing. It promised increasing prosperity and well-being for all, but it also brought hard times, wretched working conditions, and violent labor upheavals. However, critics and supporters alike agreed that the mechanization of production was inevitable and unstoppable. Therefore, Trachtenberg concludes, the changes brought by mechanization of production required adaptation, the creation of a new consensus.

In the second selection, Matthew Josephson discusses John D. Rockefeller and the Standard Oil Company, which he organized and led. For Josephson, industrialists such as Rockefeller were robber barons. Granting the ability and energy of men such as Rockefeller, Josephson finds them often to have been ruthless exploiters who brought hardship and difficulty to many. Any positive contributions they made were merely inadvertent by-products of their greedy and predatory quest for wealth and power.

Alfred D. Chandler, Jr., in the final selection, approaches the rise of big business in a very different way. He takes no moral stance as he describes how business leaders expanded their enterprises by moving into distribution and by consolidating with competitors. If the goal of such actions was higher profits, the means to that goal were increased efficiency and expanding output.

Interpretations of the Gilded Age inevitably touch on the question of morality. Are business leaders to be condemned for their moral lapses, for their greed, violence, and unfair tactics? If so, can we attack them on these grounds and find other classes in society less guilty? Or must we realize that people in the past cannot be judged by present-day moral standards?

Perhaps the moral question is not the most important question to ask. Perhaps we would do better to judge the industrialists by their contribution to the economic growth and well-being of the nation. This approach suggests a wide range of questions. Did big business give leadership to the great industrial expansion? Or did these men, through their activities, impede the full development of the economy? Did they by their unrestrained activities create more problems than they solved? If they made contributions, what specifically were they? If they did not, how specifically did they hinder progress?

Alan Trachtenberg

# Mechanization
# Takes Command

## I

Even before the Civil War, the westward trails were destined to be lined
with tracks; the pony express and the covered wagon, like the mounted Plains
Indian, would yield to the Iron Horse. For if the West of "myth and symbol,"
in Henry Nash Smith's apt terms, provided one perspective by which Americans might view their society, the machine provided another. The two images
fused into a single picture of a progressive civilization fulfilling a providential
mission. As John Kasson has shown, many Americans before the Civil War
believed that industrial technology and the factory system would serve as
historic instruments of republican values, diffusing civic virtue and enlightenment along with material wealth. Factories, railroads, and telegraph wires
seemed the very engines of a democratic future. Ritual celebrations of machinery and fervently optimistic prophecies of abundance continued throughout the Gilded Age, notably at the two great international expositions, in
Philadelphia in 1876 and in Chicago in 1893.

The image of the machine, like the image of the West, proved to be a
complex symbol, increasingly charged with contradictory meanings and implications. If the machine seemed the prime cause of the abundance of new
products changing the character of daily life, it also seemed responsible for
newly visible poverty, slums, and an unexpected wretchedness of industrial
conditions. While it inspired confidence in some quarters, it also provoked
dismay, often arousing hope and gloom in the same minds. For, accompanying

From Alan Trachtenberg, The Incorporation of America: Culture and Society in the Gilded
Age. Copyright © 1982 by Alan Trachtenberg. Reprinted by permission of Hill and Wang,
a division of Farrar, Straus, and Giroux, Inc.

the mechanization of industry, of transportation, and of daily existence, were the most severe contrasts yet visible in American society, contrasts between "progress and poverty" (in Henry George's words), which seemed to many a mockery of the republican dream, a haunting paradox. Each act of national celebration seemed to evoke its opposite. The 1877 railroad strike, the first instance of machine smashing and class violence on a national scale, followed the 1876 Centennial Exposition, and the even fiercer Pullman strike of 1894 came fast on the heels of the World's Columbian Exposition of 1893.

It is no wonder that closer examination of popular celebrations discloses bewilderment and fear. In fiction and poetry, as Leo Marx has shown in his seminal *Machine in the Garden* (1964), serious writers before the Civil War had fastened on the image of a mechanical intrusion on a pastoral setting as a characteristic expression of a deeply troubled society. In the language of literature, a machine (railroad or steamship) bursting on a peaceful natural setting represented a symbolic version of the trauma inflicted on American society by unexpectedly rapid mechanization. The popular mode of celebration covered over all signs of trauma with expressions of confidence and fulsome praise. But confidence proved difficult to sustain in the face of the evidence.

Current events instilled doubt at the very site of celebration. A period of great economic growth, of steadily rising per capita wealth, and new urban markets feeding an expanding industrial plant, the Gilded Age was also wracked with persisting crises. An international "great depression" from 1873 to 1896 afflicted all industrial nations with chronic overproduction and dramatically falling prices, averaging one-third on all commodities. "It was," writes David Landes, "the most drastic deflation in the memory of man." A severe Wall Street crash in 1873 triggered a round of bankruptcies and failures in the United States, six thousand businesses closing in 1874 alone, and as many as nine hundred a month folding in 1878. A perilously uneven business cycle continued for more than twenty years, affecting all sections of the economy: constant market uncertainties and stiffening competition at home and abroad for business; inexplicable surpluses and declining world prices, together with tightening credit for farmers; wage cuts, extended layoffs and irregular employment, and worsening conditions, even starvation, for industrial workers. Recurrent cycles of boom and collapse seemed as inexorable as the quickening pace of technological innovation. Thus, even in the shadow of glorious new machines displayed at the fairs, the public sense of crisis deepened.

No wonder modern machinery struck observers, especially those associated with the business community, as in Charles Francis Adams, Jr.'s words, "an incalculable force." The tempo of crisis accelerated in the 1870's. Farmers agitated through Granger clubs and the Greenback Party against the government's policy of supporting business through deflationary hard money and the gold standard. Industrial unrest reached a climax and a momentary catharsis in July 1877, when fears of a new civil war spread across the country during the great railroad strike. Provoked by a 10 percent wage cut announced without warning by the Baltimore and Ohio line, a measure to halt a declining rate of profit, the strike spread like wildfire to other lines, reaching from Baltimore to Pittsburgh, Chicago, St. Louis, Kansas City, and San Francisco. The apparently spontaneous work stoppages met with approval and support from local merchants, farmers, clergy, and politicians, tapping reserves of anger and wrath against the railroad companies. Workers in other industries joined the walkout, and for a short spell it seemed that the United States faced a mass rebellion, a recurrence of the Paris Commune of 1871 on an even vaster scale. In some communities (St. Louis, for example) committees of strikers briefly assumed control of government and railroad services.

The strike turned bloody and destructive, arousing a vehemence of response from big business and the national government even surpassing the wrath vented by strikers against railroad yards and equipment. The companies recruited local police and militia to protect their property, and pitched battles raged along the lines, although many militiamen refused to fire on the strikers, among whom they recognized relatives and friends. Finally, the newly inaugurated President, Rutherford Hayes, invoked his powers of military intervention and called out federal troops to protect "by force" (as he noted in his diary) the property of the railroad companies, among whose leaders he counted many of his closest friends and supporters. In the end, the strike left more than a hundred dead, millions of dollars of property destroyed, and a toughened company and government stand against unions. Strikers were very often fired and blacklisted, their leaders fined and jailed. The War Department issued a pamphlet on "riot duty" and constructed for the first time a system of armories in major cities to house a standing "national guard." Industrialization of the state's military force seemed a necessary adjunct to the mechanization of production.

The very extremes of effect lent to the machine an aura of supreme power, as if it were an autonomous force that held human society in its grip. In *The First Century of the Republic*, a book of essays published by *Harper's* magazine in celebration of the nation's centennial in 1876, the economist David Wells observed that "like one of our mighty rivers," mechanization was "beyond control." And indeed the display in Machinery Hall in Philadelphia that summer gave credence to the image of a flood, though without Wells's ominous note. Here, in an exposition of machines removed from their working location, a profusion of mechanisms seduced the eye: power looms, lathes, sewing machines, presses, pumps, toolmaking machines, axles, shafts, wire cables, and locomotives. The Remington Arms Company, declaring its versatility, displayed one of its newest products: Christopher Schole's new "typewriter", an astonishing device for producing neat, legible messages at the touch of a finger. The twenty-nine-year-old Thomas A. Edison, already the wunderkind of invention, disclosed his "multiplex" telegraph, capable of carrying several messages on the same slender wire. And, most memorably, Alexander Graham Bell here gave the world first notice of the greatest wonder of electrical communication: the telephone. For sheer grandeur and sublimity, however, the mechanisms of communication could not compete with the two most imposing structures in the Hall: the thirty-foot-high Corliss Double Walking-Beam Steam Engine, which powered the entire ensemble from a single source, and its counterpart, a 7,000-pound electrical pendulum clock which governed, to the second, twenty-six lesser "slave" clocks around the building. Unstinted but channeled power and precisely regulated time: that combination seemed to hold the secret of progress. . . .

*       *       *

## II

The idea of an autonomous and omnipotent machine, brooking no resistance against its untold and ineluctable powers, became an article of faith. The image implied a popular social theory: the machine as a "human benefactor," a "great emancipator of man from the bondage of labor." Modern technology was mankind's "civilizing force," driving out superstition, poverty, ignorance. "Better morals, better sanitary conditions, better health, better wages," wrote Carroll D. Wright, chief of the Massachusetts Bureau of Statistics of Labor, in 1882; "these are the practical results of the factory system, as compared with what preceded it, and the results of all these have been a keener intelligence." Wright's paper, originally given as an address before the American Social Science Association, bore the title "The Factory System as an Element in Civilization."

The events of the 1870's and 1880's, however, also elicited less sanguine accounts of what the factory system had wrought. Even Wright adopted a defensive tone, warning against the seductive "poetry" and "idyllic sentiment" of many critics: "I am well aware that I speak against popular impression, and largely against popular sentiment when I assert that the factory system in every respect is vastly superior as an element in civilization to the domestic system which preceded it." Wright failed to acknowledge, however, that his account of the superior benefits of the system did not include the opportunity of workers to change their status within it; his defense assumes a permanent class of wage earners, a prospect abhorrent to believers in republican enlightenment and progress. Not surprisingly, a growing number of Americans openly questioned whether industrialization was in fact, in Henry George's words, "an unmixed good." As if in pointed rebuke of Wright's arguments and images, George observed the following year, in *Social Problems* (1883), that so-called labor-saving inventions, the "greater employment of machinery," and "greater division of labor," result in "positive evils" for the working masses, "degrading men into the position of mere feeders of machines." Machines employed in production under the present system are "absolutely injurious," "rendering the workman more dependent; depriving him of skill and of opportunities to acquire it; lessening his control over his own condition and his hope of improving it; cramping his mind, and in many cases distorting and enervating

his body." True, George found the source of such evils not in machines themselves but in unjust concentrations of land ownership. In the end, he shared
Wright's vision of the potential benefits of machinery, though not his conception of a permanent class of "operatives." George plainly perceived the
process of degradation in factory labor as strictly mechanical, experienced as
an *effect* of machinery. To a wider public than Wright had addressed, George's
views seemed irrefutable. . . .

*   *   *

## III

If Americans seemed especially intense in their response to mechanization,
especially obsessed with alternating images of mechanical plenitude and devastation, an explanation lies in the special circumstances of native industrialization, its speed, its scale, its thoroughness within a brief period. Suffering fewer
social barriers, possessing the largest domestic region convertible to a national
market without internal restriction, by the end of the century American industry rapidly surpassed its chief European rivals, England and Germany. Figures
of absolute increase signified the triumph: the production of raw steel rising
from 13 tons in 1860 to near 5,000 in 1890, and of steel rails multiplying ten
times in the same years; total agricultural output tripling between 1870 and
1900. Agriculture showed the most dramatic and immediate evidence. A single
mechanized farmer in 1896 was able to reap more wheat than eighteen men
working with horses and hand equipment sixty years earlier. As output increased, more land came under cultivation (increasing almost fivefold between
1850 and 1900, from about 15 to 37 percent of the total area of the country),
and the proportion of the agricultural work force (including owners, tenants,
and managers) declined precipitously from its height of 44 percent in 1880.
In the critical decade of the 1880's, the balance began its historic shift in
favor of nonfarm labor; heavy Northern investment, in machines to produce
cash crops such as cotton, tobacco, grain, and cattle (their steep profits flowing
as capital into industrial expansion), stimulated this process of displacement
into crowded cities already bursting with rural immigrants from overseas.

But such figures of expansion tell only the outside story. The inner story
concerned not only absolute increase but a revolutionary rise in *productivity*.
"We have increased the power of production with a given amount of personal
effort throughout the country," observed David Wells in 1885, "probably at
least twenty-five, and possibly forty percent." In such figures the American
propensity for mechanical improvement seemed to bear its most impressive
fruit.

Of course, that propensity characterized the entire industrial world, but
it had been a special mark of American manufacturing since its beginnings.
With a scarcity of skilled labor, of craftsmen and artisans with accumulated
experience in nascent industrial processes such as spinning, weaving, and mill-

ing, American circumstances placed a premium on mechanical invention and improvement. Scarcity of skills together with cheapness of land had maintained a relatively high cost of labor in the young United States. Moreover, as H. J. Habakkuk has explained, the relative absence of customary work processes and of formal engineering and scientific academies provided incentives for invention, for the devising of machines and techniques to compensate for labor scarcity. Without an inherited aristocratic social order, the new country held out more hope to entrepreneurs for social acceptance as well as material rewards. Many early industrial entrepreneurs had begun their working lives as craftsmen, mechanics with a knack for invention, and had risen to wealth and status as a result of their mechanical skill and entrepreneurial expertise. With mechanical efficiency a greater economic need in the United States than in Europe, and with business a freer field of endeavor, American inventor-manufacturers such as Eli Whitney and Elias Howe developed and refined the practice of interchangeable parts (originally in the making of small arms) considerably before their European counterparts. By the 1850's, the practical Yankee inventor-entrepreneur, the tinkerer with an eye on profit, had come to seem an American type, proof of the republican principle that self-taught men of skill and ingenuity might rise to wealth and social position.

The prominence of mechanical skill made it seem to many that the dramatic increases in productivity during the years of explosive growth after the Civil War arose from the logic of invention, of mechanical improvement itself. But new economic conditions in fact marked a radical discontinuity with the past difficult for many Americans to grasp. The new breed of business leaders were often skilled in finance, in market manipulation, in corporate organization: entreprenurial skills on a scale unimaginable to most manufacturers before the war. Moreover, they conducted their daily business through a growing system of managers, accountants, supervisors, lawyers: a burgeoning structure of business offices increasingly removed from the machines and labor in the factory itself. The process of invention and technological change lay increasingly in the hands of university-trained engineers and applied scientists, representing an entire new institutional formation which had mushroomed during and after the war. And industrial laborers now tended to be men and women without traditional skills, operators and machine tenders, with little hope of significant social improvement through their own talents and efforts. In short, the increasingly rigid social stratification that accompanied the dramatic rise in industrial productivity confused, angered, and frustrated masses of Americans, a growing percentage of them recent immigrants recruited into the very industrial system which seemed destined to dash their hopes of social improvement.

Technological determinism implied that machines demanded their own improvement, that they controlled the forms of production and drove their owners and workers. Americans were taught to view their machines as independent agencies of power, causes of "progress." Machines seemed fixed in shape, definite self-propelled objects in space. In fact, however, machinery underwent constant change in appearance, in function, in design. Machines were working parts of a dynamic system. And the motives for change, the source of industrial dynamism, lay not in the inanimate machine but in the economic necessities perceived by its owners. Higher rates of productivity through economies of scale and velocity, through greater exploitation of machinery and reorganization of both factory labor and corporate structures, were deliberate goals chosen by business leaders out of economic need. "Goaded by necessity and spurred by the prospect of higher returns," as David Landes writes, industrialists undertook a concerted quest for higher productivity. That quest proved the inner engine of mechanization. . . .

*   *   *

In these years the mighty river of industrial expansion threatened to take dominion everywhere, converting all labor to mechanical labor, to the production of commodities for distant markets. The spread of the machine meant the spread of the market: more of the continent and the society brought under the domain of political economy and its unconscious logic Wells explicated so vividly. Along with regional and local autonomy, age-old notions of space and time felt the impact of mechanization as a violent wrenching of the familiar. As more efficient machine production required greater attention to uniform parts and units of measurement, standardization of basic perceptions infiltrated the society. And the chief agent of such cultural changes was, of course, the most conspicuous machine of the age: the steam-driven locomotive, with its train of cars.

It is not difficult to account for the prominence of the railroad as the age's symbol of mechanization and of economic and political change. Railroad companies were the earliest giant corporations, the field of enterprise in which first appeared a new breed of men—the Cookes, Stanfords, Huntingtons, and Hills—of unprecedented personal wealth and untrammeled power. Not only did the railroad system make modern technology visible, intruding it as a physical presence in daily life, but it also offered means of exercising unexampled ruthlessness of economic power. In railroad monopolies, combinations, conspiracies to set rates and control traffic, lobbies to bribe public officials and buy legislatures, the nation had its first taste of robber barons on a grand scale.

At the same time the railroad system provided the age with fundamental lessons in physical and economic coordination. Its physical plant in these years represented the very best mechanical invention and improvement: greater load-bearing capabilities, higher speeds, and longer trains, following from air brakes, automatic couplers, block-signaling apparatus, standard-gauge tracks. Although often overcapitalized in the 1860's (through "watered stock," a favorite device of Wall Street speculators), the railroad system expanded into several national networks, providing major stimulation to basic industries like steel, construction, and machine making. In its corporate organization the system stressed coordination and interdependence, the railroad companies being the first to rationalize their business offices into central- and regional-sales, freight, passenger, and legal divisions. Resolutely private entities, even though they thrived on outlays of public funds and privileges through government agencies, the companies organized themselves along strict military lines; indeed, former Civil War generals often served as presidents and directors of operations. They emerged by the 1870's as competing private structures employing hundreds of thousands of citizens as managers, civil and mechanical engineers, lawyers, firemen and conductors, yard and gang laborers. Models of a new corporate world, they seemed the epitome of the modern machine.

Their prominence in America also followed from unique geographical conditions: the vast spaces to be traversed as cheap land, before the Civil War, encouraged far-flung settlements. As George Taylor has shown, a revolution in transportation proved necessary before "the almost explosive rush of industrial expansion which characterized the later decades of the century." Unlike the European situation, where mechanized transport appropriated existing roads and horse tracks as it overturned an older society and culture, here the railroad seemed to "open" places for settlement, for raw materials and transport to markets. As Wolfgang Schivelbusch observes about the American difference: "The mechanization of transport is not seen, as in Europe, as the destruction of a traditional culture, but as a means to gaining a new civilization from a hitherto worthless (because inaccessible) wilderness." The American railroad seemed to create new spaces, new regions of comprehension and economic value, and finally to incorporate a prehistoric geological terrain into historical time.

The exact economic value of this massive process has been a matter of some controversy among economic historians, Robert Fogel arguing that the "net benefit" of the displacement of the canal system by the railroad being "much less than is usually presumed." But there is no doubt that the railroad "increased the *economic accessibility*" of raw material. The railroads proved decisive in this area in facilitating that "interchange of matter" from one location to another (as Karl Marx put it), essential to industrial production. This change of location of raw materials and then of goods represented a radical breaking of spatial barriers, barriers of local and regional terrain and cultural difference. Thus, the external economy provided by the railroad in its increased velocity of transport included the incorporation of space and time as factors among the elements of production: the necessary act of overcoming barriers, of virtually annihilating space or distance by reconceiving it as time (places becoming identified as scheduled moments of departure and arrival), emerging as the major capital industry in the age of steam.

The necessity of pushing aside old concepts asserted itself especially in the establishment of standard time zones in 1883. Until that year, "local mean time" ruled across the continent, as it did throughout the world. Each locale assumed responsibility for setting its own time by tested methods of solar readings. Bells and clocks struck noon, for example, when the sun stood directly overhead: never exactly the same moment from place to place or week to week. Local life arranged itself in relation to the most influential community timepieces: church bells and steeple clocks, and after the 1840's, the cupolas and stark brick bell towers of mills and factories. The latter testified to a new importance assigned to time by the factory system, to promptness, regularity of work habits, and most of all, to the conversion of work into time-wages occurring within factory walls. But stubborn local standards persisted, and overlappings of regional times set by the larger cities and local times in the hinterlands formed a crazy-quilt pattern across the nation.

The necessity of regulating times appeared with the railroad; especially after the first transcontinental hookup in 1869, the situation seemed increasingly eccentric, to the point of danger and economic loss. Obviously, a railroad passing from New York to Chicago could not adjust itself to the dozens of local times different from each other by fractions of minutes (11 minutes 45 seconds, between Boston and New York, for example). Railroad corporations set their own times. By early 1883, there were about fifty such distinct private universes of time, each streaming on wheels through the countryside, oblivious of the others. Railroad stations, which quickly became the most influential source of time in the larger cities, often displayed several clocks, each indicating the time on specific lines, and one declaring the presumed local time.

The issue came to a head in these years: not coincidentally, years of increasingly destructive competition in which the smallest factors of technical innovation in production or distribution might make the difference between success and failure. It seemed in everyone's interest to eliminate the disadvantage of eccentric time. The American Society of Civil Engineers joined with the American Association for the Advancement of Science and similar groups to give the approval of science to standard time zones. In 1882 the engineers reported: "Mistakes in the hour of the day are frequent. In every city or town, in every State, discrepancies are met which produce great aggregate inconvenience. Thousands of engagements are broken. Innumerable disappointments and losses result." In 1883 the railroads acted and, by joint decision, placed the country—without act of Congress, President, or the courts—under a scheme of four "standard time zones." This, of course, was "railroad time." Most communities adjusted their clocks at the railroad's behest (Chicago held out for a brief spell), and where local time did not immediately fall before the rush of the industrial machine, it remained only as a kind of twitch of residual "nervousness." . . .

\*   \*   \*

**IV**

In the quest for greater productivity, more efficient machines, more output per unit of cost, calculation of several kinds played an increasingly significant role. With the enlarged role of the accounting office in decisions relevant to materials and labor, transportation, advertising, and sales, mathematical considerations entered the business world in a major way. At an opposite pole to commerce, another kind of abstract calculation appeared in an enlarged and more systematic role for science, for basic research as well as applied science and engineering. Professional, white-collar personnel expanded the size and influence of office and laboratory, both increasingly distant from the shop floor but increasingly pertinent to the daily arrangements and pace of factory life. Calculations of economy and of science developed into professional processes with their own skills and rules, but in the end their effects were felt in the changing relations between human labor and machines, in the steady encroachment of mechanization on the forms of work, of everyday life, and social transactions throughout America.

The enhanced importance of refined and reliable calculations implied a position of new significance for knowledge, a critical role for trained abstract thought within the productive system. This development appeared in an intricate process of institutional change: the appearance of new schools, of new relations between formal education and corporate industries, and greater accessibility of science to industry. Events in the 1870's and 1880's prepared the way for the turn-of-the-century research laboratory as an integral component of the electrical and chemical industries. The role of scientific method and knowledge within industries expanded, however, not primarily from schools and laboratories themselves, but from new perceptions on the part of industrial managers of the advantages of scientific calculation in their quest for greater productivity, a quest itself spurred by more systematic and rationalized methods of economic calculation.

The incorporation of basic science and formal technological training with industrial production quickened dramatically during these decades of economic uncertainty. During the earlier stages of industrialization, science and technology had seemed wholly separate and often antagonistic fields, theoretical scientists (often gentlemen amateurs) holding themselves aloof from either direct mechanical application or entrepreneurship. Even as late as the early nineteenth century, craftsmen-inventors such as Elias Howe and Oliver Evans ruled over technological innovation, using an on-the-job cut-and-try technique of experimentation. Such figures predominated especially in America, where formal science bore the onus of impracticality and remoteness from human need. In fact, however, practical innovators were less ignorant and disdainful of basic principles than the popular notion recognized, and trained university scientists, particularly geologists, served as consultants for mining and railroad companies even before the Civil War. Even as the image of the self-taught cut-and-try inventor remained uppermost in popular thought as more distinctly American than the "gentleman scientist" or pure experimentalist, the currents began to converge. Graduate programs in science developed at major universities, and specialized schools of engineering supported by private funds, such as Massachusetts Institute of Technology (1866), proliferated; by 1900, the list of technical institutes included Case, Carnegie, Stevens, and Worcester Polytechnical Institute. With their close ties to private industries, their willingness to design their curricula to meet industrial needs, such schools fostered specialization of functions, a process reflected in the new professional societies splitting off from the original American Society of Civil Engineers (founded in 1852): mining, mechanical, electrical, and naval engineers all forming distinct societies with their own journals and meetings in these years.

Engineering thus transformed itself from its earlier empiricism and artisanship in order to mediate the vast structural changes in mechanical production compelled by economic need. "The artisan was replaced in the vanguard of technological progress by a new breed," writes Edwin Layton. "In place of oral traditions passed from master to apprentice, the new technologist substituted a college education, a professional organization, and a technical literature patterned on that of science." The schools, the professional societies, the new roles of responsibility within corporate hierarchies, fostered a new quality of mind and outlook: disciplined, systematic, administrative. Trained to combine the findings of formal science with economic, legal, and logistical considerations, the new engineers brought into industry an apparently detached, objective, and highly specialized approach to solving problems. But whether designing the flow of work in factories or rating the output of machines, the engineer served finally a chronic need of the industrial system: to impose system and order, through improved machinery, for the sake of assuring a reliable return on investments. As David Noble has argued, the new institutional ties between engineering and industry served that need of capitalists, more dire in time of crisis, "routinely to anticipate the future in order to survive."

The consequences were felt throughout the society and culture: most notably in the increasing specialization of knowledge, its fragmentation into arcane regions of technique and learning, and in the growing concentration of the power accompanying specialized knowledge and skills within private corporations. In the 1870's and 1880's, however, this process remained fairly hidden from view. With public attention focused on severe economic fluctuations, rising tensions between capital and labor, and the colorful if morally dubious lives of captains of industry, the steady incorporation of institutionalized rationality into the system went generally unnoticed. Moreover, persisting popular images of business success through self-help, luck and pluck, and venturesome risk taking, left little room for the concept of controlled and systematic anticipation of the future.

It remained a common belief that the system owed its dynamism and innovations to the personal "genius" of prominent individuals like Thomas A. Edison. One of the most popular Americans of his own time and since, Edison in his public guise represented a form of knowledge starkly at odds with new realities; indeed, at odds even with the truth about his own activities. Like the image of the isolated machine with its alternating demonic and Promethean currents, popular perceptions of Edison distorted the underlying logic of events, making "progress" seem both more accidental and more innocent.

Already renowned by the 1876 exposition for his multiflex telegraph, his improved ticker tape, his many patented devices, and his success as a manufacturer of his own stock-quotation printer, Edison rose to genuine fame with the invention of the phonograph in 1877 (he was then thirty years old). With his talking machine and, in 1879, the electric light bulb, Edison attracted perhaps the widest attention of the age in the press, journals, and popular books. In these years, the Edison legend took shape: the stories of his childhood experiments in rural Ohio with chemistry and electricity, his exploits as a trainboy on the Grand Truck Railroad of Canada and Central Michigan, the newspaper he published on board the train, his self-taught mastery of mechanics and electricity, his years of study, wandering, working at odd jobs, until his arrival in New York in 1868 and his invention of a stock-quotation printer which won the attention of Western Union and launched his career. The periodical literature stressed two key elements of Edison's success: his natural genius, flourishing without formal school training, and his instinctual entrepreneurship which led him unerringly to *useful*, that is to say, marketable, inventions. Thus, the public Edison seemed to embody in perfect combination precisely what many at the time felt America to be losing, its rural Protestant virtues of the self-made man, and what it was gaining in the way of material improvements. Edison seemed to hold together the old and new, the world of the tinkerer and the world of modern industry; the age of steam (his youth on the railroad) and the coming age of electricity. He made the new America of cities and complicated machinery seem to evolve in an orderly fashion from the old America of country towns and youthful high jinks on country railroads.

As a form of popular knowledge and a version of the new industrial realities, the most critical feature of the Edison image concerned the origins of invention. In 1876, Edison had sold his manufacturing business in Newark and withdrew with a small group of helpers to Menlo Park, a quiet New Jersey town about an hour by railroad from New York, where he established the first significant industrial-research laboratory in America. After five years he moved to larger, better-equipped buildings in Orange, New Jersey, but the period at Menlo Park from 1876 to 1881 proved the most fertile of his career, yielding the most dramatic products of his labors: the phonograph, the improved telephone, the incandescent lamp, and the basic elements of a central power-generating system. It was during these years, too, that Edison assumed his best-known role, as "Wizard of Menlo Park." And in their accounts of the wizard, popular stories in the press and journals portrayed a character part Prometheus, bringing light, and part Faust, tainted with satanic association. The setting itself—the mysterious fire-lit laboratories in wooden buildings within a peaceful rural landscape—enhanced the demonic aura. But demonism was no more than a whiff, dissolved by descriptions of the guileless, open-faced, wry and salty Midwestern boy-man Edison turned out to be. Instead, the wizard image served another primary function: to account for the origins of

Edison's inventions as personal "genius," out of the thin air of a fertile imagination and heroic persistence. "His inventions were calling to him with a sort of siren voice," wrote *Scribner's* in 1879. Moreover, as wizard and natural genius, Edison had no need of formal science, of mathematics and theory; the press played up his superiority to the schools, which on occasion issued scornful pronouncements upon him as a mere "mechanic."

Thus, Edison offered a reassurance that the old routes to personal success were still open, that the mass of inventions and improvements profoundly altering industry and reshaping personal lives truly emerged from a heroic wresting of the secrets of nature for human betterment. The phonograph especially, the inanimate made animate, inspired rhapsodies of technological fantasy. " 'If this can be done,' we ask, 'what is there that cannot be?' " exclaimed the writer in *Scribner's*. "We feel that there may, after all, be a relief for all human ills in the great storehouse of nature," he continued, adding pointedly: "There is an especial appropriateness, perhaps, in its occurring in a time of more than usual discontent."

With his eye to publicity, and no doubt his bemused enjoyment of so much attention, Edison seemed glad to collaborate in the image of the wizard, the wunderkind. In fact, however, Menlo Park and the later laboratories were testing grounds for the full-scale industrial research organizations which would develop within private industries such as General Electric and the American Telephone and Telegraph Company by the turn of the century. Edison hired university-trained scientists among his staff, including Francis R. Upton, a specialist in mathematical physics. Menlo Park was a team operation, the earliest research and development laboratory in America; Edison established the place as an "invention factory," a place where invention might be made to order for private industry. He differed from much of his public by having no illusions on that score. Invention was his business. . . .

\*     \*     \*

Whether acts of wizardry or genius, or sheer luck, Edison's work belonged to the evolving structure of experimental science and its alliance with industrial capitalism. To stress this obvious fact is not to debunk the myth but to place it in perspective: to see it as a myth which disguises the radical changes occurring in the origins and uses of knowledge in these years. The new relations of science to industrial technology ultimately represented a new relation of human labor to the process of production. Separated by increasingly complex and dense institutions, the shop floor and the research laboratory belonged to the same universe of production. With machines performing more of the work previously performed by people, workers themselves were required to know less in order to perform their tasks—to know less because their machines know more. Mechanization entailed, then, the transference of technical knowledge from workers to machines, a process mediated by a new corps of trained engineers. The rise of specialized skills and arcane knowledge corresponded precisely to the obliteration of traditional knowledge among skilled manual laborers. The growing numbers of trained technologists on one hand and unskilled workers on the other were two faces of the same process.

As if called forth by this prime economic motive, Frederick W. Taylor, a foreman at the Midvale Steel Company in Pennsylvania, inaugurated in the 1880's his famous "time-study" experiments, aimed at elimination of waste, inefficiency, and what he called "soldiering" on the part of workers. With his stopwatch—a further encroachment of time on physical movement—Taylor proposed to systematize exactly that process Wells had described as production through destruction: the absolute subordination of "living labor" to the machine. He envisioned a complete renovation of the production process, with standardization of tools and equipment, replanning of factories for greater efficiency, and "piece-rate" method of payment as incentive for workers. In *The Principles of Scientific Management* (1911), Taylor made explicit the heart of his program: to take possession for management of the "mass of traditional knowledge" once possessed by the workers themselves, "knowledge handed down to them by word of mouth, through the many years in which their trade has been developed from the primitive condition." For Taylor the stopwatch and flowchart were basic instruments whereby management might reduce that knowledge to measurable motions, eradicating their workers' autonomy at one stroke while enhancing their productivity.

Thus, the social distribution of knowledge begins a major shift, a transference (as far as technology and technique are concerned) from bottom to top, in these years of extensive and intensive mechanization. Just as important, and as a symbol of the process, *thought* now appears often in the dumb, mystifying shapes of machines, of standing and moving mechanical objects as incapable of explaining themselves to the unknowing eye as the standing stones of ancient peoples. The momentous event of mechanization, of science and technology coming to perform the labor most significant to the productivity of the system, reproduced itself in ambivalent cultural images of machines and inventors, and in displacements running like waves of shock through the social order.

Matthew Josephson

# *The Robber Barons*

In John D. Rockefeller, economists and historians have often seen the classic example of the modern monopolist of industry. It is true that he worked with an indomitable will, and a faith in his star à la Napoleon, to organize his industry under his own dictatorship. He was moreover a great innovator. Though not the first to attempt the plan of the pool—there were pools even in the time of Cicero—his South Improvement Company was the most impressive instance in history of such an organism. But when others had reached the stage of the pool, he was building the solid framework of a monopoly.

Rockefeller's problems were far more difficult than those for instance of Carnegie, who quickly won special economies through constructing a very costly, well-integrated, technically superior plant upon a favored site. In the oil-refining business, a small still could be thrown up in the '70's for manufacturing kerosene or lubricating oil at a tenth the cost of the Edgar Thomson steel works. The petroleum market was mercurial compared to iron, steel and even coal; there were thousands of petty capitalists competing for advantage in it. Hence the tactics of Rockefeller, the bold architecture of the industrial edifice he reared, have always aroused the liveliest interest, and he himself appeals to us for many reasons as the greatest of the American industrialists. In no small degree this interest is owing to the legend of "Machiavellian" guile and relentlessness which has always clung to this prince of oil.

After the dissolution of the South Improvement Company, Rockefeller and Flagler had come to a conference of the irate diggers of petroleum with mild proposals of peaceful coöperation, under the heading of the "Pittsburgh Plan." The two elements in the trade, those who produced the raw material in the earth and those who refined it, were to combine forces harmoniously.

"You misunderstand us," Rockefeller and Flagler said. "Let us see what combination will do."

There was much suspicion. One of Titusville's independent refiners (one of those whom Standard Oil tried to erase from the scene) made a rather warlike speech against the plan, and he recalls that Rockefeller, who had been softly swinging back and forth in a rocking chair, his hands over his face, through the conference, suddenly stopped rocking, lowered his hands and looked straight at his enemy. His glance was fairly terrifying.

*You never saw such eyes. He took me all in, saw just how much fight he could expect from me, and then up went his hands and back and forth went his chair.*

At this very moment, Rockefeller was arranging anew the secret rebates with the leading railroads of the country, which had been so loudly decried in 1872. Upon the refined oil he shipped from Cleveland he received a rebate of 50 cents a barrel, giving him an advantage of 25 percent over his competitors. Once more the railroads continued a form of espionage for his company. But all arrangements were now effected in a more complete secrecy.

Equally secret was the campaign Rockefeller pursued to amalgamate with his own company the strongest refineries in the country. According to Miss Tarbell's "History," he now constantly "bent over a map of the refining interests of the country," or hurried from one secret conference to another, at Cleveland, New York, or at Saratoga, "the Mecca of schemers," where long hours of nocturnal debate in a certain pavilion brought into his plan the refineries of Pittsburgh and Philadelphia. Look at what combination has done in one city, Cleveland, he would say. The plan now was for all the chosen ones to become the nucleus of a private company which should gradually acquire control of all the refineries everywhere, become the only shippers, and have the mastery of the railroads in the matter of freight rates. Those who came in were promised wealth beyond their dreams. The remarkable economies and profits of the Standard were exposed to their eyes. "We mean to secure the entire refining business of the world," they were told. They were urged to dissemble their actions. Contracts were entered into with the peculiar secret rites which Mr. Rockefeller habitually preferred. They were signed late at night at his Euclid Avenue home in Cleveland. The participants were besought not to tell even their wives about the new arrangements, to conceal the gains they made, not to drive fast horses or put on style, or buy new bonnets, or do anything to let people suspect there were unusual profits in oil-refining, since that might invite competition.

In this campaign perhaps fifteen of the strongest firms in the country, embracing four-fifths of the refining trade, were brought into alliance with the Standard Oil Company by 1875–78. Among them were individuals who had opposed Rockefeller most strenuously a season before: the ablest of these,

J. J. Vandergrift and John Archbold of the Pennsylvania oil regions, Charles Pratt and Henry Rogers of New York, entering the family of Standard Oil as partners by exchange of stock. They continued under their own corporate identity as "Acme Oil Company," or "Pratt & Rogers," but shared the same freight advantages as Standard Oil, used the same sources of information and surveillance, the common organization of agents and dealers in the distributing field.

"I wanted able men with me," Rockefeller said later. "I tried to make friends with these men. I admitted their ability and the value of their enterprise. I worked to convince them that it would be better for both to cooperate."

In the meantime a campaign no less elaborate and bold was pursued to eliminate from the field those firms whose existence was considered superfluous. Rockefeller did not "confiscate" his opponents outright. In the interests of his great consolidation he measured the value of their properties without sentiment, and gave his terms. Thus a plant which had cost $40,000 might in the future, after his own plans had matured, be worth little more than $15,000, or 37½ cents on the dollar. Such an offer he would make and this only. The victim, as the case might be, would surrender if timid, or attempt resistance in trade, or practice blackmail upon him, or fight him to the finish and have resort to the highest courts.

Where a "deal" across the table could not be effected, Rockefeller might try a variety of methods of expropriation. With his measured spirit, with his organized might, he tested men and things. There were men and women of all sorts who passed under his implacable rod, and their tale, gathered together reverently by Miss Tarbell, has contributed to the legend of the "white devil" who came to rule over American industry.

A certain widow, a Mrs. Backus of Cleveland, who had inherited an oil-refinery, had appealed to Mr. Rockefeller to preserve her, "the mother of fatherless children." And he had promised "with tears in his eyes that he would stand by her." But in the end he offered her only $79,000 for a property which had cost $200,000. The whole story of the defenseless widow and her orphans, the stern command, the confiscation of two-thirds of her property, when it came out made a deep stir and moved many hearts.

In another instance a manufacturer of improved lubricating oils set himself up innocently in Cleveland, and became a client of the Standard Oil for his whole supply of residuum oils. The Rockefeller company encouraged him at first, and sold him 85 barrels a day according to a contract. He prospered for three years, then suddenly when the monopoly was well launched in 1874, his supply was cut down to 12 barrels a day, the price was increased on some pretense, and the shipping cost over the railroads similarly increased. It became impossible to supply his trade. He offered to buy of Rockefeller 5,000 barrels and store it so that he might assure himself of a future supply. This was refused.

"I saw readily what that meant," the man Morehouse related to the Hepburn Committee in 1879. "That meant squeeze you out—Buy out your works. . . . They paid $15,000 for what cost me $41,000. He [Rockefeller] said that he had facilities for freighting and that the coal-oil business belonged to them; and any concern that would start in that business, they had sufficient money to lay aside a fund and wipe them out—these are the words."

In the field of retail distribution, Rockefeller sought to create a great marketing machine delivering directly from the Standard Oil's tank wagons to stores in towns and villages throughout the United States. But in the laudable endeavor to wipe out wasteful wholesalers or middlemen, he would meet with resistance again, as in the producing fields. Where unexpectedly stout resistance from competing marketing agencies was met, the Standard Oil would simply apply harsher weapons. To cut off the supplies of the rebel dealer, the secret aid of the railroads and the espionage of their freight agents would be invoked again and again. A message such as the following would pass between Standard Oil officials:

We are glad to know you are on such good terms with the railroad people that Mr. Clem [handling independent oil] gains nothing by marking his shipments by numbers instead of by names.

Or again:

Wilkerson and Company received car of oil Monday 13th—70 barrels which we suspect slipped through at the usual fifth class rate—in fact we might say we know it did—paying only $41.50 freight from here. Charges $57.40. Please turn another screw.

The process of "Turning the Screw" has been well described by Henry D. Lloyd. One example is that of a merchant in Nashville, Tennessee, who refused to come to terms and buy from Standard Oil; he first found that all his shipments were reported secretly to the enemy; then by a mysterious coincidence his freight rates on shipments of all kinds were raised 50 percent, then doubled, even tripled, and he felt himself under fire from all parts of the field. He attempted to move his merchandise by a great roundabout route, using the Baltimore & Ohio and several other connecting roads, but was soon "tracked down," his shipments lost, spoiled. The documents show that the independent oil-dealers' clients were menaced in every way by the Standard Oil marketing agency; it threatened to open competing grocery stores, to sell oats, meat, sugar, coffee at lower prices. "If you do not buy our oil we will start a grocery store and sell goods at cost and put you out of business."

By this means, opponents in the country at large were soon "mopped up"; small refiners and small wholesalers who attempted to exploit a given district were routed at the appearance of the familiar red-and-green tank wagons, which were equal to charging drastically reduced rates for oil in one town, and twice as much in an adjacent town where the nuisance of competition no longer existed. There were, to be sure, embittered protests from the victims, but the marketing methods of Standard Oil were magnificently efficient and centralized; waste and delay were overcome; immense savings were brought directly to the refining monopoly.

But where the Standard Oil could not carry on its expansion by peaceful means, it was ready with violence; its faithful servants knew even how to apply the modern weapon of dynamite.

In Buffalo, the Vacuum Oil Company, one of the "dummy" creatures of the Standard Oil system, became disturbed one day by the advent of a vigorous competitor who built a sizable refinery and located it favorably upon the water front. The offices of Vacuum conducted at first a furtive campaign of intimidation. Then emboldened or more desperate, they approached the chief mechanic of the enemy refinery, holding whispered conferences with him in a rowboat on Lake Erie. He was asked to "do something." He was urged to "go back to Buffalo and construct the machinery so it would bust up . . . or smash up," to fix the pipes and stills "so they cannot make a good oil. . . . And then if you would give them a little scare, they not knowing anything about the business. You know how . . . ." In return the foreman would have a life annuity which he might enjoy in another part of the country.

So in due time a small explosion took place in the independent plant, as Lloyd and Miss Tarbell tell the tale, from the records of the trial held several years later, in 1887. The mechanic, though on the payrolls of the Vacuum Oil Company, led a cursed existence, forever wandering without home or country, until in complete hysteria he returned to make a clean breast of the whole affair. The criminal suit against high officials of the Standard Oil monopoly included Henry Rogers and John Archbold, but the evil was laid by them to the "overenthusiasm" of underlings. Evidence of conspiracy was not found by the court, but heavy damages were awarded to the plaintiff, who thereafter plainly dreaded to reënter the dangerous business.

These and many other anecdotes, multiplied, varied or even distorted, spread through the Oil Regions of Pennsylvania and elsewhere through the country (as ogre-tales are fed to children), and were accumulated to make a strange picture of Mr. Rockefeller, the baron of oil. Miss Tarbell in her "History," written in her "muck-raking" days, has dwelt upon them with love. She has recorded them in rending tones with a heart bleeding for the petty capitalists for whom alone "life ran swift and ruddy and joyous" before the "great villain" arrived, and with his "big hand reached out from nobody knew where to steal their conquest and throttle their future."

But if truth must be told, the smaller capitalists, in the producing field especially, were themselves not lacking in predatory or greedy qualities; as Miss Tarbell herself admits, they were capable of hurrying away from church on Sundays to tap enemy tanks or set fire to their stores of oil. What they lacked, as the Beards have commented, was the discipline to maintain a producers' combination equal in strength to that of the refiners. The other factors in the industry engaged in individualistic marketing or refining ventures were very possibly "mossbacks," as one of the Standard Oil chieftains growled, "left in the lurch by progress."

The campaigns for consolidation, once launched, permitted Rockefeller little rest, and engaged his generalship on many fronts at once. In a curious interview given while he was in Europe, cited by Flynn, he himself exclaimed:

> *How often I had not an unbroken night's sleep, worrying about how it was all coming out. . . . Work by day and worry by night, week in and week out, month after month. If I had foreseen the future I doubt whether I would have had the courage to go on.*

With unblinking vigilance he conducted throughout his company an eternal war against waste. We have spoken of his unequaled efficiency and power of organization. There is a famous note to his barrel factory in his careful bookkeeper's hand which has been cited with amused contempt by his critics, to show how attention to small details absorbed his soul. It reads:

> *Last month you reported on hand, 1,119 bungs. 10,000 were sent you beginning this month. You have used 9,527 this month. You report 1,092 on hand. What has become of the other 500?*

It is not a laughing matter, this affair of 500 barrel bungs, worth at the most a dollar or two in all. Rockefeller's hatred of waste told him that in a large-scale industry the rescued pennies multiplied a million times or more represented enormous potential gains. This was to be true of all the great industrial leaders after Rockefeller's time; the spirit regarded as parsimony is a large-visioned conception of technical efficiency in handling big machines. Thus the feeding of horses, the making of his own glue, hoops, barrels, all was carefully supervised and constantly reduced in cost. Barrels were cut $1.25 apiece, saving $4,000,000 a year, cans were reduced 15 cents, saving $5,000,000 a year, and so forth. In absorbing the services of J. J. Vandergrift, in 1872, Rockefeller had acquired as an ally to his enterprise a combination of small pipe lines called the United Pipe Lines. His lieutenants then constructed more pipes; and by 1876 he controlled almost half the existing pipe lines, some running 80 to 100 miles, to the railroad terminals and shipping points. At this time the largest pipe-line interest in competition with Standard Oil's was the Empire Transportation Company, headed by Colonel Joseph Potts, but dominated by the officers of the Pennsylvania Railroad, which held an option over the entire property.

Himself an aggressive entrepreneur, Potts soon found that he must expand or suffer extinction. To the alarm of the Rockefeller organization, he purchased several big refineries in New York and proceeded to pipe crude oil from the oil fields and over the railroad to seaboard. Rockefeller vehemently petitioned the railroad to withdraw from his domain. Refused at an interview, he promised that he would take his own measures, and left his adversaries with expressions of sanctimonious regret, the form in which his most deadly threats were usually offered.

It was war, a war of rates. He moved with lightning speed. At once the other railroads, Erie and New York Central, were ordered to stand by, lowering their freight rates for him while he slashed the price of refined oil in every market which Potts reached.

But Potts, a stubborn Presbyterian, fought back harder than anyone Rockefeller had ever encountered. He replied in kind by further price cuts; he then began to build large refineries at the coast ports, lined up independent oil-producers behind him, and reserves in quantities of tank cars, in barges, ships, dock facilities. During the bitter conflict, with which, as Flynn relates, the hills and fields of Pennsylvania resounded, both sides, and the railroads supporting them as well, suffered heavy wounds. Yet Rockefeller would not desist, since Standard Oil's whole system of organization was endangered.

In the midst of this furious engagement a great blow fell upon the enemies of John D. Rockefeller, as if given by the hand of God to whom he constantly prayed. During the summer of 1877 the workers of the Baltimore & Ohio Railroad struck against wage cuts and their strike spread quickly to adjacent railroads, raging with especial violence in the Pennsylvania system. The most destructive labor war the nation had ever known was now seen in Baltimore and Pittsburgh, with militant mobs fighting armed troops and setting in flames property of great value in revenge for the many deaths they suffered. During this storm which the railroad barons had sown by cutting wages 20 percent and doubling the length of freight trains, the Pennsylvania interests quickly came to terms with Standard Oil, so that they might be free to turn and crush the rebellious workers. The entire business of Empire Transportation was sold out to the oil combination at their own terms, while Potts was called off. In Philadelphia, Rockefeller and his partners, quietly jubilant, received the sword of the weeping Potts.

The oil industry as a whole was impressed with the victory of Standard Oil over a railroad ring which had seemed invincible in the past. In a movement of fear many other interests hastened to make terms with Rockefeller. By the end of 1878 he controlled all the existing pipe-line systems; through a new freight pool he directed traffic or quantities of supplies to the various regions or cities as he pleased.

By 1876 this industry had assumed tremendous proportions. Of the annual output of nearly 10,000,000 barrels, the Standard Oil Company controlled approximately 80 percent, while exports of petroleum products to the value of $32,000,000 passed through their hands. But in 1877 the great Bradford oil field was opened with a wild boom, the uproarious coal-oil scenes of '59 were enacted anew, crowds rushed to the new fields, acreage values boomed, oil gushed out in an uncontrollable flood—half again as much oil as existed before came forth almost overnight. The markets grew demoralized again, just when Rockefeller seemed to have completed his conquest of the old Oil Regions.

What was he to do? In the two years that followed he directed his organization at the high tension of an ordnance department in wartime, so that piping, refining and marketing capacity might be expanded in time, and the almost untenable supply handled without faltering. With utmost energy a huge building program was carried on and further millions were staked on the hazardous business. Then, holding down the unruly producers, he imposed harsh terms through his pipe lines, refusing storage, forcing them to sell the oil they drilled "for immediate shipment" at the depressed prices of 64 to 69 cents a barrel, or have it run into the ground.

The overproduction could not be stopped. The oil men raged at the great machine which held them in bonds. Once more the independents gathered all their forces together to form a protective combination of their own. They founded the Parliament of Petroleum. They raised funds to construct an immense "free" pipe line running over the mountains to the seaboard, and ridding them at last of the railroads which hemmed them in. The new Tidewater Pipe Line would break Standard's control over railroad rates and bring crude oil to the sea.

Rockefeller's agents now lobbied in the state legislature of Pennsylvania to have the proposed pipe line banned. Failing of this his emissaries were thrown out over the state to buy up right of way in the path of the enemy's advance. But the Tidewater's engineers moved with equal speed and secrecy, eluded the defense which Rockefeller threw in their way and by April, 1879, completed their difficult project.

From successive stations, the great pumps were to drive oil over the very top of the Alleghenies, and down to Williamsport, touching the Reading Railroad, which had joined forces with the independents. Amid picturesque celebration—while the spies of the Standard Oil looked on incredulously—the valves were opened, the oil ran over the mountain and down toward the sea! Rockefeller was checkmated—but to whom would the producers and their free pipe line sell the crude oil at the seaboard? They had no inkling, though they berated him, of the extent of his control at the outlet.

The opposition to the Rockefeller "conspiracy" now rose to its climax of enthusiasm. The hundreds of petty oil men who fought to remain "independent" and keep their sacred right to flood the market or "hold up" consumers at their own pleasure, won sympathy everywhere; and with the aid of local politicians in New York and Pennsylvania they also had their day in court. Their tumult had grown so violent that at long last the lawmakers of

Pennsylvania moved to prosecute the monopolists for "conspiracy in restraint of trade." Writs were served and on April 29, 1879, a local Grand Jury indicted John D. Rockefeller, William Rockefeller, J. A. Bostwick, Henry Flagler, Daniel O'Day, J. J. Vandergrift and other chieftains of Standard Oil for criminal conspiracy, to "secure a monopoly of the oil industry, to oppress other refiners, to injure the carrying trade, to extort unreasonable railroad rates, to fraudulently control prices," etc. Simultaneously in New York State, the legislature appointed a committee of investigation of railroads, headed by the young lawyer A. Barton Hepburn. Forced to look at all the facts which were brought out by the Hepburn Committee, the nation was shocked. The railroad interests, as archconspirators, were at once under heavy fire. But no one understood the scope and meaning of the new phase reached in industrial life at this stage, save perhaps Mr. Chauncey Depew, who in a moment of illumination exclaimed on behalf of the railroad interests he so gallantly championed: "Every manufacturer in the state of New York existed by violence and lived by discrimination. . . . By secret rates and by deceiving their competitors as to what their rates were and by evading all laws of trade these manufacturers exist." This was God's truth and certainly true of all the other states in the Union. And of course under the prevailing circumstances there was nothing to be done, save recommend certain "regulative" laws.

With Rockefeller, there had arisen the great industrial combination in colossal and "sinister" form; he was the mighty bourgeois who was to expropriate all the petty bourgeois and his name was to be the rallying cry of parties and uprisings. The outlook for monopoly seemed dark, yet the trial, in the name of a democratic sovereignty which held "sacred" the property of the "conspirators," whatever the means by which they may have preëmpted or confiscated such property—was to be simply a comedy, and was to be enacted again and again. Before the bar of justice, Rockefeller and his brilliant lieutenants would appear, saying, "I refuse to answer on the advice of counsel." A Henry Rogers, a Flagler, would use every shift which such philosophers of the law as Joseph Choate or Samuel C. T. Dodd might counsel. They would "refuse to incriminate themselves" or evade reply on a point of technicality, or lie pointblank. Or, as in the case of the terribly cynical Archbold, they would simply jest, they would make mock of their bewildered prosecutors.

It was Rockefeller who made the most profound impression upon the public. He seemed distinguished in person; with his tall stooping figure, his long well-shaped head, his even jaw. His long, fine nose, his small birdlike eyes set wide apart, with the narrowed lids drooping a little, and the innumerable tiny wrinkles, made up a remarkable physiognomy. But his mouth was a slit, like a shark's. Rockefeller, impeccably dressed and groomed, thoroughly composed, pretendedly anxious to please, foiled his accusers with ease. Every legal subterfuge was used by him with supreme skill. Certain of his denials were legally truthful, as Flynn points out, since stockownership concerning which he was questioned was often entrusted temporarily (in time for such trials) to mere clerks or bookkeepers in his employ.

But the moment came when he was asked specifically about his connection with the notorious refiners' pool of 1872.

"Was there a Southern Improvement Company?"

"I have heard of such a company."

"Were you not in it?"

"I was not."

His hearers were amazed at the apparent perjury he made pointblank with even voice and an inscrutable movement of the eyes. But no! He had been only a director of the *South Improvement Company*, and not of the "Southern Improvement Company," as the prosecutor had named it by mistake.

If Rockefeller was embittered by the cruel fame he won, he never showed it. The silence he preserved toward all reproaches or questions may have been a matter of clever policy; yet it suggested at bottom a supreme contempt for his critics and accusers alike.

"We do not talk much—we saw wood!"

There were times when his movements were hampered, times when he dared not enter the State of Pennsylvania though the authorities there called for him impatiently; times when it was equally convenient to remain almost in hiding at his New York headquarters in Pearl Street, while the world at large howled against him. Yet he moved with unequaled agility and force against all serious attacks upon his industrial barony.

The menace of the Tidewater Pipe Line which cut through his network of railroads and refineries he must crush at all costs. This was far more important than any impeachment of his character. Fertile in expedients at a crisis, he could also be infinitely patient. It used to be said: "To Mr. Rockefeller a day is as a year, and a year as a day. He can wait, but he never gives up." Now when he perceived that the Tidewater's line to the sea was a reality, he besieged it from all sides. On the one hand he offered to buy all the oil it ran, a tempting offer which would have made the affair most profitable to the stockholders. Rebuffed here he proceeded to use the inventions of his rivals and build a long pipe line of his own to the sea. Night and day his engineers and gangs labored in the mountains, to connect the Bradford fields with the Standard Oil terminal at Bayonne. Then before the walls of Bayonne, where lay his great coastal refineries and storage tanks, his pipe line was stopped by an interested railroad from which he would have removed his freight business. The Town Council of Bayonne was induced to be friendly and grant a franchise; the Mayor who resisted for a time was suddenly won over; and in all secrecy, because of the need of haste to prevent a blocking franchise by the railroad, his gangs assembled. There were 300 men ready in the night of September 22, 1879, with all materials, tools, wagons gathered, waiting for the signal—the swift passage of an ordinance by the Town Council and its signing by the Mayor. Then with mad speed the trench across the city was dug, the pipes laid, jointed and covered, before the dawn. The National Transit Company was completed as the largest pipe-line system in the field.

His own line of communications was now secured against the enemy. But he also pursued a campaign of secret stock purchase for control, gaining a minority interest in the Tidewater company, creating dissensions within, damaging its credit, detaching its officials, instigating suits for receivership, serving writs, injunctions, and more writs, until the managers seemed to struggle for their very sanity. Day by day these blows fell mysteriously, until in 1882 the adversary surrendered and effected the best agreement possible under the circumstances. By this a minor part of the oil-transporting business was apportioned to itself and it yielded up its independence after four years of fighting an unresting, infinitely armed master. All the pipe lines were now amalgamated under Standard Oil control; the great railroads, notably the Pennsylvania, were forced by agreement and in return for a stipulated yearly ransom to retire from the business of oil transportation forever. John D. Rockefeller at the age of forty-four had accomplished his ambition—he was supreme in the oil industry, "the symbol of the American monopolist."

Up to 1881 the forty-odd companies controlled by Rockefeller and his partners formed a kind of *entente cordiale* bound by interchange of stock. This form of union being found inadequate or impermanent, the counsel of the Standard Oil Company, Samuel C. T. Dodd, came forward with his idea of the Trust. By a secret agreement of 1882, all the existing thirty-seven stockholders in the divers enterprises of refining, piping, buying or selling oil conveyed their shares "in trust" to nine Trustees: John and William Rockefeller, O. H. Payne, Charles Pratt, Henry Flagler, John Archbold, W. G. Warden, Jabez Bostwick and Benjamin Brewster. The various stockholders then received "trust certificates" in denominations of $100 in return for the shares they had deposited; while the Trustees, controlling two-thirds of all the shares, became the direct stockholders of all the companies in the system, empowered to serve as directors thereof, holding in their hands final control of all the properties. The Trustees could dissolve any corporations within the system and organize new ones in each state, such as the Standard Oil of New Jersey, or the Standard Oil of New York. Nor could any outsiders or newly arrived stockholders have any voice in the affairs of the various companies. The Trustees formed a kind of supreme council giving a centralized direction to their industry. Such was the first great Trust; thus was evolved the harmonious management of huge aggregations of capital, and the technique for large-scale industry.

Dodd, the resourceful philosopher of monopoly, defended his beautiful legal structure of the "Standard Oil Trust" both in a pamphlet of 1888 and in an argument before a Congressional committee of that year. It was but the outcome of a crying need for centralized control of the oil business, he argued. Out of disastrous conditions had come "coöperation and association among the refiners, resulting eventually in the Standard Oil Trust [which] enabled the refiners so coöperating to reduce the price of petroleum products, and thus benefit the public to a very marked degree." In these arguments, learned economists of the time, such as Professor Hadley, supported Dodd. The Trust, as perfected monopoly, pointed the way to the future organization of all industry, and abolished "ruinous competition."

From their headquarters in the small old-fashioned building at 140 Pearl Street the supreme council of an economic empire sat together in conference like princes of the Roman Church. Here in utmost privacy confidential news brought by agents or informers throughout the world was discussed, and business policies determined. The management and responsibility was skillfully divided among committees: there was a committee on Crude Oil, a committee on Marketing, on Transportation, and numerous other departments. By these new processes markets or developments everywhere in everybody's business were followed or acted upon.

Every day the astute leaders rounded together by Rockefeller lunched together in Pearl Street, and later in a large and famous office building known as 26 Broadway. No one questioned the pre-eminence of John D. Rockefeller, though Charles Pratt usually sat at the head of the table. The aggressive Archbold was closest to John D. Rockefeller. His brother William Rockefeller, an amiable mediocrity, but immensely rich as well, and long trained in the use of money, depended most upon Henry H. Rogers. Rogers took a more dominant place in the management with the passing years. He is described by Thomas Lawson as "one of the most distinguished-looking men of the time, a great actor, a great fighter, an intriguer, an implacable foe."

These, together with Brewster, Barstow, J. H. Alexander and Bostwick, were the leaders who carried on their industrial operations throughout the world like a band of conspiratorial revolutionists. But "there was not a lazy bone nor a stupid head" in the whole organization, as Miss Tarbell has said. Behind them were the active captains, lieutenants, followers and workers, all laboring with the pride, the loyalty, the discipline and the enthusiasm born of the knowledge that "they can do no better for themselves" anywhere than under the "collar" of the Standard Oil. Freed of all moral scruples, curiously informed of everything, they were prompted by a sense of the world's realities which differed strangely from that of the man in the street. They were a major staff engaged in an eternal fight; now they scrapped unprofitable plants, acquiring and locating others; or now they gathered themselves for tremendous mobilizing feats during emergencies in trade. They found ways of effecting enormous economies; and always their profits mounted to grotesque figures: in 1879, on an invested capital of $3,500,000, dividends of $3,150,000 were paid; the value of the congeries of oil companies was then estimated at $55,000,000. Profits were overwhelmingly reinvested in new "capital goods" and with the formation of the Trust capitalization was set at $70,000,000. By 1886 net earnings had risen to $15,000,000 per annum.

"Hide the profits and say nothing!" was the slogan here. To the public prices had been reduced, it was claimed. But after 1875, and more notably after 1881, despite the fluctuations of crude oil a firm tendency set in for the markets of refined oil products. Upon the charts of prices the rugged hills and valleys of oil markets turn into a nearly level plain between 1881 and 1891. Though raw materials declined greatly in value, and volume increased, the margin of profit was consistently controlled by the monopoly; for the services of gathering and transporting oil, the price was not lowered in twenty years, despite the superb technology possessed by the Standard Oil. Questioned on this, that "frank pirate" Rogers replied, laughing: "*We are not in business for our health, but are out for the dollar.*"

While the policy of the monopoly, as economists have shown, might be for many reasons to avoid *maximum* price levels—such as invited the entrance of competition in the field—it was clearly directed toward keeping the profit margin stable during a rising trend in consumption and falling "curve" in production cost. Similarly in perfecting its technology the Trust was guided by purely pecuniary motives, as Veblen points out, and it remains always a matter of doubt if the mightier industrial combinations improved their service to society at large in the highest possible degree. As often as not it happened that technical improvements were actually long delayed until, after a decade or more, as in the case of Van Syckel's pipe line of 1865, their commercial value was proved beyond a doubt. It was only after rivals, in desperation, contrived the pumping of oil in a two-hundred-mile-long pipe line that Rockefeller followed suit. So it was with the development of various by-products, the introduction of tank cars, etc.

The end in sight was always, as Veblen said, increase of ownership, and of course pecuniary gain rather than technical progress in the shape of improved workmanship or increased service to the community. These latter effects were also obtained. But to a surprising degree they seem accidental by-products of the long-drawn-out struggles, the revolutionary upheavals whence the great industrial coalitions sprang.

The greatest service of the industrial baron to business enterprise seemed to lie elsewhere, as Veblen contended. "The heroic role of the captain of industry is that of a deliverer from an excess of business management." It is a "sweeping retirement of business men as a class from service . . . a casting out of business men by the chief of business men."

John D. Rockefeller said that he wanted in his organization "only the big ones, those who have already proved they can do a big business. As for others, unfortunately they will have to die."

The obscure tumult in the Oil Regions in 1872, the subsequent expo- the railroad rebate and the oil monopoly in 1879, made a lively lear impression upon the public mind. Now the more imaginative among the mass of consumers felt fear course through them at the thought of secret combinations ranged against them, the loud demagogue was roused from his slumbers, the reformer set off upon his querulous and futile searches. But among the alert entrepreneurs of all the money marts an entirely different response must have been perceptible. With envious lust the progress of the larger, more compact industrial organizations, like that of Carnegie Brothers & Company, or the associations formed by a Rockefeller, was now studied. Ah-ha! there was the way to profits in these confused and parlous times. How quickly and abundantly those fellows accumulated cash and power! "I was surprised," confessed William Vanderbilt before a committee of New York legislators in 1878, "at the amount of ready cash they were able to provide." He referred to the oil-refiners' combination. In the twinkling of an eye they had put down 3,000,000 to buy out Colonel Potts' pipe-line company. And in the following year Vanderbilt, commenting to the Hepburn Committee at Albany on the shrewdness of the Standard Oil ring, said:

> *There is no question about it but these men are smarter than I am a great deal. . . . I never came in contact with any class of men as smart and alert as they are in their business. They would never have got into the position they now are. And one man could hardly have been able to do it; it is a combination of men.*

The storms of public indignation, as we have seen, vented themselves chiefly upon the railroad heads who "discriminated against the little fellow" by the rebate and freight pool. But far from being frightened at such protests the money-changers hastened to throw their gold at the feet of him who promised them crushing, monopolistic advantages. So Villard, in 1881, by whispering his plans to conquer all the Northwest overnight, attracted instantly a powerful following of capitalists to his "blind pool." So the lawyers or undertakers who came forward with plans for secret trade associations or pools in salt, beef, sugar or whiskey, were heard with intense excitement by men who yesterday were busy ambushing or waylaying each other in the daily routine of their business.

They would say to each other, as in the Salt Association, formed earliest of all, "In union there is strength. . . ." Or, "Organized we have prospered; unorganized not." "Our combination has not been strong enough; the market is demoralized." And others would murmur fearsomely: "But we will be prosecuted for 'restraint of trade.' There are state laws in Maryland, Tennessee and elsewhere which hold that 'monopolies are odious.' There is the common law against trade conspiracy. . . ."

Then a bolder voice among the plotters would say: "How much did you make last year? Not a cent? Are you making anything now? Well, what do you propose to do? Sit here and lose what capital you have got in the business? There is only one way to make any money in a business like the—business and that is to have a pool."

Thus the trail would be blazed. The industrialists, like the railroad barons before them, came together in furtive conferences, much mistrusting each other, but lamenting together the bad times and owning to the folly of competition among themselves; while those who made pools, as they heard by rumor, in oil or salt flourished. After much bickering and jockeying, the lawyers would draw up binding agreements by which the amount of output would be fixed, quotas and territories would be assigned to each member, and business orders proportionally allotted, with fines levied upon those who broke the rules. These planning agreements the members of the pool would promise faithfully to live by.

The first pools, crude experiments in a "federalism" of industry, were as inept as the first weak devices for union among laborers. Their tactics and results differed widely. By 1880, certain pools such as the salt pool had got the margin of profit much higher by "pegging" the market price of a barrel of salt at about double what it was formerly, and holding steadily to this level. Their procedure usually avoided raising the market price too high. This would beget fresh competition. However, they kept prices "moderately" firm, although supply might actually be abundant. The essential object in view was "to increase the margins between the cost of materials and the price of the finished product," and this was effected, according to Ripley, "in almost every case."

A variety of economies were gained by pooling, depending upon the firmness of the association. Railroads were forced to give rebates; inefficient or badly located plants were closed down; excess sales forces and labor were reduced, a "war chest" was accumulated and competitors were driven out. To intruders the cost of necessary machinery might be made more burdensome. Thus in connection with the Wire Nail Pool, independents declared to government investigators:

We found the market in which we could buy machines [to manufacture nails] was very limited, most of the machine manufacturers having entered into an agreement with the combination to stop making them for outside parties.

In some cases the pool might, as in the case of salt in 1881, decide to "slaughter the market" for a reason, giving the *coup de grâce* to overstocked competitors in some areas, then resume the even tenor of their ways. Or they would sell low in one section which was pestered by competition, and recoup off the general market. The pools, in short, claimed to represent the party of "modernity," of progress by specializing machinery, buying raw materials cheaper, utilizing more by-products, research units, export development, advertising and selling in common. While "not wishing to take the position of posing before the public as benefactors to any extent," yet they claimed that industry was more stabilized, prices were seldom raised inordinately, and labor was paid higher wages—though here one famous manufacturer, John Gates, admitted that this was done on demand, in periods of affluence, when it was seen they had high profits and desired to avoid labor troubles. Generally they assumed a marvelous command over the labor situation—here was one of their surest gains. The workman became truly their commodity; for in time of a strike, orders could be shifted to other factories in a different section of the country and these kept running full blast.

In other cases, it was also notable that a technique of central control, extremely rigid and absolute, was developed. Immediately upon formation of the Distilling & Cattle Feeding Association, as Ripley relates, prices were cut sharply to force competitors into the pool, rivals were bought up or forced out, sometimes by negotiation and sometimes by intimidation or violence. Then by 1889, from twelve to twenty whiskey distilleries were operated on behalf of eighty-three plants previously existing, great savings were effected, and profits were steady and high enough to "accumulate a surplus for purpose of contest with outsiders." Thus the "whiskey ring," as Henry Lloyd wrote at the time, regulated the liquor traffic as no government could up to then or ever since effectively do, decreeing where and how much liquor should be made, and enforcing their decree, controlling alcohol, hence the sciences, medicine, even the arts and poetry. By February, 1888, only two large independents out of eighty distilleries resisted the combination. These were in Chicago, and one of them in April of that year published in the *Chicago Tribune* the fact that they had caught a spy of the combination in their works; later, tampering with the valves of their vats was discovered; then offers of large bribes if they would sell out their plants. In December, according to Lloyd's account, this distillery became the scene of an awful explosion:

All the buildings in the neighborhood were shaken and many panes of glass were broken. . . . There were 15,000 barrels of whiskey stored under the roof that was torn open, and if these had been ignited a terrible fire would have been added to the effect of the explosion. A package of dynamite which had failed to explode, though the fuse had been lighted, was found on the premises by the Chicago police. . . .

In the meantime, the years of depression after 1893 had wrought no less signal changes in the nature of the Standard Oil Company. This industrial empire, which continued to conquer markets and sources of supply in Russia and China as well as at the frontiers of the two Americas, was in no way checked by the period of general hardship. Nor had prohibitive laws, or condemnation of the company in certain regions such as the State of Ohio, hampered its progress in any degree. The order of dissolution in Ohio had simply been resisted by every legal subterfuge conceivable to its counsels; and then after seven years the Standard Oil had simply sloughed off its skin, and appeared as a New Jersey holding corporation.

But after 1893 the Standard Oil Company had a dual character. It was no longer simply an industrial monopoly, composed of men who simply owned and managed their oil business; it became, in great part, a reservoir of money, a house of investment bankers or absentee owners. So rapid had been the increase in annual profits, from $15,000,000 per annum in 1886 to $45,000,000 in 1899, that there was always more cash than could be used as capital in the oil and kindred trades. It became inevitable that the Standard Oil men make reinvestments regularly and extensively in new enterprises which were to be carried on under their absentee ownership. By a coincidence these developments came at a time when John D. Rockefeller announced his "retirement" from active business.

Moody in his "Masters of Capital" relates:

> The Rockefellers were not the type of investors who were satisfied with five or six percent. . . . They meant to make, if possible, as large profits in the investment of their surplus cash as they had been accustomed to make in their own line of business. But to make money at so rapid a pace called for the same shrewd, superior business methods. . . . To discerning men it was clear that ultimately these other enterprises into which the Standard Oil put its funds must be controlled or dominated by Standard Oil. William Rockefeller had anticipated this development to some extent years before when he had become active in the financial management of the Chicago, Milwaukee and St. Paul Railroad. But it was not until after the panic of 1893 that he and his associates began to reach out aggressively to control the destinies of many corporations.

John D. Rockefeller at this time possessed a fortune that has been estimated at two hundred millions; his brother William owned probably half as much, while his associates who usually moved in conjunction with him or his brother, Rogers, Flagler, Harkness, Payne, and various others combined now to form a capital of a size probably unprecedented in history. Soon the money markets felt the entrance of the Standard Oil "gang" in strange ways, as they began buying and selling pieces of capital, industries, men and material. This omnipotent group had brought a "new order of things" into the world of high finance. They had introduced into Wall Street operations, according to Henry Clews, "the same quiet, unostentatious, but resistless measures that they have always employed heretofore in their corporate affairs." Where a Gould might sometimes face the chance of failure, or a Commodore Vanderbilt have to fight for his life, Clews continued wonderingly, these men seemed to have removed the element of chance:

> Their resources are so vast that they need only to concentrate on any given property in order to do with it what they please . . . that they have thus concentrated . . . is a fact well known. . . . They are the greatest operators the world has ever seen, and the beauty of their method is the quiet and lack of ostentation . . . no gallery plays . . . no scare heads in the newspapers . . . no wild

*scramble or excitement. With them the process is gradual, thorough, and steady, with never a waver or break.*

In the conduct of these far-flung undertakings the Standard Oil family had always the loyal coöperation of the captains and lieutenants who wore their "collar" so contentedly, and who sent confidential news every day from all parts of the world. The "master mind" in these investment operations nowadays would seem to have been Henry Rogers; while important alliances . . . were effected with Stillman, the astute commander of the National City Bank, and Harriman, the rising giant of railroads.

After the headquarters of Standard Oil had been removed from Pearl Street to the high building at 26 Broadway, the active leaders of The System, as Thomas W. Lawson termed it, would go upstairs every day at eleven o'clock, to the fifteenth floor, and gather together around a large table. It was the high council of a dynasty of money, and men everywhere now spoke with bated breath of the commands which went forth from this council, and of the power and relentlessness of The System. In his romantic history, "Frenzied Finance," the stock-market plunger Lawson seems to blubber at the stupendous holdings of the Standard Oil "gang" toward 1900—"its countless miles of railroads . . . in every state and city in America, and its never-ending twistings of snaky pipe lines . . . its manufactories in the East, its colleges in the South, and its churches in the North." The guarded headquarters of Standard Oil aroused and have always aroused an awe which Lawson accurately reflects:

*At the lower end of the greatest thoroughfare in the greatest city of the New World is a huge structure of plain gray-stone. Solid as a prison, towering as a steeple, its cold and forbidding facade. . . . Men point to its stern portals, glance quickly up at the rows of unwinking windows, nudge each other, and hurry onward, as the Spaniards used to do when going by the offices of the Inquisition. The building is No. 26 Broadway.*

Alfred D. Chandler, Jr.

# The Coming of the Modern
# Industrial Corporation

### Reasons for Integration

Integration of mass production with mass distribution offered an opportunity for manufacturers to lower costs and increase productivity through more effective administration of the processes of production and distribution and co-ordination of the flow of goods through them. Yet the first industrialists to integrate these two basic sets of processes did not do so to exploit such economies. They did so because existing marketers were unable to sell and distribute products in the volume they were produced. The new mass producers were keenly aware of the national and international markets opened up by the new transportation and communication infrastructure. The potential of that market had impelled them to adopt the mass production machinery. However, as long as merchandising enterprises were able to sell their goods, they saw little reason to build marketing organizations of their own. Once the inadequacies of existing marketers became clear, manufacturers integrated forward into marketing.

In the 1880s two types of mass producers embarked on such a strategy of vertical integration. One set was composed of those who adopted new continuous-process machinery that swiftly expanded the output of their industrial establishments. Such entrepreneurs found that the existing marketers were unable to move their goods quickly enough or to advertise them effectively enough to keep their high-volume production facilities operating steadily. Most of these manufacturers continued to distribute through wholesalers, but they

*Excerpted by permission of the author and publishers from* The Visible Hand: The Managerial Revolution in American Business *by Alfred D. Chandler, Jr. Cambridge, Mass.: The Belknap Press of Harvard University Press,* © 1977 by Alfred D. Chandler, Jr.

assumed responsibility for the coordination of the flow from the factory to the customer.

The second set of pioneers were manufacturers who required specialized distribution and marketing services which wholesalers, mass retailers, manufacturers' agents, and other middlemen were unable to provide. These manufacturers were, in turn, of two sorts. One included a small number of processors who had adopted refrigerated or temperature-controlled techniques for the distribution of perishable products in the national market. The other included the makers of new complex, high-priced machines that required specialized marketing services—demonstration, installation, consumer credit, after-sales service and repair—if they were to be sold in volume. The marketing of these latter products demanded a continuing after-sales contact with the customer. Existing middlemen had neither the interest nor the facilities to maintain a continuing relationship. Nearly all of the firms in this last group manufactured standardized machines that were or could be mass produced through the fabrication and assembling of interchangeable parts.

Those manufacturers who found existing marketers inadequate to meet these needs created multiunit marketing organizations of their own. They set up branch offices headed by salaried managers in major commercial centers of the country and the world. Next, to assure a high-volume continuing flow of materials into their factories, they built large purchasing establishments and smaller traffic departments and often began to supply and transport their own materials.

Because they integrated production, marketing, and purchasing, the activities of the new firms were far more varied than those of other business enterprises of their day. Whereas the railroad, telegraph, marketing, financial, or existing manufacturing firms carried on a single basic economic function, the new integrated enterprise carried on several. Because they came to own and operate many factories, many sales offices, many purchasing units, mines, forest lands, and transportation lines, their operation required even more full-time salaried managers than did the railroad and telegraph companies of the late nineteenth century. These managers handled a far wider variety of tasks and faced even greater challenges in coordinating the flow of materials through their enterprises than did those in transportation, communication, or mass marketing. With the rise of the integrated industrial enterprise, the salaried manager became a major figure in the operation of the American economy.

The new administrative hierarchies, extending as they did from the supplier of raw materials to the ultimate consumer, were from their beginning national enterprises; many soon became multinational. The railroads by the 1890s covered large regions, but there was no single nationwide railroad enterprise. The mass marketers concentrated on local urban and larger rural regional markets. Before 1880, Western Union and Montgomery Ward were among the few large firms to operate on a national scale. By the end of the 1880s, however, a number of industrial enterprises were beginning to serve the entire nation. By 1900 the names of many integrated, multifunctional enterprises had become household words. By then they were beginning to play a significant role in the transformation of the nation from what Robert Wiebe had termed a distended society of "island communities" into a far more homogeneous and integrated community.

As the twentieth century opened, the new integrated multifunctional, often multinational, enterprise was becoming the most influential institution in the American economy. It surpassed the railroad in size and in complexity and diversity of operations. The decisions of its managers affected more businessmen, workers, consumers, and other Americans than did those of railroad executives. It soon replaced the railroad as the focus for political and ideological controversy. In fact, in the first decade of the twentieth century the control of the new industrial corporations became the central domestic political issue of the day. Of more lasting importance, the techniques and procedures perfected in the first years of the century to manage these integrated enterprises have remained the foundation of modern business administration.

## Integration by Users of Continuous-Process Technology

The most dramatic examples of the integration of mass production and mass distribution came in those industries adopting continuous-process machinery during the decade of the 1880s. Such machinery was, it will be recalled, invented almost simultaneously for making cigarettes, matches, flour, breakfast cereals, soup and other canned products, and photographic film. These innovations in mechanical continuous-process machinery and plant became the basis for a number of the first of the nation's giant industrial corporations. The creation of such enterprises drastically and permanently altered the structure of the industry in which they operated. . . .

As has been suggested, innovation in these industries was in part a response to the rise of the mass market which emerged with the completion of the nation's basic transportation and communication infrastructure. By the 1880s railroad, steamship, and telegraphic networks were fully integrated. By then belt lines, standard gauges and equipment, and interroad administrative arrangements permitted the movement of goods in nearly all parts of the nation with the minimum of transshipment. And almost instantaneous communication existed between Western Union's 12,000 offices.

The potential of the national market was further enlarged by two new types of ancillary business institutions that had already become widely used by the mass marketers. The credit agency, operating on a national scale after the Civil War, permitted manufacturers to check the reliability of jobbers and retailers in all parts of the country. The advertising agency, which purchased advertising space for clients in newspapers, journals, and periodicals circulating throughout the nation, was of even more value to mass producers. Until after the Civil War such agencies concentrated on writing copy and buying space in their local communities. Until the 1870s their major customers were department stores and jobbers and wholesalers selling traditional lines of dry goods, hardware, groceries, jewelry, furniture, cards, and stationery in local and regional markets. In that decade only books, journals, and patent medicines were advertised on more than a regional basis. Nearly all other manufacturers left advertising to the wholesalers who marketed their goods.

The manufacturers adopting the new continuous-process technology differed from the producers of books, journals, and patent medicines in that the unit output of their factories was much higher. To enlarge and maintain a market for these goods, they embarked on massive advertising campaigns carried out through these advertising agencies. They learned soon, too, that the wholesaler could not be relied upon to order and maintain inventory so that the customer could be always sure of obtaining the product. So the manufacturer took charge of scheduling the flow of finished products from the factory to the customer and then of raw and semifinished materials from the suppliers to the factories.

The story of James Buchanan Duke effectively illustrates these general practices. Duke's dominance in the cigarette industry rested on his appreciation of the potential of the Bonsack cigarette machine. Duke, a manufacturer of smoking tobacco in Durham, North Carolina, had decided in 1881 to produce cigarettes because he was having difficulty in competing with a well-established neighbor, Blackwell and Company. At that date cigarettes were still a new and exotic product just beginning to find favor in the growing urban markets. Cigarette smoking was only starting to take the place of pipe smoking, chewing tobacco, cigars, or snuff. In 1881 four cigarette firms produced 80 percent of the output, primarily for nearby markets.

As a newcomer, Duke was searching for a way to break into the market. In 1884, shortly after a sharp reduction in taxes on cigarettes permitted a major price cut to consumers, Duke installed two Bonsack machines. With each machine producing 120,000 cigarettes a day, he could easily saturate the American market. To test the world market, Duke had sent a close associate, Richard M. Wright, on a nineteen-month tour overseas. In June, 1885, Duke signed a contract with Bonsack to use the machine exclusively to make all his cigarettes, high-quality as well as cheap, in return for a lower leasing charge.

Duke's gamble paid off. Output soared. Selling became the challenge. Even before Duke had made his basic contract with Bonsack, he built a factory in New York City, the nation's largest urban market, and set up his administrative offices there. He immediately intensified a national advertising campaign. Not only did Duke rely on advertising agencies but also his own staff distributed vast quantities of cards, circulars, and handbills—all proclaiming the virtues of his products.

He then began to build extensive sales organizations. Duke followed up the contacts Wright had made on his trip abroad by signing marketing agreements with wholesalers and dealers in all parts of the globe. At the same time, he and one or two other associates established a network of sales offices in the larger American cities. These offices, headed by salaried managers, became responsible for both the marketing and distributing of the product. The office kept an eye on local advertising. Its salesmen regularly visited tobacco, grocery, drug, and other jobbers, and a few large retailers to obtain orders. Duke's local sales managers worked closely with New York headquarters to assure the effective scheduling of the high-volume flow of cigarettes to jobbers and a few large retailers.

At the same time that Duke and his close associates were building their sales organization, they were creating an extensive purchasing network in southeastern United States, where bright-leaf tobacco—that used in cigarettes—was grown. Tobacco, after its annual harvest, was normally dried and cured before being sold to manufacturers. The timing of the process varied from several months to two or three years, according to the leaf and the quality desired. Because the supply of cured tobacco depended on both the size of the crop and the availability of curing facilities, prices fluctuated widely. By building its own buying, storing, and curing facilities, Duke's company was able to purchase directly from the farmers, usually at auctions, and so reduce transactions costs and uncertainties. What counted more was that the company was also assured of a steady supply of cured tobacco for its mass-producing factories in Durham and New York City.

By combining mass production with mass distribution Duke was able to maintain low prices and reap high profits. By 1889 Duke was by far the largest manufacturer in the industry, producing 834 million cigarettes with sales of over $4.5 million and profits of $400,000 annually, despite heavy advertising costs. To compete, other cigarette manufacturers had little choice but to follow Duke's strategy. They quickly turned to machine production and began to build and enlarge their sales and purchasing organizations. As packages of cigarettes were priced in 5 cent increments—5 cents for the standard package and 10 cents to 25 cents for the better brands—there was little room for price cutting, particularly in the all-important cheaper brands. The manufacturers concentrated on advertising instead. In 1889 Duke's advertising cost rose to $800,000 a year. Here his high volume and resulting cash flow gave him an advantage, for he had a larger cash surplus than the others to spend on advertising. But the cost of these sales campaigns reduced profits.

The desire to control this competition caused Duke and his four competitors to merge in 1890, forming the American Tobacco Company. For a brief time the constituent companies continued to operate independently; but after 1893 their functional activities were consolidated into the Duke manufacturing, sales, and leaf (purchasing) departments. As had been the case with the railroads and would be again in manufacturing, the largest of the early enterprises became the core organization for continuing growth. The enlarged centralized departmentalized company, operating from its New York corporate central office, proved extraordinarily profitable even during the economically depressed years of the 1890s. Profits from cigarettes allowed Duke to install new methods of production and distribution in other branches of the tobacco trade. By 1900 the American Tobacco Company had come to dominate that industry completely, except for the making of cigars. . . .

*       *       *

During a very short period in the 1880s, new processes of production and distribution had transferred the organization of a number of major American industries—tobacco, matches, grain milling, canning, soap, and photography. These changes were revolutionary, and they were permanent. The enterprises that pioneered in adopting and integrating the new ways of mass production and mass distribution became nationally known. By 1900, they were household words. Three-quarters of a century later the names American Tobacco, Diamond Match, Quaker Oats, Pillsbury Flour, Campbell Soup, Heinz, Borden, Carnation, Libby, Proctor & Gamble, and Eastman Kodak are still well known.

These enterprises were similar in that they used new continuous-process machinery to produce low-priced packaged consumer goods. Their new processes of production were so capital-intensive (that is, the ratio of workers to the quantity of units produced was so small) that production for the national and global market became concentrated in just a few plants, often only one or two. In all cases it was the massive increase in output made possible by the new continuous-process, capital-intensive machinery that caused the manufacturers to build large marketing and purchasing networks.

The national and international network of sales offices took over from the wholesaler the functions of branding and advertising. Although advertising agents continued to be used to reach the national and world markets, the sales department became increasingly responsible for the content, location, and volume of advertising. As many of these products, like cigarettes, cereals, canned milk, and canned meat, were relatively new, advertising was important to enlarge demand. It was also a major competitive weapon because a relatively low unit price per package (usually 5 cents or 10 cents) made demand inelastic. It was difficult to increase demand by reducing prices. Although in most cases, jobbers continued to be used to distribute goods to the retailers, the sales offices took over scheduling and coordinating the flow of goods from factories to jobbers and often to retailers. (At Eastman this involved the flow of exposed film for printing as well.) They also worked closely with the manufacturing departments to coordinate the flow from the suppliers of the raw material through the processes of production and distribution to the final consumers. A few of these firms, including Campbell Soup and Eastman Kodak, were soon selling and delivering directly to retailers. By the early twentieth century Eastman Kodak began to build its own retail stores in major cities.

In all these cases the high volume of output permitted by the integration of mass production with mass distribution generated an impressive cash flow that provided these enterprises with most of their working capital, as well as funds to expand capital equipment and facilities. These enterprises relied on local businessmen and commercial banks for both short-term and long-term loans. None, however, needed to go to the capital markets for funds to finance the expansion that so quickly placed them among the largest business enterprises in the world. For this reason the entrepreneurs, their families, and the associates who created these enterprises continued to control them. They personally held nearly all the voting stock in a company. Thus, although day-to-day operations had to be turned over to full-time salaried managers, long-term decisions as to investment, allocation of funds, and managerial recruitment remained concentrated in the hands of a small number of owners.

The administrative networks built to integrate the new processes of production and distribution gave the pioneering enterprises their greatest competitive advantage. Although capital-intensive in terms of the ratio of capital to labor inputs, the new machinery was not that expensive. The absolute cost of entry was not high, nor in most industries were patents a barrier to entry. The makers of cigarette, milling, canning, and soap-making machinery were eager to sell their products to as many manufacturers as possible. Nor was branding or advertising a barrier. Advertising agencies were just as intent as machinery manufacturers on finding new clients.

The most imposing barrier to entry in these industries was the organization the pioneers had built to market and distribute their newly mass-produced products. A competitor who acquired the technology had to create a national and often global organization of managers, buyers, and salesmen if he was to get the business away from the one or two enterprises that already stood astride the major marketing channels. Moreover, where the pioneer could finance the building of the first of these organizations out of cash flow, generated by high volume, the newcomer had to set up a competing network before high-volume output reduced unit costs and created a sizable cash flow. In this period of building he had to face a competitor whose economies of speed permitted him to set prices low and still maintain a margin of profit. Newcomers, of course, did appear. Kellogg and Postum in breakfast cereals and Colgate and Babbitt in soaps are examples. But all these industries were highly concentrated from the moment mass production methods were adopted. Except for flour milling, the industries in which these integrated industrial enterprises first appeared immediately became oligopolistic and have so remained.

## Integration by Processors of Perishable Products

Whereas many of the mass producers of semiperishable packaged products continued to use the wholesaler to handle the physical distribution of their goods—even after they had taken over that middleman's advertising and scheduling functions—the makers of more perishable products such as meat and beer, in building their marketing networks, began to sell and distribute directly to the retailers. The market for perishable products expanded as the railroad and telegraph networks grew. As early as the 1850s crude refrigerator cars were used to bring milk, butter, and meat to urban markets. In the 1870s, when the direct movement of cars over long distances became possible, western meat packers began to ship fresh meat to the eastern cities. Then, in 1881 the modern refrigerated car made its appearance. Gustavus F. Swift hired Andrew J. Chase, a leading refrigeration engineer, to design a car to carry Swift's dressed beef from Chicago to Boston. Again, the 1880s were the crucial years.

The refrigerator car, however, was not the reason Swift became the innovator in high-volume, year-round production of perishable products. He became the first modern meat packer because he was the first to appreciate the need for a distribution network to store meat and deliver it to the retailers. He was the first to build an integrated enterprise to coordinate the high-volume flow of meat from the purchasing of cattle through the slaughtering or disassembling process and through distribution to the retailer and ultimate consumer.

When Gustavus Swift, a New England wholesale butcher, moved to Chicago in 1875, nearly all meat went east "on the hoof." Western cattle were shipped alive by rail in cattle cars to local wholesalers who butchered and delivered to retailers. The economies of slaughtering in the West and shipping the dressed meat east were obvious. Sixty percent of an animal was inedible and cattle lost weight and often died on the trip east. Moreover, the concentration of butchering in Chicago and other western cities permitted a high-volume continuous operation which not only lowered unit cost but also made possible fuller use of by-products.

To carry out his strategy, Swift, who had begun winter shipments in 1878, not only concentrated on improving the refrigerated car but also built a network of branch houses, first in the northeast and then after 1881 in the rest of the country. Each house included refrigerated storage space, a sales office, and a sales staff to sell and deliver the meat to the retail butchers, grocers, and other food shops. Swift soon supplemented this distributing and marketing network with "peddler car routes" which distributed dressed meat in small lots by refrigerator car to towns and villages.

In executing his plan, Swift met with most determined opposition. Railroads, startled by the prospect of losing their livestock business, which was an even greater producer of revenue than grain on the west to east routes, refused to build refrigerated cars. When Swift began to construct his own, the Eastern Trunk Line Association refused to carry them. Only by using the Grand Trunk, then outside of the association, was Swift able to bring his cars east. At the same time he had to combat boycotts by local wholesalers, who in 1886 formed the National Butchers' Protective Association to fight "the trust." These butchers attempted to exploit a prejudice against eating fresh meat that had been killed days or even weeks before, more than a thousand miles away.

High quality at low prices soon overcame this opposition. Though Swift did rely on advertising to counter prejudice against his product, it was clearly the prices and quality made possible by high-volume operations and the speed and careful scheduling of product flow that won the market. Once the market was assured, Swift had to expand his production facilities to keep up with demand. He increased his speed of throughput by subdividing the processes of butchering and by using moving "disassembling" lines. In the 1880s and early 1890s, Swift & Company built new packing plants in six cities along the cattle frontier. The company then bought into adjoining stockyards where men from its purchasing department became experts in buying cattle in volume.

Other packers realized that if they were to compete with Swift in the national market they must follow his lead. By the end of 1882, Philip D. Armour of Chicago and George H. Hammond of Detroit were beginning to build comparable networks of branch houses and to compete with Swift for the best locations along the railroad lines. Nelson Morris of Chicago and the two Cudahy brothers of Omaha constructed similar networks in the mid-1880s. The oligopoly was rounded out when the New York firm of Swartschild and Sulzberger completed a comparable integated national enterprise in the early 1890s. Except for Hammond who died in 1886, all these entrepreneurs enlarged their processing facilities, built new packing plants in other western cities, bought into the stockyards, and expanded their fleet of refrigerated cars. Well before the end of the eighties a small number of very large meat-packing firms dominated the dressed meat business, and they continued to do so until well into the twentieth century.

*    *    *

## Integration by Machinery Makers Requiring Specialized Marketing Services

The other manufacturers to by-pass the wholesalers were the makers of recently invented machines that were produced in volume through the fabrication and assembling of interchangeable parts. The marketing needs of these machinery makers were even greater than those of the meat packers and brewers. They found that the volume sale of their products required more than centralized advertising and coordinated flows. Their new and relatively complex products had to be demonstrated before they could be sold. Mechanical expertise was needed to service and repair them after they had been sold. And because the machines were relatively costly, buyers often could only purchase them on credit. Independent wholesalers were rarely able or willing to provide such demonstrations, maintenance and repair, and consumer credit.

The machines requiring these close and continuing services to the customer were of two sorts. Sewing machines, agriculture equipment, and office machinery were similar to present-day consumer durables, even though they were sold primarily to produce goods and services and not for consumption by the final consumer. They were produced at a high rate, often many thousands a week, and sold to individuals as well as to business firms. The second type—

elevators, pumps, boilers, printing presses, and a variety of electrical equipment—were clearly producers' goods. They were complex, large, standardized machines that required specialized installation as well as sales and repair and long-term credit. In the eighties the makers of both sorts of machines began to expand output by pioneering in or adopting the new ways of systematic factory management. Both sold their products in national and world markets and created or reorganized extensive marketing organization in that same decade.

The first mass producers of machinery to build their own sales organizations were the makers of sewing machines. These machines could be produced commercially in the early 1850s, but the manufacturers could not begin to make them in quantity until the legal battle over patents was settled in 1854 and a patent pool formed. The winner of the court trials, Elias Howe, insisted that the pooled patents be released to twenty-four manufacturers. Nevertheless, the industry was dominated within a short time by the three firms that first acquired marketing networks—Wheeler & Wilson Co., Grover and Baker, and I. M. Singer Company. These manufacturers at first relied on full-time but independent agents who, though receiving a small salary, were paid primarily on a commission basis and were solely responsible for marketing activities within their territories. But these agents had little technical knowledge of the machines and were unable to demonstrate them properly or service and repair them. Nor were the agents able to provide credit, an important consideration if customers were to pay for these relatively expensive goods in installments.

As an alternative, Grover and Baker began to set up a company owned and operated store or branch office to provide such services. By 1856 Grover and Baker had already established such branch offices, as they were called, in ten cities. In that year Isaac Merritt Singer decided to follow suit. So, almost immediately, did Wheeler & Wilson. By 1859 Singer had opened fourteen branches, each with a female demonstrator, a mechanic to repair and service, and a salesman or canvasser to sell the machine, as well as a manager who supervised the others and handled collections and credits. Nevertheless, because finding and training personnel took time, these three enterprises continued to rely heavily on commission agents to market their goods. The swift selection of these agents and the building of branch stores permitted these three to dominate the trade. By 1860 they already produced three-fourths of the industry's output, with Wheeler & Wilson manufacturing 85,000 machines in that year and the other two 55,000 apiece.

After 1860 Singer moved more aggressively than the other two in replacing regional distributors with branch stores supervised by full-time, salaried regional agents. Edward Clark, Singer's partner and the business brains of the partnership, had become even more convinced as time passed of the value of relying on his own sales force. The independent agents had difficulty in supplying the necessary marketing services, and they failed to maintain inventories properly. They waited until their stocks were low and then telegraphed large orders, requesting immediate delivery. They seemed to be always either understocked or overstocked. Moreover, the agents were frustratingly slow in returning payments made on the machines to the central office.

Therefore, Clark was constantly on the outlook for men he could hire as salaried "general agents" or regional managers of geographical districts to supervise existing branch stores and to set up new ones. Where such men could not be found, Clark continued to rely on independent agents; but he insisted that such dealers set up branch offices similar to those in a company-managed district.

When Clark became president in 1876, a year after Singer's death, he decided to eliminate the independent agencies altogether, at home and abroad. Singer's central offices in New York and London had as yet little control over the branch stores of the independent distributors and, in fact, relatively little control over their own salaried agents. Scarcely any effort had been made to sell in any systematic or standardized way. Uniformity in sales, accounting, credit policies, and procedures was lacking. The techniques of administrative coordination had not yet been perfected. Moreover, in 1877 the last patents of the 1856 pool were to expire. After that year Singer would have to compete at home, as it had long done abroad, without patent protection.

Working closely with George Ross McKenzie, a Scotsman who helped to build Singer's overseas organization and succeeded him as president, Clark gradually reorganized and rationalized Singer's marketing and distribution network. First he completed the replacement of the independent distributors with regional offices manned by salaried executives. Then he installed everywhere similar branch offices with teams of canvassers as well as repairmen and accountants. Such offices had proved particularly successful in Great Britain, an area where Singer had never enjoyed patent protection. The network made possible aggressive marketing, reliable service and repair, and careful supervision of credits and collections; it also assured a steady cash flow from the field to the headquarters in London, Hamburg, and New York.

In the period immediately after 1878, Clark and McKenzie perfected the procedures and methods needed to supervise and evaluate this branch office network. In the United States twenty-five different regional "general agencies" reported to the central office in New York. In the United Kingdom, twenty-six regional sales offices reported to a London office. In northern and central Europe the managers of fifty-three more reported to headquarters in Hamburg. Nine others in the rest of Europe, Africa, and the Near East reported to London, while those in Latin America, Canada, and the Far East were supervised by the central New York office.

The expansion and then reformation of the marketing organization resulted in a constant increase in Singer's sales and, therefore, the daily output of its factories, and the overall size of the enterprise. In 1874 the company built by far the largest sewing machine factory in the world at Elizabethport, New Jersey. During the 1880s it grew in size; but its capacity was surpassed when the company constructed a plant in 1885 in Kilbowie, Scotland (a suburb of Glasgow). That plant, with a rated capacity of 10,000 machines a week, was constructed to replace a smaller Scottish plant built in 1867. Both plants were constructed to improve coordination between production and distribution. The filling of hundreds and then thousands of orders in Europe from the American factory became more and more difficult. Delays became the major cause for losing orders. In 1866, for example, the head of Singer's London office complained that the inability to deliver machines had "utterly ruined" the company's business in Britain. All Singer's capital facilities—its two great factories, a small cabinetmaking plant in South Bend, Indiana, and a foundry in Austria—were financed out of current earnings.

Increased demand in these years caused Singer to expand and systematize its purchasing operations. By the 1890s the company had obtained its own timberlands, an iron mill, and some transportation facilities. These purchases were also paid for from the ample cash flow provided by sale of the machines. Indeed, the company often had a surplus which it invested in railroad and government bonds, and even in other manufacturing firms. Both insiders and outsiders credited Singer's business success to its marketing organization and abilities.

\*　　\*　　\*

As the experience of all the new mass-produced machinery companies emphasizes, they could sell in volume only if they created a massive, multiunit marketing organization. All their products were new, all were relatively complicated to operate and maintain, and all relatively costly. No existing marketer knew the product as well as the manufacturer. None had the facilities to provide after-sales service and repair. Few were willing to take the risk of selling on installment, a marketing device which these machinery makers had to invent. Nor were outsiders able to maintain close control over collections, essential to assure a continued cash flow on which the financial health of the enterprise rested. Finally, by using uniform sales techniques, bringing together regularly members of a nationwide sales force, and comparing the activities and performances of the many different sales offices, the single, centrally controlled sales department was able to develop more effective marketing techniques. It was also able to obtain a constant flow of information on the changing shifts in demands and customer requirements.

Close and constant communication between the branch sales offices, the factory, and its purchasing organization made it possible to schedule a high-volume flow of goods from the suppliers of raw materials to the ultimate consumer, and so to keep the manufacturing facilities relatively full and running steadily. It also assured a steady flow of cash to the central office. Such coordination would have been exceedingly difficult if independent enterprises handled each stage of the processes of supplying, manufacturing, and marketing. The regular and increasing demand made possible in part by an aggressive sales force in turn created pressures to speed up the processes of production through improved machinery, plant design, and management. Increased speed of production in its turn reduced unit costs. The economies of speed and scale, and their national, often global, marketing organizations gave the pioneering firms an impressive competitive advantage and so made it easy for them to continue to dominate their industries.

All this was also true for the makers of new, technologically advanced, relatively standardized machinery that was sold to other manufacturers to be used in their production processes. Because these goods were even more complex and more costly, they required specialized installation as well as closer attention to after-sales service and repair. The sales force for such manufacturers required more professional training than persons selling light machines in mass markets. Salesmen often had degrees in mechanical engineering. Again, it was the decade of the 1880s when enterprises in these industries began to build or rationalize their national and global sales forces.

An excellent example of enterprises producing and marketing in volume for global markets were the makers of recently invented machinery to generate, transmit, and use electricity for power and light. The salesmen at Westinghouse, Thompson-Houston, and Edison General Electric (the last two combined into General Electric in 1892) all knew more about the technical nature of their equipment than did most of their customers. Moreover, few independent distributors could obtain a firm grasp of the rapidly changing new technology. Because of the dangers of electrocution and fire, trained salaried employees of these companies had to install and service and repair their products. Financing involved large sums, often requiring extensive credit, which independent distributors were unable to supply. Thompson-Houston and Edison Electric, and, to a lesser extent, Westinghouse, began to finance new local central power stations in order to build the market for their machinery.

In these pioneering years of the electrical equipment business, technology was developing fast. Coordination between the sales, production, and purchasing departments thus involved more than scheduling flows of material. It meant that salesmen, equipment designers, and the manufacturing executives had to be in constant touch to coordinate technological improvements with market needs so that the product could be produced at the lowest possible unit cost. It also lessened even more the opportunities for independent sales agencies to acquire the necessary skills to market the product.

*       *       *

All of the pioneering machinery firms continued to dominate their industries for decades. Administrative coordination brought lower costs and permitted manufacturers to have a more direct contact with markets. The technological complexities of their products, particularly those selling producers' goods, made their marketing organizations of trained engineers and other technical specialists even more powerful competitive weapons than were the sales departments of makers of consumer goods purchased for immediate consumption. The nature of their processes as well as products, led to the assigning of technicians to concentrate on improving both product and process and so to the formation of the first formal industrial research departments. As in the case of the first integrated manufacturers of perishable and semiperishable products, the machinery firms soon had competitors. But to compete with the established enterprise demanded the creation of a comparable national and often international marketing network. And in competing, the new enterprise had to win customers before its organization could generate the volume necessary to provide low prices and high cash flow or develop its staffs of expert marketing and research technicians. Rarely did more than a handful of competitors succeed in obtaining a significant share of the national and international markets. These industries quickly became and remained oligopolistic or monopolistic.

Makers of volume-produced standardized machinery, processors of perishable products, and those that mass produced low-priced packaged goods, internalized the activities of the wholesaler or other middlemen when these distributors were unable to provide the marketing services needed if the goods were to be manufactured in the unprecedented volume permitted by the new technologies of production and distribution. The resulting enterprises, clustered in the food and machinery industries, were then the first industrial corporations to coordinate administratively the flow of goods on a national, indeed a global, scale. They were among the world's first modern multinationals. Their products were usually new. This was true not only for sewing, agricultural, and office machinery but also for cigarettes, matches, breakfast cereals, canned milk and soup, roll film and Kodak cameras, and even fresh meat that had been butchered a thousand miles away. In all these new industries the pioneers remained dominant enterprises. Because they were the first big businesses in American industry, they defined many of its administrative practices and procedures. Their formation, organization, and growth, therefore, have significant implications for the operation and structure of American industry and the economy as a whole.

## SUGGESTIONS FOR FURTHER READING

Samuel P. Hays, *The Response to Industrialism (Chicago, 1957), argues that "the desire to create wealth possessed all Americans." Industrialism created new problems, but Americans welcomed it as they sought to adjust by creating a new consensus. Robert Wiebe, *The Search for Order (New York, 1965), shows how economic change broke down the old order based upon local authority and created a new one based upon growing centralization of authority. He describes how Americans had to adjust to these changed conditions.

Gustavus Myers, History of the Great American Fortunes (New York, 1907), like Josephson's The Robber Barons (New York, 1934), is a blistering attack on the businessmen. Henry Demarest Lloyd, *Wealth against Commonwealth (New

* Available in paperback edition.

York, 1894), is sharply critical of John D. Rockefeller, as is Ida M. Tarbell, *The History of Standard Oil Company* (New York, 1904; abridged version in paperback). The opposite approach is taken by Allan Nevins in his long biography of Rockefeller: *John D. Rockefeller: The Heroic Age of American Enterprise*, 2 vols. (New York, 1940), and *Study in Power: John D. Rockefeller, Industrialist and Philanthropist*, 2 vols. (New York, 1953). Like Nevins, Ralph W. and Muriel E. Hidy, *Pioneering in Big Business, 1882–1911: History of Standard Oil Company (New Jersey)* (New York, 1955), stress the importance of Rockefeller in organizing the oil business. Louis M. Hacker, *The Triumph of American Capitalism* (New York, 1940), places the contributions of the post-Civil War industrialists in the context of earlier economic history; although often critical of them, Hacker concludes by praising their accomplishments.

As famous (or infamous) as Rockefeller was J. P. Morgan. Two very different pictures of the great banker may be found in Frederick Lewis Allen, *\*The Great Pierpont Morgan* (New York, 1949), and Lewis Corey, *The House of Morgan* (New York, 1930).

Useful interpretive surveys of the vast literature on the "robber barons" may be found in Edward C. Kirkland, "The Robber Barons Revisited," *American Historical Review*, 66 (October 1960), pp. 68–73; Hal Bridges, "The Robber Baron Concept in American History," *Business History Review*, 32 (Spring 1958), pp. 1–13; Thomas C. Cochran, "The Legend of the Robber Barons," *The Pennsylvania Magazine of History and Biography*, 74 (July 1950), pp. 307–21; Gabriel Kolko, "The Premises of Business Revisionism," *Business History Review*, 33 (Autumn 1959), pp. 330–44.

The selection by Alfred D. Chandler, Jr., illustrates a different approach toward the rise of big business that has been adopted by some scholars in recent years. Discounting the personalities of the business leaders and avoiding the question of whether they were right or wrong, these historians give emphasis instead to problems such as management, markets, organization, and structure. Glenn Porter, *\*The Rise of Big Business, 1860–1910* (New York, 1973), provides a good brief introduction with a fine annotated bibliography. The serious student should read Chandler's *The Visible Hand* in its entirety, as well as Chandler's earlier book, *\*Strategy and Structure* (Cambridge, Mass., 1962). Valuable also is Thomas C. Cochran, *\*Business in American Life: A History* (New York, 1972). A good discussion of this work, its assumptions and its methods is found in Louis Galambos, "The Emerging Organizational Synthesis in Modern American History," *Business History Review*, 44 (Autumn 1970), pp. 279–90.

# 3

# *Farmers*
# *in an Industrial Age*

"Those who labor in the earth are the chosen people of God," wrote Thomas Jefferson. Virtue resides in the hearts of the agriculturists, he explained. "Corruption of morals in the mass of cultivators is a phenomenon of which no age nor nation has furnished an example." To this day many Americans have the vague feeling that farming is the most natural, the most virtuous occupation, that somehow those who work the land are especially important to the survival of American democracy.

Yet farmers are rarely mentioned in American history except in discussions of farmers' problems. And, indeed, over the years the American farmer has had many serious problems. In the colonial period, when most of the nation's citizens tilled the soil, the small farmers along the frontier bore the brunt of the Indian raids and lamented the lack of adequate protection for their families and lands. They complained that they were underrepresented in the assemblies, overtaxed, and given too few of the bridges and roads that they demanded. Occasionally, when they felt that their problems had gone unheeded too long, they rebelled against colonial authorities.

Independence did not end the small farmers' difficulties. Shays's Rebellion in Massachusetts and the Whiskey Rebellion in Pennsylvania, both put down quickly, represented the unhappiness and the discontent of some farmers.

Working the land may have seemed an ideal occupation to those living in the cities, but many farmers knew better. The everyday struggle to eke out a living from the soil, often without the cooperation of the elements, was hard and frequently frustrating. Nor did the passage of time solve the farmers' problems; more often new problems were added to the old.

From the colonial period to the early nineteenth century, most of those who worked the land were subsistence farmers, that is, they produced the greatest part of what they ate and wore. A few had a cash crop—potash or grain (often distilled into whiskey) or cotton or tobacco, depending on the area—but most sold very little of what they raised. With the rise of industrialism in the nineteenth century, and the improvement of transportation, first through the canal and then the railroad, subsistence farming gave way in many areas to commercial farming. Farmers concentrated on cash crops, wheat or cotton or pork, and used the proceeds to buy the food, clothing, and other items needed. With the rise of commercial farming, farmers lost their economic independence. They became increasingly dependent on the bankers, who lent them money to buy more land and machinery needed to increase production, and upon the railroad, which was often the only way to get crops to market. Moreover, their income, and hence their well-being, depended upon the vicissitudes of the worldwide market for their crops.

The spread of commercial farming and the expansion of industrialism, especially in the years after the Civil War, raised the standard of living of many farmers, who were able to purchase some of the luxuries enjoyed by the city dweller. Often, however, the price of higher living standards was great. Many went deeply in debt as they sought to increase production by purchasing new lands and more machinery. As production rose, prices went down; efforts to increase income through further increases in production compounded the problem. Fluctuations of the business cycle, as well as the natural disasters of droughts, floods, hail, and wind, added to the farmers' woes. Increasingly in the years after the Civil War, farmers felt victimized, and often they blamed the railroad or the banker for their plight. To improve their situation they attempted to organize. They joined the Patrons of Husbandry, more commonly known as the Grange. At first primarily a social organization, inevitably the Grange became involved in politics, and in several midwestern states successfully pressured for laws regulating railroads. When most of the laws proved inadequate, farmers continued to agitate, joining societies like the Agricultural Wheel in Arkansas, the Farmers' Union in Louisiana, and the Farmers' Alliances in various other states. All this organizing came to a climax in 1892 when many farmers bolted the two regular parties and formed the People's or Populist party.

The Populists regarded their movement as a weapon in their struggle against what they termed "the interests," a massive conspiracy of bankers, railroads, and big businessmen seeking to exploit the farmers. Their only defense, they concluded, was organization and struggle. For many of their opponents, the movement was a threat, for it smacked of revolution. Some historians, accepting this evaluation, have concluded that the farmers' movements represented a fundamental class conflict in American society. According to this view, farmers resisted the encroachment of big business and sought to retain their economic independence and their political influence. Some scholars add that what made the farmers' movement really revolutionary was that they were proposing an alternative path for the country to follow; they opposed the growth of big business and the centralized corporate state, favoring instead decentralized production with local controls.

Other scholars disagree, but their disagreements take different forms. Some insist that the farmers were not revolutionary at all. Like other Americans at the time, they were merely seeking a bigger slice of the economic pie. According to this view, the farmers did not resist economic change or the growth of large-scale, highly mechanized agriculture. Their complaint was that they were not sharing equitably with other businessmen in the benefits of change. Other historians argue that the Populists were in a sense counter-revolutionaries. They were suffering from their inability to adapt to changing economic conditions and longed to turn back the clock, to return to the age of subsistence agriculture, the small family farm, and the pastoral village.

Examples of these diverse interpretations are presented in the following selections. Readers should keep a number of questions in mind as they seek to sort out the various interpretations. What exactly were the farmers asking for? If they had gotten all they asked for, would the result have been a revolutionary change in American society?

In the first selection, John D. Hicks spells out the farmers' grievances against the railroads, big business, bankers, and middlemen. The picture that emerges is one of sharp class conflict, with agrarians—West and South—arrayed against eastern capitalists. Richard Hofstadter, in the next selection, finds the Populists unable to understand the problems they faced. Instead of attempting to adapt to the modern world, they looked backward to what seemed to be better days; instead of realistically assessing their problems, they viewed themselves as victims of a conspiracy. But the conspiracy, according to Hofstadter, was a product of their imagination. Lawrence Goodwyn, in the final selection, finds the farmers' grievances to be real and their solutions realistic. He insists that the farmers were proposing a more democratic path for America to follow, a path that was not taken because a newly created consensus —acceptance of the progressive, corporate state—led the majority down an alternative and less democratic path.

There can be no doubt that the farmers' life was often difficult and that they faced real problems. But did the farmers' problems stem from fundamental differences in American society? Were they victims, as they claimed, of the businessmen and bankers who controlled the country? Did their efforts to organize to improve their condition signal class war between farmer and businessman? Or were the farmers simply victims of the overproduction that drove their prices down? If so, then perhaps their complaints and their organizational efforts, despite the rhetoric involved, were merely efforts to adapt to the new industrial age. Or were the farmers rejecting the ideology of the new age, posing an alternative, more democratic ideology?

*John D. Hicks*

# The Farmers' Grievances

In the spring of 1887 a North Carolina farm journal stated with rare accuracy what many farmers in all sections of the United States had been thinking for some time.

There is something radically wrong in our industrial system. There is a screw loose. The wheels have dropped out of balance. The railroads have never been so prosperous, and yet agriculture languishes. The banks have never done a better or more profitable business, and yet agriculture languishes. Manufacturing enterprises never made more money or were in a more flourishing condition, and yet agriculture languishes. Towns and cities flourish and "boom" and grow and "boom," and yet agriculture languishes. Salaries and fees were never so temptingly high and desirable, and yet agriculture languishes.

Nor was this situation imputed to America alone. Once in an unguarded burst of rhetoric a high priest of the Alliance movement pointed out that similar conditions prevailed in all thickly populated agricultural countries, "high tariff and low tariff; monarchies, empires, and republics; single gold standard, silver standard or double standard." It was true indeed that the blessings of civilization had not fallen upon all mankind with equal bounty. To the upper and middle classes more had been given than to the lower; to the city dweller far more than to his country kinsman. The farmer had good reason to believe, as he did believe, that he worked longer hours, under more adverse conditions, and with smaller compensation for his labor than any other man on earth.

For this condition of affairs the farmer did not blame himself. Individual farmers might be lacking in industry and frugality, but farmers as a class were

From John D. Hicks, The Populist Revolt. University of Minnesota Press, Minneapolis. © 1931 by University of Minnesota; renewed 1959 by John D. Hicks. Reprinted by permission of the University of Minnesota Press.

devoted to these virtues. Those who gave up the struggle to win wealth out of the land and went to the cities so generally succeeded in the new environment that a steady migration from farm to city set in. Why should the same man fail as a farmer and succeed as a city laborer? More and more the conviction settled down upon the farmer that he was the victim of "some extrinsic baleful influence." Someone was "walking off with the surplus" that society as a whole was clearly building up and that in part at least should be his. He was accustomed to regard himself as the "bone and sinew of the nation" and as the producer of "the largest share of its wealth." Why should his burdens be "heavier every year and his gains . . . more meager?" Why should he be face to-face with a condition of abject servility? Not himself, certainly, but someone else was to blame.

The farmer never doubted that his lack of prosperity was directly traceable to the low prices he received for the commodities he had to sell. The period from 1870 to 1897 was one of steadily declining prices. As one writer put it, the farmer's task had been at the beginning of this era "to make two spears of grass grow where one grew before. He solved that. Now he is struggling hopelessly with the question how to get as much for two spears of grass as he used to get for one." Accurate statistics showing what the farmer really received for his crops are almost impossible to obtain, but the figures given by the Department of Agriculture for three major crops, given in the table below, will at least reveal the general downward trend of prices.

**AVERAGE MARKET PRICES OF THREE CROPS, 1870–1897**

| Years | Wheat (per bushel) | Corn (per bushel) | Cotton (per pound) |
|-------|--------------------|--------------------|--------------------|
| 1870–1873 | 106.7 | 43.1 | 15.1 |
| 1874–1877 | 94.4 | 40.9 | 11.1 |
| 1878–1881 | 100.6 | 43.1 | 9.5 |
| 1882–1885 | 80.2 | 39.8 | 9.1 |
| 1886–1889 | 74.8 | 35.9 | 8.3 |
| 1890–1893 | 70.9 | 41.7 | 7.8 |
| 1894–1897 | 63.3 | 29.7 | 5.8 |

These prices are subject to certain corrections. They are as of December 1, whereas the average farmer had to sell long before that time, often on a glutted market that beat down the price to a much lower figure. They make no allowance, either, for commissions to dealers, for necessary warehouse charges, nor for deductions made when the produce could not be regarded as strictly first class. They fail to show, also, the difference in prices received along the frontier, where the distance to market was great, and in the eastern states, where the market was near at hand. In 1889, for example, corn was sold in Kansas for as low a price as ten cents a bushel and was commonly burned in lieu of coal. In 1890 a farmer in Gosper County, Nebraska, it was said, shot his hogs because he could neither sell nor give them away.

So low did the scale of prices drop that in certain sections of the country it was easy enough to prove, statistically at least, that farming was carried on only at an actual loss. It was generally agreed that seven or eight cents of the price received for each pound of cotton went to cover the cost of production; by the later eighties, moreover, many cotton growers were finding it necessary to market their crops for less than they had been getting. The average price per bushel received by northwestern wheat growers dropped as low as from forty-two to forty-eight cents, whereas the cost of raising a bushel of wheat was variously estimated at from forty-five to sixty-seven cents. Statisticians held that it cost about twenty-one cents to produce a bushel of corn, but the western farmer sometimes had to take less than half that sum. Quoth one agitator:

We were told two years ago to go to work and raise a big crop, that was all we needed. We went to work and plowed and planted; the rains fell, the sun shone, nature smiled, and we raised the big crop that they told us to; and what came of it? Eight cent corn, ten cent oats, two cent beef and no price at all for butter and eggs—that's what came of it. Then the politicians said that we suffered from over-production.

Not politicians only but many others who studied the question held that overproduction was the root of the evil. Too many acres were being tilled, with the result that too many bushels of grain, too many bales of cotton, too many tons of hay, too many pounds of beef were being thrown upon the market each year. As the population increased, the number of consumers had advanced correspondingly, but the increase in production had gone on even more rapidly. It was a fact that the per capita output of most commodities had risen with each successive year. The markets of the world were literally broken down. With the supply so far in excess of the demand, prices could not possibly be maintained at their former levels.

\*     \*     \*

But the farmers and their defenders refused to place much stock in the overproduction theory. Admitting that the output from the farm had increased perhaps even more rapidly than population, they could still argue that this in itself was not sufficient to account for the low prices and the consequent agricultural depression. They pointed out that, with the general improvement of conditions among the masses, consumption had greatly increased. Possibly the demand attendant upon this fact alone would be nearly, if not quite, sufficient to offset the greater yearly output. There would be, moreover, even heavier consumption were it possible for those who needed and wanted more of the products of the farm to buy to the full extent of their ability to consume. In spite of all the advances of the nineteenth century the world was not yet free from want. "The makers of clothes were underfed; the makers of food were underclad." Farmers used corn for fuel in the West because the prices they were offered for it were so low, while at the same moment thousands of people elsewhere faced hunger and even starvation because the price of flour was so high. Why should the Kansas farmer have to sell his corn for eight or ten cents a bushel when the New York broker could and did demand upwards of a dollar for it? Were there not certain "artificial barriers to consumption?" Were there not "certain influences at work, like thieves in the night," to rob the farmers of the fruits of their toil?

Many of the farmers thought that there were; and they were not always uncertain as to the identity of those who stood in the way of agricultural prosperity. Western farmers blamed many of their troubles upon the railroads, by means of which all western crops must be sent to market. There was no choice but to use these roads, and as the frontier advanced farther and farther into the West, the length of the haul to market increased correspondingly. Sometimes western wheat or corn was carried a thousand, perhaps even two thousand, miles before it could reach a suitable place for export or consumption. For these long hauls the railroads naturally exacted high rates, admittedly charging "all the traffic would bear." The farmers of Kansas and Nebraska and Iowa complained that it cost a bushel of corn to send another bushel of corn to market, and it was commonly believed that the net profit of the carrier was greater than the net profit of the grower. The farmers of Minnesota and Dakota were accustomed to pay half the value of their wheat to get it as far towards its final destination as Chicago. Small wonder that the farmer held the railroads at least partly responsible for his distress! He believed that if he could only get his fair share of the price for which his produce eventually sold he would be prosperous enough. "How long," a Minnesota editor queried, "even with these cheap and wonderfully productive lands, can . . . any agricultural community pay such enormous tribute to corporate organization in times like these, without final exhaustion?"

Local freight rates were particularly high. The railroads figured, not without reason, that large shipments cost them less per bushel to haul than small shipments. The greater the volume of traffic the less the cost of carrying any portion of that traffic. Accordingly, on through routes and long hauls where there was a large and dependable flow of freight the rates were comparatively low—the lower because for such runs there was usually ample competition. Rates from Chicago to New York, for example, were low in comparison with rates for similar distances from western points to Chicago, while between local points west of Chicago the rates were even more disproportionate. Sometimes the western local rate would be four times as great as that charged for the same distance and the same commodity in the East. The rates on wheat from Fargo to Duluth were nearly double those from Minneapolis to Chicago —a distance twice as great. It cost as much as twenty-five cents a bushel to transport grain from many Minnesota towns to St. Paul or Minneapolis, while for less than as much more it could be transported all the way to the seaboard. Indeed, evidence was at hand to show that wheat could actually be sent from Chicago to Liverpool for less than from certain points in Dakota to the Twin Cities. Iowa farmers complained that it cost them about as much to ship in corn from an adjoining county for feeding purposes as it would have cost to ship the same corn to Chicago; and yet the Iowa rates seemed low to the farmers of Nebraska, who claimed that they paid an average of fifty percent more for the same service than their neighbors across the Missouri River.

Undoubtedly it cost the railroads more to haul the sparse freight of the West than it cost them to haul the plentiful freight of the East. Railway officials pointed out that western traffic was nearly all in one direction. During one season of the year for every car of wheat hauled out an empty car had to be hauled in, while the rest of the time about ninety percent of the traffic went from Chicago westward. They asserted that the new roads were often in thinly settled regions and were operated at a loss even with the highest rates. James J. Hill maintained that the roads were reducing rates as fast as they could, and to prove it he even declared himself "willing that the state make any rates it see fit," provided the state would "guarantee the roads six percent on their actual cost and a fund for maintenance, renewal and other necessary expenditures." President Dillon of the Union Pacific deplored the ingratitude of the farmers who grumbled about high rates. "What would it cost," he asked, "for a man to carry a ton of wheat one mile? What would it cost for a horse to do the same? The railway does it at a cost of less than a cent." Moreover, he thought that unreasonable rates could never long survive, for if a railroad should attempt anything of the sort competition would come immediately to the farmers' aid, and a parallel and competing line would be built to drive the charges down.

But critics of the railroads saw little that was convincing in these arguments. As for the regulation of rates by competition, it might apply on through routes, providing the roads had no agreement among themselves to prevent it, but competition could scarcely affect the charges for local hauls for the simple reason that the average western community depended exclusively upon a single road. Only rarely did the shipper have a choice of two or more railway companies with which to deal, and even when he had this choice there was not invariably competition. The roads reached agreements among themselves; more than that, they consolidated. "The number of separate railroad companies operating distinct roads in Minnesota was as high as twenty, three years ago," wrote the railway commissioner of that state in 1881. "Now the number is reduced to substantially one-third that number." Nor did Minnesota differ particularly in this respect from any other frontier state. Throughout the eighties as the number of miles of railroad increased, the number of railroad companies tended to decrease. Communities that prided themselves upon a new "parallel and competing line" were apt to discover "some fine morning that enough of its stock had been purchased by the older lines to give them control." Thus fortified by monopoly, the railroads, as the farmer saw it, could collect whatever rates they chose.

*　　*　　*

It was commonly believed also that the practice of stock-watering had much to do with the making of high rates. The exact extent to which the railroads watered their stock, or to which a particular railroad watered its stock, would be a difficult matter to determine, but that the practice did exist in varying degrees seems not to be open to question. A writer in Poor's *Manual* for 1884 stated that the entire four billion dollars at which the railways of the United States were capitalized represented nothing but so much "water." So sweeping a statement seems rather questionable, but the belief was general that railroad companies got their actual funds for investment from bond issues and passed out stocks to the shareholders for nothing. The roads, indeed, did not deny the existence of a certain amount of stock-watering. They argued that their property was quite as likely to increase in value as any other property—farm lands, for example—and that they were justified in increasing their capital stock to the full extent that any increase in value had taken place. Some of their apologists held also that the value of the road was determined by its earning power rather than by the amount actually invested in the enterprise. It followed, therefore, that new capital stock should be issued as fast as the earnings of the road showed that the old valuation had been outgrown.

But to those who suffered from the high rates all these arguments seemed like so many confessions of robbery. The governor of Colorado, considering especially the sins of the Denver and Rio Grande, declared it "incredible that the legitimate course of business can be healthfully promoted by any such inflated capitalization. There must be humbug, if not downright rascality, behind such a pretentious array of figures." The *Kansas Alliance* saw in the prevalent custom of stock-watering an evil "almost beyond comprehension." It placed the total amount of railway overcapitalization at a sum far in excess of the national debt and described these inflated securities as "an ever present incubus upon the labor and land of the nation." Jerry Simpson of Kansas figured that the 8,000 miles of road in his state cost only about $100,000,000, whereas they were actually capitalized at $300,000,000 and bonded for $300,000,000 more. "We who use the roads," he argued, "are really paying interest on $600,000,000 instead of on $100,000,000 as we ought to." Such statements could be multiplied indefinitely. The unprosperous farmers of the frontier saw nothing to condone in the practice of stock-watering. Honest capitalization of railroad property would, they felt, make possible a material reduction in rates. And, in spite of the assertion of one who defended the practice of stock-watering that a citizen who questioned "the right of a corporation to capitalize its properties at any sum whatever committed an 'impertinence,'" the farmers had no notion that the matter was none of their business.

High rates due to overcapitalization and other causes were not, however, the sole cause of dissatisfaction with the railways. It was commonly asserted that the transportation companies discriminated definitely against the small shipper and in favor of his larger competitors. The local grain merchant without elevator facilities or the farmer desirous of shipping his own grain invariably had greater and graver difficulties with the roads than did the large elevator companies. These latter, the farmers contended, were favored by "inside rates," by rebates, and by preferential treatment with regard to cars.

\*        \*        \*

The indictment against the railroads was the stronger in view of their political activities. It is not unfair to say that normally the railroads—sometimes a single road—dominated the political situation in every western state. In Kansas the Santa Fe was all-powerful; in Nebraska the Burlington and the Union Pacific shared the control of the state; everywhere the political power of one or more of the roads was a recognized fact. Railway influence was exerted in practically every important nominating convention to insure that no one hostile to the railways should be named for office. Railway lobbyists were on hand whenever a legislature met to see that measures unfavorable to the roads were quietly eliminated. Railway taxation, a particularly tender question, was always watched with the greatest solicitude and, from the standpoint of the prevention of high taxes, usually with the greatest of success. How much bribery and corruption and intrigue the railroads used to secure the ends they desired will never be known. For a long time, however, by fair means or foul, their wishes in most localities were closely akin to law. Beyond a doubt whole legislatures were sometimes bought and sold.

\*        \*        \*

But from the standpoint of the western pioneer the crowning infamy of the railroads was their theft, as it appeared to him, of his lands. Free lands, or at least cheap lands, had been his ever since America was. Now this "priceless heritage" was gone, disposed of in no small part to the railroads. To them the national government had donated an area "larger than the territory occupied by the great German empire," land which, it was easy enough to see, should have been preserved for the future needs of the people. For this land the railroads charged the hapless emigrant from "three to ten prices" and by a pernicious credit system forced him into a condition of well-nigh perpetual "bondage." "Only a little while ago," ran one complaint, "the people owned this princely domain. Now they are *starving for land*—starving for an opportunity to labor—starving for the right to create from the soil a subsistence for their wives and little children." To the western farmers of this generation the importance of the disappearance of free lands was not a hidden secret to be unlocked only by the researches of some future historian. It was an acutely oppressive reality. The significance of the mad rush to Oklahoma in 1889 was by no means lost upon those who observed the phenomenon. "These men want *free land*," wrote one discerning editor. "They want *free land*—the land that Congress squandered . . . the land that should have formed the sacred patrimony of unborn generations." Senator Peffer of Kansas understood the situation perfectly. "Formerly the man who lost his farm could go west," he said, "now there is no longer any west to go to. Now they have to fight for their homes instead of making new." And in no small measure, he might have added, the fight was to be directed against the railroads.

Complaints against the railways, while most violent in the West, were by no means confined to that section. Practically every charge made by the western farmers had its counterpart elsewhere. In the South particularly the sins that the roads were held to have committed differed in degree, perhaps, but not much in kind, from the sins of the western roads. Southern railroads, like western railroads, were accused of levying "freight and fares at their pleasure to the oppression of the citizens" and of making their rates according to the principle, "take as much out of the pockets of the farmers as we can without actually taking it all." Southerners believed, in fact, that the general decline in freight rates that had accompanied the development of the railroads throughout the country was less in the South than anywhere else and that their section was for this reason worse plagued by high rates than any other.

*    *    *

These common grievances of South and West against the railroads promised to supply a binding tie of no small consequence between the sections. Whether they were westerners or southerners, the orators of revolt who touched upon the railway question spoke a common language. Moreover, the common vocabulary was not used merely when the malpractices of the railroads were being enumerated. Any eastern agitator might indeed have listed many of the same oppressions as typical of his part of the country. But the aggrieved easterner at least suffered from the persecutions of other easterners, whereas the southerner or the westerner was convinced that he suffered from a grievance caused by outsiders. In both sections the description of railway oppression was incomplete without a vivid characterization of the wicked eastern capitalist who cared nothing for the region through which he ran his roads and whose chief aim was plunder. This deep-seated antagonism for a common absentee enemy was a matter of the utmost importance when the time came for bringing on joint political action by West and South. . . .

*    *    *

If the farmer had little part in fixing the price at which his produce sold, he had no part at all in fixing the price of the commodities for which his earnings were spent. Neither did competition among manufacturers and dealers do much in the way of price-fixing, for the age of "big business," of trusts, combines, pools, and monopolies, had come. These trusts, as the farmers saw it, joined with the railroads, and if necessary with the politicians, "to hold the people's hands and pick their pockets." They "bought raw material at their own price, sold the finished product at any figure they wished to ask, and rewarded labor as they saw fit." Through their machinations "the farmer and the workingman generally" were "overtaxed right and left."

One western editor professed to understand how all this had come about. The price-fixing plutocracy, he argued, was but the "logical result of the individual freedom which we have always considered the pride of our system." The American ideal of the "very greatest degree of liberty" and the "very least legal restraint" had been of inestimable benefit to the makers of the trusts. Acting on the theory that individual enterprise should be permitted unlimited scope, they had gone their way without let or hindrance, putting weaker competitors out of business and acquiring monopolistic privileges for themselves. At length the corporation "had absorbed the liberties of the community and usurped the power of the agency that created it." Through its operation "individualism" had congealed into "privilege."

The number of "these unnatural and unnecessary financial monsters" was assumed to be legion. An agitated Iowan denounced the beef trust as "the most menacing" as well as the most gigantic of "about 400 trusts in existence." A Missouri editor took for his example the "plow trust. As soon as it was perfected the price of plows went up 100 percent . . . who suffers? . . . Who, indeed, but the farmer?" Senator Plumb of Kansas held that the people of his state were being robbed annually of $40,000,000 by the produce trust. Southern farmers complained of a fertilizer trust, a jute-bagging trust, a cottonseed oil trust. Trusts indeed there were: trusts that furnished the farmer with the clothing he had to wear; trusts that furnished him with the machines he had to use; trusts that furnished him with the fuel he had to burn; trusts that furnished him with the materials of which he built his house, his barns, his fences. To all these he paid a substantial tribute. Some of them, like the manufacturers of farm machinery, had learned the trick of installment selling, and to such the average farmer owed a perpetual debt.

\*     \*     \*

It was the grinding burden of debt, however, that aroused the farmers, both southern and western, to action. The widespread dependence upon crop liens in the South and farm mortgages in the West has already been described. In the South as long as the price of cotton continued high and in the West as long as the flow of eastern capital remained uninterrupted, the grievances against the railroads, the middlemen, and the tariff-protected trusts merely smouldered. But when the bottom dropped out of the cotton market and the western boom collapsed, then the weight of debt was keenly felt and frenzied agitation began. The eastern capitalists were somehow to blame. They had conspired together to defraud the farmers—"to levy tribute upon the productive energies of West and South." They had made of the one-time American freeman "but a tenant at will, or a dependent upon the tender mercies of soulless corporations and of absentee landlords." . . .

As one hard season succeeded another the empty-handed farmer found his back debts and unpaid interest becoming an intolerable burden. In the West after the crisis of 1887 interest rates, already high, rose still higher. Farmers who needed money to renew their loans, to meet partial payments on their land, or to tide them over to another season were told, truly enough, that money was very scarce. The flow of eastern capital to the West had virtually ceased. The various mortgage companies that had been doing such a thriving business a few months before had now either gone bankrupt or had made drastic retrenchments. Rates of seven or eight percent on real estate were now regarded as extremely low; and on chattels ten or twelve percent was considered very liberal, from eighteen to twenty-four percent was not uncommon, and forty percent or above was not unknown. Naturally the number of real estate mortgages placed dropped off precipitately. Instead of the six thousand, worth nearly $5,500,000, that had been placed in Nebraska during the years 1884 to 1887, there were in the three years following 1887 only five hundred such mortgages, worth only about $650,000, while only one out of four of the farm mortgages held on South Dakota land in 1892 had been contracted prior to 1887. When the farmer could no longer obtain money on his real estate, he usually mortgaged his chattels, with the result that in many localities nearly everything that could carry a mortgage was required to do so. In Nebraska during the early nineties the number of these badges of "dependence and slavery" recorded by the state auditor averaged over half a million annually. In Dakota many families were kept from leaving for the East only by the fact that their horses and wagons were mortgaged and could therefore not be taken beyond the state boundaries.

Whether at the old rates, which were bad, or at the new, which were worse, altogether too often the western farmer was mortgaged literally for all he was worth, and too often the entire fruits of his labor, meager enough after hard times set in, were required to meet impending obligations. Profits that the farmer felt should have been his passed at once to someone else. The conviction grew on him that there was something essentially wicked and vicious about the system that made this possible. Too late he observed that the money he had borrowed was not worth to him what he had contracted to pay for it. As one embittered farmer-editor wrote,

*There are three great crops raised in Nebraska. One is a crop of corn, one a crop of freight rates, and one a crop of interest. One is produced by farmers who by sweat and toil farm the land. The other two are produced by men who sit in their offices and behind their bank counters and farm the farmers. The corn is less than half a crop. The freight rates will produce a full average. The interest crop, however, is the one that fully illustrates the boundless resources and prosperity of Nebraska. When corn fails the interest yield is largely increased.*

What was the fair thing under such circumstances? Should the farmer bear the entire load of adversity, or should the mortgage-holder help? Opinions varied, but certain extremists claimed that at the very least the interest should be scaled down. If railroads were permitted to reorganize, reduce their interest rates, and save their property when they got into financial straits, why should the farmer be denied a similar right?

The only reorganization to which the farmer had recourse, as a rule, was through foreclosure proceedings, by which ordinarily he could expect nothing less than the loss of all his property. Usually the mortgagor was highly protected by the terms of the mortgage and could foreclose whenever an interest payment was defaulted, whether the principal was due or not. In the late eighties and the early nineties foreclosures came thick and fast. Kansas doubtless suffered most on this account, for from 1889 to 1893 over eleven thousand farm mortgages were foreclosed in this state, and in some counties as much as ninety percent of the farm lands passed into the ownership of the loan companies. It was estimated by one alarmist that "land equal to a tract thirty miles wide and ninety miles long had been foreclosed and bought in by the loan companies of Kansas in a year." Available statistics would seem to bear out this assertion, but the unreliability of such figures is notorious. Many farmers and speculators, some of them perfectly solvent, deliberately invited foreclosure because they found after the slump that their land was mortgaged for more than it was worth. On the other hand, many cases of genuine bankruptcy were settled out of court and without record. But whatever the unreliability of statistics the fact remains that in Kansas and neighboring states the number of farmers who lost their lands because of the hard times and crop failures was very large.

In the South the crop-lien system constituted the chief mortgage evil and the chief grievance, but a considerable amount of real and personal property was also pledged for debt. Census statistics, here also somewhat unreliable because of the numerous informal and unrecorded agreements, show that in Georgia about one-fifth of the taxable acres were under mortgage, and a special investigation for the same state seemed to prove that a high proportion of the mortgage debt was incurred to meet current expenditures rather than to acquire more land or to make permanent improvements. Similar conditions existed throughout the cotton South. Chattel mortgages were also freely given, especially by tenants, but frequently also by small proprietors. Interest rates were as impossibly high as in the West, and foreclosures almost as inevitable. Evidence of foreclosures on chattels could be found in the "pitiful heaps of . . . rubbish" that "commonly disfigured the court house squares." Foreclosures on land, or their equivalent, were numerous, serving alike to accelerate the process of breaking down the old plantations and of building up the new "merchant-owned 'bonanzas.'" Many small farmers lapsed into tenantry; indeed, during the eighties the trend was unmistakably in the direction of "concentration of agricultural land in the hands of merchants, loan agents, and a few of the financially strongest farmers."

Taxation added a heavy burden to the load of the farmer. Others might conceal their property. The merchant might underestimate the value of his stock, the householder might neglect to list a substantial part of his personal property, the holder of taxable securities might keep his ownership a secret, but the farmer could not hide his land. If it was perhaps an exaggeration to declare that the farmers "represent but one-fourth of the nation's wealth and they pay three-fourths of the taxes," it was probably true enough that land bore the chief brunt of taxation, both in the South and in the West. Tax-dodging, especially on the part of the railroads and other large corporations, was notorious. Some North Carolina railroads had been granted special exemptions from taxation as far back as the 1830's, and they still found them useful. In Georgia the railroads paid a state tax but not a county tax. Nearly everywhere they received special treatment at the hands of assessors, state boards of equalization, or even by the law itself. Western land-grant railroads avoided paying taxes on their huge holdings by delaying to patent them until they could be sold. Then the farmer-purchaser paid the taxes. Meantime the cost of state and local government had risen everywhere, although most disproportionately in the West, where the boom was on. In the boom territory public building and improvement projects out of all proportion to the capacity of the people to pay had been undertaken, and railways, street-car companies, and other such enterprises had been subsidized by the issuing of state or local bonds, the interest and principal of which had to be met by taxation. For all this unwise spending the farmers had to pay the greater part. The declaration of one Kansas farmer that his taxes were doubled in order "to pay the interest on boodler bonds and jobs voted by nontaxpayers to railroad schemes and frauds and follies which are of no benefit to the farmer" was not without a large element of truth. The farmer was convinced that he was the helpless victim of unfair, unreasonable, and discriminatory taxation. Here was another reason why he was "gradually but steadily becoming poorer and poorer every year."

Beset on every hand by demands for funds—funds with which to meet his obligations to the bankers, the loan companies, or the tax collectors and funds with which to maintain his credit with the merchants so that he might not lack the all-essential seed to plant another crop or the few necessities of life that he and his family could not contrive either to produce for themselves or to go without—the farmer naturally enough raised the battle cry of "more money." He came to believe that, after all, his chief grievance was against the system of money and banking, which now virtually denied him credit and which in the past had only plunged him deeper and deeper into debt. There must be something more fundamentally wrong than the misdeeds of railroads and trusts and tax assessors. Why should dollars grow dearer and dearer and scarcer and scarcer? Why, indeed, unless because of the manipulations of those to whom such a condition would bring profit?

Much agitation by Greenbackers and by free-silverites and much experience in the marketing of crops had made clear even to the most obtuse, at least of the debtors, that the value of a dollar was greater than it once had been. It would buy two bushels of grain where formerly it would buy only one. It would buy twelve pounds of cotton where formerly it would buy but six. The orthodox retort of the creditor to such a statement was that too much grain and cotton were being produced—the overproduction theory. But, replied the debtor, was this the whole truth? Did not the amount of money in circulation have something to do with the situation? Currency reformers were wont to point out that at the close of the Civil War the United States had nearly two billions of dollars in circulation. Now the population had doubled and the volume of business had probably trebled, but the number of dollars in circulation had actually declined! Was not each dollar overworked? Had it not attained on this account a fictitious value?

## The Appreciating Dollar, 1865 – 1895

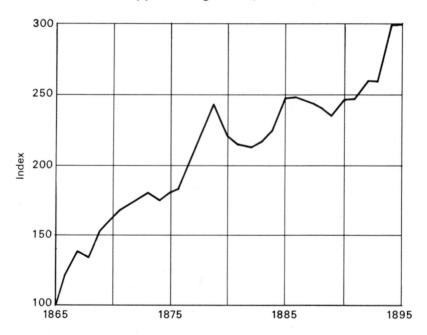

Whatever the explanation, it was clear enough that the dollar, expressed in any other terms than itself, had appreciated steadily in value ever since the Civil War. The depreciated greenback currency, in which all ordinary business was transacted until 1879, reached by that year a full parity with gold. But the purchasing power of the dollar still continued its upward course. For this phenomenon the quantity theory may be—probably is—an insufficient explanation, but in the face of the figures from which the accompanying chart has been drawn, the fact of continuous appreciation can hardly be denied.

For those farmers who were free from debt and were neither investors nor borrowers such a condition might have had little meaning. The greater purchasing power of the dollar meant fewer dollars for their crops, but it meant also fewer dollars spent for labor and supplies. Conceivably, the same degree of prosperity could be maintained on the smaller income. But in the West and in the South the number of debt-free farmers was small indeed, and for the debtor the rising value of the dollar was a serious matter. The man who gave a long-term mortgage on his real estate was in the best position to appreciate how serious it was. Did he borrow a thousand dollars on his land for a five-year term, then he must pay back at the end of the allotted time a thousand dollars. But it might well be that, whereas at the time he had contracted the loan a thousand dollars meant a thousand bushels of wheat or ten thousand pounds of cotton, at the time he must pay it the thousand dollars meant fifteen hundred bushels of wheat or fifteen thousand pounds of cotton. Interest, expressed likewise in terms of produce, had mounted similarly year by year so that the loss to the borrower was even greater than the increase in the value of the principal. What it cost the debtor to borrow under such circumstances has been well expressed by Arnett in the [following] table . . . , which is based on statistics taken from the census of 1890.

**DEBT APPRECIATION, 1865–1890**

| Average Five-year Debt Contracted in | Appreciation (in terms of dollar's purchasing power) |
| --- | --- |
| 1865–1869 | 35.2 |
| 1870–1874 | 19.7 |
| 1875–1879 | 4.5 |
| 1880–1884 | 11.7 |
| 1885–1890 | 11.6 |

Add to this the unreasonably high interest rates usually exacted and the commissions and deductions that were rarely omitted and the plight of the debtor farmer becomes painfully clear. He was paying what would have amounted to about a twenty or twenty-five percent rate of interest on a non-appreciating dollar.

It was, moreover, far from comforting to reflect that in such a transaction what was one man's loss was another's gain. Nor was it surprising that the harassed debtor imputed to the creditor, to whose advantage the system worked, a deliberate attempt to cause the dollar to soar to ever greater and greater heights. Had not the creditor class ranged itself solidly behind the

Resumption Act of 1875, by which the greenback dollar had been brought to a parity with gold? Was not the same class responsible for the "crime of 1873," which had demonetized silver and by just so much had detracted from the quantity of the circulating medium? Was there not, indeed, a nefarious conspiracy of creditors—eastern creditors, perhaps with English allies—to increase their profits at the expense of the debtors—western and southern—by a studied manipulation of the value of the dollar? "We feel," said Senator Allen of Nebraska, "that, through the operation of a shrinking volume of money, which has been caused by Eastern votes and influences for purely selfish purposes, the East has placed its hands on the throat of the West and refused to afford us that measure of justice which we, as citizens of a common country, are entitled to receive." And the grievance of the West against the East was also the grievance of the South.

Nor was this grievance confined to resentment against the steadily mounting value of the dollar. There was in addition an undeniable and apparently unreasonable fluctuation in its purchasing power during any given year. At the time of crop movements, when the farmers wished to sell—indeed, had to sell, in most cases—the dollar was dear and prices were correspondingly depressed. When, on the other hand, the crop had been marketed and the farmers' produce had passed to other hands, the dollar fell in value and prices mounted rapidly. Wall Street speculators and others bought heavily when prices were low and sold later when prices were high at handsome profits—profits which, the farmers firmly believed, should have gone to the original producer.

*    *    *

Such were the grievances of which the farmers complained. They suffered, or at least they thought they suffered, from the railroads, from the trusts and the middlemen, from the money-lenders and the bankers, and from the muddled currency. These problems were not particularly new. Always the farmer had had to struggle with the problem of transportation. He had never known a time when the price of the things he had to buy was not as much too high as the price of the things he had to sell was too low. He had had his troubles with banks and bankers. But those earlier days were the days of cheap lands, and when things went wrong the disgruntled could seek solace in a move to the West. There was a chance to make a new start. Broader acres, more fertile fields, would surely bring the desired results. And with the restless ever moving to the West, the more stable elements of society left behind made pleasing progress. Now with the lands all taken and the frontier gone, this safety valve was closed. The frontier was turned back upon itself. The restless and discontented voiced their sentiments more and fled from them less. Hence arose the veritable chorus of denunciation directed against those individuals and those corporations who considered only their own advantage without regard to the effect their actions might have upon the farmer and his interests.

Richard Hofstadter

# Populism:
# Nostalgic Agrarianism

## The Two Nations

For a generation after the Civil War, a time of great economic exploitation and waste, grave social corruption and ugliness, the dominant note in American political life was complacency. Although dissenting minorities were always present, they were submerged by the overwhelming realities of industrial growth and continental settlement. The agitation of the Populists, which brought back to American public life a capacity for effective political indignation, marks the beginning of the end of this epoch. In the short run the Populists did not get what they wanted, but they released the flow of protest and criticism that swept through American political affairs from the 1890's to the beginning of the first World War.

Where contemporary intellectuals gave the Populists a perfunctory and disdainful hearing, later historians have freely recognized their achievements and frequently overlooked their limitations. Modern liberals, finding the Populists' grievances valid, their programs suggestive, their motives creditable, have usually spoken of the Populist episode in the spirit of Vachel Lindsay's bombastic rhetoric:

> Prairie avenger, mountain lion,
> Bryan, Bryan, Bryan, Bryan,
> Gigantic troubadour, speaking like a siege gun,
> Smashing Plymouth Rock with his boulders from the West.

There is indeed much that is good and usable in our Populist past. While the Populist tradition had defects that have been too much neglected,

From The Age of Reform by Richard Hofstadter. Copyright © 1955 by Richard Hofstadter. Reprinted by permission of Alfred A. Knopf, Inc.

it does not follow that the virtues claimed for it are all fictitious. Populism was the first modern political movement of practical importance in the United States to insist that the federal government has some responsibility for the common weal; indeed, it was the first such movement to attack seriously the problems created by industrialism. The complaints and demands and prophetic denunciations of the Populists stirred the latent liberalism in many Americans and startled many conservatives into a new flexibility. Most of the "radical" reforms in the Populist program proved in later years to be either harmless or useful. In at least one important area of American life a few Populist leaders in the South attempted something profoundly radical and humane—to build a popular movement that would cut across the old barriers of race—until persistent use of the Negro bogy distracted their following. To discuss the broad ideology of the Populists does them some injustice, for it was in their concrete programs that they added most constructively to our political life, and in their more general picture of the world that they were most credulous and vulnerable. Moreover, any account of the fallibility of Populist thinking that does not acknowledge the stress and suffering out of which that thinking emerged will be seriously remiss. But anyone who enlarges our portrait of the Populist tradition is likely to bring out some unseen blemishes. In the books that have been written about the Populist movement, only passing mention has been made of its significant provincialism; little has been said of its relations with nativism and nationalism; nothing has been said of its tincture of anti-Semitism.

The Populist impulse expressed itself in a set of notions that represent what I have called the "soft" side of agrarianism. These notions, which appeared with regularity in the political literature, must be examined if we are to re-create for ourselves the Populist spirit. To extract them from the full context of the polemical writings in which they appeared is undoubtedly to oversimplify them; even to name them in any language that comes readily to the historian of ideas is perhaps to suggest that they had a formality and coherence that in reality they clearly lacked. But since it is less feasible to have no labels than to have somewhat too facile ones, we may enumerate the dominant themes in Populist ideology as these: the idea of a golden age; the concept of natural harmonies; the dualistic version of social struggles; the conspiracy theory of history; and the doctrine of the primacy of money. The last of these I will touch upon in connection with the free-silver issue. Here I propose to analyze the others, and to show how they were nurtured by the traditions of the agrarian myth.

The utopia of the Populists was in the past, not the future. According to the agrarian myth, the health of the state was proportionate to the degree to which it was dominated by the agricultural class, and this assumption pointed to the superiority of an earlier age. The Populists looked backward with longing to the lost agrarian Eden, to the republican America of the early years of the nineteenth century in which there were few millionaires and, as they saw it, no beggars, when the laborer had excellent prospects and the farmer had abundance, when statesmen still responded to the mood of the people and there was no such thing as the money power. What they meant— though they did not express themselves in such terms—was that they would like to restore the conditions prevailing before the development of industrialism and the commercialization of agriculture. It should not be surprising that they inherited the traditions of Jacksonian democracy, that they revived the old Jacksonian cry: "Equal Rights for All, Special Privileges for None," or that most of the slogans of 1896 echoed the battle cries of 1836. General James B. Weaver, the Populist candidate for the presidency in 1892, was an old Democrat and Free-Soiler, born during the days of Jackson's battle with the United States Bank, who drifted into the Greenback movement after a short spell as a Republican, and from there to Populism. His book, *A Call to Action*, published in 1892, drew up an indictment of the business corporation which reads like a Jacksonian polemic. Even in those hopeful early days of the People's Party, Weaver projected no grandiose plans for the future, but lamented the course of recent history, the growth of economic oppression, and the emergence of great contrasts of wealth and poverty, and called upon his readers to do "All in [their] power to arrest the alarming tendencies of our times."

Nature, as the agrarian tradition had it, was beneficent. The United States was abundantly endowed with rich land and rich resources, and the "natural" consequence of such an endowment should be the prosperity of the people. If the people failed to enjoy prosperity, it must be because of a harsh and arbitrary intrusion of human greed and error. "Hard times, then," said one popular writer, "as well as the bankruptcies, enforced idleness, starvation, and the crime, misery, and moral degradation growing out of conditions like the present, being unnatural, not in accordance with, or the result of any natural law, must be attributed to that kind of unwise and pernicious legislation which history proves to have produced similar results in all ages of the world. It is the mission of the age to correct these errors in human legislation, to adopt and establish policies and systems, in accord with, rather than in opposition to divine law." In assuming a lush natural order whose workings were being deranged by human laws, Populist writers were again drawing on the Jacksonian tradition, whose spokesmen also had pleaded for a proper obedience to "natural" laws as a prerequisite of social justice.

Somewhat akin to the notion of the beneficence of nature was the idea of a natural harmony of interests among the productive classes. To the Populist mind there was no fundamental conflict between the farmer and the worker, between the toiling people and the small businessman. While there might be corrupt individuals in any group, the underlying interests of the productive majority were the same; predatory behavior existed only because it was initiated and underwritten by a small parasitic minority in the highest places of power. As opposed to the idea that society consists of a number of different and frequently clashing interests—the social pluralism expressed, for instance, by Madison in the *Federalist*—the Populists adhered, less formally to be sure, but quite persistently, to a kind of social dualism: although they knew perfectly well that society was composed of a number of classes, for all practical purposes only one simple division need be considered. There were two nations. "It is a struggle," said Sockless Jerry Simpson, "between the robbers and the robbed." "There are but two sides in the conflict that is being waged in this country today," declared a Populist manifesto. "On the one side are the allied hosts of monopolies, the money power, great trusts and railroad corporations, who seek the enactment of laws to benefit them and impoverish the people. On the other are the farmers, laborers, merchants, and all other people who produce wealth and bear the burdens of taxation. . . . Between these two there is no middle ground." "On the one side," said Bryan in his famous speech against the repeal of the Sherman Silver Purchase Act, "stand the corporate interests of the United States, the moneyed interests, aggregated wealth and capital, imperious, arrogant, compassionless. . . . On the other side stand an unnumbered throng, those who gave to the Democratic party a name and for whom it has assumed to speak." The people versus the interests, the public versus the plutocrats, the toiling multitude versus the money power—in various phrases this central antagonism was expressed. From this simple social classification it seemed to follow that once the techniques of misleading the people were exposed, victory over the money power ought to be easily accomplished, for in sheer numbers the people were overwhelming. "There is no power on earth that can defeat us," said General Weaver during the optimistic days of the campaign of 1892. "It is a fight between labor and capital, and labor is in the vast majority."

The problems that faced the Populists assumed a delusive simplicity: the victory over injustice, the solution for all social ills, was concentrated in the crusade against a single, relatively small but immensely strong interest, the money power. "With the destruction of the money power," said Senator Peffer, "the death knell of gambling in grain and other commodities will be sounded; for the business of the worst men on earth will have been broken up, and the mainstay of the gamblers removed. It will be an easy matter, after the greater spoilsmen have been shorn of their power, to clip the wings of the little ones. Once get rid of the men who hold the country by the throat, the parasites can be easily removed." Since the old political parties were the primary means by which the people were kept wandering in the wilderness, the People's Party advocates insisted, only a new and independent political party could do this essential job. As the silver question became more prominent and the idea of a third party faded, the need for a monolithic solution became transmuted into another form: there was only one *issue* upon which the money power could really be beaten and this was the money issue. "When we have restored the money of the Constitution," said Bryan in his Cross of

Gold speech, "all other necessary reforms will be possible; but . . . until this is done there is no other reform that can be accomplished."

While the conditions of victory were thus made to appear simple, they did not always appear easy, and it would be misleading to imply that the tone of Populistic thinking was uniformly optimistic. Often, indeed, a deep-lying vein of anxiety showed through. The very sharpness of the struggle, as the Populists experienced it, the alleged absence of compromise solutions and of intermediate groups in the body politic, the brutality and desperation that were imputed to the plutocracy—all these suggested that failure of the people to win the final contest peacefully could result only in a total victory for the plutocrats and total extinction of democratic institutions, possibly after a period of bloodshed and anarchy. "We are nearing a serious crisis," declared Weaver. "If the present strained relations between wealth owners and wealth producers continue much longer they will ripen into frightful disaster. This universal discontent must be quickly interpreted and its causes removed." "We meet," said the Populist platform of 1892,

*in the midst of a nation brought to the verge of moral, political, and material ruin. Corruption dominates the ballot-box, the Legislatures, the Congress, and touches even the ermine of the bench. The people are demoralized. . . . The newspapers are largely subsidized or muzzled, public opinion silenced, business prostrated, homes covered with mortgages, labor impoverished, and the land concentrating in the hands of the capitalists. The urban workmen are denied the right to organize for self-protection, imported pauperized labor beats down their wages, a hireling standing army, unrecognized by our laws, is established to shoot them down, and they are rapidly degenerating into European conditions. The fruits of the toil of millions are boldly stolen to build up colossal fortunes for a few, unprecedented in the history of mankind; and the possessors of these, in turn, despise the Republic and endanger liberty.*

Such conditions foreboded "the destruction of civilization, or the establishment of an absolute despotism." . . .

## History as Conspiracy

There was . . . a widespread Populist idea that all American history since the Civil War could be understood as a sustained conspiracy of the international money power.

The pervasiveness of this way of looking at things may be attributed to the common feeling that farmers and workers were not simply oppressed but oppressed deliberately, consciously, continuously, and with wanton malice by "the interests." It would of course be misleading to imply that the Populists stand alone in thinking of the events of their time as the results of a conspiracy. This kind of thinking frequently occurs when political and social antagonisms are sharp. Certain audiences are especially susceptible to it—particularly, I believe, those who have attained only a low level of education, whose access to information is poor, and who are so completely shut out from access to the centers of power that they feel themselves completely deprived of self-defense and subjected to unlimited manipulation by those who wield power. There are, moreover, certain types of popular movements of dissent that offer special opportunities to agitators with paranoid tendencies, who are able to make a vocational asset out of their psychic disturbances. Such persons have an opportunity to impose their own style of thought upon the movements they lead. It would of course be misleading to imply that there are no such things as conspiracies in history. Anything that partakes of political strategy may need, for a time at least, an element of secrecy, and is thus vulnerable to being dubbed conspiratorial. Corruption itself has the character of conspiracy. In this sense the Crédit Mobilier was a conspiracy, as was the Teapot Dome affair. If we tend to be too condescending to the Populists at this point, it may be necessary to remind ourselves that they had seen so much bribery and corruption, particularly on the part of the railroads, that they had before them a convincing model of the management of affairs through conspiratorial behavior. Indeed, what makes conspiracy theories so widely acceptable is that they usually contain a germ of truth. But there is a great difference between locating conspiracies *in* history and saying that history *is*, in effect, a conspiracy, between singling out those conspiratorial acts that do on occasion occur and weaving a vast fabric of social explanation out of nothing but skeins of evil plots.

When conspiracies do not exist it is necessary for those who think in this fashion to invent them. Among the most celebrated instances in modern history are the forgery of the Protocols of the Elders of Zion and the grandiose fabrication under Stalin's regime of the Trotzkyite-Bukharinite-Zinovievite center. These inventions were cynical. In the history of American political controversy there is a tradition of conspiratorial accusations which seem to have been sincerely believed. Jefferson appears really to have believed, at one time, that the Federalists were conspiring to re-establish monarchy. Some Federalists believed that the Jeffersonians were conspiring to subvert Christianity. The movement to annex Texas and the war with Mexico were alleged by many Northerners to be a slaveholders' conspiracy. The early Republican leaders, including Lincoln, charged that there was a conspiracy on the part of Stephen A. Douglas to make slavery a nationwide institution. Such pre-Civil War parties as the Know-Nothing and Anti-Masonic movements were based almost entirely upon conspiratorial ideology. The Nye Committee, years ago, tried to prove that our entry into the first World War was the work of a conspiracy of bankers and munitions-makers. And now not only our entry into the second World War, but the entire history of the past twenty years or so is being given the color of conspiracy by the cranks and political fakirs of our own age.

Nevertheless, when these qualifications have been taken into account, it remains true that Populist thought showed an unusually strong tendency to account for relatively impersonal events in highly personal terms. An overwhelming sense of grievance does not find satisfactory expression in impersonal explanations, except among those with a well-developed tradition of intellectualism. It is the city, after all, that is the home of intellectual complexity. The farmer lived in isolation from the great world in which his fate was actually decided. He was accused of being unusually suspicious, and certainly his situation, trying as it was, made thinking in impersonal terms difficult. Perhaps the rural middle-class leaders of Populism (this was a movement of farmers, but it was not led by farmers) had more to do than the farmer himself with the cast of Populist thinking. At any rate, Populist thought often carries one into a world in which the simple virtues and unmitigated villainies of a rural melodrama have been projected on a national and even an international scale. In Populist thought the farmer is not a speculating businessman, victimized by the risk economy of which he is a part, but rather a wounded yeoman, preyed upon by those who are alien to the life of folkish virtue. A villain was needed, marked with the unmistakable stigmata of the villains of melodrama, and the more remote he was from the familiar scene, the more plausibly his villainies could be exaggerated.

It was not enough to say that a conspiracy of the money power against the common people was going on. It had been going on ever since the Civil War. It was not enough to say that it stemmed from Wall Street. It was international: it stemmed from Lombard Street. In his preamble to the People's Party platform of 1892, a succinct, official expression of Populist views, Ignatius Donnelly asserted: "A vast conspiracy against mankind has been organized on two continents, and it is rapidly taking possession of the world. If not met and overthrown at once it forebodes terrible social convulsions, the destruction of civilization, or the establishment of an absolute despotism." A manifesto of 1895, signed by fifteen outstanding leaders of the People's Party, declared: "As early as 1865–66 a conspiracy was entered into between the gold gamblers of Europe and America. . . . For nearly thirty years these conspirators have kept the people quarreling over less important matters while they have pursued with unrelenting zeal their one central purpose. . . . Every device of treachery, every resource of statecraft, and every artifice known to the secret cabals of the international gold ring are being made use of to deal a blow to the prosperity of the people and the financial and commercial independence of the country."

The financial argument behind the conspiracy theory was simple enough. Those who owned bonds wanted to be paid not in a common currency but in gold, which was at a premium; those who lived by lending money wanted as high a premium as possible to be put on their commodity by increasing its scarcity. The panics, depressions, and bankruptcies caused by their policies only added to their wealth; such catastrophes offered opportunities to engross the wealth of others through business consolidations and foreclosures. Hence the interests actually relished and encouraged hard times. The Greenbackers had long since popularized this argument, insisting that an adequate legal-tender currency would break the monopoly of the "Shylocks." Their demand for $50 of circulating medium per capita, still in the air when the People's Party arose, was rapidly replaced by the less "radical" demand for free coinage of silver. But what both the Greenbackers and free-silverites held in common was the idea that the contraction of currency was a deliberate squeeze, the result of a long-range plot of the "Anglo-American Gold Trust." Wherever one turns in the Populist literature of the nineties one can find this conspiracy theory expressed. It is in the Populist newspapers, the proceedings of the silver conventions, the immense pamphlet literature broadcast by the American Bimetallic League, the Congressional debates over money; it is elaborated in such popular books as Mrs. S. E. V. Emery's *Seven Financial Conspiracies which have Enslaved the American People* or Gordon Clark's *Shylock: as Banker, Bondholder, Corruptionist, Conspirator.*

Mrs. Emery's book, first published in 1887, and dedicated to "the enslaved people of a dying republic," achieved great circulation, especially among the Kansas Populists. According to Mrs. Emery, the United States had been an economic Garden of Eden in the period before the Civil War. The fall of man had dated from the war itself, when "the money kings of Wall Street" determined that they could take advantage of the wartime necessities of their fellow men by manipulating the currency. "Controlling it, they could inflate or depress the business of the country at pleasure, they could send the warm life current through the channels of trade, dispensing peace, happiness, and prosperity, or they could check its flow, and completely paralyze the industries of the country." With this great power for good in their hands, the Wall Street men preferred to do evil. Lincoln's war policy of issuing greenbacks presented them with the dire threat of an adequate supply of currency. So the Shylocks gathered in convention and "perfected" a conspiracy to create a demand for their gold. The remainder of the book was a recital of a series of seven measures passed between 1862 and 1875 which were alleged to be a part of this continuing conspiracy, the total effect of which was to contract the currency of the country further and further until finally it squeezed the industry of the country like a hoop of steel.

Mrs. Emery's rhetoric left no doubt of the sustained purposefulness of this scheme—described as "villainous robbery," and as having been "secured through the most soulless strategy." She was most explicit about the so-called "crime of 1873," the demonetization of silver, giving a fairly full statement of the standard greenback-silverite myth concerning that event. As they had it, an agent of the Bank of England, Ernest Seyd by name, had come to the United States in 1872 with $500,000 with which he had bought enough support in Congress to secure the passage of the demonetization measure. This measure was supposed to have greatly increased the value of American four percent bonds held by British capitalists by making it necessary to pay them in gold only. To it Mrs. Emery attributed the panic of 1873, its bankruptcies, and its train of human disasters: "Murder, insanity, suicide, divorce, drunkenness and all forms of immorality and crime have increased from that day to this in the most appalling ratio."

"Coin" Harvey, the author of the most popular single document of the whole currency controversy, *Coin's Financial School*, also published a novel, *A Tale of Two Nations*, in which the conspiracy theory of history was incorporated into a melodramatic tale. In this story the powerful English banker Baron Rothe plans to bring about the demonetization of silver in the United States, in part for his own aggrandizement but also to prevent the power of the United States from outstripping that of England. He persuades an American Senator (probably John Sherman, the *bête noire* of the silverites) to co-operate in using British gold in a campaign against silver. To be sure that the work is successful, he also sends to the United States a relative and ally, one Rogasner, who stalks through the story like the villains in the plays of Dion Boucicault, muttering to himself such remarks as "I am here to destroy the United States—Cornwallis could not have done more. For the wrongs and insults, for the glory of my own country, I will bury the knife deep into the heart of this nation." Against the plausibly drawn background of the corruption of the Grant administration, Rogasner proceeds to buy up the American Congress and suborn American professors of economics to testify for gold. He also falls in love with a proud American beauty, but his designs on her are foiled because she loves a handsome young silver Congressman from Nebraska who bears a striking resemblance to William Jennings Bryan!

One feature of the Populist conspiracy theory that has been generally overlooked is its frequent link with a kind of rhetorical anti-Semitism. The slight current of anti-Semitism that existed in the United States before the 1890's had been associated with problems of money and credit. During the closing years of the century it grew noticeably. While the jocose and rather heavy-handed anti-Semitism that can be found in Henry Adams's letters of the 1890's shows that this prejudice existed outside Populist literature, it was chiefly Populist writers who expressed that identification of the Jew with the usurer and the "international gold ring" which was the central theme of the American anti-Semitism of the age. The omnipresent symbol of Shylock can hardly be taken in itself as evidence of anti-Semitism, but the frequent references to the House of Rothschild make it clear that for many silverites the Jew was an organic part of the conspiracy theory of history. Coin Harvey's Baron Rothe was clearly meant to be Rothschild; his Rogasner (Ernest Seyd?) was a dark figure out of the coarsest anti-Semitic tradition. "You are very wise in your way," Rogasner is told at the climax of the tale, "the commercial way, inbred through generations. The politic, scheming, devious way, inbred through generations also." One of the cartoons in the effectively illustrated *Coin's Financial School* showed a map of the world dominated by the tentacles of an octopus at the site of the British Isles, labeled: "Rothschilds." In Populist demonology, anti-Semitism and Anglophobia went hand in hand.

The note of anti-Semitism was often sounded openly in the campaign for silver. A representative of the New Jersey Grange, for instance, did not hesitate to warn the members of the Second National Silver Convention of 1892 to watch out for political candidates who represented "Wall Street, and the Jews of Europe." Mary E. Lease described Grover Cleveland as "the agent of Jewish bankers and British gold." Donnelly represented the leader of the governing Council of plutocrats in *Caesar's Column*, one Prince Cabano, as a powerful Jew, born Jacob Isaacs; one of the triumvirate who lead the Brotherhood of Destruction is also an exiled Russian Jew, who flees from the apocalyptic carnage with a hundred million dollars which he intends to use to "revive the ancient splendors of the Jewish race, in the midst of the ruins of the world." One of the more elaborate documents of the conspiracy school traced the power of the Rothschilds over America to a transaction between Hugh McCulloch, Secretary of the Treasury under Lincoln and Johnson, and Baron James Rothschild. "The most direful part of this business between Rothschild and the United States Treasury was not the loss of money, even by hundreds of millions. It was the resignation of the country itself INTO THE HANDS OF ENGLAND, as England had long been resigned into the hands of HER JEWS."

Such rhetoric, which became common currency in the movement, later passed beyond Populism into the larger stream of political protest. By the time the campaign of 1896 arrived, an Associated Press reporter noticed as "one of the striking things" about the Populist convention at St. Louis "the extraordinary hatred of the Jewish race. It is not possible to go into any hotel in the city without hearing the most bitter denunciation of the Jews as a class and of the particular Jews who happen to have prospered in the world." This report may have been somewhat overdone, but the identification of the silver cause with anti-Semitism did become close enough for Bryan to have to pause in the midst of his campaign to explain to the Jewish Democrats of Chicago that in denouncing the policies of the Rothschilds he and his silver friends were "not attacking a race; we are attacking greed and avarice which know no race or religion."

It would be easy to misstate the character of Populist anti-Semitism or to exaggerate its intensity. For Populist anti-Semitism was entirely verbal. It was a mode of expression, a rhetorical style, not a tactic or a program. It did not lead to exclusion laws, much less to riots or pogroms. There were, after all, relatively few Jews in the United States in the late 1880's and early 1890's, most of them remote from the areas of Populist strength. It is one thing, however, to say that this prejudice did not go beyond a certain symbolic usage, quite another to say that a people's choice of symbols is of no significance. Populist anti-Semitism does have its importance—chiefly as a symptom of a certain ominous credulity in the Populist mind. It is not too much to say that the Greenback-Populist tradition activated most of what we have of modern popular anti-Semitism in the United States. From Thaddeus Stevens and Coin Harvey to Father Coughlin, and from Brooks and Henry Adams to Ezra Pound, there has been a curiously persistent linkage between anti-Semitism and money and credit obsessions. A full history of modern anti-Semitism in the United States would reveal, I believe, its substantial Populist lineage, but it may be sufficient to point out here that neither the informal connection between Bryan and the Klan in the twenties nor Thomas E. Watson's conduct in the Leo Frank case were altogether fortuitous. And Henry Ford's notorious anti-Semitism of the 1920's, along with his hatred of "Wall Street," were the foibles of a Michigan farm boy who had been liberally exposed to Populist notions.

Lawrence Goodwyn

# *Populism: Democratic Promise*

A large number of people in the United States discovered that the economic premises of their society were working against them. These premises were reputed to be democratic—America after all was a democratic society in the eyes of most of its own citizens and in the eyes of the world—but farmers by the millions found that this claim was not supported by the events governing their lives.

The nation's agriculturalists had worried and grumbled about "the new rules of commerce" ever since the prosperity that accompanied the Civil War had turned into widespread distress soon after the war ended. During the 1870s they did the kinds of things that concerned people generally do in an effort to cope with "hard times." In an occupation noted for hard work they worked even harder. When this failed to change things, millions of families migrated westward in an effort to enlist nature's help. They were driven by the thought that through sheer physical labor they might wring more production from the new virgin lands of the West than they had been able to do in their native states of Ohio and Virginia and Alabama. But, though railroad land agents created beguiling stories of Western prosperity, the men and women who listened, and went, found that the laws of commerce worked against them just as much in Kansas and Texas as they had back home on the eastern side of the Mississippi River.

So in the 1870s, the farmers increasingly talked to each other about their troubles and read books on economics in an effort to discover what had gone wrong. Some of them formed organizations of economic self-help like the

Excerpted from The Populist Moment: A Short History of the Agrarian Revolt in America by Lawrence Goodwyn. Copyright © 1978 by Lawrence Goodwyn. Reprinted by permission of the author and Oxford University Press, Inc.

Grange and others assisted in pioneering new institutions of political self-help like the Greenback Party. But as the hard times of the 1870s turned into the even harder times of the 1880s, it was clear that these efforts were not really going anywhere. Indeed, by 1888 it was evident that things were worse than they had been in 1878 or 1868. More and more people saw their farm mortgages foreclosed. As everyone in rural America knew, this statistic inexorably yielded another, more ominous one: the number of landless tenant farmers in America rose steadily year after year. Meanwhile, millions of small landowners hung on grimly, their unpaid debts thrusting them dangerously close to the brink of tenantry and peonage. Hard work availed nothing. Everywhere the explanation of events was the same: "Times were hard."

Then gradually, in certain specific ways and for certain specific reasons, American farmers developed new methods that enabled them to try to regain a measure of control over their own lives. Their efforts, halting and disjointed at first, gathered form and force until they grew into a coordinated mass movement that stretched across the American continent from the Atlantic coast to the Pacific. Millions of people came to believe fervently that a wholesale overhauling of their society was going to happen in their lifetimes. A democratic "new day" was coming to America. This whirlwind of effort, and the massive upsurge of democratic hopes that accompanied it, has come to be known as the Populist Revolt. . . .

For a number of reasons, all of them rather fundamental to historical analysis, the Populist moment has proved very difficult for Americans to understand. Under the circumstances, it is probably just as well to take these reasons up one at a time at the very outset in an effort to clear as much underbrush as possible before turning our attention to the protesting farmers of the 1890s.

There are three principal areas of interpretive confusion that bear directly on the Populist experience. First, very little understanding exists as to just what mass democratic movements are, and how they happen. Second, there are serious problems embedded in the very language of description modern Americans routinely employ to characterize political events. These problems particularly affect commonly held presumptions about how certain "classes" of people are supposed to "act" on the stage of history. Finally, and by all odds most importantly, our greatest problem in understanding protest is grounded in contemporary American culture. In addition to being central, this cultural difficulty is also the most resistant to clear explanation: we are not only culturally confused, our confusion makes it difficult for us even to imagine our confusion. Obviously, it is prudent, then, to start here.

The reigning American presumption about the American experience is grounded in the idea of progress, the conviction that the present is "better" than the past and the future will bring still more betterment. This reassuring belief rests securely on statistical charts and tables certifying the steady upward tilt in economic production. Admittedly, social problems have persisted— inequities of income and opportunity have plagued the society—but these, too, have steadily been addressed through the sheer growth of the economy. For all of its shortcomings, the system works.

This is a powerful assumption. It may be tested by reflecting upon the fact that, despite American progress, the society has been forced to endure sundry movements of protest. In our effort to address the inconvenient topic of protest, our need to be intellectually consistent—while thinking within the framework of continuous progress—has produced a number of explanations about the nature of dissent in America. Closely followed, these arguments are not really explanations at all, but rather the assertion of more presumptions that have the effect of defending the basic intuition about progress itself. The most common of these explanations rests upon what is perceived to be a temporary malfunction of the economic order: people protest when "times are hard." When times stop being "hard," people stop protesting and things return to "normal"—that is to say, progress is resumed.

Unfortunately, history does not support the notion that mass protest movements develop because of hard times. Depressed economies or exploitive arrangements of power and privilege may produce lean years or even lean lifetimes for millions of people, but the historical evidence is conclusive that they do not produce mass political insurgency. The simple fact of the matter is that, in ways that affect mind and body, times have been "hard" for most humans throughout human history and for most of that period people have not been in rebellion. Indeed, traditionalists in a number of societies have often pointed in glee to this passivity, choosing to call it "apathy" and citing it as a justification for maintaining things as they are.

This apparent absence of popular vigor is traceable, however, not to apathy but to the very raw materials of history—that complex of rules, manners, power relationships, and memories that collectively comprise what is called culture. "The masses" do not rebel in instinctive response to hard times and exploitation because they have been culturally organized by their societies not to rebel. They have, instead, been instructed in deference. Needless to say, this is the kind of social circumstance that is not readily apparent to the millions who live within it.

The lack of visible mass political activity on the part of modern industrial populations is a function of how these societies have been shaped by the various economic or political elites who fashioned them. In fundamental ways, this shaping process (which is now quite mature in America) bears directly not only upon our ability to grasp the meaning of American Populism, but our ability to understand protest generally and, most important of all, on our ability to comprehend the prerequisites for democracy itself. This shaping process, therefore, merits some attention.

Upon the consolidation of power, the first duty of revolutionaries (whether of the "bourgeois" or "proletarian" variety) is obviously to try to deflect any further revolutions that necessarily would be directed against them. Though a strong central police or army has sometimes proved essential to this stabilizing process, revolutionaries, like other humans, do not yearn to spend their lives fighting down counterrevolutions. A far more permanent and thus far more desirable solution to the task of achieving domestic tranquillity is cultural—the creation of mass modes of thought that literally make the need for major additional social changes difficult for the mass of the population to imagine. When and if achieved, these conforming modes of thought and conduct constitute the new culture itself. The ultimate victory is nailed into place, therefore, only when the population has been persuaded to define all conceivable political activity within the limits of existing custom. Such a society can genuinely be described as "stable." Thenceforth, protest will pose no ultimate threat because the protesters will necessarily conceive of their options as being so limited that even should they be successful, the resulting "reforms" will not alter significantly the inherited modes of power and privilege. Protest under such conditions of cultural narrowness is, therefore, not only permissible in the eyes of those who rule, but is, from time to time, positively desirable because it fortifies the popular understanding that the society is functioning "democratically." . . .

\* \* \*

The principal hazard to a clear understanding of the meaning of American Populism exists in this central anomaly of contemporary American culture. Reform movements such as Populism necessarily call into question the underlying values of the larger society. But if that society is perceived by its members to be progressive and democratic—and yet is also known to have resisted the movement of democratic reform—the reigning cultural presumption necessarily induces people to place the "blame" for the failure of protest upon the protesters themselves. Accordingly, in the case of the Populists, the mainstream presumption is both simple and largely unconscious: one studies Populism to learn where the Populists went wrong. The condescension toward the past that is implicit in the idea of progress merely reinforces such complacent premises.

Further, if the population is politically resigned (believing the dogma of "democracy" on a superficial public level but not believing it privately), it becomes quite difficult for people to grasp the scope of popular hopes that were alive in an earlier time when democratic expectations were larger than those people permit themselves to have today. By conjoining these two contradictory features of modern culture—the assumption of economic progress with massive political resignation—it is at once evident that modern people are culturally programmed, as it were, to conclude that past American egalitarians such as the Populists were "foolish" to have had such large democratic hopes. Again, our "progressive" impulse to condescend to the past merely reinforces such a presumption. In a society in which sophisticated deference masks private resignation, the democratic dreams of the Populists have been difficult for twentieth-century people to imagine. Contemporary American culture itself therefore operates to obscure the Populist experience.

A second obstacle to a clear perception of Populism is embedded in the language of description through which contemporary Americans attempt to characterize "politics." A central interpretive tool, derived from Marx but almost universally employed today by Marxists and non-Marxists alike, is based upon concepts of class: that is, that the intricate nature of social interaction in history can be rendered more intelligible by an understanding of the mode and extent of class conflict that was or was not at work during a given period. Needless to say, many psychological, social, and economic ingredients are embedded in concepts of class, and, when handled with care, they can, indeed, bring considerable clarity to historical events of great complexity. Nevertheless, as an interpretive device, "class" is a treacherous tool if handled casually and routinely—as it frequently is. For example, offhand "class analysis,"when applied to the agrarian revolt in America, will merely succeed in rendering the Populist experience invisible. While classes in agricultural societies contain various shadings of "property-consciousness" on the part of rich landowners, smallholders, and landless laborers ("gentry," "farmers," and "tenants," in American terminology), these distinctions create more problems than they solve when applied to the agrarian revolt. It is a long-standing assumption— not so thoroughly tested in America by sustained historical investigation as some might believe—that "landowners" must perforce behave in politically reactionary ways. The political aspirations of the landless are seen to deserve intense scrutiny, but the politics of "the landed" cannot be expected to contain serious progressive ideas. The power of this theoretical assumption can scarcely be understated. It permits the political efforts of millions of human beings to be dismissed with the casual flourish of an abstract category of interpretation. One can only assert the conviction that a thoroughgoing history of, for example, the Socialist Party of the United States, including the history of the recruitment of its agrarian following in early twentieth-century America, will not be fully pieced together until this category of political analysis is successfully transcended. The condition of being "landed" or "landless" does not, a *priori*, predetermine one's potential for "progressive" political action: circumstances surrounding the ownership or non-ownership of land are centrally relevant, too. The Populist experience in any case puts this proposition to a direct and precise test, for the agrarian movement was created by landed *and* landless people. The platform of the movement argued in behalf of the landless because that platform was seen as being progressive for small landowners, too. Indeed, from beginning to end, the chief Populist theoreticians—"landowners" all—stood in economic terms with the propertyless rural and urban people of America.

In consequence, neither the human experiences within the mass institutions generated by the agrarian revolt nor the ideology of Populism itself can be expected to become readily discernible to anyone, capitalist or Marxist, who is easily consoled by the presumed analytical clarity of categories of class. The interior life of the agrarian revolt makes this clear enough. While the economic and political threads of populism did not always mesh in easy harmony (any more than the cultural threads did), the evolution of the political ideology of the movement proceeded from a common center and a common experience and thus possessed an instructive degree of sequential consistency.

The use of the word "sequential" provides an appropriate introduction to the final hazard confronting the student of the agrarian revolt—the rather elementary problem of defining just what "mass movements" are and how they happen. The sober fact is that movements of mass democratic protest— that is to say, coordinated insurgent actions by hundreds of thousands or millions of people—represent a political, an organizational, and above all, a cultural achievement of the first magnitude. Beyond this, mass protest requires a high order not only of cultural education and tactical achievement, it requires a high order of *sequential* achievement. These evolving stages of achievement are essential if large numbers of intimidated people are to generate both the psychological autonomy and the practical means to challenge culturally sanctioned authority. A failure at any stage of the sequential process aborts or at the very least sharply limits the growth of the popular movement. Unfortunately, the overwhelming nature of the impediments to these stages of sequential achievement are rarely taken into account. The simple fact of the matter is that so difficult has the process of movement-building proven to be since the onset of industrialization in the Western world that all democratic protest movements have been aborted or limited in this manner prior to the recruitment of their full natural constituency. The underlying social reality is, therefore, one that is not generally kept firmly in mind as an operative dynamic of modern society—namely, that mass democratic movements are overarchingly difficult for human beings to generate.

How does mass protest happen at all, then—to the extent that it does happen?

The Populist revolt—the most elaborate example of mass insurgency we have in American history—provides an abundance of evidence that can be applied in answering this question. The sequential process of democratic movement-building will be seen to involve four stages: (1) the creation of an autonomous institution where new interpretations can materialize that run counter to those of prevailing authority—a development which, for the sake of simplicity, we may describe as "the movement forming"; (2) the creation of a tactical means to attract masses of people—"the movement recruiting"; (3) the achievement of a heretofore culturally unsanctioned level of social analysis—"the movement educating"; and (4) the creation of an institutional means whereby the new ideas, shared now by the rank and file of the mass movement, can be expressed in an autonomous political way—"the movement politicized."

Imposing cultural roadblocks stand in the way of a democratic movement at every stage of this sequential process, causing losses in the potential constituencies that are to be incorporated into the movement. Many people may not be successfully "recruited," many who are recruited may not become adequately "educated," and many who are educated may fail the final test of moving into autonomous political action. The forces of orthodoxy, occupying the most culturally sanctioned command posts in the society, can be counted upon, out of self-interest, to oppose each stage of the sequential process— particularly the latter stages, when the threat posed by the movement has become clear to all. In the aggregate, the struggle to create a mass democratic movement involves intense cultural conflict with many built-in advantages accruing to the partisans of the established order.

Offered here in broad outline, then, is a conceptual framework through which to view the building process of mass democratic movements in modern industrial societies. The recruiting, educating, and politicizing methods will naturally vary from movement to movement and from nation to nation, and the relative success in each stage will obviously vary also. The actions of both the insurgents and the defenders of the received culture can also be counted upon to influence events dramatically.

Within this broad framework, it seems helpful to specify certain subsidiary components. Democratic movements are initiated by people who have individually managed to attain a high level of personal political self-respect. They are not resigned; they are not intimidated. To put it another way, they are not culturally organized to conform to established hierarchical forms. Their sense of autonomy permits them to dare to try to change things by seeking to influence others. The subsequent stages of recruitment and of internal economic and political education (steps two, three, and four) turn on the ability of the democratic organizers to develop widespread methods of internal communication within the mass movement. Such democratic facilities provide the only way the movement can defend itself to its own adherents in the face of the adverse interpretations certain to emanate from the received culture. If the movement is able to achieve this level of internal communication and democracy, and the ranks accordingly grow in numbers and in political consciousness, a new plateau of social possibility comes within reach of all participants. In intellectual terms, the generating force of this new mass mode of behavior may be rather simply described as "a new way of looking at things." It constitutes a new and heretofore unsanctioned mass folkway of autonomy. In psychological terms, its appearance reflects the development within the movement of a new kind of collective self-confidence. "Individual self-respect" and "collective self-confidence" constitute, then, the cultural building blocks of mass democratic politics. Their development permits people to conceive of the idea of acting in self-generated democratic ways—as distinct from passively participating in various hierarchical modes bequeathed by the received culture. In this study of Populism, I have given a name to this plateau of cooperative and democratic conduct. I have called it "the movement culture." Once attained, it opens up new vistas of social possibility, vistas that are less clouded by inherited assumptions. I suggest that all significant mass democratic movements in human history have generated this autonomous capacity. Indeed, had they not done so, one cannot visualize how they could have developed into significant mass democratic movements.

Democratic politics hinge fundamentally on these sequential relationships. Yet, quite obviously the process is extremely difficult for human beings to set in motion and even more difficult to maintain—a fact that helps explain why genuinely democratic cultures have not yet been developed by mankind. Self-evidently, mass democratic societies cannot be created until the components of the creating process have been theoretically delineated and have subsequently come to be understood in practical ways by masses of people. This level of political analysis has not yet been reached, despite the theoretical labors of Adam Smith, Karl Marx, and their sundry disciples and critics. As a necessary consequence, twentieth-century people, instead of participating in democratic cultures, live in hierarchical cultures, "capitalist" and "socialist," that merely call themselves democratic.

All of the foregoing constitutes an attempt to clear enough cultural and ideological landscape to permit an unhampered view of American Populism. The development of the democratic movement was sequential. The organizational base of the agrarian revolt was an institution called the National Farmers Alliance and Industrial Union. Created by men of discernible self-possession and political self-respect, the Alliance experimented in new methods of economic self-help. After nine years of trial and error, the people of the Alliance developed a powerful mechanism of mass recruitment—the world's first large-scale working class cooperative. Farmers by the hundreds of thousands flocked into the Alliance. In its recruiting phase, the movement swept through whole states "like a cyclone" because, easily enough, the farmers joined the Alliance in order to join the Alliance cooperative. The subsequent experiences of millions of farmers within their cooperatives proceeded to "educate" them about the prevailing forms of economic power and privilege in America. This process of education was further elaborated through a far-flung agency of internal communication, the 40,000 lecturers of the Alliance lecturing system. Finally, after the effort of the Alliance at economic self-help had been defeated by the financial and political institutions of industrial America, the people of the movement turned to independent political action by creating their own institution, the People's Party. All of these experiences, stretching over a fifteen-year period from 1877 to 1892, may be seen as an evolutionary pattern of democratic organizing activity that generated, and in turn was generated by, an increasing self-awareness on the part of the participants. In consequence, a mass democratic movement was fashioned.

Once established in 1892, the People's Party challenged the corporate state and the creed of progress it put forward. It challenged, in sum, the world we live in today. Though our loyalty to our own world makes the agrarian revolt culturally difficult to grasp, Populism may nevertheless be seen as a time of economically coherent democratic striving. Having said this, it is also necessary to add that Populists were not supernatural beings. As theoreticians concerned with certain forms of capitalist exploitation, they were creative and, in a number of ways, prescient. As economists, they were considerably more thoughtful and practical than their contemporary political rivals in both major parties. As organizers of a huge democratic movement, Populists learned a great deal about both the power of the received hierarchy and the demands imposed on themselves by independent political action. As third party tacticians, they had their moments, though most of their successes came earlier in the political phase of their movement than later. And, finally, as participants in the democratic creed, they were, on the evidence, far more advanced than most Americans, then or since. . . .

Out of their cooperative struggle came a new democratic community. It engendered within millions of people what Martin Luther King would later call a "sense of somebodiness." This "sense" was a new way of thinking about oneself and about democracy. Thus armed, the Populists attempted to insulate themselves against being intimidated by the enormous political, economic, and social pressures that accompanied the emergence of corporate America.

*    *    *

Populism in America was not the sub-treasury plan, not the greenback heritage, not the Omaha Platform. It was not, at bottom, even the People's Party. The meaning of the agrarian revolt was its cultural assertion as a people's movement of mass democratic aspiration. Its animating essence pulsed at every level of the ambitious structure of cooperation: in the earnest probings of people bent on discovering a way to free themselves from the killing grip of the credit system ("The suballiance is a schoolroom."); in the joint-notes of the landed, given in the name of themselves and the landless ("The brotherhood stands united."); in the pride of discovery of their own legitimacy ("The merchants are listening when the County Trade Committee talks."); and in the massive and emotional effort to save the cooperative dream itself ("The Southern Exchange Shall Stand."). The democratic core of Populism was visible in the suballiance resolutions of inquiry into the patterns of economic exploitation ("find out and apply the remedy"); in the mile-long Alliance wagon trains ("The Fourth of July is Alliance Day."); in the sprawling summer encampments ("A pentecost of politics"); and, perhaps most tellingly, in the latent generosity unlocked by the culture of the movement itself, revealed in the capacity of those who had little, to empathize with those who had less ("We extend to the Knights of Labor our hearty sympathy in their manly struggle against monopolistic oppression," and "The Negro people are part of the people and must be treated as such.").

While each of these moments occurred in the 1890s, and have practical and symbolic meaning because they did occur, Populism in America was not an egalitarian achievement. Rather, it was an egalitarian attempt, a beginning. If it stimulated human generosity, it did not, before the movement itself was destroyed, create a settled culture of generosity. Though Populists attempted to break out of the received heritage of white supremacy, they necessarily, as white Americans, did so within the very ethos of white supremacy. At both a psychological and political level, some Populists were more successful than others in coping with the pervasive impact of the inherited caste system. Many were not successful at all. This reality extended to a number of pivotal social and political questions beside race—sectional and party loyalties, the intricacies of power relationships embedded in the monetary system, and the ways of achieving a politics supportive of popular democracy itself. In their struggle, Populists learned a great truth: cultures are hard to change. Their attempt to do so, however, provides a measure of the seriousness of their movement.

Populism thus cannot be seen as a moment of triumph, but as a moment of democratic promise. It was a spirit of egalitarian hope, expressed in the actions of two million beings—not in the prose of a platform, however creative, and not, ultimately, even in the third party, but in a self-generated culture of collective dignity and individual longing. As a movement of people, it was expansive, passionate, flawed, creative—above all, enhancing in its assertion of human striving. That was Populism in the nineteenth century.

*       *       *

However they were subsequently characterized, Populists in their own time derived their most incisive power from the simple fact that they declined to participate adequately in a central element of the emerging American faith. In an age of progress and forward motion, they had come to suspect that Horatio Alger was not real. In due course, they came to possess a cultural flaw that armed them with considerable critical power. Heretics in a land of true believers and recent converts, they saw the coming society and they did not like it. It was perhaps inevitable that since they lost their struggle to deflect that society from its determined path of corporate celebration, they were among the last of the heretics. Once defeated, they lost what cultural autonomy they had amassed and surrendered their progeny to the training camps of the conquering army. All Americans, including the children of Populists, were exposed to the new dogmas of progress confidently conveyed in the public school system and in the nation's history texts. As the twentieth-century recipients of this instruction, we have found it difficult to listen with sustained attention to the words of those who dissented at the moment a transcendent cultural norm was being fashioned.

In their own era, the agrarian spokesmen who talked of the "coming revolution" turned out to be much too hopeful. Though in the months of Populist collapse and for successive decades thereafter prosperity eluded those the reformers called the "producing classes," the growing industrial society preserved the narrowed boundaries of political dialogue substantially intact, as roughly one-third of America's urban workers moved slowly into the middle class. The mystique of progress itself helped to hold in muted resignation the millions who continued in poverty and other millions who, for reasons of the exclusiveness and white supremacy of the progressive society, were not permitted to live their lives in dignity.

As the first beneficiary of the cultural consolidation of the 1890s, the new Republican orthodoxy, grounded in the revolutionary (and decidedly anti-Jeffersonian) political methods of Mark Hanna, provided the mores for the twentieth century without ever having to endure a serious debate about the possibility of structural change in the American forms of finance capitalism. Political conservatives nevertheless endured intermittent periods of extreme nervousness—such as was produced in 1933 by the nation's sudden and forced departure from the gold standard. Given the presumed centrality of a metallic currency, it took a while for cultural traditionalists, including bankers, to realize that the influence of the banking community had not suffered organic disturbances—J. Laurence Laughlin to the contrary notwithstanding. Though the pattern of interest rates during and after World War II continued to transfer measurable portions of the national income from both business and labor to bankers—in the process burdening the structure of prices with an added increment of cost as well as changing the very structure of industrial capitalism—disputes over the distribution of income within the whole society did not precipitate serious social contentions as long as America maintained a favorable international trade and investment balance. It remained clear, however, that unresolved questions about the inherited financial system might well make a sudden and unexpected reappearance if, at any time in the second half of the twentieth century, shifts in world trade and the cost of imported raw materials placed severe forms of competitive pressure on the American economy and on the international monetary system. At such a moment the cultural consolidation fashioned in the Gilded Age would undergo its first sustained re-evaluation, as the "financial question" once again intruded into the nation's politics and the issues of Populism again penetrated the American consciousness. That time, while pending, has not yet come.

For their part, Gilded Age traditionalists did not view the conclusive triumph of the corporate ethos as a foregone conclusion. Themselves insecure in an era of real and apparent change, they were unable to distinguish between authentic signs of economic dislocation and the political threat represented by those who called attention to those signs. On this rather primitive level the politics of the era resolved itself, and the progressive society was born. As an outgrowth of its insularity and complacency, industrializing America wanted uncritical voices of celebration. The agrarian radicals instead delivered the warning that all was not well with the democracy. They were not thanked.

Today, the values and the sheer power of corporate America pinch in the horizons of millions of obsequious corporate employees, tower over every American legislature, state and national, determine the modes and style of mass communications and mass education, fashion American foreign policy around the globe, and shape the rules of the American political process itself. Self-evidently, corporate values define modern American culture.

It was the corporate state that the People's Party attempted to bring under democratic control.

# SUGGESTIONS FOR FURTHER READING

John D. Hicks, *The Populist Revolt* (Minneapolis, 1931), deserves to be read in its entirety. Broader in scope and sympathetic to the farmers is Fred A. Shannon's outstanding work, *The Farmers' Last Frontier: Agriculture, 1860–1897* (New York, 1945). Excellent introductions to Southern Populism are C. Vann Woodward, *The Origins of the New South, 1877–1913* (Baton Rouge, 1951, 1971), and Sheldon Hackney, *From Populism to Progessivism in Alabama, 1890–1920* (Princeton, 1969).

Especially useful examples of the vast literature dealing with farmers' problems are Allan G. Bogue, *Money at Interest: The Farm Mortgage on the Middle Border* (Ithaca, New York, 1955), and *From Prairie to Cornbelt: Farming on the Illinois and Iowa Prairies in the Nineteenth Century* (Chicago, 1963); Paul W. Gates, *Fifty Million Acres: Conflicts over Kansas Land Policy, 1854–1890* (Ithaca, New York, 1954); and Theodore Saloutos and John D. Hicks, *Twentieth Century Populism* (Lincoln, Nebraska, 1951).

In the 1950s Richard Hofstadter's *The Age of Reform* (a portion of which is reprinted here) began a reexamination of the Populists. He and others charged the Populists with some degree of responsibility for the anti-Semitism, isolationism, and antiintellectualism in American life. C. Vann Woodward discusses some of this anti-Populist literature in "The Populist Heritage and the Intellectual," *American Scholar*, 29 (Winter 1959–1960), pp. 55–72, also reprinted in C. Vann Woodward, *The Burden of Southern History* (Baton Rouge, 1960). The attack on the Populists has also produced a vigorous defense. Walter T. K. Nugent denies that the Populists were anti-Semitic and xenophobic in *The Tolerant Populists* (Chicago, 1963). Norman Pollack, in *The Populist Response to Industrial America* (Cambridge, Mass., 1962), finds them to be realistic radicals, who looked not to the past but to a future when businessmen would no longer be able to exploit farmers and workers. For Pollack, the Populists posed a kind of socialist answer, but Lawrence Goodwyn, in *The Populist Moment* (New York, 1978) (a portion of which is reprinted here), maintains that the Populist alternative was neither socialist nor bourgeois. (The volume by Goodwyn is an abridgement of his more detailed study, *Democratic Promise* [New York, 1976].) A similar point of view is found in Robert C. McMath, Jr., *Populist Vanguard: A History of the Southern Farmers' Alliance* (Chapel Hill, N.C., 1975). Michael Schwartz, *Radical Protest and Social Structure: The Southern Farmers' Allliance and Cotton Tenancy, 1880–1890* (New York, 1976), argues that the Alliance was a radical people's movement and that it was diverted from its radicalism when it was taken over by politicians whose main goal was election to office rather than real reform. John L. Thomas, *Alternative America: Henry George, Edward Bellamy, Henry Demarest Lloyd and the Adversary Tradition* (Cambridge, Mass., 1983) is a discussion of three critics who shared some of the goals of the Populists and helped to shape the social thought of the period.

* Available in paperback edition.

# 4

# *Workers in an Industrial Age*

Ultimately, the effect of America's industrialization would be added opportunities, increased wages, more and better goods and services, and improved working conditions. But behind the statistics of economic growth and rising standards of living were serious problems brought by the rapid and often chaotic economic and social changes. Workers found themselves crowded into urban slums that were marked by unspeakable filth and grossly inadequate public services. In the shops and factories hours were usually long, conditions dangerous and unhealthy, and wages woefully low. Periodic economic crises threw people out of work, giving employers a powerful weapon to force down the wages and to lengthen the working hours of those who remained employed.

In order to protect themselves, workers often united, sometimes in trade unions but often in less formal and structured organizations. When organized and determined workers used the strike in their struggle against organized and equally determined employers, the result was bitter and, at times, violent. Striking workers were often greeted at plant gates by armed guards hired by factory owners intent upon dispersing the pickets and maintaining production with unorganized labor. Workers regularly armed themselves, equally resolved to keep the struck factory closed by preventing "scabs" from entering the shops. When these two determined and armed groups met, the result was invariably a bloody clash.

Historians, of course, cannot ignore the many instances of conflict, and every labor history bristles with accounts of violent struggles between labor and management. From this, many scholars conclude that there is no tradition of consensus in this aspect of American history.

Yet others argue that conflict is not the basic underlying feature in American labor history. Without attempting to ignore the conflicts, they point to other aspects of the American labor movement. They argue that only a few American unionists have been radicals and that never has the trade union movement followed a program designed to overthrow the existing social and economic system. Those unions that have adopted a radical or revolutionary program have always been in the distinct minority; the major portion of organized labor has consistently repudiated the radical sections of the movement.

In a word, then, these historians point to consensus as the basic theme in American labor history. Labor and management, they argue, have often disagreed over wages and working conditions and these disagreements often led to strikes and conflicts; but, behind these disagreements, there existed an underlying unity based upon an acceptance of the sanctity of private property as well as the most important features of American democratic government.

Just as those historians who emphasize consensus cannot ignore the violent conflicts that often characterized labor-management relations, those who stress conflict cannot ignore the fact that the major portions of the American labor movement have not been radical and revolutionary. Still they

145

continue to insist that conflict is the basic theme. Some argue that although the labor movement is not socialistic, it has always adopted goals that would fundamentally alter our social and economic system even if they would not completely destroy it. Others argue that the American labor movement will eventually become socialistic, like its European counterparts.

Some of the problems involved in interpreting American labor history can be seen in the selections that follow. Readers should keep in mind that one's approach to the evaluation of the labor movement, including the many instances of strikes and violence, rests upon an assessment of the nature of the divisions between worker and employer. What exactly did the workers want?

One answer to this question is provided by Herbert G. Gutman in the first selection. Gutman finds sharp and bitter conflict as workers—both men and women, from rural and artisan backgrounds—were forced to modernize, that is, to adapt to the new industrial society. Workers resisted, but the ensuing conflict was not revolutionary or socialist. Workers resisted changes being forced upon them by the demands of expanding industrialism; they sought to retain many of their old ways and traditions.

In the second selection, Daniel T. Rodgers describes a different kind of conflict between workers and employers, a conflict stemming from differing attitudes toward work. The work ethic, he notes, was a "businessmen's creed." Workers did not completely repudiate the work ethic, but they did object to the long hours and the rigid discipline that employers attempted to impose upon them. The ensuing conflicts often began with agreement on the need and value of work but disagreement on the meaning and significance of that work.

It would appear that both Gutman and Rodgers find class conflict. Is this conflict potentially revolutionary? Or are the conflicts, however violent and sharp, merely reformist in nature? In other words, do workers and employers in the United States accept the fundamentals of the economic and social system with workers interested in no more than increasing their share of the nation's wealth?

A somewhat different view of matters appears in the final selection, where Alice Kessler-Harris considers problems from the perspective of women workers. To improve their working conditions and wages, women had to fight not only their employers but also the traditions that defined their proper role and the unions that were often antagonistic. Employers who wanted a cheap and docile labor force hired increasing numbers of women workers, while the unions felt that women workers took jobs that were rightly men's and that they kept wages low. In the end, women remained in the labor force, but they found themselves segregated into what was considered "women's work."

The demands discussed in these three selections do not appear to be radical or socialistic. But does it therefore follow that working men and women have simply accepted the ideas and outlook of the employers? Is it not more realistic to speak of a mutual accommodation between labor and capital than of a capitulation on the part of labor? If so, what is the nature of this accommodation?

What do answers to these questions suggest for the future? Radicals place great emphasis on the role of the working class in the overthrow of private property, in the replacement of capitalism by socialism. Does the history of American labor point in this direction?

*Herbert G. Gutman*

# Work, Culture, and Society in Industrializing America 1815-1919

With a few significant exceptions, for more than half a century American labor history has continued to reflect both the strengths and the weaknesses of the conceptual scheme sketched by its founding fathers, John R. Commons and others of the so-called Wisconsin school of labor history. Even their most severe critics, including the orthodox "Marxist" labor historians of the 1930s, 1940s, and 1950s and the few New Left historians who have devoted attention to American labor history, rarely questioned that conceptual framework. Commons and his colleagues asked large questions, gathered important source materials, and put forth impressive ideas. Together with able disciples, they studied the development of the trade union as an institution and explained its place in a changing labor market. But they gave attention primarily to those few workers who belonged to trade unions and neglected much else of importance about the American working population. Two flaws especially marred this older labor history. Because so few workers belonged to permanent trade unions before 1940, its overall conceptualization excluded most working people from detailed and serious study. More than this, its methods encouraged labor historians to spin a cocoon around American workers, isolating them from their own particular subcultures and from the larger national culture. An increasingly narrow "economic" analysis caused the study of American working-class history to grow more constricted and become more detached from larger developments in American social and cultural history and from the writing of American social and cultural history itself. . . .

The focus in these pages is on free white labor in quite different time periods: 1815–43, 1843–93, 1893–1919. The precise years serve only as

From *American Historical Review,* LXXVIII (June 1973). *Reprinted by permission of the author.*

guideposts to mark the fact that American society differed greatly in each period. Between 1815 and 1843 the United States remained a predominantly preindustrial society and most workers drawn to its few factories were the products of rural and village preindustrial culture. Preindustrial American society was not premodern in the same way that European peasant societies were, but it was, nevertheless, premodern. In the half century after 1843 industrial development radically transformed the earlier American social structure, and during this Middle Period (an era not framed around the coming and the aftermath of the Civil War) a profound tension existed between the older American preindustrial social structure and the modernizing institutions that accompanied the development of industrial capitalism. After 1893 the United States ranked as a mature industrial society. In each of these distinctive stages of change in American society, a recurrent tension also existed between native and immigrant men and women fresh to the factory and the demands imposed upon them by the regularities and disciplines of factory labor. That state of tension was regularly revitalized by the migration of diverse premodern native and foreign peoples into an industrializing or a fully industrialized society. The British economic historian Sidney Pollard has described well this process whereby "a society of peasants, craftsmen, and versatile labourers became a society of modern industrial workers." "There was more to overcome," Pollard writes of industrializing England,

> than the change of employment or the new rhythm of work: there was a whole new culture to be absorbed and an old one to be traduced and spurned, there were new surroundings, often in a different part of the country, new relations with employers, and new uncertainties of livelihood, new friends and neighbors, new marriage patterns and behavior patterns of children within the family and without.

That same process occurred in the United States. Just as in all modernizing countries, the United States faced the difficult task of industrializing whole cultures, but in this country the process was regularly repeated, each stage of American economic growth and development involving different first-generation factory workers. The social transformation Pollard described occurred in England between 1770 and 1850, and in those decades premodern British cultures and the modernizing institutions associated primarily with factory and machine labor collided and interacted. A painful transition occurred, dominated the ethos of an entire era, and then faded in relative importance. After 1850 and until quite recently, the British working class reproduced itself and retained a relative national homogeneity. New tensions emerged but not those of a society continually busy (and worried about) industrializing persons born out of that society and often alien in birth and color and in work habits, customary values, and behavior. "Traditional social habits and customs," J. F. C. Harrison reminds us, "seldom fitted into the patterns of industrial life, and they had . . . to be discredited as hindrances to progress." That happened regularly in the United States after 1815 as the nation absorbed and worked to transform new groups of preindustrial peoples, native whites among them.

The result, however, was neither a static tension nor the mere recurrence of similar cycles, because American society itself changed as did the composition of its laboring population. But the source of the tension remained the same, and conflict often resulted. It was neither the conflict emphasized by the older Progressive historians (agrarianism versus capitalism, or sectional disagreement) nor that emphasized by recent critics of that early twentieth-century synthesis (conflict between competing elites). It resulted instead from the fact that the American working class was continually altered in its composition by infusions, from within and without the nation, of peasants, farmers, skilled artisans, and casual day laborers who brought into industrial society ways of work and other habits and values not associated with industrial necessities and the industrial ethos. Some shed these older ways to conform to new imperatives. Others fell victim or fled, moving from place to place. Some sought to extend and adapt older patterns of work and life to a new society. Others challenged the social system through varieties of collective associations. But for all—at different historical moments—the transition to industrial society, as E. P. Thompson has written, "entailed a severe restructuring of working habits—new disciplines, new incentives, and a new human nature upon which these incentives could bite effectively.". . .

Men and women who sell their labor to an employer bring more to a new or changing work situation than their physical presence. What they bring to a factory depends, in good part, on their culture of origin, and how they behave is shaped by the interaction between that culture and the particular society into which they enter. Because so little is yet known about preindustrial American culture and subcultures, some caution is necessary in moving from the level of generalization to historical actuality. What follows compares and contrasts working people new to industrial society but living in quite different time periods. First, the expectations and work habits of first-generation predominantly native American factory workers before 1843 are compared with first-generation immigrant factory workers between 1893 and 1920. Similarities in the work habits and expectations of men and women who experienced quite different premodern cultures are indicated. Second, the work habits and culture of artisans in the industrializing decades (1843–93) are examined to indicate the persistence of powerful cultural continuities in that era of radical economic change. Third, evidence of premodern working-class behavior that parallels European patterns of premodern working-class behavior in the early phases of industrialization is briefly described to suggest that throughout the entire period (1815–1920) the changing composition of the American working class caused the recurrence of "premodern" patterns of collective behavior usually only associated with the early phases of industrialization. And, finally, attention is given to some of the larger implications resulting from this recurrent tension between work, culture, and society.

The work habits and the aspirations and expectations of men and women new to factory life and labor are examined first. Common work habits rooted in diverse premodern cultures (different in many ways but nevertheless all ill fitted to the regular routines demanded by machine-centered factory processes) existed among distinctive first-generation factory workers all through American history. We focus on two quite different time periods: the years before 1843 when the factory and machine were still new to America and the years between 1893 and 1917 when the country had become the world's industrial colossus. In both periods workers new to factory production brought strange and seemingly useless work habits to the factory gate. The irregular and undisciplined work patterns of factory hands before 1843 frustrated cost-conscious manufacturers and caused frequent complaint among them. Textile factory work rules often were designed to tame such rude customs. A New Hampshire cotton factory that hired mostly women and children forbade "spirituous liquor, smoking, nor any kind of amusement . . . in the workshops, yards, or factories" and promised the "immediate and disgraceful dismissal" of employees found gambling, drinking, or committing "any other debaucheries." A Massachusetts firm nearby insisted that young workers unwilling to attend church stay "within doors and improve their time in reading, writing, and in other valuable and harmless employment." Tardy and absent Philadelphia workers paid fines and could not "carry into the factory nuts, fruits, etc.; books or paper." A Connecticut textile mill owner justified the twelve-hour day and the six-day week because it kept "workmen and children" from "vicious amusements." He forbade "gaming . . . in any private house." Manufacturers elsewhere worried about the example "idle" men set for women and children. Massachusetts family heads who rented "a piece of land on shares" to grow corn and potatoes while their wives and children labored in factories worried one manufacturer. "I would prefer giving constant employment at some sacrifice," he said, "to having a man of the village seen in the streets on a rainy day at leisure." Men who worked in Massachusetts woolen mills upset expected work routines in other ways. "The wool business requires more man labour," said a manufacturer, "and this we study to avoid. Women are much more ready to follow good regulations, are not captious, and do not clan as the men do against the overseers." Male factory workers posed other difficulties, too. In 1817 a shipbuilder in Medford, Massachusetts, refused his men grog privileges. They quit work, but he managed to finish a ship without using further spirits, "a remarkable achievement." An English visitor in 1832 heard an American complain that British workers in the Paterson cotton and machine shops drank excessively and figured as "the most beastly people I have ever seen." Four years later a New Jersey manufacturer of hats and caps boasted in a public card that he finally had "4 and 20 good, permanent workmen," not one infected with "the brutal leprosy of blue Monday habits and the moral gangrene of 'trades union' principles." Other manufacturers had less good fortune. Absenteeism occurred frequently among the Pennsylvania iron workers at the rural Hopewell Village forge: hunting, harvesting, wedding parties, frequent "frolicking" that sometimes lasted for days, and uproarious Election and Independence Day celebrations plagued the mill operators. In the early nineteenth century, a New Jersey iron manufacturer filled his diary with notations about irregular work habits: "all hands drunk"; "Jacob Ventling hunting"; "molders all agree to quit work and went to the beach"; "Peter Cox very drunk and gone to bed. Mr. Evans made a solemn resolution any person or persons bringing liquor to the work enough to make drunk shall be liable to a fine"; "Edward Rutter off a-drinking. It was reported he got drunk on cheese."

Employers responded differently to such behavior by first-generation factory hands. "Moral reform" as well as what Sidney Pollard calls carrot-and-stick policies meant to tame or to transform such work habits. Fining was common. Hopewell Furnace managers deducted one dollar from Samuel York's wages "for getting intoxesitated [sic] with liquer [sic] and neglecting hauling 4 loads wash Dird at Joneses." Special material rewards encouraged steady work. A Hopewell Village blacksmith contracted for nineteen dollars a month, and "if he does his work well we are to give him a pair of coarse boots." In these and later years manufacturers in Fall River and Paterson institutionalized traditional customs and arranged for festivals and parades to celebrate with their workers a new mill, a retiring superintendent, or a finished locomotive. Some rewarded disciplined workers in special ways. When Paterson locomotive workers pressed for higher wages, their employer instructed an underling: "Book keeper, make up a roll of men . . . making *fulltime*; if they can't support their families on the wages they are now getting, they must have more. But the other men, who are drunk every Monday morning, I don't want them around the shop under any circumstances." Where factory work could be learned easily, new hands replaced irregular old ones. A factory worker in New England remembered that years before the Civil War her employer had hired "all American girls" but later shifted to immigrant laborers because "not coming from country homes, but living as the Irish do, in the town, they take no vacations, and can be relied on at the mill all year round." Not all such devices worked to the satisfaction of workers or their employers. Sometime in the late 1830s merchant capitalists sent a skilled British silk weaver to manage a new mill in Nantucket that would employ the wives and children of local whalers and fishermen. Machinery was installed, and in the first days women and children besieged the mill for work. After a month had passed, they started dropping off in small groups. Soon nearly all had returned "to their shore gazing and to their seats by the sea." The Nantucket mill shut down, its hollow frame an empty monument to the unwillingness of resident women and children to conform to the regularities demanded by rising manufacturers.

First-generation factory workers were not unique to premodern America. And the work habits common to such workers plagued American manufacturers in later generations when manufacturers and most native urban whites scarcely remembered that native Americans had once been hesitant first-generation factory workers. To shift forward in time to East and South European immigrants new to steam, machinery, and electricity and new to the United States itself is to find much that seems the same. American society, of course, had changed greatly, but in some ways it is as if a film—run at a much faster speed—is being viewed for the second time: primitive work rules for unskilled labor, fines, gang labor, and subcontracting were commonplace. In 1910 two-thirds of the workers in twenty-one major manufacturing and mining industries came from Eastern and Southern Europe or were native American blacks, and studies of these "new immigrants" record much evidence of pre-industrial work habits among the men and women new to American industry. According to Moses Rischin, skilled immigrant Jews carried to New York City town and village employment patterns, such as the *landsmannschaft* economy and a preference for small shops as opposed to larger factories, that sparked frequent disorders but hindered stable trade unions until 1910. Specialization spurred anxiety: in Chicago Jewish glovemakers resisted the subdivision of labor even though it promised better wages. "You shrink from doing either kind of work itself, nine hours a day," said two observers of these immigrant women. "You cling to the variety . . . , the mental luxury of first, finger-sides, and then, five separate leather pieces, for relaxation, to play with! Here is a luxury worth fighting for!" American work rules also conflicted with religious imperatives. On the eighth day after the birth of a son, Orthodox Jews in Eastern Europe held a festival, "an occasion of much rejoicing." But the American work week had a different logic, and if the day fell during the week the celebration occurred the following Sunday. "The host . . . and his guests," David Blaustein remarked, "know it is not the right day," and "they fall to mourning over the conditions that will not permit them to observe the old custom.". . . Slavic and Italian immigrants carried with them to industrial America subcultures quite different from that of village Jews, but their work habits were just as alien to the modern factory. Rudolph Vecoli has reconstructed Chicago's South Italian community to show that adult male seasonal construction gangs as contrasted to factory labor were one of many traditional customs adapted to the new environment, and in her study of South Italian peasant immigrants Phyllis H. Williams found among them men who never adjusted to factory labor. After "years" of "excellent" factory work, some "began . . . to have minor accidents" and others "suddenly give up and are found in their homes complaining of a vague indisposition with no apparent physical basis." Such labor worried early twentieth-century efficiency experts, and so did Slavic festivals, church holidays, and "prolonged merriment." "Man," Adam Smith wisely observed, "is, of all sorts of luggage, the most difficult to be transported." That was just as true for these Slavic immigrants as for the early nineteenth-century native American factory workers. A Polish wedding in a Pennsylvania mining or mill town lasted between three and five days. Greek and Roman Catholics shared the same jobs but had different holy days, "an annoyance to many employers." The Greek Church had "more than eighty festivals in the year," and "the Slav religiously observes the days on which the saints are commemorated and invariably takes a holiday.". . .

More than irregular work habits bound together the behavior of first-generation factory workers separated from one another by time and by the larger structure of the society they first encountered. Few distinctive American working-class populations differed in so many essentials (their sex, their religions, their nativity, and their prior rural and village cultures) as the Lowell mill girls and women of the Era of Good Feelings and the South and East European steel workers of the Progressive Era. To describe similarities in their expectations of factory labor is not to blur these important differences but to suggest that otherwise quite distinctive men and women interpreted such work in similar ways. The Boston Associates, pioneer American industrialists, had built up Lowell and other towns like it to overcome early nineteenth-century rural and village prejudices and fears about factory work and life and in their regulation of working-class social habits hoped to assure a steady flow of young rural women ("girls") to and from the looms. "The sagacity of self-interest as well as more disinterested considerations," explained a Lowell clergyman in 1845, "has led to the adoption of a strict system of moral police." Without "sober, orderly, and moral" workers, profits would be "absorbed by cases of irregularity, carelessness, and neglect." The Lowell capitalists thrived by hiring rural women who supplemented a distant family's income, keeping them a few years, and then renewing the process. Such steady labor turnover kept the country from developing a permanent proletariat and so was meant to assure stability. Lowell's busy cotton mills, well-ordered boarding houses, temples of religion and culture, factory girls, and moral police so impressed Anthony Trollope that he called the entire enterprise a "philanthropic manufacturing college." John Quincy Adams thought the New England cotton mills "palaces of the Poor," and Henry Clay marveled over places like the Lowell mills. "Who has not been delighted with the clock-work movements of a large cotton factory?" asked the father of the American System. The French traveler Michel Chevalier had a less sanguine reaction. He found Lowell "neat and decent, peaceable and sage," but worried, "Will this become like Lancashire? Does this brilliant glare hide the misery and suffering of the working girls?"

Historians of the Lowell mill girls find little evidence before 1840 of organized protest among them and attribute their collective passivity to corporation policing policies, the frequent turnover in the labor force, the irregular pace of work (after it was rationalized in the 1840s, it provoked collective protest), the freedom the mill girls enjoyed away from rural family dominance, and their relatively decent earnings. The women managed the transition to mill life because they did not expect to remain factory workers too long. Nevertheless frequent inner tension revealed itself among the mobile mill women. In an early year, a single mill discharged twenty-eight women for such reasons as "misconduct," "captiousness," "disobedience," "impudence," "levity," and even "mutiny." The difficult transition from rural life to factory work also caused tensions outside the mills. . . .

Even the *Lowell Offering* testified to the tensions between mill routines and rural rhythms and feelings. Historians have dismissed it too handily because the company sponsored it and refused to publish prose openly critical of mill policies. But the fiction and poetry of its contributors, derivative in style and frequently escapist, also often revealed dissatisfactions with the pace of work. Susan, explaining her first day in the mill to Ann, said the girls awoke early and one sang, "Morning bells, I hate to hear. / Ringing dolefully, loud and clear." . . . Ellen Collins quit the mill, complaining about her "obedience to the ding-dong of the bell—just as though we were so many living machines." In "A Weaver's Reverie," Ella explained why the mill women wrote "so much about the beauties of nature."

*Why is it that the delirious dreams of the famine-stricken are of tables loaded with the richest viands? . . . Oh, tell me why this is, and I will tell you why the factory girl sits in the hours of meditation and thinks, not of the crowded, clattering mill, nor of the noisy tenement which is her home.*

Contemporary labor critics who scorned the Lowell Offering as little more than the work of "poor, caged birds," who "while singing of the roses . . . forget the bars of their prison," had not read it carefully. Their attachment to nature was the concern of persons working machines in a society still predominantly "a garden," and it was not unique to these Lowell women. In New Hampshire five hundred men and women petitioned the Amoskeag Manufacturing Company's proprietors in 1853 not to cut down an elm tree to allow room for an additional mill: "It was a beautiful and goodly tree" and belonged to a time "when the yell of the red man and the scream of the eagle were alone heard on the banks of the Merrimack, instead of two giant edifices filled with the buzz of busy and well-remunerated industry." Each day, the workers said, they viewed that tree as "a connecting link betwen the past and the present," and "each autumn [it] remind[s] us of our own mortality."

Aspirations and expectations interpret experience and thereby help shape behavior. Some Lowell mill girls revealed dissatisfactions, and others made a difficult transition from rural New England to that model factory town, but that so few planned to remain mill workers eased that transition and hampered collective protest. Men as well as women who expect to spend only a few years as factory workers have little incentive to join unions. That was just as true of the immigrant male common laborers in the steel mills of the late nineteenth and early twentieth centuries (when multi-plant oligopoly characterized the nation's most important manufacturing industry) as in the Lowell cotton mills nearly a century earlier. David Brody has explained much about the common laborers. In those years, the steel companies successfully divorced wages from productivity to allow the market to shape them. Between 1890 and 1910, efficiencies in plant organization cut labor costs by about a third. The great Carnegie Pittsburgh plants employed 14,359 common laborers, 11,694 of them South and East Europeans. Most, peasant in origin, earned less than $12.50 a week (a family needed fifteen dollars for subsistence). A staggering accident rate damaged these and other men: nearly twenty-five per cent of the recent immigrants employed at the Carnegie South Works were injured or killed each year between 1907 and 1910, 3,723 in all. But like the Lowell mill women, these men rarely protested in collective ways, and for good reason. They did not plan to stay in the steel mills long. Most had come to the United States as single men (or married men who had left their families behind) to work briefly in the mills, save some money, return home, and purchase farm land. Their private letters to European relatives indicated a realistic awareness of their working life that paralleled some of the Lowell fiction: "if I don't earn $1.50 a day, it would not be worth thinking about America"; "a golden land so long as there is work"; "here in America one must work for three horses"; "let him not risk coming, for he is too young"; "too weak for America." Men who wrote such letters and avoided injury often saved small amounts of money, and a significant number fulfilled their expectations and quit the factory and even the country. Forty-four South and East Europeans left the United States for every one hundred that arrived between 1908 and 1910. . . . Immigrant expectations coincided for a time with the fiscal needs of industrial manufacturers. The Pittsburgh steel magnates had as much good fortune as the Boston Associates. But the stability and passivity they counted on among their unskilled workers depended upon steady work and the opportunity to escape the mills. When frequent recessions caused recurrent unemployment, immigrant expectations and behavior changed. What Brody calls peasant "group consciousness" and "communal loyalty" sustained bitter wildcat strikes after employment picked up. The tenacity of these immigrant strikes for higher wages amazed contemporaries, and brutal suppression often accompanied them (Cleveland, 1899; East Chicago, 1905; McKees Rock, 1909; Bethlehem, 1910; and Youngstown in 1915 where, after a policeman shot into a peaceful parade, a riot caused an estimated one million dollars in damages). The First World War and its aftermath blocked the traditional route of overseas outward mobility, and the consciousness of immigrant steel workers changed. They sparked the 1919 steel strike. The steel mill had become a way of life for them and was no longer the means by which to reaffirm and even strengthen older peasant and village life-styles.

Let us sharply shift the time perspective from the years before 1843 and those between 1893 and 1919 to the decades between 1843 and 1893 and also shift our attention to the artisans and skilled workers who differed so greatly in the culture and work-styles they brought to the factory from men and women bred in rural and village cultures. The focus, however, remains the same—the relationship between settled work habits and culture. This half century saw the United States (not small pockets within it) industrialize as steam and machinery radically transformed the premodern American economic structure. That so much attention has been given to the Civil War as a crucial divide in the nation's history (and it was, of course, for certain purposes) too frequently has meant neglect by historians of common patterns of behavior that give coherence to this period. . . . In the year of Abraham Lincoln's election as President, the United States ranked behind England, France, and Germany in the value of its manufactured product. In 1894 the United States led the field: its manufactured product nearly equalled in value that of Great

Britain, France, and Germany together. But such profound economic changes did not entirely shatter the older American social structure and the settled cultures of premodern native and immigrant American artisans. "There is no such thing as economic growth which is not, at the same time, growth or change of a culture," E. P. Thompson has written. Yet he also warns that "we should not assume any automatic, or overdirect, correspondence between the dynamic of economic growth and the dynamic of social or cultural life." That significant stricture applies as much to the United States as to England during its Industrial Revolution and especially to native and immigrant artisans between 1843 and 1893.

It is not surprising to find tenacious artisan work habits before the Civil War, what Thompson calls "alternate bouts of intense labour and of idleness wherever men were in control of their working lives." An English cabinetmaker shared a New York City workplace with seven others (two native Americans, two Germans, and one man each from Ireland, England, and France), and the readers of *Knight's Penny Magazine* learned from him that "frequently . . . after several weeks of real hard work . . . a simultaneous cessation from work took place." "As if . . . by tacit agreement, every hand" contributed "loose change," and an apprentice left the place and "speedily returned laden with wine, brandy, biscuits, and cheese." Songs came forth "from those who felt musical," and the same near-ritual repeated itself two more times that day. Similar relaxations, apparently self-imposed, also broke up the artisans' work day in the New York City shipyards, and a ship carpenter described them as "an indulgence that custom had made as much of a necessity in a New York shipyard as a grind-stone". . . .

Despite the profound economic changes that followed the American Civil War, Gilded Age artisans did not easily shed stubborn and time-honored work habits. Such work habits and the left-styles and subcultures related to them retained a vitality long into these industrializing decades. Not all artisans worked in factories, but some that did retained traditional craft skills. Mechanization came in different ways and at different times to diverse industries. Samuel Gompers recollected that New York City cigarmakers paid a fellow craftsman to read a newspaper to them while they worked, and Milwaukee cigarmakers struck in 1882 to retain such privileges as keeping (and then selling) damaged cigars and leaving the shop without a foreman's permission. "The difficulty with many cigarmakers," complained a New York City manufacturer in 1877, "is this. They come down to the shop in the morning; roll a few cigars and then go to a beer saloon and play pinnocio or some other game, . . . working probably only two or three hours a day." Coopers felt new machinery "hard and insensate," not a blessing but an evil that "took a great deal of joy out of life" because machine-made barrels undercut a subculture of work and leisure. Skilled coopers "lounged about" on Saturday (the regular pay day), a "lost day" to their employers. . . . Such traditions of work and leisure . . . angered manufacturers anxious to ship goods as much as it worried sabbatarians and temperance reformers. Conflicts over life- and work-styles occurred frequently and often involved control over the work process and over time. The immigrant Staffordshire potters in Trenton, New Jersey, worked in "bursts of great activity" and then quit for "several days at a time." "Monday," said a manufacturer, "was given up to debauchery.". . . Hand coopers (and potters and cigarmakers, among others) worked hard but in distinctly preindustrial styles. Machine-made barrels pitted modernizing technology and modern habits against traditional ways. To the owners of competitive firms struggling to improve efficiency and cut labor costs, the Goose Egg and Blue Monday proved the laziness and obstinacy of craftsmen as well as the tyranny of craft unions that upheld venerable traditions. To the skilled cooper, the long weekend symbolized a way of work and life filled with almost ritualistic meanings. Between 1843 and 1893, compromise between such conflicting interests was hardly possible. . . .

The persistence of such traditional artisan work habits well into the nineteenth century deserves notice from others besides labor historians, because those work habits did not exist in a cultural or social vacuum. If modernizing technology threatened and even displaced such work patterns, diverse nineteenth-century subcultures sustained and nourished them. "The old nations of the earth creep on at a snail's pace," boasted Andrew Carnegie in *Triumphant Democracy* (1886), "the Republic thunders past with the rush of an express." The articulate steelmaster, however, had missed the point. The very rapidity of the economic changes occurring in Carnegie's lifetime meant that many, unlike him, lacked the time, historically, culturally, and psychologically, to be separated or alienated from settled ways of work and life and from relatively fixed beliefs. Continuity not consensus counted for much in explaining working-class and especially artisan behavior in those decades that witnessed the coming of the factory and the radical transformation of American society. Persistent work habits were one example of that significant continuity. But these elements of continuity were often revealed among nineteenth-century American workers cut off by birth from direct contact with the preindustrial American past, a fact that has been ignored or blurred by the artificial separation between labor history and immigration history. In Gilded Age America (and afterwards in the Progressive Era despite the radical change in patterns of immigration), working-class and immigration history regularly intersected, and that intermingling made for powerful continuities. . . .

As early as the 1830s, the theme that industrialism promised to make over the United States into a "European" country had its artisan and working-class advocates. Seth Luther then made this clear in his complaint about "gentlemen" who "exultingly call LOWELL the Manchester of America" and in his plea that the Bunker Hill monument "stand *unfinished*, until the time passes away when aristocrats talk about mercy to mechanics and laborers, . . . until our rights are acknowleged." The tensions revealed in labor rhetoric between the promises of the Republic and the practices of those who combined capital and technology to build factories continued into the 1890s. In 1844 New England shoemakers rewrote the Declaration of Independence to protest that the employers "have robbed us of certain rights," and two years later New England textile workers planned without success a general strike to start on July 4, 1846, calling it "a second Independence Day." The great 1860 shoemakers' strike in Lynn started on George Washington's birthday, a celebration strikers called "sacred to the memory of one of the greatest men the world has ever produced." Fear for the Republic did not end with the Civil War. The use of state militia to help put down a strike of Northeastern Pennsylvania workers in 1874 caused *Equity*, a Boston labor weekly, to condemn the Erie Railroad as "the George III of the workingman's movement" and "the Government of Pennsylvania" as "but its parliament." ("Regiments," it added, "to protect dead things.")

Such beliefs, not the status anxieties of Progressive muckrakers and New Deal historians, gave rise to the pejorative phrase "robber baron." Discontented Gilded Age workers found in that phrase a way to summarize their worries about dependence and centralization. "In America," exploded the *National Labor Tribune* in 1874, "we have realized the ideal of republican government at least in form." "America," it went on, "was the star of the political Bethlehem which shone radiantly out in the dark night of political misrule in Europe. The masses of the old world gazed upon her as their escape." Men in America could be "their own rulers"; "no one could or should become their masters." But industrialization had created instead a nightmare: "These dreams have not been realized. . . . The working people of this country . . . suddenly find capital as rigid as an absolute monarchy." Two years later, the same Pittsburgh labor weekly asked, "Shall we let the gold barons of the nineteenth century put iron collars of ownership around our necks as did the feudal barons with their serfs in the fourteenth century?" The rhetoric surrounding the little-understood 1877 railroad strikes and riots summed up these fears. Critics of the strikes urged repressive measures such as the building of armories in large cities and the restriction of the ballot, and a few, including Elihu Burritt, even favored importing "British" institutions to the New World. But the disorders also had their defenders, and a strain in their rhetoric deserves notice. A radical Massachusetts clergyman called the strikers "the lineal descendants of Samuel Adams, John Hancock, and the Massachusetts yeomen who began so great a disturbance a hundred years ago . . . only now the kings are money kings and then they were political kings.". . .

Quite diverse patterns of collective working-class behavior (some of them disorderly and even violent) accompanied the industrialization of the United States, and certain of them (especially those related to artisan culture and to peasant and village cultures still fresh to factory labor and to the machine) deserve brief attention. Characteristic European forms of "premodern" artisan and lower-class protest in the United States occurred before (prior to 1843), during (1843–93), and after (1893–1919) the years when the country "modernized." The continuing existence of such behavior followed from the changing composition of the working-class population. Asa Briggs's insistence that "to understand how people respond to industrial change it is important to examine what kind of people they were at the beginning of the process" and "to take account of continuities as well as new ways of thinking," poses in different words the subtle interplay between culture and society that is an essential factor in explaining working-class behavior. Although their frequency remains the subject for much further detailed study, examples of premodern working-class behavior abound for the entire period from 1815 to 1919, and their presence suggests how much damage has been done to the past American working-class experiences by historians busy, as R. H. Tawney complained more than half a century ago, "dragging into prominence forces which have triumphed and thrusting into the background those which have been swallowed up." Attention is briefly given to three types of American artisan and working-class behavior explored in depth and with much illumination by European social historians ("church-and-king" crowds, machine-breaking, and food riots) and to the presence in quite different working-class protests of powerful secular and religious rituals. These occurred over the entire period under examination, not just in the early phases of industrial development.

Not much is yet known about premodern American artisan and urban lower-class cultures, but scattered evidence suggests a possible American variant of the European church-and-king phenomenon. Although artisan and lower-class urban cultures before 1843 await their historians, popular street disorders (sometimes sanctioned by the established authorities) happened frequently and increasingly caused concern to the premodern elite classes. Street gangs, about which little is yet known except the suggestion that some had as members artisans (not just casual or day laborers) and were often organized along ethnic lines, grew more important in the coastal and river towns after 1830. New York City, among other towns, had its Fly Boys, Chichesters, Plug Uglies, Buckaroos, and Slaughterhouse Gangs, and their violence against recent immigrants provoked disorderly counterthrusts. Political disorders on election days, moreover, were apparently well-organized and may have involved such gangs. The recurrence of such disorders through the pre-Civil War decades (including the nativist outbursts in nearly all major Northern and Southern cities in the 1850s) may have meant that local political parties, in their infancy, served as the American substitute for the King and the Church, a third party "protecting" artisans and even day laborers from real and imagined adversaries and winning clanlike loyalty. . . .

Available evidence does not yet indicate that machine-breaking of the "Luddite" variety was widespread in the United States. There are suggestive hints in reports that Ohio farm laborers burnt and destroyed farm machinery in 1878 and that twenty years later in Buffalo a crowd of Polish common day laborers and their wives rioted to break a street-paving machine, but the only clear evidence found of classic machine-breaking occurred early in the Civil War among rural blacks in the South Carolina Sea Islands, who resisted Yankee missionary and military efforts to make them plant cotton instead of corn and therefore broke up cotton gins and hid the iron work. "They do not see the use of cotton," said a Northern female school teacher, and a Yankee entrepreneur among them added that "nothing was more remote from their shallow pates than the idea of planting cotton for 'white-folks' again." (Some time later, this same man ordered a steam-run cotton gin. "This engine," he confided, "serves as a moral stimulus to keep the people at work at their hand-gins, for they want to gin all the cotton by hand, and I tell them if they don't by the middle of January I shall get it by steam.") If white workers rarely broke machines to protest their introduction, they sometimes destroyed the product of new technology. In the early 1830s Brooklyn ropemakers paraded a "hated machine" through town and then "committed to the flames" its product. Theirs was not an irrational act. They paid for the destroyed hemp, spun "a like quantity" to allow the machine's owner to "fulfill his engagement for its delivery," and advertised their product in a newspaper, boasting that its quality far surpassed machine-made rope "as is well known to any practical ropemaker and seaman." Silk weavers in the Hudson River towns of New Jersey broke looms in 1877 but only to prevent production during a strike. A more common practice saw the destruction of the product of labor or damage to factory and mining properties to punish employers and owners. Paterson silk weavers regularly left unfinished warps to spoil in looms. Crowds often stoned factories, burned mine tipples, and did other damage to industrial properties (as in the bitter Western Pennsylvania coke strikes between 1884 and 1894) but mostly to protest the hiring of new hands or violence against them by "police.". . .

"Luddism" may have been rare, but classic "European" food riots occurred in the United States, and two in New York City—the first in 1837 and the second in 1902—that involved quite different groups of workers are briefly examined to illustrate the ways in which traditional cultural forms and expectations helped shape working-class behavior. (Other evidence of similar disorders, including the Confederate food riots led by white women in Mobile, Savannah, and Richmond, await careful study.) In February, 1837, thousands gathered in City Hall Park to protest against "monopolies" and rising food prices. Some months before, that park had witnessed yet another demonstration against the conspiracy trial of twenty-five striking journeymen tailors. In their rhetoric the protesters identified the trial with the betrayal of the premodern "Republic." "Aristocrats" had robbed the people of "that liberty bequeathed to them, as a sacred inheritance by their revolutionary sires" and "so mystified" the laws that "men of common understanding cannot unravel them." "What the people thought was liberty, bore not a semblance to its name." Resolutions compared the tailors to that "holy combination of that immortal band of Mechanics who . . . did throw into Boston Harbor the Tea." In 1837 a crowd dumped flour, not tea, and in its behavior revealed a commonplace form of premodern protest, a complaint against what Thompson calls "the extortionate mechanisms of an unregulated market economy." The crowd in City Hall Park heard protests about the high price of rent, food, and especially flour and denunciations of "engrossers," and the New York *Herald* called the gathering "a flour meeting—a fuel meeting—a rent meeting—a food meeting—a bread meeting—every kind of a meeting except a political meeting." But a New York newspaper had printed advice from Portland, Maine, that "speculating" flour dealers be punished with "some mark of public infamy," and after the meeting adjourned a crowd (estimates range from two hundred to several thousand) paraded to Eli Hart's wholesale flour depot. A speaker advised it to "go to the flour stores and offer a fair price, and if refused take the flour." Crowd members dumped two hundred barrels of flour and one thousand bushels of wheat in the streets, broke windows, did other minor damage, and chased the city's mayor with stones and "balls of flour." At first, little looting occurred, and when wagons finally appeared to carry home sacks of flour "a tall athletic fellow in a carman's frock" shouted: "No plunder, no plunder; destroy as much as you please. Teach these monopolists that we know our rights and will have them, but d—n it don't rob them." The crowd moved on to other flour wholesalers and continued its work. It smashed the windows of B. S. Herrick and Son, dumped more flour, and finally stopped when "a person of respectable appearance" came from inside the building to promise that what remained untouched would be distributed gratis the next day to the "poor." The crowd cheered and melted away. More than twenty-eight persons were arrested (among them "mere boys," a few "black and ignorant laborers," a woman, and as yet unidentified white men), but the *Herald* found "mere humbug . . . the unholy cry of 'It's the foreigners who have done all this mischief.' " The daily press, including the *Herald*, denounced the crowd as "the very canaille of the city," but the *Herald* also pleaded for the reimposition of the assize of bread. "Let the Mayor have the regulation of it," said the *Herald*. "Let the public authorities regulate the price of such an essential of life." (In 1857, incidentally, New Yorkers again filled the City Hall Park to again demand the restoration of the assize of bread and to ask for public works.)

More than half a century later different New York City workers reenacted the 1837 food "riot." Unlike the rioters of 1837 in origins and rhetoric, the later rioters nevertheless displayed strikingly similar behavior. In 1902, and a few years before Upton Sinclair published *The Jungle*, orthodox New York City Jews, mostly women and led by a woman butcher, protested the rising price of kosher meat and the betrayal of a promised boycott of the Meat Trust by retail butchers. The complaint started on the Lower East Side and then spontaneously spread among Jews further uptown and even among Jews in Brooklyn, Newark, and Boston. The Lower East Side Jews demanded lower prices. Some called for a rabbi to fix for the entire New York Jewish community the price of meat, as in the East European *shtetl*. Others formed a cooperative retail outlet. But it is their behavior that reveals the most. The nation's financial metropolis saw angry immigrant women engage in seemingly archaic traditional protest. Outsiders could not understand its internal logic and order. These women did not loot. Like the 1837 demonstrators, they punished. Custom and tradition that reached far back in historical time gave a coherence to their rage. The disorders started on a Wednesday, stopped on Friday at sundown, and resumed the following evening. The women battered butcher shops but did not steal meat. Some carried pieces of meat "aloft on pointed sticks . . . like flags." Most poured kerosene on it in the streets or in other ways spoiled it. "Eat no meat while the Trust is taking meat from the bones of your women and children," said a Yiddish circular apparently decorated with a skull and crossbones. . . .

The perspective emphasized in these pages tells about more than the behavior of diverse groups of American working men and women. It also suggests how larger, well-studied aspects of American society have been affected by a historical process that has "industrialized" different peoples over protracted periods of time. Fernand Braudel reminds us that "victorious events come about as the result of many possibilities," and that "for one possibility which actually is realized, innumerable others have drowned." Usually these others leave "little trace for the historian." "And yet," Braudel adds, "it is necessary to give them their place because the losing movements are forces which have at every moment affected the final outcome." Contact and conflict between diverse preindustrial cultures and a changing and increasingly bureaucratized industrial society also affected the larger society in ways that await systematic examination. Contemporaries realized this fact. Concerned in 1886 about the South's "dead"—that is, unproductive—population, the Richmond *Whig* felt the "true remedy" to be "educating the industrial morale of the people." The *Whig* emphasized socializing institutions primarily outside of the working class itself. "In the work of inculcating industrial ideas and impulses," said the *Whig*, "all proper agencies should be enlisted—family discipline, public school education, pulpit instruction, business standards and requirements, and the power and influence of the workingmen's associations." What the *Whig* worried over in 1886 concerned other Americans before and after that time. And the resultant tension shaped society in important ways. Some are briefly suggested here. In a New York *Times* symposium ("Is America by Nature a Violent Society?") soon after the murder of Martin Luther King, the anthropologist Clifford Geertz warned: "Vague references to the frontier tradition, to the unsettledness of American life, to our exploitative attitude toward nature or to our 'youthfulness' as a nation, provide us with prefabricated 'explanations' for events we, in fact, not only do not understand, but do not want to understand." More needs to be said than that Americans are "the spiritual descendants of Billy the Kid, John Brown, and Bonnie and Clyde." It has been suggested here that certain recurrent disorders and conflicts relate directly to the process that has continually "adjusted" men and women to regular work habits and to the discipline of factory labor. The British economic historian Sidney Pollard reminds us that this "task, different in kind" is "at once more subtle and more violent from that of maintaining discipline among a proletarian population of long standing."

The same process has even greater implications for the larger national American culture. Hannah Arendt has brilliantly suggested that the continual absorption of distinctive native and foreign "alien" peoples has meant that "each time the law had to be confirmed anew against the lawlessness inherent in all uprooted people," and that the severity of that process helps explain to her why the United States has "never been a nation-state." The same process also affected the shaping and reshaping of American police and domestic military institutions. We need only realize that the burning of a Boston convent in 1834 by a crowd of Charlestown truckmen and New Hampshire Scotch-Irish brickmakers caused the first revision of the Massachusetts Riot Act since Shays' Rebellion, and that three years later interference by native firemen in a Sunday Irish funeral procession led to a two-hour riot involving upwards of fifteen thousand persons (more than a sixth of Boston's population), brought militia to that city for the first time, and caused the first of many reorganizations of the Boston police force. The regular contact between alien work cultures and a larger industrializing or industrial society had other consequences. It often worried industrialists, causing C. E. Perkins, the president of the Chicago, Burlington, and Quincy Railroad to confide in a friend in the late nineteenth century, "If I were able, I would found a school for the study of political economy in order to harden men's hearts." It affected the popular culture. A guidebook for immigrant Jews in the 1890s advised how to make it in the New World: "Hold fast, this is most necessary in America. Forget your past, your customs, and your ideals. . . . A bit of advice to you: do not take a moment's rest. Run, do, work, and keep your own good in mind." Cultures and customs, however, are not that easily discarded. So it may be that America's extraordinary technological supremacy—its talent before the Second World War for developing labor-saving machinery and simplifying complex mechanical processes—depended less on "Yankee know-how" than on the continued infusion of prefactory peoples into an increasingly industrialized society. The same process, moreover, may also explain why movements to legislate morality and to alter habits have lasted much longer in the United States than in most other industrial countries, extending from the temperance crusades of the 1820s and the 1830s to the violent opposition among Germans to such rules in the 1850s and the 1860s and finally to formal prohibition earlier in this century. Important relationships also exist between this process and the elite and popular nativist and racist social movements that have ebbed and flowed regularly from the 1840s until our own time, as well as between this process and elite political "reform" movements between 1850 and the First World War. . . .

These pages have fractured historical time, ranging forward and backward, to make comparisons for several reasons. One has been to suggest how much remains to be learned about the transition of native and foreign-born American men and women to industrial society, and how that transition affected such persons and the society into which they entered. "Much of what gets into American literature," Ralph Ellison has shrewdly observed, "gets there because so much is left out." That has also been the case in the writing of American working-class history, and the framework and methods suggested here merely hint at what will be known about American workers and American society when the many transitions are studied in detail. Such studies, however, need to focus on the particularities of both the group involved and the society into which they enter. Transitions differ and depend upon the interaction between the two at specific historical moments. But at all times there is a resultant tension. Thompson writes:

*There has never been any single type of "the transition." The stress of the transition falls upon the whole culture: resistance to change and assent to change arise from the whole culture. And this culture includes the systems of power, property-relations, religious institutions, etc., inattention to which merely flattens phenomena and trivializes analysis.*

Enough has been savored in these pages to suggest the particular importance of these transitions in American social history. And their recurrence in different periods of time indicates why there has been so much discontinuity in American labor and social history. The changing composition of the working population, the continued entry into the United States of nonindustrial people with distinctive cultures, and the changing structure of American society have combined together to produce common modes of thought and patterns of behavior. But these have been experiences disconnected in time and shared by quite distinctive first-generation native and immigrant industrial Americans. It was not possible for the grandchildren of the Lowell mill girls to understand that their Massachusetts literary ancestors shared a great deal with their contemporaries, the peasant Slavs in the Pennsylvania steel mills and coal fields. And the grandchildren of New York City Jewish garment workers see little connection between black ghetto unrest in the 1960s and the Kosher meat riots seventy years ago. A half century has passed since Robert Park and Herbert Miller published W. I. Thomas's *Old World Traits Transplanted*, a study which worried that the function of Americanization was the "destruction of memories." . . .

Daniel T. Rodgers

# Industrial Workers
# and Their Labor

The work ethic was in its origins a middle-class affair. Its constituent faiths reverberated most strongly among the sober, Protestant churchgoing, propertied segments of Northern society. Such men might be farmers as well as college professors, clerks as well as bankers, for the "middling classes" possessed of skill, property, and a measure of economic independence formed a broadly defined group in the nineteenth century. A Booker T. Washington or a William Jennings Bryan held to a faith in the moral centrality of work every bit as deep as that of a Theodore Roosevelt or an Andrew Carnegie. But in terms of the power to enforce, the work ethic was a businessmen's creed. In the industrial towns of the North, it was preeminently the faith of those who owned and managed the mills—of those whose comfortable houses climbed the hills above the factories and the cramped and pinched dwellings of the workers they employed.

There could be no mistaking the manufacturers' allegiance to the gospel of work. It was reiterated in voluminous testimony and driven home in the long hours and labor discipline of the factories. Even the architecture of the mill districts reflected it. In scores of nineteenth- and early twentieth-century mill towns, no feature stood out more prominently than the great, looming bell towers of the factories. Originating as simple cupolas perched on the ridgepoles of the early, barnlike textile mills, the bell towers assumed an imposing presence as the century wore on. At the model plant George Pullman constructed outside Chicago in the early 1880s, the bell tower was a massive Victorian structure, its great illuminated clock face reflected by the pool in front of it. In the textile city of Manchester, New Hampshire, the mill towers, dominated by the great brick bell tower of the Amoskeag Mills, lined the Merrimack River in a regular, imposing phalanx.

Even far less pretentious bell towers than these, their lines revealing the century's shifts in aesthetic taste, showed signs of architectural imagination rarely found elsewhere in the mill districts. Such towers rose above the utilitarian clutter of the buildings around them much like church spires in a slum; nor is the parallel farfetched. Where clocks and watches remained rare, factory bells served the essential, utilitarian function of ringing the labor force out of bed, into work, and home again at the day's end. But in the more ornate bell towers there are clearly marks of faith as well as necessity. In their great clock faces and clanging bells, the towers broadcast the mechanization of work and time, the narrowing and tightening of the injunction to diligence that was at the heart of the industrial transformation of work. They loomed as monuments to a creed of regular, untiring industry to which many of their builders held themselves accountable and which all of them hoped to impress upon the older, far less systematic work rhythms that still prevailed outside the factory gates. No other symbol caught the factory masters' revolutionary faith or the obligations it entailed for the new industrial workforce quite so vividly.

The men and women who worked within the factories left no such permanent or conspicuous record of their feelings about time and labor. Save for occasional testimony before government investigating committees and the responses gleaned by haphazard surveys of state bureaus of labor statistics, there is little recorded evidence of the opinions of rank-and-file workers. Even such basic behavioral data as rates of work attendance and labor turnover are scarce for most of the nineteenth century when many factories were run virtually as independent baronies by foremen uninterested in the tedium of record keeping. The shards of evidence historians work with contain incomparably more information about labor organizations than about the values and habits of ordinary laborers, even though the unions never managed to enroll more than a tenth of the manufacturing labor force at any time before the First World War. Labor history that would try to focus on the worker at his job is a more than usually hazardous enterprise.

Yet there is ample evidence that large numbers of industrial workers failed to internalize the faith of the factory masters. Long in advance of the hesitant middle-class recognition of the claims of leisure, workers dreamed of a workday short enough to push labor out of the center of their lives. By reporting irregularly for work, moving restlessly from job to job, or engaging in slowdowns and work restrictions, industrial laborers stubbornly resisted the new work discipline the factory masters tried to impose upon them. Such workers made industrialization a turbulent, bitterly contested process. And yet even active dissenters from middle-class models of diligence were not immune to the pervading belief in the values of hard work. Even as they fabricated visions of leisure or resisted the compulsions of factory toil, industrial workers kept up a steady insistence on the special dignity and worth of those who soiled their hands with honest labor. The phenomenon is particularly striking evidence of the ways in which the factories strained work values everywhere, wrenching habits and splitting ideas apart. But it also shows something of the ways in which a work-tied culture perpetuated its attenuated faiths, even among potential rebels in anomalous circumstances. If to probe the habits of industrial workers is to find abundant evidence of dissent from the work standards of the factories, to probe the rhetoric of the spokesmen they pushed forward from their ranks is to find a working-class version of the work ethic— albeit far from that of the bell towers.

How much of a man's life should work consume? No work-related question is more central than this, and none in the nineteenth and early twentieth centuries divided workers and employers more sharply. The early factory masters took over the traditional sun-to-sun workday, stretched it to between twelve and fourteen hours of labor winter and summer alike with the introduction of gas lighting in the 1830s and 1840s, and brought the full weight of generations of moralizing to bear in justification. "Labor is *not* a curse," they insisted; "it is not the hours per day that a person *works* that breaks him down, but the hours spent in dissipation." Give men "plenty to do, and a long while to do it in, and you will find them physically and morally better."

But among workingmen, the drive to shorten the hours of labor was a long and fervent struggle. The campaign began early in the nineteenth century with the appearance of the first self-conscious workingmen's organizations. By the 1840s the ten-hour movement had moved into the New England textile mills, producing a massive flood of shorter-hours petitions, the largest, from Lowell in 1846, containing signatures equivalent to almost two-thirds of the city's cotton mill operatives. After 1850 the shorter-hours demand—now typically put in terms of the eight-hour day—was at the forefront of every organized labor effort. The National Labor Union at its first convention in 1866 declared a federal eight-hour law "the first and grand desideratum of the hour," and, though the organization drifted shortly thereafter toward rival programs of cooperatives and currency reform, many of its member unions clung firmly to the original platform. P. J. McGuire of the Carpenters, for example, told a congressional committee in 1883 that the reduction of working hours was the "primary object" of the union he headed. The American Federation of Labor under Samuel Gompers was a still more persistent champion of the shorter workday—"eight hours to-day, fewer to-morrow," as Gompers defined the cause. The shorter workday was "the question of questions," the only one which "reaches the very root of society," Gompers declared in the 1880s, and over the next twenty years he labored tirelessly to promote strikes over the issue. Nor did the labor left disagree. For Bill Haywood of the IWW, the only fit motto for the working class was "the less work the better."

"However much they may differ upon other matters, . . . all men of labor . . . can unite upon this," Samuel Gompers wrote in defense of the eight-hour issue in 1889. If the unions, particularly the nonfactory building trades unions, led the agitation for the shorter workday, there was more than Gompers's testimony to indicate that the shorter-hours dream had a strong hold on the larger number of nonunionized workers as well. For three decades after 1869, until they turned to the neutral and duller task of compiling purely statistical data, many of the new state bureaus of labor statistics took upon themselves the task of canvassing the opinions of the workingmen they took to be their constituents. Who these often nameless workers were and how their opinions found their way into print is not clear, but, taking opinion samples as they come, none more closely approaches the rank and file of labor than these. And when they posed the working-hours question, the surveys repeatedly turned up strong, often overwhelming support for the shorter-hours demand. "We go into the factory too young and work too hard afterwards," a New Jersey glass blower put the recurrent complaint in the mid-1880s. A decade and a half later, Thomas Jones, a nonunion Chicago machinist, interrupted his testimony on the un-American and anti-Christian policies of trade unions to interject that "we nonunion men are not opposed to more pay and shorter hours; not at all."

Twice in the nineteenth century, moreover, the shorter-hours demand mushroomed into popular crusades unsurpassed in their intensity by any other of the era's labor issues. The first wave of enthusiasm began quietly in 1865 with the organization of the Grand Eight-Hour League of Massachusetts by a small group of Boston workingmen. Three years later workingmen's Eight-Hour Leagues had proliferated throughout the Northern states and, together with the trade unions, had succeeded in writing the eight-hour day in the statute books of seven states and forcing an eight-hour law for federal employees through Congress. Riddled with loopholes, the legislation proved a hollow victory, and workers angrily turned to more aggressive tactics. In Chicago some 6,000 to 10,000 workers walked off their jobs on 1 May 1867 in a massive demonstration to demand enforcement of the new Illinois eight-hour law, and strikes, rioting, and some machine breaking followed in its wake. A year later in the anthracite coalfields of Pennsylvania, similarly angered workers abandoned the coal pits and, marching from mine to mine, shut down virtually all operations in the state's leading coal-producing county in a bitter three-month strike. Only in the building trades did the first eight-hour campaign bear fruit, and many of those gains evaporated in the depression of the 1870s. But the experience suggested something of the emotional reserves behind the shorter-hours issue.

The second eight-hour crusade of the mid-1880s was still larger and more spontaneous than the first. When in 1884 the Federation of Organized Trades and Labor Unions issued a call for a general eight-hour demonstration to take place on 1 May 1886, it was a quixotic gesture on the part of a weak and barely solvent organization. But the call fell on unexpectedly fertile ground. Over the next two years, workers flocked into the labor unions filled with hopes for a shorter working day. The Knights of Labor, the chief recipient of the influx, ballooned from 104,066 members in July 1885 to 702,924 members a year later, and the newcomers threatened to overwhelm the organization. Grand Master Workman Terence Powderly waged a vigorous fight to dampen the strike fever of the local Knights assemblies. In place of a general strike, Powderly proposed an educational campaign and a nationwide essay contest on the eight-hour question and, that failing, championed a less than realistic scheme to shorten the working day through a cooperative agreement between the Knights and a yet unformed general association of the nation's manufacturers. A month before the day set for the demonstration, P. M. Arthur of the strongly organized locomotive engineers denounced the whole affair as a demand for "two hours more loafing about the corners and two hours more for drink." Yet notwithstanding such foot-dragging at the top, 190,000 workers struck for the eight-hour day in the first week of May. In Milwaukee, according to the Wisconsin Bureau of Labor and Industrial Statistics, the shorter hours issue was "*the* topic of conversation in the shop, on the street, at the family table, at the bar, [and] in the counting room." Beginning with a monster picnic on 2 May, the crusade turned grim and bloody as police opened fire on workers intent on shutting down the city's iron and steel works. In Chicago, the center of the movement, May opened with police and worker battles, some five hundred individual strikes, and still more imposing demonstrations.

Despite Samuel Gompers's best efforts over the next decade and a half, the general strike of 1886 was never repeated. Most workers who walked off their jobs in the late nineteenth and early twentieth centuries struck over wage-related issues, not working hours; and where the wage question pressed most heavily or where hours reduction meant a cut in pay, hours demands generally made little headway. Yet, larger on the average than wage strikes, shorter-hours walkouts possessed a peculiar intensity. And in the massive garment workers' strikes of 1910–11, the IWW-led silk workers' walkout in Paterson, New Jersey, in 1913, the great steel strike of 1919, and elsewhere, the shorter-hours issue smoldered under the surface of many of the era's most famous labor disputes long after the experience of 1886 had faded from memory. . . .

*     *     *

The long contest over the length of the industrial workday was the first of the workingmen's quarrels with the ethos of the bell towers. The second, far less open conflict took place over labor discipline, made tighter and more exacting as working hours shrank and employers turned to closer supervision and a faster work pace to recover their losses. How well industrial workers adjusted to the increasingly regimented labor of the factories is not easy to determine. Crisscrossed by deep lines of ethnicity, industry, and region, there was nothing uniform about the workforce in industrial America, and the evidence about their work behavior is incomplete, often inextricably mired in prejudice, and frequently contradictory.

European observers, for example, generally came away strongly impressed with the energy and discipline of American industrial workers. James Burn, an English hatter who spent an unhappy sojourn in the United States during the Civil War, returned home to pour out his complaints of the "fire-eaters" in his shop who had fallen upon their work with "ravenous appetites for labour," savagely devouring every scrap in sight. Thirty years later a delegation of French workingmen puzzled over the absence of "hurly burly" in the factories they visited. "Work in the American shops is altogether different from what it is in France," one of them remarked. "Nobody talks, nobody sings, the most rigorous silence reigns." A British trade union delegation that arrived a few years later on a more comprehensive tour was less inclined to agree. Except for the shoe factories, where by English standards the machines worked at breakneck speed, the Englishmen concluded that the Americans did not work essentially harder than the British and that the "everlasting hustle" of the American workshops was a "myth." But even the British unionists, whose report was generously self-serving, could not conceal their surprise at the absence of beer and liquor in the American shops and the general sobriety of American workers.

Yet, running counter to the Europeans' repeated stress on the peculiarly industrious temper of the Americans, there is abundant evidence that adjustment to the factory regime did not come easily. At a Lowell, Massachusetts, plant in 1867, for example, the management posted a set of new work rules stipulating that the factory gates were to be kept locked during working hours and that the men were to keep their work clothes on during the day. It seems an unexceptionable requirement by most twentieth-century standards. But to the machinists, the idea that they could not come and go from their work as free men was "a system of slavery" that threatened time-honored traditions and time-honored rights. Led by the machinist who reported the incident to the Massachusetts Bureau of Statistics of Labor, the men struck, and in the compromise that resulted the gates were left unlocked.

The incident at Lowell was unique neither in its circumstances nor its implications. In the movement from farm and artisan shop into the mills, old prerogatives and work habits clashed over and again with the factory masters' strange and galling standards of discipline and work pace. Workers unwilling to break their accustomed mores to the discipline of the mills—hard-drinking potters and cigar makers, "intractable" Polish and Italian peasants in the textile mills of southern New England, or Maine factory hands who threw over job and employer each summer for the freedom of their farms and fishing boats—could be found throughout the factories as the new economic order pushed aside the old. It was only by draconian fining policies that punished lateness or visiting and talking on the job by fines of up to half a day's pay that many employers managed to create the silence and discipline that so caught the eye of the Europeans.

For many workers in industrial America, moreover, adjustment to the employers' demand for regular, clock-disciplined work never came at all. From the highly paid, British-born mule spinners of Fall River to common, unskilled laborers, a conspicuous fraction of workers simply failed to convert to the creed of day-in and day-out labor. Irregular work patterns were most common in casually supervised piecework trades where work itself was often fitful and a day's lost pay might be partially recovered by harder work the next. But even in the highly disciplined New England textile mills, managers in the 1870s were sometimes hard-pressed to keep their machines running on the hottest days of the summer for lack of workers. As one textile manufacturer testified in 1878: "Our mill operatives are much like other people, and take their frequent holidays for pleasure and visiting." Sickness, accidents, and lack of work—dominant elements in the lives of all workers in industrial America—inflated the high absence rates found in virtually all factory payroll records before the turn of the century. As time went on and industrial discipline tightened, moreover, the places where a worker could take a day off with impunity narrowed. In the anthracite coalfields where underemployment was chronic, "blue Mondays" and a thick calendar of immigrant holidays persisted well into the twentieth century; but among the hard-pressed New York City garment workers, the prohibitions against labor on the Jewish Sabbath fell increasingly into disuse. By the turn of the century, as a Massachusetts survey made clear in 1904, the factories had succeeded in exacting far more regular attendance at work than the old hand trades and village shops. Yet in small-town textile mills from Vermont to North Carolina, managers still made the best of a bad bargain and shut down on the day the circus arrived. And where management was lax or jobs easy to come by, as at a large number of manufacturing plants during the First World War, employers found themselves missing as much as a tenth or more of their workforce on a normal workday. "The general indisposition" of factory hands "to work steady," as a Chicopee, Massachusetts, mill agent put the complaint in 1859, remained far from cured sixty years later.

A second act of rebellion was to quit. Systematic studies of labor turnover did not begin until the second decade of the twentieth century, but what they found then was a strikingly mobile workforce, rattling from job to job at a rate astonishingly high by modern standards. According to data gathered for the years from 1905 to 1917, the majority of industrial workers changed jobs at least every three years. But mobility was not evenly spread through the workforce. In normal times, one in three factory workers moved considerably faster than the norm, staying at his job less than a year and often only days or weeks. At the Armour meat-packing plant in Chicago, for example, the average daily payroll numbered about eight thousand during 1914. But to keep that many employees, the company hired eight thousand workers during the course of the year, filling and refilling the places of transients. Larger surveys of textile mills, automobile plants, steel mills, clothing shops, and machine works showed turnover rates at least as high as the 100 percent reported at Armour. In the woolen industry between 1907 and 1910, turnover varied between 113 and 163 percent, and at casually managed plants or regions troubled by labor shortages it ran still higher. It reached 232 percent among New York City cloak, suit, and skirt shops in 1912–13, 252 percent in a sample of Detroit factories in 1916, and the bewildering rate of 370 percent at Ford in 1913. The most extensive study, undertaken by the United States Bureau of Labor Statistics and using data from 1913–14, found a "normal" turnover rate in the factories of 115 percent, and, given the depressed economic conditions in those years, that figure, if it erred at all, underestimated the normal amount of job changing. . . .

*     *     *

Even those who turned up regularly for work and stuck by their jobs were not necessarily committed to the new work discipline. Throughout the industries workers maintained their own work norms and work customs, which effectively undercut the formal factory rules and the expectations of the factory masters. Like so many of the essentials of working-class history, most of the outlines of these shop cultures have been lost beyond recovery. But one aspect was brought into relief by the argument over output restriction set off by a bitter Chicago building trades dispute in 1900. In its wake, even union sympathizers like Clarence Darrow and Jane Addams joined the chorus of concern over deliberate production restriction. The Bureau of Labor's monumental effort to clarify the issue, however, reported that restrictive practices were far older and more widespread than all but the harshest critics had suggested. Only a few skilled workers at the height of their power—glassblowers, potters, iron molders, and puddlers and rollers in the iron and steel mills—maintained openly acknowledged limits on their day's work. But the report concluded that clandestine shop agreements to enforce production quotas were common throughout the factories among union and nonunion workers alike.

Such informal compacts were highly unstable, and they broke down repeatedly under pressure from employers or from workers themselves. Yet the mood behind the output agreements was dead serious, and at times the results could be dramatic. In 1901, in a brief flush of unionization, sheep and cattle butchers slowed down the lines of the Chicago packing plants by some 30 percent until the new regime fell apart in a disastrous strike. Where workers could not control the factory pace, they could at the least turn their resentments against the exceptionally fast worker. "The common sentiment of the workman is strong and severe against those whose output is materially above the average," the Bureau of Labor reported. Hog, rooter, boss's pet, bell-horse, swift, rusher—the factory names for the unusually diligent worker amounted to a string of epithets.

Thanks to the labors of investigators at the federal arsenal at Watertown, Massachusetts, we know about one of these shop cultures in some detail, and the precipitating incident, fittingly enough, was a direct clash between a group of skilled workers and the clock. In the summer of 1911, the arsenal management was in the early stages of introducing the Taylor system into the Watertown plant. The first time studies had been made in the machine shop in June. But the commandant was anxious for results and particularly anxious to see improvements made in the foundry, where he was convinced that the molders were systematically holding output down to a fraction of what it should be. On 10 August, accordingly, a Taylor-trained time-study expert appeared in the foundry to time one of the molders at a routine task. The angry molders met that evening and resolved to quit if more time studies were made. When they were resumed the next day, the entire molding force struck. The walkout at Watertown was not the first workers' protest against scientific management. Employees at the Rock Island arsenal had succeeded in halting the introduction of Taylorism there in 1908, and both the American Federation of Labor and the International Association of Machinists were actively campaigning against Taylorism in the summer of 1911. But the Watertown strike was a local, spontaneous affair, and coming in the midst of the boom of popular enthusiasm over Taylor's work it precipitated both a great deal of embarrassing publicity and two teams of investigators, who over the next two months tried to piece together what had happened.

The investigators found not only the molders but the machinists, too, in seething discontent. Many of the strikers were convinced that the time studies were a prelude to drastic rate cuts, a prospect reinforced by the fact that, in eliminating the "waste motions" from the job he observed, Taylor's man had cut the worker's time by more than a third, and aggravated by the subsequent introduction of a nonunion "rate buster" into the foundry. Several of the strike leaders, at least one of whom had read the more flamboyant claims of Taylor's "Shop Management," worried that Taylorism meant the routinization of their trade and the eventual displacement of all skilled workers from it. Others, the foremen in particular, resented taking technical instruction from abrasive, soft-handed college men who had never themselves poured a mold or run a machine. . . .

But the focus of the workers' grievances, the symbol to which their testimony returned over and again, was the time-study man's stopwatch. Whatever questions of procedure were involved, it is clear that what was essentially at stake for most of the Watertown employees was the nature of work itself. Autonomy was part of the matter. To work under continuous observation was to keep a man "in a constant state of agitation," the molders complained. "There are men standing over you all the time, and of course you are almost drove to it. You have got to keep pegging at it and working." To work under the constant eye of a boss was nerve-racking; it was "getting down to slavery." But equally threatening was the idea that a man should account for his time by seconds, that he should keep at his work with the unremitting persistence of a machine. That was not the way the Watertown employees had been accustomed to work. Machinists had had time to talk and rest while their automatic lathes and planers were running, and in the foundry the commandant complained that none of the arsenal management could tell if a molder were busy or simply keeping busy. Whatever the case in the foundry, the piecework-paid metal polishers at the arsenal did effectively enforce a common, mutually agreed upon work pace, checking out a uniform amount of material and stretching the last pieces or helping out those caught short if they finished early.

Measured against these accustomed work norms and liberties, the second-by-second accounting of scientific management came as an alien intrusion. Under the new system a man "would have to work there every second of the eight hours, and if there is any man who can do that I don't believe I ever saw him," machinist George White protested; "I never saw a man who can stand right in the same place all day and work every instant for eight hours." Labor without room for rest or talk or a moment's loafing was no longer hard work but—in a reiteration of the phrase used by Lowell machinists long before—"getting down to slavery."

Time and discipline, the lessons of the bell towers made relentlessly precise, formed the core of the matter not only at Watertown. The same quarrels ran through the shorter-hours crusade, the absenteeism and turnover, and the output quotas as well. Another machinist, thrown into prominence by the scientific management controversy, tried to sum up the mood of his fellow workers in a debate with Frederick W. Taylor in 1914: "We don't want to work as fast as we are able to. We want to work as fast as we think it's comfortable for us to work. We haven't come into existence for the purpose of seeing how great a task we can perform through a lifetime. We are trying to regulate our work so as to make it an auxiliary to our lives."

Not all industrial workers, of course, dissented so fully from middle-class ideas of time and labor. The sociology of work ideals cannot be simply reduced to two monolithic camps: work-obsessed businessmen outside the factories and restless, work-weary wage earners within them. The cotton weaver who wrote the Massachusetts Bureau of Statistics of Labor in 1879 that it should not forget that "hard, untiring labor is necessary for the prosperity and well-being of our country" was by no means unique among workingmen in his convictions. An antiunion shoe cutter in the same year complained of "idle, unthrifty, beer-drinking, don't-care sort of people, who are out at the elbows, and waiting for some sort of legislation to help them." "In this country, as a general thing," he protested, hard work and a will to succeed could get any self-reliant man ahead in the world. Unionized workers, too, were not immune from the faiths in activity and self-advancement that comprised the work ethic. The journal of the Knights of Labor in its first years was punctuated with the homilies long familiar to middle-class moralists: the ennui of idleness, the creative power of labor, the "room at the top." Offering a "Recipe for a Good Union" soon after the turn of the century, the *Journal of the Amalgamated Meat Cutters and Butcher Workmen* turned to the pushy maxims of the *Saturday Evening Post*: "Grit. Vim. Push. Snap. Energy. . . . Fire all loafers, croakers and deadbeats." Turnover studies revealed not only a core of drifters but a minority of extraordinarily steady employees in the factories. Everywhere, as at Watertown, individualistic, success-driven workers bucked the ethics of group solidarity and helped to sabotage the fragile output quotas. Just as workers' economic ideas and Sunday habits infected middle-class Northerners, so the work ideals of the middle-class moralists seeped into the factories. Discipline, sobriety, ambition, and diligence were not class monopolies in a land where the sense of class itself was unusually weak.

Much of the behavior that looks on the surface like rebellion, moreover, turns out on closer inspection to be considerably more complicated. Some of the restless job changing, for example, was due less to clashes over work values than to the fact that the industrial economy itself was highly unstable. Regularly counting out time in good years and bad alike, the factory bell towers belied the boom and bust cycle that afflicted virtually every industry in industrial America and caught up workers in repeated cycles of overtime work and unemployment. Such swings were most violent in the clothing trade, where the year was divided into two intensely busy seasons, interrupted by twelve to eighteen weeks of slack work or none at all. Boot- and shoemaking, glassmaking, meat-packing, canning, and foundry work followed similar seasonal cycles. Elsewhere, particularly in the steel mills and coal mines, irregular changes in demand brought volatile fluctuations in employment, aggravated in the steel industry by the steel-makers' policy of running their works at full production or not at all. Depressions repeated the famine and surfeit cycle on a larger and still more catastrophic scale. Of the 28,000 male wage earners in manufacturing and mining surveyed by the Immigration Commission in 1909, when the economy was still recovering from the financial panic two years before, almost half had been out of work two months or more during the preceding year. Even in 1892, notwithstanding the nation's general prosperity, Pennsylvania steel mills, carpet mills, rubber boot factories, window glass factories, and coal mines all shut down for a month or more.

The boom and bust experience had a deep impact on the workforce. "At one time they drive us like slaves, and at other times we have to beg for work," a Brooklyn Knights of Labor official protested in 1883 in the complaint that recurs again and again in the bureaus of labor statistics reports and in immigrant letters. Let the work be heavy, "but may it last without interruption," a Polish brickworks laborer pleaded. But the economics of cheap labor took precedence over steady employment, even though the result worked to undercut the factory goal of steady, clockwork labor—ingraining habits of irregular work on potentially steady workers and uprooting others in the constant scramble for jobs. A Pennsylvania miner, explaining the fact that he had changed his residence five times during 1885, argued that "if I had stopped at one place, I should not have worked half of my time." Employers complained repeatedly of their short-term workers. But men like this not only bore the stamp of the economy that made them but provided what the factory masters sorely needed—a reserve army of irregular, highly mobile workers able to iron out the gyrations of a still far from rationalized economy.

If the industrial economy was capable of making mobile, footloose employees out of potentially steady workers, it was equally capable of making exceptionally diligent employees out of some of those who came to the factories from wholly alien work experiences. Laborers drawn directly from the peasant villages of Europe to the American mills and factories could be found everywhere in the industrial North. By the end of the first decade of the twentieth century, according to the Immigration Commission's survey, one out of every three employees in the Northern cotton textile mills, the soft coal mines, the iron and steel mills, and the meat-packing plants was a European-born worker who had come to America directly from agricultural labor. Many such laborers never made the adjustment to the new and strange expectations of the factories. A sizable fraction simply left and returned home. Others, clinging to the ways they had always known—the unsteady rhythms of agricultural work and the holidays sanctified by the creeds of folk Catholicism—augmented the constant turbulence of the American factories. But with some of the migrants the experience of dislocation was just the reverse, to break down resistance to the norms of factory toil and counter some of the general restlessness of the industrial workforce with converts to the factory masters' faith. . . .

*   *   *

All these factors, then, qualified the clash of work norms in the factories. Men reared in the work ethic, migrants wrenched from the standards of the past, and workers willing to chain themselves to the long hours and discipline of the factories in exchange for its material rewards and the chance of escape all rubbed shoulders with the more restless wage earners in the mills. But they did not set the dominant temper. With time and experience many of the tradition-torn migrants assumed more independent, more assertive, and more fractious habits. Others, who began with ambitions and hopes, ultimately decided that the costs of this form of toil were too high, just as most of the middle-class sojourners who tried their hand far more briefly at factory work came to the same conclusion. Resistance to factory expectations can be found among first-generation industrial workers and the children of mill children, among the immigrant Chicago slaughterhouse workers and the native-born machinists and molders at Watertown, among highly skilled pieceworkers and the army of drifting, unskilled industrial laborers. Absenteeism, mobility, and worker slowdowns were the most obvious manifestations of values in conflict. The long tradition of surplus-based working-class economic theories was another. Most commonly of all, alienation from factory labor amounted simply to an inner turn of mind—a withdrawal of interest from work and indulgence in the dream of the day when men would no longer live to work but would make labor "auxiliary" to their lives.

Throughout the factories industrial workers chafed at their jobs and dreamed of leisure; they engaged their employers in long and bitter disputes over working conditions. But if they rallied to leaders at all, it was not to men who denigrated work but to those who insisted on its inherent value. Their mirroring of one of the central clichés of the culture they contested was not accomplished without some twinges of resentment and anxiety. William Sylvis, the iron molders' leader who dominated the labor movement in the 1860s, complained of the surfeit of appeals to the "dignity of labor" by demagogues, politicians, and "effeminate nonproducers" looking for "a stepping stone to gain notoriety or promotion." Terence Powderly likewise recalled suffering through the harangues of politicians on the nobility of the men who toiled, and a half-century after Powderly's experience Eugene Debs berated labor audiences for their susceptibility to the same flattery. Let a politician offer up some praise to the "horny handed sons of toil," Debs chided, and it "fetches you every time." Yet what made the hypocrites particularly galling to labor spokesmen like Sylvis, Powderly, or Debs was that for each of them the rhetoric was second nature. No theme was more enduring in the labor movement than an appeal to the dignity of labor and the worth of those who did the world's "real" work.

The tradition was manufactured in part out of pride and in part out of a sense of acute degradation. The rhetoric worked at all only by virtue of the very abstraction and conventionality of its premises. But for workers pushed to the wall by industrialization and often abused by the keepers of the work ethic, who found by some galling paradox that their dirty hands were a brand of inferiority in a society filled with obeisances to labor, praise of work offered too useful and too essential a weapon in the battle for status and self-respect to ignore. Thus, below the bell towers and with their own share of incongruity, workers turned a piece of the work ethic into an enduring labor tradition.

Skilled workers, acutely conscious of their declining status, were the first to turn to the language of the work ethic to protest their lot. Condemnation of "irrational, anti-republican and unchristian opinions in relation to the worth and respectability of *manual labor*," as a Massachusetts labor leader put the plea in the 1830s, begins well before the middle of the nineteenth century. When the bricklayers and masons organized in the mid-1860s, they promised to combat the sentiments that elevated wealth above usefulness and industry, the professional above the workingman; and their pledge, with variations, was a staple of nineteenth-century union platforms. Such protests were directed not only at the prejudices of outsiders. Is God "less because His mechanical hand formed the mountains?" Richard Trevellick, of the Ship Carpenters appealed to workingmen. "No fellow toilers; He is not less because He worked; neither are you." William Sylvis was one of the most effective orators in the dignity of labor vein, transforming protest into soaring, self-dignifying affirmation. Labor, he told audiences of workingmen, "is the foundation of the entire political, social, and commercial structure. . . . It is the base upon which the proudest structure of art rests—the leverage which enables man to carry out God's wise purposes—the source from which science draws the elements of its power and greatness, . . . the attribute of all that is noble and grand in civilization." As for those who labored, they were "the bone and muscle of the nation, the very pillars of our temple of liberty."

The American Federation of Labor represented a more hard-bitten style than the socialists, the Knights, or their mid-nineteenth-century predecessors. Encomiums to the dignity of labor appeared only infrequently in the *American Federationist* or the journals of the AFL's member unions, and then most frequently in the poetry columns. "All honor to the brown and skillful hand, / The swell of muscle, the nerve like steel," the *Machinists' Monthly Journal* editorialized in 1910, but more typical was the platform John F. Tobin of the Boot and Shoe Workers offered the Commission on Industrial Relations: "less work to more workers for better pay and shorter hours." Samuel Gompers, the self-conscious industrial proletarian whose drinking annoyed Powderly and whose step-at-a-time practicality angered the socialists, tirelessly preached the same antiromantic doctrine. He argued insistently for the eight-hour day, not entirely as a means of reducing unemployment and raising wages, but as the legitimate right of those "who have borne the awful strains and burdens of exacting toil." Against the cult of unchecked production he argued for cultivation of consumption and, in Herbert Spencer's phrase, for the "gospel of relaxation." Not until the antiunion movement was at its height after 1900 did Gompers compromise the dream of lessened toil by taking up the argument that eight-hour workers would make up production losses by more efficient work. Even then Gompers threw his energies against scientific management's version of the work ethic, damning Taylor's system as reducing men to "mere machines."

But Gompers's response to Taylor's charge of widespread worker malingering was to retreat into the rhetoric of pride. "The heart of the working-man is sound," Gompers insisted in the *American Federationist* in 1911, when the scientific management controversy was at its height; "he who calls him an habitual loafer, an upholder of 'soldiering,' traduces him. . . . Our wage-workers despise sneaking methods, are by training and on principle averse to taking a man's money without rendering full equivalent, and would infinitely rather 'fight it out' with an unfair employer, and have done with it, than adopt the unmanly, dishonorable, puerile methods ascribed to them by . . . 'Doctor Taylor.' . . . It is uniformly harder to pretend to work than to really work." The argument was disingenuous, but Gompers employed it over and over again in the early twentieth century for both trade-union and non-trade-union audiences. There was not "in the whole world, civilized or uncivilized, a working people who toil so hard, who give so much of their mental and physical effort in their work, as do the American people." "When European workmen come over to this country and stand beside their American fellow workingmen it simply dazes them—the velocity of motion, the deftness, the quickness, the constant strain . . . and it is some months, with the greatest endeavor, before [they] can at all come near the production of the American workingman." Other AFL chieftains involved in the fight against Taylorism seconded the theme. "The American workman, as to skill, ingenuity, and quantity of output, has no equal, let alone a peer, on the face of God's green earth," the machinists' union head argued before a congressional committee. The defensive posture of the trade unions in the decade before the First World War, under siege both from the courts and from manufacturers, does not entirely explain away the reappearance of the phrases of the Knights' initiation ritual slightly disguised in the language of labor's self-appointed pragmatists.

Certainly there were impelling reasons for those who presumed to speak for workingmen to seize upon the phrases of the work ethic. Early nineteenth-century America had offered its shop workers identities of place and trade—a fraternity of craft secrets, skills, and time-hallowed symbols. In labor parades in the 1860s and 1870s, workers still bore their trade traditions proudly. In the Chicago eight-hour parade of 1867, according to a contemporary report, "the Stone Cutters Union had three trucks with operatives cutting ornamental masonry. The Iron Molders Union truck was drawn by eight noble horses, and contained men at work on the finer branches of iron molding. The Ship Carpenters and Caulkers Union had a full rigged ship and yawl boat with busy workmen thereon." By the middle of the twentieth century, with the eight-hour day and five-day week finally realized, the hobbies a worker possessed and the way he spent his weekends had begun to fill some of the same self-defining purposes. But industrial America, in blasting skills and undermining traditions, left the majority of its industrial wage workers with only the simplest common denominator of labor. If the semiskilled factory hand did not claim his place as a worker, industrial society offered few other opportunities for assertion of his dignity. Protest movements are not successfully made on the theme of exploitation alone. Thus even those profoundly alienated from their work rallied to leaders who knew the rhetoric of pride, who defended the wage earner as the "bone and sinew" of the nation, his labor as a marvel of efficiency, and insisted that work itself was noble and honorable.

Seizing on the theme of work, industrial wage earners tried to turn the North's pervasive moralism to their own ends. But to join the factory masters on their own terms did not come without costs. One of them was, at times, to force the labor movement into a style of circumlocution. Denying against the preponderance of evidence that output quotas existed, AFL spokesmen took refuge in the considerably more ambiguous formula: a fair day's wage and a fair day's work. By the same token the Knights' pledge to defend a form of "labor (not exhaustive)" scarcely did explicit justice to the contests over labor discipline that swirled only half-acknowledged in the factories. Circumlocutions were common in all discussions of work in industrial America, but the evasions peculiar to labor spokesmen made it considerably easier for those outside the factories to miss what the noise and tumult was all about.

The second, more obvious cost was to entrench in the labor movement a schism between rhetoric and action, the language of work pride and practical alienation. From the restless industrial workers of the nineteenth century to the hard hats and survey respondents of the twentieth, the tension between pride in one's job and estrangement from it has a long and enduring history. But the final price was the most anomalous, to add the voices of men weary with work to the chorus of Carlylean phrases that pervaded industrial America. What such men meant, of course, was not the tightly supervised, clock-driven work toward which the factories were evolving. It had little in it of the ascetic obsessions of a man like Taylor. Perhaps it was not work at all. But even for those who chafed at labor, the appeal to the moral centrality of work was too useful to resist. Pitched in the abstract, it turned necessity into pride and servitude into honor; it offered a lever upon the moral sentiments of those whose power mattered. But in the process, a work-immersed culture exacted its due from its largest body of rebels.

Alice Kessler-Harris

# Technology, Efficiency, and Resistance

By the late nineteenth century there was nearly universal agreement on two scores. Women's expanding labor force participation was an unfortunate necessity that threatened to interfere with their more desirable work at home. And nothing that happened at work could be allowed to hinder the capacity of wage-earning women to resume or assume home roles at some future time. . . . Such ideas channeled women's entrance into the work force, and . . . instead of providing them with safe, clean, unpressured jobs, notions of women's place in fact reduced them to the poorest levels. Unskilled, largely unorganized, and crowded into few occupations, women found themselves subject to some of the worst conditions of any wage workers.

The pattern, once established, encouraged employers to hire women because they were said to have characteristics such as docility, attachment to family, little expectation of advancement, and no trade union consciousness. It led employers to assign women to jobs that matched their expectations of women's possibilities and performance. But in the late 1800s and early 1900s, new technology and new forms of industrial organization altered the structure of work, promising new opportunities to women. The struggle to take advantage of these jobs placed women in direct competition with male workers. To protect themselves, male workers, who were rapidly unionizing, drew on the ideology of woman's place to create obstacles for women. These efforts, along with managerial attempts to order the labor market, cemented the existing segmentation in place, defining the boundaries of men's and women's work for more than half a century.

From Alice Kessler-Harris, Out to Work: A History of Wage-Earning Women in the United States (New York: Oxford University Press, 1982). Copyright © 1982 by Alice Kessler-Harris. Reprinted by permission of Oxford University Press.

The rapidity of Gilded Age industrialization created turmoil in male and female jobs. Since only minimal respect remained for custom and ideology—traditionally the barriers inhibiting substitution of white women for more expensive male workers—employers felt free to experiment with the sexual division of labor. As they did so, the contributions of women seemed increasingly threatening to male workers. Worry began early and got worse by the turn of the century. The federal government had provoked hostility when it hired women for some clerical jobs in 1862. Until then there had been no more than a few women scattered in an occasional federal office, employed largely as copyists and low-grade clerks. Under pressure of the war, the Treasury hired some women to cut currency. And in 1862 the Post Office hired eight women among twenty-five new employees to sort mail. The new employees were ridiculed and insulted by male colleagues who "stared, blew smoke in the women's faces, spat tobacco juice, and gave cat-calls or made obnoxious remarks." The women, who earned an average of $300 a year less than men for precisely the same job, were discovered to be as productive as their colleagues, and the department promptly hired more women at the reduced rate. Though some federal officials objected on principle to hiring women, others appreciated the money saved by paying lower salaries. The end of the war brought predictable outcries. The *Workingmen's Advocate* deplored the fact that even the "government of the United States, which squanders millions uselessly every year, has stooped to the hiring of female clerks to do the work of its Departments because they could be got for a smaller sum than males."

But new machinery constituted the most typical reason to substitute women for men. Each time women entered an occupation for which training had become unnecessary, men saw it as an attack. In the pottery industry, skilled jiggermen feared, as they testified in 1900, that female labor operating new machinery would cut their wages in half and drive them out of the trade. It had happened, they said, in Great Britain, where the jobs of Englishmen had already been destroyed. The 1910 government report on the glass industry concluded that not only had certain parts of the work been readjusted so that women could be employed, but "new methods and new machines were devised with this end in view." The resulting reorganization of the work force broke up processes previously performed by skilled men into smaller tasks that "ceased to require skill. Machinery was adapted to women and much of it was and is advertised as being so adapted."

Changes in machinery, of course, had variable results. Sometimes jobs were created for women; but frequently a change had the opposite result. The textile industry witnessed both kinds of changes in the nineteenth century. In 1850, spinning jennies, operated by women in cotton mills, were widely replaced by spinning mules, heavy machines that called for physical strength and lent themselves to a male work force, according to the custom of the day. By the 1890s, when mule spinners, who then earned the relatively high wage of twelve to fourteen dollars a week, began seeking even more pay, several mills took advantage of new ring-spinning machinery to replace these demanding craftsmen with women at from six to eight dollars per week. One mill superintendent described the replacement process in his mill as follows: "A few years ago they were giving us trouble . . . so one Saturday afternoon, after they had gone home, we started right in and smashed up a room full of mules with sledge hammers. When the men came back on Monday morning, they were astonished to find that there was no work for them. That room is now full of ring frames run by girls." . . .

*   *   *

After the first breach of the office walls during the labor shortage of the Civil War, women moved quickly into most clerical positions. Their place was assured when the typewriter came into general use in the 1890s. The machine required nimble fingers—presumably an attribute of women. Its operators exercised no initiative. They were expected simply to copy. And the work was clean. Attracted by the new jobs, large numbers of women not previously employed began to look for work. These were native-born daughters of native parents, who had consistently refused jobs next to immigrant women in factories. For them, office work brought only minimal loss of dignity and offered the chance to earn decent incomes. The best-paid office workers—those who worked for the federal government, for example—might earn $900 a year in the 1870s. Though less than male wages for similar jobs, this compared favorably with other women's jobs. A teacher could make $500 a year. A stellar "typewriter" could make $7 a week, and an ordinary office clerk earned $6. A competent cap maker might earn $7 a week, but seasonal unemployment reduced her wages to less than $250 for a year's work.

Women's entry into the labor force accompanied a transition in the structure of offices. Unlike the men they replaced, women did not work primarily as personal secretaries. Rather, they found themselves doing tasks that were subdivided to produce maximal efficiency with minimal training. A year of secretarial training could turn a woman into a competent typist and stenographer. Lesser amounts were required for file clerks, telephone operators, and receptionists. But her ability to perform tasks constituted only part of a woman employee's attraction. Her personality weighed heavily. In 1916, a writer in the *Ladies' Home Journal* attributed 50 percent of the stenographer's value to her personality, quoting an employer who declared, "I expect from my stenographer the same service I get from the sun, with this exception: the sun often goes on a strike and it is necessary for me to use artificial light, but I pay my stenographer to work six days out of every seven and I expect her all the while to radiate my office with sunshine and sympathetic interest in the things I am trying to do."

The office worker's job might have made consistent sunshine difficult. Expected to possess all the sympathetic and nurturing characteristics of a good wife, she often performed tasks as routine as those of any factory worker. In the interests of efficiency, managers pooled their labor so that women might be called upon to perform their assigned job for any number of bosses. Even in this early period, managers simplified jobs, reducing tasks to the level of petty detail. One office manager declared women to be more "temperamentally reconciled" to the new jobs than ambitious men. By the 1920s attempts to systematize and control the office led to experiments with scientific management techniques. Creating systems for filing, keeping records, and corresponding became the tasks of an office manager. In a scientifically managed office the clerk or typist could no longer work according to her own methods, but according to methods and at times specified by the manager. Detailed studies were expected to reveal optimal speeds for each task and to break down the work into its simplest components. Though these techniques were never widely adopted, they influenced perceptions of systematic work and affected the tasks of numerous female office clerks.

In the given-out trades the transition first to factory work and then to efficiency techniques produced different results. As long as women made hats, garments, paper flowers, and feathers in the context of a rural family environment, they could trade off their small wages against the advantages of flexible work schedules. Supported by home-grown products, they might get through hard times without work, and they benefited from community sanction against those who cheated or did not pay as promised. These favorable conditions changed as the production of most goods shifted to factories in the 1850s, 1860s and 1870s. During the transition, home work competed with factory products, forcing middlemen to demand a speedup in manufacture at the cost of quality. And centralization of the manufacturing process meant that even the paid work that remained in the home tended to gravitate from rural to urban environments, where community sanctions had less force and women had fewer resources to fall back on. . . . Contractors who distributed work from a shop in an impersonal urban environment succumbed to temptations to cheat and to offer the lowest possible wages. They ushered in some of the worst abuses of the sweating system.

In the garment industry, the rapid spread of the sewing machine after 1860 meant that for a while women, whether they sewed at home or in a shop, had to bear the increased costs of buying a piece of equipment. But its long-run effect was to encourage the slow movement of the work force into factories, where centralized production rationalized the garment-making process.

For a while, garment manufacturers distinguished sharply between "inside" and "outside" shops. In both, manufacturers distributed cut garments to contractors who bid against each other. The lowest bid got the bundle, and the contractor who won it hired his own operators to make up the pieces. Those who worked "inside" normally supervised the work process under the roof of the manufacturer himself. Others took the bundles "outside" to their own tenement flats, or to cheaply rented quarters. Since a contractor's income depended directly on how cheaply he could get people to finish the garments, he paid as little as he possibly could, and charged for thread, heat, light, and power, if he could get away with it. The system encouraged the use of family labor—which could be employed for endless hours—and of women. Though immigrant men were sometimes as much as 40 percent of the machine operators, the core of the labor force consisted of young, often immigrant women. Whether a woman worked inside or outside, she was most often paid directly by the contractor to whom she was responsible. That contractor—perhaps a tailor—in turn got his bundles from a foreman who coordinated the work of finishing and pressing completed garments. In inside shops this relationship left the subcontracting tailor less control than might otherwise seem possible. Becky Stein, a Philadelphia garment worker, recounted to the Commission on Industrial Relations in 1916 her sense of grievance at foremen who could compel a tailor to discharge a finisher against his will by threatening, "If you won't discharge her, you can't get no work."

The sewing machine, agitation from reformers who feared the spread of disease from tenement-made goods, and a desire for closer supervision of the work process all encouraged manufacturers to bring their contractors inside, and by the early 1900s some branches of the industry began to eliminate the contractor altogether. As among telephone operators later, the increasing similarity of work and close association of workers stimulated unionization. Female sewing machine operators employed in the shirtwaist industry led the series of strikes that breathed life into the moribund International Ladies' Garment Workers' Union between 1909 and 1911. Shirtwaist manufacture —the newest branch of the garment industry—was organized in fairly large inside shops with relatively decent working conditions. The young female labor force sought freedom from the erratic decisions and often harassing behavior of foremen and supervisors. To get it, they fought for and finally won union recognition.

Not surprisingly, manufacturers, interested in rationalizing their industry, used the young union to institute some efficiency techniques that the union agreed would benefit workers as well as manufacturers. Their agreements are embodied in the Protocols of Peace—a series of compacts negotiated from 1910 to 1917 between local unions and maufacturers' associations representing various branches of the women's garment industry. The protocols normally included provisions for minimum wages, maximum hours, sanitary conditions, and arbitration mechanisms. But some went further. In New York's dress and waist industry, for example, the protocol guaranteed union cooperation in raising worker efficiency and holding manufacturers' costs down in return for guaranteed prices, mutually negotiated and agreed upon by the two parties in advance. The Board of Protocol Standards created under this industry's 1913 agreement set up union/employer time and motion study teams that would recommend appropriate wages and standard procedures and accounting methods. Since efficiency systems were then anathema to organized trade unionists, who were largely skilled, white males, the ILGWU leadership acted cautiously. But, for its semiskilled female membership, notions of efficiency and negotiated prices had tangible benefits. The union acquired a voice in the labor process. Women experienced relatively less harassment by amorous foremen and received designated and attainable tasks at prescribed prices. The ILGWU's rationale earned the support of Sidney Hillman, president of the newly formed Amalgamated Clothing Workers' Union, which organized workers in the men's clothing industry. The Amalgamated, 40 percent of whose members were female in 1920, cooperated with employers who tried to increase efficiency on the grounds that it subjected employees to less irrational behavior.

As it encouraged employers to turn to female labor for some jobs, the movement to increase worker productivity and to rationalize the work process produced an upsurge of resistance on the part of both men and women. But whereas men involved in the de-skilling process could and did unionize to defend their status, women discovered that their attempts to do so ran counter to assumptions about their social roles.

When the Knights of Labor flourished in the 1880s, women took advantage of its open membership policy to organize in large numbers. But the American Federation of Labor, founded in 1886, represented relatively privileged workers, willing to sacrifice the larger issue of working-class solidarity for the immediate gain of higher wages. In the creation of what economist Selig Perlman called "a joint partnership of organized labor and organized capital," the Federation cooperated extensively with corporation-dominated government agencies, sought to exclude immigrants, and supported an imperialist foreign policy. Its mechanisms for dealing with the huge numbers of women entering the labor force are an integral part of the puzzle surrounding the interaction of ideological and economic forces in regulating labor market participation.

In the period from 1897 to 1920, the AFL underwent dramatic expansion. It consolidated and confirmed its leadership over a number of independent unions, including the dying Knights of Labor. Membership increased from about 265,000 in 1897 to more than four million by 1920, and included four-fifths of all organized workers. In the same period, the proportion of women working in the industrial labor force climbed by about 20 percent. Rapid and heady expansion offered a golden opportunity for organizers. That they did not take advantage of it is one of the most important facts in the history of labor organizing in America.

Figures for union membership are notoriously unreliable, and estimates fluctuate widely. But something like 3.3 percent of the women who were engaged in industrial occupations in 1900 were organized into trade unions. As low as that figure was, it began to decrease around 1902 and 1903, reaching a low of 1.5 percent in 1910. Then, a surge of organization among garment workers raised it. A reasonable estimate might place 6.6 percent of wage-earning women in trade unions by 1920—nearly half of them in the clothing trades and another 25 percent in printing. The rest belonged to a variety of unions, including meat packers, electrical workers, railway clerks, textile workers, boot and shoe workers, and hotel employees. In a decade that saw little change in the relative proportion of female and male workers, the proportion of women who were trade union members quadrupled, increasing at more than twice the rate for trade union members in general. Even so, the relative numbers of wage-earning women who were trade union members remained tiny. One in every five men in the industrial work force belonged to a union, compared to one in every fifteen women. Although more than 20 percent of the labor force was female, less than 8 percent of organized workers were women.

The dearth of women in unions had historic roots. These are readily located in the personality and behavioral patterns that derived from traditional family expectations. The young, unskilled workers who looked to marriage to escape the shop or factory were not ideal candidates for unionization. At the turn of the century, 87 percent of female workers were unmarried and nearly half were under twenty-five. Wage-earning women often came from groups without a union tradition: about half were immigrants or daughters of immigrants who shared rural backgrounds. In the cities, the figure sometimes rose to 90 percent. Like immigrant and black men, women formed a large reservoir of unskilled workers. Because they offered employers the advantage of low pay and exploitative working conditions, employers had a special incentive to resist unionization among women. As John Andrews, writing in the 1911 Report on the Condition of Woman and Child Wage Earners, put it: "The moment she organizes a union and seeks by organization to secure better wages she diminishes or destroys what is to the employer her chief value." Women who wished to unionize had to fight on two fronts: against the weight of tradition and expectation, and against employers.

There was yet a third battle front—the trade union itself—and it might have been the most important of all. Instead of recognizing women as workers and encouraging them to join in organizational struggles, male unionists insisted on women's primary function in the home and remained stubbornly ambivalent about their efforts. They understood that employers had an important economic incentive for hiring women, and so their rhetoric, reflecting fears of being undercut, affirmed a commitment to unionize women wage earners and to extract equal pay for them. Yet in practice trade unionists remained locked into patriarchal attitudes that valued women's contributions to the home. Women's duties as mothers and wives, most felt, echoing the arguments of the preceding generation, were so valuable that women ought not to be in the labor force at all. This was unfortunate for women who wished to organize because it deprived them of help from the largest body of collective working-class opinion.

"The great principle for which we fight," said the AFL's treasurer in 1905, "is opposed to taking . . . the women from their homes to put them in the factory and the sweatshop." "We stand for the principle," said another AFL member, "that it is wrong to permit any of the female sex of our country to be forced to work, as we believe that the man should be provided with a fair wage in order to keep his female relatives from going to work. The man is the provider and should receive enough for his labor to give his family a respectable living." And yet a third proclaimed, "Respect for women is apt to decrease when they are compelled to work in the factory or the store. . . . More respect for women brings less degeneration and more marriages . . . if women labor in factories and similar institutions they bring forth weak children who are not educated to become strong and good citizens." No language was too forceful or too dramatic. "The demand for female labor," wrote an official of the Boston Central Labor Union in 1897, is "an insidious assault upon the home . . . it is the knife of the assassin, aimed at the family circle." The AFL journal, *American Federationist*, romanticized women's jobs at home, extolling the virtues of refined and moral mothers, of good cooking, and even of beautiful needlework and embroidery.

These arguments from home and motherhood had several effects. They sustained women's sense of themselves as temporary workers—a self-image on which their exploitation rested. In so doing they inadvertently aided employers, who relied on the notion that women were marginal to the work force to pay low wages and limit training. Trade unionists thus contributed to segmenting the labor force and crowding women into a few areas. Perhaps worst of all, the notion that women constituted a different kind of worker created barriers between the sexes that inhibited cooperation in a common struggle with employers.

The perception that women belonged in the home translated into the desire that they be eliminated from the work force entirely. "Every woman employed," wrote an editor in *American Federationist*, "displaces a man and adds one more to the idle contingent that are fixing wages at the lowest limit." "It is the so-called competition of the unorganized defenseless woman worker, the girl and the wife, that often tends to reduce the wages of the father and husband," proclaimed Samuel Gompers. . . .

\*     \*     \*

These sentiments did not entirely prevent the AFL from attempting to unionize women. Although the grim realities of exploitative working conditions and the difficulties of caring for children while working ten or more hours a day sustained the argument for eliminating women from the work force, this goal was impossible to achieve. So the AFL, supported by well-intentioned social reformers, continued to organize women and to demand equal pay for equal work. Gompers editorialized on the subject frequently: "We . . . shall bend every energy for our fellow workmen to organize and unite in trade unions; to federate their effort without regard to . . . sex." He and others conceded the "full and free opportunity for women to work whenever and wherever necessity requires," but Gompers did not address himself to the problem of how to determine which women were admissible by this standard, and his actions revealed that he thought their numbers relatively few. . . .

*    *    *

A strong union could simply cut women out of the kinds of jobs held by unionized men, a form of segmenting the labor market that sometimes contradicted the interests of employers who would have preferred cheap labor. A Binghamton, New York, printing establishment, for example, could not hire women Linotype operators because "the men's union would not allow it." This tactic excluded racial minorities as often as it restricted women; and, like appeals to racist beliefs, arguments based on the natural weakness of women worked well as a rationale. Mary Dreier, then president of the New York Chapter of the Women's Trade Union League, recalled a union of tobacco workers whose leaders refused to admit women because "they could only do poor sort of work . . . because women had no colour discrimination." A Boston metal polishers' union refused to admit women. "We don't want them," an official told an interviewer. "Women can only do one kind of work while men can polish anything from iron to gold and frame the smallest part to the largest." Besides, he added, "metal polishing is bad for the health."

Less direct methods excluded women from unions equally effectively. The International Retail Clerks' Union charged an initiation fee of three dollars and dues of fifty cents a month. Hilda Svenson, a local organizer in 1914, complained that she had been unable to negotiate a compromise with the International. "We want to be affiliated with them," she commented, "but on account of the dues and initiation fee we feel it is too high at the present time for the salaries that the girls in New York are getting." Sometimes union pay scales were set so high that the employer would not pay the appropriate wage to women. Joining the union could mean that a female printer would lose her job; so women simply refused to join.

But even membership in a union led by men guaranteed little to women. Unions often deliberately sabotaged their female members. Detroit's Amalgamated Association of Street Railway and Electrical Employees had agreed under wartime duress to admit women who were to be employed as conductors into their union in 1918. Just as their probationary period ended, men began returning from overseas and the union refused 250 women regular cards. Only an appeal to the National Labor Board, which ruled in the women's favor, saved their jobs. Supporting union men was not likely to benefit women either. Mary Anderson, newly appointed head of the U.S. Department of Labor's Women's Bureau, got a frantic telegram from a WTUL organizer in Joliet, Illinois, early in 1919. The woman in a Joliet steel plant who, in return for the promise of protection, had supported unionized men in a recent strike were fighting desperately for jobs that the union now insisted they give up. The company wanted to retain the women, but union men argued that the work was too heavy for them.

In addition, such well-known tactics as holding meetings in saloons, scheduling them at late hours, and ridiculing women who dared to speak deprived women of full participation. Italian and southern families disliked their daughters going out in the evenings. Married and self-supporting women and widows had household duties at which they spent after-work hours. Women who attended meetings usually participated reluctantly. They found the long discussions dull and were often intimidated by the preponderance of men. Men, for their part, resented the indifference of the women and further excluded them from leadership roles, thereby discouraging more women from attending. Even fines failed to spark attendance. Some women preferred to pay them rather than go to the meetings.

Cultural patterns that derived from a patriarchal society joined ethnic ties in hindering unionization. Wage-earning women, anxious to marry, were sometimes reluctant to join unions for what they felt would be a temporary period. The role conflict implicit in a young wage-earning woman's assumptions about future family life emerged in ambivalence toward unions. "No nice girl would belong to one," said one young woman. An ILGWU organizer commented that the reluctance of most women who did not want to unionize reflected the obedience they owed to fathers. "The boss is good to us" they claimed; "we have nothing to complain about and we don't want to join the union." A woman who resisted unionization told an organizer that she knew "$6 a week is not enough pay but the Lord helps me out. He always provides. . . . I won't ever join a union. The Lord doesn't want me to." A recent convert to unionism apologized for her former reluctance. She had always scabbed because church people disapproved of unions. Moreover, she and her sister, she admitted to an organizer, had only with difficulty overcome their fear of the Italian men who were organizing their factory.

For all their initial reluctance women could be devoted and successful union members, convinced that unionism would serve them as it seemed to be serving their brothers. In the words of a seventeen-year-old textile worker, "We all work hard for a mean living. Our boys belong to the miners' union so their wages are better than ours. So I figure that girls must have a union. Women must act like men, ain't?" Such attitudes occurred most often among women whose ethnic backgrounds encouraged both wage labor and a high level of social consciousness, as in the American Jewish community, for example. Young Jewish women constituted the bulk of the membership of the International Ladies' Garment Workers' Union in the period from 1910 to 1920. Their rapid organization and faithful tenure was responsible for at least one-quarter of the increased number of unionized women in those years. And yet they were unskilled and semiskilled workers, employed in small, scattered shops, theoretically among the least organizable. These women, having unionized at their own initiative, formed the backbone of the ILGWU, which had originally sought to organize the skilled male cutters in the trade. They often served as shop "chairladies" and reached positions of minor importance in the union structure. Faige Shapiro recalled that her union activity began at the insistence of a business agent but quickly became an absorbing interest. The commitment of some women was such that when arrested on picket lines, they offered to spend the night in jail in order to save the union bail costs before returning to the line in the morning.

Whether in mixed unions or segregated by sex, women often outdid men in militancy. Once organized, they could more easily rely on the families they lived with to support them in a pinch. Since women as a group tended to have fewer dependents than men, they could hold out longer in a strike. Examples abound. Iowa cigar makers reported in 1899 that striking men had resumed work, while the women stood fast. Boot and shoe workers in Massachusetts were reported in 1905 to be tough bargainers. "It is harder to induce women to compromise," said their president; "they are more likely to hold out to the bitter end . . . to obtain exactly what they want." The great 1909 uprising in which 20,000 women walked out of New York's garment shops occurred over the objections of the male leadership, striking terror into the hearts of Jewish men afraid "of the security of their jobs." Protesting a rate cut in the textile mills of Chicopee, Massachusetts, Polish "spool girls" refused their union's suggestion that they arbitrate and won a resounding victory. Swedish women enrolled in a Chicago Custom Clothing Makers local lost a battle against employers' attempts to subdivide and speed up the sewing process when the largely male United Garment Workers' Union agreed to the new conditions. The management promptly locked out the women, forcing many to come to terms and others to seek new jobs. These militant characteristics enabled women who overcame the initial barriers to organization to run highly successful sex-segregated unions. They account for the early success of such turn-of-the-century unions as those of female garment workers in San Francisco, of telephone operators in Boston, and of tobacco strippers, and overall and sheepskin workers elsewhere.

Militance was less effective where trade union ambivalence left women at the mercy of employers who were particularly eager to discourage organization among women. In these instances, employers pressed their advantage. Sometimes they used crude techniques familiar to men. Department store employees were commonly fired when their union membership became known. Many stores had spy systems so that employees could not trust each other. Blacklists were common. Members of the Retail Dry Goods Associations refused jobs to women whose names appeared on lists of troublemakers. The Association itself kept a complete record of all employees, including where they were employed and why discharged. Records were passed on to prospective employers, with no right of appeal by the employee. For fear of retaliation, a representative of the year-old Retail Clerks' Union, testifying before a congressional committee in 1914, refused to reveal the number of members in her union. To undercut trade union activities, department stores formed their own employee associations. Filene's in Boston and Bloomingdale's in New York set up welfare funds to make loans to employees in distress or to distribute turkeys at Thansgiving. Although these funds required employee contributions, and representatives to the boards that controlled them were technically elected by the workers, no employee had ever sat on the Filene's board when one worker described it to an investigative committee in 1916. . . .

*       *       *

New ideas about corporate welfare and Taylor's notions of scientific management encouraged some managers to handle disciplinary problems through personnel and welfare work. Personnel management was of course the ideal tool for intervention and control. This newly founded science purported to be able to select employees judiciously and to assign them to the work they could do most effectively. Its techniques ranged from diagnostic interviews that attempted to choose likely candidates for each job, through careful juxtaposition of workers, with due consideration for race and ethnicity, and formal procedures for promotion and termination. Welfare work promised to keep workers contented by enhancing their sense of general well-being. Plants engaged in welfare work might offer employees incentives to purchase houses, to suggest innovative techniques through formal channels, and to participate in company-sponsored recreation. As a government report on textile mills concluded: "Parks, skating rinks, baseball teams, bands, and other welfare work doubtless have as one of their objects the creation of a contented class of mill employees who will not move about."

To workers and trade union organizers, welfare work appeared as an attempt to undermine their roles. One active union organizer described welfare work as "the last stand of the intelligent employer before doing business with a trade union. . . ." The focus of such work varied, but often it seemed to workers just another form of charity. The president of the Retail Clerks' Union, employed by Bloomingdale's Department Store, complained that only married workers and male employees got turkeys at Thanksgiving. "You have got to apply for it and ask for it, say that you need it. It is given out just as a charity is handed out . . . and the turkeys are paid for out of the money of the employees."

*       *       *

The paternalism, benevolence, and welfare employers offered in compensation for foregoing unionism proved to be particularly useful tools for diverting women from organization. They promised to alleviate some of the harsh conditions under which women worked—conditions long viewed by reformers and investigators as detrimental to the preservation of home and family. These voluntary employer programs, in conjunction with government regulation, seemed to many an adequate alternative to unionism. What was more, trade unions, by allying themselves with regulators and sometimes with employers, could use appeals to women's "natural roles" to restrict their labor force participation.

*       *       *

If women were not to unionize, how were they to overcome low pay and exploitation at work? Training women in the skills appropriate to their sphere seemed like a plausible answer. Such activists in women's rights as Anna Dickinson and Mary Livermore had advocated training as a solution to women's problems for years. Early commentators on female labor—Virginia Penny, Caroline Dall, and later Annie McLean—repeatedly urged vocational training for girls. These women argued that the changing sex ratio—women already made up more than 51 percent of the population in such urban states as New York, Connecticut, Massachusetts, and New Jersey—would necessitate life-long work for many women, and that widowhood, desertion, and even divorce would force still others to fend for themselves. But acceptance of their proposals turned on the critical question of whether training would break down, or contribute to, sexual segmentation in the job market.

Skilled trades had traditionally been a province of unionized craftsmen who jealously guarded access to training in their fields. Though women frequently taught each other, and occasionally managed to "steal" a trade from a willing male relative, they were rarely admitted to the requisite apprenticeships. Where they managed to acquire skills and posed a threat to male workers, craft unions sometimes grudgingly helped women to form separate, affiliated unions. . . . To allow outsiders to train men or women, but especially women, in skilled areas posed an unending threat. When, in 1872, cigar makers faced an influx of skilled female Bohemian cigar rollers into their union, they responded by excluding the women altogether, provoking their use as strikebreakers a year later.

By the late 1890s employers began to move toward manual training programs in the public schools as a way of breaking craft monopolies. Manual training—which encouraged general skills useful for industrial work—quickly gave way to vocational education, which emphasized the skills specific to particular jobs. Such developments reflected a general shift in attitude toward all education. Initially education had been seen as useless in terms of vocation. Agnes Smedley's father expressed a general prejudice when he pronounced it worthwhile "only for women and men who were dudes." But the urban and industrial nation that had emerged out of the Civil War demanded disciplined workers with positive attitudes toward their jobs. In the words of one supervisor, the best educated of his workers were "the most capable, intelligent, energetic, industrious, economical, and moral . . . they produce the best work and the most of it, with the least injury to the machinery." Youngsters, employers thought, should be taught in school to work with their hands so that when they left school they could fit easily into an industrial framework.

For men, the issue of vocational education centered on the problem of control. But for women, it became ambiguous. To some well-meaning reformers, vocational training assumed the aspect of a panacea. Teaching women a trade opened tempting possibilities of financial security for them as well as a way out of overcrowded women's fields and up in the occupational structure. "Girls do not become apprentices or learn a trade thoroughly, and consequently they lagged behind man in the race of life," argued Ernestine Rose in 1869. "Teach girls to learn a trade as well as boys," she continued, "and then they would be independent." Jennie Cunningham Croly, feminist and socialist, concurred. To a congressional committee investigating capital and labor she declared in 1883: "Wherever a person can do anything, can do it in a proper sense, they can always earn a living by it; they can always get a certain amount for it." Sewing women earned only 50 cents a day because they were not properly competent. Even a washerwoman, who could wash, might make $1.25 a day. Raise "the standard of useful work by education and training," Croly argued, and women would earn more. The U.S. Department of Labor added fuel to the movement in 1909 when it documented what everyone already suspected. A New York City investigative committee had discovered that the average annual wage for girls without training approximated one-third of the wage of those who were trained as stenographers, and less than half of those trained as nurses.

Training would also provide access to jobs previously closed. If women "want to do a man's work," argued New York *Tribune* publisher Whitelaw Reid, "they must prepare." She would, Croly suggested, "supplement . . . common school education with technical or industrial schools where they would be made thorough mechanical draughtsmen, engravers, modelers, designers, dressmakers, embroiderers, laundresses, cooks, and tailors." Training would provide skills for middle-aged women who had worked for years. It could even, Leonora O'Reilly proposed, "act as an incentive to unionization." O'Reilly, who would later supervise machine operators for the Manhattan Trade School for Girls, wondered in 1898 whether training might not give to "working girls" that "force of character which will secure them desirable conditions of life and work." As jobs became increasingly mechanical, she touted trade schools as a way of preventing the "numbness of mind that comes with doing rote work." A trade school taught a girl "the relation between the brain and the hands."

But in practice, vocational education for women was fraught with problems. Widespread opinion held that homemaking was sufficiently complicated that all women should train to become efficient and effective housekeepers. Women entered the labor force briefly—too briefly, some thought, to be worth the time or energy of adequate training. To provide training appropriate to rewarding jobs threatened to undermine women's investment in home roles. Female college graduates, fully half of whom never married, provided a specter of the future. Should social institutions, public or private, lend themselves to such an aberration?

Advocates of vocational education for women tried to meet this objection by praising the home-related aspects of their program and obscuring its job-training potential. "Industrial education," in the words of a noted authority, should be designed "to meet the needs of the manual wage workers in the trades and industries, and in the household." Conceptually this meant that a notion of household labor as a woman's real work underlay every aspect of her vocational training. An insistent refrain accompanied preparation for even the most difficult jobs. Training would prepare female workers "for right living and right spending" in the future, said the Women's Educational and Industrial Union, whose purpose was "the advancement of women." It could teach them to be good consumers, "intelligent, discriminating, purchasing agents for themselves and their homes," said the Federal Board for Vocational Education. Out of training for a job, in short, would come not workers prepared to cope with the job market, but better house tenders. The National Society for the Promotion of Industrial Education, a coalition of small manufacturers, educators, social workers, and representatives of organized labor, waxed eloquent on this theme. "Will not the woman who has learned to systematize, to go forth rain or shine to work an eight-hour day, to stand on her own feet, taking the consequences of her own mistakes, and expecting no indulgences, have developed a respect for method, a sense of responsibility, and a discipline that are among the best gifts she could bring into the home?"

In this conspiracy to disguise what job training could accomplish, the representatives of interest groups ranging from educators and trade unionists to feminists concurred. Every plan of education for women, the manual training committee of the National Educational Association argued, should be tested "not merely with questions of immediate expediency or of personal advantage, but always with the thought of the larger contribution to the common good, and the higher functions which women can never surrender." The committee insisted that women could not only "lead happier and richer lives and will be more successful as the future homemakers of our cities" if they had some early training, but that industrial education would provide a skill with innumerable advantages. It would raise their parents' standards of living, as well as afford them protection and support if they were to lose their own partners.

Even those who sympathized most with women's needs for saleable skills defended vocational training as an adjunct to normal expectations of marriage. A national committee on women in industry, reporting on ways to educate women at the end of the war, offered a sweeping vision: vocational education would provide training for "the period previous to marriage, or if she does not marry, for the period of her working life, or for the married woman, who, because of widowhood, desertion, childlessness, or some other deviation from normal married life, returns to industry as a wage-earner." "The qualities needed in trade," wrote Mary Woolman after five years as director of the Manhattan Trade School for Girls,

*are the same as those which elevate the home. Employers ask for workers who are reliable, who respect authority, who are honest in time, in work, and in word. The development of a sense of responsibility is a difficult task to accomplish, but it is not impossible at least to lay the foundation, even though the poverty of the students necessarily limits the period of instruction. A trade school can develop character, and consequently the better homekeeper is born from the better trade worker.*

Opposition to training women for exclusively wage-earning roles led to schools and curricula that appeared distinctly defensive. Those who developed trade schools played down the remunerative aspects of the skills they were teaching. Witness Florence Leadbetter, principal of Boston's Trade School for Girls: "We have always said that we would not admit to our trade school any trade which would not help the girl in her highest vocation—homemaking—but we believe that any trade, well-taught . . . will give that discipline . . . needed to make her the ideal wife, mother, sympathetic helpmate and resourceful adviser." What had begun in the 1870s as a movement to train women in saleable skills had become a major adjunct to training for the home by 1900. . . .

*       *       *

In accepting the condition that homemaking be part of the educational process, and in acquiescing to existing job segmentation, advocates of vocational education for women fell into a predictable trap. For the new programs perpetuated familiar characteristics among women workers. They trained women expected to stay in the labor market briefly to expect little upward mobility and to deflect their ambitions into marriage. A Women's Bureau argument illustrated the tenacious effect of old prescriptions. After making the point that women were, after all, capable of doing these jobs, the Bureau said, "The increase in the use of mechanical devices in the modern home renders a knowledge of mechanics essential, if not more so, to the average woman who eventually leaves industry to take up household duties as is a knowledge of sewing, because the manufacture of clothing has ceased practically, to be a profitable household industry." If the Woman's Bureau could resort to such logic, it was small wonder that Anna Lalor Burdick, who worked for the Federal Board of Vocational Training, found it easy to argue for training women for garment and hat work, the hosiery industry, and soapmaking, on the grounds that "women's small and agile hands are especially adapted to the work of certain industries."

Despite the influx of married women into the work force, and the clear evidence that their jobs offered inadequate pay and opportunity, vocational education perpetuated the assumption that married women's work was, and would remain, peripheral. Yet for daughters of the working class, it involved a breakthrough of sorts. While denying that individual women could be permanent workers, it acknowledged a permanent role for women in general in the work force. It took women's work seriously enough to provide a few women with access to decent training and a real possibility for creative work force participation. But vocational education did not yield access to upward mobility. Rather, the skills provided more often than not led to a fixed, if slightly more comfortable, labor force position.

## SUGGESTIONS FOR FURTHER READING

For many years the study of American labor was dominated by the Wisconsin school founded by John Commons, a group of scholars who collected a great many source materials and studied the development of the trade union as an institution. They stressed the lack of class consciousness and the concern for job consciousness among most American labor organizations. Important examples of this approach are the four-volume *History of Labor in the United States* by Commons and others (New York, 1918–1935); Selig Perlman, *A Theory of the Labor Movement* (New York, 1928); and Philip Taft's massive two-volume history of the A. F. of L.: *The A. F. of L. in the Time of Gompers* (New York, 1957); *The A. F. of L. from the Death of Gompers to the Merger* (New York, 1959).

Strongly opposed to the Wisconsin group is Philip S. Foner, whose Marxist interpretation of the *History of the Labor Movement in the United States* (four volumes to date; New York, 1947–1965) emphasizes class struggle and conflict. Violent labor conflict can be seen in studies of specific strikes: Almont Lindsay, *The Pullman Strike* (Chicago, 1942) and Henry David, *History of the Haymarket Affair* (New York, 1936). Louis Adamic's theme is expressed in the title of his book, *Dynamite, The Story of Class Violence in America* (New York, 1931).

In recent years many labor historians have tried to break away from the study of organized labor and/or individual strikes and have emphasized instead the history of workers (rather than unions) in the context of social change in the United States. These historians have been strongly influenced by a pioneer study by a British scholar, E. P. Thompson, *The Making of the English Working Class* (London, 1963). An example of this influence can be seen in the article by Herbert Gutman reprinted above. Other articles by Gutman are collected in a book, *Work, Culture and Society in Industrializing America* (New York, 1976). A perceptive study with a good bibliography is Melvyn Dubofsky, *Industrialism and the American Worker, 1865–1920* (New York, 1975). Problems of social mobility among workers are dealt with in two books by Stephan Thernstrom: *Poverty and Progress: Social Mobility in a Nineteenth Century City* (Cambridge, Mass., 1964), and *The Other Bostonians* (Cambridge, Mass., 1973). The problem of working women can be followed in Rosiland Baxandall, Linda Gordon, Susan Reverby, eds., *America's Working Women* (New York, 1976); David M. Katzman, *Seven Days a Week: Women and Domestic Service in Industrializing America* (New York, 1978); and Alice Kessler-Harris, "Where are the Organized Women Workers?" *Feminist Studies* 3 (Fall 1975), pp. 92–110.

Daniel T. Rodgers, *The Work Ethic in Industrial America, 1850–1920* (Chicago, 1978), a portion of which is reprinted above, deserves to be carefully read in its entirety. For a similar approach from a different perspective see David Montgomery, *Beyond Equality: Labor and the Radical Republicans, 1862–1872* (New York, 1967). Montgomery's views for the later years may be found in his *Workers' Control in America* (Cambridge, England, 1979).

* Available in paperback edition.

# 5

# *Migrants to an Urban America*

The history of modern America is in many ways a history of urbanism. "The United States was born in the country, but has moved to the city," Richard Hofstadter has written. Of course, there were cities in America from the very beginning of the nation's history; Philadelphia, with a population of about 25,000 in 1776, was one of the largest cities in the British Empire. But in the early years of the new republic, the urban population was small. In 1790 there were only twenty-four towns in the United States with a population of 2,500 or more (the census definition of an urban place); the 201,655 urban residents in that year accounted for only about 5 percent of the total population.

The growth of trade and industry in the nineteenth century brought massive urban growth. By 1860 about 20 percent of the population resided in cities, and forty years later four Americans in ten were urban dwellers. The census of 1920 revealed that more than half the American population lived in cities.

Rapid urbanization did not bring universal approval from the nation's intellectual and cultural leaders. Some, such as Frederick C. Howe, saw the city as "The Hope of Democracy," picturing the metropolis as the center of culture, business, and opportunity. But many, recalling Thomas Jefferson's warnings, distrusted the city, seeing it as a source of corruption and sin and a threat to American democracy.

Critics found much to distrust about city life. They pointed to the filth and the smoky air, to the violence and crime, and to the political corruption. But most frightening of all, the cities seemed strangely alien with their hordes of immigrants from the farms and cities of Europe. During the century after 1820, 38 million Europeans came to America; between 1902 and 1914 well over half a million immigrants arrived every year. Most of the latter came from southern and eastern Europe and settled in the cities.

Americans had always prided themselves on being a mixture of many races and nationalities and had viewed their country as a haven for the oppressed. As early as 1782, the naturalized New Yorker, Crèvecoeur, had written: "He is an American who leaving behind him all his ancient prejudices and manners, receives new ones from the new mode of life he has embraced. . . . Here individuals of all nations are melted into a new race of men. . . ." Despite the image of the melting pot, however, newly arrived immigrants were often greeted with suspicion. In the early nineteenth century, Irish and German immigrants faced resentment that occasionally boiled over into riots and violence. Antagonism toward newcomers increased as millions of eastern and southern European immigrants flocked to America during the late nineteenth and early twentieth centuries. Many Americans—including second-generation immigrants—began to question the concept of open immigration and called for restrictions.

The melting pot did not seem to be working. Contrary to expectations, the immigrants did not become Americanized overnight. Organizing their own communities and their own national societies, they held desperately to their old ways. The problems in the cities seemed to be the result of the arrival of millions of alien people who were unable and unwilling to adopt American ways. To make matters worse, in the eyes of native-born citizens, the newcomers provided the voting support for corrupt political machines in the cities or supported radical, un-American causes.

But immigrants continued to come, lured by the hope of a better life in the New World. Often they were bitterly disappointed, finding instead crowded tenements, poor jobs, and violence in the teeming streets; they lived days of struggle and nights of loneliness in an alien land. Yet, for many, America was the land of opportunity; or at least it was better than the old country. One German wrote home: "No one can give orders to anybody here, one is as good as another, no one takes off his hat to another as you have to do in Germany."

Most newcomers to America's growing cities were not foreigners, however, but native Americans who left their rural villages and farms to seek a new life and, they hoped, new opportunities in the cities. They, too, faced the problem of adjusting to new living and working conditions. Urban migrants, whatever their nationality, suffered the hardships associated with cities that had grown too fast to provide adequate housing, streets, sewers, police protection, and transportation. One group of native migrants, the blacks, suffered additionally from racism.

There can be no doubt that the great migration to American cities in the nineteenth and twentieth centuries produced tensions and conflicts that often erupted into bloody violence. For many historians, this is the proper emphasis to give to the experience. But other historians have argued that despite the conflict, the newcomers were usually integrated into American society. The cities, they argue, offered new opportunities; the bewildered newcomers of one year became the solid citizens of the next. Still other historians, even if they accept the view that the melting pot was effective, maintain that there is one conspicuous exception. Black Americans, they argue, were prevented from seizing the opportunities available to other migrants. While antagonism against foreigners and rural whites eventually faded, racism remained an all but insurmountable obstacle blocking the progress of the blacks.

In the following selections the reader is introduced to some of the ways in which the problems of urban migration have been evaluated. In the first selection, Oscar Handlin discusses the alienation of the immigrants both from their native land and from the new world that they had entered. "Uprooted" from their own culture, they found it difficult to sink roots in a new and alien culture. They were expected to assimilate, to give up all that they understood and held dear, and they were condemned when they could not do so. But their children, Handlin concludes, had less trouble; they were "natives."

Blacks were the most recent migrants to the urban areas, and they faced many of the same problems that foreigners faced when they arrived. But, as Allan H. Spear argues in the second selection, blacks faced special problems. His analysis of the creation of the black ghetto in Chicago leads him to conclude that the experience of the blacks was unique. Unlike other migrants, black Americans were prevented from assimilating into American urban society.

In the final selection, Richard C. Wade surveys urban violence in broad historical perspective, arguing that while violence has always characterized American urban life, its causes have over the years been largely mitigated. As a result, "the level of large-scale disorder and violence is less ominous today than it has been during much of the past." The one major exception to this generalization is the violence associated with racial antagonism. Denying that race conflict is mainly class conflict, Wade argues that racism created the ghetto, limited opportunities for the blacks, and left the nation with "a growingly alienated and embittered group" in its midst.

In judging the urban experience in America, should we emphasize the violence, the riots, the crime, and the corruption, or should we stress the cultural and economic achievements of our cities? Should we stress the urban melting pot, where many ethnically diverse people came together and found an opportunity to improve themselves, or should we emphasize the alienation, the pathos, and the conflict? Is discrimination against the blacks simply the result of their being the last group to enter the cities? Or is racism a special problem that other migrants never had to face?

Oscar Handlin

# *The Uprooted*

Letters bring the low voices across the sea. The unfamiliar pens grope for the proper words. When you ask somebody to write for you, you must go and treat him. Therefore you try yourself. In the store are printed forms. Sometimes they will do to transmit information. But you wish through this lifeless paper to do more than send news. With painful effort and at the sacrifice of precious time, you express the solidarity you still feel with those who stayed behind. The sheet is then the symbol of the ties that continue to bind.

Ceremonial salutations, *to my dearest* . . . to every him and her who filled the days of the old life and whom I will never see again. By this letter I kiss you. To the aged parents who bred and nurtured, who took trouble over, shed tears for me and now have none to comfort them; to the brother who shared my tasks and bed; to my comrades of the fields; to all the kin who joined in festivals; to the whole visible communion, the oneness, of the village that I have forfeited by emigration; to each I send my greetings. And with my greetings go wishes that you may have the sweet years of life, of health and happiness, alas elusive there and here.

They are wanderers to the wide world and often yearn toward the far direction whence they have come. Why even the birds who fly away from their native places still hasten to go back. Can ever a man feel really happy condemned to live away from where he was born? Though by leaving he has cut himself off and knows he never will return, yet he hopes, by reaching backward, still to belong in the homeland.

It is to that end that the husband and wife and older children gather to assist in the composition; it is to that end that they assemble to read the reply. Little enough occurs to them that is worth recording, certainly not the

From The Uprooted. *Second Edition Enlarged by Oscar Handlin. Copyright 1951, © 1973, 1979 by Oscar Handlin. By permission of Little, Brown and Company in association with the Atlantic Monthly Press.*

monotonous struggle of getting settled. Instead their lines go to reminiscence, to the freshening of memories, to the commemoration of anniversaries. Later, when the art spreads and photographs are available at low cost, these are exchanged with great frequency.

Other acts of solidarity also absorbed the attention of the immigrants. Vivid recollections of the suffering they had left behind spurred them on in the effort to set aside from their own inadequate earnings enough to aid the ones who had not come. By 1860 the Irish alone were sending back four or five million dollars a year; a half-century later, the total remitted by all groups was well over one hundred and forty million for a twelve-month period. Often, in addition, some unusual disaster evoked a special sympathetic response— the church burned down, or famine appeared, or war. Such contributions recognized the continued connectedness with the old place. In time, that was further strengthened by involvement in nationalistic movements which established a political interest in the affairs of the Old Country, an interest the peasants had not had while they were there.

As the passing years widened the distance, the land the immigrants had left acquired charm and beauty. Present problems blurred those they had left unsolved behind; and in the haze of memory it seemed to these people they had formerly been free of present dissatisfactions. It was as if the Old World became a great mirror into which they looked to see right all that was wrong with the New. The landscape was prettier, the neighbors more friendly, and religion more efficacious; in the frequent crises when they reached the limits of their capacities, the wistful reflection came: *This would not have happened there.*

The real contacts were, however, disappointing. The requests—that back there a mass be said, or a wise one consulted, or a religious medal be sent over—those were gestures full of hope. But the responses were inadequate; like all else they shrank in the crossing. The immigrants wrote, but the replies, when they came, were dull, even trite in their mechanical phrases, or so it seemed to those who somehow expected these messages to evoke the emotions that had gone into their own painfully composed letters. Too often the eagerly attended envelopes proved to be only empty husks, the inner contents valueless. After the long wait before the postman came, the sheets of garbled writing were inevitably below expectations. There was a trying sameness to the complaints of hard times, to the repetitious petty quarrels; and before long there was impatience with the directness with which the formal greeting led into the everlasting requests for aid.

This last was a sore point with the immigrants. The friends and relatives who had stayed behind could not get it out of their heads that in America the streets were paved with gold. *Send me for a coat . . . . There is a piece of land here and if only you would send, we could buy it . . . . Our daughter could be married, but we have not enough for a dowry . . . . We are ashamed, everyone else gets . . . much more frequently than we.* Implicit in these solicitations was the judgment that the going-away had been a desertion, that unfulfilled obligations still remained, and that the village could claim assistance as a right from its departed members.

From the United States it seemed there was no comprehension, back there, of the difficulties of settlement. It was exasperating by sacrifices to scrape together the remittances and to receive in return a catalogue of new needs, as if there were not needs enough in the New World too. The immigrants never shook off the sense of obligation to help; but they did come to regard their Old Countrymen as the kind of people who depended on help. The trouble with the Europeans was, they could not stand on their own feet.

The cousin green off the boat earned the same negative appraisal. Though he be a product of the homeland, yet here he cut a pitiable figure; awkward manners, rude clothes, and a thoroughgoing ineptitude in the new situation were his most prominent characteristics. The older settler found the welcome almost frozen on his lips in the face of such backwardness.

In every real contact the grandeur of the village faded; it did not match the immigrants' vision of it and it did not stand up in a comparison with America. When the picture came, the assembled family looked at it beneath the light. This was indeed the church, but it had not been remembered so; and the depressing contrast took some of the joy out of remembering.

The photograph did not lie. There it was, a low building set against the dusty road, weather-beaten and making a candid display of its ill-repair. But the recollections did not lie either. As if it had been yesterday that they passed through those doors, they could recall the sense of spaciousness and elevation that sight of the structure had always aroused.

Both impressions were true, but irreconcilable. The mental image and the paper representation did not jibe because the one had been formed out of the standards and values of the Old Country, while the other was viewed in the light of the standards and values of the New. And it was the same with every other retrospective contact. Eagerly the immigrants continued to look back across the Atlantic in search of the satisfactions of fellowship. But the search was not rewarded. Having become Americans, they were no longer villagers. Though they might willingly assume the former obligations and recognize the former responsibilities, they could not recapture the former points of view or hold to the former judgments. They had seen too much, experienced too much to be again members of the community. It was a vain mission on which they continued to dispatch the letters; these people, once separated, would never belong again.

Their home now was a country in which they had not been born. Their place in society they had established for themselves through the hardships of crossing and settlement. The process had changed them, had altered the most intimate aspects of their lives. Every effort to cling to inherited ways of acting and thinking had led into a subtle adjustment by which those ways were given a new American form. No longer Europeans, could the immigrants then say that they belonged in America? The answer depended upon the conceptions held by other citizens of the United States of the character of the nation and of the role of the newcomers within it.

In the early nineteenth century, those already established on this side of the ocean regarded immigration as a positive good. When travel by sea became safe after the general peace of 1815 and the first fresh arrivals trickled in, there was a general disposition to welcome the movement. The favorable attitude persisted even when the tide mounted to the flood levels of the 1840's and 1850's. The man off the boat was then accepted without question or condition.

The approval of unlimited additions to the original population came easily to Americans who were conscious of the youth of their country. Standing at the edge of an immense continent, they were moved by the challenge of empty land almost endless in its extension. Here was room enough, and more, for all who would bend their energies to its exploitation. The shortage was of labor and not of acres; every pair of extra hands increased the value of the abundant resources and widened opportunities for everyone.

The youth of the nation also justified the indiscriminate admission of whatever foreigners came to these shores. There was high faith in the destiny of the Republic, assurance that its future history would justify the Revolution and the separation from Great Britain. The society and the culture that would emerge in this territory would surpass those of the Old World because they would not slavishly imitate the outmoded forms and the anachronistic traditions that constricted men in Europe. The United States would move in new directions of its own because its people were a new people.

There was consequently a vigorous insistence that this country was not simply an English colony become independent. It was a nation unique in its origins, produced by the mixture of many different types out of which had come an altogether fresh amalgam, the American. The ebullient citizens who believed and argued that their language, their literature, their art, and their polity were distinctive and original also believed and argued that their population had not been derived from a single source but had rather acquired its peculiar characteristics from the blending of a variety of strains.

There was confidence that the process would continue. The national type had not been fixed by its given antecedents; it was emerging from the experience of life on a new continent. Since the quality of men was determined not by the conditions surrounding their birth, but by the environment within which they passed their lives, it was pointless to select among them. All would come with minds and spirits fresh for new impressions; and being in America would make Americans of them. Therefore it was best to admit freely everyone who wished to make a home here. The United States would then be a great smelting pot, great enough so that there was room for all who voluntarily entered; and the nation that would ultimately be cast from that crucible would be all the richer for the diversity of the elements that went into the molten mixture.

The legislation of most of the nineteenth century reflected this receptive attitude. The United States made no effort actively to induce anyone to immigrate, but neither did it put any bars in the way of their coming. Occasional laws in the four decades after 1819 set up shipping regulations in the hope of improving the conditions of the passage. In practice, the provisions that specified the minimum quantities of food and the maximum number of passengers each vessel could carry were easily evaded. Yet the intent of those statutes was to protect the travelers and to remove harsh conditions that might discourage the newcomers.

Nor were state laws any more restrictive in design. The seaports, troubled by the burdens of poor relief, secured the enactment of measures to safeguard their treasuries against such charges. Sometimes the form was a bond to guarantee that the immigrant would not become at once dependent upon public support; sometimes it was a small tax applied to defray the costs of charity. In either case there was no desire to limit entry into the country; and none of these steps had any discernible effect upon the volume of admissions.

Once landed, the newcomer found himself equal in condition to the natives. Within a short period he could be naturalized and acquire all the privileges of a citizen. In some places, indeed, he could vote before the oath in court so transformed his status. In the eyes of society, even earlier than in the eyes of the law, he was an American.

It was not necessary that the immigrants should read deeply in the writings of political and social theorists to understand this conception of America. The idea was fully and clearly expressed in practice. The sense of being welcome gave people who had elsewhere been counted superfluous the assurance that their struggles to build a new life would be regarded with sympathy by their new neighbors. On such a foundation they could proceed to settle down in their own ways, make their own adjustments to the new conditions.

Significantly, the newcomers were not compelled to conform to existing patterns of action or to accept existing standards. They felt free to criticize many aspects of the life they discovered in the New World, the excessive concern with material goods and the inadequate attention to religion, the pushiness and restlessness of the people, the transitory quality of family relationships. The boldness of such judgments testified to the voluntary nature of immigrant adjustment. The strangers did not swallow America in one gulp; through their own associations and their own exertions they discovered how to live in the new place and still be themselves.

Until the 1880's the diverse groups in the United States got in each other's way only on very unusual occasions; generally rapid expansion made room for the unrestrained activity of all. Indeed the newcomers themselves did not then become issues; nor was there then any inclination to question the desirability of continuing the traditional open policy. But the second generation was an unstable element in the situation; as it grew in prominence, it created troublesome problems precisely because it had not a fixed place in the society. Standing between the culture of its parents and the culture of the older America, it bared the inadequacies of the assumption that the fusion of the multitude of strains in the melting pot would come about as a matter of course. The moments of revelation, though still rare, were profoundly shocking.

The discovery came most commonly in matters related to employment. However the native wage earner may have judged the effects of the immigrants upon the economy in general, he knew that these people did not directly compete with him for his job. But the children of the immigrants were Americans who were not content with the places that went to foreigners. On the labor market the offspring of the newcomers jostled the sons of well-established families. There was still no lack of space in a productive system that grew at an ever-accelerating pace. But the ambitious youngster every now and then hit upon the advertisement, No Irish need apply! The hurt would affect him, but also his father. It would disclose to these immigrants, and to many who came later, the limits of their belonging to America.

In politics also there were occasions on which the activities of the new citizens met the hostility of the old. If the consequences then were more striking, it was because there was less room for competition in the contest for political control. There were times when groups of men, unable to attain their own ends through government and unable to understand their own failure, sought to settle the blame on the foreign-born in their midst. In the 1850's, for instance, agitation of the slavery question and of a host of reform proposals put an intolerable strain upon the existing party structure. Years of compromise had produced no durable solution; instead they had given rise to grave forebodings of the calamitous Civil War that impended.

At the point of crisis, the stranger who stood in the way of attainment of some particular objective became the butt of attack. Abolitionists and reformers who found the conservative Irish arrayed against them at the polls, proslavery politicians who made much of the radicalism of some of the German leaders, and temperance advocates who regarded an alien hankering after alcohol as the main obstruction on the way to universal abstinence—such people were the backbone of the Know-Nothing Party that leaped to sudden prominence in the election of 1854. The oddly assorted elements that entered this political coalition had little in common; it took them only two years to come to know each other better, and once they did the party fell apart. Nothing positive had drawn such men together; they were attracted to each other rather by the fears that troubled them all. Incapable for the moment of confronting the real divisions within their society, many Americans achieved a temporary unity by cohering against the outsider in their midst.

The Know-Nothing movement disappeared as rapidly as it had appeared. In that respect it traced a course later followed by similar movements that flashed across the political horizon—the A.P.A. of the 1890's and the anti-German agitation of the First World War. These brief lapses in relationships that were generally peaceful had no enduring effects upon legislation or upon the attitudes of the mass of the native-born.

But even very brief glimpses of the hatred that might be generated against them disturbed the immigrants. The memory of charges violently made lingered long after the charges themselves were no longer a threat. They left behind a persistent uneasiness. The foreign-born could not forget that their rights as citizens had once been challenged. Could they help but wonder how fully they belonged in the United States? Occasional street fights among the boys that pitted group against group, from time to time more serious riots in which the unruly elements in the town attacked the aliens, and the more frequent slurs from press and platform kept alive that doubt.

Yet until the 1880's confidence outweighed the doubt. So long as those native to the country retained the faith that America would continue to grow from the addition of variety to its culture, the newcomers retained the hope, despite the difficulties of settlement and the discouragement of sporadic acts of hostility, that there would be here a home for the homeless of Europe.

As the nineteenth century moved into its last quarter, a note of petulance crept into the comments of some Americans who thought about this aspect of the development of their culture. It was a long time now that the melting pot had been simmering, but the end product seemed no closer than before. The experience of life in the United States had not broken down the separateness of the elements mixed into it; each seemed to retain its own identity. Almost a half-century after the great immigration of Irish and Germans, these people had not become indistinguishable from other Americans; they were still recognizably Irish and German. Yet even then, newer waves of newcomers were beating against the Atlantic shore. Was there any prospect that all these multitudes would ever be assimilated, would ever be Americanized?

A generation earlier such questions would not have been asked. Americans of the first half of the century had assumed that any man who subjected himself to the American environment was being Americanized. Since the New World was ultimately to be occupied by a New Man, no mere derivative of any extant stock, but different from and superior to all, there had been no fixed standards of national character against which to measure the behavior of newcomers. The nationality of the new Republic had been supposed fluid, only just evolving; there had been room for infinite variation because diversity rather than uniformity had been normal.

The expression of doubts that some parts of the population might not become fully American implied the existence of a settled criterion of what was

American. There had been a time when the society had recognized no distinction among citizens but that between the native and the foreign-born, and that distinction had carried no imputation of superiority or inferiority. Now there were attempts to distinguish among the natives between those who really belonged and those who did not, to separate out those who were born in the United States but whose immigrant parentage cut them off from the truly indigenous folk.

It was difficult to draw the line, however. The census differentiated after 1880 between natives and native-born of foreign parents. But that was an inadequate line of division; it provided no means of social recognition and offered no basis on which the true Americans could draw together, identify themselves as such.

Through these years there was a half-conscious quest among some Americans for a term that would describe those whose ancestors were in the United States before the great migrations. Where the New Englanders were, they called themselves Yankees, a word that often came to mean non-Irish or non-Canadian. But Yankee was simply a local designation and did not take in the whole of the old stock. In any case, there was no satisfaction to such a title. Its holders were one group among many, without any distinctive claim to Americanism, cut off from other desirable peoples prominent in the country's past. Only the discovery of common antecedents could eliminate the separations among the really American.

But to find a common denominator, it was necessary to go back a long way. Actually no single discovery was completely satisfactory. Some writers, in time, referred to the civilization of the United States as Anglo-Saxon. By projecting its origins back to early Britain, they implied that their own culture was always English in derivation, and made foreigners of the descendants of Irishmen and Germans, to say nothing of the later arrivals. Other men preferred a variant and achieved the same exclusion by referring to themselves as "the English-speaking people," a title which assumed there was a unity and uniqueness to the clan which settled the home island, the Dominions, and the United States. Still others relied upon a somewhat broader appellation. They talked of themselves as Teutonic and argued that what was distinctively American originated in the forests of Germany; in this view, only the folk whose ancestors had experienced the freedom of tribal self-government and the liberation of the Protestant Reformation were fully American.

These terms had absolutely no historical justification. They nevertheless achieved a wide currency in the thinking of the last decades of the nineteenth century. Whatever particular phrase might serve the purpose of a particular author or speaker, all expressed the conviction that some hereditary element had given form to American culture. The conclusion was inescapable: to be Americanized, the immigrants must conform to the American way of life completely defined in advance of their landing.

There were two counts to the indictment that the immigrants were not so conforming. They were, first, accused of their poverty. Many benevolent citizens, distressed by the miserable conditions in the districts inhabited by the laboring people, were reluctant to believe that such social flaws were indigenous to the New World. It was tempting, rather, to ascribe them to the defects of the newcomers, to improvidence, slovenliness, and ignorance rather than to inability to earn a living wage.

Indeed to those whose homes were uptown the ghettos were altogether alien territory associated with filth and vice and crime. It did not seem possible that men could lead a decent existence in such quarters. The good vicar on a philanthropic tour was shocked by the moral dangers of the dark unlighted hallway. His mind rushed to the defense of the respectable young girl: *Whatever her wishes may be, she can do nothing—shame prevents her from crying out.* The intention of the reformer was to improve housing, but the summation nevertheless was, *You cannot make an American citizen out of a slum.*

The newcomers were also accused of congregating together in their own groups and of an unwillingness to mix with outsiders. The foreign-born flocked to the great cities and stubbornly refused to spread out as farmers over the countryside; that alone was offensive to a society which still retained an ideal of rusticity. But even the Germans in Wisconsin and the Scandinavians in Minnesota held aloofly to themselves. Everywhere, the strangers persisted in their strangeness and willfully stood apart from American life. A prominent educator sounded the warning: *Our task is to break up their settlements, to assimilate and amalgamate these people and to implant in them the Anglo-Saxon conception of righteousness, law, and order.*

It was no simple matter to meet this challenge. The older residents were quick to criticize the separateness of the immigrant but hesitant when he made a move to narrow the distance. The householders of Fifth Avenue or Beacon Street or Nob Hill could readily perceive the evils of the slums but they were not inclined to welcome as a neighbor the former denizen of the East Side or the North End or the Latin Quarter who had acquired the means to get away. Among Protestants there was much concern over the growth of Catholic, Jewish, and Orthodox religious organizations, but there was no eagerness at all to provoke a mass conversion that might crowd the earlier churches with a host of poor foreigners. When the population of its neighborhood changed, the parish was less likely to try to attract the newcomers than to close or sell its building and move to some other section.

Indeed there was a fundamental ambiguity to the thinking of those who talked about "assimilation" in these years. They had arrived at their own view that American culture was fixed, formed from its origins, by shutting out the great mass of immigrants who were not English or at least not Teutonic. Now it was expected that those excluded people would alter themselves to earn their portion in Americanism. That process could only come about by increasing the contacts between the older and the newer inhabitants, by sharing jobs, churches, residences. Yet in practice, the man who thought himself an Anglo-Saxon found proximity to the other folk just come to the United States uncomfortable and distasteful and, in his own life, sought to increase rather than to lessen the gap between his position and theirs.

There was an escape from the horns of this unpleasant dilemma. It was tempting to resolve the difficulty by arguing that the differences between Americans on the one hand and Italians or Jews or Poles on the other were so deep as to admit of no conciliation. If these other stocks were cut off by their own innate nature, by the qualities of their heredity, then the original breed was justified both in asserting the fixity of its own character and in holding off from contact with the aliens.

Those who wished to support that position drew upon a sizable fund of racialist ideas that seeped deep into the thinking of many Americans toward the end of the nineteenth century. From a variety of sources there had been accumulated a body of doctrine that proclaimed the division of humanity into distinct, biologically separate races.

In the bitter years of controversy that were the prelude to the Civil War, there were Southerners who had felt the urgency of a similar justification. The abolitionists had raised the issue of the moral rightness of slavery, had pronounced it sinful to hold a fellow man in bondage. Sensitive to the criticism but bound in practice to his property, the plantation owner was attracted by the notion that the blacks were not his fellow men. Perhaps, as George Fitzhugh told him, the Negroes were not really human at all, but another order of beings, condemned by their natures to a servile status.

During the tragic reconstruction that followed the peace the argument acquired additional gravity. The formal, legal marks of subordination were gone; it was the more important to hold the colored people in submission by other means. Furthermore the section was now under the control of a national authority, dominated by Northern men; the vanquished faced the task of convincing the victors of the essential propriety of the losing cause.

For years after the end of the war, Southerners directed a stream of discussion across the Mason-Dixon line. Through their writing and talking ran an unvarying theme—the Negro was inherently inferior, did not need or deserve, could not use or be trusted with, the rights of humans. It did not matter how many auditors or readers were persuaded; the very agitation of the question familiarized Americans with the conception of race.

Eastward from the Pacific Coast came a similar gospel, also the product of local exigencies. Out of the dislocating effects of depression in 1873 and of the petering-out of the mining economy, there had developed in California a violently anti-Chinese movement. Those who regarded the Oriental as the source of all the state's difficulties were not content with what discriminatory measures the legislature could enact. They wished no less than the total exclusion of the Chinese.

Satisfaction of that demand could come only from the Federal Congress; and to get Congress to act, it was necessary to persuade representatives from every section of the reality of the menace. The attack upon the little brown rice-eaters, congenitally filthy and immoral, had the same consequences as the Southern charges against the Negro; it made current the notion of ineradicable race differences.

A third problem brought the prestige of many influential names to the support of the idea. The War with Spain had given the United States substantial new overseas possessions, government of which posed troublesome problems. In the traditional pattern of American expansion, additional lands were treated as territories, held in a transitional stage until the time when they would become states. But their residents were citizens, endowed with all the rights of residents of the older part of the Union.

Substantial bodies of opinion opposed the extension of such treatment to the newly acquired islands. The proponents of navalism and of an aggressive imperialism, businessmen interested in the possibilities of profitable investments, and Protestant clergymen attracted by the possibility of converting large numbers of Catholics and heathen preferred to have the conquered areas colonies rather than territories, preferred to have the inhabitants subjects rather than citizens protected by the Constitution. To persuade the nation that such a departure from past policy was appropriate, the imperialists argued that the conquered peoples were incapable of self-government; their own racial inferiority justified a position of permanent subordination.

By 1900, the debates over the Negro, the Chinese, and the Filipino had familiarized Americans with the conception of permanent biological differences among humans. References to the "realities of race" by then had taken on a commonplace, almost casual quality. Early that year, for instance, a distinguished senator, well known for his progressive temperament and scholarly attainments, spoke exultantly of the opportunities in the Philippines and in China's limitless markets. *We will not renounce our part in the mission of our race, trustee of the civilization of the world. God has not been preparing the English-Speaking and Teutonic People for one thousand years for nothing. He has made us the master organizers to establish system where chaos reigns. He has marked the American People as the chosen nation to finally lead in the regeneration of the world.*

These ideas were unsystematic; as yet they were only the unconnected defenses of specific positions. But there were not lacking men to give these rude conceptions a formal structure, to work them up into a scientific creed.

Sociology toward the end of the century, in the United States, was only just emerging as a discipline of independent stature. The certitude with which its practitioners delivered their generalizations covered its fundamental immaturity of outlook. The American social scientists approached their subject through the analysis of specific disorders: criminality, intemperance, poverty, and disease. Everywhere they looked they found immigrants somehow involved in these problems. In explaining such faults in the social order, the scholar had a choice of alternatives: these were the pathological manifestations of some blemish, either in the nature of the newcomers or in the nature of the whole society. It was tempting to accept the explanation that put the blame on the outsiders.

From the writings of the Europeans Gobineau, Drumont, and Chamberlain, the sociologists had accepted the dictum that social characteristics depended upon racial differences. A succession of books now demonstrated that flaws in the biological constitution of various groups of immigrants were responsible for every evil that beset the country—for pauperism, for the low birth rate of natives, for economic depressions, for class divisions, for prostitution and homosexuality, and for the appearance of city slums.

Furthermore, the social scientists of this period were not content with academic analysis. They were convinced their conclusions must be capable of practical application and often became involved in the reform movements which, by planning, hoped to set right the evils of the times. The sociologist eager to ameliorate the lot of his fellow men by altering the conditions of their lives found the newcomers intractable, slow to change, obstacles in the road to progress. Since few among these thinkers were disposed to accept the possibility they might themselves be in error, they could only conclude the foreigners were incapable of improvement. From opposite ends of the country, two college presidents united in the judgment that the immigrants were *beaten men from beaten races, biologically incapable of rising, either now or through their descendants, above the mentality of a twelve-year-old child.*

The only apparent solution was in eugenics, the control of the composition of the population through selection of proper stocks based on proper heredity. A famous social scientist expressed it as his considered opinion that *race differences are established in the very blood. Races may change their religions, their form of government, and their languages, but underneath they may continue the PHYSICAL, MENTAL, and MORAL CAPACITIES and INCAPACITIES which determine the REAL CHARACTER of their RELIGION, GOVERNMENT, and LITERATURE.* Surface conformity would only conceal the insidious subtle characteristics that divided the native from the foreign-born.

The fear of everything alien instilled by the First World War brought to fullest flower the seeds of racist thinking. Three enormously popular books by an anthropologist, a eugenicist, and a historian revealed to hundreds of thousands of horrified Nordics how their great race had been contaminated by contact with lesser breeds, dwarfed in stature, twisted in mentality, and ruthless in the pursuit of their own self-interest.

These ideas passed commonly in the language of the time. No doubt many Americans who spoke in the bitter terms of race used the words in a figurative sense or in some other way qualified their acceptance of the harsh doctrine. After all, they still recognized the validity of the American tradition of equal and open opportunities, of the Christian tradition of the brotherhood of man. Yet, if they were sometimes troubled by the contradiction, nevertheless enough of them believed fully the racist conceptions so that five million could become members of the Ku Klux Klan in the early 1920's.

Well, a man who was sixty then had seen much that was new in his lifetime; and though he had not moved from the town of his birth, still his whole world had wandered away and left him, in a sense, a stranger in his native place. He too knew the pain of unfamiliarity, the moments of contrast between what was and what had been. Often he turned the corner of some critical event and confronted the effects of an industrial economy, of an urban society, of unsettled institutions, and of disorderly personal relationships. And, as he fought the fear of the unknown future, he too yearned for the security of belonging, for the assurance that change had not singled out him alone but had come to the whole community as a meaningful progression out of the past.

It was fretfully hard, through the instability of things, to recognize the signs of kinship. In anxious dread of isolation the people scanned each other in the vain quest for some portentous mark that would tell them who belonged together. Frustrated, some created a sense of community, drew an inner group around themselves by setting the others aside as outsiders. The excluded became the evidence of the insiders' belonging. It was not only, or not so much, because they hated the Catholic or Jew that the silent men marched in hoods, but because by distinguishing themselves from the foreigner they could at last discover their common identity; feel themselves part of a meaningful body.

The activities of the Klan were an immediate threat to the immigrants and were resisted as such. But there was also a wider import to the movement. This was evidence, at last become visible, that the newcomers were among the excluded. The judgment at which the proponents of assimilation had only hinted, about which the racist thinkers had written obliquely, the Klan brought to the open. The hurt came from the fact that the mouthings of the Kleagle were not eccentricities, but only extreme statements of beliefs long on the margin of acceptance by many Americans. To the foreign-born this was demonstration of what they already suspected, that they would remain as alienated from the New World as they had become from the Old.

Much earlier the pressure of their separateness had begun to disturb the immigrants. As soon as the conception of Americanization had acquired the connotation of conformity with existing patterns, the whole way of group life of the newcomers was questioned. Their adjustment had depended upon their ability as individuals in a free society to adapt themselves to their environment through what forms they chose. The demand by their critics that the adjustment take a predetermined course seemed to question their right, as they were, to a place in American society.

Not that these people concerned themselves with theories of nationalism, but in practice the hostility of the "natives" provoked unsettling doubts about the propriety of the most innocent actions. The peasant who had become a Polish Falcon or a Son of Italy, in his own view, was acting as an American; this was not a step he could have taken at home. To subscribe to a newspaper was the act of a citizen of the New World, not of the Old, even if the journal was one of the thousand published by 1920 in languages other than English. When the immigrants heard their societies and their press described as un-American they could only conclude that they had somehow become involved in an existence that belonged neither in the old land nor in the new.

Yet the road of conformity was also barred to them. There were matters in which they wished to be like others, undistinguished from anyone else, but they never hit upon the means of becoming so. There was no pride in the surname, which in Europe had been little used, and many a new arrival was willing enough to make a change, suitable to the new country. But August Björkegren was not much better off when he called himself Burke, nor [was] the Blumberg who became Kelly. The Lithuanians and Slovenes who moved into the Pennsylvania mining fields often endowed themselves with nomenclature of the older settlers, of the Irish and Italians there before them. In truth, these people found it difficult to know what were the "American" forms they were expected to take on.

What they did know was that they had not succeeded, that they had not established themselves to the extent that they could expect to be treated as if they belonged where they were.

If he was an alien, and poor, and in many ways helpless, still he was human, and it rankled when his dignity as a person was disregarded. He felt an undertone of acrimony in every contact with an official. Men in uniform always found him unworthy of respect; the bullying police made capital of his fear of the law; the postmen made sport of the foreign writing on his letters; the streetcar conductors laughed at his groping requests for directions. Always he was patronized as an object of charity, or almost so.

His particular enemies were the officials charged with his special oversight. When misfortune drove him to seek assistance or when government regulations brought them to inspect his home, he encountered the social workers, made ruthless in the disregard of his sentiments by the certainty of their own benevolent intentions. Confident of their personal and social superiority and armed with the ideology of the sociologists who had trained them, the emissaries of the public and private agencies were bent on improving the immigrant to a point at which he would no longer recognize himself.

The man who had dealings with the social workers was often sullen and uncooperative; he disliked the necessity of becoming a case, of revealing his dependence to strangers. He was also suspicious, feared there would be no understanding of his own way of life or of his problems; and he was resentful, because the powerful outsiders were judging him by superficial standards of their own. The starched young gentleman from the settlement house took stock from the middle of the kitchen. Were there framed pictures on the walls? Was there a piano, books? He made a note for the report: *This family is not yet Americanized; they are still eating Italian food.*

The services are valuable, but taking them is degrading. It is a fine thing to learn the language of the country; but one must be treated as a child to do so. *We keep saying all the time, This is a desk, this is a door. I know it is a desk and a door. What for keep saying it all the time? My teacher is a very nice young lady, very young. She does not understand what I want to talk about or know about.*

The most anguished conflicts come from the refusal of the immigrants to see the logic of their poverty. In the office it seems reasonable enough: people incapable of supporting themselves would be better off with someone to take care of them. It is more efficient to institutionalize the destitute than to allow them, with the aid of charity, to mismanage their homes. But the ignorant poor insist on clinging to their families, threaten suicide at the mention of the Society's refuge, or even of the hospital. What help the woman gets, she is still not satisfied. Back comes the ungrateful letter. *I don't ask you to put me in a poorhouse where I have to cry for my children. I don't ask you to put them in a home and eat somebody else's bread. I can't live here without them. I am so sick for them. I could live at home and spare good eats for them. What good did you give me to send me to the poorhouse? You only want people to live like you but I will not listen to you no more.*

A few dedicated social workers, mostly women, learned to understand the values in the immigrants' own lives. In some states, as the second generation became prominent in politics, government agencies came to co-operate with and protect the newcomers. But these were rare exceptions. They scarcely softened the rule experience everywhere taught the foreign-born, that they were expected to do what they could not do—to live like others.

For the children it was not so difficult. They at least were natives and could learn how to conform; to them the settlement house was not always a threat, but sometimes an opportunity. Indeed they could adopt entire[ly] the assumption that national character was long since fixed, only seek for their own group a special place within it. Some justified their Americanism by discovery of a colonial past; within the educated second generation there began a tortuous quest for eighteenth-century antecedents that might give them a portion in American civilization in its narrower connotation. Others sought to gain a sense of participation by separating themselves from later or lower elements in the population; they became involved in agitation against the Orientals, the Negroes, and the newest immigrants, as if thus to draw closer to the truly native. Either course implied a rejection of their parents who had themselves once been green off the boat and could boast of no New World antecedents.

The old folk knew then they would not come to belong, not through their own experience nor through their offspring. The only adjustment they had been able to make to life in the United States had been one that involved the separateness of their group, one that increased their awareness of the differences between themselves and the rest of the society. In that adjustment they had always suffered from the consciousness they were strangers. The demand that they assimilate, that they surrender their separateness, condemned them always to be outsiders. In practice, the free structure of American life permitted them with few restraints to go their own way, but under the shadow of a consciousness that they would never belong. They had thus completed their alienation from the culture to which they had come, as from that which they had left.

*Allan H. Spear*

# The Making of a Negro Ghetto

The problems of class conflict, industrial strife, and corrupt politics that confronted Chicago's reformers at the turn of the century were complicated by the city's great ethnic diversity. Since the Civil War, the emerging metropolis had attracted peoples from every part of the world. By 1890, 77.9 percent of its population was foreign born or of foreign parentage. The Germans, Irish, and Scandinavians were still the largest ethnic groups in the city, but after 1880, increasing numbers of Poles, Lithuanians, Czechs, Italians, and Eastern European Jews entered the city, concentrating in Chicago's perennial area of first settlement—the near West Side. There, cultural alienation complicated the problems of poverty. Facing the baffling complexities of urban life and an alien culture, these new groups strove against difficult odds to maintain their own ethnic integrity. Although various immigrant groups met the problems of American life in diverse ways, all attempted, through the creation of community institutions or the preservation of a traditional family structure, to maintain enough of their heritage to provide identity and a sense of belonging.

There were, then, many Chicagos by the end of the century. The reformers faced not merely the problem of an exploited working class, but of numerous worker enclaves, each clinging proudly to its own traditions. The newcomers' ignorance of American economic and political life made them particularly susceptible to the blandishments of unscrupulous employers and political bosses. A few of the reformers, such as Jane Addams and Graham Taylor, attempted to bring the immigrants into the mainstream of the city's life while at the same time respecting and even encouraging their cultural

Reprinted from Black Chicago: The Making of a Negro Ghetto, 1890–1920 by Allan H. Spear, pp. 4–8, 11–27, 29–35, 48–49, 228–229. By permission of The University of Chicago Press. Copyright 1967 by The University of Chicago.

diversity. But many old-stock Chicagoans—and this included many of the sons and daughters of the earlier immigrants—were hostile, or at best patronizing, toward the ways of the newcomers.

Of Chicago's many ethnic groups, none had a longer local history than the Negroes. According to tradition, the first permanent settler on the site of Chicago was a black trader from Santo Domingo, Jean Baptiste Pointe de Saible, who built a cabin on the mouth of the Chicago River in about 1790. The beginning of Negro community life in the city can be traced to the late 1840's, when a small stream of fugitive slaves from the South and free Negroes from the East formed the core of a small Negro settlement. Soon there were enough Negroes in Chicago to organize an African Methodist Episcopal church, and within a decade several more churches and a number of social and civic clubs were flourishing. By 1860, almost a thousand Negroes lived in Chicago. A small leadership group, headed by a well-to-do tailor, John Jones, participated in antislavery activities and articulated the grievances of a people who already found themselves the victims of segregation and discrimination.

Despite the presence of an active antislavery movement, Negroes in antebellum Chicago were severely circumscribed. Residents of downstate Illinois frequently characterized Chicago as a "sinkhole of abolition" and a "nigger-loving town"; yet the sympathy that many white Chicagoans expressed for the Southern slaves was not often extended to the local Negroes. To be sure, the antislavery press, on occasion, noted approvingly the orderliness and respectability of the city's Negro community, but little was done to improve the status of the group. Chicago's Negroes could not vote, nor could they testify in court against whites. State law forbade intermarriage between the races. Segregation was maintained in the schools, places of public accommodation, and transportation. Chicago's abolitionists regarded these conditions as side issues and manifested little interest in them.

Between 1870 and 1890, the Chicago Negro community grew from less than four thousand to almost fifteen thousand and developed a well delineated class structure and numerous religious and secular organizations. After the fire of 1871, the community became more concentrated geographically. Most Negroes lived on the South Side, but were still well interspersed with whites. Although a majority of the city's Negroes worked as domestic and personal servants, a small business and professional class provided community leadership. St. Clair Drake and Horace Cayton described the Chicago Negro community of this period as

*a small, compact, but rapidly growing community divided into three broad social groups. The "respectables"—churchgoing, poor or moderately prosperous, and often unrestrained in their worship—were looked down upon somewhat by the "refined" people, who, because of their education and breeding, could not sanction the less decorous behavior of their racial brothers. Both of these groups were censorious of the "riffraff," the "sinners"—unchurched and undisciplined.*

During the postwar years, the formal pattern of segregation that had characterized race relations in antebellum Chicago broke down. By 1870, Negroes could vote. In 1874, the school system was desegregated. A decade later, after the federal civil rights bill was nullified by the United States Supreme Court, the Illinois legislature enacted a law prohibiting discrimination in public places. Despite these advances, however, the status of Negroes in Chicago remained ambiguous. They continued to face discrimination in housing, employment, and, even in the face of the civil rights law, public accommodations. But they were not confined to a ghetto. Most Negroes, although concentrated in certain sections of the city, lived in mixed neighborhoods. Negro businessmen and professional men frequently catered to a white market and enjoyed social, as well as economic, contacts with the white community. And although Negro churches and social clubs proliferated, there were still few separate civic institutions. Local Negro leaders were firmly committed to the ideal of an integrated community in which hospitals, social agencies, and public accommodations would be open to all without discrimination.

From the beginning, the experience of Chicago's Negroes had been, in significant ways, separate from the mainstream of the city's history. No other ethnic group had been legally circumscribed; no white minority had been forced to fight for legal recognition of citizenship rights. In 1890, despite the improvement in the Negroes' status since 1865, many of their problems were still unique. In a chiefly industrial city, they worked principally in domestic and service trades, almost untouched by labor organization and industrial strife. The political and economic turmoil of the late nineteenth century seemed to have little effect on the city's Negroes. No Jane Addams or Graham Taylor sought to bring them within the reform coalition that was attempting to change the life of the city. Generally ignored by white Chicagoans, Negroes were viewed neither as a threat to the city's well-being nor as an integral part of the city's social structure. Most responsible whites probably held the view quoted by Ray Stannard Baker: "We have helped the Negro to liberty; we have helped to educate him to stand on his own feet. Now let's see what he can do for himself. After all, he must survive or perish by his own efforts."

Still, the story of Chicago's Negroes in the late nineteenth and early twentieth centuries is interwoven with the general history of the city. As their numbers increased between 1890 and 1910, Negroes became ever more conspicuous, and the indifference with which they had been regarded in the nineteenth century changed to hostility. Labor strife, ethnic tension, political corruption, and inefficiency—the problems of greatest concern to white Chicagoans—all helped determine the status of the city's Negroes. So too did the rise of racist doctrines that many old-stock Chicagoans applied indiscriminately to Negroes and the "new" immigrants. The virulently anti-Negro works of Thomas Dixon, the Chautauqua addresses of South Carolina's Senator Benjamin Tillman, as well as the anti-immigrant propaganda of Prescott Hall,

Henry Pratt Fairchild, and Madison Grant epitomized an age of race chauvinism in which Anglo-Americans strove to preserve a mythical racial purity.

The profound changes that took place in the Chicago Negro community between the 1890's and 1920 had both internal and external dimensions. On the one hand, they were the result of the mounting hostility of white Chicagoans. Whites grew anxious as a growing Negro population sought more and better housing; they feared job competition in an era of industrial strife when employers frequently used Negroes as strikebreakers; and they viewed Negro voters as pawns of a corrupt political machine. All of these fears were accentuated by the rise of a racist ideology that reinforced traditional anti-Negro prejudices. On the other hand, Negroes were not passive objects in the developments of the early twentieth century. Their response to discrimination and segregation, the decisions their leaders made, and the community activities in which they engaged all helped to shape the emerging Negro ghetto. The rise of Chicago's black ghetto belongs to both urban history and Negro history; it was the result of the interplay between certain trends in the development of the city and major currents in Negro life and thought.

\*       \*       \*

Between 1890 and 1915, the Negro population of Chicago grew from less than fifteen thousand to over fifty thousand. Although this growth was overshadowed by the massive influx of Negroes during and after World War I, this was nevertheless a significant increase. By the eve of World War I, although Negroes were still a minor element in the city's population, they were far more conspicuous than they had been a generation earlier. The population increase was accompanied by the concentration of Negroes into ever more constricted sections of the city. In the late nineteenth century, while most Negroes lived in certain sections of the South Side, they lived interspersed among whites; there were few all-Negro blocks. By 1915, on the other hand, the physical ghetto had taken shape; a large, almost all-Negro enclave on the South Side, with a similar offshoot on the West Side, housed most of Chicago's Negroes.

Migration was the major factor in the growth of the Negro community, and most migrants were coming from outside of the state. Over 80 percent of Chicago's Negro population in 1900 was born in states other than Illinois. The largest portion of these migrants originated in the border states and in the Upper South: Kentucky, and Missouri, in particular, had sent large groups of Negroes to Chicago. The states of the Deep South were, as yet, a secondary source of Chicago's Negro population; only 17 percent had come from these states as opposed to 43 percent from the Upper South. The states located directly south of Chicago supplied a larger segment of the population than the southeastern states, but there were sizable groups born in Virginia and Georgia.

From the beginning of Chicago's history, most Negroes had lived on the South Side. As early as 1850, 82 percent of the Negro population lived in an area bounded by the Chicago River on the north, Sixteenth Street on the south, the South Branch of the river on the west, and Lake Michigan on the east. The famous South Side black belt was emerging—a narrow finger of land, wedged between the railroad yards and industrial plants just west of Wentworth Avenue and the fashionable homes east of Wabash Avenue. By 1900, the black belt stretched from the downtown business district as far south as Thirty-ninth Street. But there were also sizable Negro enclaves, usually of a few square blocks each, in several other sections of the city. The Thirteenth Ward Negro community stretched along West Lake Street from

### TABLE I   NEGRO POPULATION OF CHICAGO 1850–1930

| | | | | Percent Increase | |
| Date | Total Population | Negro Population | Percent Negro | Total Population | Negro Population |
| --- | --- | --- | --- | --- | --- |
| 1850 | 29,963 | 323 | 1.1 | . . . | . . . |
| 1860 | 109,260 | 955 | 0.9 | 265 | 196 |
| 1870 | 293,977 | 3,691 | 1.2 | 174 | 286 |
| 1880 | 503,185 | 6,480 | 1.1 | 68 | 75 |
| 1890 | 1,099,850 | 14,271 | 1.3 | 119 | 120 |
| 1900 | 1,698,575 | 30,150 | 1.9 | 54 | 111 |
| 1910 | 2,185,283 | 44,103 | 2.0 | 29 | 46 |
| 1920 | 2,701,705 | 109,453 | 4.1 | 24 | 148 |
| 1930 | 3,376,438 | 233,903 | 6.9 | 25 | 114 |

SOURCE: *U.S. Census Reports, 1850–1930.*

Ashland to Western. The Eighteenth Ward Negroes lived in the old immigrant neighborhood on the Near West Side near Hull House. On the Near North Side, Negroes had begun to settle in the Italian Seventeenth Ward. And on the South Side, beyond the black belt, communities of upper- and middle-class Negroes had emerged in Hyde Park, Woodlawn, Englewood, and Morgan Park.

Despite this concentration of Negroes in enclaves, the Negro population of the city was still relatively well distributed in 1900. Nineteen of the city's thirty-five wards had a Negro population of at least .5 percent of the total population of the ward and fourteen wards were at least 1 percent Negro. Only two wards had a Negro population of more than 10 percent. In 1898, just over a quarter of Chicago's Negroes lived in precincts that were more than 50 percent Negro, and over 30 percent lived in precincts that were at least 95 percent white. As late as 1910, Negroes were less highly segregated from native whites than were Italian immigrants.

The decade 1900 to 1910 saw several significant changes in the population pattern of Negroes in Chicago. The growth rate, which had far outpaced the white growth rate in the 1890's, declined from 111 percent to 46 percent, and the proportion of Negroes in the population increased from 1.9 percent to only 2 percent. Yet despite this stabilization, the Negro population was still composed largely of migrants. Over 77 percent of Chicago's Negroes were born outside of Illinois. This represents only a slight drop from 1900 and was almost five times as great as the corresponding figure for white Chicagoans. Only three major Negro communities in the country—Los Angeles, Denver, and Oklahoma City, all young Western cities with highly mobile populations—had higher proportions of out-of-state migrants than Chicago. Even such burgeoning industrial centers as Detroit, Pittsburgh, and Cleveland had a lower percentage of Negroes born in other states.

The concentration of Negroes in enclaves was clearly increasing throughout this period. By 1910, over 30 percent lived in predominantly Negro sections of the city and over 60 percent in areas that were more than 20 percent Negro. Whereas in 1900 nineteen of thirty-five wards had been over .5 percent Negro, this figure was reduced to thirteen in 1910. Furthermore, the second and third wards, which included the heart of the black belt, were now 25 percent Negro, while in 1900 only one ward had even approached that figure.

Negro residential patterns for 1910 can be seen most clearly through the use of census tract data. Of 431 census tracts in the city, Negroes could be found in all but ninety-four; eighty-eight were at least 1 percent Negro. Four tracts were over 50 percent Negro, but no tract was more than 61 percent Negro. Despite greater concentration, therefore, there were still few all-Negro neighborhoods in Chicago.

The eight or nine neighborhoods that had been distinguishable as areas of Negro settlement in 1900 remained the core of the Chicago Negro community in 1910. The principal South Side black belt was slowly expanding to accommodate the growing population. Not only did Negroes push steadily southward, but the narrow strip of land that made up the black belt began to widen as Negroes moved into the comfortable neighborhood east of State Street. By the end of the decade, Negroes could be found as far east as Cottage Grove Avenue.

Statistical data, then, reveal several definite trends in the pattern of Negro population in Chicago in the early twentieth century. The growth rate between 1900 and 1910 had decreased from the previous decade, but was still 50 percent greater than that of whites. Most of the population increase was the result of migration, particularly from the nearby border states. Negroes could be found throughout much of the city and the Negro neighborhoods were by no means exclusively black. But the concentration of Negroes in two enclaves on the South and West Sides was increasing. As the population grew, Negroes were not spreading throughout the city but were becoming confined to a clearly delineated area of Negro settlement.

The increasing physical separation of Chicago's Negroes was but one reflection of a growing pattern of segregation and discrimination in early twentieth-century Chicago. As the Negro community grew and opportunities for interracial conflict increased, so a pattern of discrimination and segregation became ever more pervasive. And perhaps the most critical aspect of interracial conflict came as the result of Negro attempts to secure adequate housing.

The South Side black belt could expand in only two directions in the early twentieth century—south and east. To the north lay the business district, which was moving south; in fact, commercial and light industrial concerns were pushing Negroes out of the area between Twelfth and Twenty-second Streets. West of Wentworth Avenue was a district of low-income immigrant homes, interspersed with railroad yards and light industry; the lack of adequate housing made this area undesirable for Negro expansion. East of State Street, on the other hand, was a neighborhood suitable for Negro residential requirements. This area, bounded by Twelfth and Thirty-ninth Streets, State Street and Lake Michigan, had, in the 1880's and early 1890's, included the most fashionable streets in the city—Prairie and Calumet Avenues. But by 1900, the wealthy residents were moving to the North Side, leaving behind them comfortable, if aging, homes. South of Thirty-ninth Street was an even more desirable residential area—Kenwood and Hyde Park —and across Washington Park from the southern extremity of the black belt were the new and attractive communities of Woodlawn and Englewood. In these areas, between 1900 and 1915, the lines were drawn in the struggle for housing that would subsequently lead to full-scale racial war. If no major battle was fought before 1915, there were at least several preliminary skirmishes that set the pattern for future, and more serious, confrontations.

Negro expansion did not always mean conflict, nor did it mean that a neighborhood would shortly become exclusively black. In 1910, not more than a dozen blocks on the South Side were entirely Negro, and in many mixed areas Negroes and whites lived together harmoniously. But as Negroes became more numerous east of State and south of Fifty-first, friction increased and white hostility grew. When a Negro family moved into a previously all-white neighborhood, the neighbors frequently protested, tried to buy the property, and then, if unsuccessful, resorted to violence to drive out the interlopers. In many cases, the residents organized to urge real estate agents and property owners to sell and rent to whites only. The whites often succeeded in keeping Negroes out, at least temporarily. When their efforts failed, they gradually moved out, leaving the neighborhood predominantly, although rarely exclusively, Negro.

Such incidents occurred with only minor variations throughout the prewar period. In 1900, three Negro families brought about "a nervous prostration epidemic" on Vernon Avenue. Five years later, an attempt to oust Negroes from a Forrestville Avenue building landed in court. In 1911, a committee of Champlain Avenue residents dealt with a Negro family in the neighborhood by the "judicious use of a wagon load of bricks"; the *Record-*

*Herald* described the affair as "something as nearly approaching the operations of the Ku Klux Klan as Chicago has seen in many years." Englewood residents, two years later, did not have to go quite so far; the objectionable party, this time a white man with a Negro wife, agreed to sell his property to a hastily organized "neighborhood improvement association." A Negro who moved into a home on Forrestville Avenue in 1915, on the other hand, termed an offer of this type "blackmail," but after several days of intimidation, he too submitted and sold his property.

Perhaps the most serious incident, and the one which provides the most insight into the nature of the housing conflict, occurred in Hyde Park—Chicago's most persistent racial trouble spot—in 1909. A separate town until 1892, Hyde Park was still an area of pleasant, tree-shaded streets, large, comfortable homes, and a vigorous cultural life centered on the campus of the new but thriving University of Chicago. Negroes were no strangers to the community: for many years a few families, mostly house servants and hotel employees who worked in the neighborhood, had clustered on Lake Avenue near Fifty-fifth Street, on the eastern edge of Hyde Park. Now this community began to expand and Negroes occupied homes in nearby white blocks.

White Hyde Parkers responded to the Negro "invasion" with a concerted drive to keep Negroes out of white areas. The Hyde Park Improvement Protective Club was organized in the autumn of 1908; headed by a prominent attorney, Francis Harper, it soon boasted 350 members, "including some of the wealthiest dwellers on the South Side." In the summer of 1909, the Club issued a manifesto: Negro residents of Hyde Park must confine themselves to the "so-called Districts," real estate agents must refuse to sell property in white blocks to Negroes, and landlords must hire only white janitors. To implement this policy, the Club appointed a committee to purchase property owned by Negroes in white blocks and to offer bonuses to Negro renters who would surrender their leases. Moreover, the Club threatened to blacklist any real estate firm that defied its edict. "The districts which are now white," said Harper, "must remain white. There will be no compromise."

Despite the efforts of the Negro residents of Hyde Park to counter the activities with indignation meetings and boycotts, the white campaign continued. The neighborhood newspaper supported the Improvement Club, and Harper maintained that he had "received hosts of letters commending the course of the organization." When the Club was unable to persuade a Negro family to move voluntarily, the neighbors used more direct tactics: vandals broke into a Negro home on Greenwood Avenue one night and broke all the windows; the family left the next day. In September, the Club announced a boycott of merchants who sold goods to Negroes living in white neighborhoods. It urged separate playgrounds and tennis courts for Negroes in Washington Park, and, in its annual report, advocated segregation of the public schools. "It is only a question of time," a Club spokesman predicted, "when there will be separate schools for Negroes throughout Illinois." The group operated more quietly after 1909, but it had achieved its major goal. The little Negro community on Lake Avenue dwindled in size and the rest of Hyde Park remained white for forty years.

The Hyde Park episode well illustrates the intensification of anti-Negro feeling in the early twentieth century. This feeling could even create strong sentiment among whites for a return to formalized segregation—separate schools and recreation facilities. Some white Chicagoans spoke of the necessity for a residential segregation ordinance. The incident also provided an early example of techniques that were to become increasingly important as whites continually tried to stem the tide of Negro residential "invasion": the neighborhood improvement association, the community newspaper, the boycott, and in the last resort, violence. Furthermore, the episode was significant because it occurred in a middle- and upper-class community, and its victims were middle- and upper-class Negroes attempting to find comfortable homes among people of their own economic status. The housing problem for Negroes was not restricted to the poor; even the affluent were blocked in their quest for a decent place to live.

The unwillingness of whites to tolerate Negroes as neighbors had far-reaching results. Because Negroes were so limited in their choice of housing, they were forced to pay higher rents in those buildings that were open to them. Real estate agents frequently converted buildings in marginal neighborhoods from white to Negro and demanded rents 10 to 15 percent higher than they had previously received. Sophonisba Breckinridge of Hull House estimated that a Negro family "pays $12.50 for the same accommodations the Jew in the Ghetto received for $9 and the immigrant for $8." One realty company inserted two advertisements for the same apartment in a daily newspaper: one read, "seven rooms, $25"; the other, "seven rooms for colored people, $37.50." High rents often forced Negro families to take in lodgers. A 1912 survey of 1,775 South Side Negroes reported that 542, or 31 percent, lived as lodgers in the homes of others.

Living conditions in much of the black belt closely resembled conditions in the West Side ghetto or in the Stockyards district. Although Negroes could find some decent homes on the fringes of the Negro section, the core of the black belt was a festering slum. Here was an area of one- and two-story frame houses (unlike the older Eastern cities Chicago had, as yet, few large tenements), usually dilapidated with boarded-up porches and rickety wooden walks. Most of the buildings contained two flats and, although less crowded than houses in the Jewish, Polish, and Bohemian slums, they were usually in worse repair. The 1912 survey revealed that in a four-block area in the black belt, only 26 percent of the dwellings were in good repair—as compared to 71 percent in a similar sampling in a Polish neighborhood, 57 percent among Bohemians, and 54 percent in the ethnically mixed Stockyards district. "Colored tenants," the survey reported, "found it impossible to persuade their landlords either to make the necessary repairs or to release them from their contracts; . . . it was so hard to find better places in which to live that they were forced to make the repairs themselves, which they could rarely afford to do, or to endure the conditions as best they might."

White real estate agents, insensitive to class differences among Negroes, made no attempt to uphold standards in middle-class Negro neighborhoods as they did in comparable white districts. They persistently rented flats in "respectable" Negro neighborhoods to members of the "sporting element," thus forcing middle-class Negroes to move continually in search of decent areas to live and rear families. As a result, neighborhood stability was at best temporary. The streets east of State, which had become the mecca of the Negro middle class in the late 1890's, began to decline by 1905. A few years later the district was characterized by "men and women half clothed hanging out of a window," "rag-time piano playing . . . far into the night," and "shooting and cutting scrapes."

Municipal policy regarding vice further complicated the situation. City authorities, holding that the suppression of prostitution was impossible, tried to confine it to certain well-defined areas where it could be closely watched. The police frequently moved the vice district so as to keep it away from commercial and white residential areas. Invariably they located it in or near the black belt, often in Negro residential neighborhoods. The chief of police declared that so long as prostitutes confined their activities to the district between Wentworth and Wabash, they would not be apprehended. Neighborhood stability, then, was threatened not only by the influx of Negro "shadies," but by the presence of an officially sanctioned vice district catering primarily to whites.

Periodic attempts to clean up the red-light district received little support from Negro leaders who believed that such campaigns would merely drive the undesirables deeper into Negro residential neighborhoods. When legal prostitution was finally abolished in 1912, these fears were fully realized; vice in Chicago continued to be centered in the black belt. Fannie Barrier Williams, a prominent Negro civic leader, summed up the plight of the middle- and upper-class Negro: "The huddling together of the good and the bad, compelling the decent element of the colored people to witness the brazen display of vice of all kinds in front of their homes and in the faces of their children, are trying conditions under which to remain socially clean and respectable."

The pattern of Negro housing, then, was shaped by white hostility and indifference: limited in their choice of homes, Negroes were forced to pay higher rents for inferior dwellings and were frequently surrounded by prostitutes, panderers, and other undesirable elements. This, together with the poverty of the majority of Chicago Negroes, produced in the black belt the conditions of slum-living characteristic of American cities by the end of the nineteenth century.

The most striking feature of Negro housing, however, was not the existence of slum conditions, but the difficulty of escaping the slum. European immigrants needed only to prosper to be able to move to a more desirable neighborhood. Negroes, on the other hand, suffered from both economic deprivation and systematic racial discrimination. "The problem of the Chicago Negro," wrote Sophonisba Breckinridge,

*is quite different from the white man and even that of the immigrants. With the Negro the housing dilemma was found to be an acute problem, not only among the poor, as in the case of the Polish, Jewish, or Italian immigrants, but also among the well-to-do. . . . Thus, even in the North, where the city administration does not recognize a "Ghetto" or "pale," the real estate agents who register and commercialize what they suppose to be a universal race prejudice are able to enforce one in practice.*

The development of a physical ghetto in Chicago, then, was not the result chiefly of poverty; nor did Negroes cluster out of choice. The ghetto was primarily the product of white hostility. Attempts on the part of Negroes to seek housing in predominantly white sections of the city met with resistance from the residents and from real estate dealers. Some Negroes, in fact, who had formerly lived in white neighborhoods, were pushed back into the black districts. As the Chicago Negro population grew, Negroes had no alternative but to settle in well-delineated Negro areas. And with increasing pressure for Negro housing, property owners in the black belt found it profitable to force out white tenants and convert previously mixed blocks into all-Negro blocks. The geographical dimensions of Black Chicago in the early twentieth century underwent no dramatic shift similar, for instance, to Negro New York, where the center of Negro life moved to previously all-white Harlem in less than a decade. Negroes in Chicago were not establishing new communities. But to meet the needs of a growing population, in the face of mounting white resistance, Negro neighborhoods were becoming more exclusively Negro as they slowly expanded their boundaries.

*       *       *

As white hostility almost closed the housing market to Negroes and created a physical ghetto, it also limited the opportunities for Negroes to secure desirable jobs and gain access to public facilities. Chicago Negroes in the early twentieth century were confined to the domestic and personal service trades and were unable to gain even a foothold in industry and commerce. In 1900, almost 65 percent of the Negro men and over 80 percent of the Negro women worked as domestic and personal servants, while only 8.3 percent of the men and 11.9 percent of the women were engaged in manufacturing (and most of the women so employed worked in their own homes as dressmakers and seamstresses). In 1910 the basic pattern remained the same. Over 45 percent of the employed Negro men worked in just four occupations—as porters, servants, waiters, and janitors—and over 63 percent of the women were domestic servants or laundresses. In both 1900 and 1910, more Negroes were engaged in the professions than their numbers would warrant, but these were concentrated in professions that required relatively little formal training —music, the theater, and the clergy. Relatively few Negroes could be found in the legal, medical, and teaching professions. A large portion of those Negroes employed in manufacturing, trade, and transportation were unskilled laborers.

Negroes entered occupations that were not desirable enough to be contested by whites. When white workers sought jobs in trades dominated by Negroes, they were usually able to drive the Negroes out. In the nineteenth century, for instance, many Negroes had worked as barbers and coachmen, but by the early twentieth century, whites had replaced most of them in these capacities. Hence Negroes "were constantly driven to lower kinds of occupations which are gradually being discarded by the white man." These jobs were generally low-paying, carried the stigma of servility, and offered few opportunities for advancement. Porters in hotels, stores, and railroads, and janitors in apartment buildings and business houses had no chance to move up to better positions because these concerns hired Negroes in no other capacities. Among the service trade employees, only waiters could look forward to promotions; the job of headwaiter, which paid as much as one hundred dollars a month, was perhaps the most lucrative to which Negroes could aspire. Negro women were particularly limited in their search for desirable positions. Clerical work was practically closed to them and only a few could qualify as school teachers. Negro domestics often received less than white women for the same work, and they could rarely rise to the position of head servant in large households—a place traditionally held by a Swedish woman.

Several factors combined to keep Negroes out of industry and trade— especially the skilled and semiskilled jobs. First, most employers were simply disposed against hiring Negroes so long as an adequate supply of white labor was available—and with open immigration from Europe there was seldom a labor shortage. These employers feared that their white employees would object to working with Negroes, and many believed that Negro workers were less efficient. Secondly, many Negroes with skills had acquired them in the South and were often unable to meet Northern standards. Moreover, they were seldom able to acquire skills in the North: apprentice programs were usually open to whites only, and Negroes had little desire to learn a trade so long as its job prospects remained uncertain. Finally, the refusal of most trade unions to admit black workers on an equal basis kept Negroes out of many trades. Some unions completely excluded Negroes through clauses in their constitutions; others admitted Negroes, but then either segregated them in separate, subordinate locals, excluded them from specific projects, or simply made no effort to find jobs for them.

\* \* \*

Most observers—both Negro and white—agreed that the status of Negroes in Chicago was deteriorating, and some saw parallels between developments in Chicago and the hardening of Jim Crow patterns in the South. Two white commentators noted that "in the face of increasing manifestations of race prejudice, the Negro has come to acquiesce silently as various civil rights are withheld him in the old 'free North.'" A Negro columnist, in 1914, took an even more pessimistic position. He noted that "Afro-American people in increasing numbers are refused the accommodations of public places . . . in . . . violation of the laws of the state of Illinois," that "discrimination is manifesting itself more and more in the courts of Chicago," and that "the police department is especially filled with the wicked and unlawful determination to degrade Afro-Americans and fix upon them the badge of inferiority." He concluded that Negroes "are more and more being reduced to a fixed status of social and political inferiority."

To compare the evolution of the Negro's status in Chicago with the crystallization of the caste system in the South during the same period was an exaggeration. Discrimination in Chicago remained unofficial, informal, and uncertain; the Negro's status did not become fixed. Nevertheless, as Negroes became more numerous and conspicuous, white hostility increased and Negroes encountered an ever more pervasive pattern of exclusion. Edward E. Wilson, a Negro attorney, noted that the growth of the Negro community "brought [Negroes] into contact with whites who hardly knew that there were a thousand Colored people in Chicago." Moreover, "Colored children have appeared in numbers in many schools," and "Colored men have pushed their way into many employments." "All these things," he concluded, "have a tendency to cause the whites to resort to jim crow tactics."

By 1915, Negroes had become a special group in the social structure of prewar Chicago. They could not be classified as merely another of Chicago's many ethnic groups. The systematic proscription they suffered in housing and jobs, the discrimination they often—although not always—experienced in public accommodations and even municipal services, the violence of which they were frequently victims, set them apart from the mainstream of Chicago life in significant ways. They were forced to work out their destiny within the context of an increasingly biracial society.

\*    \*    \*

The Chicago experience, therefore, tends to refute any attempt to compare Northern Negroes with European immigrants. Unlike the Irish, Poles, Jews, or Italians, Negroes banded together not to enjoy a common linguistic, cultural, and religious tradition, but because a systematic pattern of discrimination left them no alternative. Negroes were tied together less by a common cultural heritage than by a common set of grievances. Even those who made a major effort to emphasize the positive aspects of separate Negro development were hard-pressed. The Garveyites, for instance, were forced to glorify an African past that had no relationship to the historical experience of

American Negroes. Racial solidarity was a response rather than a positive force. It was an attempt to preserve self-respect and foster self-reliance in the face of continual humiliations and rebuffs from white society.

The persistence of the Chicago Negro ghetto, then, has been not merely the result of continued immigration from the South, but the product of a special historical experience. From its inception, the Negro ghetto was unique among the city's ethnic enclaves. It grew in response to an implacable white hostility that has not basically changed. In this sense it has been Chicago's only true ghetto, less the product of voluntary development within than of external pressures from without. Like the Jewries of medieval Europe, Black Chicago has offered no escape. Irishmen, Poles, Jews, or Italians, as they acquired the means, had an alternative: they could move their enclaves to more comfortable environs or, as individuals, leave the enclaves and become members of the community at large. Negroes—forever marked by their color —could only hope for success within a rigidly delineated and severely restricted ghetto society. No physical wall has encircled the black belt. But an almost equally impervious wall of hostility and discrimination has isolated Negroes from the mainstream of Chicago life. Under such conditions, Negroes have tried, often against impossible odds, to make the best of their circumstances by creating a meaningful life of their own. But they have done so, not out of choice, but because white society has left them no alternative.

Richard C. Wade

# *Violence in the Cities*

Violence is no stranger to American cities. Almost from the very beginning, cities have been the scenes of sporadic violence, of rioting and disorders, and occasionally virtual rebellion against established authority. Many of these events resulted in only modest property damage and a handful of arrests. Others were larger in scale with deaths running into the scores and damages into the millions. This paper attempts to survey briefly some of these outbreaks and to analyze their origins and consequences. We confine ourselves, however, to the larger ones, and omit any discussion of individual acts of violence or the general level of crime. In addition, to keep these remarks relevant to the present crisis, we have confined our analysis to disorders in urban areas.

There has been, in fact, a good deal more violence and disorder in the American tradition than even historians have been willing to recognize. The violence on the frontier is, of course, well known, and in writing, movies, and television it has been a persistent theme in our culture. Indeed, one of America's favorite novelists, James Fenimore Cooper, transformed the slaughter and mayhem of Indians into heroic, almost patriotic, action. As the literary historian David Brion Davis has observed: "Critics who interpret violence in contemporary literature as a symptom of a sick society may be reassured to know that American writers have always been preoccupied with murder, rape, and deadly combat." To be sure, violence is not "as American as cherry pie," but it is no newcomer to the national scene.

Though serious scholarship on this dimension of the American past is shamefully thin, it is already quite clear that disorder and violence in our cities were not simply occasional aberrations, but rather a significant part of urban development and growth. From the Stamp Act riots of the pre-revolutionary age, to the assaults on immigrants and Catholics in the decades before the Civil War, to the grim confrontation of labor and management at the end of the nineteenth century and its sporadic reappearance after World War I and during the depression, through the long series of racial conflicts for two centuries, American cities have known the physical clash of groups, widescale breakdown of established authority, and bloody disorder.

Nor is it hard to see why this early history had more than its share of chaos. American cities in the eighteenth and nineteenth centuries were very young. They had not yet the time to develop a system of orderly government; there was no tradition of habitual consent to local authority; there was no established police system. In addition, these cities grew at a spectacular rate. In the twentieth century, we have used the term "exploding metropolis" to convey the rapid pace of urbanization. It is not often remembered that the first "urban explosion" took place more than a century ago. Indeed, between 1820 and 1860 cities grew proportionately faster than they had before or ever would again. The very speed of this urban development was unsettling and made the maintenance of internal tranquillity more difficult.

The problem was further compounded by the fact that nearly every American city was born of commerce. This meant that there was always a large transient population—seamen engaged in overseas trade, rivermen plying the inland waters, teamsters and wagonmen using the overland routes, and a constant stream of merchants and salesmen seeking customers. At any moment the number of newcomers was large and their attachments to the community slight. Hence when they hit town, there was always some liveliness. After exhausting the cities' museums and libraries, sailors and teamsters would find other things to do. In the eighteenth and nineteenth century, transients comprised a significant portion of those who engaged in rioting and civil disorders.

In addition to being young, rapidly growing, and basically commercial, American cities also had very loose social structures. Unlike the Old World, they had no traditional ruling group, class lines were constantly shifting, and new blood was persistently pumped into these urban societies. One could say that up until the last part of the nineteenth century, mercantile leaders dominated municipal government; but even that commercial leadership changed continually. Later, immigrant groups shared high offices in municipal affairs, thus underlining the shifting nature of the social structure of most cities. Within this looseness there was always a great deal of mobility, with people rising and falling in status not only from generation to generation but within a single lifetime.

This fluid social system contrasted sharply with other, older societies, yet it contained a high incidence of disorder. For it depended on the constant acceptance of new people and new groups to places of influence and importance, and their incorporation into the system on a basis of equality with others. This acceptance was only grudgingly conceded, and often only after some abrasive episodes. The American social structure thus had a large capacity to absorb revolutionary tensions and avoid convulsive upheavals. But it also bred minor social skirmishes which were not always orderly. It is significant that in the pre-Civil War South, where slavery created a more traditional social structure, there was less rioting and civil disorder than in the North (though one ought not underestimate the individual violence against the slave built into institutional bondage).

The American social structure was also unique because it was composed not only of conventional classes, but also of different ethnic, religious, and racial groups. They had at once an internal cohesion that came from a common background and a shared American experience and also a sense of sharp differences with other groups, especially with the country's older stock. These groups, the Negro excepted, were initially both part of the system and yet outside of it. The resultant friction, with the newcomers pressing for acceptance and older groups striving for continued supremacy, was a fruitful source of disorder and often violence. Since it was in the city that these groups were thrown together, became aware of their differences, and struggled for survival and advancement, it would be on the streets rather than on the countryside that the social guerrilla warfare would take place.

If the internal controls in the American social structure were loose, the external controls were weak. The cities inherited no system of police control adequate to the numbers or to the rapid increase of the urban centers. The modern police force is the creation of the twentieth century; the establishment of a genuinely professional system is historically a very recent thing. Throughout the eighteenth and nineteenth century, the force was small, untrained, poorly paid, and part of the political system. In case of any sizable disorder, it was hopelessly inadequate; and rioters sometimes routed the constabulary in the first confrontation. Josiah Quincy, for example, in Boston in the 1820's had to organize and arm the teamsters to re-establish the authority of the city in the streets. Many prudent officials simply kept out of the way until the worst was over. In New York's draft riots, to use another instance, the mayor wandered down to see what the disturbance was all about and nearly got trampled in the melee.

Moreover, since some of the rioting was political, the partisanship of the police led official force to be applied against one group, or protection to be withheld from another. And with every turnover in the mayor's office, a substantial and often a complete change occurred in the police. In Atlanta, for instance, even where there was only one party, each faction had its own men in blue ready to take over with the changes in political fortunes. In some places where the state played a role in local police appointments, the mayor might even be deprived of any control at all for the peace of the city. In New York in the 1850's there was an awkward moment when there were two police forces—the Municipals and the Metropolitans—each the instrument of opposing parties. At the point of the most massive confusion, one group tried to arrest the mayor and an armed struggle took place between the two competing forces.

The evolution toward more effective and professional forces was painfully slow. Separating the police from patronage proved difficult, the introduction of civil service qualifications and protection came only in this century, and the development of modern professional departments came even later. To be sure, after a crisis—rioting, widescale looting, or a crime wave—there would be a demand for reform, but the enthusiasm was seldom sustained and conditions returned quickly to normal. The ultimate safety of the city thus resided with outside forces that could be brought in when local police could not handle the mob.

These general considerations account in large part for the high level of disorder and violence in American cities over the past three centuries. The larger disorders, however, often stemmed from particular problems and specific conditions and resulted in widescale bloodshed and destruction. Though these situations varied from place to place and time to time, it is perhaps useful to divide them into a few categories. Some rioting was clearly political, surrounding party struggles and often occasioned by legislation or an election. Some sprang from group conflict, especially the resistance to the rising influence of immigrant groups. Still others stemmed from labor disputes. And the largest, then as now, came out of race conflict. A few examples of each will convey some of their intensity and scale.

Politics has always been a fruitful source of disorders. Indeed, one of the most significant groups of riots surrounded the colonial break with Great Britain. In Boston, Samuel Adams and other radical leaders led the otherwise directionless brawling and gang warfare around the docks and wharfs into a political roughhouse against British policy. The Stamp Tax Riots, the Townshend Duty Riots and, of course, the Boston Massacre were all part of an organized and concerted campaign by colonial leaders. The urban middle classes initially tolerated the disorders because they too opposed certain aspects of British policy; they later pulled back when they felt that radical leadership was carrying resistance beyond their own limited objectives. Yet for nearly a decade, rioting and organized physical force was a part of the politics of the colonies.

*　　*　　*

Attacks against immigrants comprise another theme in the story. Often the assault by older, more established groups was against individuals or small groups. But in other cases it would be more general. The string of riots against Catholic churches and convents in the nineteenth century, for example, represented an attack on the symbols of the rise of the new groups. In the summer of 1834, for instance, a Charlestown (Mass.) convent was sacked and burned to the ground; scuffles against the Irish occurred in various parts of nearby Boston; some Irish houses were set afire. At the outset, the episode was carefully managed; then it got out of hand as teenage toughs got into action. Nor was this an isolated incident.

Characteristic of this period too was the resistance to the incorporation of immigrants into the public life of the city. "Bloody Monday" in Louisville in 1855 will perhaps serve as an illustration. Local politicians had become worried about the increase of the immigrant (German and Irish) vote. The Know-Nothings (a party built in part on anti-immigrant attitudes) determined to keep foreign-born residents away from the polls on election day. There was only a single voting place for every ward, thus numbering only eight in the entire city. Know-Nothing followers rose at dawn and occupied the booths early in the morning. They admitted their own reliables, but physically barred their opponents. The pre-election campaign had been tense and bitter with threats of force flying across party lines. By this time some on each side had armed themselves. Someone fired a shot, and the rioting commenced. When it was all through, "Quinn's Row," an Irish section, had been gutted, stores looted, and Catholic churches damaged. A newspaper which was accused of stirring up feeling only barely escaped destruction. The atrocities against the Irish were especially brutal, with many being beaten and shot. Indeed, some of the wounded were thrown back into the flames of ignited buildings. Estimates of the dead range from 14 to 100, though historians have generally accepted (albeit with slim evidence) 22 as the number killed.

Labor disputes have also often spawned widescale disorder. Indeed, at the turn of the century, Winston Churchill, already a keen student of American affairs, observed that the United States had the most violent industrial relations of any western country. Most of this rioting started with a confrontation of labor and management over the right to organize, or wages and hours, or working conditions. A large portion of these strikes found the workers in a vulnerable if not helpless position, a fact which has led most historians to come down on the side of labor in these early disputes. Moreover, unlike the disorders we have previously discussed, these were nationwide in scope—occurring at widely scattered points. There was no question of their being directed since a union was usually involved and it had some control over local action throughout the country. Yet the violence was seldom uniform or confined to strikers. It might flare up in Chicago and Pittsburgh, while St. Louis, where the issues would be the same, might remain quiescent. Often, as in the case of the railroad strike of 1877, the damage to life and property was large. In the Homestead lockout alone, 35 were killed and the damage (in 1892 dollars) ran to $2,500.00. In the 1930's the organizing steel, auto, and rubber unions brought a recrudescence of this earlier grisly process.

\*　　\*　　\*

Of all the sources of civil disorder, however, none has been more persistent than race. Whether in the North or South, whether before or after the Civil War, whether nineteenth or twentieth century, this question has been at the root of more physical violence than any other. There had been some sporadic slave uprisings before emancipation, the largest being the Nat Turner rebellion in 1831. But most which moved from plot to action occurred on the countryside rather than in the cities. Yet even the fear of a slave insurrection took its toll; in 1822, for instance, Charleston, South Carolina, officials, acting on tips and rumors, hanged 37 Negroes and deported many more for an alleged plot to capture and burn the city. Seven years later, in a free state, whites invaded Cincinnati's "Little Africa" and burned and killed and ultimately drove half the colored residents from town. In the same period mobs also assaulted abolitionists, sometimes killing, otherwise sacking buildings and destroying printing presses.

Even the New York City riot against the draft in 1863 took an ugly racial twist before it had run its course. The events themselves arose out of the unpopularity of the draft and the federal government's call for more men as Lee headed into Pennsylvania. The situation was further complicated by a crisis in the police department as a result of the conflicting claims of command by a Republican mayor and a Democratic governor. The rioting broke out July 13 and the first target was the provost marshal's office. Within a short time 700 people ransacked the building and then set it afire. The crowd would not let the firemen into the area and soon the whole block lay gutted. Later the mob began to spill over into the Negro area where many blacks were attacked and some killed.

The police were helpless as the riot spread. The few clashes with the mob saw the police retreat; the crowd wandered about almost at will. Political leaders did not want to take the consequences for action against the mob, and soon it started to head toward the business district. Slowly the police reorganized, by Tuesday they began to win engagements with the rioters, and in a little while they were able to confine the action to the original area. The mobs were, however, better armed and organized and gave a good account of themselves in pitched battle. On the third day federal troops arrived and the control swung over to the authorities and quiet was restored. But in three days the casualties ran to at least 74 dead and many times that number wounded. The property damage was never accurately added up, but claims against the county exceeded $1,500,000 by 1865.

Emancipation freed the Negro from bondage, but it did not grant him either equality or immunity from white aggression. From the New Orleans riot of 1866, through the long list of racial disorders to the end of World War II with datelines running through Atlanta, Springfield, East St. Louis, Washington, Mobile, Beaumont, Chicago, Detroit, and Harlem, [all these riots] reveal something of the depth of the crisis and the vulnerability of American cities to racial disorders. These riots were on a large scale, involved many deaths, millions of dollars of property damage, and left behind deep scars which have never been fully erased. Most of these riots involved the resort to outside military help for containment; all exposed the thinness of the internal and external controls within our urban society.

In fact, the war had scarcely ended before racial violence erupted in New Orleans. The occasion of the outbreak was a Negro procession to an assembly hall where a debate over enfranchising the blacks was to take place. There was some jostling during the march and a shot fired; but it was only after the arrival at the convention that police and special troops charged the black crowd. In the ensuing struggle [the] Negroes were finally routed, but guns, bricks, and stones were generously used. Many Negroes fell on the spot; others were pursued and killed on the streets trying to escape. Later General Sheridan reported that "at least nine-tenths of the casualties were perpetrated by the police and citizens by stabbing and smashing in the heads of many who had already been wounded or killed by policemen." Moreover, he added that it was not just a riot but "an absolute massacre by the police . . . a murder which the mayor and police . . . perpetrated without the shadow of necessity." Federal troops arrived in the afternoon, took possession of the city, and restored order. But 34 Negroes and 4 whites were already dead and over 200 injured.

Smaller places, even in the North, were also affected with racial disorder. In August 1908, for instance, a three-day riot took its toll in Springfield, Illinois. The Negro population in the capital had grown significantly in the years after the turn of the century, and some whites sensed a political and economic threat. On August 13th a white woman claimed she had been violated by a Negro. An arrest was made and the newspapers carried an inflammatory account of the episode. Crowds gathered around the jail demanding the imprisoned black, but the sheriff quickly transferred the accused and another Negro to a prison in a nearby town without letting the public know. "The crowd outside was in an ugly mood," writes an historian of the riot, "the sun had raised tempers; many of the crowd had missed their dinners, which added to their irritation; and the authorities seemed to be taking no heed of their presence. By sundown the crowd had become an ugly mob."

The first target of the rioters was a restaurant whose proprietor presumably had driven the prisoners from jail. Within a few minutes his place was a shambles. They then headed for the Negro section. Here they hit homes and businesses either owned by or catering to Negroes. White owners quickly put white handkerchiefs in their windows to show their race; their stores were left untouched. A Negro was found in his shop and was summarily lynched. Others were dragged from streetcars and beaten. On the 15th the first of 5,000 national guardsmen reached Springfield; very quickly the mob broke up and the town returned to normal. The death toll reached six (four whites and two blacks); the property damage was significant. As a result of the attack,

Springfield's Negro population left the city in large numbers hoping to find better conditions elsewhere, especially in Chicago.

A decade later the depredations in East St. Louis were much larger, with the riot claiming the lives of 39 Negroes and 9 whites. The best student of this episode points out that the 1917 riot was not a sudden explosion but resulted from "threats to the security of whites brought on by the Negroes' gains in economic, political and social status; Negro resentment of the attempts to 'kick him back in his place'; and the weakness of the external forces of constraint—the city government, especially the police department." Tensions were raised when the Aluminum Ore Company replaced white strikers with Negro workers. In addition to these factors, race had become a political issue in the previous year when the Democrats accused Republicans of "colonizing" Negroes to swing the election in East St. Louis. The kindling seemed only to lack the match.

On May 28 came the fire. A Central Trades and Labor Union delegation formally requested the Mayor to stop the immigration of Negroes to East St. Louis. As the men were leaving City Hall they heard a story that a Negro robber had accidentally shot a white man during a holdup. In a few minutes the word spread; rumor replaced fact. Now it was said the shooting was intentional; that a white woman was insulted; that two white girls were shot. By this time 3,000 people had congregated and the cry for vengeance went up. Mobs ran downtown beating every Negro in sight. Some were dragged off the streetcars, others chased down. The police refused to act except to take the injured to hospitals and to disarm Negroes. The next day the National Guard arrived to restore order.

Two days later the governor withdrew troops although tension remained high. Scattered episodes broke the peace, but no sustained violence developed. The press, however, continued to emphasize Negro crimes and a skirmish broke out between white pickets and black workers at the Aluminum Company. Then on July 1 some whites drove through the main Negro neighborhood firing into homes. The colored residents armed themselves, and when a similar car, this time carrying a plainclothesman and reporter, went down the street the blacks riddled the passing auto with gunshot.

The next day was the worst. At about 10:00 A.M. a Negro was shot on the main street and a new riot was underway. An historian of the event asserted that the area along Collinsville Avenue between Broadway and Illinois Avenue became a "bloody half mile" for three or four hours. "Streetcars were stopped: Negroes, without regard to age or sex, were pulled off and stoned, clubbed and kicked. . . . By the early afternoon, when several Negroes were beaten and lay bloodied in the street, mob leaders calmly shot and killed them. After victims were placed in an ambulance, there was cheering and handclapping." Others headed for the Negro section and set fire to homes on the edge of the neighborhood. By midnight the South End was in flames and black residents began to flee the city. In addition to the dead, the injured were counted in the hundreds and over 300 buildings were destroyed.

Two summers later the racial virus felled Chicago. Once again, mounting tension had accompanied the migration of blacks to the city. The numbers jumped from 44,000 in 1910 to 109,000 ten years later. Though the job market remained good, housing was tight. Black neighborhoods could expand only at the expense of white ones, and everywhere the transition areas were filled with trouble. Between July 1, 1917, and March 1921, there had been 58 bombings of Negro houses. Recreational areas also witnessed continual racial conflict.

The riot itself began on Sunday, July 27, on the 29th Street Beach. There had been some stone-throwing and sporadic fighting. Then a Negro boy, who had been swimming in the Negro section, drifted into the white area and drowned. What happened is not certain, but the young blacks charged he had been hit by stones and demanded the arrest of a white. The police refused, but then arrested a Negro at a white request. When the Negroes attacked the police, the riot was on. News of the events on the beach spread to the rest of the city. Sunday's casualties were 2 dead and 50 wounded. On Monday, attacks were made on Negroes coming from work; in the evening cars drove through black neighborhoods with whites shooting from the windows. Negroes retaliated by sniping at any white who entered the Black Belt. Monday's accounting found 20 killed and hundreds wounded. Tuesday's list was shorter, a handful dead, 139 injured. Wednesday saw a further waning and a reduction in losses in life and property. Rain began to fall; the Mayor finally called in the state militia. After nearly a week a city which [had] witnessed lawlessness and warfare quieted down and began to assess the implications of the grisly week.

The Detroit riot of 1943 perhaps illustrates the range of racial disorders that broke out sporadically during World War II. There had been earlier conflicts in Mobile, Los Angeles, and Beaumont, Texas, and there would be some others later in the year. No doubt the war with its built-in anxieties and accelerated residential mobility accounted for the timing of these outbreaks. In Detroit, the wider problem was compounded by serious local questions. The Negro population in the city had risen sharply, with over 50,000 arriving in the 15 months before the riot; this followed a historical increase of substantial proportions which saw black residents increase from 40,000 to 120,000 in the single decade between 1920 and 1930. These newcomers put immense pressures on the housing market, and neighborhood turnover at the edge of the ghetto bred bitterness and sometimes violence; importantly, too, recreational areas became centers of racial abrasiveness.

On June 20 the riot broke out on Belle Isle, a recreational spot used by both races, but predominantly by Negroes. Fistfighting on a modest basis soon escalated, and quickly a rising level of violence spread across the city. The Negro ghetto—ironically called Paradise Valley—saw the first wave of looting and bloodshed. The area was, as its historians have described it, "spat-tered with blood and littered with broken glass and ruined merchandise. The black mob had spared a few shops owned by Negroes who had chalked COL-ORED on their windows. But almost every store in the ghetto owned by a white had been smashed open and ransacked." Other observers noted that "crudely organized gangs of Negro hoodlums began to operate more openly. Some looters destroyed property as if they had gone berserk."

The next morning saw the violence widen. The police declared the situation out of control and the mayor asked for state troops. Even this force was ineffective, and finally the Governor asked for federal help. Peace returned under the protection of 6,000 men; and the troops remained for more than a week. The dead numbered 34, 25 Negroes and 9 whites; property damage ex-ceeded $2,000,000. And almost as costly was the bitterness, fear, and hate that became part of the city's legacy.

*      *      *

This survey, which is only suggestive and not exhaustive, indicates that widescale violence and disorder have been man's companion in the American city from the outset. Some generalizations out of this experience might be useful in the light of the present crisis.

*First,* most of the rioting has usually been either limited in objective or essentially sporadic. This, of course, is not true of racial conflict, but it is characteristic of a large number of the others. In those, the event was discrete; there was no immediate violent sequel. After a labor dispute, especially if it involved union recognition, bitterness and hate persisted, but there was no annual recurrence of the violence. Attacks on immigrants seldom produced an encore, though they might have an analogue in some other city in the same month or year. In short, though there was enough disorder and mob action to create a persistent anxiety, the incidence of overt conflict was ir-regular enough to preclude predictions of the next "long hot summer."

*Second,* this sporadic quality meant that the postmortems were usually short and shallow. It was characteristic to note the large number of teenagers who got involved; to attribute the disruption to outsiders (especially anar-chists and communists); to place a large responsibility on the newspapers for carrying inflammatory information and spreading unfounded rumors; to blame the local police for incompetence, for prejudice, for intervening too soon or too late, or at all. After any episode, the urge to fix blame led to all kinds of analyses. The historian of the 1877 railroad violence, for example, observes that "the riots were variously ascribed to avarice, the expulsion of the Bible from the schools, the protective tariff, the demonetization of silver, the ab-sence of General Grant, the circulation of the *Chicago Times* and original sin." Others saw in it a labor conspiracy or a communist plot. And the *New York Times* could assert after the Chicago riot in 1919 that: "The outbreak of race riots in Chicago, following so closely on those reported from Washington, shows clearly enough that the thing is not sporadic (but has) . . . intelligent direction and management . . . (It seems probable) that the Bolshevist agitation has been extended among the Negroes."

There were a few exceptions. After the Chicago race riot, for example, an Illinois commission studied the event in some detail and also examined the deteriorating relations between the races which lay at the bottom. Others occasionally probed beneath the surface [to get] at the deeper causes of unrest. But most cities preferred to forget as soon as possible and hoped for an end to any further disorder. Indeed, even the trials that followed most riots show how rapidly popular interest faded. The number of people brought to trial was small and the number of convictions extremely small; and, most significantly, there was little clamor for sterner measures.

*Third*, if the analyses of the riots were shallow, the response of cities and legislatures was not very effective. After quiet was restored, there would almost certainly be a discussion of police reform. Customarily little came of it, though in Louisville the utter ineptness and obvious partisanship of the police in 1855 prompted a change from an elective to an appointive force. Legislation usually emphasized control. As early as 1721, Massachusetts responded to growing disorders with an anti-riot act. And Chicago's Commercial Club made land available for Fort Sheridan after the events of 1877 in order to have troops nearby for the protection of the city. But most cities rocked back to normal as soon as the tremors died down.

*Fourth*, there was a general tendency to rely increasingly on outside forces for containing riots. Partly, this resulted from the fact that in labor disorders local police and even state militia fraternized with strikers and could not be counted on to discipline the workers. Partly, it was due to inadequate numbers in the face of the magnitude of the problem. Partly, too, it stemmed from the fact that sometimes the police were involved in the fighting at the outset and seemed a part of the riot. The first resort was usually to state troops; but they were often unsatisfactory, and the call for federal assistance became more frequent.

*Fifth*, while it is hard to assess, it seems that the bitterness engendered by riots and disorders was not necessarily irreparable. Though the immigrants suffered a good deal at the hands of nativists, it did not slow down for long the process of their incorporation into American life. Ten years after Louisville's "Bloody Monday" the city had a German mayor. The trade unions survived the assaults of the nineteenth century and a reduction of tension characterized the period between 1900 and the depression (with the notable exception of the post-war flare-ups). And after the violence of the 1930's, labor and management learned to conduct their differences, indeed their strikes, with reduced bloodshed and violence. It is not susceptible of proof, but it seems that the fury of the defeated in these battles exacted a price on the victors that ultimately not only protected the group but won respect, however grudgingly, from the public.

At any rate, the old sources of major disorders, race excepted, no longer physically agitate American society. It has been many years since violence has been a significant factor in city elections and no widespread disorders have even accompanied campaigning. Immigrant groups have now become so incorporated in American life that they are not easily visible and their election to high offices, indeed the highest, signals a muting of old hostilities. Even when people organized on a large scale against minority groups—such as the Americans' Protective Association in the 1890's or the Ku Klux Klan in the 1920's—they have seldom been able to create major riots or disorders. And though sporadic violence occasionally breaks out in a labor dispute, what is most remarkable is the continuance of the strike as a weapon of industrial relations with so little resort to force. Even the destruction of property during a conflict has ceased to be an expectation.

*Sixth*, race riots were almost always different from other kinds of disorders. Their roots went deeper; they broke out with increasing frequency; and their intensity mounted rather than declined. And between major disorders the incidence of small-scale violence was always high. Until recently, the Negro has largely been the object of the riot. This was true not only in northern cities where changing residential patterns bred violence, but also in the South where this question was less pervasive. In these riots the lines were sharply drawn against the Negroes, the force was applied heavily against them, and the casualties were always highest among blacks.

Finally, in historical perspective, if racial discord be removed, the level of large-scale disorder and violence is less ominous today than it has been during much of the past. As we have seen, those problems which have produced serious eruptions in the past no longer do so. In fact, if one were to plot a graph, omitting the racial dimension, violence and disorder over a long period have been reduced. Indeed, what makes the recent rioting so alarming is that it breaks so much with this historical trend and upsets common expectations.

Yet to leave out race is to omit the most important dimension of the present crisis. For it is race that is at the heart of the present discord. Some analysts, of course, have argued that the problem is class and they emphasize the numbers caught in widening poverty, and the frustration and envy of poor people in a society of growing affluence. Yet it is important to observe that though 68 percent of the poor people in this country are white, the disorders stem almost wholly from black ghettoes. The marginal participation of a few whites in Detroit and elsewhere scarcely dilutes the racial foundations of these disorders.

In fact, a historical survey of disorders only highlights the unique character of the present problem. For the experience of the Negro in American cities has been quite different from any other group. And it is in just this difference that the crisis lies. Because the black ghetto is unlike any ghettoes that our cities have known before. Of course, other groups knew the ghetto experience too. As newcomers to the city they huddled in the down-town areas where they met unspeakably congested conditions, occupied the worst housing, got the poorest education, toiled, if fortunate enough to have a job, at the most menial tasks, endured high crime rates, and knew every facet of deprivation.

The urban slum had never been a very pleasant place, and it was toler-able only if the residents, or most of them, thought there was a way out. To American immigrants generally the ghetto was a temporary stage in their incorporation into American society. Even some of the first generation es-caped, and the second and third generation moved out of the slums in very large numbers. Soon they were dispersed around the metropolitan area, in the suburbs as well as the pleasant residential city wards. Those who remained behind in the old neighborhoods did so because they chose to, not because they had to. By this process, millions of people from numberless countries, of different national and religious backgrounds, made their way into the main current of American life.

It was expected that Negroes would undergo the same process when they came to the city. Thus, there was little surprise in the first generation when black newcomers did indeed find their way into the central city, the historic staging ground for the last and poorest arrivals. But the ghetto proved to be not temporary. Instead of colored residents dispersing in the second genera-tion, the ghetto simply expanded. Block by block it oozed out into the nearby white neighborhoods. Far from breaking up, the ghetto grew. In fact, housing became more segregated every year; and the walls around it appeared higher all the time. What had been temporary for other groups seemed permanent to Negroes.

The growth of the Negro ghetto created conditions which had not ex-isted before and which generated the explosiveness of our present situation. In the first place, the middle-class Negroes became embittered at their exclu-sion from the decent white neighborhoods of the city and suburbs. These people, after all, had done what society expected of them; they got their edu-cation, training, jobs, and income. Yet even so they were deprived of that essential symbol of American success—the home in a neighborhood of their own choosing where conditions would be more pleasant and schools better for their children. For this group, now about a third of all urban Negroes, the exclusion seemed especially cruel and harsh.

As a result they comprise now a growingly alienated and embittered group. The middle-class blacks are now beginning to turn their attention to organizing among the poor in the worst parts of the ghetto. Their children make up the cadres of black militants in the colleges. And when the riots come, they tolerate the activity even though they usually do not themselves participate. In short, the fact of the ghetto forces them to identify with race, not class. When the riots break, they feel a bond with the rioters, not white society. This had not been true of the emerging middle class of any immigrant group before.

If the ghetto has new consequences for the middle class, it also creates a new situation among the poorer residents of the ghetto, especially for the young people. They feel increasingly that there is no hope for the future. For other groups growing up in the ghetto there had always been visible evidence that it was possible to escape. Many before had done it; and everyone knew it. This produced the expectation that hard work, proper behavior, some schooling, and a touch of luck would make it possible to get ahead. But the young Negro grows up in increasing despair. He asks himself—"What if I do all they say I should—stay in school, get my training, find a job, accumulate some money—I'll still be living here, still excluded from the outside world and its rewards." He asks himself, "What's the use?" Thus, the hopelessness, despair, and frustration mounts, and the temperature of the ghetto rises. Nearly all of our poverty programs are stumbling on the problem of motivation. To climb out of the slum has always required more than average incentive. Yet this is precisely what is lacking in the ghetto youth.

The present riots stem from the peculiar problems of the ghetto. By confining Negroes to the ghetto we have deprived them of the chance to enter American society on the same terms as other groups before them. And they know increasingly that this exclusion is not a function of education, training, or income. Rather, it springs from the color of their skin. This is what makes race the explosive question of our time; this is what endangers the tranquillity of our cities. In the historian's perspective, until the ghetto begins to break, until the Negro middle class can move over this demeaning barrier, until the young people can see Negroes living where their resources will carry them and hence get credible evidence of equality, the summers will remain long and hot.

## SUGGESTIONS FOR FURTHER READING

The literature on urban history and the urban crisis has expanded rapidly in the past decade. General introductions are Charles N. Glaab and A. Theodore Brown, *A History of Urban America* (New York, 1967); Sam Bass Warner, *The Urban Wilderness: A History of the American City* (New York, 1972). A valuable analysis of recent trends in the writing of urban history, along with bibliographic information, is Richard C. Wade, "An Agenda for Urban History," in George Athan Billias and Gerald N. Grob, eds., *American History: Retrospect and Prospect* (New York, 1971), pp. 367–98. (The same essay also appears in Herbert J. Bass, ed., *The State of American History* [New York, 1971].) Arthur M. Schlesinger, *The Rise of the City* (New York, 1933), is an early effort to direct historians' attention to urban history; Schlesinger finds a developing urban consensus in the late nineteenth century. The antiurban tradition in America can be approached through Morton and Lucia White, *The Intellectual versus the City* (Cambridge, Mass., 1962). On the contemporary urban crisis, Jeanne Lowe, *Cities in a Race with Time* (New York, 1967), and Mitchell Gordon, *Sick Cities: Psychology and*

* Available in paperback edition.

*Pathology of American Urban Life* (New York, 1965), are pessimistic, while Jane Jacobs, *The Death and Life of Great American Cities* (New York, 1961), and Robert Weaver, *The Urban Complex: Human Values in Urban Life* (New York, 1964) find more hope. There are a number of books on the problems of governing cities, problems that often led to conflicts. For the problem of law enforcement, see Robert N. Fogelson, *Big-City Police* (Cambridge, Mass., 1977). A survey of the literature is Jon C. Teaford, "Finis for Tweed and Steffens: Rewriting the History of Urban Rule," *Reviews in American History*, 10 (December 1982), 133–49.

The best place to begin a study of immigration is Maldwyn Allen Jones, *American Immigration* (Chicago, 1960). John Higham, *Strangers in the Land: Patterns of American Nativism, 1860–1925* (New Brunswick, N.J., 1955) describes some of the sharp conflicts between the immigrants and native Americans. On the problems of assimilation, see Nathan Glazer and Daniel Patrick Moynihan, *Beyond the Melting Pot: The Negroes, Puerto Ricans, Jews, Italians and Irish of New York City* (Cambridge, Mass., 1963). An important study of New York City blacks is Gilbert Osofsky, *Harlem: The Making of a Ghetto* (New York, 1965). Kenneth L. Kusmer, *A Ghetto Takes Shape: Black Cleveland, 1870–1930* (Champagne, Ill., 1976), and Thomas Lee Philpott, *The Slum and the Ghetto: Neighborhood Deterioration and Middle-Class Reform, Chicago 1880–1930* (New York, 1978), are two excellent studies. Florette Henri, *Black Migration: Movement North, 1900–1920* (Garden City, N.Y., 1975), traces the movement of southern blacks to northern cities.

In recent years the study of both urban and immigration history has moved away from attempts to define an urban or an ethnic consensus in America to efforts to examine the diversity of ethnic experience and the complexity of the city in many times and places. Examples of the new approach can be found in three collections of essays: Stephan Thernstrom and Richard Sennett, eds., *Nineteenth-Century Cities* (New Haven, 1969); Allen F. Davis and Mark Haller, eds., *The Peoples of Philadelphia: A History of Ethnic Groups and Lower-Class Life, 1790–1940* (Philadelphia, 1973); and Richard L. Ehrlich, ed., *Immigrants in Industrial America* (Charlottesville, Va., 1977). One example of many specialized studies is Thomas Kessner, *The Golden Door: Italian and Jewish Immigrant Mobility in New York City 1880–1915* (New York, 1977). Leonard Dinnerstein, Roger L. Nichols, and David M. Reimers, *Natives and Strangers: Ethnic Groups and the Building of America* (New York, 1979), is a comprehensive general account. Thomas Sowell, *Ethnic America: A History* (New York, 1981) is a controversial book that examines nine ethnic groups including blacks and argues that all groups can get ahead through hard work not federal aid.

# 6

# The Progressive Movement

Progressivism was a broad and diverse reform movement that had its roots in the 1890s but came to a climax on the national level during the administrations of Theodore Roosevelt and Woodrow Wilson. It affected all areas of American life, including art, literature, religion, and education; but it was also a political movement founded on the idea that the problems arising in an industrialized America could be solved only by expanding democracy and social justice. Reformers in the cities sought to promote clean, honest, efficient government and to end boss rule. Reformers in the states paraded under the banner of "give the government back to the people," seeking the initiative, the referendum, the recall, the direct election of senators, and many other reforms that had been supported by the Populists. Muckrakers sought to expose corruption in the world of business and politics. Social workers and other reformers fought to regulate child labor, to clean up the slums, and to promote better working conditions for both men and women. On the national level, leaders of both political parties, seeking ways to deal with the giant industrial combinations, turned to regulation, control, and "trust busting." Everywhere progressives were concerned with solving the many problems created by industrialism.

Not all progressives agreed on the objectives of the movement or even the best methods for reform; historians have also disagreed about the meaning and nature of progressivism. To some historians the progressive era was a time of fundamental conflict between reformers on one side and businessmen and political bosses on the other. Some stress the Populist origins of progressivism. These scholars agree with William Allen White, a leading midwestern progressive, who remarked that the progressives "caught the Populists in swimming and stole all their clothing except the frayed underdrawers of free silver." They see the movement as drawing its chief support from the midwestern farmers and small businessmen who were engaged in a bitter struggle for survival with the eastern bankers and corporation presidents.

Another group of historians interpret the progressive movement as much more than an extension of populism; indeed, its dominant spirit becomes not "rural and provincial" but "urban, middle-class and nationwide." These historians often explain the movement in terms of what Richard Hofstadter has called "the status revolution." This thesis attempts to show that a group of middle-class, well-educated citizens, including lawyers, doctors, preachers, educators, and small businessmen, who had usually held positions of leadership, were being displaced in the late nineteenth century by the rising power of labor union leaders, corporation executives, and political bosses. Frustrated by their loss of status and power, driven by a sense of responsibility or guilt when confronted by the problems of urbanism and industrialism, they became reformers in an effort to hold on to a society that they deemed good but rapidly disappearing.

Whatever their motivations, the progressives, as the name they gave themselves makes clear, believed in progress. They were certain that they could improve the quality of life. But would progress come through minor adjustments and reforms in a system that was fundamentally sound, or would it come through bitter conflict with the forces of evil? The progressives themselves were not sure—or at least they did not always agree with one another. Historians who have studied them also disagree, as the following selections make clear.

George Mowry, in the first selection, denies that progressivism was a class conflict between rich and poor, and he sees no real link between the populist and the progressive reformers. Instead he finds that the progressive impulse came from those who found it difficult to adjust to the changes brought by the industrial age. He concludes by suggesting that the progressives were divided in their goals, some looking backward to conditions that were disappearing, others looking forward to a highly centralized government that could institute needed changes.

In the second selection, Paul Boyer sees progressivism as a moral crusade against sin and evil. The progressives, he writes, had "an infinite capacity for moral indignation" in their battle for social justice and against corporate wrongdoing, governmental corruption, and immorality of all kinds. Progressives fought for better housing, parks and playgrounds, and improved schools; they were appalled by child labor and the unsafe condition of the cities. Here, however, Boyer concentrates on the moral crusades of the progressives against liquor and prostitution.

If Mowry finds some Progressives opposed to the system as it was developing, he finds others favoring a strong government that could correct evils. For the latter group, the evils were real and important, but they were not endemic to the system. Similarly, Boyer argues that the system required adjustment to correct evils, but that the system itself was not fundamentally evil.

Readers should note that both Mowry and Boyer find a coercive strain in progressivism. People often had to be forced to give up their evil ways. What implications does such an attitude have for democracy? Can coercion and democracy exist together? In the third selection, David J. Rothman directly addresses these questions. He sees the progressives as liberal reformers who sought to ameliorate wrongs but who in the process often trampled on the rights of those they were helping. Using the power of the state, they sought to impose a middle-class consensus; like parents, they thought they knew what was best for the disadvantaged "children." Rothman argues that the current concern with liberty and the appearance of adversary politics and social relations mark a revolt against the pervasive liberalism that had its origins in the progressive era.

How important were the differences that divided reformers from their opponents during the progressive period? Was there a widespread agreement on fundamentals that led progressives merely to seek minor adjustments in a basically sound society? Or did progressive reformers recognize deep-seated problems and seek major changes?.

Were the liberal reformers illiberal in their goals and methods? Did they, in seeking their goals, infringe upon the rights of those they were supposed to be helping? Or does such a view do an injustice to a group of people who spent their time, money, and energy to help people in distress?

George Mowry

# Progressivism:
# Middle-Class Disillusionment

As a group, the reform mayors and governors, their prominent supporters, and the muckrakers were an interesting lot. Considering the positions they held, they were very young. Joseph W. Folk was only thirty-five when elected governor, Theodore Roosevelt forty, Charles Evans Hughes and Hiram Johnson forty-four, and Robert La Follette forty-five. The average age of the important progressive leaders who upset the Southern Pacific Railroad machine in California was a little over thirty-eight. The tale of a rather typical young reformer was that of Joseph Medill Patterson of the Chicago *Tribune* family. Patterson's grandfather founded the *Tribune*, his father was general manager of the paper, and his cousin was Robert McCormick, who controlled the paper for over thirty years. Patterson sharply reacted against the reigning conservatism by winning a seat in the Illinois legislature at the age of twenty-four on a platform advocating the municipal ownership of all city utilities in the state. Two years later he resigned from the Chicago Commission of Public Works to become a Socialist because, he announced, it was impossible to reform the city and the country under capitalism. In 1906 he published a diatribe against wealth in the *Independent* entitled "The Confessions of a Drone," and followed it two years later with a book of similar tone.[1] Obviously, this was a period, like the ones after the War of 1812 and in the 1850's,

From pages 85–93, 98–105, The Era of Theodore Roosevelt by George Mowry. Copyright © 1958 by George E. Mowry. By permission of Harper & Row, Publishers.

[1] George E. Mowry, *The California Progressives* (Berkeley and Los Angeles, 1952), p. 87; *The Public*, April 8, 1905; *Independent*, LXI (1906), pp. 493–495; Joseph Medill Patterson, *Little Brother of the Rich* (Chicago, 1908).

when energetic and incautious youth took command. And in each instance the departure of the elder statesmen portended great changes.

Some of these reformers, like Golden Rule Jones, Charles Evans Hughes, and Tom Johnson, were self-made men, although Hughes's father was a minister, and Johnson's, a Confederate colonel, had come from the upper stratum of Kentucky society. A surprising number of them came from very wealthy families, with names like du Pont, Crane, Spreckels, Dodge, Morgenthau, Pinchot, Perkins, McCormick, and Patterson. The quip was made that this was a "millionaire's reform movement." But the great majority of the reformers came from the "solid middle class," as it then was called with some pride. That their families had been of the economically secure is indicated by the fact that most of them had had a college education in a day when a degree stamped a person as coming from a special economic group. It is interesting to note that most of the women reformers and social workers had gone to college. Occupationally also the reformers came from a very narrow base in society. Of a sample of over four hundred a majority was lawyers, as might be expected of politicians, and nearly 20 percent of them newspaper editors or publishers. The next largest group was from the independent manufacturers or merchants, with the rest scattered among varied occupations, including medicine, banking, and real estate. A statistical study of sixty of the wealthier reformers reveals that the largest single group of twenty-one was manufacturers or merchants, ten lawyers, six newspaper publishers, while nineteen more had inherited their wealth. Quite a few among the latter group had no definite occupation save that of preserving their family fortune and indulging in reform. Of the sixty only about half attended college, a figure much lower than that for the entire group of reformers. Of this number just 50 percent came from three institutions, Harvard, Princeton, and Yale.[2]

If names mean anything, an overwhelming proportion of this reform group came from old American stock with British origins consistently indicated. Except for the women, who were predominantly Midwestern, the reformers' places of origin were scattered over the country roughly in proportion to population densities. Practically all of them by 1900, however, lived in northern cities, most of the Southerners having left their section during early manhood. Religious affiliations were surprisingly difficult to get, and no really trustworthy national sample was obtained. The figures collected were not at all consonant with national church membership statistics. Representatives of the Quaker faith bulked large among the women reformers, as did members of the Jewish religion among the very wealthy. But for the group as a whole the religious descendants of Calvin and Knox predominated, with the Congregationalists, Unitarians, and Presbyterians in the vast majority. Thus it seems likely that the intellectual and religious influence of New England was again dominating the land.

---

[2] These statistics and the ones following came from a series of studies in the writer's seminar. The figures were rechecked and are in the author's possession.

Whether Democrats or Republicans, the overwhelming number of this group of twentieth-century reformers had been conservatives in the nineties. If Republican, they had almost to a man followed the way of Theodore Roosevelt, Robert La Follette, Lincoln Steffens, and William Allen White to support William McKinley. Most of the progressive Democrats had not been supporters of Bryan, but, like Woodrow Wilson, John Johnson, and Hoke Smith of Georgia, had either followed the Gold Democratic ticket or had remained silent during the election of 1896. Yet from four to six years later most of these men were ardent advocates of municipal gas and water socialism, and were opposed to their regular party machines to the extent of leading either nonpartisan movements in the municipalities or rebellious splinter groups in the states. Moreover, the new century found most of them, except on the currency issue, supporting many of the 1896 Populist and Bryanite demands. Before the Progressive years were finished they and their kind had not only secured the inception of a host of the Populists' reforms, but had contributed a few of their own.

Obviously, a good many questions arise about the motivation of this economically secure, well-educated, middle-class group. On the surface it looked as if the progressive movement was simply a continuation under different leadership of the Populist cause. According to William Allen White, Populism had "shaved its whiskers, washed its shirt, put on a derby, and moved up into the middle class. . . ." But White's remark scarcely probed beneath the surface. Populism arose from farmer distress in a period of acute depression. Its reforms were belly reforms. The movement was led by angry men and women not too far removed from the Grange hall. Except for the western silver men, they were incensed at the mounting figures of farm foreclosures and a withering countryside. To the contrary, progressivism arose in a period of relative prosperity. Its reforms were more the results of the heart and the head than of the stomach. Its leaders were largely recruited from the professional and business classes of the city. A good many were wealthy men; more were college graduates. As a group they were indignant at times, but scarcely ever angry. What caused them to act in the peculiar way they did? A part of the answer lies in the peculiar economic and social position in which this middle-class group found itself at about the turn of the century, a part in the intellectual and ethical climate of the age, a part in the significant cluster of prejudices and biases that marked the progressive mind.

"The world wants men, great, strong, harsh, brutal men—men with purpose who let nothing, nothing, nothing stand in their way," Frank Norris wrote in one of his novels. This worship of the strong man, so characteristic of the age, produced a cult of political leadership with ominous overtones for later years. Tempered at this time with the ethics of the social gospel, the cult produced an image far less frightening: an image of men dedicated to the social good, an image approximating the hope of Plato for his guardians. These strong good men, "the change-makers," Harold Frederic wrote, were the protectors of morality, the originators of progress. They were ambitious men and ruthless, but only ruthless in their zeal for human advancement. They were supremely alone, the causative individuals. Far from being disturbed when isolated, David Graham Phillips's hero Scarborough was only concerned when he was "propped up" by something other than his own will and intelligence. "I propose," he commented, "never to 'belong' to anything or anybody."[3]

In 1872 a future progressive, Henry Demarest Lloyd, confessed that he wanted power above all things, but "power unpoisoned by the presence of obligation." That worship of the unfettered individual, the strong pride of self, the strain of ambition, and the almost compulsive desire for power ran through progressive rhetoric like a theme in a symphony. From Frank Norris's strong-minded heroes to Richard Harding Davis's men of almost pure muscle these feelings were a badge of a restless, sensitive, and troubled class. They were never far below the surface in the character of Theodore Roosevelt. Robert La Follette knew them, and Woodrow Wilson had more than his share of them. While still a scholar and teacher, Wilson poured out his frustration with the contemplative life: "I have no patience with the tedious world of what is known as 'research,' " he wrote to a friend. "I should be complete if I could inspire a great movement of opinion. . . ."[4]

A few progressive leaders like William Jennings Bryan and Golden Rule Jones really thought of themselves as servants of the people,[5] and almost completely identified themselves with their constituents. But most progressives set themselves apart from the crowd. Mankind was basically good and capable of progress, but benign change scarcely issued from the masses. Rather it was only accomplished through the instrumentality of a few great and good men. Woodrow Wilson believed that efficient government could come only from "an educated elite," William Kent thought that progress never came from the bottom, and Roosevelt often spoke of government as the process of "giving justice from above." Occasionally, when the electorate disagreed with them, the progressives contented themselves with the thought that truth "was always in the minority" and a possession alone of the "few who see." In 1912 Walter Lippmann wrote that since men could do anything but govern themselves, they were constantly looking for some "benevolent guardian." To the progressive politician that guardian, of course, was patterned after his image of himself.[6] . . .

A small reform-minded minority in 1900 was outspoken in defense of

[3] Frank Norris, *A Man's Woman* (New York, 1900), p. 71; David Graham Phillips *The Cost* (Indianapolis, 1904), p. 17.

[4] Quoted in Daniel Aaron, *Men of Good Hope* (New York, 1951), p. 139; Richard Hofstadter, *The American Political Tradition and the Men Who Made It* (New York, 1948), p. 243.

[5] Frances G. Newland, *Public Papers* (New York, 1932), p. 311.

[6] Theodore Roosevelt, "Who Is a Progressive?" *The Outlook*, C (1912), 2; *The Public*, April 18, 1903; Walter Lippmann, *Drift and Mastery* (New York, 1914), p. 189.

the large industrial and commercial city as the creator of the good life. Some of them saw the city as a place of refuge from an ugly countryside and from a hostile natural environment. Remembering his own bleak and lonely boyhood on an upstate New York farm, the novelist Harold Frederic condemned a daily communion with nature that starved the mind and dwarfed the soul. Theodore Dreiser bluntly described the natural processes as inimical to man as a species. Others felt the fascination of the city, a place of excitement and of opportunity. Lincoln Steffens recalled that he felt about the concrete canyons of New York as other youths felt about the wild West. For people like Jane Addams, Jacob Riis, and Hutchins Hapgood the city offered a place to work and an avenue to opportunity.

For the great majority of the new century's reformers, however, the city contained almost the sum of their dislikes. It was a "devilsburg of crime" sucking into its corrupt vortex the "young, genuine, strong and simple men from the farm." There, if successful, they became "financial wreckers" who made their money strangling legitimate enterprises and other human beings. If they were failures—that is, if they remained factory workers—they gradually became like the machine they tended, "huge, hard, brutal, strung with a crude blind strength, stupid, unreasoning." At the worst such unfortunates became the flotsam of the slums, making the saloon their church and the dive their home. The native American lost not only his morals in the city but also his talent for creative work and his sense of beauty. "Sometimes, I think, they'se poison in th' life in a big city," Mr. Dooley remarked, "the flowers won't grow there. . . ." If a man stayed in the city long enough, one of David Graham Phillips' characters remarked, he would almost inevitably lose those qualities that made him an American: one had to go West to see a "real American, a man or a woman who looks as if he or she would do something honest or valuable. . . ."[7]

With such intense antiurban feelings, it is small wonder that the United States began to romanticize its pioneer past and its agrarian background. Following the Spanish War historical novels fairly poured from the publishers. The public appetite for western stories had one of its periodic increases, and the virtues of the countryside were extolled in even the best literature. In one of Ellen Glasgow's first novels the country, "with its ecstatic insight into the sacred plan of things," is contrasted with the city's "tainted atmosphere." Almost repeating William Jennings Bryan in 1896, Miss Glasgow wrote that the country was the world as God had planned it, the city as man had made it. The cult of the frontier, first introduced into historical scholarship by

---

[7] For varied expressions of this antiurbanism, see Irving Bacheller, *Eben Holden* (Boston, 1900), p. 336; Alice H. Rice, *Mrs. Wiggs of the Cabbage Patch* (New York, 1901), p. 29; Winston Churchill, *The Dwelling-Place of Light* (New York, 1917), p. 79; Finley Peter Dunne, *Mr. Dooley in Peace and War* (Boston, 1898), p. 125; D. G. Phillips, *Golden Fleece* (New York, 1903), pp. 57–58.

Frederick Jackson Turner in 1890, and the new emphasis upon agrarian virtues were zealously reflected by the more sensitive politicians. William Jennings Bryan, Theodore Roosevelt, Robert La Follette, and Woodrow Wilson all showed to varying degrees this national nostalgia, this reactionary impulse. Roosevelt in particular saw the great city as the creator of national weakness and possible disintegration, and the countryside as the nation's savior. It was the man on the farm, he wrote, who had consistently done the nation the "best service in governing himself in time of peace and also in fighting in time of war." Dangerous elements to the commonwealth lurked in every large city, but among the western farmers of the West "there was not room for an anarchist or a communist in the whole lot." What Professor Richard Hofstadter has called the agrarian myth, but which might better be called the agrarian bias, was one of the more important elements that went into the making of the progressive mind.[8]

A part of the progressive's romantic attraction to the countryside at this particular time can be explained by the alien character of the urban population. In 1903 the Commissioner of Immigration reported that the past year had witnessed the greatest influx of immigrants in the nation's history. But far from being pleased, the Commissioner was plainly worried. An increasing percentage of these newcomers, he pointed out, belonged to an "undesirable foreign element," the "indigestible" aliens from south Europe. The public was neither surprised at the figures of the report nor shocked by its adjectives. It had been made increasingly sensitive to the changing patterns of immigration by numerous periodical articles and newspaper items calling attention to the alien nature of the eastern seaboard cities. As the immigrant tide welled stronger each year, the nativist spirit that had been so obviously a part of the mental complex leading to the Spanish War increased in intensity. Throughout the decade editors, novelists, and politicians competed with each other in singing the praises of the "big-boned, blond, long-haired" Anglo-Saxon with the blood of the berserkers in his veins, and in denigrating Jack London's "dark pigmented things, the half castes, the mongrel bloods, and the dregs of long conquered races. . . ." In Frank Norris's novels the really despicable characters run all to a type. Braun, the diamond expert in *Vandover*; Zerkow, the junk dealer in *McTeague*; the flannel-shirted Grossman in *The Pit*; and Behrman in *The Octopus* were all of the same religion and approximately from the same regions in Europe. One of the themes in Homer Lea's *The Vermillion Pencil* was the extra-national loyalty of the Catholic bishop who intrigued endlessly for the Church and against the State. Although Chester Rowell frankly admitted that

---

[8] Ellen Glasgow, *The Descendant* (New York, 1897), p. 254; Roosevelt to George Otto Trevelyan, March 9, 1905, and to Kermit Roosevelt, January 1, 1907, Roosevelt MSS.; *The Public*, November 14, 1903.

California needed "a class of servile labor," he was adamantly opposed to the admission of Orientals, who were dangerous to the state and to "the blood of the next generation."[9]

The progressives, of course, had no monopoly of this racism. Such conservatives as Elihu Root, Henry Cabot Lodge, and Chauncey Depew, and even radicals like Debs, shared their views to a degree. But for one reason or another neither conservative nor radical was as vocal or as specific in his racism as was the reformer. No more eloquent testimony to the power of racism over the progressive mind is evident than in the writings of the kindly, tolerant Middle Westerner William Allen White. In a book published in 1910 White explained nearly all of America's past greatness, including its will to reform, in terms of the nation's "race life" and its racial institutions, "the home and the folk moot." Nor would this genius, this "clean Aryan blood," White promised, be subjected to a debilitating admixture in the future despite the incoming hordes. "We are separated by two oceans from the inferior races and by an instinctive race revulsion to cross breeding that marks the American wherever he is found."[10] Such diverse reformers as Theodore Roosevelt, Albert J. Beveridge, Chester Rowell, Frank Parsons, Hoke Smith, Richard W. Gilder, and Ray Stannard Baker, with more or less emphasis, echoed White's sentiments. . . .

Since the progressive usually came from a comfortable part of society and a general attack upon property was usually furthest from his mind, this assault upon great wealth put him in a rather ambiguous position. The one way out of the paradox was to draw a line between good and bad wealth. For some the limit of private fortunes was the total that man could "justly acquire." For others the measurement was made in terms of service to society. Tom Johnson, for example, believed that the law could be so drawn that men would be able "to get" only the amount "they earned." Still others argued that there must be a point where additional money ceased to be salubrious for a man's character and became instead a positive evil force. Wayne MacVeagh, Garfield's Attorney General, suggested that all people could be divided into three classes: those who had more money than was good for them, those who had just enough, and those who had much less than was morally desirable. Just where the exact lines should be drawn, most progressives would not say. But the imputation that the state ought to redivide wealth on a morally desirable basis found a receptive audience. To George F. Baer's claim that coal prices should be the sum of "all the traffic will bear," the editors of *The Outlook* replied that property was private not by any natural right but by an "artificial arrangement made by the community." "If under those artificial arrangements," the editorial continued, "the community

[9] *Literary Digest*, XXVII (1903), p. 158; Jack London, *The Mutiny of the Elsinore* (New York, 1914), pp. 197–198. See also John Higham, *Strangers in the Land, Patterns of American Nativism, 1860–1925* (New Brunswick, N.J., 1955), pp. 131 ff.

[10] William Allen White, *The Old Order Changeth* (New York, 1910), pp. 128, 197, 253.

is made to suffer, the same power that made them will find a way to unmake them." Thus in the progressive mind the classical economic laws repeatedly described in the past as natural had become artificial arrangements to be re-arranged at any time the community found it morally or socially desirable. Admittedly the formulations of new ethical standards for a division of national wealth were to be extremely difficult. But once the progressive had destroyed the popular sanction behind the "laws" of rent, prices, and wages, there was to be no complete turning back. A revolution in human thought had occurred. Man, it was hoped, would now become the master and not the creature of his economy. And the phrases punctuating the next fifty years of history—the "square deal," the New Deal, the Fair Deal, the just wage, the fair price—attested to his efforts to make the reality square with his ambitions.[11]

After revisiting the United States in 1905, James Bryce, the one-time ambassador from Great Britain, noted that of all the questions before the public the ones bearing on capital and labor were the most insistent and the most discussed. Certainly for many a progressive the rise of the labor union was as frightening as the rise of trusts. True, he talked about them less because nationally they were obviously not as powerful as were the combines of capital. But emotionally he was, if anything, more opposed to this collectivism from below than he was to the collectivism above him in the economic ladder.[12]

"There is nothing ethical about the labor movement. It is coercion from start to finish. In every aspect it is a driver and not a leader. It is simply a war movement, and must be judged by the analogues of belligerence and not by industrial principles." This statement by a Democratic progressive illustrates the ire of the small and uncertain employer who was being challenged daily by a power he often could not match. In their lawlessness and in their violence, remarked another, unions were "a menace not only to the employer but to the entire community."[13] To the small employer and to many middle-class professionals unions were just another kind of monopoly created for the same reasons and having the same results as industrial monopoly. Unions, they charged, restricted production, narrowed the available labor market, and raised wages artificially in the same manner that trusts were restricting production, narrowing competition, and raising their own profits. "Every step in trade unionism has followed the steps that organized capital has laid down before it," Clarence Darrow observed in a speech before the Chicago Henry George Association. The ultimate direction of the two monopolies was as clear to the individual entrepreneur as it was to Darrow.

[11] *The Public*, September 23, 1905, and February 3, 1906; Wayne MacVeagh, "An Appeal to Our Millionaires," *North American Review*, June, 1906; *The Outlook*, LXXVI (1904), 240.

[12] James Bryce, "America Revisited," *The Outlook*, LXXIX (1905), p. 848.

[13] *The Public*, June 13, 1903; *The Outlook*, LXVIII (1901), p. 683.

Either trade unionism would break down, a Midwestern editor argued, or it would culminate in "a dangerously oppressive partnership" with the stronger industrial trusts. The end result was equally obvious to such men: a steady decrease in opportunity for the individual operating as an individual, an economy of statics, an end to the open society. The burden of the industrial evolution, Darrow said in concluding his speech, "falls upon the middle class."[14] And Howells' traveler from Altruria put the case even more graphically: "the struggle for life has changed from a free fight to an encounter of disciplined forces, and the free fighters that are left get ground to pieces between organized labor and organized capital." . . .

" 'I am for labor,' or 'I am for capital,' substitutes something else for the immutable laws of righteousness," Theodore Roosevelt was quoted as saying in 1904. "The one and the other would let the class man in, and letting him in is the one thing that will most quickly eat out the heart of the Republic." Roosevelt, of course, was referring to class parties in politics. Most progressives agreed with Herbert Croly that a "profound antagonism" existed between the political system and a government controlled by a labor party.[15] In San Francisco in 1901, in Chicago in 1905, and in Los Angeles in 1911, when labor used or threatened direct political action, the progressive reacted as if touched by fire. Chicago was a "class-ridden" city, remarked one progressive journal, which would not redeem itself until the evil pretensions of both organized capital and labor had been suppressed. In Los Angeles, where a Socialist labor group came within a hair's breadth of controlling the city, the progressives combined with their old enemies, the corporation-dominated machine, to fight off the challenge, and as a result never again exerted the power they once had in the city. Apropos of that struggle punctuated by a near general strike, dynamite, and death, the leading California progressive theorist, Chester Rowell, expostulated that no class as a class was fit to rule a democracy; that progress came only from the activities of good citizens acting as individuals. Class prejudice and class pride excused bribery, mass selfishness, lawlessness, and disorder. This class spirit emanating from both business and labor was "destroying American liberty." When it became predominant, Rowell concluded, American institutions would be dead, for peaceful reform would no longer be possible, and "nothing but revolution" would remain.[16]

At various times and places the progressive politician invited the support of organized labor, but such co-operation was almost invariably a one-way

[14] Chicago *Record Herald*, June 26, 1903; *The Public*, June 11, 1903.

[15] Charles H. Cooley, *Human Nature and the Social Order* (New York, 1902), p. 72; Ray Stannard Baker, "The Rise of the Tailors," *McClure's*, XXIV (1904), p. 14. For other expressions of the same spirit, see Simon Patten, *The New Basis of Civilization* (New York, 1907), p. 84; John N. McCormick, *The Litany and the Life* (Milwaukee, 1904), p. 93; H. B. Brown, "Twentieth Century," *Forum*, XIX (1895), p. 641; *The Public*, November 26, 1914; Jacob A. Riis, "Theodore Roosevelt, The Citizen," *The Outlook*, LXXVI (1904), p. 649; Croly, *Promise*, p. 129.

[16] *The Public*, May 13, 1905, and June 17, 1905; *Fresno Republican*, November 20, 1911.

street. Somewhat reminiscent of the early relations between the British Liberal and Labor parties, it worked only if the progressive rather than the labor politician was in the driver's seat. In Maine, for example, when labor attempted to lead a campaign for the initiative and referendum, it was defeated in part by progressives, who two years later led a successful campaign on the same issues.[17] In the progressive literature the terms "captain of industry" and "labor boss" were standard, while "labor statesman" was practically unknown. Roosevelt's inclination to try labor lawbreakers in a criminal court is well known; his administration's failure to indict criminally one corporation executive is eloquent of the limits of his prejudice. Progressive literature contained many proposals for permitting corporations to develop until they had achieved quasi-monopoly status, at which time federal regulation would be imposed. No such development was forecast for labor. Unions were grudgingly recognized as a necessary evil, but the monopolistic closed shop was an abomination not to be tolerated with or without government regulation. In the Chicago teamsters' strike of 1905 Mayor Dunne ordered the city police to be "absolutely impartial" toward both capital and labor. But he also insisted that the strikers not be allowed to block the teams of nonunion men or the delivery of nonunion-marked goods.[18]

A few progressives, of course, hailed the rise of labor unions as an advance in democracy. But the majority, while sincerely desirous of improving the plight of the individual workingman, was perhaps basically more hostile to the union than to corporate monopoly. If the progressive attention was mostly centered on the corporation during the decade, it was largely because the sheer social power of the corporation vastly overshadowed that of the rising but still relatively weak unions. When confronted with a bleak either-or situation, progressive loyalties significantly shifted up and not down the economic ladder.

Emotionally attached to the individual as a causative force and to an older America where he saw his group supreme, assaulted economically and socially from above and below, and yet eager for the wealth and the power that flowed from the new collectivism, the progressive was at once nostalgic, envious, fearful, and yet confident about the future. Fear and confidence together for a time inspired this middle-class group of supremely independent individuals with a class consciousness that perhaps exceeded that of any other group in the nation. This synthesis had been a long time developing. Back in the early 1890's Henry George had remarked that the two dangerous classes to the state were "the very rich" and "the very poor." Some years afterward a Populist paper referred to the "upper and lower scum" of society. At about the same time the acknowledged dean of American letters had inquired just where the great inventions, the good books, the beautiful pictures, and the

---

[17] J. William Black, "Maine's Experience with the Initiative and Referendum," *Annals of the American Academy of Political Science*, XLII, pp. 164–165.

[18] *The Public*, April 15, 1905.

just laws had come from in American society. Not from the "uppermost" or "lowermost" classes, Howells replied. They had come mostly from the middle-class man. In the first decade of the twentieth century the progressive never questioned where ability and righteousness resided. Nor was he uncertain of the sources of the nation's evils. "From above," one wrote, "come the problems of predatory wealth. . . . From below come the problems of poverty and pigheaded and brutish criminality."[19]

As the progressive looked at the sharply differentiated America of 1900, he saw "pyramids of money in a desert of want." For William Allen White the world was full of "big crooks" and the "underprivileged." The polar conditions of society assaulted the progressive conscience and threatened progressive security. Supremely individualistic, the progressive could not impute class consciousness, or, as he would have phrased it, class selfishness, to himself. His talk was therefore full of moral self-judgments, of phrases like "the good men," "the better element," "the moral crowd." From the Old Source, he paraphrased, "Thou shalt not respect the person of the poor, nor honor the person of the great; in righteousness shalt thou judge thy neighbor." His self-image was that of a "kind-hearted man" dealing in justice. William Kent publicly stated that he could not believe in the class struggle because every great reform of the past had been wrought by men who were not "selfishly interested." "I believe," he concluded, "altruism is a bigger force in the world than selfishness."[20]

Since the progressive was not organized economically as was the capitalist and the laborer, he chose to fight his battles where he had the most power —in the political arena. And in large terms his political program was first that of the most basic urge of all nature, to preserve himself, and secondly to refashion the world after his own image. What the nation needed most, wrote a Midwestern clergyman, was an increase in the number of "large-hearted men" to counteract the class organization of both capital and labor. "Solidarity," Herbert Croly stated, "must be restored." The point of reconcentration around which the hoped-for solidarity was to take place, of course, was the middle class. It was to "absorb" all other classes, thought Henry Demarest Lloyd. It was to be both the sum and substance of the classless state of the future.[21]

The progressive mentality was a compound of many curious elements. It contained a reactionary as well as a reform impulse. It was imbued with a burning ethical strain which at times approached a missionary desire to create a heaven on earth. It had in it intense feelings of moral superiority over both

---

[19] Aaron, *Men of Good Hope*, pp. 84, 193; Jackson (Michigan) *Industrial News*, March 8, 1894; *California Weekly*, December 18, 1908.

[20] William Allen White to Henry J. Allen, July 28, 1934, in Walter Johnson (ed.), *Selected Letters of William Allen White, 1899–1943* (New York, 1947), p. 348; San Francisco *Bulletin*, September 8, 1911.

[21] William J. McCaughan, *Love, Faith and Joy* (Chicago, 1904), p. 206; Croly, *Promise of American Life*, p. 139; Aaron, *Men of Good Hope*, p. 160.

elements of society above and below it economically. It emphasized individual dynamism and leadership. One part of it looked backward to an intensely democratic small America; another looked forward to a highly centralized nationalistic state. And both elements contained a rather ugly strain of racism.

The progressive mentality was generated in part from both a fear of the loss of group status and a confidence in man's ability to order the future. Had progressive militancy come in a more despondent intellectual and ethical climate and in a bleaker economic day, group fear might have won over group hope. Its more benign social ends might then have been transmuted into something more malignant. But in the warm and sunny atmosphere of 1900 the optimistic mood prevailed. . . .

Paul Boyer

# Battling the Saloon and the Brothel: The Great Coercive Crusades

On June 25, 1910, President William Howard Taft signed into law a bill introduced by Congressman James Mann of Illinois making it a federal offense to transport a woman across a state line for "immoral purposes." A death blow had been struck, so the framers of the Mann Act claimed, against prostitution, the brothel, and the dread "white-slave traffic."

Seven and a half years later, on December 22, 1917, in the midst of a world war, Congress submitted to the states a constitutional amendment barring the manufacture, sale, or importation of intoxicating liquor within the United States. In January 1919, the necessary thirty-six states having ratified, prohibition became the law of the land. (By the terms of the Eighteenth Amendment, actual enforcement began a year later: a final crumb tossed to the liquor interests by the triumphant prohibitionists.)

These two measures were among the crowning achievements of the great Progressive-era crusades against the "liquor evil" and the "prostitution evil." . . . The brothel and the saloon were widely perceived as the great bastions of urban vice. So long as they stood, the dream of an urban moral awakening would be no more than that; if they could be subdued, the purified, morally homogeneous city might at last become a reality.

Intemperance and prostitution were not, of course, discoveries of the Progressives. Both had been the object of reformist attention since the days of Lyman Beecher and John R. McDowall. In the Gilded Age, the Woman's Christian Temperance Union (1874) had revived the temperance cause, and the antiprostitution banner had been upheld by "social purity" leaders like

Abby Hopper Gibbons of New York and the Philadelphia Quaker Aaron Macy Powell, as well as by local civic organizations campaigning against municipal regulation (and hence tacit acceptance) of prostitution. The decade of the 1890s saw an intensification of both antialcohol and antiprostitution effort, including state campaigns to raise the legal age of consent, national temperance conventions and "purity" congresses, the formation of the Anti-Saloon League (1895) and the American Purity Alliance, and the organization of rescue work aimed at prostitutes and unwed mothers.

For all this, the dawning century found both vices still deeply entrenched. In 1900 only three states had prohibition laws on the books; saloons, liquor stores, and the infamous "bucket shops" flourished in every major city; and per capita alcohol consumption—augmented by the new national favorite, German lager beer—stood at nearly twice the 1860 figure. As for prostitution, every city had its red-light district, including some now bathed in a nostalgic glow: Gayosa Street in Memphis; the Levee in Chicago; San Francisco's Barbary Coast; New Orleans' Storyville (named for the alderman who drafted the statute establishing its boundaries); "Hooker's Division" in Washington, an appelation immortalizing the Civil War general who had confined prostitutes to that section. In 1900, two Omaha madams, Ada and Minna Everleigh, felt confident enough of their prospects to invest thousands of dollars in a luxurious Chicago brothel, the Everleigh Club, which soon became the showplace of the Levee.

In focusing attention on these evils—indeed, in making them stand symbolically for much that was unsettling about city life—urban moral reformers of the Progressive era succeeded in channeling the urban uplift enthusiasm of the 1890s into highly organized efforts involving specific goals and carefully planned strategies. In the prohibition drive, the Anti-Saloon League—supported by innumerable small contributors and a few very large ones like John D. Rockefeller, Jr., and dime-store baron S. S. Kresge—played the crucial organizational role. From the first, the ASL's single-minded goal was legal prohibition, and its major target, the cities. In counties and townships where prohibitionist sentiment was strong, the league organized local-option campaigns and worked for the election of sympathetic state legislators. The local groundwork laid, it moved to the state level, exhibiting the same skill in legislative lobbying that it displayed in marshaling public opinion. By concentrating on state legislatures (where the cities were underrepresented), the Anti-Saloon League gradually isolated urban America. In the campaign's final stages, thousands of ASL speakers promoted the cause in the nation's Protestant pulpits, and oceans of propaganda (including the League's principal organ, the *American Issue*) poured from ASL presses in Westerville, Ohio. The triumph of 1919 was thus the culmination of more than two decades of grass roots effort, reinforced by wartime fervor, grain-conservation enthusiasm, and anti-German-brewer sentiment.

While the ASL was orchestrating the prohibition campaign, a more complex organizational effort was focusing diffuse sexual-purity impulses on a specific issue: urban prostitution. The issue first surfaced in New York City, where the number of saloons harboring prostitutes had increased sharply after 1896, when a revision of the state licensing code—dubbed the Raines Law after its sponsor—had inadvertently made it advantageous for them to add bedrooms and transform themselves into "hotels." The spread of these "Raines Law hotels" into well-to-do neighborhoods aroused a storm of indignation, and in November 1900 Episcopal Bishop Henry C. Potter penned a stinging protest to Tammany mayor Robert Van Wyck. (Unruffled, Van Wyck declared that New York had "the highest standard of morality in the world"; Tammany boss Richard Croker, taking a rather contradictory tack, argued that in any city there were "bound to be some unusually vile places.")

A few days after Potter's letter, the New York Committee of Fifteen was formed. This organization of businessmen, publishers, academics, and other elite figures—the prototype of antiprostitution commissions that would soon emerge in scores of cities—set out quietly to investigate vice conditions and develop legislative remedies. It soon became involved in more stirring matters, however, through its support for a flamboyant young special-sessions judge, William T. Jerome—the "second Theodore Roosevelt," his admirers claimed—who had won celebrity for his dramatic raids on brothels and other vice dens. In the municipal elections of 1901, thanks in part to the support of the Committee of Fifteen and the Reverend Charles Parkhurst's City Vigilance League, Jerome was elected district attorney while Seth Low, a "fusion" candidate backed by the reformers, defeated Tammany's man in the mayoral race.

Meanwhile, a team of prostitution investigators had been recruited by the Committee of Fifteen, and in 1902 its findings were published as *The Social Evil, with Special Reference to Conditions Existing in the City of New York*. A 1909 *McClure's* exposé, "The Daughters of the Poor: A Plain Story of the Development of New York City as a Leading Center of the White Slave Trade of the World, under Tammany Hall," helped sustain the cause, as did the 1910 investigations of a special grand jury under John D. Rockefeller, Jr.

At the same time, Chicago was emerging as a second major center of the antiprostitution campaign. In a 1907 *McClure's* article, "The City of Chicago: A Study of the Great Immoralities," muckraker George Kibbe Turner accorded prostitution a prominent place in his catalog of evils. ("As in the stock-yards, not one shred of flesh is wasted.") Soon an ambitious assistant state's attorney named Clifford G. Roe was organizing a series of white-slave prosecutions. Thwarted by his superiors, Roe resigned, secretly arranged financial backing from a group of sympathetic Chicagoans, and proceeded with his investigations as a private citizen. In 1911 Roe organized the National Vigilance Society (with himself as director, secretary, and general counsel) and over the next few years published several lurid books on prostitution.

Meanwhile, in January 1910, under pressure from the Chicago church federation, Mayor Fred Busse had appointed a thirty-member vice commission (twenty-eight men, two women), under the chairmanship of Walter T. Sumner, dean of the Cathedral of Saints Peter and Paul (Episcopal), to investigate prostitution in the city. Given a $5,000 appropriation, the Commission in 1911 produced *The Social Evil in Chicago*, a 394-page report ending with a set of recommendations aimed at implementing its motto: "Constant and Persistent Repression of Prostitution the Immediate Method; Absolute Annihilation the Ultimate Ideal." The report was based on data compiled by a research team under George J. Kneeland, a Yale Divinity School dropout who had worked as an editor with several New York magazines before becoming director of investigations for New York's Committee of Fifteen in 1908.

Also involved in the antiprostitution crusade were the American Society of Sanitary and Moral Prophylaxis (founded 1905), a medical group headed by the prominent dermatologist Prince A. Morrow, whose influential *Social Diseases and Marriage* had appeared in 1904, and the Bureau of Social Hygiene (1910), a small, New York-based agency financed with Rockefeller money. Among the latter's publications was *Commercialized Prostitution in New York* (1913), a somewhat popularized version of the various vice reports already in circulation.

Some order emerged in this organizational thicket in 1913 when the Rockefeller and Morrow groups, together with several other societies (including the old American Purity Alliance), merged to form the American Social Hygiene Association. While no single group ever dominated the antiprostitution movement as the Anti-Saloon League did the prohibition crusade, the ASHA and its magazine *Social Hygiene* played a central role.

Sparked by all this organizational activity, the antiprostitution drive had assumed the characteristics of a national crusade. "No movement devoted to the betterment and uplift of humanity has advanced more rapidly within recent years," reported the *New Encyclopedia of Social Reform* in 1909. From 1902 to 1916, 102 cities and 3 states conducted vice investigations modeled on those of New York and Chicago. By 1920 practically every state had outlawed soliciting, and more than 30 had passed Injunction and Abatement laws empowering the courts to close brothels upon the filing of citizens' complaints. At the federal level, the reform found expression not only in the Mann Act but also in President Roosevelt's 1908 announcement of America's adherence to an internal white-slave convention recently adopted in Paris, as well as a series of reports on prostitution—"the most accursed business ever devised by man"—by the United States Immigration Commission.

"White slavery" proved a gold mine to journalists, editors, moviemakers, and publishers. George Kibbe Turner's exposés are merely the best remembered of many in the periodicals of the day. *Traffic in Souls*, a film purporting to document the nationwide prostitution business, appeared in 1913. As for books, the scores of vice commission reports simply added to a torrent of works including such diverse titles as Clifford Roe's *Horrors of the White*

*Slave Trade* (1911), with its 448 pages and thirty-two illustrations; Jane Addams's thoughtful *A New Conscience and an Ancient Evil* (1912); and David Graham Phillips's novel *Susan Lenox; Her Fall and Rise* (1917).

Just as it provided the final impetus for prohibition, the wartime mood of 1917–18 also intensified the antiprostitution crusade. With the support of Secretary of War Newton D. Baker (who as mayor of Cleveland had taken a strong antiprostitution stand), the wartime Commission on Training Camp Activities closed a number of red-light districts hitherto resisting purification—an achievement perhaps praised more heartily in *Social Hygiene* than in the barracks.

## Moralism and Expertise: The Links between the Great Coercive Crusades and Progressivism

Historians have engaged in a lively debate over whether prohibition—and, by implication, the antiprostitution crusade—should be included within the canon of legitimate Progressive reforms. Writing in 1955, Richard Hofstadter said no. Prohibition, he contended, was "a ludicrous caricature of the re-forming impulse"—a "pinched, parochial substitute" for genuine reform, imposed by spiteful rural folk upon the more tolerant and urbane cities. In the same vein, Egal Feldman in 1967 described the coercive aspects of the antiprostitution crusade as "irrational, evangelical, uncompromising, and completely divorced from the humanitarianism of the early twentieth century." Other historians have challenged this thesis. Demonstrating the close connections—in terms of personnel, mutual affirmations of support, and overlapping organizational commitments—that can be established between the moral-control crusades and other strands of progressivism, they argue that the former must be considered an authentic expression of the broader Progressive impulse.

Interestingly, the Progressives themselves had trouble reaching a consensus on this question. Although some reformers and ideologues welcomed the prohibition and antiprostitution campaigns, others denied any kinship between what they stood for and the coercive moral-control crusades. Walter Lippmann, for example, ridiculed the "raucous purity" of some antivice campaigners, and Charles A. Beard in 1912 criticized the "moral enthusiasts" who were "pushing through legislation which they are not willing to uphold by concentrated and persistent action." Herbert Croly in *The Promise of American Life* declared that reformers who functioned merely as "moral protestants and purifiers" were engaged in a fundamentally "misdirected effort." Only "personal self-stultification," he insisted, could result from such an "illiberal puritanism." True reform, Croly characteristically added, involved "an intellectual as well as a moral challenge."

The answer depends in large part, of course, on where one looks on the Progressive spectrum and, indeed, on how one defines progressivism. . . . But one trait common to most reformers of these years—and one which helped establish a bond between the coercive reformers and other Progressives—was an infinite capacity for moral indignation. For Progressives of all stripes, as for their predecessors in the 1890s, questions of social injustice, corporate wrongdoing, governmental corruption, and personal morality were inextricably linked. Almost every Progressive cause had its moral dimension; almost every condition Progressives set out to change was seen as contributing to a debilitating social environment that made it easier for people to go wrong and harder for them to go right. Child labor and the exploitation of women workers were evil not only because they were physically harmful, but also because they stunted the moral and spiritual development of their victims. (Society had the right to limit the hours of women in industry, Louis D. Brandeis argued before the United States Supreme Court in 1908, because the fatigue of long hours was undermining their moral fiber and driving them to "alcoholic stimulants and other excesses.") Urban graft and misgovernment were evil not only because they wasted taxpayers' money but also because they debased the moral climate of the city. ("The influence and example of bad municipal government . . . , of public servants dishonest with impunity and profit," cried an officer of the National Municipal League in 1904, echoing his reform predecessors of the Gilded Age, "constitutes a disease against which we have greater need of a quarantine than we ever had against yellow fever.") As Stanley K. Schultz has written of progressivism's journalistic advance guard the muckrakers, their writings often "assumed the nature of a moral crusade, . . . because ultimately their search was a moral endeavor."

The moral substratum of progressivism is heavily underscored in the autobiography of Frederic C. Howe, in many respects a prototypical Progressive, in which he describes his intensely evangelical upbringing and its shaping influence on his later reform career: "Physical escape from the embraces of evangelical religion did not mean moral escape. From that religion my reason was never emancipated. By it I was conformed to my generation and made to share its moral standards and ideals. . . . Early assumptions as to virtue and vice, goodness and evil remained in my mind long after I had tried to discard them. This is, I think, the most characteristic influence of my generation."

Some historians have drawn sharp distinctions between progressivism's various facets, opposing the economic and political reforms to those that were explicitly moralistic. Such an approach, if too literally applied, does violence to the powerful moral thrust underlying *all* these reforms. For the Progressives, society had the right—indeed the duty!—to intervene at any point where the well-being of its members was threatened, since every such threat had its moral aspect. A 1914 article in a reform journal edited by Josiah Strong and W. D. P. Bliss put the matter plainly: "We are no longer frightened by that ancient bogy—'paternalism in government.' We affirm boldly, it is the business of government to be just that—paternal. . . . *Nothing human can be foreign to a true government.*"

Within this intensely moralistic ambience, it was easy to see the coercive social-control crusades as simply one piece in the larger reform mosaic. In *The Shame of the Cities* (1904), for example, muckraker Lincoln Steffens frequently called attention to organized gambling and prostitution as by-products of municipal political corruption. Similarly, a leading San Francisco Progressive, newspaper editor Fremont Older, in fighting boss Abraham Ruef in 1907–1909, revealed many seamy details of Ruef's involvement with organized vice.

Those who were seeking to rid urban America of these vices, for their part, never doubted that they were in the mainstream of the era's broader reform current. "We are tired of poverty, of squalor, of ignorance . . . , of the wretchedness of women and the degradation of men," wrote a prohibition leader in 1908. "Our hearts bleed when we look upon the misery of child life." Convinced that intolerable conditions of work and habitation were driving men into the saloons and women into the streets, they supported such Progressive reforms as wage-and-hour laws, tenement codes, and factory-safety legislation. "Is it any wonder," asked the Chicago Vice Commission rhetorically, "that a tempted girl who receives only six dollars per week working with her hands sells her body for twenty-five dollars per week when she learns there is a demand for it and men are willing to pay the price?"

A second important respect in which the coercive moral reformers were closely attuned to the broader Progressive impulse was in their reliance on statistics, sociological investigation, and "objective" social analysis to buttress their cause—a strategy characteristic of many otherwise quite disparate Progressive reforms. For the antisaloon and antiprostitution forces, this represented a significant shift from earlier approaches. Through much of the Gilded Age, the temperance and social-purity enthusiasts had concentrated on moral appeals to the individual, assuming that they and the objects of their benevolent attention shared, at some level, a common body of values and standards. (There were exceptions to this personalistic approach—the state drives to raise the legal age of consent, the quadrennial electoral campaigns of the Prohibition party—but in general the personal moral appeal was the preferred strategy.)

By the end of the century, as the old assumptions faded, overtly moralistic personal appeals were being supplanted by a more generalized emphasis on the reformers' technical expertise and superior factual grasp of urban issues. Moral reform must be rooted in careful investigation and social analysis, insisted Benjamin Flower in *Civilization's Inferno*. "Mere sentimentality will not answer. We must have incontrovertible data upon which to base our arguments." The first step of a prestigious Committee of Fifty for the investigation of the Liquor Problem formed in New York City in 1893 was to "secure a body of facts which may serve as a basis for intelligent public and private actions." Even the WCTU established a Department of Scientific Temperance Instruction that lobbied for alcohol-education programs in the public schools.

In the Progressive years this shift accelerated, and the personalistic approach was largely abandoned. Now, by contrast, intemperance and sexual deviation came to be viewed less as personal failings than as products of an urban environment that needed to be purified—by force of law if necessary. The Chicago Vice Commission expressed the prevailing view when it dismissed as "naive" those who looked for the sources of prostitution in the individual prostitute's flaws of character. The emphasis was now on eliminating from the urban environment those institutions that undermined individual moral resistence—especially the saloon and the brothel.

With this development, the "scientific" aura of urban moral reform intensified. A *Scientific Temperance Journal* was established in Boston in 1906 by Cora Frances Stoddard. Muckraking journalists like George Kibbe Turner marshaled facts, statistics, dates, and names to buttress their indictment of the saloon, and the antiprostitution crusaders similarly strove for a tone of objective expertise as remote as possible from the thundering moral denunciations of earlier years. Indeed, in a number of cities the antiprostitution groups called themselves "Morals Efficiency Commissions." The 1902 report of New York's Committee of Fifteen exuded the scholarly aura appropriate to what its secretary called in the preface "a valuable scientific contribution," and *The Social Evil in Chicago*, a forbiddingly dry compendium of charts, statistics, appendixes, medical data, and analyses of interviews with 2,420 prostitutes, was similarly described by its sponsors as a "scientific study" based on the findings of "experts and trained investigators."

The fetish of scientific objectivity took many forms. One national group concentrated on assigning exact numerical ratings to various cities' success in eradicating prostitution: Chicago, 37 percent; New York, 41 percent; Houston, 86 percent; and so on. In many vice commission reports, the antiseptic aura was heightened by the substitution of numbers and letters for actual names: "One woman, Mollie (X61), lives near Oak Park and solicits in (X62). Her husband is dying in (X62a)." The point of view underlying all this was summed up by the chairman of the Moral Survey Committee of Syracuse, New York. "It is a waste of time and energy to begin dealing with commercialized vice with talk, talk, talk," he wrote. "What we need is facts, facts, facts." The ASL's *National Issue* and its hefty annual *Yearbook* fairly bristled with charts, tables, and graphs purporting to establish positive or negative correlations between the saloon and death rates, arrest rates, tax rates, divorce rates, wages, insanity, pauperism, bank deposits, industrial efficiency, housing investment, and public-school enrollment. Drawing upon data compiled by Cora Frances Stoddard, the ASL in 1917 reported—with the usual flourish of graphs—that studies undertaken in Germany and Finland had proved conclusively a link between drinking, sloppy typing, and the inability to thread needles.

This obsession with technical expertise and factual data completed the secularization of the urban moral-control movement. To be sure, these reforms ultimately depended on the moral energy of Protestant America, and denominational agencies like the Methodist Board of Temperance and Morals played an important role in rallying support. Yet appeals to the evangelical moral code do not figure strongly in either the prohibition or the antiprostitution movements, and the organizations promoting these reforms were not by any means overweighed with clergymen. The top ASL men were ministers, to be sure, but during the prohibition struggle they functioned almost entirely as secularized managers, lobbyists, and propagandists rather than as latter-day Jeremiahs pronouncing God's judgment on the saloon. The lower echelons of ASL administration were even more completely secular. The organization's general superintendent, Purley A. Baker, set the tone. "The narrow, acrimonious and emotional appeal is giving way," he declared in 1915, "to a rational, determined conviction that the [liquor] traffic . . . has no rightful place in our modern civilization."

The antiprostitution movement, despite the prominence of an occasional cleric like Chicago's Dean Sumner, was even more completely divorced from the Protestant establishment. Indeed, by around 1910, antivice zealots among the clergy had become a distinct embarrassment. The Chicago Vice Commission roundly condemned an evangelist who was conducting prayer meetings in front of the city's leading brothels. An *Arena* writer in 1909 urged that the cause be pursued "sanely and scientifically" and not through " 'moral' rant from the pulpits." The local vice commissions usually had only token ministerial representation, and many delegated the actual investigative work to the team of New York–based researchers originally put together by George Kneeland for the Committee of Fifteen. As an older generation of urban moral reformers passed from the scene, the movement came to exude more of the aura of the laboratory, law library, and university lecture hall than the pulpit.

Indeed, the very shift in terminology in the antiprostitution movement, from "social *purity*" to "social *hygiene*," is significant. The entire urban moral-control effort in these years was suffused with public-health terminology and rhetoric. A writer in *Social Hygiene* in 1917 predicted that New Orleans would soon conquer prostitution just as she had eradicated yellow fever, and in *The Challenge of the City*, Josiah Strong suggested that the polluters of the city's "moral atmosphere" should be considered as deadly as the "vermin of an Egyptian plague." In Boston, the Watch and Ward Society won praise in these years from Harvard professor Francis G. Peabody for "unobtrusively working underground, guarding us from the pestiferous evil which at any time may come up into our faces, into our homes, into our children's lives." Picking up on these cues, the Watch and Ward, like similar moral-control agencies elsewhere, increasingly defined its mission in public-health terms. "The old idea of 'charity' . . . has gradually given way to a larger conception," it declared in 1915, "to prevent . . . the moral diseases which lead to misery and crime."

The fullest elaboration of the public-health analogy in this period was probably that offered by the Massachusetts prohibitionist Newton M. Hall in *Civic Righteousness and Civic Pride* (1914). "The moral evil of the community does not remain in the foul pools in which it is bred," he wrote. "A moral miasma arises from those pools, and . . . enters not the poorest homes of the city alone, but the most carefully guarded, and leaves its trail of sorrow and despair. . . . Why should the community have any more sympathy for the saloon . . . than . . . for a typhoid-breeding pool of filthy water, . . . a swarm of deadly mosquitoes, or . . . a nest of rats infected with the bubonic plague?" For Hall, the logic of the analogy was irresistible: "Cut off the impure water and the typhoid epidemic is conquered"; destroy the saloon and the urban "moral epidemic" would vanish.

The ubiquitous medical terminology in the utterances of these reformers had more than rhetorical significance, because recent advances in venereal disease research had made clear the ravages of the disease's advanced stages, the process of transmission, and the clear link with sexual promiscuity. For the antiprostitution reformers, the moral implications of these findings were no less important than the medical. "In all previous efforts to safeguard the morality of youth," wrote one reformer in *Social Hygiene*, "the ethical barrier was alone available," and "the situation seemed . . . hopeless"; now, happily, the "ethical ideal" could be "grounded upon the most convincing facts." Jane Addams welcomed these findings as a powerful force in the emergence of a "new conscience" on prostitution, and Dr. Prince A. Morrow expressed his pleasure that "punishment for sexual sin" no longer need be "reserved for the hereafter."

Through lectures, tracts, posters, exhibits, and graphic films, the antiprostitution reformers warned of promiscuity's grim consequences—for the wrongdoer and his innocent progeny alike. The Chicago Vice Commission vividly spelled out VD's long-range effects—"the blinded eyes of little babes, the twisted limbs of deformed children, degradation, physical rot and mental decay"—and demanded that every brothel be quarantined forthwith as a "house of contagious disease." The control of sexual expression, in short, was simply another of the social constraints essential to modern urban life. Just as "the storage of gasoline and other combustibles is controlled by the city," argued the Louisville Vice Commission, so dance halls and other "vice combustibles" had to be "carefully watched and controlled."

One significant if inadvertent by-product of this preoccupation with establishing the scientific legitimacy of the urban moral-control effort—particularly through the accumulation of statistical data—was that the researchers often achieved a fragile but authentic intimacy with the objects of their study, and their reports provided glimpses of otherwise obscure facets of turn-of-the-century urban social history. Budding young sociologists danced and talked for hours with prostitutes and girls of the street . . . though always (so far as we know) holding back from the actual sexual encounter. One woman investigator, in particular, was praised by George Kneeland as "extraordinarily successful in winning the confidence of the girls with whom she associated on easy and familiar terms."

In the thousands of pages of vice commission reports lie buried fascinating details illuminating the reality of urban prostitution in this period: the business practices and domestic details of brothel life; the prevalence of oral sex in the "better" houses ("$3.00 straight, $5.00 French"); the slang (in some cities, the police assigned to the red-light district were called "fly cops"); the euphemistic advertising. (One madam who had moved sent out postcards urging her former patrons to renew their "membership in the library." A selection of "new books," she promised, could be found "on file in our new quarters.")

Striving for objectivity, these investigators often evoked the complexity of the urban sexual scene in ways that contradicted the simplistic certitude of the antivice leadership. Even William T. Stead, a first-rate journalist as well as an antivice crusader, offered considerable evidence undermining the stereotyped image of the brothel as a den of wild revels and unbridled sensuality. "The rules and regulations . . . posted in every room," he wrote of one Chicago brothel in *If Christ Came to Chicago*, "enforce decorum and decency with pains and penalties which could hardly be more strict if they were drawn up for the regulation of a Sunday School."

Such observations, with their implication that organized prostitution might sometimes function as a stabilizing and conservative urban social force, appear frequently in the early-twentieth-century vice reports. In *Commercialized Vice in New York*, for example, George Kneeland reported that many of the city's brothels were "cozy and homelike" institutions presided over by madams who possessed not only considerable business acumen but also keen psychological insight and great capacity for human warmth: "It is not uncommon for the girls as well as the customers to call her 'mother.' Strange as it may seem, some men marry these women and find them devoted wives." Describing the various classes of men who patronized brothels, Kneeland wrote:

*A numerous but pathetic group is that made up of young clerks who, living alone in unattractive quarters, find in professional prostitutes companions in the company of whom a night's revel offsets the dullness of their lives at other times. There are thousands of these men in New York. No home ties restrain them; no home associations fill their time or thought. Their rooms are fit only to sleep in; close friends they have few or none. You can watch them on the streets any evening. Hour after hour they gaze at the passing throng; at length they fling themselves into the current,—no longer silent and alone.*

What YMCA leader of the 1850s could have described the plight of the young man in the city more eloquently?

Furthermore, one finds in these vice reports insights into the motivations of the prostitutes that go beyond such stock explanations as alcohol, slum life, early seduction and abandonment, or even the perils of the industrial order. This is particularly true of the often verbatim summaries of interviews with individual prostitutes that are included by the hundred—for no apparent reason except perhaps the investigators' wish that the rich complexities of their findings not be flattened out into a few pat conclusions and recommendations. What emerges most strongly from these interviews with women of the turn-of-the-century city is how many of them, old and young, appear reasonably well satisfied with their lot, insist that they are performing a useful social function for a satisfactory return, and reveal little sense of regret or inclination to reform. "No. 3 is refined looking; no one would take her for a public woman. She is fond of drink. She states, 'I have a lovely boss. He often takes me out in his car. Have made many friends in this town. If a girl is careful she can make good money here.'"

What initially led these women to become prostitutes? The reasons that emerge in these interviews are varied, personal, and unpredictable. Sometimes, to be sure, it was economic, as with twenty-two-year-old Paulette, "interviewed on the corner of Curtis and West Madison" in Chicago, "who 'hustles' to support a two-year-old baby," or nineteen-year-old Tantine who snapped: "It is easier than waiting on table for $1.00 per day." More frequently, however, the impetus was a more complex combination of factors: the lure of the city, the fascination of activity and glitter ("I loved the excitement and a good time"), the drive to achieve a higher living standard, the unwillingness to pass one's life in subservient, deferential roles: "The ladies when they got money to hire servants imagine they have some kind of a dog to kick around, and I didn't want to be kicked around."

Time and again in these interviews one encounters real-life parallels to David Graham Phillips's Susan Lenox—spirited women who have chosen prostitution in preference to boring, demeaning, or otherwise intolerable situations: Bessie, the Indiana farm girl who "prefers city life"; another rural girl who "did not want to live among a lot of 'dead ones'"; the two small-town girls who "ran away from home so they would not have to go to school"; the Hartford young woman just beginning in the street life: "I want nice clothes and a good time . . . I am crazy to get to New York." Many had walked out on husbands they found improvident, inadequate, or simply tiresome:

"I was always fond of life. Married a dead one; he never goes out."

"I married a fellow in Pennsylvania. He is all right but damn slow. He doesn't know he is alive; not the right kind of man for me."

Her husband is employed in the AB164 store as salesman. "Too dumb to be alive. All he knows is work and he makes no money at that."

Her husband is cold; she longs for affection, clothes and pleasure; he never leaves the house. She comes to Hartford two or three times a week from B155. She will go out with a man for a glass of soda.

In the more lurid rhetorical flights of the antivice crusaders, to become a prostitute was to enter a life of "white slavery"; from the perspective of many of the women themselves (as revealed in the very reports generated by the crusade!), the decision represented a liberating escape from bondage.

Thus, buried in the interstices of the vice reports, one comes upon observations, insights, and personal revelations that suddenly illuminate the human reality of urban prostitution two generations ago—a complex reality that resists easy summation or judgment. Seeking to validate their moral-control impulse through sociological investigation, the urban moral reformers of the Progressive era unwittingly sponsored the collection of a wealth of social data that reveals far more about the actual contours of urban "vice" than they perhaps intended.

David J. Rothman

# The State as Parent

The Progressive tradition that took hold in the United States during the first two decades of the twentieth century and persisted right through the middle of the 1960s gave a remarkable primacy to the idea of the state as parent. Far more than a rhetorical flourish or convenient metaphor with which to galvanize public support, this concept shaped reformers' definitions of the proper realm for state action and, perhaps even more important, the appropriate methods for the state to adopt in fulfilling its goals. The ideal dictated not only the ends but the means of doing good.

As one would expect from such an orientation, Progressives were far more attentive to the "needs" of disadvantaged groups than to their "rights." Needs were real and obvious—the poor were overworked and underpaid, living in unhealthy tenements and working in miserable sweatshops. Rights, on the other hand, were "so-called"—the right of the poor to sleep under the bridge or the right of the laborer to fix his own contract with an all-powerful corporation. Clearly, a reform platform that looked to needs expanded the boundaries of political intervention, legitimating a wide range of ameliorative action; the state as parent had a lengthy agenda to accomplish. But the concept cut two ways: those in need of help were more or less like children. The disadvantaged were the objects of care, they were to be done for. They did not require protection against the well-meaning parent, rights to be exercised against the paternalistic state.

It is not claiming too much to assert that this perspective was at the core of liberalism in modern America, uniting, for all their minor differences, the first settlement-house workers with later New and Fair Dealers. One can identify a mainstream reform position in the period 1900–1965 that shared a basic agreement on the principles that should guide a benevolent social policy. To be sure, there were critics to either side, socialists and Marxists to the left who defined Progressives as no more than tinkerers with a fundamentally corrupt capitalist organization, and conservatives to the right who saw their interventions as destructive of the essential integrity of the system. Nevertheless, the Progressives enjoyed a centrality and an influence that marked them off in a special way and that enables us to talk meaningfully, if in shorthand terms, of *the reformers*. Then, rather suddenly, beginning in the mid-1960s and continuing to our day, this tradition came under a novel, vigorous, and even bitter attack emanating not from the far left or far right, but—and in more than a metaphorical sense—from the children of Progressivism. We are now, in ways and for reasons that this essay will explore, in a post-Progressive period. A new generation of reformers, drawn to an unprecedented degree from the ranks of lawyers and the dependent groups themselves, are pitting rights against needs, or, to put it more broadly, are challenging the wisdom and propriety of an ideal of the state as parent and the dependent as child. They are highly critical of Progressivism not merely for pragmatic reasons— for what it did or did not manage to accomplish—but for conceptual reasons: for importing a misguided and ultimately mischievous model into the political arena.

Given the centrality of Progressive thinking in this country, it is appropriate to place the contemporary objections to this tradition in still another light. An arrow that the late critic Lionel Trilling once aimed at the far left would now seem to many observers an appropriate barb to hurl against liberalism itself. In 1947 Trilling published an essay, "Manners, Morals and the Novel," in which he elegantly set out his case against Marxist reform. (Indeed, in his novel of the same period, *The Middle of the Journey*, Trilling had Gilbert Maxim, his disillusioned ex-Communist character, voice a variant on this same argument.) Trilling defended the novel for its ability to strip away illusions, to go beyond hyperbolic rhetoric so as to uncover the hidden realities. His praise for such novelists as Balzac, James, and Forster—indeed for the whole genre—reflected a commitment to what he called "moral realism." Moral realism, he explained, taught us "that to act against social injustice is right and noble but that to choose to act so does not settle all moral problems but on the contrary generates new ones of an especially difficult sort." We have so many books, Trilling commented, "that praise us for taking progressive attitudes." We sorely lack those that "ask what might lie behind our good impulses." He fully appreciated that "anything that complicates our moral fervor in dealing with reality . . . must be regarded with some impatience." Yet it was just this impatience that worried him and must worry us. "Moral passions are even more willful and imperious and impatient than the self-seeking passions. All history is at one in telling us that their tendency is to be not only liberating but restrictive." And so he concluded in a sentence that has taken on a new relevance: "Some paradox in our nature leads us, once we have made our fellow men the objects of our enlightened interest, to go on to make them the objects of our pity, then of our wisdom, ultimately of our coercion."

This phrase brings us to the very heart of the current dissatisfactions with Progressivism, for to its critics the movement suffered deeply from an absence of moral realism. Its proponents were so attached to a paternalistic model that they never concerned themselves with the potential of their programs to be as coercive as they were liberating. In their eagerness to play parent to the child, they did not pause to ask whether the dependent had to be protected against their own well-meaning interventions. It was as if the benevolence of their motives together with their clear recognition of the wretchedness of lower-class social conditions guaranteed that ameliorative efforts would unambiguously benefit the poor. The problem, it now appears, is not only that Progressives could not accomplish their grand designs but that policies whose legitimacy rested on their promise to do good may actually have produced substantial harms.

Each generation has its own favorite brand of horror stories, its own special set of circumstances that prick its conscience and goad it to action. For Progressives, it was instances of neglect; the state had to intervene to correct inequities. The Jacob Riis and Lewis Hine photographs revealed little waifs selling newspapers on street corners or tending oversized mill looms. The tracts of Jane Addams and Lillian Wald pointed to the desperate need of widows left to their own devices, the horrors of families broken up with the mother entering an almshouse and her children an orphan asylum. Surely men and women of good will ought to be able to halt such practices, and public resources had to be devoted to improving their living conditions. To choose to act against such gross social injustice had to be right and noble, and anything that complicated one's response to these wretched circumstances seemingly had to be treated with impatience.

Now a new kind of horror story has gained popularity. It is aptly represented in the case of Mrs. Lake, a Washington "bag lady," who carried her worldly possessions in two shopping bags. Mrs. Lake went out one day to the Department of Justice to press a claim for a pension; her efforts were unsuccessful, and as she left the Justice building, a police officer, a woman police officer at that, spotted her as someone who might be in need of assistance. Mrs. Lake appeared disoriented in the downtown district. The policewoman asked her for her home address, which Mrs. Lake was unable to supply; and although she had found her way to the Justice Department, the officer believed she could not find her way back home again. In short order, Mrs. Lake was confined to St. Elizabeth's Mental Hospital for "wandering," in mind and body, and despite her persistent efforts to be released from the institution, she remained there, for the rest of her days, ostensibly for her own good. Betty Higden won her battle; Mrs. Lake lost.

That Mrs. Lake's misfortune typifies the prevailing horror stories is another indication of the nature of the attack now being mounted against Progressivism. Put most succinctly, the commitment to paternalistic state intervention in the name of equality is giving way to a commitment to restrict intervention in the name of liberty. If our predecessors were determined to test the maximum limits for the exercise of state power in order to correct imbalances, we are about to test the minimum limits for the exercise of state power in order to enhance autonomy. The dialogue between these two approaches now dominates social policy discussions on dependency, and a close analysis of the assumptions and records of each position may well clarify, and perhaps even advance, the debates.

The Progressives' allegiance to a model of the state as parent rested on a series of propositions all of which seemed to confirm the validity and desirability of their approach. For one, Progressives were convinced that the sum of individual self-interested actions could no longer be counted upon to produce the common good. The nineteenth-century assumption of such a coincidence disappeared with the rise of the cities, business trusts, and immigrant ghettos. As Herbert Croly brilliantly argued, "No preestablished harmony can then exist between the free and abundant satisfactions of private needs and the accomplishment of a morally and socially desirable result." Rather, he insisted, "the American problem is a social problem"; the nation stood in need of "a more highly socialized democracy." To realize the promise of American life, the public sector would have to dominate the private sector. The state, not the individual, would define the common good and see to its fulfillment. In short, the major tenet of Progressive thought was that only the state could make the individual free. Only the enlarged authority of the government could satisfy the particular needs of all the citizens.

Further, Progressives had little doubt of the state's ability to fulfill this charge or, put another way, of the ability of their programs to accomplish their goals. For one, their ranks were composed of the graduates of the new universities, those who had typically spent most of their classroom hours learning the canons of social science. They had been taught to investigate social reality with a clear eye to its improvement. The facts of the case— whether the rates of tuberculosis in the slums or the number of families poverty-stricken because of industrial accidents—would not only locate the source of the problem but at once compel ameliorative action. Progressive tracts and testimony at hearings were filled with statistical tables—as if the data would insure the success of their legislative efforts.

Progressives, in ways that cannot help but make contemporary analysts nostalgic, also shared a remarkable consensus on the goals for reform. There was no crisis of values that had to be debated, no agonizing consideration of the comparative worth of different life-styles. To Progressives, all Americans were to enter the ranks of the middle class. The melting-pot metaphor implied not only an amalgam of immigrants into a common mold, but an amalgam of classes into a common mold. Everyone was to respect private property, send their children to school, and give up whatever vices—particularly intemperance—that they might have brought with them from the old world, in order to become hardworking and law-abiding. "It is fatal for a democracy to permit the formation of fixed classes," argued that leading Progressive reformer, John Dewey; and one Progressive institution after another, from schools to settlement houses, set out to bridge the gap between the upper classes and the lower classes, between native-born and immigrants. The traffic across this bridge, of course, was to move only in one way, from them to us, from alien to American, from lower class to middle class.

This certain sense of direction among Progressives testified finally, and most significantly, to their keen sense of the essential viability—indeed superiority—of the American system. They stood ready to make immigrants over in their own image because ultimately they did not doubt that this course was in everyone's best interest. No sense of conflict of interests among classes or even among different groups within the same class complicated their analysis. Yes, some greedy businessmen would have to give up excess profits; some greedy speculators would have to be curbed. But no one's "true" or "real" interests (at least as reformers defined them) would be violated. The economic pie was infinitely expandable. The poor need not rise up against the rich to obtain their fair share. Social mobility promised that all of the deserving would climb the ladder; no one had to remain stuck at the bottom. Thus, that which promoted the stability of the society promoted the welfare of its members. Social cohesion and individual betterment went hand in hand.

Armed with these principles, Progressives enacted a series of novel measures designed to prevent and to relieve dependency and deviancy. Between 1900 and 1920 practically every state passed widow-pension laws, what we know today as Aid to Dependent Children. Heretofore, unless rescued by a private charitable society, the mother and her children had entered institutions; now public funds were to be expended to keep the family together at home. At the same time, practically every major city organized juvenile courts to handle cases of dependency and delinquency. In informal hearings, these special courts would decide, at their own discretion, what was in the best interests of the neglected or delinquent child. Moreover, juvenile courts as well as adult criminal courts began to organize and administer probation departments. Instead of sending youthful or minor offenders to an institution, the court could now sentence them to probation, leaving them in the community under the supervision of an officer.

It is clear that the Progressives were the first American reformers to perceive and to be outraged by the miseries that were endemic to the modern industrial system. The wretchedness of the almshouses—let alone the cruelty of separating the widow from her children, and the injuries inflicted by locking ten-year-olds in a stinking and filthy jail—were terribly real. No one is belittling the good conscience of the Progressives or their effort to go beyond a simple moralism that blamed the poor for their poverty. But what is at issue is how they moved to correct these evils. It is not so much their definitions of what constituted a social problem as the assumptions with which they attempted to ameliorate it that are now controversial.

The design of each of the Progressives' programs assumed a nonadversarial relationship between the state and the client. Since the state, whether in the guise of the juvenile court judge or probation officer or welfare administrator, was to help and not to punish the poor or the criminal, it was unnecessary—in fact it was counterproductive—to limit or to circumscribe officials' discretionary powers. Indeed, since no conflicts of interest divided the welfare of society from that of the dependent or deviant, Progressives were still more determined to endow the state with all necessary authority to fulfill its goals. The great discovery of the juvenile court, noted one reformer, was that "individual welfare coincided with the well-being of the state. Humanitarian and social considerations thus recommended one and the same procedure. . . . Sympathy, justice, and even the self-interest of society were all factors in bringing about the changed attitude." The state could do good without sacrificing anyone's interests, without having to make trade-offs.

In each instance, therefore, enabling legislation and agency practice enhanced the prerogatives of state officials and reduced—and almost eliminated—legal protections and rights for those coming under their authority. To call the acts "widow pensions" was really a misnomer. The widows did not receive their allowance as a matter of right, the way a pensioner received his. Rather, the widow had to apply for her stipend, demonstrate her qualifications, her economic need, and her moral worth, and then trust to the decision of the welfare board. At their pleasure, and by their reckoning, she then obtained or did not obtain help. By the same token the juvenile court proceedings gave no standing to the whole panoply of rights that offenders typically enjoyed, from a trial by jury to assistance from counsel, to protections against self-incrimination. There was nothing atypical about the juvenile court judge who openly admitted that in his Minnesota courtroom "the laws of evidence are sometimes forgotten or overlooked." So too, probation officers were not bound by any of the restrictions that might fetter the work of police officers. They did not need a search warrant to enter a probationer's home, for as another juvenile court judge explained: "With the great right arm and force of the law, the probation officer can go into the home and demand to know the cause of the dependency or the delinquency of a child. . . . He becomes practically a member of the family and teaches them lessons of cleanliness and decency, of truth and integrity." So caught up were reformers with this image of officer as family member that they gave no heed to the coercive character of their programs. To the contrary, they frankly declared that "threats may be necessary in some instances to enforce the learning of the lessons that he teaches, but whether by threats or cajolery, by appealing to their fear of the law or by rousing the ambition that lies latent in each human soul, he teaches the lesson and transforms the entire family into individuals which the state need never again hesitate to own as citizens."

With the state eager and able to accomplish so beneficent a goal, there appeared no reason to restrict its actions.

The prevalence of such judgments among Progressives practically blinded them to the realities that followed on the enactment of their proposals. Not only did they fail to see the many inadequacies that quickly emerged in day-to-day operations, worse yet, they could not begin to understand that the programs might be administered in the best interests of officials, not clients. In the case of widow pensions, state legislatures appropriated niggardly amounts of funds for relief, so that only a handful of needy cases were served, and the monies that even they received were too limited to allow them to subsist. In effect, the widow had to open her life to the investigatory impulses of her social worker and at the same time still find work to supplement her dole. And those ineligible for even these paltry funds had to bear both the stigma of being labeled unworthy while they too desperately tried to make ends meet. The widow-pension program may have soothed the conscience of reformers—the state was now committed to the care of the worthy widow and her children—but it certainly did not solve the problem that they had originally addressed.

The operation of the juvenile court was no more satisfactory. Judges had unbounded discretion to do as they saw fit, and there was little recourse from their decisions. They still relied upon state reformatories and training schools to discipline the young, only now they justified their sentences, and not cynically either, in the language of rehabilitating the offender instead of punishing him. To incarcerate the young, a Pennsylvania court ruled in upholding the constitutionality of juvenile court sentences, was not to deprive them of their liberty. Commitments to reformatories under the new laws do not contemplate "restraint upon the natural liberty of children." The state was merely assuming the privileges that parents enjoy, exercising the "wholesome restraint which a parent exercises over his child. . . . No constitutional right is violated but one of the most important duties which organized society owes to its helpless members is performed." And the administration of probation was still less successful. Reformers had looked to a group of well-trained officers counseling a small number of clients. In fact, the probation officers were poorly trained, ill-equipped to do very much good at all, and, in any event, there was little that the best-intentioned of them could accomplish when carrying case loads of two to three hundred.

It may well also be that probation, which presented itself as an alternative to incarceration, served more frequently as a supplement to incarceration. The same numbers still went to institutions; the difference was that cases which had once been dismissed or suspended now came under the supervisory network of probation officers. To be sure, the encroachments on the civil liberties of many but certainly not all of the clients were generally not egregious because of the incredible case loads that probation officers carried. But that simply meant that the coerciveness of the state was limited only by the unwillingness of legislators to spend taxpayer money. It is an odd but perhaps accurate conclusion to note that the dependent and deviant may owe what freedom they have more to the fiscal conservatism of elected officials than to the benevolent motives of reformers.

Finally, Progressives' sense of paternalism enabled them to move in harsh and stringent ways against those that they believed to be irreformable and beyond rehabilitation—namely, the recidivist, the defective, the mentally retarded, and the unworthy poor. Since they had designed programs that would keep reformable types out of institutions and in the community, those that they defined as beyond help deserved incarceration, and incarceration for very long periods of time. Accordingly, many Progressives accepted the eugenic arguments of the time and were eager to confine the retarded for life, particularly the borderline retarded who might pass as normals and so go on to propagate a race of defectives. Some Progressives were also ready to sterilize the retarded, to make that operation the prerequisite for release into the community. And in a similar spirit, almost all Progressives were prepared to define broadly the category of PINS, persons in need of super-vision, so that the state could move quickly to remove children from parents deemed unworthy, those children, in the language of one reformer, who had been raised in homes "in which they had been accustomed from their earliest infancy to drunkenness, immorality, obscene and vulgar language, filthy and degraded conditions of living."

This sketch of the Progressive tradition has a dual relevance to our understanding of contemporary American attitudes and policies toward the dependent. First, and most obviously, we are today well aware of the record of failure of these programs. We recognize that widow pensions did not reduce or eliminate poverty, that the juvenile court did not eradicate delin-quency, that probation was hardly a panacea for crime. But such knowledge is really of minor import. Merely because programs did not work in the past does not mean that they might not work in the future. In no simple sense does history repeat itself. Perhaps less stingy legislatures, perhaps a more munificent federal government, would fund these programs fully and we would then witness their achievements.

Far more important, therefore, to the contemporary sense of dependency is the fact that the underlying assumptions of the Progressive stance no longer seem valid. What is remarkable about current reformist thinking is how far it has moved from these premises, how fundamentally it has rejected every major point in the synthesis.

To characterize this transformation in summary fashion there now exists a widespread and acute suspicion of the very notion of doing good among widely divergent groups on all points of the political spectrum. To claim to act for the purposes of benevolence was once sufficient to legitimate a pro-gram; at this moment it is certain to create suspicion. To announce that you are prepared to intervene for the best interests of some other person or party is guaranteed to provoke the quick, even knee-jerk, response that you are masking your true, self-interested, motives. Whereas once historians and policy analysts were prone to label some movements reforms, thereby assuming their humanitarian aspects, they are presently far more comfortable with a designation of social control, thereby assuming their coercive quality. Not that one or the other approach is necessarily more intellectually faithful. Rather, fashions have changed. The prevailing perspective looks first to how a measure may regulate the poor, not relieve them.

So too, we share a very acute sense of the failure of institutions to fulfill their caretaker responsibilities. Whereas Progressive reformers did recognize, indeed, by the recurring nature of scandals were compelled to recognize, the inadequacy of institutions—whether reformatories, orphan asylums, or almshouses—invariably they blamed the frugality of legislators, or the incompetence of administrators, or the cupidity of superintendents for the failures. The system was benign; the problem was with its implementation. Now, to the contrary, the system, the very idea of incarceration for the purposes of rehabilitation, is suspect among a surprisingly diverse group of observers, from federal judges to members of state investigatory commissions on nursing homes and juvenile corrections. And not only do a host of more or less well-designed research projects unanimously report on the failure of institutions to be rehabilitative, but a strong and compelling theoretical analysis, such as offered by Erving Goffman in *Asylums*, insists that incarceration by its very nature will inevitably infantilize the inmate and make his future adaptation to society more problematic.

This suspicion of benevolence and antiinstitutionalism has encouraged and is reinforced by an acute distrust of discretionary authority. It no longer seems appropriate to endow public or private officials with a wide latitude for the exercise of their authority. Since neither their motives, which are assumed to be social control, nor their decisions, which might well involve commitment to an institution, now seem acceptable, their prerogatives and powers must be carefully defined, bound in and circumscribed through detailed and precise laws and regulations. The formula is clear: better that a few should suffer from the inflexibility of a code than that the many should suffer through the discretion of an administrator.

Of the fact of this reversal there can be no question. We are in full revolt against the Progressive synthesis. But the more complicated and intriguing question, the answers to which must be more suggestive than definitive, is why this change should have occurred. Why is it that reformers in the 1970s are far more receptive to Trilling's call for moral realism? Why are they so much more comfortable with labels like "social control" and titles like "Regulating the Poor"? Why are they more prepared to rely upon procedural protections than purity of motive? Why is it that while they may grant the accuracy of a biological or psychoanalytic finding of the significance of altruism in many species, they are terribly reluctant to allow such a conclusion to structure social policy? Or, finally, why are they leaving an equality model to test the limits of a liberty model?

To begin to formulate an answer to these questions (or at least to recast them in a still broader context), it is appropriate to note first that these developments are part of a pervasive distrust of all constituted authorities, a general decline in the legitimacy of the authority of a whole series of persons and institutions. The list of those who have suffered this loss is as lengthy as it is revealing: college presidents and deans, high school principals and teachers, husbands and parents, psychiatrists, doctors, research scientists, and, obviously, prison wardens, social workers, hospital superintendents, and mental hospital superintendents. Many of us, either as objects of power or as wielders of power, have experienced this diminution quite directly. To choose but one example, many of us can remember from our own college days the phenomenon of dean's discipline. Having broken some rule or other, a rule which we had probably learned of through an informal student network, we shuffled into the dean's office, sheepishly, head hanging. We told our story, bringing up every exculpatory fact we could imagine, and then sat back hoping for the best. The dean pronounced the punishment, and, mumbling our apologies, we more or less backed out of the office. Such times are over. The student appears not before a dean in the privacy of his office but before a tribunal, whose composition reflects the working of a mathematical formula that brings so many administrators together with so many professors and so many students from the several university divisions. If the charge is of any significance, the student comes with his lawyer. Examination and cross-examination goes on: did the student have a printed, formally distributed listing of the college rules? Was his identity in the incident established beyond a reasonable doubt? And once the hearing is over, the tribunal retires, like a jury, to make its deliberations and reach its verdict. If the student is unhappy with the finding, he will move the case immediately into the courts, where the attention to procedural protections will be only somewhat more rigorous than what was practiced at the original hearing.

So too, the freewheeling exercise of disciplinary authority by high school officials is under challenge. Hearings and legal representation may well become the rule here. And more and more patients are refusing to sign the blanket release form that gives a doctor and his hospital the right to do whatever they think "necessary" to the person's body. Some research scientists are even discovering that their research protocols have to be carefully negotiated not just with the university and government committees on experimentation, but with the community at large. And if the community does not like what is afoot, as was the case, for example, with research into minimal brain dysfunction in Boston's schools, they will exercise political power, often successfully, to terminate the work. Marriage contracts that once vaguely spelled out duties of loving, cherishing, and, yes, obeying, may give way to contracts that detail who will carry out household duties on alternate days. And whereas once it was assumed that parents would invariably act in the best interests of the child, even in the midst of divorce proceedings, now it seems the better part of wisdom to have children represented by their own attorney. Indeed, before parents can commit their child to a mental hospital, it is becoming obligatory that the child be represented separately by an attorney.

In effect, reform policy presupposes a conflict of interests among these parties, conflicts which before were never admitted to or acknowledged. The assumption is that deans will act for the best interest of the university, not the student; that husbands will further their own needs, not their wives'; that parents will satisfy their own desires, not necessarily their children's; that research scientists have their own agenda of priorities that need not fit with the welfare of their subjects; that wardens' first thought is to the prison and not the inmate; and that psychiatrists will be more concerned with the health of the hospital than with the health of the patient. The Progressives' assumption that interests coincided, that the welfare of all parties could be satisfied, has become a thing of the past. Now the game seems to be a zero-sum game: if one party wins, another loses; if you are not one up, you are one down.

To put these changes into still another framework, we are witnessing the dissolution of the Progressive version of community as a viable concept, indeed, the breakdown of normality as a viable concept. To many critics, there no longer seems to be a common weal that can be defined or appealed to as a justification for action. The very notion of a harmony of interests seems deceptive and mischievous. Not only can no one agree on what is good for all of us, no one can agree on what is proper behavior for any one of us. No consensus allows for a clear and uncontroversial division between sane and insane behavior, no unity exists around the once self-evident proposition that it is better to be sane rather than insane. As to any effort to define what constitutes normal sexual behavior—one has only to raise this point to recognize immediately how absurd any such attempt would be.

There is far more agreement on the reality of this state of affairs than on its merits. Some observers describe these developments in terms of loss and corruption, searching, logically enough, for a way to restore a sense of community, to revive the social contract, or, in Daniel Bell's formulation, to rebuild a sense of civitas among citizens. Somehow or other, through the family, or the church, or a new ideology, we will recreate bonds of trust, commonality of goals, a system in which all institutions and individuals will know and take their place. To others, these changes represent something quite different, a coming of wisdom, an ability to see farther than our predecessors, an unmasking of a reality that had been obfuscated for too long by a rhetoric of reform and benevolence.

But in effect, this description has only pushed the question back one stage. Why this loss of civitas? Or, alternately, why this new-found wisdom? We may well be too close to the issues to be able to formulate compelling hypotheses, but nevertheless, some of the elements promoting the change can be sketched. The bridge between the Progressive ideology and this new sense of things may well be the civil rights movement. In its origins, this movement was prototypically Progressive, its leaders confident that the attainment of equality for blacks would in no way conflict with the interest of society as a whole. Throughout the several decades of litigation that led up to the 1954 Supreme Court decision in *Brown* v. *Board of Education*, and down until 1966, the civil rights movement assumed that no basic clash of interests existed. Yes, some Southern bigots, the likes of bull-headed sheriffs, would lose out. But apart from the lunatic-fringe racists, there would be no victims.

The finest expression of this optimism came from Martin Luther King. And no speech of his, or perhaps more properly, no sermon of his, better captured this quality than his famous "I have a dream," delivered August 28, 1963. He spoke from the steps of the Lincoln Memorial; the band struck up the "Battle Hymn of the Republic" as he rose; and King opened appropriately enough with the words "Five score years ago." There was no need, King told his rapt audience, "to satisfy our thirst for freedom by drinking from the cup of bitterness and hatred." He went on: "Our white brothers . . . have come to realize that their destiny is tied up with our destiny and their freedom is inextricably bound to our freedom." "My dream," declared King, "is a dream deeply rooted in the American dream. I have a dream that one day on the red hills of Georgia the sons of former slaves and the sons of former slave owners will be able to sit down together at the table of brotherhood. . . . This is our hope. This is our faith. . . . With this faith we will be able to transform the jangling discords of our nation into a beautiful symphony of brotherhood." King ended his speech with the lines: "We will be able to speed up that day when all of God's children, black men and white men, Jews and Gentiles, Protestants and Catholics, will be able to join hands and sing in the words of the old Negro spiritual, Free at Last! Free at Last! Thank God almighty, we are free at last!"

It is almost embarrassing to read King's words today. Not only because we have fallen so far short of living up to his dream, but because his very announcement of his dream seems so very soft, so very tender, so very out of keeping with the realities of the world as we perceive them. Most dramatically, it is his notions of the possibility of brotherhood, or to put it into more mundane terms, the ability to satisfy at once the interests of everyone, that now seems so problematic. The turning point was probably 1966. After a series of impressive legislative victories, the civil rights movement met its first defeat that year—and the issue upon which it met its defeat is still very much with us today, the issue of open housing. 1966 was also the year that the formulations of "black power" first came to the fore. And black power, unlike King's rhetoric, looked first not to brotherhood, but to separatism; it premised itself not upon a mutuality of interests that all members of this society shared, but upon basic conflicts within this society. It announced in no uncertain terms that blacks had better organize themselves, get control of their own economic institutions, their own political institutions, their own community, if they would ever achieve substantial gains. And in all so many ways, the changeover from dreams of brotherhood to black power is paradigmatic of the changes that have transformed our society from 1966 until the present.

The ranks of black power may well have never amounted to more than a fraction of the black community. But far more important, black power became the strategy that every minority group in our society attempted to emulate. One finds this in the organization of welfare rights, with equal clarity, and with direct historical continuities, in the movements for prisoners' rights, mental patients' rights, the rights of the retarded, and the rights of children. The commonalities are clear: organize one's own special-interest group; press one's demands. The perspective is not the perspective of common welfare but the needs of the particular group. The intellectual premises are not unity but conflict. It is "us" versus "them."

In many ways, it was the dissatisfaction among blacks themselves with the advances made by the civil rights movement that helped generate this changed outlook. Rightly or wrongly, they believed that progress was too slow to come, that commonality of interests was not serving their own welfare. And that assumption, based upon the black experience, has fueled the various protest movements of other minority groups. So too, one should not minimize the implications of the changes in the American economy between the pre- and post-1965 period. The slowdown in economic growth that occurred after the mid-1960s, and the recessions that followed, to an extraordinary degree shook people's faith in the idea that an expanding economy would ultimately solve all of America's social problems. Added to this, of course, was a new concern for the allocation of scarce resources. Even before the oil shortages, conservationists and ecologists were warning us that our resources were finite and limited. And finally, every cynical judgment about the nature of American society seemed to be confirmed by the course of the Vietnam war. Here was a moment when a posture of "us" versus "them" seemed to make the best of sense.

One of the leading Progressive social planners, Charles Merriam of the University of Chicago, once wrote: "The most tragic moments in human life are those in which the value systems are unreconciled—when one cries out against another; the family against the state, the state against the church, the neighborhood against the distant capitol, life in the broader sense against nonlife or narrow life—against the end of life." Merriam was ever thankful that his times, he believed, were not so tragic. No final conflict, he insisted, separated "self interest and the public interest." But in Merriam's sense of the term, we do indeed face tragedy. We can no longer entertain the simple hope that interests can be reconciled, that public interest and self-interest will necessarily coincide.

In light of this record and these prevailing assumptions, one can well appreciate how appealing and attractive a host of constituencies find a "liberty" model. Convinced that paternalistic state intervention in the name of the common good has all too typically worked to their disadvantage, they are now determined to rid themselves of the onus of ostensibly protective and benevolent oversight and substitute instead a commitment to their own autonomy. Thus, the emergence of a series of liberation and rights movements, from women's liberation to welfare rights. In all these cases the goal is to reduce state power, to define the groups' aims in terms of rights that should be immune from interference, not needs that ought to be fulfilled. And in many instances this strategy makes fundamental good sense and does further the particular interests of the group. Do not deprive us of our liberty to follow our own life-styles because we are women, or ostensibly in need of treatment, or committed to a different sexual orientation, or because we are young, or because we are poor. A liberty model is most effective and appropriate in removing fetters that have blocked freedom of choice and action.

But the expansion of rights solves only part of the problem, for there do remain, like it or not, needs as well, imbalances in economic and social power, in inherited physical constitutions, that demand redress. It is not the goal of a liberty model to promote neglect, to legitimate cruelty and inattention in the name of rights. Rather, this camp recognizes that state intervention may often be necessary, but must take place with a minimum of discretionary authority, with the objects of protection or improvement having a determinative voice in the shaping of the program itself. To this end, advocates of the liberty model are far more comfortable with an adversarial approach, an open admission of conflict of interest, than with an equality model with its presumption of harmony of interests.

In practice, such a commitment means that liberty-minded groups will advocate a clear delineation of the powers of the state, more prepared to trust to a political process that carefully spells out authority and responsibility than to an open-ended grant of authority to administrators to do as they please. Assuming that the players are competitive, that the game will be won by some and lost by others, it seems best to keep the rules clear, to know in advance how the action will proceed. So, better to list what welfare mothers are entitled to, rather than let the social worker act in her mysterious ways. Import all procedural protections into the juvenile court, rather than trust to the benevolence of its judge. Fix the terms for juvenile delinquents, make them consistent with adult ones, rather than allow the judge to pass indeterminant sentences that could stretch through the years of one's minority.

By the same token, better to trust to the skills of a lawyer in court than to the good intentions of the state or the agency or the institution. Presupposing conflict, let the battle be fought with both sides armed. Hence, the call for lawyers for children so that their wishes can be represented in custody cases, and their needs fully considered before they are institutionalized in the name of treatment. Hence, the call for lawyers inside the mental hospital, so that those diagnosed and committed as mentally ill will be fully informed of their rights and their ability to exercise choice expanded. Hence, the call for lawyers for students, so that their self-interests and not that of the high school or the college will be defended. And hence, the call for lawyers for welfare recipients and prisoners, so that their rights will be promoted, and the authority of social workers, probation officers, wardens, and guards will be reduced.

There is no denying that a liberty model and an adversarial stance may pose as many questions as they solve about the problems of dependency in American society. For one, a focus on rights may well give a new legitimacy to neglect, allowing conservatives to join in the chorus for rights, not for the sake of maximizing choice but for reducing tax-based expenditures. For another, the traits of the lawyers are not those that would necessarily warm anybody's heart, let alone those who stand in need of support. It was Willard Gaylin who commented, with all sarcasm intended, that he finally understood the motive impulse of the adversarial movement: to substitute for the hardnosed, belligerent, and tough-minded psychiatrist the attention of the gentle, understanding, empathetic lawyer! For still another, an adversarial model, setting interest off against interest, does seem to run the clear risk of creating a kind of ultimate shoot-out in which, by definition, the powerless lose and the powerful win. How absurd to push for confrontation when all the advantages are on the other side. Finally, courts are not the most reliable or consistent institutions to trust to in an effort to advance the claims of minorities. The new reformers themselves are fully aware of the grimmer prospects they face as the Warren Court gives way to the Burger Court.

But it is not the point of this essay to predict how a liberty model and adversarial tactics will fare in the future so much as to make clear how far the post-1960s reformers have moved from the Progressive tradition. The optimism and confidence that Progressives shared, both about the wisdom and potential effectiveness of their social policies, their firm sense of having diagnosed the problems of dependency and formulated the right programs to eliminate it, their belief in the superiority of their values and all that meant to their ability to define and to attempt to implement the proper life-styles in all citizens and classes, have disappeared and can hardly be resurrected. To try to recapture their vision of things, to assume as they did that the state should act as parent, is to misread in the most basic way the realities of our own particular social situation and to embark on a futile and probably dangerous endeavor.

Rather than trying to revive an older type of social contract, under which the better sort, the expert and the professional, was to act benevolently toward others and on their behalf, we would do better to address a very different series of issues. Will we as a society be able to recognize and respect rights and yet not ignore needs? Can we do good to others, but on their terms? Rather than wondering how professional expertise and discretionary authority can be exercised in the best interest of the client or the patient, we should ponder how the objects of authority can protect themselves against abuse without depriving themselves of the benefits that experts can deliver— and to turn the matter around in this way represents more than just a stylistic revision. Or to revert to the modern horror stories, is there some way that we can give Mrs. Lake her freedom and yet not breed cruelty? These are the right questions to be confronting, even if the record of American reform gives little reason to be confident that we will answer them well.

## SUGGESTIONS FOR FURTHER READING

Much of the writing on American history in the twentieth century has been influenced by the progressive movement. Beard and Parrington, of course, felt the impact directly, but later writers like Eric Goldman in *Rendezvous with Destiny* (New York, 1952) are also sympathetic to the progressive point of view. George E. Mowry, *The Era of Theodore Roosevelt, 1900–1912* (New York, 1958), and Arthur S. Link, *Woodrow Wilson and the Progressive Era, 1910–1917* (New York, 1954), are balanced studies that fit the two major progressive politicians into the larger progressive movement and in the process reduce some of the conflict that earlier writers emphasized. Samuel P. Hays, *The Response to Industrialism* (Chicago, 1957), and Robert Wiebe, *The Search for Order, 1877–1920* (New York, 1967), see adjustment, consolidation, order, and efficiency, rather than conflict, as the keys to the period. Gabriel Kolko, *The Triumph of Conservatism: A Reinterpretation of American History, 1900–1916* (New York, 1963), sees progressivism as a movement dominated by businessmen who believed that "the general welfare of a community could be best served by satisfying the concrete needs of business." Robert Wiebe, *Businessmen and Reform: A Study of the Progressive Movement* (Cambridge, Mass., 1962), finds business support for progressivism, but, unlike Kolko, describes the business community as divided during the period. James Weinstein, *The Corporate Ideal in the Liberal State, 1900–1918* (Boston, 1968), finds a conservative business consensus; but Allen F. Davis, *Spearheads for Reform* (New York, 1967), still finds the quest for social justice a part of the movement. For convenient selections of writings and good bibliographies see David M. Kennedy, ed., *Progressivism: The Critical Issues* (Boston, 1971), and Arthur Mann, *The Progressive Era: Major Issues of Interpretation*, 2nd ed., (New York, 1975). Interesting and provocative general accounts are David W. Noble, *The Progressive Mind, 1890–1917* (Chicago, 1970); William O'Neill, *The Progressive Years* (New York, 1975); and Robert M. Crunden, *Ministers of Reform: The Progressive Achievement in American Civilization, 1889–1920* (New York, 1982). Arthur S. Link and Richard L. McCormick, *Progressivism* (Arlington Heights, Ill., 1983), is an excellent brief summary and an historiographic overview of the movement.

Progressive reformers—or at least reformers during the progressive period—seemed to be everywhere, concerning themselves with a wide variety of problems. The following books provide examples of this variety as well as discussions of how reformers viewed the problems and their causes: Aileen S. Kraditor, *The Ideas of the Woman Suffrage Movement, 1890–1929* (New York, 1965); Robert H. Bremner, *From the Depths: The Discovery of Poverty in the United States* (New York, 1956); Lawrence A. Cremin, *The Transformation of the School: Progressivism in American Education, 1876–1957* (New York, 1961); Samuel P. Hays, *Conservation and the Gospel of Efficiency: The Progressive Conservation Movement, 1890–1920* (Cambridge, Mass., 1959).

Even the South had its progressive reformers, but as C. Vann Woodward has put it, southern progressivism was "for whites only." See his chapter with that title in *Origins of the New South* (Baton Rouge, La., 1951). The same point is

* Available in paperback edition.

made in more detail in George B. Tindall, *The Emergence of the New South, 1913–1945* (Baton Rouge, La., 1967). A good study of what this meant for blacks is John Dittmer, *Black Georgia in the Progressive Era, 1900–1920* (Urbana, Ill., 1977). The varying responses of black leaders are brilliantly discussed in August Meier, *Negro Thought in America, 1880–1915* (Ann Arbor, Mich., 1969).

# 7

# The
# Twenties

The decade between the end of World War I and the stock market crash of 1929 was filled with paradoxes and contradictions. The American people overwhelmingly elected Republicans Warren G. Harding, Calvin Coolidge, and Herbert Hoover president, but chose as their heroes such different figures as Charles A Lindbergh and Babe Ruth. Americans self-righteously proclaimed prohibition; then, patronizing speak-easies and bootleggers, they increased the amount of social drinking. The 1920s were marked by provincialism, immigration restriction, and fundamentalist rejection of modern science, but this same decade was the occasion for a great burst of literary and artistic activity. It was a period of seeming isolation as the United States pulled back from political involvement with Europe, but it was also a time that saw increasing expansion of American investment overseas. It was a time of unprecedented business prosperity that important groups such as farmers and unorganized workers did not share, and the decade ended with the collapse of the stock market and the onset of a major depression. It was an era when progressivism and reform all but disappeared on the national level but remained alive in a number of states and cities.

These paradoxes and contradictions were the source of much conflict during the twenties. A group of intellectuals and writers, alienated from the mainstream of American life, rejected the materialism and the social and political values that they associated with the small-town Midwest. For some, such as Ernest Hemingway and F. Scott Fitzgerald, this "revolt against the village" led them to leave the country to become expatriates in France or Spain. Others, such as H. L. Mencken and Sinclair Lewis, stayed at home, leading an attack on the "booboisie" and the Babbitts. Out of the disillusionment of this "lost generation" came some of the most searching critiques of American life and some of the most creative and enduring of American art and literature.

Other manifestations of conflict were also evident in the twenties. The Scopes trial in Dayton, Tennessee, in 1925, trying and convicting a high school biology teacher for teaching Darwinian ideas, symbolized the conflict between fundamentalists and modernists, between the small town and the city. The trial, conviction, and eventual execution of two Italian immigrants, Nicola Sacco and Bartolomeo Vanzetti, for a robbery-murder in Massachusetts elicited widespread protest among many who believed that they were convicted on inadequate evidence because of prejudice against immigrants and radicals. A resurgent Ku Klux Klan, boasting some five million members, North and South, carried on an intensive campaign directed against blacks, Catholics, Jews, and immigrants. Organized labor lost many of its wartime gains and suffered a decline in membership in the face of a renewed employer offensive often supported by the courts and local law enforcement agencies.

If class, religious, racial, and ethnic conflict seemed close to the surface in the 1920s, when viewed another way, the decade seemed to represent a time of unprecedented national unity and consensus based on prosperity, smug isolation from the evils of Europe, and the enjoyment of an expanding consumer society that made available the radio, the refrigerator, the automobile, and other material symbols of the jazz age. Indeed, it was against this self-satisfied complacency that the critics often railed. Americans enjoyed more telephones, automobiles, good roads, and electrical appliances than any other people in the world. Critics were easily dismissed as sour, alien, and un-American.

These varied views are reflected in the selections that follow. The first selection is from Frederick Lewis Allen's Only Yesterday, written during the depression that followed the 1920s. His nostalgic view of the twenties does not rule out conflict, but it emphasizes a national consensus that lasted until it was shattered by the stock market crash and the depression. He argues that there was a revolution in manners and morals, an overturning of the dominant mores of the pre-World War I years that created a new consensus marked by sexual freedoms and just plain fun (at least for the young). In the second selection, John Higham explores a much different aspect of the 1920s. He describes a time of racial and ethnic conflict, a period of hate and distrust of radicals and immigrants. Eric Goldman, in the final selection, describes a conservative consensus that rejected Progressive reform. But he also sees the 1920s as a time of rising nationalism and of increasing black identity. In the midst of the conservative consensus he sees a number of reformers who fought a delaying action "staving off the complete triumph of the Babbitts."

In trying to understand this fascinating time, should we emphasize a national consensus based on prosperity, isolation, and the luxuries of the jazz age? Or should we stress the racial, ethnic, and class conflicts that were also present during the 1920s?

Perhaps the most satisfying and meaningful interpretation would be one that combined the two features so evident in the twenties, that is, an explanation of the conflict amidst the general prosperity. Why were critics so unhappy with their society? And why did such critics receive a sympathetic hearing from some but not other Americans?

Frederick Lewis Allen

# *The Revolution in Manners and Morals*

A first-class revolt against the accepted American order was certainly taking place during those early years of the Post-war Decade, but it was one with which Nikolai Lenin had nothing whatever to do. The shock troops of the rebellion were not alien agitators, but the sons and daughters of well-to-do American families, who know little about Bolshevism and cared distinctly less, and their defiance was expressed not in obscure radical publications or in soap-box speeches, but right across the family breakfast table into the horrified ears of conservative fathers and mothers. Men and women were still shivering at the Red Menace when they awoke to the no less alarming Problem of the Younger Generation, and realized that if the Constitution were not in danger, the moral code of the country certainly was.

This code, as it currently concerned young people, might have been roughly summarized as follows: Women were the guardians of morality; they were made of finer stuff than men and were expected to act accordingly. Young girls must look forward in innocence (tempered perhaps with a modicum of physiological instruction) to a romantic love match which would lead them to the altar and to living-happily-ever-after; and until the "right man" came along they must allow no male to kiss them. It was expected that some men would succumb to the temptations of sex, but only with a special class of outlawed women; girls of respectable families were supposed to have no such temptations. Boys and girls were permitted large freedom to work and play together, with decreasing and well-nigh nominal chaperonage, but only because the code worked so well on the whole that a sort of honor system was supplanting supervision by their elders; it was taken for granted that if they had been well brought up they would never take advantage of this freedom. And although the attitude toward smoking and drinking by girls differed widely in different strata of society and different parts of the country, majority opinion held that it was morally wrong for them to smoke and could hardly imagine them showing the effects of alcohol.

The war had not long been over when cries of alarm from parents, teachers, and moral preceptors began to rend the air. For the boys and girls just growing out of adolescence were making mincemeat of this code.

The dresses that the girls—and for that matter most of the older women —were wearing seemed alarming enough. In July, 1920, a fashion-writer reported in the *New York Times* that "the American woman . . . has lifted her skirts far beyond any modest limitation," which was another way of saying that the hem was now nine inches above the ground. It was freely predicted that skirts would come down again in the winter of 1920–21, but instead they climbed a few scandalous inches farther. The flappers wore thin dresses, short-sleeved and occasionally (in the evening) sleeveless; some of the wilder young things rolled their stockings below their knees, revealing to the shocked eyes of virtue a fleeting glance of shin-bones and knee-cap; and many of them were visibly using cosmetics. "The intoxication of rouge," earnestly explained Dorothy Speare in *Dancers in the Dark*, "is an insidious vintage known to more girls than mere man can ever believe." Useless for frantic parents to insist that no lady did such things; the answer was that the daughters of ladies were doing it, and even retouching their masterpieces in public. Some of them, furthermore, were abandoning their corsets. "The men won't dance with you if you wear a corset," they were quoted as saying.

The current mode in dancing created still more consternation. Not the romantic violin but the barbaric saxophone now dominated the orchestra, and to its passionate crooning and wailing the fox-trotters moved in what the editor of the Hobart College *Herald* disgustedly called a "syncopated embrace." No longer did even an inch of space separate them; they danced as if glued together, body to body, cheek to cheek. Cried the *Catholic Telegraph* of Cincinnati in righteous indignation, "The music is sensuous, the embracing of partners—the female only half dressed—is absolutely indecent; and the motions—they are such as may not be described, with any respect for propriety, in a family newspaper. Suffice it to say that there are certain houses appropriate for such dances; but those houses have been closed by law."

Supposedly "nice" girls were smoking cigarettes—openly and defiantly, if often rather awkwardly and self-consciously. They were drinking—somewhat less openly but often all too efficaciously. There were stories of daughters of the most exemplary parents getting drunk—"blotto," as their companions cheerfully put it—on the contents of the hip-flasks of the new prohibition regime, and going out joyriding with men at four in the morning. And worst of all, even at well-regulated dances they were said to retire where the eye of the most sharp-sighted chaperon could not follow, and in darkened rooms or in parked cars to engage in the unspeakable practice of petting and necking.

It was not until F. Scott Fitzgerald, who had hardly graduated from Princeton and ought to know what his generation were doing, brought out *This Side of Paradise* in April, 1920, that fathers and mothers realized fully what was afoot and how long it had been going on. Apparently the "petting party" had been current as early as 1916, and was now widely established as an indoor sport. "None of the Victorian mothers—and most of the mothers were Victorian—had any idea how casually their daughters were accustomed to be kissed," wrote Mr. Fitzgerald. ". . . Amory saw girls doing things that even in his memory would have been impossible: eating three-o'clock, after-dance suppers in impossible cafés, talking of every side of life with an air half of earnestness, half of mockery, yet with a furtive excitement that Amory considered stood for a real moral let-down. But he never realized how wide-spread it was until he saw the cities between New York and Chicago as one vast juvenile intrigue." The book caused a shudder to run down the national spine; did not Mr. Fitzgerald represent one of his well-nurtured heroines as brazenly confessing, "I've kissed dozens of men. I suppose I'll kiss dozens more"; and another heroine as saying to a young man (*to a young man!*), "Oh, just one person in fifty has any glimmer of what sex is. I'm hipped on Freud and all that, but it's rotten that every bit of real love in the world is ninety-nine percent passion and one little *soupçon* of jealousy"?

It was incredible. It was abominable. What did it all mean? Was every decent standard being thrown over? Mothers read the scarlet words and wondered if they themselves "had any idea how often their daughters were accustomed to be kissed." . . . But no, this must be an exaggerated account of the misconduct of some especially depraved group. Nice girls couldn't behave like that and talk openly about passion. But in due course other books appeared to substantiate the findings of Mr. Fitzgerald: *Dancers in the Dark, The Plastic Age, Flaming Youth.* Magazine articles and newspapers reiterated the scandal. To be sure, there were plenty of communities where nice girls did not, in actual fact, "behave like that"; and even in the more sophisticated urban centers there were plenty of girls who did not. Nevertheless, there was enough fire beneath the smoke of these sensational revelations to make the Problem of the Younger Generation a topic of anxious discussion from coast to coast.

The forces of morality rallied to the attack. Dr. Francis E. Clark, the founder and president of the Christian Endeavor Society, declared that the modern "indecent dance" was "an offense against womanly purity, the very fountainhead of our family and civil life." The new style of dancing was denounced in religious journals as "impure, polluting, corrupting, debasing, destroying spirituality, increasing carnality," and the mothers and sisters and church members of the land were called upon to admonish and instruct and raise the spiritual tone of these dreadful young people. President Murphree of the University of Florida cried out with true Southern warmth, "The low-cut gowns, the rolled hose and short skirts are born of the Devil and his angels, and are carrying the present and future generations to chaos and destruction."

A group of Episcopal church-women in New York, speaking with the authority of wealth and social position (for they included Mrs. J. Pierpont Morgan,
Mrs. Borden Harriman, Mrs. Henry Phipps, Mrs. James Roosevelt, and Mrs.
E. H. Harriman), proposed an organization to discourage fashions involving
an "excess of nudity" and "improper ways of dancing." The Y. W. C. A.
conducted a national campaign against immodest dress among high-school
girls, supplying newspapers with printed matter carrying headlines such as
"Working Girls Responsive to Modesty Appeal" and "High Heels Losing
Ground Even in France." In Philadelphia a Dress Reform Committee of
prominent citizens sent a questionnaire to over a thousand clergymen to ask
them what would be their idea of a proper dress, and although the gentlemen
of the cloth showed a distressing variety of opinion, the committee proceeded
to design a "moral gown" which was endorsed by ministers of fifteen denominations. The distinguishing characteristics of this moral gown were that it
was very loose-fitting, that the sleeves reached just below the elbows, and
that the hem came within seven and a half inches of the floor.

Not content with example and reproof, legislators in several states introduced bills to reform feminine dress once and for all. The *New York American*
reported in 1921 that a bill was pending in Utah providing fine and imprison-
ment for those who wore on the streets "skirts higher than three inches above
the ankle." A bill was laid before the Virginia legislature which would forbid
any woman from wearing shirtwaists or evening gowns which displayed "more
than three inches of her throat." In Ohio the proposed limit of decolletage
was two inches; the bill introduced in the Ohio legislature aimed also to prevent the sale of any "garment which unduly displays or accentuates the lines
of the female figure," and to prohibit any "female over fourteen years of age"
from wearing "a skirt which does not reach to that part of the foot known as
the instep."

Meanwhile innumerable families were torn with dissension over cigarettes and gin and all-night automobile rides. Fathers and mothers lay awake
asking themselves whether their children were not utterly lost; sons and
daughters evaded questions, lied miserably and unhappily, or flared up to reply
rudely that at least they were not dirty-minded hypocrites, that they saw no
harm in what they were doing and proposed to go right on doing it. From
those liberal clergymen and teachers who prided themselves on keeping step
with all that was new, came a chorus of reassurance: these young people were
at least franker and more honest than their elders had been; having experimented for themselves, would they not soon find out which standards were
outworn and which represented the accumulated moral wisdom of the race?
Hearing such hopeful words, many good people took heart again. Perhaps
this flare-up of youthful passion was a flash in the pan, after all. Perhaps in
another year or two the boys and girls would come to their senses and everything would be all right again.

They were wrong, however. For the revolt of the younger generation
was only the beginning of a revolution in manners and morals that was al-

ready beginning to affect men and women of every age in every part of the country.

A number of forces were working together and interacting upon one another to make this revolution inevitable.

First of all was the state of mind brought about by the war and its conclusion. A whole generation had been infected by the eat-drink-and-be-merry-for-tomorrow-we-die spirit which accompanied the departure of the soldiers to the training camps and the fighting front. There had been an epidemic not only of abrupt war marriages, but of less conventional liaisons. In France, two million men had found themselves very close to filth and annihilation and very far from the American moral code and its defenders; prostitution had followed the flag and willing mademoiselles from Armentières had been plentiful; American girls sent over as nurses and war workers had come under the influence of continental manners and standards without being subject to the rigid protections thrown about their continental sisters of the respectable classes; and there had been a very widespread and very natural breakdown of traditional restraints and reticences and taboos. It was impossible for this generation to return unchanged when the ordeal was over. Some of them had acquired under the pressure of war-time conditions a new code which seemed to them quite defensible; millions of them had been provided with an emotional stimulant from which it was not easy to taper off. Their torn nerves craved the anodynes of speed, excitement, and passion. They found themselves expected to settle down into the humdrum routine of American life as if nothing had happened, to accept the moral dicta of elders who seemed to them still to be living in a Pollyanna land of rosy ideals which the war had killed for them. They couldn't do it, and they very disrespectfully said so.

"The older generation had certainly pretty well ruined this world before passing it on to us," wrote one of them (John F. Carter in the *Atlantic Monthly*, September, 1920), expressing accurately the sentiments of innumerable contemporaries. "They give us this thing, knocked to pieces, leaky, red-hot, threatening to blow up; and then they are surprised that we don't accept it with the same attitude of pretty, decorous enthusiasm with which they received it, way back in the 'eighties."

The middle generation was not so immediately affected by the war neurosis. They had had time enough, before 1917, to build up habits of conformity not easily broken down. But they, too, as the let-down of 1919 followed the war, found themselves restless and discontented, in a mood to question everything that had once seemed to them true and worthy and of good report. They too had spent themselves and wanted a good time. They saw their juniors exploring the approaches to the forbidden land of sex, and presently they began to play with the idea of doing a little experimenting of their own. The same disillusion which had defeated Woodrow Wilson and had caused strikes and riots and the Big Red Scare furnished a culture in which the germs of the new freedom could grow and multiply.

The revolution was accelerated also by the growing independence of the American woman. She won the suffrage in 1920. She seemed, it is true, to be very little interested in it once she had it; she voted, but mostly as the unregenerate men about her did, despite the efforts of women's clubs and the League of Women Voters to awaken her to womanhood's civic opportunity; feminine candidates for office were few, and some of them—such as Governor Ma Ferguson of Texas—scarcely seemed to represent the starry-eyed spiritual influence which, it had been promised, would presently ennoble public life. Few of the younger women could rouse themselves to even a passing interest in politics: to them it was a sordid and futile business, without flavor and without hope. Nevertheless, the winning of the suffrage had its effect. It consolidated woman's position as man's equal.

Even more marked was the effect of woman's growing independence of the drudgeries of housekeeping. Smaller houses were being built, and they were easier to look after. Families were moving into apartments, and these made even less claim upon the housekeeper's time and energy. Women were learning how to make lighter work of the preparation of meals. Sales of canned foods were growing, the number of delicatessen stores had increased three times as fast as the population during the decade 1910–20, the output of bakeries increased by 60 percent during the decade 1914–24. Much of what had once been housework was now either moving out of the home entirely or being simplified by machinery. The use of commercial laundries, for instance, increased by 57 percent between 1914 and 1924. Electric washing-machines and electric irons were coming to the aid of those who still did their washing at home; the manager of the local electric power company at "Middletown," a typical small American city, estimated in 1924 that nearly 90 percent of the homes in the city already had electric irons. The housewife was learning to telephone her shopping orders, to get her clothes ready-made and spare herself the rigors of dress-making, to buy a vacuum cleaner and emulate the lovely carefree girls in the magazine advertisements who banished dust with such delicate fingers. Women were slowly becoming emancipated from routine to "live their own lives."

And what were these "own lives" of theirs to be like? Well, for one thing, they could take jobs. Up to this time girls of the middle classes who had wanted to "do something" had been largely restricted to school-teaching, social-service work, nursing, stenography, and clerical work in business houses. But now they poured out of the schools and colleges into all manner of new occupations. They besieged the offices of publishers and advertisers; they went into tearoom management until there threatened to be more purveyors than consumers of chicken patties and cinnamon toast; they sold antiques, sold real estate, opened smart little shops, and finally invaded the department stores. In 1920 the department store was in the mind of the average college girl a rather bourgeois institution which employed "poor shop girls"; by the end of the decade college girls were standing in line for openings in the misses' sports-wear department and even selling behind the counter in the hope that some day fortune might smile upon them and make them buyers or stylists. Small-town girls who once would have been contented to stay in Sauk Center all their days were now borrowing from father to go to New York or Chicago to seek their fortunes—in Best's or Macy's or Marshall Field's. Married women who were encumbered with children and could not seek jobs consoled themselves with the thought that house-making and child-rearing were really "professions," after all. No topic was so furiously discussed at luncheon tables from one end of the country to the other as the question whether the married woman should take a job, and whether the mother had a right to. And as for the unmarried woman, she no longer had to explain why she worked in a shop or an office; it was idleness, nowadays, that had to be defended.

With the job—or at least the sense that the job was a possibility—came a feeling of comparative economic independence. With the feeling of economic independence came a slackening of husbandly and parental authority. Maiden aunts and unmarried daughters were leaving the shelter of the family roof to install themselves in kitchenette apartments of their own. For city-dwellers the home was steadily becoming less of a shrine, more of a dormitory —a place of casual shelter where one stopped overnight on the way from the restaurant and the movie theater to the office. Yet even the job did not provide the American woman with that complete satisfaction which the management of a mechanized home no longer furnished. She still had energies and emotions to burn; she was ready for the revolution.

Like all revolutions, this one was stimulated by foreign propaganda. It came, however, not from Moscow, but from Vienna. Sigmund Freud had published his first book on psychoanalysis at the end of the nineteenth century, and he and Jung had lectured to American psychologists as early as 1909, but it was not until after the war that the Freudian gospel began to circulate to a marked extent among the American lay public. The one great intellectual force which had not suffered disrepute as a result of the war was science; the more-or-less educated public was now absorbing a quantity of popularized information about biology and anthropology which gave a general impression that men and women were merely animals of a rather intricate variety, and that moral codes had no universal validity and were often based on curious superstitions. A fertile ground was ready for the seeds of Freudianism, and presently one began to hear even from the lips of flappers that "science taught" new and disturbing things about sex. Sex, it appeared, was the central and pervasive force which moved mankind. Almost every human motive was attributable to it: if you were patriotic or liked the violin, you were in the grip of sex—in a sublimated form. The first requirement of mental health was to have an uninhibited sex life. If you would be well and happy, you must obey your libido. Such was the Freudian gospel as it imbedded itself in the American mind after being filtered through the successive minds of interpreters and popularizers and guileless readers and people who had heard guileless readers talk about it. New words and phrases began to be bandied about the cocktail-tray and the Mah Jong table—inferiority complex, sadism, masochism, Œdipus complex. Intellectual ladies went to Europe to be analyzed; analysts plied their new trade in American cities, conscientiously transferring the affections of their fair patients to themselves; and clergymen who preached about the virtue of self-control were reminded by outspoken critics that self-control was out-of-date and really dangerous.

The principal remaining forces which accelerated the revolution in manners and morals were all 100 percent American. They were prohibition, the automobile, the confession and sex magazines, and the movies.

When the Eighteenth Amendment was ratified, prohibition seemed, as we have already noted, to have an almost united country behind it. Evasion of the law began immediately, however, and strenuous and sincere opposition to it—especially in the large cities of the North and East—quickly gathered force. The results were the bootlegger, the speakeasy, and a spirit of deliberate revolt which in many communities made drinking "the thing to do." From these facts in turn flowed further results: the increased popularity of distilled as against fermented liquors, the use of the hip-flask, the cocktail party, and the general transformation of drinking from a masculine prerogative to one shared by both sexes together. The old-time saloon had been overwhelmingly masculine; the speakeasy usually catered to both men and women. As Elmer Davis put it, "The old days when father spent his evenings at Cassidy's bar with the rest of the boys are gone, and probably gone forever; Cassidy may still be in business at the old stand and father may still go down there of evenings, but since prohibition mother goes down with him." Under the new régime not only the drinks were mixed, but the company as well.

Meanwhile a new sort of freedom was being made possible by the enormous increase in the use of the automobile, and particularly of the closed car. (In 1919 hardly more than 10 percent of the cars produced in the United States were closed; by 1924 the percentage had jumped to 43, by 1927 it had reached 82.8.) The automobile offered an almost universally available means of escaping temporarily from the supervision of parents and chaperons, or from the influence of neighborhood opinion. Boys and girls now thought nothing, as the Lynds pointed out in *Middletown*, of jumping into a car and driving off at a moment's notice—without asking anybody's permission—to a dance in another town twenty miles away, where they were strangers and enjoyed a freedom impossible among their neighbors. The closed car, moreover, was in effect a room protected from the weather which could be occupied at any time of the day or night and could be moved at will into a darkened byway or a country lane. The Lynds quoted the judge of the juvenile court in "Middletown" as declaring that the automobile had become a "house of prostitution on wheels," and cited the fact that of thirty girls brought before his court in a year on charges of sex crimes, for whom the place where the offense had occurred was recorded, nineteen were listed as having committed it in an automobile.

Finally, as the revolution began, its influence fertilized a bumper crop of sex magazines, confession magazines, and lurid motion pictures, and these in turn had their effect on a class of readers and movie-goers who had never heard and never would hear of Freud and the libido. The publishers of the sex adventure magazines, offering stories with such titles as "What I Told My Daughter the Night Before Her Marriage," "Indolent Kisses," and "Watch Your Step-Ins," learned to a nicety the gentle art of arousing the reader without arousing the censor. The publishers of the confession magazines, while always instructing their authors to provide a moral ending and to utter pious sentiments, concentrated on the description of what they euphemistically called "missteps." Most of their fiction was faked to order by hack writers who could write one day "The Confessions of a Chorus Girl" and the next day recount, again in the first person, the temptations which made it easy for the taxi-driver to go wrong. Both classes of magazines became astonishingly numerous and successful. Bernarr McFadden's *True-Story*, launched as late as 1919, had over 300,000 readers by 1923; 848,000 by 1924; over a million and a half by 1925; and almost two million by 1926— a record of rapid growth probably unparalleled in magazine publishing.

Crowding the news stands along with the sex and confession magazines were motion-picture magazines which depicted "seven movie kisses" with such captions as "Do you recognize your little friend, Mae Busch? She's had lots of kisses, but she never seems to grow *blasé*. At least you'll agree that she's giving a good imitation of a person enjoying this one." The movies themselves, drawing millions to their doors every day and every night, played incessantly upon the same lucrative theme. The producers of one picture advertised "brilliant men, beautiful jazz babies, champagne baths, midnight revels, petting parties in the purple dawn, all ending in one terrific smashing climax that makes you gasp"; the venders of another promised "neckers, petters, white kisses, red kisses, pleasure-mad daughters, sensation-craving mothers, . . . the truth—bold, naked, sensational." Seldom did the films offer as much as these advertisements promised, but there was enough in some of them to cause a sixteen-year-old girl (quoted by Alice Miller Mitchell) to testify, "Those pictures with hot love-making in them, they make girls and boys sitting together want to get up and walk out, go off somewhere, you know. Once I walked out with a boy before the picture was even over. We took a ride. But my friend, she all the time had to get up and go out with her boy friend."

A storm of criticism from church organizations led the motion-picture producers, early in the decade, to install Will H. Hays, President Harding's Postmaster-General, as their arbiter of morals and of taste, and Mr. Hays promised that all would be well. "This industry must have," said he before the Los Angeles Chamber of Commerce, "toward that sacred thing, the mind of a child, toward that clean virgin thing, that unmarked slate, the same responsibility, the same care about the impressions made upon it, that the best clergyman or the most inspired teacher of youth would have." The result of Mr. Hay's labors in behalf of the unmarked slate was to make the moral ending as obligatory as in the confession magazines, to smear over sexy pictures with pious platitudes, and to blacklist for motion-picture production many a fine novel and play which, because of its very honesty, might be construed as seriously or intelligently questioning the traditional sex ethics of the small town. Mr. Hays, being something of a genius, managed to keep the churchmen at bay. Whenever the threats of censorship began to become ominous he would promulgate a new series of moral commandments for the producers to follow. Yet of the practical effects of his supervision it is perhaps enough to say that the quotations given above all date from the period of his dictatorship. Giving lip-service to the old code, the movies diligently and with consummate vulgarity publicized the new.

Each of these diverse influences—the post-war disillusion, the new status of women, the Freudian gospel, the automobile, prohibition, the sex and confession magazines, and the movies—had its part in bringing about the revolution. Each of them, as an influence, was played upon by all the others; none of them could alone have changed to any great degree the folkways of America; together their force was irresistible. . . .

A time of revolution, however, is an uneasy time to live in. It is easier to tear down a code than to put a new one in its place, and meanwhile there is bound to be more or less wear and tear and general unpleasantness. People who have been brought up to think that it is sinful for women to smoke or drink, and scandalous for sex to be discussed across the luncheon table, and unthinkable for a young girl to countenance strictly dishonorable attentions from a man, cannot all at once forget the admonitions of their childhood. It takes longer to hard-boil a man or a woman than an egg. Some of the apostles of the new freedom appeared to imagine that habits of thought could be changed overnight, and that if you only dragged the secrets of sex out into the daylight and let every one do just as he pleased at the moment, society would at once enter upon a state of barbaric innocence like that of the remotest South Sea Islanders. But it couldn't be done. When you drag the secrets of sex out into the daylight, the first thing that the sons and daughters of Mr. and Mrs. Grundy do is to fall all over themselves in the effort to have a good look, and for a time they can think of nothing else. If you let every one do just as he pleases, he is as likely as not to begin by making a nuisance of himself. He may even shortly discover that making a nuisance of himself is not, after all, the recipe for lasting happiness. So it happened when the old codes were broken down in the Post-war Decade.

One of the most striking results of the revolution was a widely pervasive obsession with sex. To listen to the conversation of some of the sons and daughters of Mr. and Mrs. Grundy was to be reminded of the girl whose father said that she would talk about anything; in fact, she hardly ever talked about anything else. The public attitude toward any number of problems of the day revealed this obsession: to give a single example, the fashionable argument against women's colleges at this period had nothing to do with the curriculum or with the intellectual future of the woman graduate, but pointed out that living with girls for four years was likely to distort a woman's sex life.

The public taste in reading matter revealed it: to say nothing of the sex magazines and the tabloids and the acres of newspaper space devoted to juicy scandals like that of Daddy Browning and his Peaches, it was significant that almost every one of the novelists who were ranked most highly by the post-war intellectuals was at outs with the censors, and that the Pulitzer Prize juries had a hard time meeting the requirement that the prize-winning novel should "present the wholesome atmosphere of American life and the highest standard of American manners and manhood," and finally had to alter the terms of the award, substituting "whole" for "wholesome" and omitting reference to "highest standards." There were few distinguished novels being written which one could identify with a "wholesome atmosphere" without making what the Senate would call interpretive reservations. Readers who considered themselves "modern-minded" did not want them: they wanted the philosophical promiscuity of Aldous Huxley's men and women, the perfumed indiscretions of Michael Arlen's degenerates, Ernest Hemingway's unflinching account of the fleeting amours of the drunken Brett Ashley, Anita Loos's comedy of two kept women and their gentlemen friends, Radclyffe Hall's study of homosexuality. Young men and women who a few years before would have been championing radical economic or political doctrines were championing the new morality and talking about it everywhere and thinking of it incessantly. Sex was in the limelight, and the Grundy children could not turn their eyes away.

Another result of the revolution was that manners became not merely different, but—for a few years—unmannerly. It was no mere coincidence that during this decade hostesses—even at small parties—found that their guests couldn't be bothered to speak to them on arrival or departure; that "gate-crashing" at dances became an accepted practice; that thousands of men and women made a point of not getting to dinners within half an hour of the appointed time lest they seem insufficiently *blasé*; that house parties of flappers and their wide-trousered swains left burning cigarettes on the mahogany tables, scattered ashes light-heartedly on the rugs, took the porch cushions out in the boats and left them there to be rained on, without apology; or that men and women who had had—as the old phrase went—"advantages" and considered themselves highly civilized, absorbed a few cocktails and straightway turned a dinner party into a boisterous rout, forgetting that a general roughhouse was not precisely the sign of a return to the Greek idea of the good life. The old bars were down, no new ones had been built, and meanwhile the pigs were in the pasture. Some day, perhaps, the ten years which followed the war may aptly be known as the Decade of Bad Manners.

Nor was it easy to throw overboard the moral code and substitute another without confusion and distress. It was one thing to proclaim that married couples should be free to find sex adventure wherever they pleased and that marriage was something independent of such casual sport; it was quite another thing for a man or woman in whom the ideal of romantic marriage had been ingrained since early childhood to tolerate infidelities when they actually took place. Judge Lindsay told the story of a woman who had made up her mind that her husband might love whom he pleased; she would be modern and think none the less of him for it. But whenever she laid eyes on her rival she was physically sick. Her mind, she discovered, was hard-boiled only on the surface. That woman had many a counterpart during the revolution in morals; behind the grim statistics of divorce there was many a case of husband and wife experimenting with the new freedom and suddenly finding that there was dynamite in it which wrecked that mutual confidence and esteem without which marriage—even for the sake of their children—could not be endured.

The new code had been born in disillusionment, and beneath all the bravado of its exponents and the talk about entering upon a new era the disillusionment persisted. If the decade was ill-mannered, it was also unhappy. With the old order of things had gone a set of values which had given richness and meaning to life, and substitute values were not easily found. If morality was dethroned, what was to take its place? Honor, said some of the prophets of the new day: "It doesn't matter much what you do so long as you're honest about it." A brave ideal—yet it did not wholly satisfy; it was too vague, too austere, too difficult to apply. If romantic love was dethroned, what was to take its place? Sex? But as Joseph Wood Krutch explained, "If love has come to be less often a sin, it has also come to be less often a supreme privilege." And as Walter Lippmann, in *A Preface to Morals*, added after quoting Mr. Krutch, "If you start with the belief that love is the pleasure of a moment, is it really surprising that it yields only a momentary pleasure?" The end of the pursuit of sex alone was emptiness and futility—the emptiness and futility to which Lady Brett Ashley and her friends in *The Sun Also Rises* were so tragically doomed.

There were not, to be sure, many Brett Ashleys in the United States during the Post-war Decade. Yet there were millions to whom in some degree came for a time the same disillusionment and with it the same unhappiness. They could not endure a life without values, and the only values they had been trained to understand were being undermined. Everything seemed meaningless and unimportant. Well, at least one could toss off a few drinks and get a kick out of physical passion and forget that the world was crumbling. . . . And so the saxophones wailed and the gin-flask went its rounds and the dancers made their treadmill circuit with half-closed eyes, and the outside world, so merciless and so insane, was shut away for a restless night. . . .

It takes time to build up a new code. Not until the decade was approaching its end did there appear signs that the revolutionists were once more learning to be at home in their world, to rid themselves of their obsession with sex, to adjust themselves emotionally to the change in conventions and standards, to live the freer and franker life of this new era gracefully, and to discover among the ruins of the old dispensation a new set of enduring satisfactions.

John Higham

# The Tribal Twenties

*The old Americans are getting a little panicky, and no wonder. . . . America,
Americans and Americanism are being crowded out of America. It is inevitable
that there should be silly forms of protest and rebellion. But the Ku Klux Klan
and the hundred percenters are fundamentally right from the standpoint of an
American unity and destiny.*
—Ltr. to ed., New Republic, 1924

*. . . not nostrums but normalcy . . . not experiment but equipoise, not submergence
in internationality but sustainment in triumphant nationality.*
—Warren G. Harding, 1920

During the night of August 5, 1920, and all through the following day hundreds of people laden with clothing and household goods filled the roads
leading out of West Frankfort, a mining town in southern Illinois. Back in
town their homes were burning. Mobs bent on driving every foreigner from
the area surged through the streets. Foreigners of all descriptions were beaten
on sight, although the Italian population was the chief objective. Time and
again the crowds burst into the Italian district, dragged cowering residents
from their homes, clubbed and stoned them, and set fire to their dwellings.
The havoc went on for three days, although five hundred state troops were
rushed to the scene.

The immediate background of the affair was trivial enough. Thousands
of workers were idle and restless owing to a strike in the coal mines where
the Italians and a large part of the native population were employed. A series
of bank robberies, popularly attributed to a Black Hand Society, had lately
occurred; this was followed by the kidnapping of two boys. The discovery of
their bodies touched off the civic explosion. The region, to be sure, had a

bloody history. Violent anti-foreign incidents had occurred there during and before the war. But never on this scale.

About the same time, an exuberance not wholly unrelated to the miners' frenzy sprang up elsewhere on the national scene in sundry ways. In California anti-Japanese hysteria, quiescent during the war, broke out again in the latter part of 1919 and rose to unprecedented heights during the election of 1920. A new law forbidding Japanese ownership of land passed by popular initiative; a fearful clamor against Japanese "picture brides" went up; and for the first time the agitation was beginning to have a real effect on eastern opinion. In Georgia the 1920 primaries brought the old warrior, Tom Watson, back to the hustings to end his career with a successful campaign for a seat in the United States Senate. The issue was popery. Silenced by the federal government during the war because of his anti-war attitudes, Watson now heaped ridicule on the authors of the discredited Red Scare while crying up the peril of Catholic domination. Not to be outdone, the adjoining state of Alabama had recently set up a convent-inspecting commission to ensure that no Protestant maidens were held under durance vile. Out of the Midwest in May 1920 came the opening blast of a propaganda campaign against Jews launched by Henry Ford, America's leading industrialist and a man idolized by millions. Almost simultaneously the most widely read magazine in the United States, the *Saturday Evening Post*, began to quote and urgently commend the doctrines of Madison Grant. At another intellectual level one of the country's foremost literary arbiters instigated a general critical assault on writers of alien blood and spirit for corrupting American literature. And during that same summer, quite outside the public eye, an insignificant little society named the Ku Klux Klan was feeling a sudden flutter of life. The upheaval in West Frankfort was only the gaudiest of the portents signaling another great nativist wave that was boiling up in the wake of the Red Scare.

## Blighted New World

In its basic patterns, the new ferment of 1920–1924 was far from new. The nativisms that came to the fore in 1920 essentially continued prewar trends. They consisted largely of hatreds—toward Catholics, Jews, and southeastern Europeans—that had gathered strength in the late Progressive era, reaching a minor crescendo in 1914. The war had simply suspended these animosities while American nationalism vented itself in other directions. Once the war and immediate postwar period passed, the two leading nativist traditions of the early twentieth century, Anglo-Saxonism and anti-Catholicism, reoccupied the field. Anti-radicalism, their historic partner, had grown hugely under the conditions which temporarily blocked the other two, but its collapse cleared the way for their revival.

As they passed into the 1920's, the Anglo-Saxon and anti-Catholic traditions retained the distinctive character that the prewar decade had stamped upon them. Racial nativism remained fixed on the new immigration (together with the Japanese), rooted in primitive race-feelings, and rationalized by a scientific determinism. It owed to the early twentieth century its prophet, Madison Grant, its southern and western political leadership, and its nation-wide appeal. Anti-Catholic nativism similarly exhibited the characteristics it had developed just before the war. Whereas racism knew no limits of section or class and preserved an air of respectability, anti-Romanism throve outside of the big cities and the cultivated classes. Reborn after 1910 in the small towns of the South and West, religious nativism resumed its prewar pattern of growth, feeding on the continuing surge of rural fundamentalism and the deepening frustration of progressive hopes. Despite the incongruities between religious and racial xenophobias, they had begun to intersect before the World War in the demagoguery of Tom Watson and, less melodramatically, in the program of the Junior Order United American Mechanics. After the war, the two traditions flowed together in the comprehensive nativism of the Ku Klux Klan, an organization which itself dated from 1915.

Yet the tempestuous climate of the early twenties is not to be accounted for simply as a resumption of storms after a temporary lull. The very fact that the lull did prove temporary, that old hatreds came to life after the war instead of being consumed by it, needs explanation. In some degree the causes lay in the objective circumstances of 1920. That year, as part of a general adjustment to peacetime conditions, two factors which time and again in American history encouraged anti-foreign outbreaks vividly reappeared. One was economic depression, the other a fresh wave of immigration. During the latter months of the year the war and postwar boom collapsed. For a year and a half businessmen, farmers, and workers felt the pinch of hard times, with all the consequences of unemployment, credit stringencies, and tobogganing prices. Unfortunately for the immigrants, the economic downswing synchronized with a sudden revival of immigration. Virtually halted by the war, immigration had remained at low ebb through 1919 and into the early months of 1920. In the second half of 1919 so many aliens, flushed with wartime savings and embittered toward America, had returned home to Europe that immigration figures showed a net loss. But the tide turned decisively around the end of May 1920. By early September an average five thousand arrivals per day were pouring into Ellis Island. Before the year was out newspapers teemed with hostile comment on the relation between this torrential influx and the worsening unemployment problem. Some thought that immigration was undermining the whole economic system.

A third well-known irritant to ethnic relations intruded into the postwar era, assuming somewhat more importance than it had hitherto displayed. Whereas the scale of immigration and the state of the economy had often contributed significantly to nativist movements, the association of foreigners with crime had not affected their reception to a comparable degree. Crime had helped to make anti-foreign stereotypes rather than anti-foreign hatreds.

Prohibition, however, created a much more highly charged situation, for it precipitated a head-on collision between mounting lawlessness and a new drive for social conformity.

On the one hand, the Eighteenth Amendment attempted an unprecedented regimentation of morality by law. Although a tradition of reform originally sired the prohibition movement, its national triumph awaited the strenuous spirit of conformity which the war unleashed. Riding the wave of 100 percent Americanism, the Drys identified their crusade to regulate behavior with preservation of the American way of life. On the other hand, constraint bred revolt. Prohibition aggravated the normal lawlessness of a postwar era by opening a vast illicit traffic in alcohol. The immigrants, whose own cultures imposed no alcoholic taboos, were Wets by habit and conviction. The dazzling opportunities that prohibition created for organized gangsterism thrust immigrant children into a special notoriety, for city gangs had long recruited a high proportion of their members in the disorganizing environment of foreign slum quarters. Thus the ban on alcohol hit the immigrants two ways: it increased their conspicuousness as lawbreakers and brought down upon their heads the wrath of a 100 percent American morality.

By the end of 1919 the press was commenting on a rising "crime wave" and speculating on its alien origins, but it remained for the eruption at West Frankfort to demonstrate the intensity of the hatred of foreign lawlessness. In the years ahead similar feelings would find a powerful outlet through the hooded legions of the Ku Klux Klan; in the Midwest the Klan delivered more real assaults on the bootleggers than on any other target. At the same time, one state after another tackled the specter of the foreign criminal with legislation to disarm all aliens. Wyoming took particular care to forbid the possession by aliens of "any dirk, pistol, shot gun, rifle, or other fire arm, bowie knife, dagger, or any other dangerous or deadly weapon."

The resumption of immigration, the onset of depression, a wave of crime —each of these formed part of a social pattern shaped by a return to peace, and all three had precedents in the circumstances of earlier peacetime eras in which nativism flourished. But if these events help to account for the regeneration of historic xenophobias in 1920, in themselves they can hardly explain the peculiar force and magnitude that the reawakened hatreds now displayed. Indeed, the alien lawbreaker owed his new significance as an anti-foreign symbol more largely to a state of mind that had crystallized during the war than to the objective circumstances of the postwar period. In many respects the level of hysteria in the early twenties was a heritage of mind and spirit from the World War. Pre-1914 traditions supplied the massive roots of that hysteria; post-1919 conditions provided fertile soil for a new season of growth; but 100 percent Americanism was the vital force that gave it abundant life.

On first thought one may wonder how the new nationalism survived so vigorously the transition from war to peace, when many other wartime ideals were shipwrecked. It is important to realize that during the years from 1915 to 1919, 100 percent Americanism shared in the heady optimism that flourished during the war and collapsed soon after. If the guardians of an exclusive loyalty had nothing else in common with the cosmopolitan, democratic nationalists, at least they felt a common exaltation. Despite the obsessive fears that tortured the 100 percenters, they too looked forward to a brave new world once the nation had passed through its ordeal. To be sure, their assurance was a grimmer and narrower thing than that of their liberal opponents; real victory would require iron resolution and heroic measures. But a crusading idealism formed a fundamental part of the 100 percent American outlook. The millennial expectations dominant in public opinion since 1898 had reached a culmination during the war period, deeply affecting almost the whole spectrum of American thought, and 100 percenters acquired much of their evangelical zeal from the general hope that the war's turmoil would usher in a purified, regenerate society. So Americanizers set about with a will to transform the immigrants; patriotic clergymen testified to the spiritually ennobling results of warfare; prohibitionists carried the point that outlawing alcohol would accomplish a general moral improvement and call for little enforcement at that; few seriously challenged President Wilson's vision of a new reign of peace founded on a league of nations.

Perhaps this utopian spirit could not long have survived unsullied under any circumstances. Certainly the harsh facts of the postwar world produced, during 1919 and 1920, a general disillusion. The quarreling at Versailles and the class strife that broke out at home and abroad began the process of deflation and embitterment. It went forward under the influence of partisan wrangling in Congress, economic depression, the manifest failure of Americanization, and the scandalous consequences of prohibition. The letdown seriously undermined democratic, cosmopolitan values, for many who held them abandoned a crusading stance, repudiating their ideals as delusive, nationalism as nasty, and society as unsalvageable. One hundred percent Americanism, on the other hand, had a built-in shock-absorber which not only saved it from disintegrating but converted every disappointment into rebounding aggressiveness. Believing implicitly that the great source of evil lay outside of their own society, super-nationalists could not hold their own principles at fault when failure mocked them. The trouble must come instead from the tenacity and secret cunning of alien influences, together with a lack of sufficient solidarity on the part of true Americans in resisting them. The nation must gird anew against protean forces working in ever grander and more mysterious ways. Thus, instead of crippling the force of 100 percent Americanism, the discouragements of 1919–1920 broadened the fears which it expressed and turned it against enemies vaguer and more elusive than either the German or the Bolshevik.

The persistence, then, of the fundamental premises of wartime nationalism was crucial to the nativist climate of the early twenties, but equally important was the loss of the spirit of confidence characteristic of the war years. In their own fashion, 100 percenters reflected the general psychological letdown. They ceased on the whole to look forward to a total defeat of the forces of darkness. The evil was too great, the world too deeply infected. Americans must concentrate their efforts on holding their present ground. In short, 100 percent Americanism passed entirely to the defensive. Its aggressions took the form not of conquest but of a holding operation to save "the last best hope of earth." The result was an intense isolation that worked hand in hand with nativism. By mid-1920 a general revulsion against European entanglements was crystallizing. In the debate over the Versailles Treaty an afterglow of Wilsonian ideals had lingered through 1919, and the League of Nations commanded immense support in public opinion (though with increasing qualifications) until the early months of 1920. By autumn not 10 percent of the daily press, and hardly a single national magazine, still backed the league. America now seemed vulnerable to European influences of every kind. Policies of diplomatic withdrawal, higher tariffs, and more stringent immigration restriction were all in order.

## Flowering of Racism

Logically, a nationalism so committed to isolation, so distrustful of entanglements with Europe, should find expression in a general revulsion against all foreigners. Indeed, an indiscriminate antiforeignism did extend far and wide in the early twenties. It echoed through the debate on the League of Nations; it swayed the policies of the American Legion and rumbled in the "konklaves" of the Ku Klux Klan; it unloosed a new torrent of state legislation excluding aliens from a great many occupations. Nevertheless the most intense and significant anti-foreign feelings still focused on symbols of hatred more specific than the whole foreign population. One hundred percent Americanism had greatest impact through interaction with older cultural traditions.

As the Red Scare subsided, the Anglo-Saxon tradition displayed more than ever the special magnetism it acquired in the prewar period. No other nativism spoke with equal authority or affected so much of American society. This was the flowering time of the semi-scientific racism that had burgeoned in the decade before the war. Although this ideology had the limitation (from a 100 percent point of view) of not rejecting all Europeans, it was peculiarly well suited as a channel for the defensive nationalism of an age undergoing disillusion. In the nineteenth and early twentieth centuries racial nativism had developed in minds of a gloomy cast; it registered a failure of nerve on the part of an exhausted elite. Explicitly, racism denied the regnant optimism of the Progressive era; a pessimistic determinism imprisoned ideals within iron laws of heredity. Thus, when the utopian hopes of the war years dissolved, the harsh racial doctrines fitted a prevailing mood. Those doctrines not only explained the apparent imperviousness of the immigrant to Americanization. They also accounted for the failure of all efforts at universal uplift. And they showed that the United States could trust in no ideals save those that rested upon and served to protect the nation's racial foundations. . . .

## The International Jew

Of all the European groups that lay outside of the charmed Nordic circle none was subjected to quite so much hatred as the Jews. They had always played a special role in the American imagination, but until the postwar period anti-Jewish sentiment, though unique in kind, probably did not exceed in degree the general level of feeling against other European nationalities. The fear of a Jewish money-power during the 1890's and Georgia's emotional debauch at the height of the Frank Case in 1914 were merely preludes to the much more widespread and tenacious anti-Semitism that developed after the World War. No pogrom has ever stained American soil, nor did any single anti-Jewish incident in the 1920's match the violence of the anti-Italian riot in southern Illinois. Nevertheless the Jews faced a sustained agitation that singled them out from the other new immigrant groups blanketed by racial nativism—an agitation that reckoned them the most dangerous force undermining the nation.

During a period of a general weakening in democratic values social discrimination against Jews would undoubtedly have spread even if no new ideological attack on them had occurred. After the war a flood of Jewish students into private eastern colleges resulted in restrictions on admission similar to those earlier adopted by preparatory schools and college fraternities. Beginning in 1919, New York University instituted stringent restrictions. Columbia soon cut the number of Jews in her incoming classes from 40 to 22 percent. At Harvard, where Brahmin students feared that the university was becoming a new Jerusalem, President Lowell in 1922 moved, with unseemly frankness, to raise the bars. At the same time job opportunities were continuing to shrink. By the end of the twenties one informed estimate indicated that Jews were excluded from 90 percent of the jobs available in New York City in general office work.

What was startling, however, was not so much the steady growth of discrimination as the rise of a new anti-Semitic nationalism. On the whole the wartime spirit of fraternity had repressed and inhibited anti-Semitic ideas. Nevertheless, the seeds of a new movement against Jews were to be found in the 100 percent Americanism of the war years. The more wealthy and prominent Jews in the United States were of German background. Certain 100 percenters, therefore, applied to the Jews the suspicion of all things German. Among some of the bitter, overwrought men who believed that the Wilson administration was dealing laxly, perhaps treasonably, with traitors within and enemies without, dark rumors circulated concerning German-Jewish influence in high places. Henry Cabot Lodge and others whispered about secret ties between Wilson and Germany through Paul Warburg, a recent Jewish immigrant who sat on the Federal Reserve Board. "The government," a Texas businessman exploded, "seems to be permeated with the atmosphere of different kinds of Jews."

The growth of anti-radical nativism during the war opened another channel for anti-Semitic feelings—one that broadened enormously after the armistice. Morris Hillquit's remarkably strong showing as the Socialist, anti-war candidate for mayor of New York City in 1917 gave a good many people a glimpse of the radical ferment at work in Lower East Side tenements. Leon Trotsky's departure for Russia in 1917, after a brief stay in New York, and the sympathy with which other Russian Jews in the United States greeted the Bolshevik revolution sharpened an emerging image of the Jew as a subversive radical. In September 1918, Brooklyn witnessed the debut of a periodical "Devoted to the Defense of American Institutions Against the Jewish Bolshevist Doctrines of Morris Hillquit and Leon Trotsky."

The Big Red Scare turned these surreptitious by-products of the war into a thriving anti-Jewish agitation. Most commonly, of course, the nativists of 1919 identified radicalism with foreigners generally, so that anti-Semitism remained a subordinate aspect of an attack upon the larger immigrant community. Nevertheless, the Jew offered the most concrete symbol of foreign radicalism, and his significance as such increased very greatly when 100 percent Americanism burst through the confining dikes of wartime unity. Stories circulated about the streets of New York to the effect that every Jewish immigrant would become a soldier in the revolutionary army assembling in America. A Methodist clergyman testified before a Senate committee that Bolshevism in Russia was drawing much of its inspiration and support from the Yiddish sections of New York. The same doctrine that Bolshevism was a Jewish movement echoed from public meetings and from the pulpits of many churches. A powerful propaganda organization of conservative businessmen in the Midwest, the Greater Iowa Association, spread word throughout the state that Russian Jewish peddlers were disseminating Bolshevik literature. . . .

The new anti-Semitism secured its standard-bearer and its prophet in one of the commanding figures of the day, Henry Ford. In the *Dearborn Independent*, a general magazine which he published and distributed through his thousands of dealerships, Ford, in May 1920, launched an offensive against the International Jew which continued off and on for several years. Then and after, the "Flivver King" was enormously popular (and not a little feared) as America's greatest industrialist, as a folk philosopher, and as a potential politician. In 1923 he was one of the most popular and widely discussed candidates for the next Presidential nomination. That he was a food faddist, a suspicious factory-master, a man of mercurial mood swings and dogmatic opinions, and a quixotic crusader who once sent a boatload of pacifists to Europe to stop the World War, counted for little in the public eye. To millions he embodied the old pioneer virtues: a farm-bred simplicity contemptuous of elegance or intellect, a rugged individualism, a genius for practical achievement.

Ford carried over into the industrial field not only the personal traits but also the social ideas typical of his rustic background. The son of Michigan tenant farmers, he looked upon big cities as cesspools of iniquity, soulless and artificial. He hated monopoly and special privilege. He jealously guarded his enterprises from banker influence and was regarded, in the words of the Detroit *News*, as "the recognized crusader against the money changers of Wall Street." In short, Ford, for all of his wealth, typified some of the key attitudes for which Watson had stood. It is hardly surprising that in Ford and in many others with an agrarian background, nativism took a violently anti-Semitic turn at a time of depression, isolation, and disillusion.

Each of the factors that apparently impelled the extension of anti-Semitism after the Red Scare affected Henry Ford in an acute and special way. The economic slump of 1920 hit him hard and early. Swallowing his scruples, he had borrowed $75,000,000 in 1919 from eastern bankers in order to buy out his partners. The decline of sales in 1920 left him loaded with debts and unsold cars. His anti-Jewish campaign began in the midst of this crisis, and at first his propaganda presented the International Jew solely in the role of financier. Jewish bankers, according to the *Dearborn Independent*, operating through a vast international network, dominate the American economy. The great struggle of the hour lies between the contending forces of "international Finance" and "creative Industry," and apparently the latter cannot triumph until control of the world is wrested from the Jewish money-kings. . . .

Another index of the locus and relative importance of the anti-Semitic theme may be found in the chief organization that fostered it, the Ku Klux Klan. Since all of the xenophobias of the 1920's flowed into this central apotheosis of a tribal spirit, the Klan furnishes a kind of litmus-paper test of rural nativism. Significantly, the Klan's home was not in the great cities. Its strength came chiefly from the towns, from the villages, and from the ordinarily tranquil countryside. Through the theory and practice of a "noble Klannishness," anti-Semitism achieved, for the first time in American history, substantial organizational expression.

Klan propaganda echoed the Ford attack on the Jewish banker-Bolshevik, adding a special emphasis on vice that reflected the powerful strain of evangelical morality in the organization. To the Klan the Jew stood for an international plot to control America and also for the whole spectrum of urban sin—for pollution of the Sabbath, bootlegging, gambling, and carnal indulgence. Thus Klan publications described the Jew as a subversive radical, a Shylock seeking power through money, and a "Christ-killing" monster of moral corruption. All of these destructive forces radiated from the centers of population, and Klansmen had the assurance—in the words of one Oregon spellbinder—that in some cities "the Kikes are so thick that a white man can hardly find room to walk on the sidewalk."

Still, later generations of Americans, remembering the Hitlerite groups of the 1930's, can easily exaggerate the part that anti-Semitism played in the organized nativism of the postwar decade. The Jew occupied, on the whole, a distinctly secondary rank in the Klan's demonology. On the level of ideas, other passions outweighed, other hatreds outreached the attack on the Jew.

As for direct action, he suffered largely from sporadic economic proscriptions. In southern as well as western towns boycotts harassed long-established Jewish merchants; sometimes enterprising Klansmen launched their own proudly labeled "100 per cent American" clothing stores. But personal violence was quite rare. Klan energies found larger outlet in the older, more massive traditions of American nativism. It is time to turn to the whole range of the Klan's operations, and to its central meaning. . . .

## The Klan Rides

The first acknowledged public appearances of the Klan in the postwar period reflected its underlying racial spirit. On the eve of the election of 1920, Klansmen paraded in many southern towns as a silent warning against Negro voting. A large number of anti-Negro outrages were committed in the next few months under Klan auspices, provoked partly by fear that a "New Negro" had emerged from the war. (In point of fact, Negro veterans returning from France in 1919 and 1920 were often determined to stand militant and upright.) The men in white bludgeoned employers into downgrading or discharging Negro employees, intimidated Negro cotton-pickers into working for wages they would not otherwise accept, forced Negro residents out of a part of South Jacksonville coveted by whites, and branded the letters "KKK" on the forehead of a Negro bellboy. In these early months of expansion the organization presented itself very largely as a means for keeping "the nigger in his place."

White supremacy remained an important theme even when the Klan spread into the North, but it would be a mistake to regard the Negro issue as the mainspring of its career. Fear of the "New Negro" rapidly declined as he either accepted his old place or moved to northern cities. By mid-1921 the Klan was specializing in attacking white people, and thereafter the great bulk of its disciplinary activities in all parts of the country had to do with whites. This shift of emphasis by no means indicated a slackening of the racial imperative. To a considerable degree, however, it suggested that race-thinking was more and more taking a nativistic and nationalistic direction. The Klan's snowballing advance in the early twenties paralleled the upthrust of racial nativism in public opinion generally. And within the order an insistence on preserving the superiority of the old Anglo-Saxon stock over foreigners of every description became pronounced. Edward Y. Clarke exemplified this trend in 1922 by defining the Klan's mission as one of creating national solidarity by protecting "the interest of those whose forefathers established the nation." Other Klan leaders, in particularizing on the old stock's interest, called immigration restriction the most momentous legislative issue of the day, asserted that only Anglo-Saxons or Nordics had an inherent capacity for American citizenship, damned "the cross-breeding hordes" of the new immigration, and trembled lest the "real whites" fail to keep the nation "free from all mongrelizing taints." This emphatic Anglo-Saxonism did not, of course, prevent the same men from ranting loudly at foreigners as such, on the plea that America must be made safe for Americans.

If the Ku Klux Klan had mobilized only this much of the emotional ferment of the period, if it had functioned only through an Anglo-Saxon version of 100 percent Americanism and through related fears of Jews and of foreigners generally, it would have incarnated a very large part of the current tribal spirit. Yet the Klan had another big side. By embracing the anti-Catholic tradition along with the racial tradition and the new anti-Semitism, it comprehended the whole range of post-1919 nativism. Anti-Catholicism did not prevail as widely in American public opinion as did the Anglo-Saxon ideas reflected in the organization; an urban, materialistic culture had stifled in too many Americans the religious feelings on which Protestant xenophobia fed. Due, however, to the semirural base of the Klan, within its ranks anti-Catholicism actually grew to surpass every other nativistic attitude. In fact, a religious impulse, perverted but not devoid of idealistic implications, accounts for much of the Klan's distinctive energy, both as a nativist organization and as an agent of other kinds of repressions too.

Although the Klan was Protestant from the day its first cross burned on Stone Mountain, an anti-Catholic emphasis came into the order only in the course of its expansion in 1920 and 1921. Simmons, Clarke, and Tyler had not at first expected to sell the organization as a bulwark against Rome. The Klan's stress on religious nativism, even more than the parallel expansion of its Anglo-Saxon agitation, reflected the passions of the people who joined it. By 1920 the anti-Catholic crusade that had appeared in the South and West after 1910 was reasserting itself more powerfully than ever. Under a prohibitionist governor, Alabama pointed the way as early as 1919. While laying plans for inspecting convents, the state also challenged Catholic (and secular) sentiment by requiring daily Bible reading in the public schools, thus reviving a trend begun in Pennsylvania in 1913. The following year the tide came in strongly. Tom Watson's Senatorial campaign spread about Georgia an impression that President Wilson had become a tool of the Pope; Governor Sidney J. Catts stomped up and down Florida warning that the Pope planned to invade the state and transfer the Vatican there; an able journalist reported that anti-Catholicism had become "second only to the hatred of the Negro as the moving passion of entire Southern communities"; Michigan and Nebraska debated constitutional amendments banning parochial schools; and in Missouri the once-mighty anti-Catholic weekly, *The Menace*, revived under a new name, *The Torch*.

Sentiment of this kind amounted to a standing invitation to secret societies. The first to respond prominently was not the Klan but rather the True Americans, a local southern organization. The T.A.'s acquired such influence in Birmingham in 1920 that they dominated the city administration and secured a purge of Catholic municipal employees. Before long Ku Kluxers eclipsed and very likely absorbed the True Americans. Klan propaganda, reviving all of the old stories about arms stored in Catholic church basements, began to lay special stress on the menace of Rome to the nation. Instead of relying entirely on professional organizers, the Klan engaged itinerant preachers as heralds of its message. Increasingly its arrival in a new area was signaled by public lectures on popish conspiracies to destroy *"the only truly Christian nation . . . where prophecy is being fulfilled."* As if to demonstrate that the hatred transcended rhetoric, in the summer of 1921 a Methodist minister who belonged to the Klan shot to death a Catholic priest on his own doorstep, and incendiaries destroyed a Catholic church in Illinois two hours after a monster Klan initiation.

The storm of anti-Catholic feeling, for which the Klan proved a wonderfully sensitive barometer, was closely related to the growth of fundamentalism. This militant repudiation of a liberalized gospel and a secularized culture was making itself felt in the closing years of the Progressive era, but only after the World War did it become a major force in American Protestantism. In truth, fundamentalism owed so much to the emotional aftermath of the war that one may almost define it as the characteristic response of rural Protestantism to the disillusion following America's international crusade. The wartime hope for a new and beatific world had produced nothing but crime, moral chaos, and organized selfishness on a grander scale than before. Surely here was proof that the nation had misplaced its faith, that the only true salvation for a sinful society lay in blotting out the whole spirit of innovation and returning to the theological and moral absolutism of an earlier day. Insistence on a Biblical Christianity naturally sharpened the historic lines of Protestant-Catholic cleavage, but the vigor of anti-Catholicism in the twenties could only result from the affiliations between fundamentalism and 100 percent Americanism. The fundamentalist determination to fix and purify a Protestant orthodoxy followed the same channels and obeyed the same laws that governed the course of 100 percent Americanism. Both epitomized a kind of crusading conformity, reacted to a common disillusion, and represented an urge for isolation from an evil world. Who can wonder that the two movements intermingled in rural areas, or that fundamentalism energized a religious version of postwar nationalism? . . .

The Klan torrent rolled onward through 1923, reaching a high point late in the year. By that time the organization had enrolled an aggregate membership probably close to three million. Arkansas and Oklahoma fell vassal to it, and a spectacular expansion in the Midwest made Indiana and Ohio the leading Klan states in the nation. Except for Colorado, the order touched the Rocky Mountain states only negligibly; it left no considerable impression on the Atlantic seaboard outside of Pennsylvania and upstate New York. In Indiana and Texas, however, it could organize vast public gatherings attended by seventy-five thousand people. . . .

At the same time, anti-Klan mobs were beginning to lash back at the organization in areas where the immigrants were strongly entrenched. A bomb wrecked the offices of the Klan newspaper in Chicago. In a suburb of Pittsburgh an angry throng pelted a white-robed parade with stones and bottles, killing one Klansman and injuring many others. In the small indus trial city of Steubenville, Ohio, a mob of three thousand attacked a meeting of one hundred Klansmen. In Perth Amboy, New Jersey, a mob six-thousand-strong, led by Jews and Catholics, closed in on a Klan meeting place, over-whelmed the entire police and fire departments, and fell upon some five hundred Ku Kluxers, kicking, stoning, and beating them as they fled.

Such, from the West Frankfort riots of 1920 to the collapse of civil government in Oklahoma three years later, from the triumphant demonstrations of racist scholarship to the nightmares of Henry Ford, were some of the fruits of nativism in a postwar world neither brave nor new.

Eric F. Goldman

# *The Shame of the Babbitts*

It was shortly before Christmas 1920, and William Allen White was writing to his old friend Ray Stannard Baker, but the best the genial White could manage in the way of season's cheer was: "What a God-damned world this is! . . . If anyone had told me ten years ago that our country would be what it is today . . . I should have questioned his reason."

Something or somebody had certainly damned the world of reformer William Allen White. In the White House a bitter, broken Wilson awaited death and Harding. Too ill to know much of what was going on, too changed to care very deeply, the one-time progressive hero headed a country that was racing to the right. Congress whooped through pro-corporation legislation, the courts interpreted New Freedom laws in a way that harassed unions and encouraged trusts, official and unofficial Red-hunts hounded reformers even more relentlessly than the wartime inquisition. In the midst of it all, the crowning symbol of the drive for conformity, the nation decreed that anyone who drank a liquid containing as much as one two-hundredth part of alcohol was a criminal. From the sickroom in the White House came a weakly worded veto of the Prohibition enforcement act. It was the last gasp of Wilsonian progressivism.

A few months later Warren Harding's amiable smile broke over the inaugural crowd. The new President's father once spoke a three-sentence biography of his son. "Warren, it's a good thing you wasn't born a gal," the old man said. ". . . You'd be in the family way all the time. You can't say No." Harding couldn't say no to politicians wheedling privileges for corporations. He couldn't say no to jobseekers like the Reverend Heber H. Votaw, whose qualifications to be Superintendent of Federal Prisons consisted of having been a missionary in Burma and a Republican in Ohio. He couldn't

From Rendezvous with Destiny, by Eric F. Goldman. Copyright 1952 by Alfred A. Knopf, Inc. Reprinted by permission of Alfred A. Knopf, Inc.

say no to a gang of thieves that swept into Washington with him, including jolly Jesse Smith, who used to hum "My God, how the money rolls in" while he sold federal favors from the notorious little green house at 1625 K Street. Jesse Smith's friend in the White House did manage three positive achievements. The President, according to his mistress, left behind an illegitimate daughter, conceived in the Senate Office Building shortly before his nomination. He added "back to normalcy" to the American language because he misread the correct phrase that a professor had written for him. And he took a firm stand on the tariff. "We should," the President of the United States told a reporter, "adopt a protective tariff of such a character as will help the struggling industries of Europe to get on their feet." The reporter rose and left the room, speechless.

After Harding there was Coolidge and after Coolidge there was Hoover. As President, Coolidge permitted no flagrant boodling, made no additions to the language or to the population. Hoover was not only virtuous and grammatical; he was intelligent. He had, besides, entered the White House something of a darling among reformers. He wore the garland of a humanitarian for his war relief work, and had shown his interest in new thinking by offering to purchase stock in the *New Republic*. Hoover's Presidential candidacy was first pushed by progressive journalists, against the strong opposition of old-guard Republicans (even Mary Ellen Lease, in the early Twenties, was hailing Hoover as "one sent by God"). But reformers soon discovered that intelligence, or respectability, or even feeding the Belgians was not quite the point. Under Hoover and Coolidge, no less than under Harding, government proved increasingly responsive to the will of corporations.

Economists have long since made plain the real nature of the prosperity of the Twenties. The national income was fabulously high, unemployment was relatively low, but the control of the country's industries was steadily concentrating and the returns from the increased national wealth were not proportionately distributed. The Twenties were another intensive period of trust-building, new combines constantly forming, old combines gaining new power through the holding-company device or through establishing links with international cartels. By their ability to control prices, these giants brought unprecedented wealth to a few and substantial gain to thousands of skilled workers and white-collar employees, while small business was also generally prosperous. For the rest of the nation the glow of prosperity was largely reflected heat. Statisticians with no strong ideological bent have agreed that about $2,000 was the minimum necessary to provide a family with the decencies during the Twenties, and almost one third of the breadwinners received less than $2,000—one fifth, less than $1,000. Child labor was increasing; all industrial laborers had to face new dangers to their health from the speed-up of mass production and new risks of unemployment from the onrushing technology.

To the farmers the Twenties brought another disaster. In the years immediately after the Armistice farm prices took the sharpest drop in American history. In 1919 a bushel of corn bought five gallons of gasoline; a year later it bought one gallon; one year more and it bought half a gallon. Throughout the Twenties, farm prices never went up enough to stop an ominous increase of tenant farming in the South and in the Midwest. The distress of the farmers was so great and their political power so concentrated that a number of governmental moves were made to aid them. But even the farmers never got the legislation they wanted most, the McNary-Haugen bill, and the general reaction of government to the maldistribution of prosperity was to aid in distributing it still more unequally.

Business triumphant, of course, included a reconquest of the American mind by conservatism. With no widespread protest, an official United States Government publication defined democracy as "a government of the masses. . . . Results in mobracy. Attitude toward property is communistic—negating property rights. Attitude toward law is that the will of the majority shall regulate, whether it be based upon deliberation or governed by passion, prejudice, and impulse, without restraint or regard to consequences. Results in demagogism, license, agitation, discontent, anarchy." Conservative Darwinism reasserted itself in a thousand sleek apostrophes to the economic jungle. Walter Rauschenbusch's Jesus of low food prices had become Bruce Barton's Jesus as the prototype of the go-getting businessman. Magazines that only a few years before were deploring the unbridled competitiveness of the market-place now featured articles on "It Is Up to You," "What a Whale of a Difference an Incentive Makes," and "The Bookkeeper Who Refused to Stay Put."

If any one man was the American folk hero of the Twenties, unquestionably the man was the winner in the race for automobile millions, Henry Ford. The peevish, erratic manufacturer did his best to fray the halo. He conducted his business with a coarse tyranny. He succumbed to a whole menagerie of fads, announcing that crime could be cured by changes in diet, and that cows, which were lazy besides being crime-breeding, "must go." He proved himself an ignoramus by financing assaults on a supposed Jewish conspiracy to rule the world, and a coward by wriggling for weeks to avoid appearing in the libel trial that ensued. The halo simply would not fray. The American people played mah jong, devoured five million telegraphed words on the murder of the Reverend Mr. Hall and his choir-singer mistress, repeated with M. Coué: "Day by day in every way I am getting better and better," and made Henry Ford a major threat for the Presidency of the United States.

For progressives, here was certainly a post-Civil War all over again, only worse. Reform in the Seventies and Eighties had the buoyancy of a movement that was just taking the offensive. Progressivism of the Twenties was a beaten army, muscles aching, its ranks seriously depleted. As the new era opened, so the story goes, Herbert Croly went home and refused to see anyone for three days. On the fourth day he summoned his editors to his office and told them that progressivism was finished. "From now on we must work for the redemption of the individual." Then Croly began bringing to *New Republic* luncheons a bearded Englishman named Orage, who explained that what the world needed was the self-discipline of yoga. Croly's death in 1930, some of his friends believed, was hastened by forcing his frail body through the rigors of the cult.

Others found a less strenuous escape. Thousands were like the progressive the authors of *Middletown* talked to in Muncie, Indiana. With witch-hunters thrashing through the state, this man was no longer signing petitions or making speeches at the town meeting. "I just run away from it all to my books," he explained resignedly. Still other progressives turned to the cushion of cynicism, or to expatriation, which offered the delights of disillusionment on a devaluated franc, or to the exhilaration of Socialism or Communism. The varieties of Marxism that were winning American converts before 1917 were certainly not made less attractive by the progressive debacle at Paris and at home. Besides, as Robert Morss Lovett has remarked in his autobiographical account of the Twenties, only from Russia did there seem to be any light breaking on the world.

In the middle of the Twenties, the remaining progressive aspirations, ignored by the leaders of both the Republican and the Democratic organizations, found their natural outlet in the third-party effort headed by Robert La Follette. The election of 1924 was La Follette's last campaign, and pathos surrounded the exit of the gallant old battler. Two generations of reformers swung to his support; the famous pompadour, now totally gray, bristled as belligerently as ever, flame still leaped from his words. But when the votes were counted, the ticket had polled only seventeen percent of the total—about ten percent less than Roosevelt's third-party vote in 1912. In seven months La Follette was dead, finally exhausted by his thirty years' crusade, scarcely concealing his bitterness that progressivism had become a nagging aunt unwanted in the cozy rendezvous of business and America.

Why the failure of progressivism in the Twenties, reformers asked themselves then and have continued to ask. The most common explanation boiled down to two points: the effects of the war and of an atmosphere of general prosperity. Unquestionably these factors were important. In the modern history of many countries war has frequently exalted the large-scale businessman and smothered discontent; hard times certainly have increased the appeal of programs for change. But it is possible to make these explanations carry too heavy a load, as Professor Arthur M. Schlesinger has suggested in an essay on "The Tides of National Politics." From the beginnings of political parties in the United States to the anti-Fair Deal Congressional landslide in 1946, Professor Schlesinger maintained, the country has shifted eleven times from "conservative" governments to those which represented an inclination for change. Analysis of the eleven instances indicates that "the worsening of material conditions invariably disturbs the political waves, but, unless reinforced by other factors, does not affect the deeper waters." Foreign wars, he continued, offer no more satisfying an explanation. "These conflicts have taken place about equally in conservative and liberal periods, sometimes coming at the start, sometimes at the end and sometimes midway."

What's more, explaining progressive weakness in the Twenties by prosperity and war suggests the same type of incomplete analysis as explaining the progressive debacle at the peace conference by blaming Woodrow Wilson. Both explanations were the natural kind for progressives to make—they assigned the whole fault, or almost the whole fault, to factors external to progressivism. But placing Jeffersonian, New Freedom progressivism alongside Crolyite, New Nationalist progressivism has revealed important deficiencies in both varieties of reform. Going at the problem in this way suggests that war and prosperity, in addition to being causes of the progressive decline in the Twenties, provided the circumstances that brought out progressivism's own inner difficulties. These difficulties lost followers for reform, rendered less effective certain factors on which the progressives had depended heavily, and made the rule of conservatives more disastrous to progressive purposes.

## II

At the heart of traditional, Jeffersonian progressivism had been a faith in the people, or, more specifically, in the majority. The trouble with America was that the people did not really rule, most reformers had argued; democratize government, and government would really serve the whole community. The years immediately surrounding the war brought climactic successes in the drive for more democracy. By the time of the Armistice, the direct election of United States senators had been made mandatory by a Constitutional amendment. Direct primaries were in operation in all but four of the states; the initiative and referendum, in almost a half; the recall, in scores of state and municipal governments. Within a year after the Armistice, and partly as a result of the war, the woman-suffrage amendment was ratified. With that, a far larger percentage of American citizens could participate in the processes of government than ever before in the history of the country. And the results that appeared during the Twenties in no way justified the hopes and the claims of the progressives.

The most conspicuous result was the lack of any result. The initiative, referendum, and recall were invoked sparingly, and to a lessening extent. When the techniques were used, they produced no significant change in the political and economic situation. The experience of California, probably the most active direct-democracy state during the Twenties, was revealing. The initiative was employed in attempts to license "naturopaths," to close barbershops on Sunday, and to create the Klamath Fish and Game District; referendums were staged in efforts to get rid of laws enforcing the Volstead Act, to increase the registration fee on trucks, and to prohibit shingle roofs in incorporated places. A wide variety of groups, practical-minded and crackpot, turned to the new devices. But when the decade was over, two political scientists reviewed the California experience and emerged with this "indubitable fact": direct democracy had changed California very little.

No more perceptible effect came from the direct elections of senators, unless it was in increasing the chances of a candidate with a talent for demagogy. As early as 1912 the reform-minded political scientist Charles Merriam had sighed: "Some bosses are wondering why they feared the law; and some reformers why they favored it." The primary did seem to make political bosses interested in picking a candidate who could appeal to the general public more than the rival faction's candidate. But one of the shrewdest and most intensive students of democratic processes, Professor V. O. Key, Jr., has concluded that in general the direct primary left elections where they had always been, in the hands of party managers. If reform forces were strong enough to make the bosses recognize them within the primary, Professor Key pointed out, they were also strong enough to force approximately the same degree of recognition under any nominating system.

Woman suffrage made the most spectacular lack of difference. Elections became no cleaner, no glow of motherly kindness spread over the industrial scene. In election after election large numbers of women failed to use their hard-won ballots. (In 1924 the estimated percentages of males and females voting were sixty-five and thirty-five, respectively.) When women did vote, the fact that they were women did not seem to matter particularly. Using the data available after a decade of woman suffrage, observers concluded that sex had less to do with determining a vote than place of residence, wealth, occupation, race, nationality, or religion. . . .

## III

A few years before La Follette was defeated, Bagdasar K. Baghdigian walked up to the registration desk of a Kansas City school and struggled through an application for courses. The teacher glanced at the Armenian name and snapped: "Oh, give that up and change your name to Smith, Jones or a name like that and become Americanized. Give up everything you brought with you from the Old Country. You did not bring anything worth while anyway."

Baghdigian froze into group consciousness. "The Turkish sword," he told himself, "did not succeed in making me become a Turk, and now this hare-brained woman is trying to make an American out of me. I defy her to do it." After that, Baghdigian recalled later, "I was more of an Armenian patriot than I had ever thought of being." And after that he was a perfect symbol of the rapid accentuation of another type of special interest in the United States.

The trend had been spurred on by two quite different developments. Wilson's appeal to nationalism during the war had an electric effect within the United States. Czech, Slovak, and Polish immigrants, pouring funds into movements for the creation of an independent Czechoslovakia and Poland, became a good deal more nationality-conscious in all their attitudes, and every other American group felt the surge of nationality feeling. This positive effect of Wilsonianism, important as it was, proved less significant than the kickback from another wartime phenomenon.

Until 1917, most Americans, progressive or conservative, had glided along in the happy illusion that the melting-pot was working with great efficiency. But as soon as the foreign-policy issue became acute, the country split into a babble of groups, many of them obviously influenced by Old World ties. Suddenly it was plain that the melting-pot had failed in important respects, and this revelation provoked the campaign that made sure the melting-pot would fail still more. After the Armistice a call for "Americanization" sounded across the country. To informed and humane people, Americanization might still mean the old progressive policy, the two-way procedure of bringing all the American people into a common community. But for an overwhelming percentage of the Americanizers, the campaign quickly turned into the process that Baghdigian met; the whole population was to be insulted and browbeaten into "one-hundred-percent Americanism," which meant what the local guardians of Americanism defined as the ways of white, Protestant Americans who were not recent immigrants. Such Americanization stimulated all racial, religious, and nationality prejudices, and the resulting discrimination hurried all minorities along the way to minority chauvinism.

The Twenties saw the reaction of Bagdasar Baghdigian repeated time and again. Scores of organizations sprang up to assert that their members, no matter how much the Americanizers shrilled, were still Armenian patriots, Irish patriots, or Scandinavian patriots. In the previous generation it was not difficult to find prominent Catholics who were so leery of marking out Catholics from the general population that they opposed parochial schools; by the mid-Twenties the newly created National Catholic Welfare Conference was busily co-ordinating the segregation of Catholics, hurrying them toward parochial schools, a Catholic Boy Scouts, a Catholic Daughters of America, and a Catholic Total Abstinence Union, not to speak of the election of a Catholic Mother of the Year. Among the Jews and Negroes, the groups hit hardest by the intolerance of the Twenties, the long-running trends toward inward-looking minority feeling speeded up two- or three-fold. "Until the Twenties," one Zionist leader, Stephen Wise, has recalled, "we were a movement. Then we became an avalanche, and we tumbled along with us many a boulder of Jewish respectability."

Negro nationalism leaped ahead to its own full-blown Zionism. The leader was a chubby, elegantly mustached immigrant from the West Indies, Marcus Aurelius Garvey, who had organizational abilities worthy of a Gompers and a flair for publicity which no muckraker had excelled. Establishing himself in Harlem in 1916, Garvey summoned his fellow Negroes to have done with "boot-licking" organizations like the National Association for the Advancement of Colored People, and mulattoes like William Du Bois, who could not possibly understand the national glories of the black man. "As much as the white man may boast of his glorious deeds to-day," Garvey blustered, "the fact remains that what he now knows was inherited from the original mind of the black man who made Egypt, Carthage and Babylon, the centres of civilization, that were not known to the unskilled and savage men of Europe." So glorious a race deserved its own home. The immediate necessity for the Negroes was a "Back to Africa" movement, which would give all the black men of the world their "motherland." When "the Jew said, 'We shall have Palestine,' " Garvey added, "we said, 'We shall have Africa.' "

Soon Garvey had churned black America into a chauvinistic froth by his inflammatory speeches, wild receptions for Negro dignitaries, and resplendent parades in which uniformed troops and "Black Cross" nurses chanted:

> *Oh, glorious race of mighty men*
> *The homeland calls to you.*

An estimated one hundred thousand Negroes were buying subscriptions to Garvey's journal, and, according to Garvey's wife, ten million dollars poured in to pay for the "Black Star" ships that were to carry the American Negroes "home." At the height of Garvey's influence, about 1921, his organization boasted the largest membership of any Negro society in American history: four million dues-paying enthusiasts. In Europe, nervous chancelleries pondered the possible effects of the "Back to Africa" movement on their delicate colonial arrangements.

The leader never quite got around to mundane details. He was too busy making his ornate offices still more ornate, supporting a bevy of very nationalistic and very good-looking women, equipping, gazetting, and knighting the aristocracy of the coming black empire. The United States Government, skeptical about Garvey's use of the mails, sent him to Atlanta Penitentiary in 1925, but even this did not entirely quash him. Negro political pressure secured Garvey's release in return for his deportation, and he went on agitating in the freedom of Jamaica. When Garvey died, in 1940, the decorous *Journal of Negro History*, which lived conspicuously above sex and parades, chose to point out that if Garvey was a criminal, "he was no more a criminal . . . than thousands of other persons in the business world." Besides, he was the only well-known American Negro who did not owe his prominence "mainly to white men."

Few educated Negroes were captured by the rococo Garvey, but many went on sympathetically reading W. E. B. Du Bois, who, in one important sense, was an honest and a sophisticated Marcus Garvey. Though the brilliant official of the NAACP showed no sympathy for "repatriating" Negroes to Africa, he was increasing his emphasis on the point that Negroes were a separate people and should act as one. For all of Garvey's scurrilous attacks on him, Du Bois could never quite get himself to repudiate the Negro Zionist completely. Garvey's methods were "bombastic, wasteful, illogical," but he was also a "sincere" leader, speaking for "one of the most interesting spiritual movements of the modern world." Du Bois's intense racialism became most clear in 1919, when he began organizing "Pan-African Congresses," where representatives of Negroes from all nations were to plan "concerted thought and action." The trouble with progressivism among white Americans, Du Bois declared, was that it "did not envisage Africa and the colored peoples of the world. They [the progressives] were interested in America and securing American citizens of all and any color, their rights." Most Negroes made the same mistake. "They felt themselves Americans, not Africans. They resented and feared any coupling with Africa."

Pan-Africanism easily blended into the more general movement that is often called the "Black Renaissance." On the surface, this Renaissance was simply an exciting and long overdue recognition of Negro talent. Publishers suddenly found that Negroes could write highly salable books, Negro musicals became the vogue, night-rounders discovered that many ebony clubs offered a better show than the monotonous gyrations of white thighs on Broadway. But in the mind of the Negro, the Renaissance increasingly became an expression of the chauvinism that was marking all minority life. Negroes complained about the white invasion of "our" night clubs, campaigned to have Negroes deal only in Negro stores and read only Negro newspapers, and started a drive to substitute the term "Afro-American" for "American Negro." An Association for the Study of Negro Life, headed by a man who announced that he hated "interracialists," made rapid progress among Negro intellectuals.

The psychology of many of the Negro writers was expressed by James Weldon Johnson, a major literary figure in the Renaissance as well as the executive secretary of the NAACP. The writing of which Johnson was most proud was his "Negro National Hymn," which he wrote in a "feverish ecstasy" and could never hear performed without reliving the ecstasy. Editing a group of Negro poems in 1922, Johnson asserted that the Negro was "the creator of the only things artistic that have yet sprung from American soil and been universally acknowledged as distinctive American products." When some readers were aghast at the statement, Johnson compounded his racialism by adding a footnote in the second edition which conceded, perhaps, that skyscrapers were of some importance and not an invention of Negroes. Nor did Johnson fail to get around to the argument that always seems to creep into embittered chauvinisms—our women are better-looking than your women anyhow. Writing his autobiography at the end of the Black Renaissance, Johnson paused to emphasize that Negroes too often accepted white ideals of beauty. He had once actually compared the types, said Johnson, and it was clear that "the Negro woman, with her rich coloring, her gayety, her laughter and song, her alluring, undulating movements—a heritage from the African jungle—is a more beautiful creature than her sallow, songless, lipless, hipless, tired-looking, tired-moving white sister."

And the progressive in the midst of all this? By the Twenties, urban influences had marked reform so deeply that the progressive who spoke Anglo-Saxonism was rare and was promptly denied the label "progressive" by most reformers. Edward Ross, still alive, was already history, and was bluntly told so every time he bemoaned "race suicide." The progressive of the Twenties was outraged by the blatant bigotry of the period, and out of outrage, his sympathies, his admiration, went to the Negro or Jew or Armenian immigrant who reared back and tried to declare his self-respect. Since declaring self-respect so often took the form of minority chauvinism, the progressive's emotions easily swept him toward acceptance of, or at least failure to attack, the mounting glorification of group.

The effect of this acquiescence on progressivism during the Twenties was mixed. To the extent that minorities identified the interests of their group with a reform cause, the reform received the additional impetus of powerful clan feelings. Al Smith, a much more progressive candidate than Herbert Hoover, was aided in the Presidential election of 1928 by thousands of conservative Catholic votes, which went to him only or primarily because he was a Catholic. La Guardia was ardently backed in his campaigns for Congress by many slum-dwelling Italians and Jews, whose fervor for him was compounded of an approval for his program and an enthusiasm for his descent.

But the available evidence on the point suggests that progressivism was hurt rather than helped by the rising group consciousness. The more employees felt identified with the homeland or a particular race or religion, the easier it was for employers to divide and conquer them. "We want you," the United States Steel Corporation displayed the pattern in sending out instructions during a strike, "to stir up as much bad feeling as you possibly can between the Serbians and the Italians. . . . Call up every question you can in reference to racial hatred between these two nationalities." In the political field, closer identification with a nationality group, the Negro community, or the Catholic Church—the minority attachments that were, numerically, the most important in the Twenties—brought the citizen more under conservative influences. The popular picture of the immigrant community as more inclined to radicalism than the older settlers was incorrect, and came from a few conspicuous exceptions. Both Negro and Catholic leadership were markedly conservative. (Clarence Darrow, with pardonable hyperbole, called the hierarchy "the right wing of the right wing," and when the depression struck, it was not surprising that the only Negro Congressman, De Priest, of Chicago, fought federal relief funds.) Most important from the long-range view, the increased tendency toward religious, racial, and nationality feeling was a tendency toward thinking which asked not the progressive question: what is good for "the people" as a whole? but rather: what is good for us special few? The question could, by coincidence, aid reform, but movements do not keep their power by coincidence. . . .

## IV

The progressive practice of not seeing progressivism's inherent difficulties reached a high point in the La Follette campaign of 1924. A few leaders in the third party effort, like the attorney, Donald Richberg, worked hard to have the campaign based on something beyond the traditional reform cries, but their efforts were wasted. The La Follette campaign song, Richberg remarked as he looked back at the election, should have been "Tenting Tonight on the Old Camp Ground."

Simultaneously, many urban progressives of the better-educated group were giving their enthusiasm to a cause that involved no nagging difficulties. Even before the campaign of 1924 was over, they were neglecting La Follette's speeches for the invective that came once a month in a newly founded journal, the *American Mercury*. The magazine's editor, Henry L. Mencken, was hardly in the usual progressive tradition. He looked like a German burgher out of the eighteenth century and, in many ways, he thought like one. Suspicious of anything new, even New York, Mencken valued Pilsner, Beethoven, a sharp sally, or a workmanlike job of bricklaying far more than any plans to change society. Violently contemptuous of ordinary men, he pronounced democracy "the worship of jackals by jackasses," and the American people, "the most timorous, sniveling, poltroonish, ignominious mob of serfs and goose-steppers ever gathered under one flag in Christendom." He flayed all reformers and their "bilge of idealism," lauded "free competition . . . to the utmost limit," advocated wars, aristocracy, and a frank recognition that it made no difference whether the union or the employer won a strike. The *Nation*, Mencken merely "deplored"; the *New Republic*, because it was subsidized by the Straights, had coined for it the famous sneer "kept idealists." As for the *American Mercury*, the first issue made emphatically plain that "the Editors have heard no Voice from the burning bush. . . . The world, as they see it, is down with at least a score of painful diseases, all of them chronic and incurable."

Of course, Mencken, who was at least half Puck, loved to hear the rumble of his own hyperboles, and at bottom he was as much of a reformer as any cornfield Populist. No one outside an insane asylum ever stayed so vitriolic for so long out of sheer cussedness, and Mencken was anything but crazy. He simply had no use for much of the program that had become associated with American progressivism. He was devoted, and passionately so, to the essence of the 1872 liberalism which had been assumed with little discussion by succeeding generations of reformers until the ruthless standardization of the Twenties placed it in real jeopardy—the freedom of the individual to think and act as an individual. Simeon Strunsky was quite right when he suggested that the Mencken approach was really a kind of latter-day muckraking, exposing and assailing The Shame of Prohibition, The Shame of Comstockery, The Shame of the Babbitts.

With powers of scorn unexcelled in American letters, Mencken flailed away at Prohibitionists, Fundamentalists, book-censors, Rotarians, Ku-Kluxers, farm-bloc leaders—anyone who wanted to cajole or force anyone into a pattern. The existence of Prohibition gave Mencken's bastinado a daily workout. The Scopes trial in Tennessee brought his campaign to a rollicking climax. Here was a state forbidding by law the teaching of a doctrine that more than two generations of scientists had accepted. Here was William Jennings Bryan, a three-time nominee for the Presidency of the United States, defending the law to the cheers of thousands. Mencken hurried down to Tennessee, agonized through the insistence that all schoolchildren should accept as literal truth every word in the Bible, and wired back descriptions of rule by "gaping primates" which brought him an avalanche of invitations to leave the United States on the next boat.

Mencken's china-blue eyes took on their most ingenuous softness. Why did he continue to live in America, he catechized himself. "Why do men go to zoos?"

After a few years of the *American Mercury*, Walter Lippmann could call Mencken "the most powerful influence on this whole generation of educated people," and not a few of these educated people were men and women who in 1914 had been busy pushing the political and economic program of progressivism. Reform in the Twenties, as always, included an enormous variety of dissidents, but unquestionably the group that was most articulate and most effective were those who adopted the Mencken-type emphasis. Unlike Mencken, the typical reformer of the Twenties did not actually oppose the political and economic program of progressivism; he simply gave less stress to these problems and more stress to the battle against conformity. Appropriately enough, with the change in emphasis came a change in title, and the group that had called itself "progressive" was now more and more using the old term "liberal." In part, this shift was attributable to a desire to shake free from the clammy aftermath of Wilsonianism. In part, it reflected concern over getting rid of any connection that could play into the hands of the witch-hunters. (Vernon Louis Parrington, coming to appreciate the well-aged respectability of the term "liberal," went through his manuscript substituting it for "radical.") But most significantly, the revival of the term "liberal" corresponded to the revival of the major concern of dissidence in the late Sixties and early Seventies. Whatever the squeezings of opportunity in the days of Ulysses Grant and of Calvin Coolidge, lack of opportunity was not the problem that protruded most conspicuously. In both periods individual liberty was in danger, and plainly so.

Prewar and entirely new reform figures now engaged in a brilliantly varied campaign for personal and intellectual freedom. The effort was most noticeable in the literary field. Harold Stearns, restless in "the shadows . . . of intolerance," delayed his European exile long enough to edit *Civilization in the United States*, which made each aspect of American life a self-convicting pursuit of sameness. Sherwood Anderson, a puzzled manager of a paint factory before the war, emerged in the Twenties a mordant analyst of the village twisting under respectability. The cherubic W. E. Woodward, a frolicsome socialist in 1912, a restless employee of the Morris Plan Bank in 1920, invented a word and a profession by gaily "debunking" all the icons of the Rotaries and the ladies' clubs. Theodore Dreiser, grimly portraying Sister Carrie in the early 1900's, was grimmer still in his 1927 *American Tragedy* of a boy, a girl, and an illegitimate baby in Lycurgus, New York. Most widely read of all, as savage as Mencken, as wistful as Fitzgerald, as impish as Woodward, Sinclair Lewis came out of a socialist past to assail the Twenties in terms of the pathetic conformity of George F. Babbitt.

"I really didn't have any answers to it all," Lewis once said of his thinking in the Twenties. "I only knew that the answers could come only from free men." The dominant liberalism of the Twenties offered few answers, except from those who found an answer in despair, but at that it served a vital function in the history of American reform. It fought a magnificent delaying action, staving off the complete triumph of the Babbitts, trading positive thinking for sorely needed time.

## SUGGESTIONS FOR FURTHER READING

Anyone interested in the 1920s should begin with Frederick Lewis Allen, *Only Yesterday: An Informal History of the Nineteen Twenties* (New York, 1931), from which a selection is reprinted here. Another account, better-balanced, which sees more conflict and diversity, is William E. Leuchtenburg, *The Perils of Prosperity, 1914–1932* (Chicago, 1958). Frederick Hoffman, *The Twenties: American Writing in the Postwar Decade* (New York, 1955) is the best account of the rebellion of writers and intellectuals. In addition to books about the literature of the twenties, much can be learned by sampling the literature itself. The works of F. Scott Fitzgerald, Ernest Hemingway, H. L. Mencken, Sinclair Lewis, and other writers are readily available in paperback. The important black literary and artistic achievement known as the Harlem Renaissance is discussed in Nathan Irvin Huggins, *Harlem Renaissance* (New York, 1971); the same author's *Voices from the Harlem Renaissance* (New York, 1976) gives the reader a more direct taste of the work of the black writers. On the economic aspects of the decade, especially the problems leading to the stock market collapse, see John Kenneth Galbraith, *The Great Crash, 1929* (Boston, 1954), and Robert Sobel, *The Great Bull Market: Wall Street in the 1920's* (New York, 1968).

Two accounts that find a survival of progressivism during the decade are Arthur M. Schlesinger, Jr., *The Crisis of the Old Order* (Boston, 1957), and Clarke A. Chambers, *Seedtime of Reform: American Social Service and Social Action, 1918–1933*. Paul Murphy, "Sources and Nature of Intolerance in the 1920's," *Journal of American History*, 51 (June 1964), pp. 60–76, deals with nativism, prejudice, and conflict. Two collections of essays contain more information on some of the problems suggested here: Milton Plesur, *The 1920's: Problems and Paradoxes* (Boston, 1969); and John Braeman, Robert H. Bremner, and David Brody, *Change and Continuity in Twentieth Century America: 1920's* (Columbus, Ohio, 1968). A useful introduction to the historical writing on the period is Burl Noggle, "The Twenties: A New Historiographical Frontier," *Journal of American History*, 53 (September 1966), pp. 299–314. Two recent interpretations are Paul A. Carter, *Another Part of the Twenties* (New York, 1977), and Paula S. Fass, *The Damned and the Beautiful: American Youth in the 1920's* (New York, 1978).

* Available in paperback edition.

# The
# New Deal

The depression following the stock market crash in the fall of 1929 was the longest and most devastating the nation had ever faced. Millions lost their jobs and their savings; many, unable to meet mortgage payments or to pay rent, found themselves homeless. Hungry men and women stood in bread lines awaiting meager meals from charity organizations and churches. Farmers burned their corn for fuel because it did not pay to haul it to market, and they watched sullenly as their creditors came to evict them from their farms. Many of the homeless, hungry, and unemployed listened to radicals who urged massive social and economic change, even revolution. When a group of unemployed army veterans marched on Washington in the summer of 1932 to demand a bonus payment, a panicky President Hoover ordered them driven out of town by troops, tanks, and tear gas.

As the depression deepened, the two political parties prepared for the 1932 election. The results were inevitable. The voters rejected President Herbert Hoover and the Republican party, turning to the Democrats and their candidate, Franklin Delano Roosevelt. "Only a foolish optimist can deny the dark realities of the moment," declared the newly elected President in his inaugural address. Roosevelt went on to announce that he interpreted his victory in the elections of the previous November as a "mandate" for "direct, vigorous action" under active leadership. This leadership he promised to give.

The result was the New Deal, a period of intensive legislative activity lasting roughly from 1933 to 1938. Virtually no part of the economy failed to feel the effects of the New Deal legislation. Newly formed government agencies provided relief and work for the unemployed; farmers were paid to cut production in order to raise crop prices; workers organized trade unions under the protection of federal law. The banks and the stock exchange came under strict government supervision. Federal funds paid for flood control, rural electrification, and other forms of natural resource conservation. Federal legislation established the Social Security program, the minimum wage, and unemployment insurance.

New Deal legislation won Franklin D. Roosevelt and the Democratic party a great deal of support among the American people. But at the same time, the New Deal program elicited some of the sharpest opposition in American political history. When New Dealers noted that their goals were the Three R's—Relief, Recovery, and Reform—many opponents bitterly insisted that a fourth "R," Revolution, be added, arguing that the New Deal had turned the country toward socialism.

Few historians accept the view that the New Deal was socialistic either in its goals or its results, but some do argue that it was revolutionary in that it marked a radical break with the traditions and methods of the past. They maintain that the reforms so altered the nature of the relationship between government and society that they marked a fundamental change to which the term revolutionary may be aptly applied. Others, however, argue that the

New Deal was in reality conservative, that the legislation passed in the early thirties was really designed to conserve the American system, which was facing a dangerous crisis. From this viewpoint, the New Deal was radical neither in intent nor in method, having borrowed its techniques, its personnel, and its goals from a long tradition of American reform. Examples of these views may be seen in the following selections.

In the first selection, Frank Freidel, the biographer of Franklin Roosevelt, views the New Deal in historical perspective, deciding that it borrowed much from the progressive era. In total, Freidel concludes, the New Deal represents a conservative solution to the problems of the thirties. Some businessmen, of course, thought that Roosevelt was endangering the American way of life and leading the country toward socialism. Freidel argues that most of the businessmen's problems were of their own making; Roosevelt certainly preferred to be, and usually was, conciliatory rather than hostile toward the business community. To Freidel, the fact that the opposition party as well as the business community has in recent years accepted most of the New Deal measures proves that the Roosevelt reforms were in the tradition of the American consensus.

In tracing the connection between New Deal reforms and the reforms of earlier years, Freidel is able to stress continuity. To evaluate this interpretation, one must ask how much change is necessary before the results can be seen as a radical alteration of the status quo. Must any change short of, say, a socialist revolution be deemed conservative? Carl Degler, in the second selection, thinks not. He, like Freidel, views the New Deal sympathetically, but he finds Roosevelt's reforms revolutionary. In fact, he sees a fundamental political reorientation caused by the depression and the New Deal. While Freidel finds continuity and a conservative consensus, Degler sees a sharp break with the past and a radical consensus.

Ronald Radosh, in the third selection, presents a very different picture of the New Deal. He disagrees with both Degler and Freidel. The New Deal, he argues, was neither a sharp break with past practices nor a conservative reform movement. Rather, it was a successful effort by leading businessmen to modernize corporate capitalism. They recognized that conditions had changed and that therefore the system had to be altered to reflect these changes. Radosh concludes that only socialism would mark a truly radical change, and only socialism would really solve the problems faced by the people.

Without question, the legislation of the New Deal years had a great impact on American life, an impact that continues today. But what was the exact nature of that impact? Did the New Deal legislation mark a radical change in American society? Did the problems of the depression bring about a revolutionary break with the past? Or was the New Deal a conservative reform movement seeking to make only those innovations that would prevent revolutionary change? Is it fair to judge the New Deal from the perspective of the present, or should we view its accomplishments and limitations within the context of the 1930s?

One possible way to answer these questions is to consider the needs and demands of various groups. Was there a real possibility of revolution coming from workers or farmers or other groups? If so, how was this possibility handled by political leaders? If not, how can its absence be explained in the context of the suffering and hardship people faced? There are some historians (for example, David Rothman in Chapter 6) who argue that Progressive–New Deal liberalism came to an end in 1965. Does any part of that tradition survive today?

*Frank Freidel*

# Conservative Reform Movement

In less than a generation, the New Deal has passed into both popular legend and serious history. The exigencies of American politics long demanded that its partisans and opponents paint a picture of it either in the most glamorous whites or sinister blacks. Long after the New Deal was over, politicians of both major parties tried at each election to reap a harvest of votes from its issues.

Gradually a new generation of voters has risen which does not remember the New Deal and takes for granted the changes that it wrought. Gradually too, politicians have had to recognize that the nation faces new, quite different problems since the second World War, and that campaigning on the New Deal has become as outmoded as did the "bloody shirt" issue as decades passed after the Civil War. At the same time, most of the important manuscript collections relating to the New Deal have been opened to scholars so rapidly that careful historical research has been possible decades sooner than was true for earlier periods of United States history. (The Franklin D. Roosevelt papers and the Abraham Lincoln papers became available for research at about the same time, just after the second World War.)

It has been the task of the historians not only to analyze heretofore hidden aspects of the New Deal on the basis of the manuscripts, but also to remind readers of what was once commonplace and is now widely forgotten. A new generation has no firsthand experience of the depths of despair into which the depression had thrust the nation, and the excitement and eagerness

From The New Deal in Historical Perspective, Service Center #25, by Frank Freidel, 2nd ed. (Washington, D.C., 1965), pp. 1–20. Reprinted by permission of the American Historical Association.

with which people greeted the new program. Critics not only have denied that anything constructive could have come from the New Deal but they have even succeeded in creating the impression in the prosperous years since 1945 that the depression really did not amount to much. How bad it was is worth remembering, since this is a means of gauging the enormous pressure for change.

Estimates of the number of unemployed ranged up to thirteen million out of a labor force of fifty-two million, which would mean that one wage-earner out of four was without means of support for himself or his family. Yet of these thirteen million unemployed, only about a quarter were receiving any kind of assistance. States and municipalities were running out of relief funds; private agencies were long since at the end of their resources. And those who were receiving aid often obtained only a pittance. The Toledo commissary could allow for relief only 2.14 cents per person per meal, and the Red Cross in southern Illinois in 1931 was able to provide families with only seventy-five cents a week for food. It was in this crisis that one of the most flamboyant members of the Hoover administration suggested a means of providing sustenance for the unemployed: restaurants should dump left-overs and plate scrapings into special sanitary cans to be given to worthy unemployed people willing to work for the food. It was a superfluous suggestion, for in 1932 an observer in Chicago reported:

*Around the truck which was unloading garbage and other refuse were about thirty-five men, women, and children. As soon as the truck pulled away from the pile, all of them started digging with sticks, some with their hands, grabbing bits of food and vegetables.*

The employed in some instances were not a great deal better off. In December 1932 wages in a wide range of industries from textiles to iron and steel, averaged from a low of 20 cents to a high of only 30 cents an hour. A quarter of the women working in Chicago were receiving less than 10 cents an hour. In farming areas, conditions were equally grim. In bitter weather on the Great Plains, travelers occasionally encountered a light blue haze that smelled like roasting coffee. The "old corn" held over from the crop of a year earlier would sell for only $1.40 per ton, while coal cost $4 per ton, so many farmers burned corn to keep warm. When Aubrey Williams went into farm cellars in the Dakotas in the early spring of 1933 farm wives showed him shelves and shelves of jars for fruits and vegetables—but they were all empty. Even farmers who could avoid hunger had trouble meeting payments on their mortgages. As a result a fourth of all farmers in the United States lost their farms during these years.

Despairing people in these pre-New Deal years feared President Herbert Hoover had forgotten them or did not recognize the seriousness of their plight. As a matter of fact he had, more than any other depression president in American history, taken steps to try to bring recovery. But he had functioned largely through giving aid at the top to prevent the further collapse of banks and industries, and the concentric rings of further collapses and unemployment which would then ensue. Also he had continued to pin his faith upon voluntary action. He felt that too great federal intervention would undermine the self-reliance, destroy the "rugged individualism" of the American people, and that it would create federal centralization, thus paving the way for socialism.

President Hoover was consistent in his thinking, and he was humane. But it would have been hard to explain to people like those grubbing on the Chicago garbage heap, why, when the Reconstruction Finance Corporation was loaning $90,000,000 to a single Chicago bank, the President would veto a bill to provide federal relief for the unemployed, asserting, "never before has so dangerous a suggestion been seriously made in this country." It was not until June 1932 that he approved a measure permitting the RFC to loan $300,000,000 for relief purposes.

It seems shocking in retrospect that such conditions should have existed in this country, and that any President of either major party should so long have refused to approve federal funds to alleviate them. It adds to the shock when one notes that many public figures of the period were well to the right of the President—for instance, Secretary of the Treasury Andrew Mellon —and that almost no one who was likely to be in a position to act, including Governor Roosevelt of New York, was ready at that time to go very far to the left of Hoover.

Roosevelt, who was perhaps the most advanced of the forty-eight governors in developing a program to meet the depression, had shown little faith in public works spending. When he had established the first state relief agency in the United States in the fall of 1931, he had tried to finance it through higher taxes, and only later, reluctantly, abandoned the pay-as-you-go basis. He was, and he always remained, a staunch believer in a balanced budget. He was never more sincere than when, during the campaign of 1932, he accused the Hoover administration of having run up a deficit of three and three-quarters billions of dollars in the previous two years. This, he charged, was "the most reckless and extravagant past that I have been able to discover in the statistical record of any peacetime Government anywhere, any time."

Governor Roosevelt's own cautious record did not exempt him from attack. In April 1932, seeking the presidential nomination, he proclaimed himself the champion of the "forgotten man," and talked vaguely about raising the purchasing power of the masses, in part through directing Reconstruction Finance Corporation loans their way. This little was sufficient to lead many political leaders and publicists, including his Democratic rival, Al Smith, to accuse Roosevelt of being a demagogue, ready to set class against class.

Smith and most other public figures, including Roosevelt, favored public works programs. A few men like Senators Robert F. Wagner of New York and Robert M. La Follette of Wisconsin visualized really large-scale spending on public construction, but most leaders also wanted to accompany the spending with very high taxes which would have been deflationary and thus have defeated the program. None of the important political leaders, and none of the economists who had access to them, seemed as yet to visualize the decisive intervention of the government into the economy of the sort that is considered commonplace today. The term "built-in stabilizers" had yet to be coined.

The fact was that Roosevelt and most of his contemporaries, who like him were products of the Progressive Era, were basically conservative men who unquestioningly believed in the American free enterprise system. On the whole, they were suspicious of strong government, and would indulge in it only as a last resort to try to save the system. This was their limitation in trying to bring about economic recovery. On the other hand, part of their Progressive legacy was also a humanitarian belief in social justice. This belief would lead them to espouse reforms to improve the lot of the common man, even though those reforms might also take them in the direction of additional government regulation. Roosevelt as governor had repeatedly demonstrated this inconsistency in his public statements and recommendations. He had ardently endorsed states rights and small government in a truly Jeffersonian way. Then in quite contrary fashion (but still in keeping with Jeffersonian spirit applied to twentieth-century society) he had pointed out one or another area, such as old age security, in which he believed the government must intervene to protect the individual.

At this time, what distinguished Governor Roosevelt from his fellows were two remarkable characteristics. The first was his brilliant political skill, which won to him an overwhelming proportion of the Democratic politicians and the general public. The second was his willingness to experiment, to try one or another improvisation to stop the slow economic drift downward toward ruin. During the campaign of 1932, many a man who had observed Roosevelt felt as did Harry Hopkins that he would make a better president than Hoover, "chiefly because he is not afraid of a new idea."

Roosevelt's sublime self-confidence and his willingness to try new expedients stood him in good stead when he took over the presidency. On that grim March day in 1933 when he took his oath of office, the American economic system was half-paralyzed. Many of the banks were closed; the remainder he quickly shut down through presidential proclamation. Industrial production was down to 56 percent of the 1923–25 level. Yet somehow, Roosevelt's self-confidence was infectious. People were ready to believe, to follow, when he said in words that were not particularly new, "The only thing we have to fear is fear itself." He offered "leadership of frankness and vigor," and almost the whole of the American public and press—even papers like the

Chicago *Tribune* which soon became bitter critics—for the moment accepted that leadership with enthusiasm.

For a short period of time, about one hundred days, Roosevelt had behind him such overwhelming public support that he was able to push through Congress a wide array of legislation which in total established the New Deal. It came in helter-skelter fashion and seemed to go in all directions, even at times directions that conflicted with each other. There was mildly corrective legislation to get the banks open again, a slashing of government costs to balance the budget, legalization of 3.2 beer, establishment of the Civilian Conservation Corps, of the Tennessee Valley Authority, and of a wide variety of other agencies in the areas of relief, reform, and, above all in those first months, of recovery.

What pattern emerged in all of this legislation? How sharply did it break with earlier American political traditions? The answer was that it represented Roosevelt's efforts to be President to all the American people, to present something to every group in need. And it was based squarely on American objectives and experience in the Progressive Era and during the first World War. It went beyond the Hoover program in that while the word "voluntary" remained in many of the laws, they now had behind them the force of the government or at least strong economic incentives.

It has been forgotten how basically conservative Roosevelt's attitudes remained during the early period of the New Deal. He had closed the banks, but reopened them with relatively little change. Indeed, the emergency banking measure had been drafted by Hoover's Treasury officials. What banking reform there was came later. His slashing of the regular government costs was something he had promised during his campaign, and in which he sincerely believed and continued to believe. He kept the regular budget of the government low until the late thirties. While he spent billions through the parallel emergency budget, he did that reluctantly, and only because he felt it was necessary to keep people from starving. He was proud that he was keeping the credit of the government good, and never ceased to look forward to the day when he could balance the budget. For the first several years of the New Deal he consulted frequently with Wall Streeters and other economic conservatives. His first Director of the Budget, Lewis Douglas, parted ways with him, but late in 1934 was exhorting: "I hope, and hope most fervently, that you will evidence a real determination to bring the budget into actual balance, for upon this, I think, hangs not only your place in history but conceivably the immediate fate of western civilization." (Douglas to FDR, November 28, 1934).

Remarks like this struck home with Roosevelt. Douglas's successors as Director of the Budget held much the same views, and Henry Morgenthau, Jr., who became Secretary of the Treasury at the beginning of 1934, never failed to prod Roosevelt to slash governmental expenditures.

We should add parenthetically that Roosevelt always keenly resented the untrue newspaper stories that his parents had been unwilling to entrust him with money. As a matter of fact he was personally so thrifty when he was in the White House that he used to send away for bargain mail-order shirts, and when he wished summer suits, switched from an expensive New York tailor to a cheaper one in Washington. This he did despite the warning of the New York tailor that he might thus lose his standing as one of the nation's best-dressed men.

Financial caution in governmental affairs rather typifies Roosevelt's economic thinking throughout the entire New Deal. He was ready to go much further than Hoover in construction of public works, but he preferred the kind which would pay for themselves, and did not think there were many possibilities for them in the country. His estimate before he became president was only one billion dollars worth. In 1934, he once proposed that the government buy the buildings of foundered banks throughout the nation and use them for post-offices rather than to construct new buildings. This is how far he was from visualizing huge public works expenditures as a means of boosting the country out of the depression. His course in this area was the middle road. He wished to bring about recovery without upsetting the budget any further than absolutely necessary. He did not launch the nation on a program of deliberate deficit financing.

When Roosevelt explained his program in a fireside chat at the end of July 1933, he declared:

> It may seem inconsistent for a government to cut down its regular expenses and at the same time to borrow and to spend billions for an emergency. But it is not inconsistent because a large portion of the emergency money has been paid out in the form of sound loans . . . ; and to cover the rest . . . we have imposed taxes. . . .
>
> So you will see that we have kept our credit good. We have built a granite foundation in a period of confusion.

It followed from this that aside from limited public works expenditures, Roosevelt wanted a recovery program which would not be a drain on governmental finances. Neither the Agricultural Adjustment Administration nor the National Recovery Administration were. He had promised in the major farm speech of his 1932 campaign that his plan for agricultural relief would be self-financing; this was achieved through the processing tax on certain farm products. The NRA involved no governmental expenditures except for administration.

Both of these programs reflected not the progressivism of the first years of the century, but the means through which Progressives had regulated production during the first World War. This had meant regulation which would as far as possible protect both producers and consumers, both employers and employees. Here the parallel was direct. The rest of Roosevelt's program did not parallel the Progressives' wartime experience, for during the war, in terms of production regulation had meant channeling both factories and farms into the maximum output of what was needed to win the war. Now the problem in the thirties was one of reducing output in most areas rather than raising it, and of getting prices back up rather than trying to hold them down.

Certainly the nation badly needed this sort of a program in 1933. The products of the fields and mines and of highly competitive consumers' goods industries like textiles were being sold so cheaply that producers and their employees alike were close to starvation. The overproduction was also wasteful of natural resources. In an oilfield near Houston, one grocer advertised when 3.2 beer first became legal that he would exchange one bottle of beer for one barrel of oil. They were worth about the same. In other heavy industries like automobiles or farm machinery, production had been cut drastically while prices remained high. One need was to bring prices throughout industry and agriculture into a more equitable relationship with each other, and with the debt structure.

The NRA scheme in theory would help do this. Its antecedents were in the regulatory War Industries Board of the first World War, and indeed it was run by some of the same men. The War Industries Board had functioned through industrial committees; in the twenties these committees had evolved into self-regulatory trade associations. Unfortunately, as Roosevelt had found when he headed the association created to discipline one of the largest and most chaotic of industries, the American Construction Council, self-regulation without the force of law behind it, had a tendency to break down. When the depression had hit, some businessmen themselves had advocated the NRA scheme, but Hoover would have none of it. Roosevelt was receptive.

The theory was that committees in a few major fields like steel, textiles, bituminous coal and the like, would draw up codes of fair practice for the industry. These would not only stabilize the price structure, but also protect the wages and working conditions of labor. Even consumers would benefit, presumably through receiving more wages or profits, and thus enjoying larger purchasing power with which to buy goods at somewhat higher prices.

In practice, the NRA program went awry. Too many committees drew up too many codes embodying many sorts of unenforceable provisions. There was a code even for the mopstick industry. What was more important, some manufacturers rushed to turn out quantities of goods at the old wage and raw material level before the code went into effect, hoping then to sell these goods at new higher prices. Consequently during the summer of 1933 there was a short NRA boom when industrial production jumped to 101 percent of the 1923–25 level, and wholesale prices rose from an index figure of 60.2 in March to 71.2 by October. The crop reduction program of the AAA led to a corresponding rise in agricultural prices.

Had consumers at the same time enjoyed a correspondingly higher purchasing power, the recovery scheme might well have worked. Some of its designers had visualized pouring the additional dollars into consumers' pockets through a heavy public works spending program. Indeed the bill which created the NRA also set up a Public Works Administration with $3,300,000,000 to spend. This money could have been poured here and there into the economy where it was most needed to "prime the pump." But Roosevelt and his most influential advisers did not want to give such an enormous spending power to the administrator of the NRA, nor had they really accepted the deficit spending school of thought. Hence while some of the money being spent by the New Deal went for immediate relief of one form or another, it went to people so close to starvation that they were forced to spend what they received on bare necessities. This was of little aid in priming the pump. The public works fund, which could have served that purpose, went to that sturdy old Progressive, "Honest Harold" Ickes. He slowly went about the process of allocating it in such a way that the government and the public would get a return of one hundred cents (or preferably more) on every dollar spent. Raymond Moley has suggested that if only the cautious Ickes had headed the NRA and the impetuous Johnson the Public Works Administration the scheme might have worked.

Without a huge transfusion of dollars into the economy, the industrial and agricultural recovery programs sagged in the fall of 1933. Roosevelt turned to currency manipulation to try to get prices up. He explained to a critical Congressman, "I have always favored sound money, and do now, but it is 'too darned sound' when it takes so much of farm products to buy a dollar." Roosevelt also accepted a makeshift work relief program, the Civil Works Administration, to carry the destitute through the winter.

Already the New Deal honeymoon was over, and in 1934 and 1935 a sharp political struggle between Roosevelt and the right began to take form. To conservatives, Roosevelt was shattering the constitution with his economic legislation. Al Smith was attacking the devaluated currency as "baloney dollars," and was writing articles with such titles as "Is the Constitution Still There?" and "Does the Star-Spangled Banner Still Wave?" Former President Hoover published his powerful jeremiad, *The Challenge to Liberty.*

Many businessmen complained against the NRA restrictions, the favoritism allegedly being shown to organized labor, and the higher taxes. Although some of them had advocated the NRA, the significant fact was that the thinking of most businessmen seems to have remained about what it had been in the 1920's. They were eager for aid from the government, as long as it involved no obligations on their part or restrictions against them. They wanted a government which could protect their domestic markets with a high tariff wall, and at the same time seek out foreign markets for them, a court system which could discipline organized labor with injunctions, and a tax structure which (as under Secretary of the Treasury Mellon) would take no enormous bite of large profits, and yet retain disciplinary levies on the lower-middle income groups. All these policies they could understand and condone. The New Deal, which would confer other benefits upon them, but require corresponding obligations, they could not.

This hostile thinking which began to develop among the business community was sincere. Businessmen genuinely believed that under the New Deal program too large a share of their income had to go to organized labor, and too much to the government. They freely predicted federal bankruptcy as the deficit began to mount. If they had capital to commit, they refused to expend it on new plants and facilities (except for some introduction of labor-saving machinery). They were too unsure of the future, they complained, because they could not tell what that man in the White House might propose next. Business needed a "breathing spell," Roy Howard wrote Roosevelt, and the President promised one. Nevertheless, the legislative requests continued unabated.

All this, important though it is in delineating the ideology of businessmen, is not the whole story. The fact is that during the long bleak years after October 1929 they had slipped into a depression way of thinking. They regarded American industry as being over-built; they looked upon the American market as being permanently contracted. By 1937 when industrial production and stock dividends were up to within ten percent of the 1929 peak, capital expenditures continued to drag along the depression floor. Industrialists did not engage in the large-scale spending for expansion which has been a significant factor in the boom since 1945. As late as 1940 to 1941, many of them were loathe to take the large defense orders which required construction of new plants. Unquestionably the pessimism of businessmen during the thirties, whether or not linked to their hatred of Roosevelt and fear of the New Deal, was as significant a factor in perpetuating the depression, as their optimism since the war has been in perpetuating the boom.

The paradox is that some of the New Deal measures against which the businessmen fought helped introduce into the economy some of the stabilizers which today help give businessmen confidence in the continuation of prosperity. These came despite, not because of, the businessmen. Roosevelt long continued to try to co-operate with the leaders of industry and banking. Their anger toward him, and frequently-expressed statements that he had betrayed his class, at times bewildered and even upset him. For the most part he laughed them off. He hung in his bedroom a favorite cartoon. It showed a little girl at the door of a fine suburban home, apparently tattling to her mother, "Johnny wrote a dirty word on the sidewalk." And the word, of course, was "Roosevelt."

To some of his old friends who complained to him, he would reply with patience and humor. Forever he was trying to point out to them the human side of the problem of the depression. Perhaps the best illustration is a witty interchange with a famous doctor for whom he had deep affection. The doctor wired him in March 1935:

"Pediatricians have long been perplexed by difficulty of weaning infant from breast or bottle to teaspoon or cup. The shift often establishes permanent neurosis in subsequent adult. According to report in evening paper twenty-two million citizen infants now hang on federal breasts. Can you wean them, doctor, and prevent national neurosis?"

Roosevelt promptly replied:

As a young interne you doubtless realize that the interesting transitional process, which you describe in your telegram, presupposes that the bottle, tea-spoon, or cup is not empty. Such vehicles of feeding, if empty, produce flatulence and the patient dies from a lack of nutrition.

The next question on your examination paper is, therefore, the following:

Assuming that the transitional period has arrived, where is the Doctor to get the food from to put in the new container?

As time went on, and the attacks became virulent from some quarters, at times even passing the bounds of decency, Roosevelt struck back vigorously. During his campaign in 1936 he excoriated the "economic royalists." When he wound up the campaign in Madison Square Garden, he declared:

We had to struggle with the old enemies of peace—business and financial monopoly, speculation, reckless banking, class antagonism, sectionalism, war profiteering. They had begun to consider the Government of the United States as a mere appendage to their own affairs. And we know now that Government by organized money is just as dangerous as Government by organized mob.

Never before in all our history have these forces been so united against one candidate as they stand today. They are unanimous in their hate for me—and I welcome their hatred.

To these sharp words Roosevelt had come from his position early in the New Deal as the impartial arbiter of American economic forces. He had come to them less because of what he considered as betrayal from the right than through pressure from the left. How had this pressure applied between 1934 and the campaign of 1936?

Back in 1934, while the economic temperature chart of the near frozen depression victim had fluctuated up and down, still dangerously below normal, the dispossessed millions began to look at the New Deal with despair or even disillusion. Those workers going on strike to obtain the twenty-five or thirty-five cents an hour minimum wage or the collective bargaining privi-leges promised by the NRA began to wisecrack that NRA stood for the National Run-Around. Some of them and of the unemployed millions in northern cities still dependent upon meager relief handouts, began to listen to the stirring radio addresses of Father Charles Coughlin. Old people began to pay five cents a week dues to Dr. Francis Townsend's clubs, which promised them fantastically large benefits. Throughout the South (and even in parts of the North) the dispossessed small farmers listened with enthusiasm to the exhortations of the Louisiana Kingfish, Huey Long, that he would share the wealth to make every man a king.

Many Democratic politicians were surprisingly oblivious to these rumblings and mutterings. Much of the private conversation of men like Vice President John Nance Garner sounded like the public demands of the Liberty Leaguers: cut relief and balance the budget. Garner, who spent the 1934 campaign hunting and fishing in Texas, predicted the usual mid-term loss of a few congressional seats back to the Republicans. Instead the Democrats picked up a startling number of new seats in both houses of Congress. The dispossessed had continued to vote with the Democratic party—but perhaps because there was no alternative but the Republicans who offered only retrenchment. Charles Beard commented that the 1934 election was "thunder on the left."

President Roosevelt, who was brilliantly sensitive to political forces, sensed fully the threat from the left. At the beginning of that crisis year 1935 he proposed in his annual message to Congress the enactment of a program to reinforce "the security of the men, women, and children of the nation" in their livelihood, to protect them against the major hazards and vicissitudes of life, and to enable them to obtain decent homes. In this increased emphasis upon security and reform, Professor Basil Rauch sees the beginnings of a second New Deal.

Certainly the pattern as it emerged in the next year was a brilliant one. Roosevelt neutralized Huey Long with the "soak the rich" tax, the "holding company death sentence," and with various measures directly of benefit to the poorer farmers of the South. Before an assassin's bullet felled Long, his political strength was already undercut. Similarly Roosevelt undermined the Townsend movement by pressing passage of the Social Security Act, which provided at least small benefits for the aged, at the same time that a congressional investigation disclosed how men around Townsend were fattening themselves on the nickels of millions of the aged. As for Father Coughlin, the Treasury announced that money from his coffers had gone into silver speculation at a time he had been loudly advocating that the government buy more silver at higher prices. More important, Coughlin had less appeal to employed workers after the new National Labor Relations Act raised a benign federal umbrella over collective bargaining. For the unemployed, a huge and substantial work relief program, the Works Progress Administration, came into existence.

Partly all this involved incisive political counterthrusts; partly it was a program Roosevelt had favored anyway. In any event, combined with Roosevelt's direct and effective appeal in radio fireside chats, it caused the dispossessed to look to him rather than to demagogues as their champion.

Millions of them or their relations received some direct aid from the New Deal, whether a small crop payment or a WPA check. Millions more received wage boosts for which they were more grateful to Roosevelt than to their employers. Others through New Deal mortgage legislation had held onto their farms or homes. All these people, benefitting directly or indirectly, looked to Roosevelt as the source of their improved economic condition, and they were ready to vote accordingly. Roosevelt, who had been nominated in 1932 as the candidate of the South and the West, the champion of the farmer and the middle-class "forgotten man," after 1936 became increasingly the leader of the urban masses and the beneficiary of the growing power of organized labor.

What happened seems sharper and clearer in retrospect than it did at the time. Secretary Ickes, recording repeatedly in his diary during the early months of 1935 that the President was losing his grip, was echoing what many New Dealers and part of the public felt. They did not see a sharp shift into a second New Deal, and that is understandable. Roosevelt ever since he had become president had been talking about reform and from time to time recommending reform measures to Congress. He seems to have thought at the outset in two categories, about immediate or short-range emergency recovery measures to bring about a quick economic upswing, and also in terms of long-range reform legislation to make a recurrence of the depression less likely. Some of these reform measures like TVA had been ready for immediate enactment; others, like a revision of banking legislation and the social security legislation, he had planned from the beginning but were several years in the making. Frances Perkins has vividly described in her memoirs the lengthy task she and her associates undertook of drafting and selling to Congress and the public what became the Social Security Act of 1935.

Then Roosevelt had to face the additional factor that the emergency legislation had not succeeded in bringing rapid recovery. He had to think in terms of more permanent legislation with which to aim toward the same objectives. That meant he ceased trying to save money with a temporary program of cheaper direct relief, and switched instead to work relief (in which he had always believed) to try to stop some of the moral and physical erosion of the unfortunates who had been without employment for years.

In part the Supreme Court forced the recasting of some of his legislation. It gave a mercy killing in effect to the rickety, unwieldy NRA code structure when it handed down the Schechter or "sick chicken" decision of May 1935. On the whole the NRA had been unworkable, but it had achieved some outstanding results—in abolishing child labor, in bringing some order in the chaotic bituminous coal industry, and the like. Roosevelt was furious with the court, since the decision threatened to undermine all New Deal economic regulation. He charged that the justices were taking a horse and buggy view of the economic powers of the government. There followed six months later the court invalidation of the Triple-A processing tax, which for the moment threw out of gear the agricultural program.

The answer to these and similar Supreme Court decisions was Roosevelt's bold onslaught against the court after he had been re-elected in the great landslide of 1936. He had carried every state but Maine and Vermont; he considered himself as having a great mandate from the people to continue his program. Nor had he any reason to doubt his ability to push a court reform program through Congress, since the already bulging New Deal majorities had become still bigger. He was wrong; he failed. His failure came as much as anything through a great tactical error. He disguised his program as one to bring about a speedier handling of cases, when he should have presented it frankly as a means of ending the court obstruction of the New Deal. This obstruction was real. Many corporations openly flaunted the National Labor Relations Act, for example, they were so confident that the Supreme Court would invalidate it.

However laudable the end, to many a well-educated member of the middle class who had supported Roosevelt even through the campaign of 1936, Roosevelt's resort to subterfuge smacked of the devious ways of dictators. In 1937, Americans were all too aware of the way in which Hitler and Mussolini had gained power. It was not that any thinking man expected Roosevelt to follow their example, but rather that many objected to any threat, real or potential, to the constitutional system including the separation of powers. After Roosevelt, they argued, the potential dictator might appear. It may be too that times had improved sufficiently since March 1933 so that constitutional considerations could again overweigh economic exigencies. In any event, Roosevelt lost his battle—and won his war.

While the struggle was rocking the nation, the justices began exercising the judicial self-restraint which one of their number, Harlan F. Stone, had urged upon them the previous year. They surprised the nation by upholding the constitutionality of the National Labor Relations Act and the Social Security Act. In large part this eliminated the necessity for the New Dealers to make any change in the personnel of the court, and thus helped contribute to Roosevelt's defeat in Congress. Further, the fight had helped bring into existence a conservative coalition in Congress which from this time on gave Roosevelt a rough ride. Many old-line Democratic congressmen now dared proclaim in public what they had previously whispered in private. All this added up to a spectacular setback for Roosevelt—so spectacular that it is easy to overlook the enormous and permanent changes that had come about.

In the next few years the Supreme Court in effect rewrote a large part of constitutional law. The federal and state governments were now able to engage in extensive economic regulation with little or no court restraint upon them. The limits upon regulation must be set for the most part by the legislative branch of the government, not the judiciary. Not only were the National

Labor Relations Act and Social Security constitutional, but a bulging portfolio of other legislation.

These laws were not as spectacular as the measures of the Hundred Days, but in the bulk they were far more significant, for they brought about lasting changes in the economic role of the federal government. There was the continued subsidy to agriculture in order to maintain crop control—based upon soil conservation rather than a processing tax. There were all the agricultural relief measures which came to be centralized in the Farm Security Administration. Although that agency has disappeared, most of its functions have continued in one way or another. There was a beginning of slum clearance and public housing, and a continuation of TVA, held constitutional even before the court fight. There was a stiffening of securities regulation. There was a continuation of much that Roosevelt had considered beneficial in the NRA through a group of new laws usually referred to as the "little NRA." These perpetuated the coal and liquor codes, helped regulate oil production, tried to prevent wholesale price discriminations and legalized the establishment of "fair trade" prices by manufacturers. Most important of all, the Fair Labor Standards Act of 1937 set a national minimum of wages and maximum of hours of work, and prohibited the shipping in interstate commerce of goods made by child labor. These are lasting contributions of the New Deal, either substantial laws in themselves or the seeds for later legislation.

What then, is to be said of the recession and the anti-monopoly program? A Keynesian point of view is that public works spending, the other New Deal spending programs, and the payment of the bonus to veterans of the first World War (over Roosevelt's veto, incidentally), all these together had poured so such money into the economy that they brought about a substantial degree of recovery, except in employment, by the spring of 1937. At this point Roosevelt tried to balance the budget, especially by cutting public works and work relief expenditures. The result was a sharp recession. Roosevelt was forced to resort to renewed pump-priming, and in a few months the recession was over.

Even this recession experience did not convert Roosevelt to Keynesianism. Keynes once called upon Roosevelt at the White House and apparently tried to dazzle him with complex mathematical talk. Each was disappointed in the other. In 1939, after the recession when a protégé of Mrs. Roosevelt's proposed additional welfare spending, Roosevelt replied by listing worthwhile projects in which the government could usefully spend an additional five billions a year. Then he pointed out that the deficit was already three billions, which could not go on forever. How, he inquired, could an eight billion dollar deficit be financed.

As for economists, many of them saw the answer in the enormous spending power which would be unleashed if the government poured out billions in time of depression. To most of them the lesson from the recession was that the only way to right the economy in time of upset was through spending.

As for businessmen, they could see in the recession only the logical outcome of Roosevelt's iniquitous tinkering with the economy. They had been especially angered by the protection the Wagner Act had given to protective bargaining with the resulting militant expansion of organized labor. Roosevelt reciprocated the businessmen's feelings and blamed the recession upon their failure to co-operate. To a considerable degree he went along with a powerful handful of Progressive Republicans and Western Democrats in the Senate, like William E. Borah of Idaho and Joseph O'Mahoney of Wyoming, in attacking corporate monopoly as the villain. There are some indications, however, that the anti-monopoly program that he launched in the Department of Justice through the urbane Thurman Arnold was intended less to bust the trusts than to forestall too drastic legislation in the Congress. Roosevelt gave his strong backing to Arnold's anti-trust division only for the first year or two, and Arnold functioned for the most part through consent decrees. These in many instances allowed industries to function much as they had in the NRA days. The new program was in some respects more like a negative NRA than the antithesis of the NRA.

Thus from the beginning of the New Deal to the end, Roosevelt functioned with a fair degree of consistency. He heartily favored humanitarian welfare legislation and government policing of the economy, so long as these did not dangerously unbalance the budget. He preferred government co-operation with business to warfare with it.

Many of the New Dealers went far beyond Roosevelt in their views, and sometimes saw in his reluctance to support them, betrayal rather than a greater degree of conservatism. They had valid grievances some of the time when Roosevelt stuck to a middle course and seemed to them to be compromising away everything for which they thought he stood, in order to hold his motley political coalitions together. It is a serious moral question whether he compromised more than necessary, and whether at times he compromised his principles. It has been charged that his second four years in the White House represented a failure in political leadership.

In terms of gaining immediate political objectives, like the fiasco of the court fight, and the abortive "purge" in the 1938 primaries, this is undoubtedly true. In terms of the long-range New Deal program, I think the reverse is the case. These were years of piecemeal unspectacular consolidation of the earlier spectacular changes. It was many years before historians could say with certainty that these changes were permanent. By 1948 various public opinion samplings indicated that an overwhelming majority of those queried, even though Republican in voting habits, favored such things as social security and the TVA. The election of a Republican President in 1952 did not signify a popular repudiation of these programs. In the years after 1952 they were accepted, and in some instances even expanded, by the Republican administration. The only serious debate over them concerned degree, in which the Republicans were more cautious than the Democrats. The New Deal changes have even come for the most part to be accepted by the business community, although the United States Chamber of Commerce now issues manifestoes against federal aid to education with all the fervor it once directed against Roosevelt's proposals. The fact is that the business community in part bases its plans for the future upon some things that began as New Deal reforms. It takes for granted such factors as the "built-in stabilizers" in the social security system—something, incidentally, that Roosevelt pointed out at the time the legislation went into effect.

In January 1939 Roosevelt, concerned about the threat of world war, called a halt to his domestic reform program. What he said then, concerning the world crisis of 1939, is remarkably applicable to the United States more than two decades later:

> We have now passed the period of internal conflict in the launching of our program of social reform. Our full energies may now be released to invigorate the processes of recovery in order to preserve our reforms, and to give every man and woman who wants to work a real job at a living wage.
>
> But time is of paramount importance. The deadline of danger from within and from without is not within our control. The hour-glass may be in the hands of other nations. Our own hour-glass tells us that we are off on a race to make democracy work, so that we may be efficient in peace and therefore secure in national defense.

Carl N. Degler

# The Third American Revolution

Twice since the founding of the Republic, cataclysmic events have sliced through the fabric of American life, snapping many of the threads which ordinarily bind the past to the future. The War for the Union was one such event, the Great Depression of the 1930's the other. And, as the Civil War was precipitated from the political and moral tensions of the preceding era, so the Great Depression was a culmination of the social and economic forces of industrialization and urbanization which had been transforming America since 1865. A depression of such pervasiveness as that of the thirties could happen only to a people already tightly interlaced by the multitudinous cords of a machine civilization and embedded in the matrix of an urban society.

In all our history no other economic collapse brought so many Americans to near starvation, endured so long, or came so close to overturning the basic institutions of American life. It is understandable, therefore, that from that experience should issue a new conception of the good society.

### "Hunger Is Not Debatable"

The economic dimensions of the Great Depression are quickly sketched—too quickly perhaps to permit a full appreciation of the abyss into which the economy slid between 1929 and 1933. The value of stocks on the New York Exchange, for example, slumped from a high of $87 billion in 1929 to a mere $19 billion in 1933. Wholesale prices dropped 38 percent by 1933 and farm prices seemed almost to have ceased to exist: they were 60 percent

From Out of Our Past by Carl N. Degler, pp. 379–93, 410–16. Copyright © 1959 by Carl N. Degler. Reprinted with the permission of Harper & Row, Publishers.

below the low level of 1929. Within less than three years, realized national income plummeted to almost half of what it had been in the last boom year; and the same was true of industrial production. The human cost of this catastrophic breakdown in the complicated industrial machine, *Fortune* magazine estimated in September, 1932, was 10 million totally unemployed or 25 million people without any source of income.

To worsen matters, the industrial stagnation was accompanied by a spreading fever of bank failures. First here and there, then all over the country, the banks began to close their doors in the faces of their depositors. By the beginning of 1933, the financial self-confidence of the nation reached a dangerously low level, requiring the new administration of Franklin Roosevelt, as its first official act, to order the closing of all banks. In all, more than 10,000 deposit banks failed in the five years after 1929. If the banks, the custodians of the measure of value, proved to be unsound, men might well wonder what was left to cling to as the winds of disaster gained in fury.

Unnerving as the failure of the banks undoubtedly was, for most people the Great Depression became starkly real only when unemployment struck. No one knew whom it would hit next; the jobless were everywhere—in the cities, in the towns, on the farms. Their helplessness, their bewilderment, were often written in their faces, reflected in their discouraged gaits, and mirrored in their run-down dwellings. John Dos Passos reported seeing the unemployed of Detroit in 1932 living in caves scooped out of giant abandoned sand piles. Though it was said that no one would be allowed to starve, *Fortune*, in September, 1932, suggested that some had already. The magazine counted the millions of the unemployed and told of families subsisting on a single loaf of bread for over a week or of going without food for two or three days on end. Discarded and spoiled vegetables or wild dandelions were the substance of meals for some families. Other reports in 1933 told of at least twenty-nine persons who died of starvation in New York City. Moreover, thousands must have died from diseases which gained an easy foothold in weakened and underfed bodies; but these unfortunates were never counted. Food, casually consumed in good times, suddenly became the focus of existence for thousands. In their desperation some urban folk actually tried to wring their food from the barren soil of the city. In Gary, Indiana, for example, 20,000 families were raising food on lots lent by the city; Robert and Helen Lynd reported that in Middletown in 1933, 2,500 of the town's 48,000 people eked out their food budgets with relief gardens.

The spreading unemployment generated new and deep-seated fears. When the unkempt veterans of the First World War camped in Washington in 1932, demanding a bonus to tide them over their joblessness, a fearful and unsure President had them dispersed by troops armed with tear gas. And when Congress in that same year voted a 10 percent cut in government salaries, President Hoover sent a secret message urging that the enlisted men of the Army and the Navy be excluded from such decreases so that in case of domestic troubles the federal government would not be compelled to rely upon disgruntled troops.

Nor was it only the federal government that felt uneasy in the presence of the specter which was stalking the land. Malcolm Cowley, in an eyewitness account, described how the trucks bearing the disillusioned veterans out of Washington were quickly sped through town after town, the local authorities fearing that some of the unemployed veterans would jump off and become burdens on already overtaxed communities. Cowley tells of one citizen in Washington, not a marcher at all, who was hurriedly bundled into a truck by mistake and could not get off until he reached Indianapolis!

Driven by their desperation, some Americans began to talk of violence. Mutterings of revolution and threats to return with rifles were heard among the bonus marchers as they left Washington. Out on the farms, the dissatisfaction of the veterans was matched by sullen farmers who closed the courts and disrupted mortgage auctions to save their homes. The ugly turn which the discontent could take was revealed by the arrest of a man in Wisconsin in 1932 on suspicion of having removed a spike from the railroad track over which President Hoover's train was to pass. In that bleak year it was not uncommon for the President of the United States to be booed and hooted as he doggedly pursued his ill-starred campaign for re-election. To Theodore Dreiser, as the cold night of the depression settled over the land, it seemed that Karl Marx's prediction "that Capitalism would eventually evolve into failure . . . has come true."

Even for the Lords of Creation, as Frederick Lewis Allen was to call them, the Great Depression was an unsettling and confusing experience. "I'm afraid, every man is afraid," confessed Charles M. Schwab of United States Steel. "I don't know, we don't know, whether the values we have are going to be real next month or not." And in the very early months of the Roosevelt administration, Harold Ickes, attending a dinner of the Chamber of Commerce of the United States, could sense the pitiable impotence to which the nation's industrial leaders had sunk. "The great and the mighty in the business world were there in force," he rather gleefully noted in his diary, "and I couldn't help thinking how so many of these great and mighty were crawling to Washington on their hands and knees these days to beg the Government to run their businesses for them."

But it was the unspectacular, the everyday dreariness of unemployment that must have cut the deepest and endured the longest as far as the ordinary American was concerned. The simplest things of life, once taken for granted, now became points of irritation. "I forget how to cook good since I have nothing to cook with," remarked one housewife. Children lost their appetites upon seeing the milk and mush "that they have seen so often." Even the rare treat of fresh meat could not awaken an appetite long accustomed to disappointment and pallid food.

The routine entertainments of the poor were casualties to unemployment. "Suppose you go to a friend's house and she gives you a cup of tea and something," the wife of an unemployed worker told a social worker. "You feel ashamed. You think, now I got to do the same when she comes to my house. You know you can't so you stay home." Shifts in entertainment patterns among the unemployed were revealed in a study made of some 200 families in New Haven. Before the breadwinner lost his job, some 55 percent went to the movies; once unemployment hit, however, only 16 percent did. In the days when work was to be had, only 13 percent found recreation in "sitting around the house," but now 25 percent did so. With the loss of their jobs, 12 percent of the men admitted they "chatted and gossiped" for recreation, although none of them did when they had work.

Unemployment's effect upon the family was often more profound and far-reaching. In recounting the case history of the Raparka family, one sociologist wrote that when Mr. Raparka "lost his job in the fall of 1933, he dominated the family. Two years later it was Mrs. Raparka who was the center of authority." Again and again social workers chronicled the alteration in the father's position in the family during a period of unemployment. Humiliation settled over many a father no longer able to fulfill his accustomed role in the family. "I would rather turn on the gas and put an end to the whole family than let my wife support me," was the way one unemployed father put it. One investigator found that one-fifth of her sample of fifty-nine families exhibited a breakdown in the father's authority, particularly in the eyes of the wife. For example, one wife said, "When your husband cannot provide for the family and makes you worry so, you lose your love for him."

Fathers discovered that without the usual financial power to buy bikes or bestow nickels, their control and authority over children were seriously weakened and sometimes completely undermined. In one family where the father was unemployed for a long time, his role was almost completely taken over by the eldest son. The father himself admitted: "The son of twenty-two is just like a father around the house. He tries to settle any little brother-and-sister fights and even encourages me and my wife." In the same family, a younger son who was working summed up his relationship to his parents in a few words. "I remind them," he said, "who makes the money. They don't say much. They just take it, that's all. I'm not the one on relief." In such circumstances, it is no exaggeration to say that the massive weight of the depression was grinding away at the bedrock of American institutions.

The ties of a home struck by unemployment were weak and the opportunities for fruitful and satisfying work were almost totally absent in 1932–33. *Fortune* reported in February, 1933, that something like 200,000 young men and boys were traveling around the country on railroad trains for lack of anything better to do. Tolerated by the railroads because of their obvious poverty and lack of jobs, the boys were often suffering from disease and malnutrition. The authorities in Los Angeles asserted, for example, that 25 percent of those coming into the city needed clinical attention and 5 percent required hospitalization. During a single season, one railroad announced, fifty such footloose boys were killed and one hundred injured. From Kansas City it was reported that girl wanderers, dressed in boy's clothing, were on the increase. To many such young people, now grown, the Great Depression must still seem the most purposeless, the most enervating period of their lives.

What Robert and Helen Lynd concluded for their study of Middletown in 1935 can be applied to America as a whole: ". . . the great knife of the depression had cut down impartially through the entire population cleaving open lives and hopes of rich as well as poor. The experience has been more nearly universal than any prolonged recent emotional experience in the city's history; it has approached in its elemental shock the primary experiences of birth and death."

## The End of Laissez Faire

Perhaps the most striking alteration in American thought which the depression fostered concerned the role of the government in the economy. Buffeted and bewildered by the economic debacle, the American people in the course of the 1930's abandoned, once and for all, the doctrine of laissez faire. This beau ideal of the nineteenth-century economists had become, ever since the days of Jackson, an increasingly cherished shibboleth of Americans. But now it was almost casually discarded. It is true, of course, that the rejection of laissez faire had a long history; certainly the Populists worked to undermine it. But with the depression the nation at large accepted the government as a permanent influence in the economy.[1]

Almost every one of the best-known measures of the federal government during the depression era made inroads into the hitherto private preserves of business and the individual. Furthermore, most of these new measures survived the period, taking their places as fundamental elements in the structure of American life. For modern Americans living under a federal government of transcendent influence and control in the economy, this is the historic meaning of the great depression.

Much of what is taken for granted today as the legitimate function of government and the social responsibility of business began only with the legislation of these turbulent years. Out of the investigation of banking and bankers in 1933, for example, issued legislation which separated commercial

---

[1] A complementary and highly suggestive way of viewing this trend away from laissez faire, of which the events of the 1930's are a culmination, is that taken in K. William Kapp, *The Social Costs of Private Enterprise* (Cambridge, Mass., 1950). Kapp observes that for a long time private enterprise had shifted the social costs of production—like industrially polluted water, industrial injuries, smoke nuisances and hazards, unemployment, and the like—onto society. The decline of laissez faire has, in this view, actually been a movement to compel industry to pay for those social costs of production which it has hitherto shirked.

banking from the stock and bond markets, and insured the bank deposits of ordinary citizens. The stock market, like the banks, was placed under new controls and a higher sense of responsibility to the public imposed upon it by the new Securities and Exchange Commission. The lesson of Black Tuesday in 1929 had not been forgotten; the classic free market itself—the Exchange—was hereafter to be under continuous governmental scrutiny.

The three Agricultural Adjustment Acts of 1933, 1936, and 1938, while somewhat diverse in detail, laid down the basic lines of what is still today the American approach to the agricultural problem. Ever since the collapse of the boom after the First World War, American agriculture had suffered from the low prices born of the tremendous surpluses. Unable to devise a method for expanding markets to absorb the excess, the government turned to restriction of output as the only feasible alternative. But because restriction of output meant curtailment of income for the farmer, it became necessary, if farm income was to be sustained, that farmers be compensated for their cut in production. Thus was inaugurated the singular phenomenon, which is still a part of the American answer to the agricultural surplus, of paying farmers for *not* growing crops. The other device introduced for raising farm prices, and still the mainstay of our farm policy, came with the 1938 act, which provided that the government would purchase and store excess farm goods, thus supporting the price level by withdrawing the surplus from the competitive market. Both methods constitute a subsidy for the farmer from society at large.[2]

Though the Eisenhower administration in the 1950's called for a return to a free market in farm products—that is, the removal of government supports from prices—very few steps have been taken in that direction, and probably very few ever will.[3] A free market was actually in operation during the twenties, but it succeeded only in making farmers the stepchildren of the golden prosperity of that decade. Today the farm bloc is too powerful politically to be treated so cavalierly. Moreover, the depression has taught most Americans that a free market is not only a rarity in the modern world but sometimes inimical to a stable and lasting prosperity.

Perhaps the most imaginative and fruitful of these innovations was the Tennessee Valley Authority, which transformed the heart of the South. "It was and is literally a down to earth experiment," native Tennesseean Broadus

[2] On the day that the first AAA was declared unconstitutional, a Gallup poll revealed that, although the nation as a whole did not like the AAA, the farmers of the South and Midwest did. As a result, invalidation of the act by the Court did not mean the end of such a policy, but only the beginning of a search to find a new way of accomplishing the same end. Hence there were successive AAA's, whereas, when NRA was declared unconstitutional in 1935, it was dropped, primarily because neither business nor labor, for whose interests it had been organized, found much merit in its approach to their problems.

[3] As reported in the *New York Times*, July 2, 1958, forecasts for the fiscal year 1958–59 see government subsidies to agriculture reaching $6 billion—an all-time high.

Mitchell has written, "with all that we know from test tube and logarithm tables called on to help. It was a union of heart and mind to restore what had been wasted. It was a social resurrection." For the TVA was much more than flood and erosion control or even hydroelectric power—though its gleaming white dams are perhaps its most striking and best-known monuments. It was social planning of the most humane sort, where even the dead were carefully removed from cemeteries before the waters backed up behind the dams. It brought new ideas, new wealth, new skills, new hope into a wasted, tired, and discouraged region.

At the time of the inception of the TVA, it was scarcely believable that the "backward" South would ever utilize all the power the great dams would create. But in its report of 1956, the Authority declared that the Valley's consumption of electricity far exceeded that produced from water sites: almost three-quarters of TVA's power is now generated from steam power, not from waterfall. In large part it was the TVA which taught the Valley how to use more power to expand its industries and to lighten the people's burdens. Back in 1935, Drew and Leon Pearson saw this creation of consumer demand in action. "Uncle Sam is a drummer with a commercial line to sell," they wrote in *Harper's Magazine*. "He sold liberty bonds before, but never refrigerators."

Measured against textbook definitions, the TVA is unquestionably socialism. The government owns the means of production and, moreover, it competes with private producers of electricity.[4] But pragmatic Americans—and particularly those living in the Valley—have had few sleepless nights as a consequence of this fact. The TVA does its appointed job and, as the recent fight over the Dixon and Yates contract seemed to show, it is here to stay. It, too, with all the talk of "creeping socialism," has been absorbed into that new American Way fashioned by the experimentalism of the American people from the wreckage of the Great Depression.

Undoubtedly social security deserves the appellation "revolutionary" quite as much as the TVA; it brought government into the lives of people as nothing had since the draft and the income tax. Social security legislation actually comprises two systems: insurance against old age and insurance in the event of loss of work. The first system was completely organized and operated by the federal government; the second was shared with the states—

---

[4] The extent of the intellectual changes which the depression measures introduced can be appreciated by a quotation from President Hoover's veto in 1931 of a bill to develop a public power project in what was later to be the TVA area. "I am firmly opposed to the Government entering into any business the major purpose of which is competition with our citizens." Emergency measures of such a character might be tolerated, he said. "But for the Federal government deliberately to go out and build up and expand such an occasion to the major purpose of a power and manufacturing business is to break down the initiative and enterprise of the American people; it is destruction of equality of opportunity amongst our people; it is the negation of the ideals upon which our civilization has been based."

but the national government set the standards; both were clear acknowledgment of the changes which had taken place in the family and in the business of making a living in America. No longer in urban America could the old folks, whose proportion in the society was steadily increasing, count on being taken in by their offspring as had been customary in a more agrarian world. Besides, such a makeshift arrangement was scarcely satisfying to the self-respect of the oldsters. With the transformation of the economy by industrialization, most Americans had become helpless before the vagaries of the business cycle. As a consequence of the social forces which were steadily augmenting social insecurity, only collective action by the government could arrest the drift.

To have the government concerned about the security of the individual was a new thing. Keenly aware of the novelty of this aim in individualistic America,[5] Roosevelt was careful to deny any serious departure from traditional paths. "These three great objectives—the security of the home, the security of livelihood, and the security of social insurance," he said in 1934, constitute "a minimum of the promise that we can offer to the American people." But this, he quickly added, "does not indicate a change in values."

Whether the American people thought their values had changed is not nearly as important as the fact that they accepted social security. And the proof that they did is shown in the steady increase in the proportion of the population covered by the old-age benefit program since 1935; today about 80 percent of nonfarm workers are included in the system. Apart from being a minimum protection for the individual and society against the dry rot of industrial idleness, unemployment insurance is now recognized as one of the major devices for warding off another depression.

It is true, as proponents of the agrarian life have been quick to point out, that an industrialized people, stripped as they are of their economic self-reliance, have felt the need for social insurance more than people in other types of society. But it is perhaps just as important to recognize that it is only in such a highly productive society that people can even dare to dream of social security. Men in other ages have felt the biting pains of economic crisis, but few pre-industrial people have ever enjoyed that surfeit of goods which permits the fat years to fill out the lean ones. But like so much else concerning industrialism, it is not always easy to calculate whether the boons it offers exceed in value the burdens which it imposes.

For the average man, the scourge of unemployment was the essence of the depression. Widespread unemployment, permeating all ranks and stations in society, drove the American people and their government into some of

---

[5] Characteristically enough, as his memoirs show, President Hoover had long been interested in both old-age and unemployment insurance, but always such schemes were to be worked out through private insurance companies, or at best with the states—never under the auspices of the federal government. "It required a great depression," he has written somewhat ruefully, "to awaken interest in the idea" of unemployment insurance.

their most determined and deliberate departures from the hallowed policy of "hands off." But despite the determination, as late as 1938 the workless still numbered almost ten million—two thirds as great as in 1932 under President Hoover. The governmental policies of the 1930's never appreciably diminished the horde of unemployed—only the war prosperity of 1940 and after did that—but the providing of jobs by the federal government was a reflection of the people's new conviction that the government had a responsibility to alleviate economic disaster. Such bold action on the part of government, after the inconclusive, bewildered approach of the Hoover administration, was a tonic for the dragging spirits of the people.[6]

A whole range of agencies, from the Civil Works Administration (CWA) to the Works Progress Administration (WPA), were created to carry the attack against unemployment. It is true that the vast program of relief which was organized was not "permanent" in the sense that it is still in being, but for two reasons it deserves to be discussed here. First, since these agencies constituted America's principal weapon against unemployment, some form of them will surely be utilized if a depression should occur again. Second, the various relief agencies of the period afford the best examples of the new welfare outlook, which was then in the process of formation.

Though in the beginning relief programs were premised on little more than Harry Hopkins' celebrated dictum, "Hunger is not debatable," much more complex solutions to unemployment were soon worked out. The relief program of the WPA, which after 1935 was the major relief agency, was a case in point. In 1937, *Fortune* magazine commented on "the evolution of unemployment relief from tool to institution"—a recognition of the importance and duration of relief in America. "In 1936, the federal government was so deeply involved in the relief of the unemployed," *Fortune* contended, "that it was not only keeping them alive, but it was also giving them an opportunity to work; and not only giving them an opportunity to work but giving them an opportunity to work at jobs for which they were peculiarly fitted; and not only giving them an opportunity to work at jobs for which they

---

[6] It was the misfortune of Herbert Hoover to have been President at a time when his considerable administrative and intellectual gifts were hamstrung by his basic political philosophy, which, instead of being a guide to action, served as an obstacle. Much more of an old-fashioned liberal than a reactionary, and deeply attached to the Jeffersonian dogma of the limited powers of the federal government, Hoover was psychologically and philosophically unable to use the immense powers and resources of his office in attacking the urgent threat of unemployment. Back in 1860–61, another President—James Buchanan —had been paralyzed in the midst of a national crisis by his limited conception of the federal power, but in that instance his inaction was palliated by the fact that his successor was to take office within less than three months. Hoover, however, wrestled with the depression for three years, and all during that trying period he stoutly held to his rigid intellectual position that federally supplied and administered relief would destroy the foundations of the nation. Never has an American President, including the two Adamses, defied overwhelming popular opinion for so long for the sake of his own ideals as Herbert Hoover did then; and never has a President since Buchanan fallen so quickly into obscurity as Hoover did after March 4, 1933.

were peculiarly fitted, but creating for them jobs of an interest and usefulness which they could not have expected to find in private employment." The statement somewhat distorts the work of the WPA, but it sums up the main outlines of the evolution of the relief program.

The various artistic and cultural employment programs of the WPA are excellent examples of how relief provided more than employment, though any of the youth agencies like the Civilian Conservation Corps or the National Youth Administration (it subsidized student work) would serve equally well. At its peak, the Federal Writers' Project employed some 6,000 journalists, poets, novelists, and Ph.D.'s of one sort or another; unknowns worked on the same payroll, if not side by side, with John Steinbeck, Vardis Fisher, and Conrad Aiken. The $46 million expended on art—that is, painting and sculpture—by the WPA in 1936–37 exceeded the artistic budget of any country outside the totalitarian orbit—and there art was frankly propagandistic. *Fortune*, in May, 1937, found the American government's sponsorship of art singularly free of censorship or propaganda. The magazine concluded that "by and large the Arts Projects have been given a freedom no one would have thought possible in a government run undertaking. And by and large that freedom has not been abused." During the first fifteen months of the Federal Music Project, some fifty million people heard live concerts; in the first year of the WPA Theater, sixty million people in thirty states saw performances, with weekly attendance running to half a million. T. S. Eliot's *Murder in the Cathedral*, too risky for a commercial producer, was presented in New York by the Federal Theater to 40,000 people at a top price of 55 cents.

"What the government's experiments in music, painting, and the theater actually did," concluded *Fortune* in May, 1937, "even in their first year, was to work a sort of cultural revolution in America." For the first time the American audience and the American artist were brought face to face for their mutual benefit. "Art in America is being given its chance," said the British writer Ford Madox Ford, "and there has been nothing like it since before the Reformation. . . ."

Instead of being ignored on the superficially plausible grounds of the exigencies of the depression, the precious skills of thousands of painters, writers, and musicians were utilized. By this timely rescue of skills, tastes, and talents from the deadening hand of unemployment, the American people, through their government, showed their humanity and social imagination. Important for the future was the foresight displayed in the conserving of artistic talents and creations for the enrichment of generations to come.

The entrance of the federal government into a vast program of relief work was an abrupt departure from all previous practice, but it proved enduring. "When President Roosevelt laid it down that government had a social responsibility to care for the victims of the business cycle," *Fortune* remarked prophetically in 1937, "he set in motion an irreversible process." The burden of unemployment relief was too heavy to be carried by local government or private charities in an industrialized society; from now on, the national government would be expected to shoulder the responsibility. "Those who are on relief and in close contact otherwise with public matters realize that what has happened to the country is a bloodless revolution," wrote an anonymous relief recipient in *Harper's* in 1936. The government, he said, has assumed a new role in depressions, and only the rich might still be oblivious to it. But they too "will know it by 1940. And in time," they will "come to approve the idea of everyone having enough to eat."[7] Few people escaped the wide net of the depression: "Anybody sinks after a while," the anonymous reliefer pointed out. "Even you would have if God hadn't preserved, without apparent rhyme or reason, your job and your income." That the depression was a threat to all was perhaps the first lesson gained from the 1930's.

The second was that only through collective defense could such a threat be met. By virtue of the vigorous attack made upon the economic problems of the thirties by the government, the age-old conviction that dips in the business cycle were either the will of God or the consequence of unalterable economic laws was effectively demolished. As recently as 1931, President Hoover had told an audience that some people "have indomitable confidence that by some legerdemain we can legislate ourselves out of a world-wide depression. Such views are as accurate as the belief that we can exorcise a Caribbean hurricane." From the experience of the depression era, the American people learned that something could and ought to be done when economic disaster strikes. No party and no politician with a future will ever again dare to take the fatalistic and defeatist course of Herbert Hoover in 1929–33.

As the enactment of the Employment Act of 1946 showed, the prevention of depression now occupies top listing among the social anxieties of the American people. The act created a permanent Council of Economic Advisers to the President, to keep him continuously informed on the state of the economy and to advise him on the measures necessary to avoid an economic decline. And the Joint Committee on the Economic Report does the same for Congress.

Today political figures who indignantly repudiate any "left-wing" philosophy of any sort readily accept this inheritance from the depression. "Never again shall we allow a depression in the United States," vowed Republican candidate Eisenhower in 1952. As soon as we "foresee the signs of any recession and depression," he promised, ". . . the full power of private industry, of municipal government, of state government, of the Federal Government will be mobilized to see that that does not happen." Ignoring the fact that as a

---

[7] The providing of work relief instead of the dole did more than fill hungry stomachs; it re-established faith in America and in one's fellow man. "I'm proud of our United States," said one relief recipient. "There ain't no other nation in the world that would have sense enough to think of WPA and all the other A's." The wife of one WPA worker was quoted as saying, "We aren't on relief any more—my man is working for the government."

prospective federal official he had promised more than he could deliver, he innocently and accurately added, "I cannot pledge you more than that." Sensing the tremendous importance of the matter to the American people, Eisenhower made substantially the same statement three other times—at Yonkers, Peoria, and Pittsburgh. At Yonkers he said that he had "repeated this particular pledge over and over again in the United States" and that he and his associates were "dedicated to this proposition. . . ."

In the White House, Eisenhower continued to reflect this underlying and persistent fear that a depression would once again stride through the land. According to the account in Robert Donovan's semiofficial *Eisenhower: The Inside Story*, at session after session of the Cabinet during the recession of 1953–54, it was the President who stressed the urgency of the economic situation. It was he who constantly prodded Arthur F. Burns of the Council of Economic Advisers to prepare plans with which to forestall a serious drop in the economic indicators. Indeed as late as June, 1954, just after Burns had delivered an optimistic report on the condition and future of the economy, as Donovan tells it, "The President . . . was still concerned about whether the administration was doing enough. Even though it jarred the logic of some members of the Cabinet, he insisted, everything possible must be done to restore vigor to the economy. It was important, the President said, to produce results and to err on the side of doing too much rather than too little."

In the midst of the recession of 1957–58, Vice-President Nixon, speaking on April 24, 1958, specifically repudiated the Hoover approach of permitting the economy to right itself without government intervention. "Let us recognize once and for all," he told his audience, "that the time is past in the United States when the Federal Government can stand by and allow a recession to be prolonged or to deepen into depression without decisive Government action." Though Eisenhower was obviously worried that hasty measures might bring on further inflation, on May 20, in a public address, he agreed with the Vice-President that the government had "a continuing responsibility . . . to help counteract recession." In the same speech the President enumerated concrete measures already taken, such as extension of unemployment benefits, speeding up of defense and civilian procurement, acceleration of government construction projects, and the easing of credit by the Federal Reserve.

The Republican administration's evident acceptance of the new obligations of government in the economy is strikingly suggestive of the shock which the depression dealt conventional economic thought in America. . . .

## Was It a New or Old Deal?

One of the most enduring monuments to the Great Depression was that congeries of contradictions, naïveté, humanitarianism, realistic politics, and economic horse sense called the New Deal of Franklin D. Roosevelt. As the governmental agent which recast American thinking on the responsibilities of government, the New Deal was clearly the offspring of the depression. As we have seen, it was also more than that: it was a revitalization of the Democratic party; it was the political manifestation of that new spirit of reform which was stirring among the ranks of labor and the Negro people.

In their own time and since, the New Deal and Franklin Roosevelt have had a polarizing effect upon Americans. Probably at no time before Roosevelt has the leader of a great democratic nation come to symbolize as he did the hopes and the fears of so many people.[8] Not even Jackson, in whom Roosevelt himself recognized a President of his own popularity- and hatred-producing caliber, could rival him. Over a decade after Roosevelt's death, the mention of his name still evokes emotions, betrayed by the wistful look in the eye or in the hard set of the jaw. The election of 1956, moreover, demonstrated once again that the Old Guard of the Republican party still fights the dead Roosevelt while the Democratic party wanders leaderless in his absence. This too is a measure of the political revolution he led.

For the Democratic party, Roosevelt was like a lightning rod, drawing to himself all the venom and hatred of the opposition, only to discharge it harmlessly; nothing, it seemed, could weaken his personal hold on the affections of the majority of Americans. That something more was involved than sheer popularity is shown by the example of Dwight Eisenhower. Though held in even greater popular esteem, Eisenhower has been unable to invest his party with his own vote-getting power; Republicans lose though Eisenhower wins. The difference between F.D.R. and Ike is that one stood for a program, a hope, and a future, while the other stands for himself as a good, well-intentioned man whom all instinctively trust and perhaps even admire. The one is a leader of a nation, the other a popular hero. Roosevelt is already a member of that tiny pantheon of great leaders of Americans in which Washington, Jackson, Lincoln, and Wilson are included; it is difficult to believe that Eisenhower will be included. His monument is more likely to be inscribed: "The best-liked man ever to be President."

In the thirties, as now, the place of the New Deal in the broad stream of American development has been a matter of controversy. Historians and commentators on the American scene have not yet reached a firm agreement —if they ever will—as to whether the New Deal was conservative or radical in character, though it does appear that the consensus now seems to lean

---

[8] According to Harold Ickes, Roosevelt was profoundly struck by the adoration which was bestowed upon him by his admirers. During the 1936 campaign, the President told Ickes "that there was something terrible about the crowds that lined the streets along which he passed. He went on to explain what he meant, which was exclamations from individuals in the crowd, such as 'He saved my home,' 'He gave me a job,' 'God bless you, Mr. President,' etc." In May, 1936, Marquis Childs published an article in *Harper's*, entitled "They Hate Roosevelt," in which he described and tried to account for the unreasoning hatred for the President on the part of what Childs called the upper 2 percent of the population.

toward calling it conservative and traditional.[9] Certainly if one searches the writings and utterances of Franklin Roosevelt, his own consciousness of conservative aims is quickly apparent. "The New Deal is an old deal—as old as the earliest aspirations of humanity for liberty and justice and the good life," he declared in 1934. "It was this administration," he told a Chicago audience in 1936, "which saved the system of private profit and free enterprise after it had been dragged to the brink of ruin. . . ."

But men making a revolution among a profoundly conservative people do not advertise their activity, and above all Franklin Roosevelt understood the temper of his people.[10] Nor should such a statement be interpreted as an insinuation of high conspiracy—far from it. Roosevelt was at heart a conservative, as his lifelong interest in history, among other things, suggests. But he was without dogma in his conservatism, which was heavily interlaced with genuine concern for people.[11] He did not shy away from new means and new approaches to problems when circumstances demanded it. His willingness to experiment, to listen to his university-bred Brains Trust, to accept a measure like the TVA, reveal the flexibility in his thought. Both his lack of theoretical presuppositions and his flexibility are to be seen in the way he came to support novel measures like social security and the Wagner Act. Response to popular demand was the major reason. "The Congress can't stand the pressure of the Townsend Plan unless we have a real old-age insurance system," he complained to Frances Perkins, "nor can I face the country without having . . . a solid plan which will give some assurance to old people of systematic assistance upon retirement." In like manner, the revolutionary NLRA was adopted as a part of his otherwise sketchy and rule-of-thumb philosophy of society. Though ultimately Roosevelt championed the Wagner bill in the House, it was a belated conversion dictated by the foreshadowed success of the measure and the recent invalidation of the NRA. In his pragmatic and common-sense reactions to the exigencies of the depression, Roosevelt, the easygoing conservative, ironically enough became the embodiment of a new era and a new social philosophy for the American people.

"This election," Herbert Hoover presciently said in 1932, "is not a mere

---

[9] For example, one of the most recent short evaluations of the New Deal, by a most knowledgeable historian, Arthur Link, concludes as follows: "The chief significance of the reform legislation of the 1930's was its essentially conservative character and the fact that it stemmed from a half century or more of discussion and practical experience and from ideas proposed as well by Republicans as by Democrats." *American Epoch* (New York, 1955), p. 425.

[10] It is significant that only once during the 1932 campaign, according to Ernest K. Lindley, did Roosevelt call for "a revolution"; and then he promptly qualified it to "the right kind, the only kind of revolution this nation can stand for—a revolution at the ballot box."

[11] When an economist suggested to F.D.R. that the depression be permitted to run its course and that then the economic system would soon right itself—as Frances Perkins tells the story—the President's face took on a "gray look of horror" as he told the economist: "People aren't cattle you know!"

shift from the ins to the outs. It means deciding the direction our nation will take over a century to come." The election of Franklin Roosevelt, he predicted, would result in "a radical departure from the foundations of 150 years which have made this the greatest nation in the world." Though Hoover may be charged with nothing more than campaign flourishing, it is nevertheless a fact that his speech was made just after Roosevelt's revealing Commonwealth Club address of September. Only in this single utterance, it should be remembered, did Roosevelt disclose in clear outline the philosophy and program which was later to be the New Deal. "Every man has a right to life," he had said, "and this means that he has also a right to make a comfortable living. . . . Our government, formal and informal, political and economic," he went on, "owes to everyone an avenue to possess himself of a portion of that plenty [from our industrial society] sufficient for his needs, through his own work." Here were the intimations of those new goals which the New Deal set for America.

Accent as heavily as one wishes the continuity between the reforms of the Progressive era and the New Deal, yet the wide difference between the goals of the two periods still remains. The Progressive impulse was narrowly reformist: it limited business, it assisted agriculture, it freed labor from some of the shackles imposed by the courts, but it continued to conceive of the state as policeman or judge and nothing more. The New Deal, on the other hand, was more than a regulator—though it was that too, as shown by the SEC and the reinvigoration of the antitrust division of the Justice Department. To the old goals for America set forth and fought for by the Jeffersonians and the Progressives the New Deal appended new ones. Its primary and general innovation was the guaranteeing of a minimum standard of welfare for the people of the nation. WPA and the whole series of relief agencies which were a part of it, wages and hours legislation, AAA, bank deposit insurance, and social security,[12] each illustrates this new conception of the federal government. A resolution offered by New Deal Senator Walsh in 1935 clearly enunciated the new obligations of government. The resolution took notice of the disastrous effects of the depression "upon the lives of young men and women . . ." and then went on to say that "it is the duty of the Federal Government to use every possible means of opening up opportunities" for the youth of the nation "so that they may be rehabilitated and restored to a *decent standard of living* and ensured proper development of their talents. . . ."

But the guarantor state as it developed under the New Deal was more active and positive than this. It was a vigorous and dynamic force in the so-

[12] Social security is an excellent example of how, under the New Deal, reform measures, when they conflicted with recovery, were given priority. In siphoning millions of dollars of social security taxes from the purchasing power of the workers, social security was a deflationary measure, which must have seriously threatened the precariously based new economic recovery. For this reason and others, Abraham Epstein, the foremost authority in America on social security, denounced the act as a "sharing of poverty."

ciety, energizing and, if necessary, supplanting private enterprise when the general welfare required it. With the Wagner Act, for example, the government served notice that it would actively participate in securing the unionization of the American worker; the state was no longer to be an impartial policeman merely keeping order; it now declared for the side of labor. When social and economic problems like the rehabilitation of the Valley of the Tennessee were ignored or shirked by private enterprise, then the federal government undertook to do the job. Did private enterprise fail to provide adequate and sufficient housing for a minimum standard of welfare for the people, then the government would build houses. As a result, boasted Nathan Straus, head of the U.S. Housing Authority, "for the first time in a hundred years the slums of America ceased growing and began to shrink."

Few areas of American life were beyond the touch of the experimenting fingers of the New Deal; even the once sacrosanct domain of prices and the valuation of money felt the tinkering. The devaluation of the dollar, the gold-purchase program, the departure from the gold standard—in short, the whole monetary policy undertaken by F.D.R. as a means to stimulate recovery through a price rise—constituted an unprecedented repudiation of orthodox public finance. To achieve that minimum standard of well-being which the depression had taught the American people to expect of their government, nothing was out of bounds.

But it is not the variety of change which stamps the New Deal as the creator of a new America; its significance lies in the permanence of its program. For, novel as the New Deal program was, it has, significantly, not been repudiated by the Eisenhower administration, the first Republican government since the reforms were instituted. Verbally, it is true, the Republican administration has had to minimize its actual commitments to the New Deal philosophy, and it tends to trust private business more than the New Dealers did— witness, for example, its elimination of the minor governmental manufacturing enterprises which competed with private firms. But despite this, the administration's firm commitment to the guaranteeing of prosperity and averting depression at all costs is an accurate reflection of the American people's agreement with the New Deal's diagnosis of the depression. Nor has the Republican party dared to repeal or even emasculate the legislation which made up the vitals of the New Deal: TVA, banking and currency, SEC, social security, the Wagner Act, and fair treatment of the Negro. The New Deal Revolution has become so much a part of the American Way that no political party which aspires to high office dares now to repudiate it.

It may or may not be significant in this regard (for apothegms are more slippery than precise) but it is nonetheless interesting that Roosevelt and Eisenhower have both been impressed with the same single sentence from Lincoln regarding the role of government. "The legitimate object of Government," wrote Lincoln, "is to do for a community of people whatever they need to have done but cannot do at all or cannot do so well for themselves in their separate or individual capacities." Twice, in 1934 and again in 1936, F.D.R. in public addresses used this expression to epitomize his own New Deal, and Robert Donovan in his officially inspired book on the Eisenhower administration writes that this same "fragment of Lincoln's writing . . . Eisenhower uses time and again in describing his own philosophy of government." Between Lincoln and Eisenhower there was no Republican President, except perhaps Theodore Roosevelt, who would have been willing to subscribe to such a free-wheeling description of the federal power; in this can be measured the impact of the New Deal and the depression.

The conclusion seems inescapable that, traditional as the words may have been in which the New Deal expressed itself, in actuality it was a revolutionary response to a revolutionary situation. In its long history America has passed through two revolutions since the first one in 1776, but only the last two, the Civil War and the depression, were of such force as to change the direction of the relatively smooth flow of its progress. The Civil War rendered a final and irrevocable decision in the long debate over the nature of the Union and the position of the Negro in American society. From that revolutionary experience, America emerged a strong national state and dedicated by the words of its most hallowed document to the inclusion of the black man in a democratic culture. The searing ordeal of the Great Depression purged the American people of their belief in the limited powers of the federal government and convinced them of the necessity of the guarantor state. And as the Civil War constituted a watershed in American thought, so the depression and its New Deal marked the crossing of a divide from which, it would seem, there could be no turning back.

Ronald Radosh

# The Myth of the New Deal

Great Depression, labor unrest, massive unemployment, growing consciousness among the working classes, bitter hostility toward the multimillion-dollar
corporations, failure of the reigning Republican Administration to quiet the
brewing explosion—and then the New Deal. The social revolution, which
many expected and others feared, failed to materialize. Why? Was it because
the New Deal, in its own special way, was indeed a third American Revolution?

From the perspective of the 1970s, with the stark realization that the
United States had failed to deal with the race question, or to eradicate poverty, or even to begin to deal with the urban crisis, or to handle the general
malaise and cultural poverty, or to adapt itself to the growing realization that
revolutions abroad would have to be accepted and dealt with on their own
terms—all of these events of the past ten years seemingly provided living
evidence that a revolution had not occurred.

The new generation of New Left historians has asserted cogently that
the New Deal instituted changes that only buttressed the corporate-capitalist
order; that the vaunted Welfare State reforms hardly addressed themselves
to the existing social needs of the 1930s, not to speak of working to end
poverty, racism, and war. Historians Howard Zinn and Barton J. Bernstein
have already written critical essays seeking to evaluate the New Deal from a
radical perspective, and this essay shall not seek to repeat the critique advanced therein. The essence of their critical view has been best expressed by
Bernstein:

From A New History of Leviathan: Essays on the Rise of the American Corporate State,
edited by Ronald Radosh and Murray Rothbard. Copyright © 1972 by Ronald Radosh and
Murray H. Rothbard. Reprinted by permission of the publisher, E. P. Dutton, Inc.

*The liberal reforms of the New Deal did not transform the American system; they conserved and protected American corporate capitalism, occasionally by absorbing parts of threatening programs. There was no significant redistribution of power in American society, only limited recognition of other organized groups. . . . The New Deal failed to solve the problem of depression, it failed to raise the impoverished, it failed to redistribute income, it failed to extend equality and generally countenanced racial discrimination and segregation.*

Once having presented this argument, however, the radical critic has in effect merely chastised the New Deal for what it failed to achieve. This does not work to answer the counterargument that Franklin D. Roosevelt and the New Dealers wanted more, but were stopped short because of the power of the congressional conservative bloc and other impenetrable obstacles.

It is undeniable that to many of the over-forty generation, Franklin D. Roosevelt was and remains the unassailable hero—the man who used all the powers at his command to ease the plight of the dispossessed, and who introduced dramatic reforms that would soon be accepted by the most staunch Old Guard Republican. That generation remembers the animosity with which many in the business community greeted Roosevelt, and the way in which Roosevelt condemned the forces of organized wealth that were out to destroy him. They did not have the tools of historical perspective to evaluate F.D.R.'s actual performance, or to understand what historian Paul Conkin has noted: that the New Deal policies actually functioned in a probusiness manner. . . .

*       *       *

What Conkin was suggesting is that the anger of some businessmen was misdirected; another example of how members of the governing class can be so shortsighted that they will oppose their own best long-range interests. The confusion of the businessmen had its mirror image in the high regard in which so many members of the underclass held F.D.R. and the New Deal. Roosevelt was able, for a while, to build and maintain the famous New Deal coalition that swept him into office in 1936. White workers from the North, blacks from the urban ghettos, and farmers from the Midwest all responded to the New Deal and claimed it as their own. Explaining this success as a result of the "powers of rhetoric," as did Bernstein, evades the real question. How could rhetoric alone convince so many that their lives had changed, if indeed, life was the same as it had always been? Perhaps reality did change just enough so that the failure of the New Deal to make substantive structural changes remained hidden.

Before we can begin to deal with these questions, it may be wise to start by citing the answer presented to the New Left historians by the dean of American corporate liberalism, Arthur M. Schlesinger, Jr., author in 1948 of the theory of a crucial "vital center" in American politics. Schlesinger has carefully presented his generation's answer to the New Left, and has defended the traditional view that the New Deal was a major watershed in American history.

A young radical told him, Schlesinger wrote, that all F.D.R. did was

"abort the revolution by incremental gestures." At the same time, he dangerously cultivated a mood for charismatic mass policies, dangerously strengthened the Presidency, dangerously concentrated power in the national government. In foreign affairs, he was an imperialist who went to war against Germany and Japan because they were invading markets required by American capitalism.

Claiming that Roosevelt "will survive this assault from the left as he has survived the earlier assault from the right," Schlesinger ended with his own brief estimate of F.D.R.'s policies and times. Roosevelt

led our nation through a crisis of confidence by convincing the American people that they had unsuspected reserves of decency, steadfastness and concern. He defeated the grand ideologists of his age by showing how experiment could overcome dogma, in peace and in war.

Schlesinger's writings help us to understand how those who only mildly benefited from the New Deal praised it, defended it, and allowed their experience during the 1930s to shape their social and political attitudes for more than a decade. Undoubtedly, many Americans have the same analysis of Social Security as does Schlesinger.

No government bureau ever directly touched the lives of so many millions of Americans—the old, the jobless, the sick, the needy, the blind, the mothers, the children—with so little confusion or complaint. . . . For all the defects of the Act, it still meant a tremendous break with the inhibitions of the past. The federal government was at last charged with the obligation to provide its citizens a measure of protection from the hazards and vicissitudes of life. . . . With the Social Security Act, the constitutional dedication of federal power to the general welfare began a new phase of national history.

The assumptions behind Schlesinger's evaluation of Social Security are those he revealed years earlier. Writing in his classic *The Age of Jackson,* Schlesinger noted that "Liberalism in America has been ordinarily the movement of the part of the other sections of society to restrain the power of the business community." This statement assumes that a popular movement, opposed by business, continually arises in America to challenge the one-sided power of large corporate business. But new historical research by a generation of revisionists has all but wiped out this assumption. William Appleman Williams, Gabriel Kolko, James Weinstein, and Murray N. Rothbard have argued that liberalism has actually been the ideology of dominant business groups, and that they have in reality favored state intervention to supervise corporate activity. Liberalism changed from the individualism of laissez-faire to the social control of twentieth-century corporate liberalism. Unrestrained ruthless competition from the age of primitive capital accumulation became an anachronism, and the new social and political regulatory measures emanating from the Progressive Era were not so much victories for the people over the interests, as examples of movement for state intervention to supervise corporate activity on behalf of the large corporate interests themselves.

Just as all historians used to look at the accomplishments of the Progressive Era as antibusiness, equating state regulation with regulation over business, and with the assumption that corporate business opposed the new regulatory acts, so do many historians of the New Deal view the achievements of F.D.R.'s first two terms as a continuation of the Progressive tradition. The New Deal thus becomes the culmination of a "progressive" process that began with the age of Jackson. Once again, it is assumed that the "money changers" whom Roosevelt supposedly drove out of the temple were the New Deal's major opposition, and that government programs were per se progressive and part of a new phase of our history.

This analysis was stated most strongly by Carl N. Degler, when he referred to the New Deal as the "Third American Revolution." Seeing in the various New Deal measures "a new conception of the good society," Degler claimed pathbreaking significance once the "nation at large accepted the government as a permanent influence in the economy." Is such an influence sufficient to describe the New Deal as revolutionary?

To Degler it was. Like Schlesinger, historian Degler saw the Social Security Act as revolutionary because "it brought government into the lives of people as nothing had since the draft and the income tax." Yet another proof of revolutionary effect, even more important, was the "alteration in the position and power of labor." Noting that the decline in union growth had come to an end, and that the new spurt in unionism was that of the industrial unionism of the CIO, Degler argued that it was Robert F. Wagner's National Labor Relations Act that "threw the enormous prestige and power of the government behind the drive for organizing workers." The "placing of the government on the side of unionization," Degler wrote, "was of central importance in the success of many an organizational drive of the CIO, notably those against Ford and Little Steel."

In summation, the Wagner Act was depicted as revolutionary because, prior to the Act, no federal law prevented employers from discharging workers for exercising their rights or from refusing to bargain with a labor union, whereas after the Act was passed, workers had new rights against their employers. The result, according to Degler, was a truly pluralistic structure to American society. "Big Labor now took its place beside Big Business and Big Government to complete a triumvirate of economic power." The Wagner Act particularly revealed that:

*the government served notice that it would actively participate in securing the unionization of the American workers; the state was no longer to be an impartial policeman merely keeping order; it now declared for the side of labor.*

Although the New Deal used traditional rhetoric, Degler asserted, "in actuality it was a revolutionary response to a revolutionary situation."

This estimate was upheld by even such a critical historian as William E. Leuchtenburg. Although he modified Degler's analysis a degree, by noting that the Wagner Act was partially motivated by a desire to "contain 'unbalanced and radical' labor groups," Leuchtenburg agreed that the New Deal was a "radically new depature." But to Leuchtenburg, the New Deal had major shortcomings. It failed to demonstrate "that it could achieve prosperity in peacetime," perhaps its greatest failure. The fact that the unemployed disappeared only with war production meant to Leuchtenburg that the New Deal was only "a halfway revolution; it swelled the ranks of the bourgeoisie but left many Americans—sharecroppers, slum dwellers, most Negroes—outside of the new equilibrium." But, argued Leuchtenburg, it was a revolution anyway. Here, we might raise the question of what type of "revolution" is it that fails to deal with the most basic problems produced by the old order, especially when an end to unemployment was the key task confronting the first New Deal, and while there were still by Leuchtenburg's count six million unemployed "as late as 1941."

The myth of a New Deal revolution, or a new departure, or a basic watershed, call it what you will, dies hard. New Left critics have correctly emphasized the New Deal's failures to destroy some part of the myth. But their critique, valuable as it has been, has failed to take up a more essential question. How does one confront the truth that the New Deal obviously did move in new directions, in some ways quite dramatically, and still keep the old order intact? And how is it that, although the old order remained basically untouched and even preserved, Roosevelt and the New Dealers were able to win the everlasting gratitude of the dispossessed and the white working class?

Rather than discuss all of the policies of the New Deal, we can begin to cope with this question by a more thorough look at a few key areas, particularly the National Recovery Administration (NRA), the birth of the Congress of Industrial Organizations (CIO) and the origins of the Wagner or National Labor Relations Act, and the passage of the Social Security Act. These three areas have been pointed to as evidence for the pathbreaking if not revolutionary character of the New Deal. Close attention to them should therefore prove most helpful in arriving at a more historically accurate assessment of what the New Deal wrought.

Most historians have discussed the Social Security Act in terms of what it offered American citizens for the first time, not in terms of how and why it was passed. Fortunately, sociologist G. William Domhoff has enabled us to take a new look at what lay behind some of the major New Deal reforms. Domhoff, following the lead supplied by the New Left revisionist historians, put his emphasis on the sponsorship of major reforms by leading moderate big businessmen and liberal-minded lawyers from large corporate enterprises. Working through reform bodies such as the American Association for Labor

Legislation (AALL) and the Fraternal Order of Eagles, model bills for social insurance had been proposed and discussed in the United States as early as 1910–15.

These proposals had come to naught. But when the Great Depression hit, the need for reform was clear to all. The first unemployment bill in the United States passed the Wisconsin State Legislature in 1932, and it had evolved from a bill drafted by John R. Commons for the AALL in 1921. In the discussions in Washington, which eventually led to the Social Security Act, AALL members taking part included Paul A. Raushenbush and his wife Elizabeth Brandeis, Henry Dennison, and three New Dealers trained in corporate law, Charles W. Wyzanski, Jr., Thomas H. Eliot, and Thomas G. Corcoran. Wyzanski was graduated from Harvard and Exeter and was with the Boston law firm Ropes, Grey, Boyden and Perkins. Eliot was graduated from Brown, Nichols preparatory school, and Harvard College, and was a grandson of a former president of Harvard. Corcoran was graduated from Harvard Law School and was with the New York corporate law firm Cotton and Franklin.

In June 1934, Roosevelt appointed a Committee on Economic Security, headed by Secretary of Labor Frances Perkins. It included Treasury Secretary Henry Morgenthau, Jr., Secretary of Agiculture Henry A. Wallace, Attorney General Homer Cummings, and F.D.R.'s chief aide, Harry Hopkins. They met for the purpose of working on a comprehensive social security and old-age pensions bill. Like any other committee, they depended on advisors, and among their chief aides were men identified closely with the work of the AALL. But the basic outlines of the plan were put forth by F.D.R. himself in his June 6, 1934, message to Congress. The President called for federal-state cooperation, a contributory plan rather than a government subsidy through a tax increase, and he stressed the need for employment stabilization.

The Committee on Economic Security got to work after F.D.R.'s speech, and met eleven times. On January 15, 1935, they presented the President with their report. Two days later, Roosevelt sent his own report to Congress. Roosevelt's proposal was essentially the one prepared by corporate lawyers like Thomas Eliot, who played the major role in drafting the "bill to carry out the committee's recommendations." Yet large-scale opposition to the proposed bill came immediately from other business circles, especially from the National Association of Manufacturers.

What is important is that liberal historians have traditionally equated the NAM and small-business opposition to social reform legislation as business-community opposition. They have depicted an all-out fight between the forces of big business versus the people; the former opposing and the latter supporting reform. In his book Schlesinger wrote as follows:

*While the friends of social security were arguing out the details of the program, other Americans were regarding the whole idea with consternation, if not with horror. Organized business had long warned against such pernicious notions. "Unem-*

ployment insurance cannot be placed on a sound financial basis," said the National Industrial Conference Board; it will facilitate "ultimate socialist control of life and industry," said the National Association of Manufacturers. . . . One after another, business leaders appeared before House and Senate Committees to invest such dismal prophecies with what remained of their authority.

Republicans in the House faithfully reflected the business position.

Of significance are Schlesinger's last words, "the business position." This telling phrase reveals the ideological mask on reality that helps to hide the manner in which the corporate state maintains its hegemony over the country. Schlesinger not only overstated big-business opposition; he did not account for the support given Social Security by moderate yet powerful representatives of the large-corporation community. Particularly important is the backing given the Act by the Business Advisory Council, which formed a committee on Social Security headed by Gerard Swope, president of General Electric, Walter Teagle of Standard Oil, Morris Leeds of the AALL, and Robert Elbert. These men were major corporate leaders, or as Domhoff put it, "some of the most powerful bankers and industrialists in the country." . . .

\* \* \*

Despite the support given the Act by these key corporate figures, the original bill was to be watered down by the Congress. This was because many congressmen and senators reflected their local constituencies, which included local antilabor and small-town mentality NAM business-types. Congress, in other words, did not have the political sophistication of the corporate liberals. Once the bill got to Congress, the setting of minimum state standards in old-age assistance was discarded, as was the concept that states had to select administering personnel on a merit basis. Workers were to contribute half of the old-age pension funds, while employers paid unemployment compensation. But the large corporations would still be able to pass the costs of their contribution to the consumer. Finally, the rich were not to be taxed to help pay for the program.

As Domhoff showed, the Social Security Act was the measured response of the moderate members of the power elite to the discontent of the thirties. These moderates took their program, based on models introduced by various corporate policy-making bodies during the previous twenty years, to the Congress. Congress, however, listened more to the NAM-type businessmen. The result was a legislative compromise between the original moderate and conservative position on the Act. Radicals among labor who wanted a comprehensive social-insurance program remained unsatisfied. It was their pressure, however, that induced the moderates to present their plan to Congress. The demands of the poor and the working class provided the steam that finally brought the modified Act to fruition.

The result, as Domhoff wrote:

*from the point of view of the power elite was a restabilization of the system. It put a floor under consumer demand, raised people's expectations for the future and directed political energies back into conventional channels. The difference between what could be and what is remained very, very large for the poor, the sick, and the aged. The wealth distribution did not change, decision-making power remained in the hands of upper-class leaders, and the basic principles that encased the conflict were set forth by moderate members of the power elite.*

Social Security may have been a symbolic measure of the new Welfare State. But, to the corporate liberals in the governing class, it served as the type of legislation that eased tension, created stability, and prevented or broke any movements for radical structural change. Hence, it served an essentially conservative purpose because it helped maintain the existing system of production and distribution.

The pattern of corporate support to New Deal programs is even more vivid when we consider the first great program initiated by the New Deal to produce recovery, the National Recovery Administration. NRA arose from a background of collectivist plans such as the one proposed in 1931 by Gerard Swope, president of General Electric. Presented to a conference of the National Electrical Manufacturers Association, the plan, as Murray N. Rothbard has described it, "amounted to a call for compulsory cartelization of American business—an imitation of fascism and an anticipation of the NRA." . . .

\*    \*    \*

It is no accident that the early New Deal was characterized by the introduction of planning techniques that had antecedents in trade associations developed within industry during the Hoover years. Bernard Baruch's War Industries Board and the Hoover trade associations reached fruition with F.D.R.'s NRA. Men who had been involved with wartime planning were brought back to government service. "In quest of a precedent for government-business cooperation," Leuchtenburg wrote,

*the draftsmen of the recovery bill turned to the experience with industrial mobilization in World War I. Swope himself had served in a war agency, and his plan was one of many . . . which drew on recollections of government coordination of the economy during the war. Since they rejected laissez-faire, yet shrank from embracing socialism, the planners drew on the experience of the War Industries Board because it offered an analogue which provided a maximum of government direction with a minimum of challenge to the institutions of a profit economy.*

\*    \*    \*

. . . As Leuchtenburg went on to state, the New Dealers also rejected class struggle, as well as "mass action and socialist planning, and assumed a community of interest of the managers of business corporations and the directors of government agencies." They feared not discredited conservatives, but the "antiplutocratic movements," or we might put it, the forces of the radical left. Hence the New Deal cartelization efforts, which culminated in NRA.

One of NRA's major architects was Donald Richberg, who had been chosen for his position because of his prolabor background. But again, Richberg's commitment to labor lay within the framework of the corporate state. As a young Chicago lawyer, Richberg had written both the Railway Labor Act of 1926 and later the Norris-LaGuardia Act of 1932. He was chosen to help frame the NRA, Schlesinger pointed out, because Hugh Johnson wanted Richberg because "he assumed that Richberg had the confidence of labor and liberals." No other early appointment of F.D.R.'s, Schlesinger concluded, gave "more satisfaction to labor and liberals than that of Richberg."

As a prolabor formulator of the NRA, Richberg revealed his private vision of a new corporate state, but one in which industrial unions would have to become the prerequisite for an American corporatism. "If industrial workers were adequately organized," he explained, "it would be entirely practical to create industrial councils composed of representatives of managers, investors and workers and then to create a national council composed of similar representatives of all essential industries." In this council, "all producing and consuming interests would be so represented that one group could hardly obtain sanction for a policy clearly contrary to the general welfare." Richberg was critical of craft-union leaders. He wished they had "seized" labor's great "opportunity to organize the unemployed," and simply ignored "the hampering tradition of craft unionism" by organizing men and women "denied their inherent right to work." Labor should have demanded that "their government should no longer be controlled by rulers of commerce and finance who have utterly failed to meet their obligations." If such a movement had been built, if labor had created one "mighty arm and voice" of the "unemployed millions," Congress would have listened to the dispossessed.

Richberg also forecast the conservative role that industrial unions would play. "Let me warn those who desire to preserve the existing order," he cautioned, "but intend to do nothing to reform it, that if this depression continues much longer the unemployed will be organized and action of a revolutionary character will be demanded." To avoid that, people had to be put back to work and mass purchasing power had to be increased. The solution was to mobilize the nation "through the immediate creation of a national planning council, composed of representatives of major economic interests who recognize the necessity of a planned economy." The need: to avoid radicalism. The means: a formal American corporate state, or the NRA.

The NRA, which became law on June 16, 1933, was the agency meant to evolve into a corporate state. The NRA, John T. Flynn perceptively noted in 1934, was based on the need of businessmen to have the government control prices, production, and trade practices. "Industry wanted not freedom from regulation," he wrote, "but the right to enjoy regulation." Modification of antitrust laws was desired "so that employers might unite to fabricate and enforce regimentation of industry through trade associations." The NRA also developed plans for shorter working hours and payment of minimum wages; but Flynn noted that it was "pure fiction" that such legislation was forced on big business against its will. Actually, the corporations wanted the opportunity to force the NRA on the "unwilling ten percent" of smaller operators who competed unfairly by cutting costs through wage reductions. The NRA, Flynn remarked, represented almost "entirely the influence and ideal of big businessmen." . . .

\*        \*        \*

The NRA reformers, unlike our contemporary liberal historians, understood that their program was meant to be a conservative prop to the existing order. They also realized the dire need to include social reform as an essential component of the corporate state. They understood that many liberals and even political radicals would overlook the conservative origin and effect of the NRA if reform, especially public works, was offered as part of a package deal. Hence Title I of the NRA promoted the organization of industry to achieve cooperative action among trade associations, and it included the codes of fair competition and exemption of industry from prosecution under the antitrust laws. Title II set up a Public Works Association with a federal appropriation of three billion dollars. It should be understandable why Henry I. Harriman, president of the United States Chamber of Commerce, argued that there was "ample justification for a reasonable public works program" in conjunction with a corporate plan that would free industry from antitrust restrictions. If there was any doubt that the large corporations would support a program that would result in wage increases along with a fair return on dividends, Harriman assured reluctant congressmen that the "big ones will rush to it."

But the problem was to win the allegiance not of the big ones, but of the "liberals." The means to this end was the technique of public works. Of all the New Deal reforms, public works seemed to most people to have the aura of "socialism" or at least of an attack on private interests. To the hungry and unemployed, it symbolized a direct concern by the government for their plight. That public works, as Murray N. Rothbard has shown, was introduced effectively by the Hoover Administration was unrecognized. That the New Deal's public works was of a limited nature and did not interfere with private business prerogatives went unnoticed. In the area in which public-works development was most needed, housing, the New Deal program was hardly successful and in many ways a total failure. All this was ignored. The name *public works* and the PWA itself produced a sympathetic response from the populace, the "liberal" political groups, and the organized political left. . . .

\*        \*        \*

. . . In the words of William Appleman Williams, our leading radical historian:

*the New Deal saved the system. It did not change it. Later developments and characteristics of American society which suggest an opposite conclusion are no more than the full extension and maturation of much earlier ideas and policies that were brought together in what a high New Dealer called a shotgun approach to dealing with the depression.*

Unlike . . . Williams, most of our contemporary historians do not seem to realize that institution of "a new set of plans" is conservative, not to speak of not being radical or revolutionary. But what happens when an area emerges where the "old methods" are entirely done away with? Can one rightly call such an area of innovation revolutionary? As Degler has argued, this is indeed the case with organized labor, and the passage of the Wagner or National Labor Relations Act. More than any other piece of New Deal legislation, the policy toward labor seemed to suggest a new revolutionary stance toward the worker on the part of government.

In reality, the role played by the Wagner Act was the same as that of the NRA and the other conservative New Deal programs. It was the Wagner Act that allowed the Administration to obtain the final integration of organized labor into the existing political economy of corporation capitalism. Unions, which had a sudden revival under the NRA, even before the Wagner Act period, were industrial in nature—the United Mine Workers and the Amalgamated Clothing Workers showing exceptional growth. Craft unions grew only 13 percent between 1933 and 1935, as against 132 percent by the AF of L's four industrial unions and 125 percent for their semi-industrial unions. The NRA provided the original impetus to organization. Between July and August, 1933, the AF of L issued 340 new charters to affiliated local trade and federal labor unions, and Green estimated that in two months AF of L membership increased by about 1,500,000 members.

With the NRA, the federal government took over the traditional organizing function that had previously been an exclusive union domain. The old AF of L craft unions had refused to initiate a widespread program of unionization in unorganized basic industries. But now the New Deal was seeking a labor movement that would gain working-class support and provide the necessary structural parallel to industry that would allow integration of the labor force into the new system. The New Deal, contemporary reporter Benjamin Stolberg observed, "needed organized labor to save big business." While the NRA was a "price fixing mechanism to enable big industry to regain the control of scarcity," it needed big labor to police "the 'social planning' of stabilizing prices in an economic system" that was "partly irresponsibly competitive and partly dictatorially monopolistic." Thus the NRA turned the labor movement "into a semipublic unionism whose organization was part of a government program." . . .

\* \* \*

The leading figure among the moderates was Gerard Swope, president of General Electric. As chieftain of one of the key multimillion-dollar corporations, Swope was quite an important figure in the corporate community. Herbert Hoover had stood fast against introduction of his plan, viewing it as a stepping stone toward a business fascism. But during F.D.R.'s Administration, Swope began to get results. . . .

\*      \*      \*

Swope understood what many contemporary historians do not. Industrial unionism was not inherently radical, and its recognition by government was not revolutionary. Rather, industrial unions functioned in the era of corporate capitalism to exert discipline on the work force so that labor productivity would be improved and cooperative relations with employers would emerge. The existence of such an industrial unionism benefited the long-range interests of the corporations. It was precisely for this reason that so many employers ignored section 7-a of the NRA, and continued to build their own company unions. They simply preferred to deal with their own unions organized industrially rather than with "legitimate" trade unions organized on a craft basis. . . .

\*      \*      \*

. . . The New Dealers devised, in this case, a means to integrate big labor into the corporate state. But only unions that were industrially organized, and which paralleled in their structure the organization of industry itself, could play the appropriate role. A successful corporate state required a safe industrial-union movement to work. It also required a union leadership that shared the desire to operate the economy from the top in formal conferences with the leaders of the other functional economic groups, particularly the corporate leaders. The CIO unions, led by Sidney Hillman of the Amalgamated Clothing Workers, provided such a union leadership.

It was for this reason that the moderates in the governing class pushed for passage of the Wagner Act. As Domhoff noted, the antiunion diehards did have leverage for one major reason.

*From the point of view of the employers, it had to be an all or nobody proposition, for any holdouts would supposedly have the competitive advantage brought about by lower wage costs. Thus, the diehards held great power over the majority, making it ultimately necessary to legislate against them. Perhaps there is something to the claim that most employers would go along with union recognition if all their compatriots would. But not every employer would go along, which set the stage for the battle over the Wagner Act, a battle which precipitated a serious split in the power elite.*

As Domhoff showed, the moderate members of the power elite played shrewd politics. After a vast amount of strikes occurred, they refused to heed the many calls for sending in troops. The result was that the diehards were forced into negotiation and compromise. Roosevelt even accused the NAM forces of trying to precipitate a general strike. But in refusing to stand with the antilabor groups, Roosevelt was not the master broker, a man who favored "a balance between business and labor"; rather, he was an

*integral member of the upper class and its power elite. However, he was a member of that part of the power elite that had chosen a more moderate course in attempting to deal with the relationship of labor and capital. . . . While he did not encourage unionism, his record during the thirties makes very clear, he was nonetheless unwilling to smash it in the way the NAM had hoped to do since 1902.*

Referring back to Roosevelt's prolabor ideology formed during World War I, when he was a member of the Executive Board of the National Civic Federation, Domhoff noted that when the "time came for choosing, he and the moderate members of the power elite chose bargaining rather than repression."

\*     \*     \*

Even if a majority of businessmen opposed the Wagner Act, the moderate group within the elite was able to use political power to its own advantage. Once the Supreme Court voted in favor of the Act, the NLRB [National Labor Relations Board], an administrative body, became the final arbitrator of all labor disputes. This was, as Domhoff wrote, the "favorite solution of the moderate members of the power elite, the 'nonpolitical' administrative body or regulatory agency." Thus Biddle noted that

*the feature of the act attacked as the most radical was in fact the least novel—the provisions authorizing the Board to request a court to enforce its order, which derived from the Federal Trade Commission Act of 1914.*

Even before the Court decision favorable to the Act, F.D.R. had moved to conciliate diehards among the elite. Working through Thomas Lamont, Roosevelt made overtures toward United States Steel. Lamont brought F.D.R. and U.S. Steel president Myron Taylor together, and a contract with the Steelworkers was signed on March 3, 1937, one month before the Court decision. Only Little Steel held out on its antiunion course. Roosevelt similarly worked with Bill Knudsen, head of General Motors, and with Walter P. Chrysler, who backed him in the 1936 election. According to Perkins, F.D.R. was able to gain help from Averell Harriman and Carl Grey of the Union Pacific Railroad, Daniel Willard of the Baltimore & Ohio, Walter Teagle of Standard Oil, Thomas Lamont of J. P. Morgan, Myron Taylor of U.S. Steel, Gerard Swope of General Electric, and textile manufacturer Robert Amory. "It may be surprising to some people," Perkins wrote:

*to realize that men looked upon as the conservative branch of the Roosevelt Administration were cooperative in bringing about a new, more modern, and more reasonable attitude on the part of employers toward collective bargaining agreements.*

But the final goal for which these conservative industrialists worked was the creation of an American corporate state. This was made clear in the 1960s by Leon Keyserling, who had been legislative assistant to Robert F. Wagner during the 1930s and who helped the group that formulated the Wagner Act's principles. In 1960, economist Keyserling called for a "new national agency to embody top level discussions among those who hoped that such a body would move the country away from fruitless wrangles between competing groups." He hoped that a new agency would bring the "organized powers in our enterprise system," unions and trade associations, into a "relationship of participation and concert with the efforts of government." He then noted that this was the goal fought for by Wagner during the 1930s.

This detailed examination of the roots of the Wagner Act, as well as the NRA and the Social Security Act, should help us to assess the meaning of the New Deal. We now should be able to answer some of the questions raised earlier. First, it is clear that nonelite groups—the unemployed, workers, farmers—were the beneficiaries of many of the new social reforms. Social Security did produce benefits despite its limitations, NRA did eliminate sweatshops, and organized labor was able to strengthen its position in society. Reform, after all, would be a meaningless word if it did not have any partial effect. That is, indeed, the very meaning of reform.

But reform is not revolution. Revolution means a substantive fundamental change in the existing social structure, a massive dislocation and revamping of the existing system of production and distribution. Schlesinger's "New Left" student, if he is quoted correctly, has emphasized the wrong issue. The New Deal reforms were not mere "incremental gestures." They were solidly based, carefully worked out pieces of legislation. They were of such a character that they would be able to create a long-lasting mythology about the existence of a pluralistic American democracy, in which big labor supposedly exerts its countering influence to the domination that otherwise would be undertaken by big industry.

One cannot explain the success of the New Deal by pointing to its rhetoric. The populace responded to F.D.R.'s radical rhetoric only because it mirrored their own deeply held illusions. They could not comprehend how the reforms that changed their lives only worked to bolster the existing political economy, and they did not realize that many sponsors of the reforms came from the corporation community themselves. The integration of seemingly disparate elements into the system was successful. Labor did get its share and it did benefit from·the development of a permanent war economy and the military-industrial complex. Many of those who lived through and benefited from the New Deal most likely view its accomplishments in much the same way as Schlesinger or Carl Degler. One can never be sure whether they reflect the explanations offered by the "vital center" historians, or whether these historians merely reflect the false consciousness of their own epoch.

The New Deal policies, as that conservative Chicago lawyer so aptly put it, were only a change in the way of doing things. They were a means of working out new arrangements to bolster the existing order. That so many businessmen were shortsighted and rejected acting in terms of the system's long-term interests does not change that truth. One cannot judge the meaning of an era's policies by pointing to the opposition these policies generated. The NAM and small-business types, with their own conservative mentality, responded to the epoch in terms of the consciousness of a previous era. The moderates in the governing class had to put up a stubborn, prolonged fight until the law would be able to reflect the realities of the new epoch of corporation capitalism.

That many on the political left viewed the New Deal as "progressive" or "neosocialist" is also no clue to the meaning of New Deal policies. Like the small businessmen, the left was a victim of its own particular myths, and its support of F.D.R. cannot tell us anything about New Deal policies either. It may reveal the essential liberalism of the 1930s left, but this is another story. The failure of contemporaries properly to evaluate the epoch in which they live is traditional. One can never, as Karl Marx warned, evaluate an era by concentrating on the consciousness of an era's major protagonists. The New Deal was conservative. Its special form of conservatism was the development of reforms that modernized corporate capitalism and brought corporate law to reflect the system's changed nature. To many, these New Deal reforms seemingly proved that the system had changed its basic essentials. As we move into the era of a fully matured corporate capitalism, whose contradictions are just beginning to emerge, it has become easier to see what the New Deal accomplished. Only in an epoch where consciousness begins to soar beyond the capitalist marketplace can a critique of the major reform era that marketplace had to offer emerge. This is such an epoch. Understanding how the New Deal worked will enable us to resist policies based on further extensions of the Welfare State, and to commit ourselves instead to the collective effort to forge a socialist community in America.

## SUGGESTIONS FOR FURTHER READING

The New Deal has already inspired more writing than many periods in American history, and most of it has been favorable. A balanced, general account, tightly packed and entertainingly written, is William E. Leuchtenburg, *Franklin Roosevelt and the New Deal* (New York, 1963). Leuchtenburg emphasizes the change in American life brought about by the New Deal, but not to the extent that Mario Einaudi does in *The Roosevelt Revolution* (New York, 1959). Arthur Schlesinger, Jr., has completed three volumes of his major study of *The Age of Roosevelt* (*The Crisis of the Old Order*, *The Coming of the New Deal*, and *The Politics of Upheaval* [Boston, 1957, 1959, 1960]). Schlesinger writes exciting history as he shows Roosevelt, the pragmatic-idealist, moving from cooperation with the business community early in his first term to a more critical attitude after 1935.

The best one-volume biography of Roosevelt is James MacGregor Burns, *Roosevelt: The Lion and the Fox* (New York, 1956). Burns, like most historians, views Roosevelt as essentially conservative on political and economic issues. Edgar Robinson, *The Roosevelt Leadership, 1933–45* (Philadelphia, 1955) is the best evaluation of the New Deal from the right. Much recent writing looks at the New Deal from the left and is critical, arguing that the reforms of the 1930s did not go far enough. See Paul K. Conkin, *The New Deal* (New York, 1967) and Barton Bernstein, "The New Deal: The Conservative Achievement of Liberal Reform," in Bernstein, ed., *Towards a New Past: Dissenting Essays in American History* (New York, 1968). Richard S. Kirkendall, *The United States, 1929–1945: Years of Crisis and Change* (New York, 1974), denies that the New Deal was either conservative or revolutionary: "The New Deal did not revolutionize American life: yet the changes that it produced were not insignificant."

The debate is given a slightly different twist in two books by economists. Lester V. Chandler, *America's Greatest Depression, 1929–1941* (New York, 1970), discusses the economic impact of the depression and the response of the government to it and concludes that the experience brought a "revolutionary change in our state of economic understanding," creating a "popular consensus that government can and must promote economic stability." Charles P. Kindleberger, *The World in Depression, 1929–1939* (Berkeley, Calif., 1973), discusses the depression and its effects in a world context, concluding that the depression took hold and spread throughout most of the world because significant changes had taken place in the Western economic community. Britain was unable and the United States was unwilling to take economic leadership, and the resulting economic instability allowed the depression to spread and become prolonged.

Harvard Sitkoff, *A New Deal for Blacks: The Emergence of Civil Rights as a National Issue, The Depression Decade* (New York, 1978), describes the gradual emergence of blacks as part of the New Deal political coalition, although they were in other ways left out of the American consensus. Richard H. Pells, *Radical Visions and American Dreams* (New York, 1973), discusses some of the radicals who did not fit into the New Deal consensus. Alan Brinkley, *Voices of Protest: Huey Long, Father Coughlin and the Great Depression* (New York, 1982), examines two critics of the New Deal.

Alonzo L. Hamby, *The New Deal: Analysis and Interpretation* (New York, 1980), and Otis L. Graham, Jr., *The New Deal: The Critical Issues* (New York, 1971) are convenient collections of essays; Howard Zinn, ed., *New Deal Thought* (Indianapolis, 1966) is a good collection of contemporary documents; Richard S. Kirkendall, "The New Deal as Watershed," *Journal of American History*, 14 (March 1968), is a guide to the literature.

* Available in paperback edition.

# 9

# The
# United States as
# a World Power

Americans have always been deeply involved with the rest of the world. As colonials they often found themselves participants in England's wars. By taking advantage of the antagonism against England, they were able to secure military and financial aid from the Continent during the Revolution. In the early years of national independence, American merchants attempted to wend their way through the clashing interests of France and England, a profitable yet dangerous venture that ultimately led the new nation into a second war with England. After 1815, Americans turned their attention inward, opening and settling new lands and building a national market. Nevertheless, relations with foreign countries remained important. Foreign investment as well as income from lucrative foreign trade helped to finance the westward movement and the building of canals and roadways. The annexation of Texas and victory in the ensuing war with Mexico put over one million square miles of Mexican territory within U.S. borders.

Although America was never isolated from the rest of the world, it was not until the end of the nineteenth century that the nation emerged as a major world power. The outcome of a short but successful war with Spain in 1898 symbolized America's new position in the world. Spain ceded Guam and Puerto Rico to the United States; the Philippines, although promised independence, remained under U.S. control; and Cuba received only nominal independence, remaining virtually a protectorate of the United States. The United States had embarked upon an imperialist venture.

More important than the actual acquisition of new territories was the growing influence and power of the United States in world affairs. In 1904, the so-called Roosevelt corollary to the Monroe Doctrine announced to the world that the United States reserved to itself the right to intervene in Latin America: ". . . in the Western Hemisphere the adherence of the United States to the Monroe Doctrine may force the United States, however reluctantly, in flagrant cases of . . . wrongdoing or impotence, to the exercise of an international police power." Nor was this simply a paper declaration. In the years that followed, the United States intervened in the internal affairs of a number of Latin American countries including the Dominican Republic, Nicaragua, and Haiti.

While the United States was building a canal at the Isthmus of Panama and establishing and protecting its influence in Latin America, there were growing signs of tension among the great European powers. Yet few Americans envisioned a full-scale world war; after all, all of Europe had not been locked in conflict since the defeat of Napoleon in 1815. Thus, when war did come in 1914, most Americans were shocked. If they tended to favor Britain and its allies, they were adamant in their opinion that the United States should not become involved. But the United States was again unable to stay out of Europe's wars. On April 2, 1917, President Wilson read a war message to Congress. The issue at stake, the President argued, was democracy: "The world must be made safe for democracy."

Making the world safe for democracy proved more elusive than military victory over the central powers. A League of Nations, designed to solve international differences peaceably, was established as part of the peace treaties; but the United States Senate refused to ratify the treaties, and the United States never became a member of the League. The result, however, was not complete isolation of the United States from the rest of the world. The United States government aided in working out a solution to the reparations question, participated in conferences designed to limit naval armaments, cooperated with a number of League of Nations agencies, and jointly sponsored the Kellogg-Briand pact in which some sixty-three nations renounced "recourse to war for the solution of international controversies." In Latin America the dominance of the United States continued under the Republican administrations of the 1920s. At the same time, American businessmen took Warren G. Harding seriously when he urged them to "operate aggressively; go on to the peaceful commercial conquest of the world."

The Great Depression revealed grave domestic problems that occupied the energies of Americans during the 1930s. News from abroad, however, was disquieting: the rise of Hitler and Mussolini and the obvious expansionist aims of Japan aroused alarm. Nevertheless, Americans were determined not to repeat the mistake of becoming involved in the wars of the great powers. The Neutrality Acts passed by Congress beginning in 1935 legislated noninvolvement. Arms shipments to either side in a war were prohibited, and Americans were warned that they traveled on belligerent ships at their own risk.

Isolation, however, could not be maintained. By mid-1940 Hitler had overrun western Europe, and Britain was threatened by invasion; in September an aggressive Japan signed a military and economic alliance with Germany and Italy. In the United States rearmament quickened, and strict neutrality gave way to support for England and opposition to Japan as Americans began to realize the growing menace to their security. Then on Sunday, December 7, 1941, Japan attacked Pearl Harbor. On the following day Congress declared war on Japan. Three days later Italy and Germany declared war on the United States, and Congress responded with a declaration of war against these powers.

The attitude of the United States after World War II was very different from that following World War I. Isolationism was all but dead. Although most American envisioned a postwar world of peace and friendship among the wartime allies—Britain, the USSR, and the United States— they also seemed to realize that the nation's participation in the postwar world was essential. The onset of the cold war led not to disillusionment, disgust, and a withdrawal into isolation, but rather to a fuller participation of the United States in world affairs.

Thus it is clear that in the last three-quarters of a century the United States has emerged as a major economic and military power—a power, moreover, that has played an increasingly large role in world affairs. Less obvious are the reasons for this change. Some historians have emphasized the connection between economic development and foreign relations. They have seen the nation's foreign policy basically as an accommodation to the needs of the business community and particularly of big business. Businesses engaged in foreign trade and foreign investment needed support and protection; they received it from the politicians. Other historians find little relationship between economics and foreign policy. They emphasize instead moral fervor born of nationalism or the desire to extend democracy, or they point to strategic requirements such as the need to protect our borders from real or potential enemies.

American diplomatic relations have always been the subject of debate, but never has this debate assumed the proportions and intensity that it did with the start of the cold war. The reason is obvious enough. Military technology has reached the point where total destruction of the world is possible; diplomacy therefore deals with matters of life or death not only for Americans but for a large portion of the world's population. The following selections offer examples of the debate surrounding America's foreign policy.

In the first selection, John Spanier argues that American security after World War II required the establishment of a balance of power in Europe and Asia that would serve to block Communist expansion. This required, Spanier continues, a realistic foreign policy, one that recognized, and was willing to use, the weapons of power politics and one that accepted the necessity of "a happy marriage between diplomacy and force." But the American experience worked against such a realistic view; Americans tended to think of foreign relations in moral terms and to ignore the realities of power politics. New conditions, he concludes, demanded a change in American attitudes. Spanier denies that foreign policy is determined by the needs of an economic elite. He stresses national interests rather than class interests as the determining force and argues that a basic American consensus at home often continues to create difficulties in the formulation of an effective and realistic foreign policy.

To evaluate Spanier's analysis the reader must determine what he means by the "national interest." Is there really a national interest? Or do different groups in the nation have different interests? In the second selection, Gabriel Kolko addresses these questions. He finds that what is called the national interest is really the economic interest of big business. He denies that foreign policy arises from "capriciousness, accident, and chance," maintaining instead that it is the result of the "predominance of the economic ruling class which is the final arbiter and beneficiary" of both domestic and foreign policies. Opposition is tolerated only when it is neither serious nor effective; if necessary, a consensus is maintained by repression exercised by the ruling elite.

In the third selection, Irving Louis Horowitz looks at economic interests in an international context by investigating the effects of the multinational corporation. He finds that these massive corporations transcend national boundaries and put the conflicts described by Kolko on the international scene. The multinationals, he concludes, have brought a new international consensus among businessmen, third world nationalist leaders, and Communist bureaucrats, while at the same time bringing a new, international clash between workers and employers.

In the final selection, Walter LaFeber looks at foreign policy from a different perspective. He considers the views of a number of recent writers whom he terms the "new revisionists." He notes that these writers argue that the war in Vietnam was lost because of domestic opposition, a view LaFeber insists is incorrect. The United States failed in Vietnam because it could not win without destroying the object for which it was fighting. Thus, according to LaFeber, American policy is hobbled not by a failure to understand the true national interest and not by domestic opposition, but rather by the real limitations of American power in the modern world.

According to a popular cliché in American politics, partisan debate stops at our borders. While there is ample justification for debate on domestic issues, our foreign relations—where the security of the nation is at stake—must be bipartisan if the best interests of the country are to be served. Although often expressed, this attitude has seldom been followed in practice. Few major foreign policy decisions have been made without intense debate. Yet how significant are the issues that have divided Americans? More important, are there basic divisions of interest determining foreign policy even when these divisions are not publicly expressed? Has American diplomacy derived from a basic consensus of American opinion? Or has it arisen from the interests of particular classes in American society? If foreign policy is in the interests of the few, how do policy makers gain acceptance of their policies from the masses of the American people and their representatives? What means—if any—are available to those who oppose particular policies and who wish to bring about changes?

What accounts for recent moves toward better relations between the United States and the Soviet Union and China? Is it mutual fear of destruction? Or a diminishing of real differences between the United States and the Communist countries? Or a desire by big business to tap the markets in these countries? Or the realistic, if reluctant, recognition of the limits of American power?

John Spanier

# The American Approach
# to Foreign Policy

Following World War I, the English geopolitician Halford MacKinder wrote: "Who rules East Europe commands the Heartland [largely Russia and China, plus Iran and Afghanistan]: Who rules the Heartland commands the World-Island [Eurasia and Africa]: Who rules the World-Island commands the World." Some years later, an American geopolitician, Nicolas Spykman, paraphrased MacKinder in a reply to his thesis: "Who controls the Rimland [the peripheral areas of the Eurasian continent] rules Eurasia; who rules Eurasia controls the destinies of the world."

No two maxims could have summed up the history of the post-World War II era more aptly. The Soviet Union and Communist China now occupy most of the Heartland; surrounding them along a 20,000-mile periphery lie the exposed and weaker Rimland nations—the Scandinavian and West European countries, Italy, Greece, Turkey, the Arab countries, Iran, Afghanistan, India, Burma, Thailand, Malaya, Indochina, and Korea (with Britain, Indonesia, and Japan lying just off the Eurasian continent). It is the Communists' aim to extend their control to these nations. This would leave the United States and the Americas—the Western Hemisphere—a lone island in a totalitarian sea. American security would then be, at best, very precarious and could be maintained only by the organization of our society as a "garrison state," a condition incompatible with any interpretation of the "American way of life." At worst, the United States would be at the mercy of the Soviet bloc controlling the Eurasian continent. The ability of the United States to ensure its own security—indeed, its survival—under these circumstances depends upon its

From American Foreign Policy Since World War II, 6th rev. ed., by John Spanier. Copyright © 1977 by Praeger Publishers, Inc. Reprinted by permission of Holt, Rinehart and Winston, CBS College Publishing.

capacity to establish a balance of power in Eurasia in order to prevent the Communists from expanding into the Rimland or neutralizing those nations.

As far back as the 1830's, a prophetic Frenchman, Alexis de Tocqueville, had foreseen this struggle which dominates our age:

> There are, at the present time, two great nations in the world which seem to tend toward the same end, although they started from different points: I allude to the Russians and the Americans. . . . The Anglo-American relies upon personal interest to accomplish his ends and gives free scope to the unguided exertions and common sense of the citizens; the Russians center all the authority of society in a single arm: the principal instrument of the former is freedom; of the latter is servitude. Their starting point is different, and their courses are not the same; yet each of them seems to be marked out by the will of Heaven to sway the destinies of half the globe.

Yet, the United States in 1945 could not have been less equipped to conduct the struggle and to assume the global responsibilities involved. American experience in foreign affairs, in comparison with that of the other great powers of the world, had been limited. Consequently, the United States was essentially a novice in the art she now had to practice—the art of "power politics." For over a century the nation had cut itself off from Europe and pursued a policy of isolationism, or what today would be called neutralism or nonalignment. Like the new nations of the post-World War II era, the United States, as the world's first new nation to emerge from colonial subjection, refused to involve herself in the quarrels of Britain, France, and the other European powers. "Europe has a set of primary interests, which to us have none, or a very remote relation. Hence she must be engaged in frequent controversies, the causes of which are essentially foreign to our concerns," said George Washington in his Farewell Address. Therefore, he continued, it would be unwise

> to implicate ourselves, by artificial ties, in the ordinary vicissitudes of her politics, or the ordinary combinations and collisions of her friendships, or enmities: Our detached and distant situation invites and enables us to pursue a different course. . . . Why forego the advantages of so peculiar a situation? Why quit our own to stand upon foreign ground? Why, by interweaving our destiny with that of any part of Europe, entangle our peace and prosperity in the toils of European ambition, Rivalship, Interest, Humour or Caprice?

Why, indeed?

The republic was young, hardly yet conscious of its national identity. American nationalism had been aroused during the War of Independence. But once the British had been defeated and ejected, each of the thirteen colonies had become more interested in its own affairs than in those of the Confederation. The Confederation was a "league of states" in which loyalty to the states took precedence; it was a "firm league of friendship," not a united nation. For example, when Jefferson talked of "my country," he was referring to Virginia, not to the United States. The resulting interstate rivalries and conflicts, the absence of any effective central government, and the lack of an international status for the Confederation led to the formation of the "more perfect union." But once the colonial master who had formerly united the people in common opposition had been removed, how could this new union gain its sense of identity as a new nation? The answer given by the leaders of the young republic—and this answer is still given by the leaders of most of today's new nations—was to continue pursuing an anticolonial policy. This is essential for a new nation's national cohesion. It was colonial subjugation that first kindled the spirit of revolt and awakened the people's sense of national consciousness. It is by continuing to "fight colonialism"—both the specific former colonial ruler and colonialism in general—that this feeling of nationalism is strengthened. Since it was Europe that colonized the world, the rejection of Europe is essential to the formation of the new nation's sense of identity. Therefore, it cannot realign itself with the old colonial master, even when its security is threatened. Whether this threat comes from the Holy Alliance or Communism, the newborn state cannot in most circumstances "stand up and be counted." It must remain independent, for only its assertion against Europe—or, as we say today, "the West"—will foster its growth of national consciousness.

Avoiding "foreign entanglements," as Jefferson called it, is also necessary for the young nation's "economic development." How will it become strong enough to defend the country against possible foreign attacks or assert its prestige against disrespectful, "neocolonial" treatment by the older nations of the world? How can it tie the various parts of the nation together into an effective union and subordinate local and regional loyalties to a primary national loyalty? And finally, how can it provide a better life and standard of living for its new citizens? These are the three vital questions that confront the leaders of all new states, for the government must prove to its people that the recently formed nation is worthy of their support and allegiance because it can furnish them with a secure and decent life. Hamilton, the father of American industrialism, was keenly aware of these needs, particularly the security of the nation. Industrialization thus became a necessity if the United States was to defend her national security, safeguard her independence, and gain the respect of those states who still considered her a colonial weakling and inferior. The continuing friction with Britain during the first years after independence made this clear. The British treated the young republic in an arrogant and high-handed fashion as if it were still a colony; they refused to vacate the Northwest frontier and impressed American sailors by stopping American ships on the high seas and taking the sailors off. Not surprisingly, the lesson of the War of 1812 (also known as the Second War of Independence) was the need for industrialization and strength. But the purpose of industrialization is to do more than augment national power; it is also to strengthen the still fragile political bonds of union with economic bonds. Industrialization, with its high degree of specialization and division of labor, welds together the many areas of a country and binds the people living therein into a closer union; once strangers to each other—hardly thinking of one another as countrymen and fellow nationals—they will be compelled to travel and communicate as the imperative of economic interdependence envelops the entire nation in one large market. The people thereby become "nationalized" as industrialization molds the consciousness of the new citizens and impresses upon them an awareness that they are members of one nation who will all have to work together if their common aspirations are to be fulfilled. Finally, it enables the new nation to raise its people's standard of living. This is the ultimate test of the new political order—its ability to confer economic benefits, or, more succinctly, its ability to "pay off." This is not to deny the importance of such other values as national independence and self-government. However, if man does not live by bread alone, he cannot survive without bread either; and the crucial issue therefore becomes the new order's capacity to furnish its citizens with at least the basic necessities of life, if not a degree of affluence and leisure. It was precisely the opportunities the American political and economic system afforded to its people to improve their material condition that drew the millions of immigrants to these shores. Freedom alone would not have proved such a powerful magnet. Indeed, it is doubtful that freedom can be established, let alone survive, in conditions of poverty. A degree of affluence and a reasonably equitable distribution of income seem to be prerequisites for the blossoming of a democracy, although they are not the sole prerequisites. In any case, the conclusion is clear: Economic development is vital if the new nation is to grow strong, united, and prosperous. In fact, the term "economic development" is a misnomer. It is the *political* results of this development that are essential to the future of the new state. Economic development might more appropriately be called "nation-building."

Granted that, in the American instance—as for new nations after 1945 —the avoidance of foreign entanglements was thus a realistic policy, the subsequent American understanding of international relations proved to be unrealistic. For the priority of internal political and economic tasks, all of which were reinforced by the opening of the West and the subsequent transcontinental drive to the Pacific, led to the depreciation of the importance of foreign policy and the role that power plays in protecting the nation's interests. The ability of the United States to live in isolationism during the nineteenth century and a good part of the twentieth century was attributed, not to the nation's geographic distance from Europe or to the Royal Navy as the protector of the *Pax Britannica*, but to the nature of democracy. The United States was more than just the world's first "new nation"; it was also the world's first democracy and, as such, the first country in history that would devote itself to improving the lot of the common man, granting each individual the opportunity to enrich and ennoble his life. ("Give me your tired, your poor, your huddled masses yearning to be free," reads the inscription on the Statue of Liberty.) The more perfect union was to be an egalitarian society. European concepts of social hierarchy, nobility and titles, and bitter class struggles were not to be planted in its democratic soil. "Here the free spirit of mankind, at length, throws its last fetters off," exclaimed one writer. America was to be a "beacon lighting for all the world the paths of human destiny," wrote Emerson. From the very beginning of their national life Americans believed strongly in their destiny—to spread, by example, the light of freedom to all men and to lead mankind out of the wicked ways of the Old World. The massive immigration of the nineteenth century—particularly after 1865—was to reinforce this sense of destiny. "Repudiation of Europe," as John Dos Passos once said, "is, after all, America's main excuse for being." Europe stood for war, poverty, and exploitation; America for peace, opportunity, and democracy. But the United States was not merely to be a beacon of a superior democratic domestic way of life. It was also to be an example of a morally superior democratic pattern of international behavior. The United States would voluntarily reject power politics as unfit for the conduct of its foreign policy. Democratic theory posits that man is a rational and moral creature, and that differences among men can be settled by rational persuasion and moral exhortation. Indeed, granted this assumption about man, the only differences that could arise would simply be misunderstandings; and since man is endowed with reason and a moral sense, what quarrels could not be settled, given the necessary good will? Peace—the result of harmony among men—was thus the natural or normal state.

Conversely, conflict was considered a deviation from this norm, caused primarily by wicked statesmen whose morality and reason had been corrupted by the exercise of uncontrolled authority. Power politics was an instrument of selfish and autocratic rulers—that is, men unrestrained by democratic public opinion—who loved to wield it for their own personal advantage. To them, war was a grand game. They could remain in their palatial homes, continuing to eat well and to enjoy the luxuries of life. They suffered none of the hardships of war. These hardships fell upon the ordinary people; it was they who had to leave their families to fight, to endure the higher taxes made necessary by the costs of war, possibly to see their homes destroyed and their loved ones maimed or killed. It was only the despot who thought of war as a sport, as a sort of "bully" fox hunt; the common man, who had to endure all the cruelties of war, was therefore by his very nature peaceful. The conclusion was clear: Undemocratic states were inherently warlike and evil; democratic nations, in which the people controlled and regularly changed their leaders, were peaceful and moral.

American experience seemed to support this conclusion. The United States was a democracy and she was at peace. Furthermore, peace seemed to be the normal state of affairs. It was therefore logical that democracy and peaceful behavior and intentions should be thought of as synonymous. Americans never asked themselves whether democracy was really responsible for the peace they enjoyed, or whether this peace they assumed to be a natural condition was the product of other forces. The constant wars of Europe appeared to provide the answer: European politics were power politics, and this was because of the undemocratic nature of European regimes. Americans were therefore relieved that they had long ago, at the time of the Revolutionary War, cut themselves off from Europe and its constant class conflicts and power politics. America had to guard her democratic purity and abstain from any involvement in the affairs of Europe lest she be soiled and corrupted. Nonalignment was therefore the morally correct policy which allowed the United States to quarantine herself from contact with Europe's hierarchical social structures and immoral international habits. At the same time, by confusing the results of geography and international politics with the supposed consequence of democracy, Americans could smugly enjoy a self-conferred moral superiority. It was the Monroe Doctrine, proclaimed in 1823, which first stressed, officially and explicitly, this ideological difference between the New and Old Worlds. It declared specifically that the American political system was "essentially different" from that of Europe, whose nations were constantly engaged in warfare. The implication was very clear: Democratic government equals peace, and aristocratic government—which was identified with despotism—means war.

But this association of peace with democracy was not the only reason for the American depreciation of power politics. Another was that the United States was an overwhelmingly one-class society in which almost all men shared the same set of middle-class, capitalistic, and democratic values or beliefs. America was unique among nations in this respect. The European countries were, by contrast, three-class societies. In addition to the middle-class, they contained in their bodies politic an aristocratic class whose energies were devoted either to maintaining itself in power or to recapturing power in order to return to the glorious days of a feudal past. Moreover, European urbanization and industrialism during the nineteenth century gave birth to a proletariat which, because it felt that it did not receive a fair share of the national income, became a revolutionary class. The nations of the Old World were, in short, a composite of three elements: a reactionary aristocracy, a democratic middle class, and a revolutionary proletariat. Or, to put it another way, these nations had, in an intellectual as well as a political sense, a right, a center, and a left. The United States had only a center, both intellectually and politically. This country had never experienced a feudal past and therefore possessed no large and powerful aristocratic class on the right; and because it was, by and large, an egalitarian society, it also lacked a genuine left-wing movement of protest, such as socialism or Communism. America was, as De Tocqueville had said, "born free" as a middle-class, individualistic, capitalistic, and democratic society. We were not divided by the kind of deep ideological conflicts which in France, for instance, set one class of Frenchmen against another. No one class was ever so afraid of another that it preferred national defeat to domestic revolution—as in France in the late 1930's, when the bourgeoisie was so apprehensive of a proletarian upheaval that its slogan became "Better Hitler than Blum [the French Socialist leader]."

Americans are, in fact, in such accord on their basic values that whenever the nation is threatened from the outside, the public becomes fearful of internal disloyalty. It is one of the great ironies of American society that although Americans possess this unity of shared beliefs to a greater degree than any other people, their apprehension of external danger leads them, first, to insist upon a general and somewhat dogmatic reaffirmation of loyalty to the "American way of life," and then to a hunt for internal groups or forces that might betray this way of life. Disagreement tends to become suspect as disloyalty; men are accused of "un-American" thinking and behavior, and labeled "loyalty or security risks." Perhaps only a society so overwhelmingly committed to one set of values could be so sensitive to internal subversion and so fearful of internal betrayal; perhaps only a society in which two or more ideologies have long since learned to live together could genuinely tolerate diverse opinions. Who has ever heard of "un-British" or "un-French" activities? The United States has often been called a "melting pot" because of the many different nationality groups it comprises; but before each generation of immigrants has been fully accepted into American society, it has had to be "Americanized." Few Americans have ever accepted diversity as a value. American society has, in fact, taken great pride in destroying diversity through assimilation.

It was precisely this overwhelming agreement on the fundamental values of American society and Europe's intense class struggles that reinforced the American misunderstanding of the nature and functions of power on the international scene. Dissatisfied groups never developed a revolutionary ideology because the growing prosperity spread to them before they could translate their grievances against the capitalistic system into political action. America —politically secure and economically prosperous—therefore remained unaware of two important principles: that conflict is the natural offspring of clashing interests and groups, and that power plays a vital role in protecting, promoting, and compromising interests. By contrast, the European states, with their internal class struggles and external conflicts among themselves, never failed to appreciate the nature and role of power.

Politics did not, in any event, seem very important to Americans. The United States matured during the nineteenth century, the era of *laissez-faire* capitalism, whose basic assumption was that man was economically motivated. It was self-interest that governed the behavior of man; it might be referred to as "enlightened self-interest," but it was nevertheless self-interest. Each individual, seeking to maximize his wealth, responded to the demand of the free market. In an effort to increase his profit, he supplied the product the consumers wanted. The laws of demand and supply therefore transformed each person's economic selfishness into socially beneficial results. The entire society would prosper. The free market was thus considered the central institution that provided "the greatest good of the greatest number." Politics mattered little in this self-adjusting economic system based upon individuals' actions whose combined efforts resulted in the general welfare. The best government was the government that governed least. Arbitrary political interference with the economic laws of the market would only upset the results these laws were intended to produce. Private property, profit, the free market were thus the keys to assuring the happiness of mankind by providing him with abundance. Capitalism, in short, reflected the materialism of the age of industrialization.

To state the issue even more bluntly: Economics was good, politics was bad. This simple dichotomy came naturally to the capitalist middle class. Were the benefits of economic freedom not as "self-evident" as the truths stated in the Declaration of Independence? And had this economic freedom not been gained only by a long and bitter struggle of the European middle class to cut down the authority of the powerful monarchical state, and finally to overthrow it by revolution in France? The middle class, as it had grown more prosperous and numerous, had become increasingly resentful of paying taxes from which the aristocracy was usually exempt, of the restrictions placed upon trade and industry, of the absence of institutions in which middle-class economic and political interests were represented, of the class barriers to the social status that came with careers in the army and in the bureaucracy, and of the general lack of freedom of thought and expression. Since the middle class identified the power of the state with its own lack of freedom, its aim was to restrict this power. Only by placing restraints upon the authority of the state could it gain the individual liberty and, above all, the right to private enterprise it sought. Democratic philosophy stated these claims in terms of the individual's "natural rights" against the state. The exercise of political authority was thus equated with the abuse of that authority and the suppression of personal freedoms. The power of the state had therefore to be restricted to the minimum to ensure the individual's maximum political and economic liberties. It was with this purpose in mind that the American Constitution divided authority between the states and the Federal Government, and, within the latter, among the executive, legislative, and judicial branches. Federalism and the separation of powers were deliberately designed to keep all governments—and especially the national government—weak. Man's secular problems would be resolved not by the state's political actions but by the individual's own economic actions in society.

Again, both man's economic motivation and the benefits of a government that acts least were considered to be reflected in the American experience. Millions came to the United States from other lands to seek a better way of life. America was the earthly paradise where all men, no matter how poor or humble they had been in the old country, could earn a respectable living. A virgin and underdeveloped land, America presented magnificent opportunities for individual enterprise. First, there was the Western frontier with its rich soil; later, during the Industrial Revolution, the country's bountiful natural resources were exploited. The environment, technology, individual enterprise, and helpful governmental policies enabled the American people to become the "people of plenty." But to earn money was not only economically necessary in order to attain a comfortable standard of living; it was also psychologically necessary in order to gain social status and to earn the respect of one's fellow citizens.

Individual self-esteem is determined by the community in every society, for the individual can only judge his own worth by the standards of that society. In a class society, status can be easily recognized by certain upper-class traits, such as the clothes a man wears, the manners with which he conducts himself, and the way he pronounces his words. His education is, in fact, the key to his status. But in an egalitarian society, the successful man can be recognized only by his affluence; only the fact that he is richer than his peers, that he has more possessions, that he can afford to indulge in "conspicuous consumption" distinguishes him from other men. It follows logically that if material gain is the exclusive or at least principal sign of differentiation among men and if it confers upon them social respect and position, everyone will preoccupy himself with the pursuit and accumulation of the "almighty dollar." If men are judged primarily by their economic achievements, they will concentrate on "getting ahead." It is not surprising, therefore, that money comes closer to being the common standard of value in the United States than in any other country. For money is the symbol of power and prestige; it is the sign of success, just as failure to earn enough money is a token of personal failure. It has been said, not without some justice, that the American prefers two cars to two mistresses.

It was hardly surprising that in these circumstances the solution to international problems should be thought of in economic terms. Economics was identified with social harmony and the welfare of all men; politics was equated with conflict and war and death. Just as the "good society" was to be the product of free competition, so the peaceful international society would be created by free trade. An international *laissez-faire* policy would benefit all states just as a national *laissez-faire* policy benefited each individual within these states. Consequently, people all over the world had a vested interest in peace in order to carry on their economic relations. Trade and war were incompatible. Trade depended upon mutual prosperity (the poor do not buy much from one another). War impoverishes and destroys and creates ill-will among nations. Commerce benefits all the participating states; the more trade, the greater the number of individual interests involved. Commerce was consequently nationally and individually profitable and created a vested interest in peace. War, by contrast, was economically unprofitable and therefore obsolete. Free trade and peace, in short, were one and the same cause.

Thus the United States entered the twentieth century with a relative unawareness of the role that power plays in the relations among nations, even though as a highly industrialized and powerful nation she was at the turn of the century increasingly exerting a dominating influence in the Western Hemisphere. At no time was this attitude more vividly demonstrated than at the point of our entry into World War I and during the interwar period. It was Germany's unrestricted submarine warfare in early 1917 that brought us into that conflict; it was thus the German High Command's fatal decision that propelled the United States into the war. Yet, our security demanded this entry. The balance of power in the European battlefield was about to collapse: Britain and France were nearing financial exhaustion; Britain's food supply had reached near-starvation level because of the effectiveness of the German submarine campaign; the French Army had suffered such enormous casualties during a series of offensives that it had mutinied; and above all, the Czarist Empire was about to collapse, and this would allow the Germans to transfer some 2 million troops to the Western Front for their 1918 spring offensives. If the Western Allies had then been defeated, as seemed quite likely, the United States would have had to confront a Germany astride the whole continent, dominating European Russia, and in alliance with Austria-Hungary and the Ottoman Empire, extending her influence over the Balkans and the Middle East as far as the Persian Gulf. This would have posed a grave threat to American security, since Germany would have been in substantial control of the Heartland and the European Rimland. The United States, therefore, had good reason to ally herself with Britain and France to safeguard her own security before this menacing situation matured. But she did not—and would not have, if Germany had not launched its unrestricted submarine warfare in the spring of 1917.

The United States thus entered the war in a political vacuum. The American people were never aware of the power realities and security interests which made American participation in the war absolutely necessary. Rather, they believed they were fighting a war for freedom and democracy, conducting a crusade to destroy German despotism and militarism and to banish power politics forever. It is hardly surprising, therefore, that once the war had burned out this crusading spirit, the American public, still blissfully unaware of the relationship between American independence and the balance of power, should again wish to retire into its prewar isolationist state. The United States thus refused to help protect herself, although Britain and France had been exhausted by the four years of fighting and Germany remained second only to the United States as potentially the most powerful country in the world. We refused to face the responsibility that attended the possession of great power. Instead of playing our proper role in world affairs and attempting to preserve the international balance, thereby heading off the next war, we buried our head in the sand for more than twenty years. The result was that a renascent Germany—allied this time with Italy and Japan (plus the Soviet Union from 1939 to 1941)—once again sought to dominate the world. In December, 1941, Japan's attack on Pearl Harbor precipitated the American entry into World War II. Our ostrich policy had not prevented the waves of world politics from once more lapping our shores.

This American depreciation of power, so evident in these events, has meant that the United States draws a clear-cut distinction between war and peace in its approach to foreign policy. Peace is characterized by a state of harmony among nations; power politics, or war, is considered abnormal. In peacetime, one need pay little or no attention to foreign problems; indeed, to do so would divert men from their individual materialistic concerns and upset the whole scale of social values. The effect of this attitude is clear: Americans turn their attention toward the outside world only with the greatest reluctance and only when provoked—that is, when the foreign menace has become so clear that it can no longer be ignored. Or, to state it somewhat differently, the United States rarely initiates policy; the stimuli which are responsible for the formulation of American foreign policy come from beyond America's frontiers.

Once Americans are provoked, however, and the United States has to resort to force, the employment of this force can be justified only in terms of the universal moral principles with which the United States, as a democratic country, identifies itself. Resort to this evil instrument, war, can be justified only by presuming noble purposes and completely destroying the immoral enemy who threatens the integrity, if not the existence, of these principles. American power must be "righteous" power; only its full exercise can ensure salvation or the absolution of sin. The national aversion to violence thus becomes transformed into a national glorification of violence, and our wars become ideological crusades to make the world safe for democracy—by democratizing it or by converting the authoritarian or totalitarian states into peaceful, democratic states and thereby banishing power politics for all time. Once that aim has been achieved, the United States can again withdraw into itself, secure in the knowledge that American works have again proved to be "good works." In this context, foreign affairs are an annoying diversion from more important domestic matters. But such diversions are only temporary, since maximum force is applied to the aggressor or warmonger to punish him for his provocation and to teach him that aggression is immoral and will not be rewarded. As a result, American wars are total wars—that is, wars aimed at the total destruction of the enemy.

Not only does the American approach to international politics consider peace and war as two mutually exclusive states of affairs; it also divorces force from diplomacy. In peacetime, diplomacy unsupported by force is supposed to preserve the harmony among states. But in wartime, political considerations are subordinated to force. Once the diplomats have failed to keep the peace with appeals to morality and reason, military considerations become primary. During war, the soldier is placed in charge. Just as the professional medical man has the responsibility for curing his patients of their several maladies, so the military "doctor" must control the curative treatment of the international society when it is infected with the disease of power politics. General Douglas MacArthur has aptly summed up this attitude: when diplomacy has failed to preserve the peace, he said, "you then go to force; and when you do that, the balance of control . . . is the control of the military. A theater commander, in any campaign, is not merely limited to the handling of his troops; he commands the whole area politically, economically, and militarily. . . . when politics fail, and the military take over, you must trust the military."

The United States, then, has traditionally rejected the concept of war as a political instrument and the Clausewitzian definition of war as the continuation of politics by other means. Instead, it has regarded war as a politically neutral operation which should be guided by its own professional rules and imperatives. The military officer is a nonpolitical man who conducts his campaign in a strictly military, technically efficient manner. And war is a purely military instrument whose sole aim is the destruction of the enemy's forces and of his despotic regime so that his people can be democratized.

War is thus a means employed to abolish power politics; war is conducted to end all wars. This same moralistic attitude which is responsible for our all-or-nothing approach to war—either to abstain from the dirty game of power politics or to crusade for its complete elimination—also militates against the use of diplomacy in its classical sense: to compromise interests, to conciliate differences, and to moderate and isolate conflicts. While, on the one hand, Americans regard diplomacy as a rational process for straightening out misunderstandings between nations, they are, on the other hand, extremely suspicious of diplomacy. If the United States is by definition moral, it obviously cannot compromise; for a nation endowed with a moral mission can hardly violate its own principles. That would constitute appeasement and national humiliation. The nation's principles would be transgressed, the nation's interests improperly defended, the national honor stained. For to compromise with the immoral enemy is to be contaminated with evil. Moreover, to reach a settlement with him, rather than wiping him out in order to safeguard our principles, would be a recognition of our weakness. This attitude toward diplomacy which, in effect, prevents its use as an instrument of compromise thus reinforces our predilection for war as a means of settling our international problems. For war allows us to destroy our evil opponent, while permitting us to keep our moral mission intact and unsullied by any compromises which could infect our purity.

The result of this depreciation of power and moralistic approach to foreign policy is the inability of the United States to relate military power to political objectives. Yet, only if the two are combined can a nation conduct an effective foreign policy. Diplomacy, as an instrument by which the nation's interests are guarded without resort to force, cannot achieve its aims unless it is supported by military strength. It is precisely this strength which safeguards a nation's interests and enables it to head off crises, instead of having to pay the terrible costs of war involved in actually applying this force once the threat has become clear. Power can be employed in administering pressure upon an opponent, forcing him to be conciliatory if he wishes to avoid a clash. Military strength, in short, can act as an incentive for an adversary to compromise; for if he is unwilling to be conciliatory, he is faced with the prospect of defeat in battle. A diplomacy unsupported by a proper military power and strategy thus spells impotence. Good intentions by themselves are insufficient and must be supplemented by power. It may be true, as some like to say, that right is might; but superior moral ideals, unsupported by a political and military strategy, inevitably lead to their self-defeat. Faith without works, as Christianity has taught us, is not enough.

In the past, American foreign policy has not been characterized by such a happy marriage between diplomacy and force. Even when the United States has been involved in foreign affairs, its policy has featured the divorce of political aims from military strategy. In peacetime, the United States has, at best, possessed a skeleton military establishment; and during hostilities, it has simply maximized its strength to achieve total defeat of the enemy. American diplomacy in peacetime has been paralyzed by a lack of strength; during war, purely military objectives have become paramount. The American approach to foreign policy has been an all-or-nothing affair, characterized by either complete abstention and impotence or total commitment and strength.

The situation which faced the United States in 1945, however, no longer allowed her to abstain from this struggle. The Soviet threat required a long-range policy which would effectively combine the political, military, and economic factors of power; above all, it demanded a permanent commitment. There could be no disengagement from this conflict if the United States wished to survive as a free nation. Engagement was the only course.

Gabriel Kolko

# *The Limits of Consensus*

For a growing number of Americans the war in Vietnam has become the turning point in their perception of the nature of American foreign policy, the traumatizing event that requires them to look again at the very roots, assumptions, and structure of a policy that is profoundly destructive and dangerous. Vietnam is the logical outcome of a consistent reality we should have understood long before the United States applied much of its energies to ravaging one small nation.

We can only comprehend Vietnam in the larger context of the relations of the United States to the Third World, removing from our analytic framework superfluous notions of capriciousness, accident, and chance as the causal elements in American foreign and military policy. For the events in Vietnam expose in a sustained and systematic manner those American qualities that have led to one of the most frightful examples of barbarism of mechanized man against man known to modern history. The logical, deliberative aspects of American power at home and its interest abroad show how fully irrelevant are notions of accident and innocence in explaining the diverse applications of American power today, not only in Vietnam but throughout the Third World. If America's task of repressing the irrepressible is doomed to failure because it is impossible for six percent of the world's population to police and control the globe, critics of American policy should not attribute the undertaking to omission or ignorance. For if the United States can impose its will on the recalcitrant revolutionaries everywhere it will gain immensely thereby, and its losses will be proportionately great if it fails.

*   *   *

From The Roots of American Foreign Policy, pp. xi–xii, 3–26, 83–87. Copyright © 1969 by Gabriel Kolko. Reprinted by permission of Beacon Press.

## The Men of Power

To comprehend the nature and function of power in America is to uncover a critical analytic tool for assessing the character of the American historical experience and the role of the United States in the modern world. The failure of most of an entire generation of American intellectuals and scholars to make the phenomenon of power a central concern has permitted a fog of obscurantism and irrelevance to descend upon the study of American life in the twentieth century.

Stated simply, the question is: What are the political and economic dimensions of power in American society, how does power function, and who benefits from it? The correlations of these structural aspects of power are either curious or critical, incidental, and perhaps colorful, or of decisive importance. The structure of power may be described empirically, but power may also reflect a more elusive configuration of social attitudes and forces that makes it possible for one class to prevail in American history—or it may involve aspects of both the tangible and the intangible.

For the most part, the handful of students of American power have concentrated on the investigation of the social status and origins of men of power, an exercise that has meaning only if one can show distinctive political behavior on the part of men of power with lower social status. Indeed, one must assess the psychology of decision-makers, the genesis of their power, and the source of their conduct in the context of the structure and function of American power at home and in the world, a critical evaluation that permits one to determine whether a "military-industrial complex," a unique bureaucratic mentality, or something more substantial is the root of American policy nationally and internationally. It forces us to determine whether, for example, the presence of a Harriman-family lawyer in one key post is, in itself, crucial to understanding the goals and motives of his behavior and American policies, or whether powerful men freely use one decision-making mechanism or another in a situation in which the results are largely the same because more fundamental interests and goals define the range of action and objectives of all decision-makers. The permanence and continuity in American national and international policy for the better part of this century, scaled to the existence and possibilities of growing national strength, suggests that the study of power in America must also define the nature and function of American interests at the same time.

If, in the last analysis, the structure of power can only be understood in the context in which it functions and the goals American power seeks to attain, the fact that the magnitude of such a vast description requires a full history of twentieth century America should not deter social analysts from highlighting the larger contours of the growth of modern American bureaucracies, if only to make the crucial point that these bureaucratic structures are less the source of power than the means by which others direct power in

America for predetermined purposes. That society is one in which bureaucrats do not represent their own tangible interests, save if they wear other and more important hats, but those of what one must tentatively call that of the "power system," and when their own aspirations become dysfunctional, leaders remove them on behalf of more pliable men. For behind the bureaucrats exist levels of economic and political power, whether latent or exercised, the objectives and maintenance of which no one can abandon without far-reaching, indeed revolutionary, alterations in policy and the very nature of American society itself. It is this ultimate power that defines the limits of bureaucratic conduct and the functions of the state.

Politicians create bureaucracies for specific purposes, and that these structures develop their own administrative codes and techniques, or complex mystifying rationales, is less consequential than their objective and functions. Congress created such bureaucratic power in the United States first during the era 1887–1917 as a result of class-oriented elements seeking to rationalize via political systems the unpredictable elements of economic life in a modern technology. To study *how* rather than *why* political power operates in a class society, a formalism that Max Weber contributed to conservative descriptive social analysis, is to avoid the central issue of the class nature and function of the modern state. After the turn of the century the political parties cultivated bureaucracy purely as an instrumentality serving and reflecting class interests—bureaucracy with no independent power base and nowhere to find one within the American power structure. Given the decisive role of the businessmen in the creation of modern American bureaucracy and the "positive state," it should be neither surprising nor impractical that they staff the higher levels of the bureaucratic mechanisms of American power with men from business.

Policy, in brief, preceded bureaucratic rationalism, with Congress serving as a lobby for, and objective of, various business interests. Given the consensual nature of social and political priorities in America, and the essentially repressive manner in which the authorities handle nonconformity to consensus when it becomes a potential threat, political power in American society is an aspect of economic power—economic power often sharply in conflict by region or size or interest, but always operative within certain larger assumptions about the purposes of victory for one side or the other. Often this disunity among competing economic interests is so great as to mean mutual neutralization and ineffectuality, and frequently the divergent factions couch their goals in rhetorical terms—"anti-monopoly" being the most overworked—which has made "liberal" phraseology the useful ideology of corporate capitalism.

This diversity and conflict within the ranks of business and politicians, usually described as a pluralist manifestation, has attracted more attention than it deserves and leads to amoebic descriptions of the phenomenon of interbusiness rivalry in a manner that obscures the much more significant dimensions of common functions and objectives. The critical question for the study of what passes as conflict in American society must be: What are the major positions, and who wins and why? The motives of the losers in the game of politics, or of those who created pressures others redirected for their own ends, is less critical than the actual distribution of power in society. It is in this context of the nature of power and its function that the scholar should study bureaucracies, with less concern for social mobility than the concept of purpose and goals the bureaucracy serves. Only in this manner can we understand the interests and actions that are functional and irrevocable as part of the logic of American power and not the result of mishap, personalities, or chance. If powerful economic groups are geographically diffuse and often in competition for particular favors from the state, superficially appearing as interest groups rather than as a unified class, what is critical is not who wins or loses but what kind of socioeconomic framework they *all* wish to compete within, and the relationship between themselves and the rest of society in a manner that defines their vital function as a class. It is this class that controls the major policy options and the manner in which the state applies its power. That they disagree on the options is less consequential than that they circumscribe the political universe.

Despite the increasingly technical character of modern political and economic policy, and the need to draw on individuals with appropriate backgrounds for the administration of policy—especially businessmen—it is the structural limits and basic economic objectives of policy that define the thrust of American power nationally and internationally. The source of leadership is important, and has been since the turn of the century, but it may not be decisive. What is ultimately of greatest significance is that whether leadership comes from Exeter-Harvard or Kansas, the results have been the same, and an outcome of the nature of power in America and the role of the United States in the world.

*The Limits of Consensus.* American politics in the twentieth century has been a process of change and shifting rewards within predictable boundaries and commitments that are ultimately conservative and controlled as to the limited social and economic consequences it may achieve. No decisive or shattering social and economic goals have cracked the basic structure and distribution of power in all its forms, and if some have used democratic and liberal rhetoric to explain motion within these boundaries it is less consequential than the functional material contours of the system itself. Indeed, it is the illusion of the possibility of significant change—of true freedom in society—that helps make possible its practical suppression via liberal politics and gradualism which, as historical fact, never exceed predetermined orbits and assumptions.

One must never infer that such illusions are the sole source of conservative order—as witnessed by the response of those with power during rare periods when genuine opposition shatters the mythologies. For though freedom is a posture decision-makers tolerate among the politically impotent, those in power act to make certain that all others remain ineffectual. When their own policies are subject to severe trials, or appear to be failing, they cannot afford the luxury of organized opposition and functional freedoms which can shatter their hegemony over the normal, usually passive social apathy. The history of civil liberties in the United States is testimony to the fact that when freedom moves from rhetoric to social challenge it is suppressed insofar as is necessary. Functional freedom is the ability to relate to power or forces with the potential for achieving authority, that is, the decision-making establishment or those who seek to transform or replace it. So long as intellectuals or the people exercise this right "responsibly," which is to say to endorse and serve the consensus their rulers define, abstract freedoms flourish in public pronouncements and slogans because they lead nowhere. Hence the dissenter has the freedom to become a victim in the social process and history, and a battery of sedition, espionage, criminal anarchy, or labor laws exist in readiness for the appropriate moment of social tension and the breakdown in the social and ideological consensus which exists during periods of peace and stability. The celebrants of American freedom rarely confront the concepts of order that underlie the large body of law for suppression that always exists in reserve.

A theory of consensus is indispensable for comprehending the nature of decision-making and power in American society, but a social analyst must always consider that theory from the viewpoint of its role when some socially critical and potentially dynamic groups and classes cease to endorse or sanction the consensus, because then consensus is based on discipline and becomes, for practical purposes, authoritarian on matters of measurable power. For only challenges to a political and social system and crises reveal its true character—when established power threatens to break down and formal democracy is nearly transformed into functional, true freedom.

The essential, primary fact of the American social system is that it is a capitalist society based on a grossly inequitable distribution of wealth and income that has not been altered in any essential manner in this century. Even if there has not been *decisive* class conflict within that structure, but merely conflict limited to smaller issues that were not crucial to the existing order, one can accurately describe American society as a static class structure serving class ends. A sufficiently monolithic consensus might voluntarily exist on the fundamental questions indispensable to the continuation of the existing political and economic elites, and the masses might respect or tolerate the primary interest of a ruling class in the last analysis. The prevailing conception of interests, the critical values of the society, did not have to be essentially classless, as Louis Hartz and recent theorists of consensus have argued, but merely accepted by those segments of society without an objective stake in the constituted order. This dominant class, above all else, determines the nature and objectives of power in America. And for this reason no one can regard business as just another interest group in American life, but as the keystone of power which defines the essential preconditions and functions of the larger American social order, with its security and continuity as an institution being the political order's central goal in the post-Civil War historical experience.

On the national level, reform and legislation have led to class ends and the satisfaction of class needs, and that the purposes of decision-makers in 1968 should be any different than in 1888 makes sense only if one can posit and prove a drastic alteration in the distribution of economic power.

One may base such an analysis on a functional view of American reform, on the consequences of legislation rather than the motives of all reformers, motives that are ultimately paramount among those who are to be regulated and who have power. Social theory, muckrakers, and intellectuals did not and do not influence important businessmen, who have never aspired to have reforming crusaders regulate and direct their affairs. Businessmen have always preferred that their own lawyers and direct representatives play that role in matters of the most intimate relevance to their economic fortunes, though not necessarily in lesser affairs, and it is a fact that the government has ultimately drawn most critical political decision-makers from, or into, the higher reaches of economic life. In this setting, we should see American reform primarily as a question of technical and efficiency engineering—of social rationalization— to advance the welfare and interests of specific business interests first and society generally, but always within critical ideological boundaries and assumptions. With only occasional differences on tangential points, political authorities have shared, or conformed to, the practical applications of this conservative consolidation usually called "progressivism" or "liberalism."

Yet the critical question arises as to why, in such an economic context of inequality, poverty, and many years of unemployment, there has never been a class opposition to constituted politics and power. In brief, quite apart from the efficacy of the alternatives, why has no anti-capitalist mass movement emerged, as in Western Europe, to create that essential political option which is the indispensable precondition for true pluralism and freedom in America? For the United States is a class society, with measurable oppression, but also without decisive class conflict as of this time. It is also a society serving class ends with the consensual support or apathetic toleration of the dispossessed classes. This consensus, which serves the interest of a single class rather than all of society, exists in an altogether different situation than what theorists of consensus have described, but the social and historic outcome is the same.

The phenomenon of consensus and its causes are simply too complex to describe in light of existing evidence. But it is necessary to pose certain critical questions in order to comprehend whether consent alone is important in explaining the nature and durability of American power and the decision-making structure. What happens when the consensus is shattered and ceases to receive traditional adherence or toleration? Does the fact that all of society may at times share an ideology legitimate it? Or is it more consequential that the economically critical and powerful class endorses the ideology that serves it best—a fact that makes the ideology operate during those rare periods when consensus breaks down? And can core commitments of the public be evaluated by any measurable techniques that permit valid social generalization?

If the history of Left politics in the United States is co-option for some, it is also repression for many others: grandfather clauses, poll taxes, and other means for applying the stick when the carrot was insufficient or deemed inappropriate. The history of the militant labor movement, black struggles, southern populism, socialism, and even the current anti-war and civil rights movements all bear testimony to the fact that when politics and social movements do not legitimize the existing order consensus becomes mandatory conformity and suppression. Authority and power exist quite beyond general social sanctions and rest on specific interests and the ability to impose restraints, and the ruling class has never permitted decision-makers in the governmental apparatus who do not advance and conform to the interests of the state—for psychological reasons or whatever—to introduce dysfunctional elements or policies into governmental affairs. This enforced consensus from above and social cohesion due to the relatively rare exercise of ever latent authority and repression has been the truly revealing aspect of the nature and purpose of American power and capitalist interests. Yet whether voluntaristic or otherwise, these shared values make the origins of decision-makers, or the identity of their special governmental agencies, less consequential than the binding and permanent commitments of ruling groups and their social and economic system.

For this reason, mass consent in a society based on a relatively small elite predominance is less significant, and the operative causal agents in society are the interests and goals of men of power—and their will and ability to retain their mastery—rather than [the] masses who also endorse those objectives. It is the commitments of those able to implement their beliefs and goals, rather than of the powerless, that creates racism in the employment practices of corporations; and it is elite authoritarianism, which remains constant in the historical process, rather than working class biases—which vary with circumstances and interest and often disappear functionally—that leads to authoritarian institutions.

Yet even if the social and power weight of specific opinion and class interests, as opposed to its existence among all sectors of society, is primary, it is still vital to comprehend the elusive character of what is now called "public opinion" or "consensus." What is more significant than opinion is the ultimate implications of apathy and ignorance of elite-sanctioned policies, a condition that reveals the limits of the integrative possibilities of elite-controlled "mass culture" from above. For the most part, in matters of foreign affairs, workers are no more or less belligerent or pacifistic than executives and professionals—when they are forced to register an opinion. The theory of public attitudes as the fount of the decision-making process reinforces a democratic theory of legitimacy, which, for reasons of sentimental tradition at home and ideological warfare abroad, is a useful social myth. But the close and serious student of modern American foreign relations will rarely, if ever, find an instance of an important decision made with any reference to the alleged general public desires or opinions. What is more significant is the fact of ignorance and lack of interest among the vast majority of the population during a period of crisis as to the nature of essential issues and facts, a condition that neutralizes their role in the decision-making process even more and cultivates an elitist contempt for the inchoate role of "the people" as nothing more than the instrument or objective, rather than the source, of policy. The persistent fluctuations in such mass attitudes alone assure that for practical guidance the decision-makers must refer to their own tangible and constant values and priorities. Yet what no one has ever shown is the extent to which this mass apathy reflects the manipulative and moronizing impact of modern communications, or a superior intelligence based on the individual's awareness that he has no power or influence after all, and that he has a very different identity and interest in the social process than the managers and rulers of society.

*The Versatile Rulers.* If the manipulated values and consensual ideology coincide with the objective and material interests of the decision-makers, the fact is important but not necessarily the sole causal factor of their conduct, for even where personal interests do not exist the policies are the same. The function of bureaucracy is to serve constituted power, not itself. While it often can be relevant that an individual in government is directly connected with a business interest, even one in a field deeply concerned with the topic over which he has jurisdiction, we can determine the ultimate significance of this connection only if more disinterested men adopt different policies. Historically, by and large, they have not. In our own era the reasons for this continuity in policy and action are critical, and they reveal the institutional and interest basis of American power in the world, a power that transcends factions and men.

American diplomacy has traditionally been the prerogative of the rich and well placed. Even if they had a lifetime career in government, the intrinsic nature of the structure until 1924 required professional diplomats to be men of independent means, and that tradition persisted until today in various forms. In 1924 the Diplomatic Corps, which paid salaries so low that only the sons of the well-to-do and rich could advance very far in it, was merged with the Consular Corps into the Foreign Service to establish a merit system. In 1924, 63 percent of the diplomatic officers were Harvard-Princeton-Yale graduates, as opposed to 27 percent of the ambassadors for the years 1948, 1958, and 1963. Of the 1,032 key federal executive appointees between March 4,

1933, and April 30, 1965, 19 percent had attended these three elite schools, ranging from 16 percent under Roosevelt to 25 percent during the Johnson Administration. Somewhat lower on the scale of rank, in 1959 the three universities produced 14 percent of all Foreign Service executives, while nearly two-thirds of those in the Service were the sons of business executives and owners or professionals. At the level of all civilian federal executives above GS-18 ranking, or the very highest group, 58 percent were the sons of this upper income and status occupational category.

Sociologists such as C. Wright Mills, and often journalists as well, have made too much of these social origins, for while interesting and important there is no proof such connections are decisive. Twenty-six percent of the highest federal executives come from working class and farmer origins, and an increasingly larger percentage from the non-Ivy League schools, and there is no evidence whatsoever to prove that social and educational origins determine policies of state. That elite origins and connections accelerated personal advancement is now sufficiently self-evident not to warrant excessive attention, much less to make these standards the key criterion for explaining the sources and purposes of American power. In brief, the basic objectives, function, and exercise of American power, and not simply its formal structure and identity, are paramount in defining its final social role and significance. Without denigrating the important contribution of Mills, which was brilliant but inconsistent, such an approach fails to come to grips with the dynamics of American power in its historical setting.

A class structure, and predatory rule, can exist within the context of high social mobility and democratic criteria for rulership, perhaps all the better so because it co-opts the elites and experts of the potential opposition and totally integrates talent into the existing society. The major value in essentially static structural studies of key decision-makers is to illustrate the larger power context in which administrators made decisions, but not to root the nature of those decisions in the backgrounds or individual personalities of an elite. In brief, correlation may not be causation in the power structure, and should high status, rich men ever seek to make decisions dysfunctional to the more permanent interests of dominant power interests, even more powerful leaders would immediately purge them from decision-making roles. The point is that while such men are unlikely to make socially dysfunctional decisions, so is anyone else who rises to the top of a structure with predetermined rules and functions. To measure power that is latent as well as active, it is often easier to study the decision-makers themselves. The other approach, and by far the more difficult, is to define objective and impersonal interests and roles for the larger classes and sectors of American society, their relationship to each other and to the world, and the manner in which they have exercised their relative power.

The analyst must utilize both approaches, and should consider everything useful, including the investigation of status, celebrities, core elites, military elites—the important and trivial, as Mills discovered—and he should discount the trivial and establish the correlations in the hope of revealing causes. If Mills made it clear that there were levels of power among those who shared it, and an inner power core that transcended local society and celebrities, he slighted the economic basis of American politics and exaggerated the causal and independent importance of the military. To him, the social and educational origins of the elite were too critical, thereby excluding the possibility of a power elite "democratized" within its own ranks or selection process but still in the traditional dominant relationship to the remainder of society. Offhand, I assume that in this process it is worth striking a final balance and integration and rejecting certain factors. Social origins and education, and the possibility of the existence of an Establishment based on common heritage and interests, are of lesser concern than the currently operative ties of decision-makers, for the father's words or the impressions of old school days wear off, and the responsibilities of men are measurable in the present rather than in the past.

A more select group reveals far more than a collection as large as W. Lloyd Warner's 12,929 federal executives, and on this assumption I investigated the career cycles and origins of the key American foreign policy decision-makers from 1944 through 1960, excluding the Presidents. My major premise was that even if I could show that such men neither began nor ended in business, there were still many other and more valid ways of gauging the nature of foreign policy. We examined the State, Defense or War, Treasury and Commerce Departments, plus certain relevant executive level agencies . . . and considered only those with the highest ranks. The study included 234 individuals with all their positions in government during 1944–60, comprising the lesser posts if an individual attained the highest executive level. As a total, these key leaders held 678 posts and nearly all of them were high level and policy-making in nature.

The net result of this study, however imperfect, revealed that foreign policy decision-makers are in reality a highly mobile sector of the American corporate structure, a group of men who frequently assume and define high level policy tasks in government, rather than routinely administer it, and then return to business. Their firms and connections are large enough to afford them the time to straighten out or formulate government policy while maintaining their vital ties with giant corporate law, banking, or industry. The conclusion is that a small number of men fill the large majority of key foreign policy posts. Their many diverse posts make this group a kind of committee government entrusted to handle numerous and varied national security and international functions at the policy level. Even if not initially connected with the corporate sector, career government officials relate in some tangible manner with the private worlds predominantly of big law, big finance, and big business.

Of the 234 officials examined, 35.8 percent, or eighty-four individuals, held 63.4 percent of the posts. Thirty men from law, banking, and investment firms accounted for 22 percent of all the posts which we studied, and another fifty-seven from this background held an additional 14.1 percent—or a total of 36.1 percent of the key posts. Certain key firms predominated among this group: members of Sullivan & Cromwell, or Carter, Ledyard & Milburn, and Coudert Brothers, in that order among law firms, held twenty-nine posts, with other giant corporate-oriented law firms accounting for most of the remainder. Dillon, Read & Co., with four men, and the Detroit Bank, with only Joseph M. Dodge, accounted for eighteen and ten posts, respectively, and two men from Brown Brothers, Harriman held twelve posts—or forty posts for three firms. It was in the nature of their diverse functions as lawyers and financiers for many corporate industrial and investment firms, as Mills correctly perceived, that these men preeminently represented the less parochial interests of all giant corporations, and were best able to wear many hats and play numerous roles, frequently and interchangeably as each corporate or government problem—or both—required. Nothing reveals this dual function more convincingly than their career cycles. Despite the fact that Sullivan & Cromwell and Dillon, Read men tended to go into the State Department, or lawyers from Cahill, Gordon, Zachry & Riendel to the Navy Department, general patterns of distribution by economic interests—save for bankers in the governmental banking structure—are not discernible. And with one possible exception, all the men from banking, investment, and law who held four or more posts were connected with the very largest and most powerful firms in these fields.

In the aggregate, men who came from big business, investment, and law held 59.6 percent of the posts, with only forty-five of them filling 32.4 percent of all posts. The very top foreign policy decision-makers were therefore intimately connected with dominant business circles and their law firms. And whether exercised or not, scarcely concealed levels of economic power exist beneath or behind the government, and indeed high mobility in various key posts reinforces such interlockings. This continuous reality has not altered with successive administrations, as the state has called upon Fair Dealers and modern Republicans alike to serve as experts in running a going operation which they are asked to administer efficiently within certain common definitions of its objectives. Whether Democrats, such as James Forrestal of Dillon, Read, or Republicans, such as John Foster Dulles of Sullivan & Cromwell, the continuous contact and advice they have received from their colleagues in the world of finance, law, and business have always colored their focus. The operative assumption of such men, as Forrestal once put it, is that "What I have been trying to preach down here is that in this whole world picture the Government alone can't do the job; it's got to work through business. . . . That means that we'll need to, for specific jobs, be able to tap certain people. . . ." It is this process of "tapping" for high level policy tasks that has accounted for high mobility and the concentration of posts in few hands.

Perhaps of even greater interest is the special nature of the government career officials and their relationship to business during their extended professional lives. These sixty men, 25.6 percent of the total, held 31.7 percent of the posts considered, in part because, being full-timers, they were available for a greater number of tasks. But for many of these men government became a stepping stone toward business careers, and we can only speculate on how this possible aspiration influenced their functional policies on economic and other questions while they were in government. "The lure of industry was such that I couldn't pass it up," a former career officer and head of the C.I.A. for fourteen months, Admiral William F. Raborn, Jr., confessed in discussing why he had taken his government post in the first place. "I went there with the thought I could go when I wanted to." Over half these men, perhaps enticed in the same manner, later took up nongovernmental posts, though a significant fraction returned to government for special tasks. Conversely, however, any government employee thwarting the interests of American businesses, as expressed in foreign and national security affairs, risks losing possible future posts, even if he goes to foundations or university administrations. Most of these new private positions were in law firms and industry. But certain of these key career officials who never left for business or new careers the State Department had selected under its pre-1924 or conventional rules, where independent wealth and social connections were always helpful. The fact that John M. Cabot, Assistant Secretary of State and a Boston Cabot, also held the largest number of posts among the twenty-six full-time career officials we examined is not inconsequential. It is within this career group that the conventional elite social background predominates.

For the most part, the technical and policy nature of foreign policy and military security issues has necessitated the selection of men with requisite business backgrounds. The choice of William L. Clayton, rags-to-riches head of the largest world cotton export firm, to deal with United States foreign economic policy between 1944–47 was rational and both a cause and reflection of policy. What is most instructive was that Woodrow Wilson and Cordell Hull, President and Secretary of State (1933–44), a professor and small town politician, formulated the essential foreign economic policy, and it is here that we must see the larger ideological and consensual definition of foreign policy as ultimately transcending the decision-maker recruitment process.

*Business as the Fount.* The organizational rungs of governmental power take many other businessmen into the lower hierarchies of administration in much the same manner as their seniors function at the very highest levels. These lower tiers of operation are too extensive to measure in their entirety here, but it is sufficient to point to several readily documented expressions. Such lines of contact are perfectly logical, given the objectives of American policy abroad, and given the fact that Washington generally assigns the management of the government's relationship to various problems to the businessmen or their representatives with business connections or backgrounds in the various areas. And it is both convenient and more than logical that key federal executives recruit former associates for critical problem-solving posts for which they have responsibility. There is no conflict of interest because the welfare of government and business is, in the largest sense, identical.

This will mean that key law firm executives with major corporate connections will draw on former clients, whom they may again soon represent at the termination of their governmental service; it will simplify the task of the business representatives in Washington—about two-thirds of the top two hundred manufacturing firms maintain them on a full-time basis—who may wish assistance with marketing, legislative, or legal matters. The Government will invariably choose advisers to international raw materials and commodity meetings from the consuming industries, and will select key government executives concerned with specific issues—such as oil—from the interested industry. The existence of businessmen and their lawyers in government, in short, gives the lobbyists and those not in government something to do—successfully—insofar as it is to their interest. These men interact in different roles and at various times, for today's assistant secretary may be tomorrow's senior partner or corporate president. However much such men may have competing specific economic objectives, conflicts that may indeed at times neutralize their mutual goals, what is essentially common among such elites, whether or not they are cooperative, makes them a class with joint functions and assumptions and larger economic objectives that carry with it the power to rule. This is not to say such well placed officials with industry backgrounds are the only source of government policy, but that they exist and, more important, given the larger aims of government it is entirely rational to select personnel in this fashion. From this viewpoint the nature of the bureaucracy is essentially an outcome rather than a cause of policy.

Examples of interlocking government-business leadership are numerous even below the highest decision-making echelons. In the Department of the Interior, to cite one instance, the large majority of key personnel in the Office of Oil and Gas or the Petroleum Administration for Defense in the decade after 1946 came from the industry, often just on loan for fixed periods of time. These bodies, which are largely a continuation of wartime boards, have permitted the regulation of the petroleum industry via governmental agencies, free from the threat of antitrust prosecution and for the welfare of the industry. Pleased with the arrangement, the industry has supplied many of the key administrators and consultants the government needs on a no-compensation basis.

No less typical is the Business and Defense Services Administration of the Department of Commerce (BDSA), created in the fall of 1953. Composed of 184 industry groups during the period 1953–55, the BDSA committees dealt with a vast number of goods and the problems of their industry, recommending action to the government that was the basis of profitable action and regulation of various economic sectors. These ranged from the division of government purchases among industry members to the review of proposed Export-Import Bank and World Bank loans for the construction of competing industries abroad. In effect, BDSA committees have served themselves via the government in a classic fashion, the precedents for which range back to the early nineteenth century. In this regard they are no different in genesis and function from the federal regulatory movement initiated in 1887.

At every level of the administration of the American state, domestically and internationally, business serves as the fount of critical assumptions or goals and strategically placed personnel. But that this leadership in foreign and military affairs, as integrated in the unified hands of men who are both political and economic leaders, comes from the most powerful class interests is a reflection as well as the cause of the nature and objectives of American power at home and abroad. It is the expression of the universality of the ideology and the interests and material power of the physical resources of the ruling class of American capitalism, the latter being sufficient should consensus break down. The pervasiveness of this ideological power in American society and its measurable influence on mass culture, public values, and political opinions is the most visible reality of modern American life to the contemporary social analyst. It means that one can only assess the other institutional structures, the military in particular, in relation to the predominance of the economic ruling class which is the final arbiter and beneficiary of the existing structure of American society and politics at home and of United States power in the world.

*   *   *

## A Theory of United States Global Role

In their brilliant essay on the political economy of nineteenth-century British imperialism, John Gallagher and Ronald Robinson have described a process that parallels the nature of the United States expansion after 1945:

> Imperialism, perhaps, may be defined as a sufficient political function of this process of integrating new regions into the expanding economy; its character is largely decided by the various and changing relationships between the political and economic elements of expansion in any particular region and time. Two qualifications must be made. First, imperialism may be only indirectly connected with economic integration in that it sometimes extends beyond areas of economic development, but acts for their strategic protection. Secondly, although imperialism is a function of economic expansion, it is not a necessary function. Whether imperialist phenomena show themselves or not, is determined not only by the factors

*of economic expansion, but equally by the political and social organization of the regions brought into the orbit of the expansive society, and also by the world situation in general.*

*It is only when the politics of these new regions fail to provide satisfactory conditions for commercial or strategic integration and when their relative weakness allows, that power is used imperialistically to adjust those conditions. Economic expansion, it is true, will tend to flow into the regions of maximum opportunity, but maximum opportunity depends as much upon political considerations of security as upon questions of profit. Consequently, in any particular region, if economic opportunity seems large but political security small, then full absorption into the extending economy tends to be frustrated until power is exerted upon the state in question. Conversely, in proportion as satisfactory political frameworks are brought into being in this way, the frequency of imperialist intervention lessens and imperialist control is correspondingly relaxed. It may be suggested that this willingness to limit the use of paramount power to establishing security for trade is the distinctive feature of the British imperialism of free trade in the nineteenth century, in contrast to the mercantilist use of power to obtain commercial supremacy and monopoly through political possession.*

In today's context, we should regard United States political and strategic intervention as a rational overhead charge for its present and future freedom to act and expand. One must also point out that however high that cost may appear today, in the history of United States diplomacy specific American economic interests in a country or region have often defined the national interest on the assumption that the nation can identify its welfare with the profits of some of its citizens—whether in oil, cotton, or bananas. The costs to the state as a whole are less consequential than the desires and profits of specific class strata and their need to operate everywhere in a manner that, collectively, brings vast prosperity to the United States and its rulers.

Today it is a fact that capitalism in one country is a long-term physical and economic impossibility without a drastic shift in the distribution of the world's income. Isolated, the United States would face those domestic backlogged economic and social problems and weaknesses it has deferred confronting for over two decades, and its disappearing strength in a global context would soon open the door to the internal dynamics which might jeopardize the very existence of liberal corporate capitalism at home. It is logical to regard Vietnam, therefore, as the inevitable cost of maintaining United States imperial power, a step toward saving the future in something akin to its present form by revealing to others in the Third World what they too may encounter should they also seek to control their own development. That Vietnam itself has relatively little of value to the United States is all the more significant as an example of America's determination to hold the line as a matter of principle against revolutionary movements. What is at stake, according to the "domino" theory with which Washington accurately perceives the world, is the control of Vietnam's neighbors, Southeast Asia and, ultimately, Latin America.

The contemporary world crisis, in brief, is a by-product of United States response to Third World change and its own definitions of what it must do to preserve and expand its vital national interests. At the present moment, the larger relationships in the Third World economy benefit the United States, and it is this type of structure America is struggling to preserve. Moreover, the United States requires the option to expand to regions it has not yet penetrated, a fact which not only brings it into conflict with Third World revolutions but also with an increasingly powerful European capitalism. Where neocolonial economic penetration via loans, aid, or attacks on balanced economic development or diversification in the Third World are not sufficient to maintain stability, direct interventions to save local compradors and oligarchies often follow. Frequently such encroachments succeed, as in Greece and the Dominican Republic, but at times, such as Vietnam, it is the very process of intervention itself that creates its own defeat by deranging an already moribund society, polarizing options, and compelling men to choose— and to resist. Even the returns to the United States on partial successes have warranted the entire undertaking in the form not just of high profit ratios and exports, but in the existence of a vast world economic sector which supplies the disproportionately important materials without which American prosperity within its present social framework would eventually dry up.

The existing global political and economic structure, with all its stagnation and misery, has not only brought the United States billions but has made possible, above all, a vast power that requires total world economic integration not on the basis of equality but of domination. And to preserve this form of world is vital to the men who run the American economy and politics at the highest levels. If some of them now reluctantly believe that Vietnam was not the place to make the final defense against tides of unpredictable revolutionary change, they all concede that they must do it somewhere, and the logic of their larger view makes their shift on Vietnam a matter of expediency or tactics rather than of principle. All the various American leaders believe in global stability which they are committed to defend against revolution that may threaten the existing distribution of economic power in the world.

When the day arrives that the United States cannot create or threaten further Vietnams, the issue at stake will be no less than the power of the United States in the world. At that point, both the United States and the rest of the world will undergo a period of profound crises and trauma, at home as well as abroad, as the allocation of the earth's economic power is increasingly removed from American control. If, in the process of defending their prerogatives, the leaders of the United States during those trying years do not destroy the globe, piecemeal as in Vietnam or in a war with China or Russia, we shall be on the verge of a fundamentally new era for the United States and mankind. The elimination of that American hegemony is the essential precondition for the emergence of a nation and a world in which mass hunger, suppression, and war are no longer the inevitable and continuous characteristics of modern civilization.

Irving Louis Horowitz

# Capitalism, Communism, and Multinationalism

An advertisement in *The New York Times* (October 1, 1972), placed by the
World Development Corporation, read as follows:

*A well-known party is looking for revolutionary ideas. It may come as a surprise,
but the communists are no longer claiming they've invented every good idea under the sun. On the contrary, they're eagerly hoping that Westerners may have
invented a few before them. The fact is that the communists—in particular the
East Europeans—are building a broad consumer society. They're in a hurry. And
they're in the market for advanced technology in a staggering number of fields.
The point is this: if you own the patented or proprietary technology that East European countries need, you could work out some highly profitable arrangements.
Sell technology to the communists? Can it even be done? The answer is that today it finally can be done. And is being done. In fact, over the past couple of
years, major American corporations have been doing it with increasing frequency.
Naturally, the technology must be non-strategic. Exactly how do you go about it?
You go about it with infinite patience. As you can imagine, selling American technology in Eastern Europe is a highly complex economic, political and technical
problem. Obviously, it's absolutely crucial to develop the right contacts and the
right communication. That's where we, World Patent Development Corp. come
in. For years now, we've maintained close technological contacts with the proper
governmental agencies in all East European countries. Because of our unique position, we've been able to locate markets and negotiate licensing agreements for the
sale of almost every kind of technology. Conversely, we're also presiding over the
transfer of East European technology to the West. In fields ranging from syn-
thetic copolymers to pollution control equipment. From advanced textile equipment to natural cosmetics.*

Excerpted from Ideology and Utopia in the United States, 1956–1976 by Irving Louis
Horowitz. Copyright © 1977 by Irving Louis Horowitz. Reprinted by permission of the
author and Oxford University Press, Inc.

This is a far cry from Cold War rhetoric; and helps place in perspective the obvious thaw *cum* rapprochement reached between Nixon and Kissinger for the American side and Brezhnev and Kosygin for the Soviet side. The emergence of the multinational corporation is the paramount economic fact of the present epoch and helps to explain current trends in the political sociology of world relations.

*       *       *

## The Nature of Multinationalism

Definitions of the term "multinational corporation" vary. . . . Nonetheless, for the most part, there is agreement on the following operational guidelines:

(1) Multinationals are corporations that operate in at least six foreign nations.

(2) Multinationals are corporations whose foreign subsidiaries account for at least 10 to 20 percent of total assets, sales, or labor force.

(3) Multinationals have annual sales or incomes of more than 100 million dollars (which effectively reduces the number of firms we are dealing with to approximately 200, of which 75 percent are primarily affiliated with the United States).

(4) Multinationals have an above average rate of growth and profit margins when measured against exclusively national firms.

(5) Multinationals are found most often in high technology industries, specifically those that devote a high proportion of their resources to research, advertising, and marketing.

On the assumption that the term multinational may still be strange to some, let us try a simple definition: a multinational corporation is one that does a sizable portion of its business outside the borders of the nation in which it has its primary headquarters. . . .

*       *       *

## Multinationalism and the End of Classical Imperialism

The rise of multinationalism corresponds to a concomitant transformation of imperialist relations. What commenced as the classical military occupation of foreign territories in the preimperial, colonial period, shifted to the export of banking and industrial wealth owned by the advanced powers and exchanged for the mineral wealth and natural resources of the peripheral colonized area. Whatever the merits of economic arguments concerning the relative value of agricultural and industrial products, the historical fact is that underdeveloped areas were, and still are, characterized by an agrarian base dependent on export of raw materials and the import of finished goods and commodities. Over time this pattern has begun to break down, the first piece of evidence of this breakdown being the failure of the masses to participate in the selective distribution of commodities, creating huge riots and revolutions in overseas developing areas. Thus, the contradictions between the national middle classes and the rest of these underdeveloped societies subjected classical imperialism to intense pressures by indirection. National liberation and socialist movements of various types and structures simply invalidated the classical model of colonialism.

To stop the erosion of their international position, the imperial powers altered their strategies, and beyond that, altered their profit picture. Marx pointed out in *Das Kapital* that within a domestic context the percentage of profitability is less decisive than the maintenance of profits. The increase in product utilization is a means of stabilizing and increasing profits in absolute terms, in monetary amounts rather than in percentile units. Hence, capital-intensive industries permit less overt exploitation without a systemic collapse. This same phenomenon has occurred in an international context: a shift occurs lowering the percent of profits but not the actual flow of funds. The multinational corporations establish local participation in factory and industrial management, train local talent to assume tasks requiring special technical competence, move toward joint ownerships with local middle classes or local bureaucratic classes (if dealings are with the socialist bloc), transfer factories and technicians when necessary; and in short do everything other than surrender their positions as profit-making units operating in an overseas climate. This overseas climate has become increasingly antagonistic to the signs and symbols of imperial enterprises, while desperately demanding more of the goods and uses of these same foreign firms. Hence, the multinationals become involved in bridging the gap between revolutionary nationalism and establishment internationalism. They do this by acquiescing to the symbolic demands of nationalists and revolutionists, while satisfying the very real economic demands of the conservative middle-sector elements in Third World societies.

The rise of the multinational corporation has given increased weight to Lenin's initial focus on imperialism, albeit in a manner perhaps not entirely foreseeable by the master builder of Russian Bolshevism. At the turn of the twentieth century, the basic imperial powers engaged in banking-industrial capitalism were the United States, England, France, Germany, Japan, and Russia. After the Soviet revolution, the Marxists postulated that Russia would be out of the imperialist orbit for all time. After World War One it was further postulated that the imperialist powers would redivide Europe so as to limit and minimize German participation in the Imperial Club. After World War Two, this same set of theories further deduced that the back of Western European capitalism had been broken, and that certainly both German and Japanese capitalism had been brought to heel. Now, a quarter-century later, we have witnessed a certain Grand Restorationism, of which the multinational corporation is merely the advance guard. For what we now witness is precisely the same cluster of nations that prevailed at the turn of the century controlling the overwhelming bulk of the international economy. The economic mix has changed; it is now far more favorable to the United States than it was in 1900. But also, curiously, it is now more favorable to Japan and Germany than it was at the turn of the century.

After two immense world wars, both presumably involving, if not entirely defined by, the imperialist inner struggle, and after a presumed social revolution that shook the earth's foundations for ten days at least, we are faced with a curious similitude that takes us back to the century's starting point. This is not to suggest at all that the world has stood still. It is to say that the staying power of powerful nations has remained quite durable, whatever the rotation of political power may have been at any given time span within the twentieth century. One might say that all political revolutions have a very similar concern for the maintenance and eventual extension of economic dominion—a fact of life that was as true for German fascism and Japanese militarism as it is for Soviet communism and American capitalism. Here we have one of those long-run secular trends displaying the remarkable potency of economic factors in social life; whatever the exigencies of political game-playing may necessitate.

The multinationals, by serving to alter the fundamental relationships between the bourgeoisie of advanced countries and the bourgeoisie of the peripheral countries, have also served to change the terms of the international game. The difficulty with much Marxian thinking in the current era is the supposition that dependence and underdevelopment are the handmaidens of backwardness whereas in fact what one observes increasingly throughout the Third World is a correlation of dependence *and* development. And this is as true of Soviet penetration in Cuba as it is of United States' penetration in Brazil. For what is involved is the internationalization of the notion of the senior and junior partner arrangement, which more fittingly and accurately describes present developmental realities than does the conventional model of superordination and subordination. By internationalizing capital relations, multinationals have also internationalized class relationships. Obviously, the situation with Soviet satellites is more complex, since all trade and aid relations are filtered through a grid of political and military tradeoffs; yet the same principle clearly obtains. This means that multinationalism permits development while at the same time maintains a pattern of benign dependence.

This new situation is made perfectly plain by Richard Barnet in drawing our attention to the elimination of world war as a mixed blessing: one that permits world order within a multinationalist context sanctioned by the major powers.

*The essence of imperialism, regardless of the economic system from which it proceeds, is the unjust bargain. Human beings are used to serve ends that are not their own and in the process they pay more than they receive. The effort by two hundred multinational corporations (or twenty or two thousand) to rationalize* the world economy is part of an imperialist pattern of a new dimension. The mineral resources of the earth will soon be under the control of four centers of power: the predominantly American multinational corporations, the predominantly European multinational corporations, the Soviet state enterprise, and the Chinese state enterprise. If the attempt of a few hundred corporate managers in multinational private and state enterprises to determine how and where the resources of the whole earth shall be developed is successful, these members of the new international managerial class will for practical purposes be the first world conquerors in history.

While it is claimed by the apologists for the multinational corporation that the peaceful division of the world is the most "rational" way to exploit resources, expand productivity, and promote the good life for the greatest number, the interests of the great corporate units conflict with the basic human needs of a majority of the world's population. The supreme value pursued by the new breed of corporate managers is efficiency. This is an improvement, to be sure, over glory, machismo, and the excitement of winning, which, it will be recalled, are so important to the national security managers. For those who can make a contribution to the rationalized world economy there will be rewards. But the stark truth is that more than half of the population of the world is literally useless to the managers of the multinational corporation and their counterparts in Soviet and Chinese state enterprises, even as customers.

It need only be added that since these large masses of no importance to the multinational and state enterprises have no apparent mechanism for realizing their own aspirations through official channels, new forms of political and economic competition may emerge in this epoch.

## The Reemergence of Proletarian Internationalism as a Function of Multinationalism

The strangest, or certainly the least anticipated, consequence of the multinational corporation is the reappearance of militant unionism. The emergence of worker resistance to the multinationalist attempt to seek out the cheapest supply of labor as well as raw materials wherever that condition might obtain is still in an infant stage, but clearly on the rise. Highly paid West German optical workers must compete against low-paid workers from the same industries in Eastern Europe. Auto workers in Western Europe find themselves competing against workers in Latin America producing essentially the same cars. Chemical plants of wholly owned United States subsidiaries are put up in Belgium and England to capitalize on the cheaper wage scales of European chemical workers and to gain greater proximity to retail markets. Even American advertising agencies are protesting the manufacturing of commercials in Europe. Such stories can be repeated for every major multinational firm and every nation.

One may well appreciate the rationale offered by the multinationals. They can take advantage of the protectionist system of closed markets in the United States while pursuing an antiprotectionist approach for trading abroad.

They can thereby derive the payoffs of selling to the American worker at American market prices while employing workers overseas at lower European wage scales. Investment abroad is also a way to get beyond antitrust laws that apply fully within the United States but scarcely at all in other countries. As Gus Tyler has observed: "For all these reasons—cheap labor, tax advantages, protected markets, monopoly control—as well as for other reasons of proximity to materials or markets, the giant conglomerates of America are moving their investments massively overseas. The result has been a rising threat to American employment and trade: jobs have not kept up with either our growing population or market; exports have not kept up with an expanding world trade." In a fierce critique, he sees the situation created by multinationalism as destructive of nationalism no less than of unionism.

*The multinationals have turned this old-fashioned world topsy-turvey. The modern "cosmo-corporations" are stateless, reaching across national boundaries, often owned jointly by major corporate investors of several countries. By their integrated international organization, they have made the phrase "comparative advantage" for any nation a meaningless term. Capital, technology, management know-how, merchandizing, machinery, invention—all these "advantages" can be shipped anywhere anytime. Even raw material is hardly an advantage as multinationals of many nations move in on the lands that have natural resources, such as oil. The "advantages" offered by various locations are primarily "political," like low wages, tax benefits, protected markets, government subsidies or market monopolies.*

This new situation, whatever the merits or demerits of the rationalizing capacity of multinationals, has created a partially revivified working class that shows, unlike its responses to earlier periods, greater class solidarity than cross-class national solidarity. Certainly, in the major wars of the twentieth century, the working classes consistently lined up behind nationalism and patriotism and in so doing have frustrated just about every prediction made on their behalf by left-wing intellectuals. Now, precisely at that moment when so much left-oriented rhetoric has itself become infused with an antiworking-class bias, we bear witness to the emergence of proletarian militance; this time as a function of self-interest rather than lofty ideology.

The organization of working-class life is still along national lines; but when confronted with middle-class internationalism, i.e., as represented by the multinationals, it must either create new trade union mechanisms or revitalize old and existing ones.

*Foreign resentment against U.S. multinationals flares up most dangerously when these corporations do to the workers of other countries what they have been doing to American workers all along: shut down a plant for company reasons. Within two weeks, General Motors closed down a plant with 685 employees in Paris, because of Italian competition, and Remington Rand closed down a plant with 1,000 employees to relocate in Vienna. The French government—then under Charles de Gaulle—decided to get tough with the U.S. multinationals; so GM opened a plant in Belgium instead of France and proceeded to ship the product into France—duty free.*

It is intriguing to note how a relatively insular trade-union movement such as the British Trades Union Congress (TUC) has vigorously responded to multinationals as a threat. It has put forth demands for making union recognition a precondition for setting up foreign subsidiaries in the United Kingdom; and likewise to have organizations such as the Organization for Economic Cooperation and Development (OECD) serve as agencies for funneling and channeling working-class demands on wider multinationals. . . .

But while British responses have been legalist and proffered through government agencies, European workers on the mainland have become more direct and forthright in their dealings with multinational-led strike actions and corporate lockouts.

*The International Federation of Chemical and General Workers' Union has acted as a coordinating body for different unions in various countries in negotiations with St. Gobain, a French-owned glass manufacturing multinational. Some success for international action coordinated through International Trade Secretariats has been achieved; for example: In 1970, strikers at May and Baker, a British subsidiary of Rhone-Poulenc, won a 16 percent pay rise "largely due to large-scale international intervention" at the company's French headquarters and at other May and Baker plants in the Commonwealth. Peugeot workers in Founee threatened a 15-minute stoppage in 1968 to back 1,000 workers suspended in an Argentinian subsidiary. After two days, the company agreed to take back nearly all the suspended workers.*

This renewed working-class activity has had a stunning effect on East-West trade union relations. It is axiomatic that socialism does not tolerate or permit strikes since, in the doctrine of its founders, socialism is a workers' society, and a strike against the government is a strike against one's own interest. That such reasoning is a palpable hoax has never been denied. Indeed, the leaders of Poland, Hungary, and other East European states have become quite sensitized to such mass pressure from below. Yet the impact of this reasoning is that strike actions have been rare, and met most often with repressive measures. The concept of working-class international action between laborers in "capitalist" and "socialist" countries has been virtually nonexistent. Nevertheless, such is the force of multinationalism that even these deep political inhibitions are breaking down. We may be entering an era of working-class collaboration across systemic lines, not unlike the coalescence between the bourgeois West and bureaucratic East.

*     *     *

Several important features of this special variant of proletarian internationalism must be distinguished: (1) It cuts across national lines for the first time in the twentieth century. (2) It cuts across systemic lines, being less responsive now to Cold War calls for free labor or socialist labor than it ever was at any earlier time in the post-World War Two period. (3) The vanguard role in this effort is being assumed by the workers in the better-paid and better-organized sectors of labor; in the specialized craft sector more than in the assembly-line industrial sector. (4) While new mechanisms are being created to deal with multinational corporations, the more customary approach is to strengthen the bargaining position of available organizations, such as the International Metal Workers' Federation and the International Federation of Chemical and General Workers' Unions.

What we have then is an intensification of class competition, but on a scale and magnitude unlike the conventional national constraints. It is still difficult to demonstrate or to predict whether such class struggles can be as readily resolved short of revolution in the industrial areas as those in the previous epoch were resolved in the national areas. In effect, if Marxism as a triumphal march of socialism throughout the world has been thoroughly discredited, it manages to rise, phoenixlike, out of the bitter ashes of such disrepair. The intensification of class struggles at the international level remains muted by the comparative advantages of multinationalism to countries like Japan and the United States. But if such comparative advantages dissipate themselves over the long pull of time (and this is beginning to happen as less-developed nations begin to catch up), then the quality of class competition might well intensify.

## The Theory of Big-Power Convergence and Multinational Realities

Multinationalism has served to refocus attention on the theory of convergence: that particular set of assumptions that holds that over time the industrial and urbanizing tendencies of the United States and the Soviet Union will prevail over systemic and ideological differences and will form a convergence, or at least enough of a similitude, to prevent major grave international confrontations. The convergence theory does not postulate that the two systems will become identical but rather that what will take place is a sort of political twin-track coalition network. Convergence more nearly represents a parallelism than a true merging. In this sense, multinational corporation interpenetration is quite distinct from convergence, since what are involved are the linkages of the two superstates at the functional economic levels but continued disparity at the political organization level. In an interpenetration such as that being brought about by the multinationals, systems of society do indeed meet and cross over. The lines of intersection are clearly evident as the data show; and the implications of such a development extend far beyond a formal proof for any doctrine of political science or economics.

The evidence for the convergence theory has been generally made much stronger by the rise of multinationals. And without entering into an arid debate about whether capitalism and socialism can remain pure and noble if this can take place, the empirics of the situation are clear enough: the United States and the Soviet Union (whatever their economic systems can be called) have shown a remarkable propensity to fuse their interests at the economic level and collapse their differences at a diplomatic level, for the purpose of forming a new big-power coalition that dwarfs the dreams of Metternich for a United Europe in the nineteenth century. Indeed, we now have a situation in which the doctrine of national self-interest has been superseded by one of regional and even hemispheric spheres of domination by the two major world superpowers.

The issue of systemic convergence is certainly not new. The pros and cons of this debate have been well articulated by intellectuals and politicians alike. The existence of commonalities between the major political and economic powers has long been evident. Geographical size, racial and religious similitudes, even psychological properties of the peoples of the USA and the USSR, all conspire to fuse American and Soviet interests. What has been in dispute is whether such root commonalities are sufficient to overcome long-standing differences in the economic organization of society, ideological commitments, and political systems of domination. This argument remained largely unanswered and unanswerable as long as the mechanism, the lever, for expressing any functional convergence remained absent. The unique contribution of multinationalism to the debate over convergence between the major superpowers is precisely its functional rationality, its place in contemporary history as the Archimedean lever lifting both nations out of the Cold War. Multinational links take precedence over political differences in prosaic but meaningful ways. They serve to rationalize and standardize international economic relationships. They demand perfect interchangeability of parts; a uniform system of weights and measurements; common auditing languages for expression of world trade and commerce; standard codes for aircraft and airports, telephonic and telegraphic communications; and banking rules and regulations that are adhered to by all nations. Convergence takes place not so much by ideological proclamation (although there has even been some of this) but primarily by organizational fiat; that is, by seeming to hold ideological differences constant, while rotating every other factor in international relations.

What lies ahead? Even as we enter the multinational era, questions arise as to the efficacy of this resolution for world society. Some critics see the social structures of modern business as being in contradiction with the larger value complex of society, while crusaders see the multinational corporation as the beginning of a true internationalism. Most recently, it has been suggested that the multinationals may resolve certain issues in relationship to the underdeveloped regions and the Third World as a whole. . . .

\*    \*    \*

Multinationalism has played a major role in establishing détente as the central thrust in big-power settlements. Its doing so has profoundly lessened the bargaining power of smaller nations vis-à-vis the superpowers. But whatever problems this leaves in its wake, this myth-breaking development at least makes possible a more realistic international political climate.

## Pax Americana Plus Pax Sovietica:
## The Politics of Multinationalism

The politics of multinationalism is not so much an illustration of convergence as it is an example of pragmatic parallelism. One has only to compare and contrast the position of Michael Harrington on Nixon's program with Weisband and Franck's approach to Brezhnev's program to see how this parallelism operates—with or without a broad solution to theoretical disputations on convergence.

Harrington points out that underlying the Nixon-Kissinger position is a shared metaphysical belief that the division of the world is both necessary and desirable.

*Internationally, then Nixonism has a profoundly conservative, shrewd yet utterly flawed approach. It seeks a Metternichian arrangement among the superpowers, capitalist and communist, according to which change would be relegated to controllable channels. In pursuit of this goal it is, unlike the moralistic policy of Dulles, willing to strengthen the power of its enemies if only they will accept the model of a global equilibrium. Nixonism is rhetorically dedicated to the virtues of the global division of labor but actually committed to utilizing America's state power to socialize the enormous advantage of our corporations on the world market. . . . Capitalist collectivism, in other words, wants to make a deal with bureaucratic collectivism to preserve the status quo.*

Weisband and Franck, aside from assigning causal priority for this doctrine to the West, assert nonetheless that the Brezhnev approach to peaceful coexistence represents a similar attitude toward big-power sovereignty over smaller areas.

*The Brezhnev doctrine, which continues to govern the policies of the Warsaw Pact governments, to some degree represents a trade-off or division of the world by the Soviet Union and the United States into spheres of influence or "regional ghettos." Not that our policy-makers in Washington planned it that way: little or no evidence has been adduced to show that the U.S. government ever willfully intended to trade control over Latin America for recognition of absolute Soviet dominance over Eastern Europe. Nor can it be said that any actions we have taken in relation to Latin America are the same as Russia's brutal suppression of Czechoslovakia. . . . What we do wish to assert is that virtually every concept of the Brezhnev doctrine can be traced to an earlier arrogation of identical rights by the United States vis-à-vis Latin America. . . . it is important to realize that the search for new norms in the world must begin with a clear understanding that we, as much as the Russians, bear responsibility for conceptualizing the Brezhnev norms. . . . In the Soviet view, regional determination and prerogatives take precedence over those of the international community including the United Nations.*

Curiously enough, the connection between international politics and the rise of multinationalism was clearly articulated, even by the above prescient commentators on international affairs. Lesser analysts seem to prefer to think of the new Nixonism as some sort of magical mystery tour: a transformation of high spiritual beliefs into policy matters. My contention is that the current foreign-policy initiatives of Henry Kissinger derive directly from a new awareness of the consequences—political and economic—of the changes in corporate relationships brought about by the power of the multinationals. American policymakers have finally recognized that this industrial change has necessitated an end to the Cold War and the substitution of a new détente based on economic realities. President Nixon, throughout the 1972 year, clearly articulated such a geopolitical realignment based on economic realities.

As early as January, 1971, Nixon articulated the point of view that he sustained on his diplomatic initiatives in Moscow and Peking:

*We must remember that the only time in the history of the world that we had any extended periods of peace is when there has been a balance of power. It is when one nation becomes infinitely more powerful in relation to its potential competitor that the danger of war arises. So I believe in a world in which the United States is powerful. I think it would be a safer world and a better world if we have a strong, healthy United States, Europe, Soviet Union, China, and Japan, each balancing the other, not playing one against the other, an even balance.*

The peculiar linkage is China, since it alone has yet to participate fully in the multinational system. Further, it can be said to be by far the poorest of the countries with which power balance has to be sought. But with that admittedly crucial exception, and this can be argued to be a requirement of political trade-off preventing undue Soviet impact on the Western world and undue Japanese presence in the Eastern world, what Nixon has outlined is quite clearly the politics of multinationalism, and not of capitalism triumphant or socialism defeated. The trade and aid agreements between East and West during this period serve to confirm the accuracy of this appraisal. Even China is entering the multinational race with its increased sale of specialized consumer goods to the United States and its purchase from Boeing Aircraft of an international fleet of advanced jets.

This new Metternichian arrangement among the superpowers is precisely a repudiation of the earlier moral absolutism of anticommunism and anticapitalism. In a sense, and one step beyond an acknowledged end of the Cold War, this geopolitical redistribution may also solve a major problem of the multinational corporation, its transcendence of the limits and encumbrances placed by national sovereignty. By an international linkage of the superpowers, the problems of multinational regulation, which loom so large in the established literature, can be rationalized, if not entirely resolved, by appeals to commercial rationality rather than political sovereignty.

The thesis presented by George Kennan that the end of the Cold War came about as a result of a series of victories of the United States over the Soviet empire is simply untenable. The plain fact is that Stalinism was remarkably legalistic in its foreign policy, whatever its extralegalities were internally. Beyond that, the Soviet empire has neither shrunk nor disappeared. Current Soviet policy, especially as it affects Eastern Europe, can only be described as extremely aggressive. It is precisely the absence of victory, the existence of a thoroughly stalemated situation, that led the major powers to reconsider their collision course—a course that could threaten both empires at the expense of outsider factions in the Third World, China, and even nonaligned nations like India, waiting in the wings to pick up the pieces.

What has happened is that advances in both the political and social realms have come about in rapid succession as a result of the multinational economics; namely, arms control agreements, direct executive rapprochement, new trade and purchasing agreements, and exchanges of research and development technology in basic fields. These have signaled the real termination of the Cold War. Multinationalism, in its very extranational capacities, has served to rationalize this new foreign-policy posture on both sides. Terms like "have" versus "have-not" states have come to replace and displace an older rhetoric of capitalism versus socialism, not simply as an expression of the uneven international distribution of wealth, but as an indication of the current sponginess of any concept of capitalism or socialism. Precisely the inability of the Cold War to be resolved through victory has led to a feeling on the part of elite leadership in powerful states that the coalition of the big against the small, of wealthy against impoverished, and even of white-led nations against colored-led nations can alone guarantee the peace of the world and the tranquility of potential sources of rival power like China in the East or Germany and France in the West. With one fell swoop the mutual winding down of the Cold War settles the hash of rival powers and determines the subordinate position of the Third World for the duration of the century. The cement for this new shift in fundamental policy is the multinational corporation. An end to ideology? No. An end to capitalist and communist rhetoric? Perhaps. An end to the Cold War epoch? Probably.

Walter LaFeber

# The Last War,
# the Next War, and
# the New Revisionists

As if to prove Lord Acton's dictum that "the strong man with the dagger is followed by the weak man with the sponge," a remarkable rewriting of the Vietnam war's history is under way. It is especially remarkable because the new revisionists are either ignorant of American policy in the conflict or have chosen to forget past policies in order to mold present opinion. More generally, they are rewriting the record of failed military interventionism in the 1950 to 1975 era in order to build support for interventionism in the 1980s. More specifically, the new revisionists are attempting to shift historical guilt from those who instigated and ran the war to those who opposed it.

Immediately after South Vietnam fell in 1975, Secretary of State Henry Kissinger urged Americans to forget the quarter-century-long war. That advice was no doubt related to his other concern at the time: committing U.S. military power to Angola and the Horn of Africa. Congress had fortunately learned from experience and stopped Kissinger from involving the country in an African Vietnam. The next year, however, influential authors began to discover that Vietnam's history was more usable than Kissinger had imagined. General William Westmoreland, who commanded U.S. forces during the worst months of fighting in the 1960s, set the line when he argued in his memoirs and public speeches that the conflict was not lost on the battlefield, but at home where overly sensitive politicians followed a "no-win policy" to accommodate "a misguided minority opposition . . . masterfully manipulated by Hanoi and Moscow." The enemy, Westmoreland claimed, finally won "the war politically in Washington."

Part of Westmoreland's thesis was developed with more scholarship and cooler prose by Leslie H. Gelb and Richard K. Betts in *The Irony of Vietnam: the System Worked.* It was not the "system"—that is, the cold war national security establishment—that failed, the authors argued. Failure was to be blamed on the American people, who never understood the war and finally tired of it, and on the Presidents who supinely followed the people. Thus the "system" worked doubly well: the professional bureaucrats gave the correct advice, as they were paid to do, and the Presidents followed the public's wishes, as democratic theory provides that they should.

Westmoreland's argument that the antiwar groups wrongly labeled Vietnam an illegal and immoral conflict was developed by Guenter Lewy's *America in Vietnam*. Lewy, however, was so honest that his own evidence destroyed the thesis. Although he wrote that U.S. soldiers followed civilized modes of war even though this sometimes meant virtual suicide, Lewy also gave striking examples of how the troops ruthlessly destroyed villages and civilians. "It is well to remember," he wrote, "that revulsion at the fate of thousands of hapless civilians killed and maimed" because of American reliance upon high-technology weapons "may undercut the willingness of a democratic nation to fight communist insurgents." That becomes a fair judgment when "thousands" is changed to "hundreds of thousands." Lewy nevertheless held grimly to his thesis about the war's morality and legality, even as he reached his closing pages: "the simplistic slogan 'No more Vietnams' not only may encourage international disorder, but could mean abandoning basic American values." It apparently made little difference to Lewy that those basic American values had been ravaged at My Lai, or at Cam Ne, where a Marine commander burned down a village and then observed in his after-action report that "It is extremely difficult for a ground commander to reconcile his tactical mission and a people-to-people program." Lewy's conclusions, not his evidence, set a tone that was widely echoed, particularly after the foreign policy crises of late 1979.

The Soviet invasion of Afghanistan was seized upon with almost audible sighs of relief in some quarters. *Commentary*, which had publicly introduced Lewy's argument in 1978, published a series of essays in early 1980 that developed some of his conclusions, especially the view that if the Vietnam experience inhibited future U.S. interventions, it "could mean abandoning basic American values." In an essay that thoughtfully explored the meaning of his own antiwar protests in the 1960s, Peter Berger nevertheless drew the conclusion that the American defeat in Vietnam "greatly altered" the world balance of power, and that "American power has dramatically declined, politically as well as militarily." Charles Horner condemned President Jimmy Carter's early belief that Vietnam taught us the limits of U.S. power. "That view," Horner claimed, "is the single greatest restraint on our capacity to deal with the world, and that capacity will not much increase unless the view behind it is changed, thoroughly and profoundly." Horner did his best to reinterpret the meaning of Vietnam, but it was *Commentary's* editor, Norman Podhoretz, who best demonstrated how history could be rewritten to obtain desired conclusions.

"Now that Vietnam is coming to be seen by more and more people as an imprudent effort to save Indochina from the horrors of Communist rule rather than an immoral intervention or a crime," Podhoretz wrote in the March 1980 issue, "the policy out of which it grew is also coming to be seen in a new light." He believed that the "policy—of defending democracy [sic] wherever it existed, or of holding the line against the advance of Communist totalitarianism by political means where possible and by military means when necessary," was based on the Wilsonian idea that "in the long run," U.S. interests depended on " 'the survival and the success of liberty' in the world as a whole." This revisionist view of Vietnam, Podhoretz argued, is helping to create a "new nationalism"—the kind of outlook that "Woodrow Wilson appealed to in seeking to 'make the world safe for democracy' and that John F. Kennedy echoed."

Podhoretz's grasp of historical facts is not reassuring; the essay has three major errors in its first three pages. George A. Carver, Jr.'s, essay subtitled "The Teachings of Vietnam," in the July 1980 issue of *Harper's*, only adds to that problem. An old C.I.A. hand who was deeply involved in Vietnam policy planning, Carver is identified in *Harper's* only as "a senior fellow" at Georgetown University's Center for Strategic and International Studies. That identification is nevertheless of note, for the Center serves as an important source of personnel and ideas for what passes as Ronald Reagan's foreign policy program. In the article, Carver set out to "dispel Vietnam's shadows" so the United States could again exercise great power and influence. When he mentioned earlier policy, Carver simply postulated that South Vietnam fell to North Vietnamese conventional forces, not to "any popular rebellion," and that "the press and media, and their internal competitive imperatives" misrepresented the real progress the U.S. forces were making in the war. Beyond that, the analysis consists of empty generalizations (Americans are encumbered in their foreign policy by "theological intensity" and "childlike innocence"), and it climaxes with the insight that "the world is cruel."

Read closely, Carver's warning about the dangers of "theological intensity" contradicts Podhoretz's call for a new Wilsonianism. But in the wake of the Iranian and Afghanistan crises, few read these calls to the ramparts of freedom very closely. The essays were more valuable for their feelings than for their historical accuracy. The new revisionists wanted to create a mood, not recall an actual past, and their success became dramatically apparent when that highly sensitive barometer of popular feelings, commercial television, quickly put together a new sitcom on the war, "The Six O'Clock Follies." One reviewer labeled it a "gutlessly cynical comedy," signaling that "suddenly we are supposed to be able to laugh at Vietnam." As the *Washington Post's* critic observed, however, since the conflict has "been deemed a safe zone . . . all three networks have Vietnam sitcoms in the works" for 1980–1981. Television was placing its seal of approval on a revisionism that promised to be commercially as well as ideologically satisfying.

Given this new mood, it was natural that those who wielded, or planned to wield, power were also prepared to help wring the sponge. In 1978 Zbigniew Brzezinski had lamented privately to Senate staff members that the floundering administration needed a *Mayaguez* incident so Carter, as Ford had in 1975, could get tough with Communists (preferably, apparently, from a small country), and rally Americans behind a battle flag. By the end of 1979, Carter had not one but two such opportunities with the Iranian hostage issue and the Soviet invasion of Afghanistan, and as usual Americans indeed closed ranks behind the President. In mid-December, Brzezinski observed that the country was finally getting over its post-Vietnam opposition to military spending and overseas intervention.

Three months later, Ronald Reagan, in his only major foreign policy speech prior to the Republican Convention, urged a return to Wilsonianism— what one reporter characterized as a belief that Americans have "an inescapable duty to act as the tutor and protector of the free world in confronting . . . alien ideologies." To carry out this mission, Reagan proclaimed, "we must rid ourselves of the 'Vietnam syndrome.'" He of course meant the old "syndrome," not the new syndrome of the revisionists that the war was to be admired for its intent if not its outcome. A frustrated job seeker at the Republican Convention best captured the effects of the new revisionism. A reporter teased Henry Kissinger about his prediction in the early 1970s that if the war did not end well for Americans there would be a fierce right-wing reaction. "It turned out just about the way I predicted it would," Kissinger replied. The former Secretary of State, however, contributed to the mood that threatened to confine him to academia. In recent writings and speeches, Kissinger has argued that if the Watergate scandal had not driven Nixon from office, South Vietnam would not have been allowed to fall. His claim cannot, of course, be completely disproved, but it is totally unsupported by either the post-1973 military and political situation in Vietnam, or the anti-war course of American policies, including Nixon's, that appeared long before the Watergate scandal paralyzed the administration.

The arguments of the new revisionists—or the new nationalists, as some prefer to be called (in perhaps unconscious reference to the New Nationalism of Theodore Roosevelt and Herbert Croly that pledged an imperial "Big Stick" foreign policy)—dominated the foreign policy debates and, indeed, the Carter-Brzezinski foreign policies in early 1980. Because those arguments rest heavily on interpretations of the Vietnam conflict, their use of the war's history deserves analysis. This can be done on two levels: the new revisionists' explicit claims, and the events they choose to ignore.

The most notable explicit theme is captured by Westmoreland's assertion that the war was lost because of pressure from a "misguided minority opposition" at home, or by Peter Berger's more careful statement that "the anti-war movement was a primary causal factor in the American withdrawal from Indochina." Since at least the mid-1960s, detailed public opinion polls have existed that show that Americans supported a tough policy in Vietnam.

In this, as in nearly all foreign policies, the public followed the President. As Herbert Y. Schandler concluded after his careful study of public opinion between 1964 and 1969, "If the administration is using increasing force, the public will respond like hawks; if it is seeking peace, the public responds like doves." When Lyndon Johnson tried to convince doubters by whipping out the latest opinion polls showing support for the war, he did not have to make up the figures. George Ball has testified that the antiwar protests only "dug us in more deeply" and intensified the administration's determination to win. Ball, who served as Under Secretary of State under Johnson, rightly calculated that "only late in the day did widespread discontent . . . appreciably slow the escalation of the war." Even those who dissented in the 1960s were more hawk than dove. Richard Scammon and Ben Wattenberg's analysis of the 1968 election concluded that a plurality of the Democrats who voted for Eugene McCarthy in the primaries supported George Wallace in November, and that finding is corroborated by polls revealing that a majority of those who opposed the conduct of the war also opposed protests against the war. Westmoreland's "misguided minority opposition" was of significantly less importance than a much larger group that wanted him to have whatever he needed to end the war. It simply is not true, as Barry Goldwater claimed at the 1980 Republican Convention, that the "will" to win the war was missing in the 1960s.

By 1970–1971, antiwar opposition had increased, but it did not stop Nixon from expanding the conflict into Cambodia and Laos. One statistic stands out: before Nixon sent in the troops, 56 percent of college-educated Americans wanted to "stay out" of Cambodia, and after he committed the forces, 50 percent of the same group supported the Cambodian invasion. When Nixon carpet-bombed North Vietnam two years later and for the first time mined the North's ports, 59 percent of those polled supported the President, and only 24 percent opposed him, even though it was clear that the mining could lead to a confrontation with the Russians and Chinese, whose ships used the harbors.

The effectiveness of the antiwar movement has been greatly overrated by the new revisionists, and the movement has consequently served as the scapegoat for them as well as for the national security managers whose policies failed in Vietnam. Given the new revisionist arguments, it needs to be emphasized that the United States lost in Vietnam because it was defeated militarily, and that that defeat occurred because Americans could not win the war without destroying what they were fighting to save—or, alternatively, without fighting for decades while surrendering those values at home and in the Western alliance for which the cold war was supposedly being waged. The antiwar protesters only pointed up these contradictions; they did not create them.

The new revisionists argue that the nation has largely recovered from the disaster. Carl Gershman writes that "as the polls reveal, the American people have now overwhelmingly rejected the ideas of the new [Carter-Vance-

Young] establishment." The strategy of the post-Vietnam "establishment" is to contain communism only in selected areas, and by using nonmilitary means if possible. The polls actually reveal considerable support for this strategy. In January 1980, after the invasion of Afghanistan, a CBS/*New York Times* survey showed that about two-fifths of those polled wanted to respond with nonmilitary tactics, two-fifths wanted to "hold off for now," and less than one-fifth favored a military response. Lou Harris discovered that within six weeks after the seizure of the hostages in Iran, support for military retaliation dropped off sharply. Quite clearly, if the new nationalists hope to whip up public sentiment for using military force wherever they perceive "democracy" to be threatened, they have much work yet to do. Most Americans have not overwhelmingly rejected nonmilitary responses, even after being shaken by the diplomatic earthquakes of 1979–1980. And they appear too sophisticated to agree with Podhoretz's Wilsonian assumption that "American interests in the long run [depend] on the survival and the success of liberty in the world as a whole." A majority of Americans seem to agree with that part of the post-Vietnam "establishment" represented by Vance and Young that it is wiser to trust nationalisms in the Third World than to undertake a Wilsonian crusade to rescue those nationalisms for an American-defined "liberty."

There is a reason for this confusion among new revisionist writers. They focus almost entirely on the Soviet Union instead of on the instability in Third World areas that the Soviets have at times turned to their own advantage. Such an approach allows the new revisionists to stress military power rather than the political or economic strategies that are most appropriate for dealing with Third World problems. The new nationalists, like the old, pride themselves on being realists in regard to power, but their concept of power is one-dimensional. Once this military dimension becomes unusable, nothing is left. A direct military strategy is appropriate for dealing with the Soviets in certain cases—for example, if the Red Army invaded Western Europe or Middle East oil fields. That strategy, however, has existed since the days of Harry Truman; the Vietnam war, regardless of how it is reinterpreted, has nothing new to teach us about that kind of massive response. A quarter-century ago, when the United States took its first military steps into Vietnam, Reinhold Niebuhr warned that the policy placed "undue reliance on purely military power" and therefore missed the fundamental political point: a U.S. military response was incapable of ending "the injustices of [Asia's] decaying feudalism and the inequalities of its recent colonialism." Niebuhr's advice was of course ignored. The supposed realists of the day proceeded to commit military power in Vietnam—*to contain China*. For, in the mid-1960s, China was the villain for the national security managers, as the Soviets are now for the new revisionists.

The reason for the failure of U.S. military power was not that it was severely limited. Lyndon Johnson bragged that he put 100,000 men into Vietnam in just one hundred and twenty days. Those troops were supported by the most powerful naval and air force ever used in Asia. Laos became the most heavily bombed country in history, North Vietnam's ports and cities were bombed and mined almost yard by yard, and Nixon dropped a ton of bombs on Indochina for every minute of his first term in the White House. Neither the will nor the power was missing. As Michael Herr wrote in *Dispatches,* "There was such a dense concentration of American energy there, American and essentially adolescent, if that energy could have been channeled into anything more than noise, waste and pain, it would have lighted up Indochina for a thousand years." Vietnam provides a classic lesson in the misuse of military power, but that lesson is being overlooked by the new revisionists.

And if they have misunderstood the conflict's central political and military features, so have the new revisionists lost sight of the historical context. They stress that Vietnam caused the decline of American power. It is quite probable, however, that when historians look back with proper prospective on the last half of the twentieth century, they will conclude that U.S. foreign policy problems in the 1970s and 1980s resulted not from the Vietnam experience, but more generally from political misperception and from an overestimation of American power. The *hubris* produced by the American triumph in the Cuban missile crisis contributed to such misestimation, but the problems also resulted from the failure to understand that U.S. power began a relative decline in the late 1950s and early 1960s. It was during those earlier years that the American economy and international trade began a decline that only accelerated—not started—in the 1970s; that such important allies as Japan and West Germany directly attacked American markets and helped to undermine the dollars; that the Western alliance displayed its first signs of slipping out of Washington's control; and that the Third World rapidly multiplied its numbers and decided—as the creation of OPEC in 1960 demonstrated—that it no longer had to join either one of the superpower camps. Future historians will consequently see the Vietnam war as one result, not a cause, of the relative decline of American power that began in the late 1950s. They will also probably conclude that space ventures, and the achievement of independence by nearly one hundred nations in the Third World, were of greater historical significance than the Vietnam conflict or the U.S.-USSR rivalry that obsesses the new revisionists.

Even with their narrow focus on the lessons of Vietnam, it is striking how much the new revisionists omit from their accounts of the war. They say relatively little about the South Vietnamese. The war is viewed as an eyeball-to-eyeball confrontation between Americans and Communists, and the turn comes when the Americans, undone by what Carver calls their "childlike innocence," blink. This approach resembles watching two football teams but not noticing the ball that is being kicked and passed around. The new revisionists have down-played the inability of the South Vietnamese to establish a stable and effective government amid a massive U.S. buildup, the

Vietnamese hatred for the growing American domination, and the massive desertions from the South's army in 1966–1967, even when the U.S. forces arrived to help. As early as 1966, non-Communist student leaders accurately called the country's presidential elections "a farce directed by foreigners." By 1971, a Saigon newspaper ran a daily contest in which readers submitted stories of rape or homicide committed by Americans. As Woodrow Wilson learned in 1919, some people just do not want to be saved—at least by outsiders with whom they have little in common.

The new revisionists also overlook the role the allies played in Vietnam. There is a good reason for this omission: of the forty nations tied to the United States by treaties, only four—Australia, New Zealand, South Korea, and Thailand—committed any combat troops. The major European and Latin American allies refused to send such forces. We later discovered that the South Koreans, whom Americans had saved at tremendous cost in 1950, agreed to help only after Washington bribed them with one billion dollars of aid. The key Asian ally, Japan, carefully distanced itself from the U.S. effort. This was especially bitter for American officials, for Truman and Eisenhower had made the original commitment to Vietnam in part to keep the area's raw materials and markets open for the Japanese. Relations between Tokyo and Washington deteriorated rapidly. When Lyndon Johnson asked whether he could visit Japan in 1966, the answer came back, "inconceivable." An article in the authoritative *Japan Quarterly* stated that if the United States became involved in another war with China, divisions in Japanese public opinion "would split the nation in two" and lead to "disturbances approaching a civil war in scale."

As Jimmy Carter admitted in early 1980, the United States needs strong support from allies if it hopes to contain the Soviets in the Middle East. It would be well, therefore, to note carefully the allied view of U.S. policy in Vietnam and elsewhere before embarking on a Wilsonian crusade to make "democracy" safe everywhere. Having chosen to ignore the lesson that Vietnam teaches about the allies, the new revisionists resemble traditional isolationists, who, as scholars have agreed, were characterized by a desire for maximum freedom of action, minimum commitment to other nations ("no entangling alliances"), and a primary reliance on military force rather than on the compromises of political negotiations.

Finally, these recent accounts neglect the war's domestic costs. The new revisionists stress the decline of the American "will" to win, but they say little about how the economic disasters and a corrupted presidency produced by the war influenced that "will." As early as January 1966, Lyndon Johnson admitted that "Because of Vietnam we cannot do all that we should, or all that we would like to do" in building a more just society at home. As the phrase went at the time, Americans—those "people of plenty"—suddenly discovered they could not have both guns and butter. The butter, or, more generally, the Great Society program, was sacrificed. A Pentagon analysis drawn up under the direction of Secretary of Defense Clark Clifford after the

1968 Tet offensive faced the problem squarely. It concluded that militarily the war could not be won, "even with the 200,000 additional troops" requested by Westmoreland. A drastic escalation, moreover, would result not only in "increased defiance of the draft," but in "growing unrest in the cities because of the belief that we are ignoring domestic problems." A "domestic crisis of unprecedented proportions" threatened. If the new revisionists and Reagan Republicans plan to manipulate the war's history to obtain higher defense budgets and unilateral commitments overseas, they should discuss this crucial characteristic of the war's course: it was determined less by campus protesters than by the growing realization that the costs worsened the conditions of the poorest and most discriminated against in American society until an "unprecedented" crisis loomed. Clifford turned against the war after businessmen he respected suddenly became scared and dovish. Clifford learned, but there is little evidence that the new revisionists understand the choices that were embedded in what they dismiss as the "Vietnam syndrome."

As persons who attack centralized power in the federal government, the new revisionists and the Reagan Republicans should at least discuss the effect of Vietnam on the imperial presidency. They could note, for example, that nothing centralizes power more rapidly than waging the cold war militarily, unless it is waging hot war in Korea and Vietnam. In 1967, Under Secretary of State Nicholas Katzenbach told the Senate that the power given by the Constitution to Congress to declare war was "an outmoded phraseology." In 1969–1972, Nixon used "national security" as the rationale for ordering a series of acts that resulted in nearly forty criminal indictments. Vietnam raised the central question in American foreign policy: How can the nation's interests be defended without destroying the economic and political principles that make it worth defending? In their extensive study of Vietnam, the new revisionists have chosen to ignore that question.

They have instead concentrated on an objective that is as simple as it is potentially catastrophic: the removal of the restraints of history, so that the next war can be waged from the start with fewer limitations. They are offering a particular interpretation of the last war, so the next war can be fought differently. This purpose helps explain why these writers stress the narrow military aspects of the war and ignore the larger problems of historical context, the Western allies, economic costs, and political corruption. Westmoreland again set the tone with his remark that "If we go to war . . . we need heed the old Oriental saying, 'It takes the full strength of a tiger to kill a rabbit' and use appropriate force to bring the war to a timely end." In his reassessment of the tragedy, Ambassador Robert Komer condemned the "institutional factors—bureaucratic restraints" that made success impossible. Lewy argued that the struggle was considered a mistake at the time because of "the conviction that the war was not being won and apparently showed little prospect of coming to a successful conclusion." If only the restraints had been lifted, the new revisionists imply, the war—which they consider morally and politically justified—could have been fought to a successful conclusion. This inference is drawn with little attention to either the inherent contradictions in Vietnam military strategy (for example, that villages had to be destroyed to be saved) or the nonmilitary aspects of the conflict. It comes perilously close to an end-justifies-the-means argument.

By trying to make the last war more acceptable, the new revisionists are asking us to make the next war legitimate, even before we know where it will be or what it will be fought over. A Chinese official once told Henry Kissinger that "One should not lose the whole world just to gain South Vietnam." Nor, it might be added, should men with sponges try to legitimize their global cold-war policies by whitewashing the history of the war in South Vietnam.

## SUGGESTIONS FOR FURTHER READING

A short and readable interpretive survey that attacks Americans' moralistic approach to foreign policy is George F. Kennan, *American Diplomacy, 1900–1950* (Chicago, 1953). A scholar and career diplomat, Kennan played an instrumental role in American policy formation after World War II. Kennan's influence is clearly reflected in the work of Spanier, part of which is reprinted above. For a related view emphasizing post-World War II foreign policy, see Hans J. Morgenthau, *In Defense of the National Interest* (New York, 1951). The notions of idealism and realism in American diplomacy are surveyed perceptively by Robert E. Osgood, *Ideals and Self-Interest in America's Foreign Relations* (Chicago, 1953).

In two influential books, William Appleman Williams stresses the connection between domestic economic development and diplomacy: *The Tragedy of American Diplomacy* (Cleveland, 1959; revised edition, New York, 1962) and *The Roots of the Modern American Empire* (New York, 1969). Important also is C. Wright Mills, *The Power Elite* (New York, 1956).

The conflict of opinion discussed here may be followed in detailed studies of other periods. For the period leading up to the Spanish-American War, see Walter LaFeber, *The New Empire* (Ithaca, 1963), which considers economic developments; and Julius W. Pratt, *Expansionists of 1898* (Baltimore, 1936), which denies the influence of the business community. Charles C. Tansill, *America Goes to War* (New York, 1938), emphasizes economic factors that brought the United States into World War I, while Ernest R. May, *World War and American Isolation, 1914–1917* (Cambridge, Mass. 1959), minimizes economics.

Ernest R. May has written a perceptive bibliographical essay, "Emergence to World Power," in John Higham, *The Reconstruction of American History* (New York, 1962). A short, but useful annotated bibliography dealing with the post-World War II period is included in John Spanier's *American Foreign Policy Since World War II* (6th revised edition; New York, 1977). See also Alexander De Conde, *American Diplomatic History in Transformation* (1976), a pamphlet published by the American Historical Association's Service Center for Teachers of History.

Robert A. Divine, ed., *American Foreign Policy Since 1945* (New York, 1969); Walter LaFeber, *America, Russia and the Cold War, 1945–1966* (New

York, 1967); David Halberstam, *The Best and the Brightest* (New York, 1972); and Daniel Yerkin, *Shattered Peace: Origins of the Cold War and the National Security State* (Boston, 1972), provide various approaches to recent American foreign policy.

There is a growing literature on the multinational corporation. For examples from very different points of view, see Raymond Vernon, *Sovereignty at Bay: The Multinational Spread of U.S. Enterprise* (New York, 1971); the same author's *Storm Over the Multinationals* (Cambridge, Mass., 1977); and Ernest Mandel, *Europe versus America? Contradictions of Imperialism* (London, 1970). A fine historical survey of the rise of American multinational companies is Mira Wilkins, *Emergence of Multinational Enterprise: American Business Abroad from the Colonial Era to 1914* (Cambridge, Mass., 1970), and the same author's continuation of this survey in *The Maturing of Multinational Enterprise: American Business Abroad from 1914–1970* (Cambridge, Mass., 1974). Richard J. Barnet and Ronald Müller, *Global Reach: The Power of the Multinational Corporations* (New York, 1974), is a persuasive popular account. Stephen E. Ambrose, *Rise to Globalism: American Foreign Policy, 1938–1980* (New York, 1983), is a provocative account of recent American policy.

* Available in paperback edition.

# 10

# Liberalism and the Turbulent 1960s

The optimism generated by the victory over fascism quickly gave way to a combination of frustration, fear, and anger as the nation faced the uncertainties of the post–World War II years. The end of wartime controls and the slowness of conversion from wartime to peacetime production meant skyrocketing prices and shortages. The war had brought prosperity, but those who had lived through the hardships of the Great Depression wondered if prosperity could be sustained once the war was over. Even more frightening was the prospect of another world war. The alliance with the Soviet Union collapsed into a crisis-ridden cold war, and then, in 1950, just five years after the end of World War II, the United States entered a hot war in Korea.

Uncertainties and fears led to a polarization in politics. Disturbed by a cold war that seemed impossible to end and by a war in Korea that could not be won, some Americans imagined that the nation's problems stemmed from subversive agents who were undermining American democracy. New Deal liberalism was put on the defensive when rightist organizations linked it to Communism and labeled any criticism or dissent as subversion. In the mid-fifties, Senator Joseph McCarthy led a witch hunt designed to search out the Communists in government, but he succeeded only in threatening the basic American rights of free speech and free association. Harry Truman, who became President after the death of Franklin D. Roosevelt, promised to extend the New Deal reforms, but he was unable to stem the conservative tide. Liberals took heart when Truman won an upset victory over Thomas Dewey in 1948, but he had little success in getting Congress to extend the social legislation of the New Deal.

The election of General Dwight D. Eisenhower in 1952 appeared to usher in a period of conservatism, complacency, and conformity. Both the left and the right collapsed, and there was a noticeable absence of any meaningful ideological conflict in American politics. Prosperity continued and seemed to be the answer to all of America's problems. Our stability and prosperity were in marked contrast to the situation in the rest of the world, and seemed to signal the beginning of an era of American supremacy. A few complained of the "silent generation" of American youth and of the conformity of "organization men" in their gray flannel suits, but many more celebrated the beginning of an "American Century."

But beneath the smug conservatism was a growing restiveness. By the late 1950s there were signs of fading optimism: American economic growth was slowing; the Russians launched a space vehicle before the United States was capable of doing so; prosperity turned out to have been for middle- and upper-class whites only; and democracy was reserved for white conformists.

John F. Kennedy's narrow victory over Richard Nixon in 1960 brought a new era of idealism and change but at the same time tended once again to polarize politics. While Kennedy promised government action, many—especially the blacks and the young—organized themselves for direct action through boycotts, protest marches, and sit-ins. At the same time, the right, fearing a growing communist conspiracy at work in the country, also organized and gained in strength.

The polarization of politics was reflected in the aftermath of Kennedy's murder in 1963. During the presidential campaign of 1964, Barry Goldwater of Arizona mobilized the conservative and rightist discontent and, to the surprise of many, won the Republican nomination. He promised "a choice not an echo," but the voters, in the largest presidential landslide to that date, chose his opponent, Lyndon B. Johnson. A new, liberal majority seemed to prevail. Provided with a cooperative Congress and a powerful coalition that included not only labor, the farmers, the blacks, and the intellectuals, but a large portion of the business community as well, Johnson in 1965 pushed through Congress a program of social legislation that in many ways completed the New Deal.

But the Johnson consensus faded as rapidly as it had grown. Critics from both the left and the right became more vociferous and more active. Opposition to the war in Vietnam and increasing militancy among blacks and students elicited a "backlash" response from the conservatives. Johnson's withdrawal from the 1968 presidential race did not stem the growing bitterness and violence. The country seemed hopelessly divided; and when civil rights leader Martin Luther King and presidential hopeful Robert F. Kennedy were gunned down by assassins, many concluded that the country was sick with hate and violence. When the Democratic convention met in Chicago to nominate Hubert H. Humphrey, television viewers alternately watched the delegates select a candidate and the police and young people battle outside the convention hotels.

Richard M. Nixon was elected by a narrow margin in 1968; but, with George Wallace running on an independent ticket and taking 13 percent of the vote, Nixon was a minority president. Though he promised to work to bring the country back together, the war went on and the country remained sharply divided. When in the spring of 1970 American forces invaded Cambodia, thousands of students protested. Violence broke out on hundreds of campuses; on two of them—Kent State in Ohio and Jackson State in Mississippi—several students were killed in clashes with the National Guard. Urban strife also continued, as a portion of the black militants and New Left resorted to planned violence. The police responded in kind; indeed, many charged that the police sometimes initiated the violence against militant students and blacks. "There is in the American psyche today an alienation from the central government that is new in our experience," Richard Rovere announced. And George Reedy, a former aide to President Johnson and clearly a member of the Establishment, wrote: "The question is raised: Can our political system cope with the strains? The answer is probably not."

Yet this pessimistic statement became irrelevant almost as soon as it was made. Once again the political temper of the country changed abruptly. Militancy abated as quickly as it had arisen. Some argued that most Americans were convinced that change could come within the system; others maintained that Nixon's withdrawal of Americans from Vietnam and his ending of the draft removed the main basis for opposition; some said that the excesses of the militants brought Americans to their senses; others argued that the relative calm was the result of an apathy born of discouragement, frustration, and fear of repression.

Whatever the reasons, the American voters gave President Nixon the greatest landslide victory in American history in the election of 1972. A new conservative coalition appeared to have given Nixon an overwhelming mandate. Analysts spoke of the new Republican majority and of the end of the dominant Democratic coalition that had been forged in the New Deal.

Writing the history of the decade and a half following World War II is a formidable task. Historians must describe and explain what seems to be bewilderingly erratic behavior marked by rapid shifts in political outlook and sharply contradictory attitudes. Adding to the problems of interpretation is the fact that many of the historians were participants in the events they write about. If this gives them special insights denied to those who write about events long past, it also raises problems of objectivity, of the historian's ability to distance himself from events in which he took part. Readers should bear this in mind as they read the following selections.

In the first selection, Arthur M. Schlesinger, Jr., calls for a revitalized, tough-minded liberalism. Written in the late 1940s and reissued with new material in the early 1960s, The Vital Center is both a historical analysis of what Schlesinger considers to be true liberalism and an impassioned plea for liberalism. Schlesinger, therefore, writes as both historian and advocate, and he makes this dual role clear to his readers. Although he repudiates both radical and conservative solutions to the problems facing the nation, he views his liberalism not as a moderate, middle position between the extremes but, rather, as a "new radicalism." He calls for a continued reliance on liberal solutions to problems, and for the support of individualism and individual welfare through a more active role for government in domestic affairs. In short, he calls for a continuation of the New Deal.

In the second selection, Godfrey Hodgson describes the cultural revolution sought by the young, radical activists of the 1960s. Supporters of the counter-culture seemed to repudiate not only the solutions of the left and the right to the nation's problems but also Schlesinger's liberalism. Whereas Schlesinger called for a new consensus based upon an up-dating and extension of the liberal consensus, the members of the counter-culture called for revolution to achieve a new consensus. For them the old radical, conservative, and liberal solutions were irrelevant. Hodgson concludes, however, that the movement was not revolutionary at all, that it was well within the middle-class consensus. According to his view, the problems the young members of the counter-culture were seeking to solve were not real social problems; rather, they were the personal complaints of a bored and pampered middle class.

To evaluate Hodgson's point of view the reader must consider first whether Hodgson's consideration of drugs, rock music, and the underground media truly captures the main features of the counter-culture. Was the movement little more than a youth cult using outrageous methods to make superficial criticisms? Or were these features merely a part, and not the most important part, of a larger movement that mounted a real challenge to the prevailing consensus?

Sheila Rothman, in the third selection, suggests a possible answer to these questions by investigating the women's liberation movement. She argues that, although the movement brought substantial and lasting changes in the role of women, at the same time it caused "intense antagonism and conflicts" not only among men but also among women. She shows how many of the reforms sought by some women implied massive social changes regarding employment, the family, and abortion. Those favoring women's liberation, she concludes, have become a powerful interest group in American politics. This interest group has sparked other, opposing interest groups. The ensuing conflict over social policy is fundamental and will remain an important element in American politics. The reader might consider whether other reform movements of the 1960s had similar results.

Samuel P. Huntington, in the final selection, uses the theme of a 1969 commencement address at Harvard University to assess the meaning of the turmoil of the 1960s and, by extension, the nature of political conflicts throughout American history. He finds that theories of conflict, consensus, and pluralism, the three ways in which historians have sought to explain the nature of political developments in the United States, are all inadequate. He points instead to what he calls a disharmony that arises from the constant striving to perfect American life so that it reaches American ideals. Thus, a kind of consensus exists about ideals, but conflict arises because of the varied attempts to reach these ideals. He sees the conflict as primarily ideological and not arising from social and economic differences.

Is it possible to build a better America through traditional politics, by working within the system, or does worthwhile reform and change in domestic and foreign policy come only after sharp and fundamental conflict? Is it possible—or desirable—to build a viable liberal coalition, or has coalition politics reached a point of bankruptcy in the United States? Do the radicals on the right and left make constructive contributions to the political system, or are they dangerous enemies?

Obviously, these are fundamental questions about the recent American past and about contemporary society. The debate is not just of historical significance, for its outcome will affect the lives of all who pick up this book.

Arthur M. Schlesinger, Jr.

# *The Vital Center*

This work is not designed to set forth novel or startling political doctrines. It is intended rather as a report on the fundamental enterprise of re-examination and self-criticism which liberalism has undergone in the last decade. The leaders in this enterprise have been the wiser men of an older generation. But its chief beneficiaries have been my own contemporaries; and its main consequence, I believe, has been to create a new and distinct political generation.

This new generation can be briefly defined by a few historical—and biographical—notations. If I may use myself as a convenient example, I was born in 1917. I heard Franklin Roosevelt's first inaugural address as a boy at school, fifteen years old. Since that March day in 1933, one has been able to feel that liberal ideas had access to power in the United States, that liberal purposes. in general, were dominating our national policy. For one's own generation, then, American liberalism has had a positive and confident ring. It has stood for responsibility and for achievement, not for frustration and sentimentalism; it has been the instrument of social change, not of private neurosis. During most of my political consciousness this has been a New Deal country. I expect that it will continue to be a New Deal country.

The experience of growing up under the New Deal meant too that Communism shone for few of one's generation with the same unearthly radiance that it apparently shone for other young men a decade earlier. It was partly the fact that we did not need so desperately to believe in the Soviet utopia. Franklin Roosevelt was showing that democracy was capable of taking care of its own; the New Deal was filling the vacuum of faith which we had inherited from the cynicism and complacency of the twenties, and from the breadlines of the early thirties. Partly too the Soviet Union itself was no longer the bright dream of the twenties—the land of hope encircled by capitalist aggressors and traduced by newspapermen sending lies out of Riga. What we saw in the Russia of the thirties was a land where industrialization was underwritten by mass starvation, where delusions of political infallibility led to the brutal extermination of dissent, and where the execution of heroes of the revolution testified to some deep inner contradiction in the system. This conclusion was not, for most of us, a process of disillusionment for which we had to pay the psychological price of a new extremism. We were simply the children of a new atmosphere: history had spared us any emotional involvement in the Soviet mirage.

The degeneration of the Soviet Union taught us a useful lesson, however. It broke the bubble of the false optimism of the ninteenth century. Official liberalism had long been almost inextricably identified with a picture of man as perfectible, as endowed with sufficient wisdom and selflessness to endure power and to use it infallibly for the general good. The Soviet experience, on top of the rise of fascism, reminded my generation rather forcibly that man was, indeed, imperfect, and that the corruptions of power could unleash great evil in the world. We discovered a new dimension of experience—the dimension of anxiety, guilt and corruption. (Or it may well be, as Reinhold Niebuhr has brillantly suggested, that we were simply rediscovering ancient truths which we should never have forgotten.)

Mid-twentieth-century liberalism, I believe, has thus been fundamentally reshaped by the hope of the New Deal, by the exposure of the Soviet Union, and by the deepening of our knowledge of man. The consequence of this historical re-education has been an unconditional rejection of totalitarianism and a reassertion of the ultimate integrity of the individual. This awakening constitutes the unique experience and fundamental faith of contemporary liberalism.

This faith has been and will continue to be under attack from the far right and the far left. In this book I have deliberately given more space to the problem of protecting the liberal faith from Communism than from reaction, not because reaction is the lesser threat, but because it is the enemy we know, whose features are clearly delineated for us, against whom our efforts have always been oriented. It is perhaps our very absorption in this age-old foe which has made us fatally slow to recognize the danger on what we carelessly thought was our left—forgetting in our enthusiasm that the totalitarian left and the totalitarian right meet at last on the murky grounds of tyranny and terror. I am persuaded that the restoration of business to political power in this country would have the calamitous results that have generally accompanied business control of the government; that this time we might be delivered through the incompetence of the right into the hands of the totalitarians of the left. But I am persuaded too that liberals have values in common with most members of the business community—in particular, a belief in free society—which they do not have in common with the totalitarians.

The experience with Communism has had one singularly healthy effect: it has made us reclaim democratic ideas which a decade ago we tended to regret and even to abandon. The defense of these ideas against both right and left will be a continuous and exacting commitment. But there lies in that commitment the possibility of recharging the faith in democracy with some of its old passion and principle. I am certain that history has equipped modern American liberalism with the ideas and the knowledge to construct a society where men will be both free and happy. Whether we have the moral vigor to do the job depends on ourselves. . . .

Industrialism is the benefactor and the villain of our time: it has burned up the mortgage, but at the same time sealed us in a subtler slavery. It has created wealth and comfort in undreamed-of abundance. But in the wake of its incomparable economic achievement it has left the thin, deadly trail of anxiety. The connecting fluids of industrial society begin to dry up; the seams harden and crack; and society is transformed into a parched desert, "a heap of broken images, where the sun beats, and the dead tree gives no shelter, the cricket no relief, and the dry stone no sound of water"—that state of social purgatory which Durkheim called "anomie" and where Eliot saw fear in a handful of dust.

Under industrialism the social order ceases to be society in faith and brotherhood. It becomes the waste land, "asocial society," in Alex Comfort's phrase—"a society of onlookers, congested but lonely, technically advanced but utterly insecure, subject to a complicated mechanism of order but individually irresponsible." We live on from day to day, persisting mechanically in the routine of a morality and a social pattern which has been switched off but which continues to run from its earlier momentum. Our lives are empty of belief. They are lives of quiet desperation.

Who can live without desperation in a society turned asocial—in a social system which represents organized frustration instead of organized fulfillment? Freedom has lost its foundation in community and become a torment; "individualism" strips the individual of layer after layer of protective tissue. Reduced to panic, industrial man joins the lemming migration, the convulsive mass escape from freedom to totalitarianism, hurling himself from the bleak and rocky cliffs into the deep, womb-dark sea below. In free society, as at present constituted, the falcon cannot hear the falconer, the center cannot hold. Anarchy is loosed upon the world, and, as in Yeats's terrible vision, some rough beast, its hour come round at last, slouches toward Bethlehem to be born.

Through this century, free society has been on the defensive, demoralized by the infection of anxiety, staggering under the body blows of fascism and Communism. Free society alienates the lonely and uprooted masses; while totalitarianism, building on their frustrations and cravings, provides a structure of belief, men to worship and men to hate and rites which guarantee salvation. The crisis of free society has assumed the form of international collisions between the democracies and the totalitarian powers; but this fact should not blind us to the fact that in its essence this crisis is internal.

Free society will survive, in the last resort, only if enough people believe in it deeply enough to die for it. However reluctant peace-loving people are to recognize that fact, history's warning is clear and cold; civilizations which cannot man their walls in times of alarm are doomed to destruction by the barbarians. We have deeply believed only when the issue of war has reduced our future to the stark problem of self-preservation. Franklin Roosevelt read the American people with his usual uncanny accuracy when he named the Second War, not the "war for freedom," but the "war for survival." Our democracy has still to generate a living emotional content, rich enough to overcome the anxieties incited by industrialism, deep enough to rally its members to battle for freedom—not just for self-preservation. Freedom must become, in Holmes's phrase, a "fighting faith."

Why does not democracy believe in itself with passion? Why is freedom not a fighting faith? In part because democracy, by its nature, dissipates rather than concentrates its internal moral force. The thrust of the democratic faith is away from fanaticism; it is toward compromise, persuasion and consent in politics, toward tolerance and diversity in society; its economic foundation lies in the easily frightened middle class. Its love of variety discourages dogmatism, and its love of skepticism discourages hero-worship. In place of theology and ritual, of hierarchy and demonology, it sets up a belief in intellectual freedom and unrestricted inquiry. The advocate of free society defines himself by telling what he is against: what he is for turns out to be certain *means* and he leaves other people to charge the means with content. Today democracy is paying the price for its systematic cultivation of the peaceful and rational virtues. "Many a man will live and die upon a dogma; no man will be a martyr for a conclusion."

Democracy, moreover, has not worn too well as a philosophy of life in an industrial age. It seemed more solid at the high noon of success than it does in the uncertainties of falling dusk. In its traditional form, it has presupposed emotional and psychological stability in the individual. It has assumed, much too confidently, that the gnawing problems of doubt and anxiety would be banished by the advance of science or cured by a rise in the standard of living. The spectacular reopening of these problems in our time finds the democratic faith lacking in the profounder emotional resources. Democracy has no defense-in-depth against the neuroses of industrialism. When philosophies of blood and violence arise to take up the slack between democracy's thin optimism and the bitter agonies of experience, democracy by comparison appears pale and feeble.

Yet it seems doubtful whether democracy could itself be transformed into a political religion, like totalitarianism, without losing its characteristic belief in individual dignity and freedom. Does this mean that democracy is destined to defeat, sooner or later, by one or another of the totalitarian sects?

The death pallor will indeed come over free society, unless it can recharge the deepest sources of its moral energy. And we cannot make democracy a fighting faith merely by exhortation nor by self-flagellation; and certainly not by renouncing the values which distinguish free society from totalitarianism. Yet we must somehow dissolve the anxieties which drive people in free society to become traitors to freedom. We must somehow give the lonely masses a sense of individual human function, we must restore community to the industrial order.

There is on our side, of course, the long-run impossibility of totalitarianism. A totalitarian order offers no legitimate solution to the problem of freedom and anxiety. It does not restore basic securities; it does not create a world where men may expect lives of self-fulfillment. It enables man, not to face himself, but to flee himself by diving into the Party and the state. Only he cannot stay there; he must either come up for air or drown. Totalitarianism has scotched the snake of anxiety, but not killed it; and anxiety will be its undoing.

An enduring social order must base itself upon the emotional energies and needs of man. Totalitarianism thwarts and represses too much of man ever to become in any sense a "good society." Terror is the essence of totalitarianism; and normal man, in the long run, instinctively organizes himself against terror. This fact gives the champions of freedom their great opportunity. But let no one deceive himself about the short-run efficacy of totalitarian methods. Modern technology has placed in the hands of "totalitarian man" the power to accomplish most of his ends of human subjection. He may have no enduring solution, but neither, for example, did the Dark Ages. Yet the darkness lasted a longer time than the period which has elapsed since the discovery of America.

We cannot count upon totalitarian dynamism running down of its own accord in a single generation. Man is instinctively anti-totalitarian; but it is necessary for wise policies to mobilize these instincts early enough to do some good. Our problem is to make democracy the fighting faith, not of some future underground movement, but of us all here today in the middle of the twentieth century.

The essential strength of democracy as against totalitarianism lies in its startling insight into the value of the individual. Yet, as we have seen, this insight can become abstract and sterile; arrogant forms of individualism sometimes discredit the basic faith in the value of the individual. It is only so far as that insight can achieve a full social dimension, so far as individualism derives freely from community, that democracy will be immune to the virus of totalitarianism.

For all the magnificent triumphs of individualism, we survive only as we remain members of one another. The individual requires a social context, not one imposed by coercion, but one freely emerging in response to his own needs and initiatives. Industrialism has inflicted savage wounds on the human sensibility; the cuts and gashes are to be healed only by a conviction of trust and solidarity with other human beings.

It is in these fundamental terms that we must reconstruct our democracy. Optimism about man is not enough. The formalities of democracy are not enough. The fact that a man can cast a secret ballot or shop in Woolworth's rather than Kresge's is more important to those free from anxiety than it is to the casualties of the industrial order. And the casualties multiply: the possessors are corrupted by power, the middling undone by boredom, the dispossessed demoralized by fear. Chamber-of-commerce banalities will no longer console industrial man.

We require individualism which does not wall man off from community; we require community which sustains but does not suffocate the individual. The historic methods of free society are correct so far as they go; but they concentrate on the individual; they do not go far enough. . . . We know now that man is not sufficiently perfect to shape good means infallibly to good ends. So we no longer describe free society in terms of means alone: we must place ends as well in the forefront of our philosophy of democracy. . . .

Do the people have a relative security against the ravages of hunger, sickness and want?

Do they freely unite in continuous and intimate association with like-minded people for common purposes?

Do they as individuals have a feeling of initiative, function and fulfillment in the social order?

It has become the duty of free society to answer these questions—and to answer them affirmatively if it would survive. The rise of the social-welfare state is an expression of that sense of duty. But the social welfare state is not enough. The sense of duty must be expressed specifically and passionately in the heart and will of men, in their daily decisions and their daily existence, if free men are to remain free.

The contemporary schism between the individual and the community has weakened the will of man. Social conditions cannot, of course, make moral decisions. But they can create conditions where moral decisions are more or less likely to be made. Some social arrangements bring out the evil in man more quickly than others. Slavery, as we knew well in America, corrupts the masters; totalitarian society, placing unbearable strains on man's self-restraint, produces the most violent reactions of fanaticism and hatred; the unchecked rule of the business community encourages greed and oppression. So the reform of institutions becomes an indispensable part of the enterprise of democracy. But the reform of institutions can never be a substitute for the reform of man.

The inadequacy of our institutions only intensifies the tribute that society levies from man: it but exacerbates the moral crisis. The rise of totalitarianism, in other words, signifies more than an internal crisis for democratic society. It signifies an internal crisis for democratic man. There is a Hitler, a Stalin in every breast. "Each of us has the plague within him," cries Tarrou in the Camus novel; "no one, no one on earth is free from it. And I know, too, that we must keep endless watch on ourselves lest in a careless moment we breathe in somebody's face and fasten the infection on him. What's natural is the microbe. All the rest—health, integrity, purity (if you like)—is a product of the human will, of a vigilance that must never falter."

How to produce a vigilance that never falters? how to strengthen the human will? Walt Whitman in his later years grew obsessed with the moral indolence of democracy. Once he had hymned its possibilities with unequaled fervor. Now he looked about him and saw people "with hearts of rags and souls of chalk." As he pondered "the shallowness and miserable selfism of these crowds of men, with all their minds so blank of high humanity and aspiration," then came "the terrible query . . . Is not Democracy of human rights humbug after all?" The expansion of the powers of government provided no solution. "I have little hope of any man or any community of men, that looks to some civil or military power to defend its vital rights.—If we have it not in ourselves to defend what belongs to us, then the citadel and heart of the towns are taken."

Wherein lies the hope? In "the exercise of Democracy," Whitman finally answered. ". . . to work for Democracy is good, the exercise is good—strength it makes and lessons it teaches." The hope for free society lies, in the last resort, in the kind of men it creates. "There is no week nor day nor hour," wrote Whitman, "when tyranny may not enter upon this country, if the people lose their supreme confidence in themselves,—and lose their roughness and spirit of defiance—Tyranny may always enter—there is no charm, no bar against it—the only bar against it is a large resolute breed of men."

In times past, when freedom has been a fighting faith, producing a "large resolute breed of men," it has acquired its dynamism from communion in action. "The exercise of Democracy" has quickened the sense of the value of the individual; and, in that exercise, the individual has found a just and fruitful relation to the community. We require today exactly such a rededication to concrete democratic ends; so that the exercise of democracy can bring about a reconciliation between the individual and the community, a revival of the *élan* of democracy, and a resurgence of the democratic faith.

The expansion of the powers of government may often be an essential part of society's attack on evils of want and injustice. The industrial economy, for example, has become largely inaccessible to the control of the individual; and, even in the field of civil freedom, law is the means society has for registering its own best standards. Some of the democratic exhilaration consequently has to be revived by delegation: this is why we need the Franklin Roosevelts. Yet the expansion of the powers of government, the reliance on leadership, as Whitman perceived, have also become a means of dodging personal responsibility. This is the essential importance of the issues of civil rights and civil liberties. Every one of us has a direct, piercing and inescapable responsibility in our own lives on questions of racial discrimination, of political and intellectual freedom—not just to support legislative programs, but to extirpate the prejudices of bigotry in our environment, and, above all, in ourselves.

Through this joint democratic effort we can tap once again the spontaneous sources of community in our society. Industrialism has covered over the springs of social brotherhood by accelerating the speed and mobility of existence. Standardization, for example, while it has certainly raised levels not only of consumption but of culture, has at the same time cut the umbilical cord too early; it has reduced life to an anonymity of abundance which brings less personal fulfillment than people once got from labor in their own shop or garden. More people read and write; but what they read and write tends to have less connection with themselves. We have made culture available to all at the expense of making much of it the expression of a common fantasy rather than of a common experience. We desperately need a rich emotional life, reflecting actual relations between the individual and the community.

The cultural problem is but one aspect of the larger problem of the role of independent groups, of voluntary associations, in free society. There is an evident thinness in the texture of political democracy, a lack of appeal to those irrational sentiments once mobilized by religion and now by totalitarianism. Democracy, we have argued, is probably inherently incapable of satisfying those emotions in the apparatus of the state without losing its own character. Yet a democratic society, based on a genuine cultural pluralism, on widespread and spontaneous group activity, could go far to supply outlets for the variegated emotions of man, and thus to restore meaning to democratic life. It is the disappearance of effective group activity which leads toward emptiness in the individual, as it also compels the enlargement of the powers of the state.

People deprived of any meaningful role in society, lacking even their own groups to give them a sense of belonging, become cannon fodder for totalitarianism. And groups themselves, once long established, suffer inevitable tendencies toward exclusiveness and bureaucratization, forget their original purpose and contribute to the downfall of freedom. If the American Medical Association, for example, had given serious attention to the problem of meeting the medical needs of America today, Doctor Fishbein would not be dunning his membership for funds to support a lobby against national health insurance. In the short run, the failure of voluntary initiative invites the spread of state power. In the long run, the disappearance of voluntary association paves the way for the pulverization of the social structure essential to totalitarianism. By the revitalization of voluntary associations, we can siphon off emotions which might otherwise be driven to the solutions of despair. We can create strong bulwarks against the totalitarianization of society.

Democracy requires unremitting action on many fronts. It is, in other words, a process, not a conclusion. However painful the thought, it must be recognized that its commitments are unending. The belief in the millennium has dominated our social thinking too long. Our utopian prophets have always supposed that a day would come when all who had not worshiped the beast nor received his mark on their foreheads would reign for a thousand years. "And God shall wipe away all tears from their eyes; and there shall be no more death, neither sorrow, nor crying, neither shall there be any more pain: for the former things are passed away."

But the Christian millennium calls for a catastrophic change in human nature. Let us not sentimentalize the millennium by believing we can attain it through scientific discovery or through the revision of our economic system. We must grow up now and forsake the millennial dream. We will not arise one morning to find all problems solved, all need for further strain and struggle ended, while we work two hours a day and spend our leisure eating milk and honey. Given human imperfection, society will continue imperfect. Problems will always torment us, because all important problems are insoluble: that is why they are important. The good comes from the continuing struggle to try and solve them, not from the vain hope of their solution.

This is just as true of the problems of international society. "What men call peace," Gilson has well said, "is never anything but a space between two wars; a precarious equilibrium that lasts as long as mutual fear prevents dissension from declaring itself. This parody of true peace, this armed fear . . . may very well support a kind of order, but never can it bring mankind anything of tranquillity. Not until the social order becomes the spontaneous expression of an interior peace in men's hearts shall we have tranquillity." Does it seem likely (pending the millennium) that we shall ever have an interior peace in the hearts of enough men to transform the nature of human society? The pursuit of peace, Whitehead reminds us, easily passes into its bastard substitute, anesthesia.

So we are forced back on the reality of struggle. So long as society stays free, so long will it continue in its state of tension, breeding contradiction, breeding strife. But we betray ourselves if we accept contradiction and strife as the total meaning of conflict. For conflict is also the guarantee of freedom; it is the instrument of change; it is, above all, the source of discovery, the source of art, the source of love. The choice we face is not between progress with conflict and progress without conflict. The choice is between conflict and stagnation. You cannot expel conflict from society any more than you can from the human mind. When you attempt it, the psychic costs in schizophrenia or torpor are the same.

The totalitarians regard the toleration of conflict as our central weakness. So it may appear to be in an age of anxiety. But we know it to be basically our central strength. The new radicalism derives its power from an acceptance of conflict—an acceptance combined with a determination to create a social framework where conflict issues, not in excessive anxiety, but in creativity. The center is vital; the center must hold. The object of the new radicalism is to restore the center, to reunite individual and community in fruitful union. The spirit of the new radicalism is the spirit of the center— the spirit of human decency, opposing the extremes of tyranny. Yet, in a more fundamental sense, does not the center itself represent one extreme?

while, at the other, are grouped the forces of corruption—men transformed by pride and power into enemies of humanity.

The new radicalism, drawing strength from a realistic conception of man, dedicates itself to problems as they come, attacking them in terms which best advance the humane and libertarian values, which best secure the freedom and fulfillment of the individual. It believes in attack—and out of attack will come passionate intensity.

Can we win the fight? We must commit ourselves to it with all our vigor in all its dimensions: the struggle within the world against Communism and fascism; the struggle within our country against oppression and stagnation; the struggle within ourselves against pride and corruption: nor can engagement in one dimension exclude responsibility for another. Economic and political action can help restore the balance between individual and community and thereby reduce one great source of anxiety. But even the most favorable social arrangements cannot guarantee individual virtue; and we are far yet from having solved the social problem.

The commitment is complex and rigorous. When has it not been so? If democracy cannot produce the large resolute breed of men capable of the climactic effort, it will founder. Out of the effort, out of the struggle alone, can come the high courage and faith which will preserve freedom.

[When his book was reissued in 1962, Mr. Schlesinger added the following:]

*The Vital Center* was written in the autumn and winter of 1948–49. This was a moment of transition in the postwar history of American liberalism —a moment when the liberal community was engaged in the double task of redefining its attitude toward the phenomenon of Communism and, partly in consequence, of reconstructing the bases of liberal political philosophy.

In the years since, the process of redefinition has been completed: I believe that all American liberals recognize today that liberalism has nothing in common with Communism, either as to means or as to ends.

As for the process of reconstruction, this is by its nature continuous: if liberalism should ever harden into ideology, then, like all ideologies, it would be overwhelmed by the turbulence and unpredictability of history— especially in an age when science and technology have made the velocity of history so much greater than ever before. The continuing enterprise of reconstruction has consequently brought new phases of liberal thought to the forefront in the thirteen years since this book was published. It may be worthwhile to note some of these later developments.

So far as Communism is concerned, in the confused years immediately after the end of the Second World War, and in spite of Stalin's notable record in the thirties of internal terror and international betrayal, the Soviet Union retained for some people traces of the idealistic fervor of the Russian Revolution. By 1962, it seems safe to say that postwar Soviet policy has extinguished any remaining elements of idealism in the Communist appeal. No one with any knowledge of history can believe in the Soviet Union on the supposition that Communist victory would usher in a generous and beneficent society. Where people believe in the Soviet Union today, it is on quite other grounds: it is basically because they are persuaded that, whether they like it or not, Communism is going to win, and that they had therefore better make their terms with a Communist world. The essence of contemporary Soviet policy is to enhance this impression of the inevitability of Communist triumph, to employ every resource of science and politics to identify Communism with the future and to convince people everywhere that they must accept the necessity of Communism or face the certainty of obliteration. They have addressed this policy especially to the southern half of the world where the awakening of underdeveloped countries from centuries of oblivion is discharging new and incalculable energies into human society.

The irony is that the very eagerness with which intellectuals in emergent nations often embrace Communism itself suggests that Communism is *not* the wave of the future and is, if it is anything, a passing stage to which some may temporarily turn in the quest for modernity. Where Marx portrayed Communism as the fulfillment of the process of modernization, history seems abundantly to show that, if the world avoids thermonuclear suicide, the modernization process, contrary to Marxist prophecy, will vindicate the mixed society and render Communism obsolete.

The Marxist contention has been (a) that capitalism is the predestined casualty of the modernization process, and (b) that Communism is its predestined culmination. In these terms Communism has boasted the certification of history. But history quite plainly refutes the Communist case. It shows (a) that the mixed society, as it modernizes itself, can overcome the internal contradictions which in Marx's view doomed it to destruction, and (b) that Communism is historically a function of the prefatory rather than the concluding stages of the modernization process.

Marx rested his case for the inevitability of Communist triumph on the theory that capitalism contained the seeds of its own destruction. He argued that the capitalist economy generated inexorable inner tendencies—"contradictions"—which would infallibly bring about its downfall. One inexorable tendency was the increasing wealth of the rich and the increasing poverty of the poor. Another was the increasing frequency and severity of economic crisis. Together these tendencies would infallibly carry society to a point of revolutionary "ripeness" when the proletariat would rise in its wrath, overthrow the possessing classes and install a classless society. Marx saw no way of denying this process, because he believed that the capitalist state could never be anything but the executive committee of the capitalist class.

This was Marx's fatal error. The capitalist state in developed societies, far from being the helpless instrument of the possessing class, has become the means by which other groups in society have redressed the balance of social power against those whom Hamilton called the "rich and well-born." This has been true in the United States, for example, since the age of Jackson. The liberal democratic state has accomplished two things in particular. It has brought about a redistribution of wealth which has defeated Marx's prediction of progressive immiseration; and it has brought about an economic stabilization which has defeated Marx's prediction of ever-worsening economic crisis. What the democratic parties of the developed nations have done, in short, has been to use the state to force capitalism to do what both the classical capitalists and the classical Marxists declared was impossible: to control the business cycle and to reapportion income in favor of those whom Jackson called the "humble members of society."

The champions of the affirmative state, in their determination to avert Marxist revolution, had to fight conservatism at every step along the way. Nonetheless, they persevered; and the twentieth century in America and Great Britain saw the rejection of laissez-faire, the subjugation of the business cycle, the drowning of revolution in a torrent of consumer goods, and the establishment of the "affluent society." The revolutionary fires within capitalism, lit by the great industrialists in the nineteenth century, were put out in the twentieth by the triumphs of industry—and by the liberal politicians, by Theodore Roosevelt and Woodrow Wilson and Franklin D. Roosevelt. Such men ignored the dogmatists, the philosophers of either/or, and created the mixed society. Both classical socialism and classical capitalism were products of the nineteenth century, and their day is over. As a result, capitalism can no longer be relied upon to dig its own grave; and Communism, if it ever comes to developed countries, will come, not as a consequence of social evolution, but only on the bayonets of the Red Army.

At the same time, history has thrown sharp light on the actual function of Communism. Marx, regarding Communism as the climax of the development process, prophesied that it would come first in the most developed nations. On the contrary, it has come to nations in the early phases of development, like Russia and China; and it has appealed to activists in such nations precisely because they see it as the means of rapid and effective modernization. Instead of being the culmination of the modernization effort, Communism would seem to be a form of social organization to which some countries aspiring to development have resorted in the hope of speeding the pace of modernization. We do not know what will happen to Communism in a Communist state which achieves full development; but, if it should then survive in anything like its present form, it would be because of the efficiency of its apparatus of control and terror, not because it is the natural organizational expression of the institutions of affluence.

History thus shows plainly that Communism is not the form of social organization toward which all societies are irresistibly evolving. Rather it is a phenomenon of the transition from stagnation to development, a "disease" (in Walt Rostow's phrase) of the modernization process. Democratic, regulated capitalism—the mixed society—will be far more capable of coping with the long-term consequences of modernization. "The wave of the future,"

Walter Lippmann has well said, "is not Communist domination of the world. The wave of the future is social reform and social revolution driving us toward the goal of national independence and equality of personal status."

If this is so, it emphasizes more than ever the need to keep abreast of history in our own social ideas and programs. We are all indebted to J. K. Galbraith for his demonstration that the affluent society compels a sweeping reconsideration of social and economic policies. The problems of the New Deal were essentially quantitative problems—problems of meeting stark human needs for food, clothing, shelter and employment. Most of these needs are now effectively met for most Americans; but a sense of spiritual disquietude remains nevertheless. A full dinner pail turns out to be something less than the promised land. The final lesson of the affluent society is surely that affluence is not enough—that solving the quantitative problems of living only increases the importance of the quality of the life lived. These qualitative problems seem next on the American agenda.

The qualitative aspects of life are only marginally within the reach of government. Yet public policy surely has its contribution to make to the elevation of American civilization. "The great object of the institution of civil government," said John Quincy Adams in his first message to Congress, "is the improvement of the condition of those who are parties to the social compact, and no government, in whatever form constituted, can accomplish the lawful end of its institution but in proportion as it improves the condition of those over whom it is established . . . Moral, political, intellectual improvement are duties assigned by the Author of Our Existence to social no less than to individual man. For the fulfillment of those duties governments are invested with power, and to the attainment of the end—the progressive improvement of the condition of the governed—the exercise of delegated powers is a duty as sacred and indispensable as the usurpation of powers not granted is criminal and odious."

A central issue of contemporary domestic polity is a variation on the question which concerned Adams—that is, the question of the balance between the amount of our national wealth we reserve for private satisfaction and the amount we dedicate to public need. In the thirties "recovery" was the catchword of our national economic philosophy; in the forties, "full employment"; in the fifties, "economic growth"; in the future, it is likely to become "allocation of resources." No one would argue that steering more resources into the public sector would cure the spiritual ailments of the affluent society; but it seems possible that the resulting improvements in opportunities in education, medical care, social welfare, community planning, culture and the arts will improve the chances for the individual to win his own spiritual fulfillment.

The impending shift from quantitative to qualitative liberalism emphasizes once again the hazards involved in the degeneration of liberalism into ideology. By tradition American liberalism is humane, experimental and pragmatic; it has no sense of messianic mission and no faith that all problems have final solutions. It assumes that freedom implies conflict. It agrees with Madison, in the Tenth Federalist, that the competition among economic interests is inherent in a free society. It also agrees with George Bancroft, who wrote: "The feud between the capitalist and laborer, the house of Have and the house of Want, is as old as social union, and can never be entirely quieted; but he who will act with moderation, prefer fact to theory, and remember that everything in the world is relative and not absolute, will see that the violence of the contest may be stilled."

Its empirical temper means that American liberalism stands in sharp contrast to the millennial nostalgia which still characterizes both the American right and the European left—the notion that the day will come when all conflict will pass, when Satan will be cast into the lake of fire and brimstone, and mankind will behold a new heaven and a new earth. José Figueres, the Latin American patriot, calls his finca in the Costa Rican uplands "La Lucha San Fin"—the struggle without end. Freedom is inseparable from struggle; and freedom, as Brandeis said, is the great developer; it is both the means employed and the end attained. This, I believe, states the essence of the progressive hope—this and the understanding that the struggle itself offers not only better opportunities for others but a measure of fulfillment for oneself.

Godfrey Hodgson

# Triumph and Failure of a Cultural Revolution

## 1

The heyday of the counter culture coincided with the buildup of the Vietnam War from the President's decision to escalate in the spring of 1965 to the Tet offensive of 1968. It also coincided with the climax of racial confrontation, from Selma to the death of Martin Luther King. But if the twin crises in foreign policy and the cities were the occasion of the youth rebellion, the actual process of recruitment to the counter culture probably owed more to three factors that had little enough to do with politics except as symbols— to drugs, to rock music, and to the underground media: the sacrament, the liturgy and the gospel of a religion that failed.

The youth culture liked to remind older Americans that they, too, were insatiable consumers of various stimulants and depressants. . . .

There was no getting away from the fact that, lashed on by advertising agencies, distillers, brewers, cigarette manufacturers and pharmaceutical companies, the ordinary American had long thought it perfectly normal to be more or less addicted to alcohol, nicotine, barbiturates and tranquilizers. American physicians were prescribing more and more drugs, and sometimes, indeed, behaving almost as if they were drug salesmen. Neither the U.S. Army nor the CIA, those two pillars of the "straight" society, saw anything wrong with using LSD long before it had become a fashion in the counter culture. The drug culture of the 1960s certainly did not grow out of a society that was totally new to the idea of chemical aids to the pursuit of happiness. . . .

. . . From a historical point of view, four drugs or groups of drugs are relevant to the spread of the counter culture: marijuana, the hallucinogens, the amphetamines, and heroin. The use of all these increased dramatically during the second half of the 1960s.

The amphetamines ("speed") can be dismissed with merciful brevity. "Speed kills," the lore of the drug subculture warned, and it did not exaggerate.

Each of the other three drugs, or groups of drugs, had a special symbolic importance: the hallucinogens, especially "acid" (LSD), for the "hippies," that is, for those who were fully committed to the counter culture; marijuana for the great army of lukewarm converts and partial sympathizers; heroin for its enemies.

From the early days of the Beat Movement, the idea that hallucinogenic drugs could create a new consciousness had been "at the crux of the futurist revolt." In America, it was never in the cards that such an idea could long survive as the prerogative of an initiate elite. If Ginsberg had been the prophet of using chemistry to change consciousness, and Leary the salesman of the idea, its Henry Ford was "Owsley"—a University of California student, grandson of a United States senator from Kentucky, with the sonorous name of Augustus Owsley Stanley III. It was on February 21, 1965, ten days before Operation Rolling Thunder began, and the month before the first teach-in, that Owsley's primitive acid factory in Berkeley was raided. In March he moved to Los Angeles and went into mass production of lysergic acid monohydrate. The business was profitable by any standards: he is said to have paid twenty thousand dollars for the first shipment, of five hundred grams, which was converted into one and a half million tabs at one to two dollars apiece *wholesale!*

With massive supplies of acid guaranteed by this pioneering venture in hip capitalism, the next three years—those same three years of schism from 1965 to 1968, when the war and the urban crisis seemed to be tearing the country in two—saw the illusion that chemistry could free the human mind spin through the full cycle from frenzied hope and bombastic prophecy to panic, paranoia, and catastrophe.

In the spring of 1965 the word went out that they had discovered peace and love in San Francisco. To a depressing extent, this was an illusion resulting from the chemical effects of lysergic acid. People tried it, one researcher has concluded, as "a relief from boredom, an enhancement of sentience, a source of fusion, an escape from the sheltered life, an initiation, a way to express anger or withdrawal, an answer to loneliness, a substitute for sex, a moving psychological, philosophical or religious experience, and, most importantly [for] fun." It was all of those things, no doubt. It was also a supreme example of the power of fashion in American life.

The speed with which the craze took hold is a tribute to the needs of a generation that "had everything." It was also a remarkable illustration of the fine-tuned efficiency of the American social machine for distributing any new idea, fashion or product.

LSD was launched by a handful of Berkeley and San Francisco bohemians. Madison Avenue itself could not have handled the launch more successfully.

"It all came straight out of the Acid Tests," according to Tom Wolfe, the social historian of anti-fashion, "in a straight line leading to the Trips Festival of January, 1966. That brought the whole thing out in the open." In other words, the craze was publicized by the spectacular mass turn-ons organized by Kesey and his friends. In 1965 and 1966, LSD was still the esoteric rite of initiation into a relatively small company of the enlightened in the Haight-Ashbury district in San Francisco and the East Village in New York. That was still true even as late as January, 1967, when Allen Ginsberg, Timothy Leary and the Zen poet Gary Snyder were among the organizers of the Great Human Be-In at Golden Gate Park. Thousands of devotees, in a state of beatific hallucination, turned to face the sunset over the Pacific while Ginsberg blew on a ram's horn and recited a propitious mantra.

The omens were not favorable. The Summer of Love in 1967 turned into a nightmare. The runaways poured into the Haight-Ashbury and the East Village from every campus and suburb in the United States: the bored, the delinquent, the psychotic, and the mere followers of fashion. They were followed by tourists, journalists, sociologists and undercover agents. And they met bad acid, bad vibrations, uptight cops, Mafia peddlers, chiselers, stranglers, hepatitis, and VD.

There was a phrase the acid freaks used about a bad trip: they called it a "horror show." By 1968 the psychedelic paradise itself was turning into a horror show. The older and more serious seekers were horrified at what publicity was doing to their private cult. They began to move out physically from the hippie ghettoes, and to experiment with less instant paths to truth, with communal living, macrobiotic diets, group therapy, and transcendental meditation.

One way station on the road out of the Haight-Ashbury that summer was Esalen, in the Big Sur country, which emerged as a kind of ashram where a bizarre assembly of sadhus and disciples searched for peace and wisdom with the help of LSD, folk and rock music, naked bathing, Tai Chi exercises, and the *Gestalt* therapy of Dr. Fritz Perls as interpreted by Paul Goodman. But even on the sunny cliffs of Big Sur, the quest for truth and beauty was haunted by bad vibrations. One disciple recalls a sinister evening at Esalen that summer when one of the flower children around the campfire was heard to be muttering "Blood! Blood! Blood! Hate! Hate!" And no less a symbol of the dark potentialities of Dionysian rebellion than Charles Manson was lurking around Esalen that same summer.

"If I had to summarize in one word what has happened to the street scene in the last two years," said one literate hippie in 1969, "it would be 'decay.' It's not so much love any more, it's survival." That was the year of the Woodstock festival. Three hundred thousand turned up, and the media discovered the "Woodstock Nation." But in fact, by 1969, the use of hallucinogens had already started to level off among college students in the trend-setting regions, California and the Northeast. Not long afterward college students elsewhere and high school students followed suit. As a pilgrimage in search of new freedom, the great acid trip was over before the end of the sixties.

It was during precisely these same three years, from 1965 to 1968, that marijuana first caught on as a mass habit, first among students and then among young people generally. The first studies of drug use among college students date from 1965. In that year a survey of graduating seniors from Brooklyn College found that only 4.2 percent had ever used marijuana, and in a sample of graduate students at "a large urban university in Southern California," where the habit was most deeply established, the proportion who had ever tried marijuana was still only 10.7 percent.

By 1969 the lowest reported incidence of marijuana use in *high schools*, in conservative Utah, was higher than the rate for graduate students in Los Angeles only four years before. By the last week of 1969, a survey of full-time college students on fifty-seven campuses in the United States conducted by The Gallup Organization and reported in *Newsweek* found that 31.9 percent said that they had used marijuana.

Surveys of students at individual universities reported even higher rates of response: 44 percent, for example, at Michigan in the autumn of 1969, and 48 percent at four Massachusetts colleges, one of them Harvard, the following spring. The higher the social class from which young people came and the higher the standing of the college they attended, the more likely they were to have tried marijuana. The Massachusetts study found that only 26 percent of young people between sixteen and twenty-three in jobs had smoked marijuana, as against 48 percent of those who were in college. And a 1970 survey of students at a wide variety of educational institutions in the Denver-Boulder area of Colorado found that the percentage who had used the drug declined roughly in proportion to the academic and social standing of the college: from 35 percent at the University of Colorado at Boulder, to 16 percent at Loretto Heights College, a small local girls' college. While the craze for LSD was beginning to die down, the marijuana habit was steadily spreading to new groups of the youth population.

This remarkable change in taste, involving as it did, at last, the symbolic rejection of many of society's strongest values, was essentially spontaneous. The great majority of those who used marijuana were first given it, for free, by a friend. No large commercial organization for handling the trade and distribution ever seems to have developed. Some 80 percent of the weed was brought in over the Mexican border. The rest was grown locally, either wild, or in cultivation in Oregon and California communes, city window boxes or, once, with heroic bravado, in the median strip on Park Avenue in New York.

Some small-scale "hip capitalists" did organize shipments of grass from Mexico and of hashish from the Near East and India. But the stereotype of the evil pusher luring adolescents into the grip of addiction for his own profit was always, as far as marijuana was concerned, a myth.

Even an official publication put out by the Nixon administration in 1971, at the height of its crusade to stamp out drugs, conceded, "In general adolescents are introduced to marijuana by others in their groups. There is little evidence to confirm the belief that 'pushers' are needed to 'turn on' a novice. His friends do it for him."

Once a boy or girl had tried marijuana, he or she was automatically a potential recruit for the culture of opposition, not because of the pharmacological effects of the drug but because of its cultural associations and above all because it remained illegal. And since, unlike LSD or the amphetamines, marijuana is mild, pleasant, no more harmful than coffee or wine, and relatively cheap, the human chain effect by which millions of young people were introduced to it by their friends became a powerful recruiting network for the counter culture.

Heroin had never been central to the ideas of the counter culture, as the hallucinogenic drugs were. Nor was it ever anything like as popular as marijuana. The major prophets disapproved of it (though they disapproved more vocally of punishing people for using it), and few hippies used it. A study of the drug subculture in the East Village in 1967, at the height of the acid craze, for example, found that where 100 percent of those sampled had used marijuana and 90 percent had used acid, only 13 percent had ever experimented with heroin. No mass survey of college students ever found that as many as 0.5 percent admitted to having ever tried heroin.

As an opiate, heroin is a "depressant," a "downer," like alcohol. At best, it induces not excitement or visions but a sense of relaxed satiation. Nobody would ever take it in search of enlightenment; nobody could seriously argue that it expanded the field of human consciousness.

Except at the lowest levels of the capillary system by which it reached the addict on the street, the supply of heroin, unlike the supply of marijuana, was always firmly controlled by professional criminals operating on a fairly large scale. For this reason, and because there was no competition from domestic production, heroin remained extremely expensive. It therefore notoriously became connected with crime in a second sense: the addict was driven to steal in order to support his habit.

Leaving aside the special and apparently temporary problem of heroin use in the military services, which was related to special factors such as fear, boredom and the availability of cheap supplies in Vietnam, heroin addiction was essentially a problem of the ghetto. In 1969 just under half the known heroin addicts in the country were black. Well over one third of the rest were either Puerto Rican or Mexican.

Indeed heroin was above all a problem of the New York ghettoes. Almost half the sixty-two thousand narcotics addicts known to the authorities in 1967 were in New York, and while the spread of heroin apparently accelerated subsequently in other cities, notably in Detroit, it was still true in 1971 that thirty-three thousand out of eighty-two thousand known addicts in the whole country were in the single city of New York. Unknown addicts presumably bore approximately the same relation in numbers to those known in New York as they did elsewhere. A whole series of studies reported that heroin users overwhelmingly came from the most underprivileged, crowded and dilapidated sections of the city, and spelled out the connection between heroin and the whole syndrome of crisis in the inner city.

After about 1969 some middle-class white graduates from other drugs did experiment with heroin. "Everyone just got so that they weren't turned on to tripping [i.e., to LSD] any more," a New Jersey teen-ager explained, with all the moronic logic of the man who explains that he drinks in order to forget that he is an alcoholic; "they just decided that downs were the best kind of experience to have." But these young white boys and girls who drifted into heroin because they had tried everything else remained a small minority among heroin users. More typically, heroin was just one among the many ways in which those at the very bottom of urban society, and especially urban black society, exploited each other's desire to escape, to the ultimate profit of others outside the trap. If the LSD craze was an episode in the mythology of bohemia, heroin was part of the psychic and social pathology of the ghetto.

Unfortunately, however, those whom the counter culture dismissed as "the straight world" made no such distinction. For middle-aged conservatives, drugs were drugs. Among slightly less rigid sectors of public opinion, any awareness of differences between various drugs was canceled out by the power of the myth that all drugs were one great slippery slope; that once you took the first drag at a joint of marijuana, you would be lucky not to slide all the way down to end up as a heroin addict.

The specter conjured up by the word "drugs" in the minds of middle-class parents was above all the specter of heroin: the Big H. The myth of the insidious pusher and the innocent victim crystallized into a morality play of enticement, addiction, withdrawal, relapse, overdose, and death. There was just enough truth in this melodramatic stereotype to give it the power to trouble the sleep of half the parents of teen-age children in the country. It *did* happen that kids from "nice homes," having first tried marijuana, ended up dead in a pool of vomit after an overdose of heroin. But it happened infinitely less often than middle-class families, in their terror, imagined. Perhaps the myth, on balance, did more harm than the drug.

By the early 1970s, heroin had clearly become a surrogate target for the fears and anger of a society that was passing through a terrifying period of shocks and disillusionment. The Nixon administration—in this, at least, reflecting the feelings of a large majority of middle-class opinion—had become almost obsessional on the subject. Few issues occupied more time in the White House. In the State Department, a high official there told me late in 1971, roughly one third of the cable traffic in and out of the department was about drugs. Nelson Rockefeller, supposed champion of Republican liberalism, proposed to introduce a mandatory death penalty for selling drugs. Not that the situation did not justify serious concern: it did. But the form the hysteria about heroin took was largely unrelated to the real problems of increasing addiction in the ghetto.

Heroin had become the convenient outward symbol for deep, irrational fears: for the white man's fear of the black man, for the fear (never far below the surface in a society of immigrants) of losing beloved children to an alien culture, for the Puritan's Manichaean fear of the lurking powers of darkness. In a way, heroin had taken the place of communism.

Not the least of the ways in which America was divided in this period was by the emotional harmonics of the word "drugs." To millions of younger people, drugs meant first and foremost marijuana, which in turn meant nothing much more than fun. To some few of the intellectuals of the counter culture, drugs meant the hallucinogens, which seemed to offer the hope of achieving a "new consciousness." But to by far the largest number of Americans, drugs meant heroin. And heroin symbolized all they most hated and feared. . . .

**2**

Throughout the sixties, the changing phases of popular music did coincide uncannily with changing political moods. First came the unworldly moralizing and naïve political idealism of the folk-music movement: Judy Collins, Joan Baez, Pete Seeger, and Dylan the folk singer were at the height of their popularity between 1963 and 1965, the years of high hopes for the New Frontier and the Great Society.

Then, in 1965, came rock. The words of the folk songs had been full of radical implications. The singers themselves were men and women of the Left. They sang about peace and war, poverty and injustice, and sometimes, as in *The Times They Are A-Changin'*, they looked forward to the coming of revolution.

The rock singers sometimes sang about revolution, too. But the word meant something different for them from the literal, political revolution of such New York Marxist folk singers as Pete Seeger and Phil Ochs. The music itself was to be the revolution. In the first dizzy years of rock, in 1965 and 1966, and above all in 1967, the promise that intoxicated initiates was that of a wider revolution of consciousness and culture, of which political revolution would come as a by-product.

Rock music is American on both sides of the family if you trace its pedigree far enough. Its technical elements have come down through the commercial rock-and-roll and rhythm-and-blues of the 1950s from the two deepest fountains of American popular music, black blues and white country music. But, in 1965, two traditions fused to create the rock music of the late sixties: one come back to America from Britain, and one out of San Francisco.

Beginning, like so much else, in 1963, first the Beatles, and then a succession of other British pop groups, of whom the Rolling Stones eventually became almost as important as the Beatles themselves, re-exported American popular music to America and proved that their kind of it could be a commercial success on a far bigger scale than the originals it came from. Folk music, rock-and-roll, and urban blues all sold to fractional markets: to campus and coffee house and to the black "race" market. The Beatles' formula, compounded of driving rhythm, sophisticated musical craftsmanship, fresh and often exquisite melody, and literate, irreverent lyrics about real life, unlocked the American youth market as a whole. After the Beatles had made the breach, a host of imitators, British and American, poured through it.

Technical and economic factors contributed to the staggering commercial success of rock music. The improvement in electronic amplifying; the development of eight- and sixteen-track tape recorders; the spread of FM radio; the marketing shift from 45-rpm singles to 33-rpm albums (itself predicated on the new prosperity which meant that even teen-agers were used to spending four dollars on an album once a week or more and could afford elaborate stereo equipment); the rise of such aggressive new recording companies as the Ertegun brothers' Atlantic Records to compete with the stodgy giants of the industry—these made the rock boom possible.

But in the end the phenomenal success of the Beatles was due to psychological compatibility. They came from an Irish working-class background in Liverpool, where irreverence toward all established authority, and especially toward national and military authority, is endemic. They grew up knowing some of the things that young Americans were discovering with pained surprise in the 1960s: that industrial society uses people as well as makes them more affluent, that there is a good deal of hypocrisy about politicians' patriotism, that a lot of middle-class virtue is a sham. When a generation of young Americans emerged from Birmingham and Dallas, Mississippi and Vietnam, into disillusionment and cynicism, the Beatles were waiting there with a grin on their faces. They were as disillusioned and cynical as anyone, but they were cheerful about it; they had never expected that life would be any different.

It would be hard to exaggerate the influence the Beatles had on the generation of Americans who grew up in the sixties. But the Beatles were influenced by America, too, and in particular by the other stream that went into creating the vitality of rock music. That was the San Francisco influence.

In San Francisco in 1965, 1966, and 1967, Jon Landau of *Rolling Stone* has written, "rock was not only viewed as a form of entertainment." It was "an essential component of a 'new culture,' along with drugs and radical politics." That hardly does justice to the fervid claims that were made on behalf of the new music. The leading San Francisco band, The Grateful Dead, was at the very center of the general ferment in the Bay Area in those years. It had played at Ken Kesey's legendary "acid tests." Augustus Owsley Stanley III had personally bought the band its equipment out of his LSD profits. And the Dead had actually lived in a commune in the Haight-Ashbury until driven out by the sheer squalor into which that neighborhood declined after 1967. The other San Francisco bands, such as the Jefferson Airplane, shared this "underground" style. In 1967, for their own various reasons, the three unarguable superstars of the new music—Bob Dylan, the Beatles, and the Rolling Stones—all stopped touring America. In their absence, after the Monterey festival of that summer, it was the "underground," San Francisco style that emerged triumphant. Soon even the Beatles were imitating the San Francisco underground style: a peculiar blend of radical political rhetoric, of allusions to the drug culture, and of the excited sense of imminent, apocalyptic liberation. After 1967 the equation between rock music and "revolution" became firmly anchored in the minds of all those who listened to the one or hankered after the other.

It was perhaps always an absurd idea that a new kind of music could change society as Hamelin was changed by the Pied Piper. It was in any case a short-lived idea. The episode which, more than any other, revealed the sheer nastiness that was the antithesis to the claim that rock music was liberating came at the Rolling Stones' concert at Altamont, California, in the last month of the sixties.

It was part of the Stones' carefully polished image to be "their satanic majesties," the naughtiest boys in the world. That winter, they toured the United States. Audiences and critics agreed that their music was as exciting as ever. To end the tour, they planned to give a free concert in San Francisco. It was to be a royal gesture, and at the same time their acknowledgment of the city's role in the culture that had crowned them.

The coronation was as satanic as any press agent could have wished. "Hustlers of every stripe," wrote the relatively sympathetic Michael Lydon in *Ramparts*, "swarmed to the new scene like piranhas to the scent of blood." And so did three hundred thousand for them to prey off. Lydon saw "the dancing beaded girls, the Christlike young men and smiling babies familiar from countless stories on the Love Generation." But another side of the culture was unmistakable, too: "speed freaks with hollow eyes and missing teeth, dead-faced acid-heads burned out by countless flashes, old beatniks clutching gallons of red wine, Hare Krishna chanters with shaved heads and acned cheeks."

Four people died. One, a young man with long hair and a metal cross around his neck, was so stoned that he walked unregarding into an irrigation ditch and drowned. Another was clubbed, stabbed and kicked to death by the Hell's Angels. What were those dangerous pets of the San Francisco *avant-garde* supposed to be doing at the concert? It turned out that they had been hired as "security guards" by the Rolling Stones, on the advice of none other than The Grateful Dead, the original troubadours of love, peace and flowers. "Regrettable," commented the Rolling Stones' manager, "but if you're asking me for a condemnation of the Angels . . ." It sounded eerily like President Nixon discussing Lieutenant Calley's conviction for the massacre at My Lai.

"Altamont showed everyone," wrote one of the most levelheaded of the rock critics, Jon Landau, in *Rolling Stone*, "that everything that had been swept under the rug was now coming into the open: the greed, the hustle, the hype. . . ." Only four months earlier, the national media, always quick to seize on some dramatic but complex event and shape its ambiguities into the oversimplified symbol of a new trend, had celebrated the Woodstock Festival as the birth of a new "nation." Then, after Altamont, the boom jibed brutally over onto a new tack. Where the news magazines, the networks and the commentators had managed to ignore the hype, the hustle and even the mud, and had portrayed Woodstock as a midsummer night's dream of idyllic innocence, Altamont was painted as Walpurgisnacht, a witches' sabbath.

Those who were most sympathetic to the counter culture had been aware of its deep and dangerous ambiguities even long before Woodstock. It was as if, wrote Andrew Kopkind, a wholehearted convert to the alternative life style, "some monstrous and marvelous metaphor had come alive, revealing itself only in terms of its contradictions: paradise and concentration camp"—it was quite typical of the fashion of the time in radical journalism to compare a wet weekend with the Final Solution—"sharing and profiteering, sky and mud, love and death. The urges of the ten years' generation roamed the woods and pastures, and who could tell whether it was rough beast or speckled bird slouching through its Day-Glo manger to be born?" For Landau, more realistically, Woodstock was not a new birth but an ending. It was "the ultimate commercialization" of the underground culture at the very moment when it seemed to be in process of being transformed into a mass culture, and perhaps indeed into *the* mass culture. Since it demonstrated "just how strong in numbers the rock audience had become, and just how limited its culture was," he thought Woodstock "a fitting end to the sixties" and the satanic events at Altamont only a parody and an anticlimax.

One reason why it was absurd to equate rock music with revolution, political or cultural, was because it was so very much a commercial product and one that was marketed with single-minded cynicism by individual entrepreneurs and corporate business alike. Behaving in this instance, for once, just as pragmatically as Marxist lore would have predicted, the entertainment industry put up with whatever the musicians and their admirers chose to inflict on it. It tolerated outrageous arrogance, boorishness, and unreliability. It raised no demur at long hair on stage and clouds of marijuana in recording studios. It even shelled out royalties far higher than the deferential blacks and crooners who ground out the hits of the past had ever been paid. It would have put up with far more—just so long as the records kept selling. And sell they did.

In the very month of Woodstock *The Wall Street Journal*, no friend of revolution, psychic or political, looked upon rock music and found it good. Over the past several years, it reported, record sales had been rising at the rate of between 15 percent and 20 percent annually. The previous year, they had passed the $1 billion mark. The fundamental cause of this sales boom, no doubt, was prosperity: that very "Great Society" prosperity that the counter culture so bitterly affected to despise. But it was rock that was making those burgeoning sales. "Five years ago," the *Journal* found, meaning 1964, "Columbia Records . . . did about 15 percent of its business in rock. Today rock (using the term loosely) accounts for 60 percent or more of the vastly increased total."

In 1967 *Rolling Stone* magazine was founded, by Jann Wenner, age twenty-one, with seventy-five hundred dollars borrowed from family and friends. He could not have been a more characteristic product of the counter culture. He had dropped out of Berkeley, where he had been caught up in the Free Speech Movement. He knew Ken Kesey. He had been one of the early hippies. He had been involved with drugs. By the end of its first year *Rolling Stone* had a circulation of sixty thousand. By the end of the decade, with a circulation of over a quarter of a million, it was attracting lush advertising from the big record companies. Less than three years after it was floated, *Rolling Stone* was spending a sum of money roughly equivalent to its original capitalization in order to advertise on the back page of the New York *Times*. "If you are a corporate executive," the ad said, "trying to understand what is happening to youth today, you cannot afford to be without *Rolling Stone*."

"Several large Establishment-oriented corporations," the New York *Times* reported as if to confirm the effectiveness of this pitch, "are interested in cashing in on the youth market that Woodstock proved exists. These firms are hiring highly paid youth consultants to advise them on forthcoming trends that percolate from the deepest underground to . . . the silk-shirt hippie types from Forest Hills who do so much of the buying." "The Establishment," one underground journalist complained in 1970, "is slowly but steadily finding ways to exploit the radical movement." . . .

Rock music was never, except in the minds of a handful of its adherents, an attack on the values of "privatism, competition, commercialism, profitability, and elitism." By the end of the decade it was hard even for them to deny that it had become a glorification of each and every one of those.


## 3

Like the counter culture itself, the underground press of the sixties could trace its pedigree back to the handful of bohemian intellectuals and political radicals who held out against the consensus of the late 1950s. Like rock music, it developed as it did because of technological innovations. But it caught on because in the high years of the Great Schism, from 1964 to 1969, millions of people no longer believed what the television networks and the established papers and magazines were telling them.

The grandfather of the underground papers was *The Village Voice*, which first appeared in January, 1956. Norman Mailer was one of its founders and wrote a column for the first eighteen issues, after which he fell out with the other editors. "They wanted it to be successful," he complained later; "I wanted it to be outrageous." It did in fact become immensely successful only after it had ceased to be outrageous: which only goes to show that the consensus of the time was real enough. But it did make one crucial connection. The socialist weeklies of the Old Left had been remorselessly heavy in style and timidly puritan about such matters as drugs, art, and sexual freedom. The *avant-garde* magazines, on the other hand, were utterly apolitical. What was new about the Voice was that it always understood that the hip style and the nascent civil rights and peace movements had their sources in the same emotions. Its stance, however, was analogous to that of the folk songs of protest that were being sung around the corner from the Voice's office; like them, it had a minority audience mainly concentrated in what had become the very prosperous heirs of New York radicalism. By the middle sixties, the heartland of the Voice's readership had moved uptown from Greenwich Village to the West Side of Manhattan. In the same years two publications that combined superb journalistic quality with a consistently radical stance acquired great influence with the same educated, upper-middle-class readership: *The New York Review of Books*, closely associated with major New York publishing houses, and *I. F. Stone's Weekly*, which became more and more widely admired by journalists within the established media the more often its dogged skepticism about the Johnson administration proved justified.

But both the review and the newsletter were created by men (and women) trained in the old media. The possibility of an entirely new kind of journalism, made by a new kind of journalist for a new readership, was opened up by the development, also originally in 1956, of photo-offset typesetting. Photo offset did away with the need for [the]expensive printing plant and for highly skilled linotype operators on high union wages. Any intelligent eighteen-year-old could learn in a couple of days to make up a page with bold headlines and elaborate artwork, and after about two thousand copies, an attractive, professional-looking paper produced by photo offset was cheaper than mimeograph. . . .

In 1965 and 1966 the new papers sprang up like mushrooms in the lush manure of bad news. Their epidemiology followed the familiar pattern. The capitals of the counter culture in California and New York came first, with the *Oracle* in the Haight-Ashbury and the *East Village Other*. Then the big university centers: the Boston *Phoenix*, *The Paper* in East Lansing, home of Michigan State. Then the metropolitan cities away from the East and West coasts: the *Seed* in Chicago, the *Fifth Estate* in Detroit, the *Great Speckled Bird* in Atlanta. By 1968 there was hardly a city or a campus of any size in the country that did not boast at least one underground paper. Their mortality rate was fairly high, but by the early 1970s it was calculated that there were three–four hundred underground or alternative papers, with a total of some 9 million readers.

In 1962 a group of liberal Catholic laymen began to publish a review called *Ramparts*. Originally it was mainly literary, printing poetry by John Berryman and Conrad Aiken as well as by Allen Ginsberg and Lawrence

Ferlinghetti, and its political aims stopped short at chiding the hierarchy for its reticence on such issues as racism, poverty, and nuclear weapons. In October, 1964, however—the month after the birth of the Free Speech Movement—it changed its format, and began to tackle major political stories. *Ramparts* was in the forefront of the revival of investigative journalism, which had virtually atrophied in conventional U.S. newspapers except for periodic razzias against trivial corruption in local politics. The recurrent themes of *Ramparts'* concern were the civil rights struggle and the Vietnam War, but a survey of the major articles it published over the next four and a half years is a sound guide to the evolving political interests of the counter culture. In 1964 and 1965 *Ramparts* printed long, committed reports from Selma, from Mississippi and from Harlem. In July, 1965, it published Robert Scheer's classic analysis of the "Vietnam lobby"; in April, 1966, it revealed the involvement of Michigan State University in training President Diem's secret police in South Vietnam; and in January, 1967, in an illustrated twenty-five-page report called "the Children of Vietnam," it did much to set off national discussion of how U.S. tactics in the war were causing unnecessary civilian casualties.

Gradually *Ramparts'* political interests broadened from the specific issues of racism and war to a more generalized suspicion of "the system." In March, 1967, it published perhaps the most influential scoop of the decade: an exposé of how the National Student Association had been secretly financed for fifteen years by the CIA. In 1968 it followed that with its last two major coups: the revelation that the CIA had engineered the death of Che Guevara, and the publication of his diary. Over this same period *Ramparts* also showed a remarkable flair for social trends and fashions. To take examples almost at random, it published the first major articles on Marshall McLuhan, on LSD, on the hippies, the Black Panthers (whose Eldridge Cleaver was a *Ramparts* editor for a time), and on the women's liberation movement.

Unlike *Ramparts*, which always aspired to a national readership, the proliferating underground papers were essentially neighborhood papers. Their small ads provided the basic network of information for those who lived in the East Village, in Berkeley, in the Haight-Ashbury, or in Chicago's Old Town: they were sold by hand at street corners. They also served a community that was defined by its decision to live the new life; and so they provided such useful information as where to live, and whom you could live with, as well as what was on at the neighborhood movies and how to get a ride to a rock concert. The *Barb's* Dr. Hip Pocrates, and a hundred imitators, offered advice on the little inconveniences of liberation: what to do if you got pregnant, or if the dog swallowed some marijuana, and how to cure nonspecific vaginitis. They catered to their readers' inexhaustible fascination with drugs: the Los Angeles *Free Press* never fully recovered from the effects of a $25 million lawsuit brought against it by the state of California for identifying some hundreds of its undercover narcotics agents by name. At their best, they also reported superbly the news of the community: the *Free Press's* coverage of the Watts riot and the *Barb's* coverage of the People's Park episode were models, because virtually every bystander was not only a reader but a potential reporter. This was not only community journalism, it was participatory journalism. At its best, it produced perceptive and moving reporting. At its worst, it was a prescription for exhibitionism, parochialism, lying and chaos. . . .

As the radical movements proliferated and new causes competed with each other for the attention, the support and the money of the radical community, each movement and cause brought new papers into existence. Originally, for example, SDS published the intellectually distinguished *New Left Notes*, showing underground influence in format and style but a serious political review in content. Then local SDS chapters started their own papers, such as *Notes from Maggie's Farm*, in Ohio, its name taken from a Dylan song. By 1969 the Weathermen (their name taken from another Dylan song) were tussling openly with the Progressive Labor faction in SDS for the body of *New Left Notes*. The Black Panthers had their paper, *Black Panther*, and then, when the Eldridge Cleaver faction broke with Huey Newton, they started their own paper and called it *Right On!* There were high school underground papers, and underground papers on army bases, and American Indian papers, and *Chicano* papers in Spanish, and truly underground papers in prisons. There were homosexual papers, one with the happy name of *Fag Rag*. Then a whole crop of women's papers came along; one of them was called *Off Our Backs!*

As the underground papers got angrier, and more numerous, and less united, and smaller, they began to run into economic pressures. . . . The papers that survived in the end were those that found some way of making themselves useful to the rich, capitalist society they had failed to overthrow. *Rolling Stone* continued to thrive on advertising from CBS and the other record companies, and it was painfully noticeable that its tone was more kindly, even deferential about even the most mediocre new issues than on any other subject. Stewart Brand's *Whole Earth Catalogue*, bible of the flight from commercialism, was sold to Random House and duly became a national bestseller. The *New Times* in Phoenix raised one hundred thousand dollars by a stock issue, helped by local financiers, few of whom, no doubt, could be called totally committed to a radical position. And the *Straight Creek Journal*, in Denver, hit upon an even more ingenious scheme: it sold part of its stock to businessmen who needed tax losses. . . .

**4**

The years from 1965 to 1968 were years of polarization for America partly because they were years of unity for the counter culture. In the beginning, those who played rock music or took LSD, even those who smoked marijuana, bought a rock album or read an underground newspaper, felt themselves part of the same great army as those who went to jail for resisting the draft or dropped out to work for radical political change. Indeed, the cultural revolutionaries and the political radicals often were the same people, in the beginning. They had a single enemy, as they saw it in the first, innocent days, whether they called it capitalism, or the System, or Pig Nation, or Amerika. There was a conviction that all rebellions, however trivial or bizarre, were parts of one grand war of liberation against the infanticidal thing that Carl Oglesby, the politician, called Leviathan, and Allen Ginsberg, the poet, called Moloch.

It was in 1967 that the underground papers first began to talk about "the Revolution." The confusion between the political and the cultural was compounded by the popularity of this metaphor. At its silliest, it led to the sad delusion that you could change society by smoking marijuana and listening to amplified electric guitars (provided they were loud enough). Neither Ginsberg's mantras nor the Fugs' chords budged the walls of the Pentagon. It was a revolution that existed only in rhetoric, a linguistic escalation born of the radicals' shame at their impotence to do anything in practice either to help the blacks or to end the war, let alone to change any society but their own.

In political terms, the counter culture's claim to be revolutionary was always tenuous. Even in its political aspect, it was a subjective culture, more interested in the ethics and feelings of its members than in changing the outside world; more concerned for the morality of American policies toward Vietnam, for example, than by the future fate of the actual Vietnamese. Even the political radicals, we saw, had often been formed by a sense of alienation from a society that seemed to have gone tragically wrong in moral terms, rather than by adherence to even the broadest of programs for action.

The schism between political radicals and cultural rebels opened very gradually. As early as 1965 the underground papers were already showing signs of boredom with political issues. In the same year, Dylan, admittedly always a pathfinder, turned from his political ballads to the smoke rings of his mind. Increasingly, those who were serious about political change became exasperated by the dreamy narcissism of those who sought a personal salvation, while those whose hearts were set on a new consciousness and a new style of living were repelled by the obsessional commitments, the squalid compromises, of those whose goal was revolution.

That was one axis: between the search for salvation and the hope of revolution. But there was another sense in which both the heavily committed political radicals and those who took seriously the search for a private salvation were tiny minorities surrounded by the half-serious multitudes of their occasional followers. While an inner minority plunged deeper and deeper into alienation from society either through commitment to political extremism or through withdrawal to the north woods of Oregon or to some Oregon of the mind, for the majority the counter culture soon degenerated into a complex of fashions and attitudes. The fashions and the attitudes were not without powerful symbolic content. It was not for nothing that the mystic signs for peace and love became the most banal decorative motifs. You could even say that if the counter culture failed to change American society in any more definite way, it did make both militarism and racism unfashionable. Still, by the end of the decade, for a majority the counter culture had degenerated into a mere youth cult. Its values were often no longer determined by the aspiration to build a free society so much as by an Oedipal hostility to the older generation. . . .

The one idea that seemed never to occur to either side in these Freudian wars of the suburbs was how much the parents and the children were alike. The children said they loathed the uniformity of the suburbs, where your personality was defined by the size and style of your house and by the make and year of your car. But they allowed the record industry and the fashion trade to define their collective personality every bit as rigidly as Detroit had ever done for their parents. Their long hair, their blue denim, were every bit as much a uniform as the crew cuts and chinos of the fifties. Even their alienation from their parents may have owed more than they realized to their similarity. If children felt that their parents didn't understand them, it may have been less because of any deep clash of values than because the parents were often too busy having a good time or getting on in the world to spare much time for their children. . . .

By the end of the sixties it was plain enough that whatever the people who flocked to rock concerts or read underground newspapers wanted, it would be doing violence to the language to call it revolution. Their problem was the no-problem society—not of the United States but of the relatively privileged part of American society from which they came. They were bored because there was no problem about money, no problem about sex, no problem about college, and no great problem if you dropped out; only the inescapable bleakness of being young and insignificant, a pebble on the infinite beach of America, but a pebble bombarded with information about the gratifications of others. They turned to the life style of the counter culture for all the things they had missed in the sheltered, affluent suburbs where they grew up: excitement, purpose, a feeling of community, and some measure of individual worth. When Mick Jagger swayed in the spotlight and promised them, "We're gonna get some satisfaction," dams burst. A frightening intensity of emotion flooded normally sulky faces. It was hardly the fault of the musicians if all they had to give was excitement without purpose, an illusion of community, when the individual's yearnings were lost in the contrived explosions of mass hysteria. It wasn't revolution; it was only show business. But, then, bored, lonely, angry though they might intermittently be with a world they never made, the Superkids of the second generation wanted to change it as little as their parents had. Telegraph Avenue was indeed the child of Madison Avenue.

Sheila M. Rothman

# The Politics of
# Women's Liberation

Feminist efforts to translate the new definition of womanhood into social policy have sparked intense antagonism and conflicts. To the women's movement, equality in employment, provisions for day care, and reproductive freedom are all logical and appropriate programs; competent and energetic women have the same rights as men to privileges and opportunities in the labor force; federal assistance for day care could facilitate working and mothering. And certainly women have the right to control their own bodies, to decide for themselves when to bear children and whether a pregnancy should or should not be terminated. But to others, each of these demands represents a challenge. Will women's entrance into the work force cost men jobs? Who exactly will control day care and pay the bill? Does a right to an abortion mean that women can command a doctor to perform the procedure? What of the moral sensibilities of the Catholic Church and other religious groups? In effect, proposals designed to advance the interests of women do threaten other vested interests—the interests of males, experts, professionals, union leaders, clergymen, and all who feel a personal stake in the perpetuation of older values.

None of these developments ought to have been particularly surprising, for in unmistakable fashion, the fate of the women's movement recapitulated the fate of the civil rights movement. Martin Luther King's dream of cooperation between the races and the hope of black leaders for a rapid desegregation of schools and other facilities were among the last major efforts

Excerpted from Chapter 7 of Woman's Proper Place: A History of Changing Ideals and Practices, 1870 to the Present, by Sheila M. Rothman, © 1978 by Sheila M. Rothman, Basic Books, Inc., Publishers, New York.

to achieve social change within a Progressive framework—that is, with the assumption that one group's demands for equality would not conflict with another's; that all Americans had a stake in an equitable system; that people could be partners, not adversaries, in the march for justice. But by 1966 this dream had faded, replaced by the much harsher and combative doctrines of black power. Progress, it seemed, was coming too slowly; opposition to civil rights was far more entrenched and powerful than had been imagined. It was time to talk not of brotherhood but of group interests, not of equality but of rights, not of a balance of interests but of competing claims. In many ways, black power advocates were the first to assert the primacy of a rights model, to attack a whole network of American institutions as fundamentally corrupt (in their terms, "racist"), and to denigrate the professionals and the experts who bolstered them. And black power set the tone and became the model for the protest movements of other minority groups. In short order, prisoners' rights, mental patients' rights, students' rights, and gay rights organizations were challenging the prerogatives of administrative experts—be they psychiatrists, wardens, college presidents, deans, or high school principals—and the legitimacy of their institutions—be they mental hospitals, prisons, or universities.

The women's movement became part of this reaction. By the 1970s it, too, asserted self-interest as vigorously as possible; it, too, organized to lobby, to sue, to agitate, to put pressure on the legislature, to influence the media—and to try to do all of this more systematically, more energetically, and more effectively than its adversaries were. If Progressive reformers appealed to the national interest, feminists now appealed to women's interests. To be sure, one could still hear rhetorical flourishes that the ERA would "symbolize and effect a new era of humanhood," that it would benefit men as well as women. But when it came down to the core of things—to realizing women's equality in the work force—the strategy was to advance women's interest first and last, to obtain for women their share of the positions, pay, and promotions, no matter how costly their effort was to other claimants. The question was, and remains, whether the women's movement will be sufficiently professional, cohesive, and organized to win not only the first round but also, when the counterattacks inevitably come, the second and the third as well. This is what it means to treat politics as a zero-sum game.

## Equal Rights in the Workplace

One of the first political bodies to feel the effects of the women's movement was the Ninety-Second Congress (1971–1973). Lobbyists for NOW and other women's groups worked vigorously to accomplish their priorities. First, to promote sexual equality, they persuaded Congress to approve the passage of an equal rights amendment to the Constitution and at the same time to amend specific federal laws so as to prohibit discrimination on the basis of sex in Health Manpower Training Programs and in educational institutions receiving federal funds. Then, to facilitate women's advancement in the labor force, they were able to effect legislation that not only revised the tax codes to permit families earning under $18,000 a year to deduct child care costs but that also provided federal funds under the Comprehensive Child Development Act for the construction of day care centers. It was a good beginning, made even better by the fact that the initial reception among the states to the ERA was highly favorable. Within two years of Congressional passage, thirty-three states ratified the amendment. The ERA represented to its proponents "the culmination of the 'women rights' segment of the Movement, which works for normative changes in society through legal and institutional means," and even more, it embodied "the 'liberation' issue, for in denying that sex is a valid legal classification of persons, it implicitly denies societal values based on biological differences between the sexes and recognizes that social roles are learned, and therefore relative." It seemed not at all fanciful to imagine that sexism would die a quick death, that a new "era of humanhood" was about to be ushered in.

Before very long, however, a far grimmer reality intruded. Opposition to the ERA coalesced, attacking both its symbolic and institutional character, protesting its effort to implement new kinds of "societal values" and "normative changes." The symbolic objections were not very complicated—although they certainly were intense and effective enough to stall the amendment's passage. A group of women, supported with funds from the most conservative organizations in the country, were able to mount a campaign that carried broad appeal. They defined the amendment, appropriately enough, as an attack upon the primacy of domestic roles for women. The ERA threatened to undermine "some of those precious necessary rights particularly affecting women who wish to be full-time wives and mothers." Not that they could ever frame the character of this challenge in very specific terms, for what was at stake was not law but values. So, when pressed, the groups tried to argue (altogether incorrectly) that the ERA would abolish alimony payments (or, conversely, compel women to support lazy men) or prohibit separate-sex restrooms. But what the opposition was really concerned about was that the ERA elevated a new definition of womanhood to a national norm. It legitimated the idea that married women should work—that women had to find fulfillment in their own accomplishments, not in their husbands' or childrens'. And that message was one that a good number of housewives did not want to hear or to countenance. "We feel the family is under attack in America," declared one of them, "and we feel the Equal Rights Amendment could be the turning point on whether family life as we know it will survive." At stake was woman's proper role. "Personally," this woman went on, "nothing makes me happier than when my little boy comes home from school and says, 'Is my mother home?' and I'm there." Thus, just as Americans had once insisted that a constitutional amendment enshrine temperance as a national norm, these women were saying that a constitutional amendment should *not* establish feminism as a national norm. Status in the office should not be elevated over status in the home. Housework should not be a stigmatized calling. Full-time mothers and wives should not become obsolete.

A backlash movement was bound to come when the full implications of the ERA premises were understood. The ERA does at the least carry enormous symbolic significance. Its passage would signal the triumph of a novel definition of woman as person, putting to rest both Progressive notions that women needed special protection and the 1920s notions that women were first and foremost their husbands' helpers. But this opposition, even if successful in the short run, even if capable of blocking or preventing passage of the ERA, is ultimately not very important. The ERA has pitted the professional woman against the volunteer, the working mother against the housewife—but it has also pitted the present life style of the mother against the future life choices of her daughter. In 1975 and 1976, the victory went to the mother, but it will very likely be a temporary one. There is every indication that the preferences expressed in the ERA are going to have a much firmer hold on the coming generation than they enjoy in the passing generation. (Indeed, proponents of the amendment probably missed a critical point in strategy by not making an open appeal to mothers to vote on behalf of their daughters. The movement might well have gained far more grassroots strength by asking: "Do you want your daughter kept out of college because of a quota on women? Do you want your daughter passed over for promotion because she is a woman?") For women as well as for men, prestige is more and more going to be distributed on the basis of personal, not surrogate, achievements. No matter what the outcome of this ERA battle, the feminists are likely to win the symbolic war.

The evidence supporting such a statement is pervasive. There is no mistaking that consciousness has been raised, at least in the upper middle classes, with a ripple effect downward already evident. Advertisements have begun to lose some of their sexist characteristics (women, too, need life insurance and should buy Adidas sneakers for jogging). Dolls now show women as doctors as well as nurses (even if they do not yet present men as nurses). "Ms." as a form of address is no longer a joke; "chairperson" has lost its awkwardness. Some newspapers think it is even news, and worthy of Sunday supplement coverage, when a woman decides to quit her job and raise her baby. Indeed, that some people find it necessary to argue (and the New York Times on its "Op-Ed" page finds it fit to print) that women should be free to be mothers as well as office workers testifies to the fact that the new norm is competing well with the old—although it is highly doubtful whether the women's movement has, or will, become so powerful as to justify fears of its tyranny.

But the most important evidence of the substantial differences between daughters' and mothers' life styles comes from the admissions rates to professional schools. In recent years the number of women attending law schools and medical schools has climbed dramatically. In 1973, there were three and one-half times the number of. women enrolled in law schools (16,760) than there were in 1969 (4,715). So, too, the number of women in medical school has almost doubled. In 1969, there were 3,392 women who made up 9 percent of the students; by 1973, women had increased to 7,824, or 15 percent of the group. More women also entered traditionally male white-collar occupations. Between 1960 and 1970, the number of women accountants rose from 80,400 to 183,000; the number of engineers climbed from 7,000 in 1960 to 19,600 in 1973. The number of female real estate sales agents jumped from 46,000 to 83,600, and the number of female insurance agents and brokers rose from 35,300 (or almost 10 percent of the group) to 56,600 (or almost 12.4 percent). As the image of the working woman has changed, women have entered occupations that Progressive protective legislation had closed off. Over the 1960s, the number of women guards and bus drivers tripled; the number of policewomen doubled. Women entered the skilled trades too in unprecedented force. The percentage of woman carpenters rose from 0.4 to 1.3, the percentage of electricians from 0.7 to 1.8, and the percentage of auto mechanics from 0.5 to 1.4. Clearly, women were leaping traditional barriers, and in many cases traditional barriers were coming down.

But the conflict over values and the inroads that the younger generation has made into positions that were once exclusively male is only one part of the story—and not necessarily the most significant part. When one turns to institutional change, from the achievements of a few pioneers in the man's world to a structural analysis of the position of women in the labor force, the gains become far less notable and the clash of competing claims far more intense. It may only be tokenism that is marking women's progress. Even more disturbing, the efforts to enforce rules against sexual discrimination have been neither wholehearted nor effective. The passage of the ERA may well represent a victory for the values of the women's movement, but whether it will help to advance their actual position is acutely problematic.

For one, a reduction of sex stereotyping in jobs at the very moment when unemployment in the economy has been rising has had the effect of bringing more men into positions that were once exclusively women's. Although an absence of discrimination on grounds of sex properly cuts both ways, it does mean that the gains that women have made in some occupations is offset by losses in others. Thus, the number of male elementary school teachers rose from 140,000 (or 14 percent of the total) in 1960 to 231,000 (or 16 percent of the total) in 1970—counterbalancing advances made among women carpenters and electricians. So, too, between 1972 and 1976, the attempts to end job stereotyping in the Bell Telephone System led to an increase in the number of women in managerial positions as well as a decrease in the total number of women working for the company. The number of male telephone operators has climbed far more rapidly than the number of female operators. In all, Bell now employs 15,000 women—four years ago it employed 25,000 women.

More important, the disparity in wages between men and women did not decline over the past decade—in fact, it widened! In 1963, the median earnings of full-time, year-round women workers were 63 percent of those of men workers. In 1973 the figure dropped to 57 percent. To be sure, the gap varied from occupation to occupation. Among clerical workers, women in 1965 earned 72 percent of the salaries of the men; in 1973 they earned 61 percent. Women in professional and technical work earned 66 percent of men's salaries in 1962 and 63.6 percent in 1973. These figures, it should be noted, do not indicate in any simple fashion that employers were biased against women. Market forces were at play: the number of women entering the work force, particularly in the less skilled positions, has been so great as to depress the pay scale; women with higher educational achievements are in greater demand for skilled positions and hence have fared better. Yet, as Caroline Shaw Bell explains, if one cause "of the worsening position of women's work in terms of earned income has been the influx of women into the labor force," the other cause is "stringent occupational barriers." Sex stereotyping of jobs remains strong enough to crowd women into a few occupations and thus to reduce their wages. A very rigid sense of what constitutes women's work still dominates in the work force and in the society, and the consequences of that rigidity are apparent in the lower earning power of women.

*    *    *

Another of the barriers to equality for working women is the sluggish state of the economy. A contraction in the job market does hurt newcomers, be they women or blacks or members of other minority groups. Some feminists fear that a persistent recession will not only impede progress but also cancel gains already made. "The economic environment," notes one analyst, "may prove to be the major determinant of women's role in 1980. . . . Scarcity of jobs in the next decade [will] produce a greater competition in the labor market and a tremendous backlash against women."

Despite the persistence of these problems, ample room does exist for optimism about future prospects. The economist Victor Fuchs argues persuasively that the very fact that women did not *lose* considerable ground in their earning powers during a period of marked expansion of participation in the work force augurs very well. "Able to hold their own . . . the long-run prospects for women must be viewed as favorable." Nor is it naïve to believe that token advances can encourage real ones. The publicity that accompanies advancement of a few secretaries into higher-paying and more responsible administrative positions may well prompt others to compete for these jobs. The delight with which the media covers "the first woman who . . ." is probably helping to raise women's expectations and to alter sexist images. The token woman may turn out to be a model for the young.

The prospect for change through federal agencies is not altogether bleak, either. The presence of a large pool of women in the law schools today may mean that the EEOC will be staffed tomorrow by a group far more sympathetic to enforcing compliance. Reformers understand quite clearly the need to "capture" federal bureaucracies through a variety of stratagems. Thus, Jo Freeman, a political scientist and feminist, has counseled women's organizations not only to carry out more litigation and public education campaigns but also to make certain that an agency knows full well what women clients want of it. "Government agencies are subject to a sufficient number of demands to effectively prevent them from looking for any problems they don't already have." Women activists recognize that one of their tasks is to keep administrators alert to their problems.

The ease with which progress can be measured in this field simplifies such efforts. The difficult task is not to define what constitutes discrimination but to implement corrective actions. The response of a corporation or a university that the available pool of qualified women is too small to permit promotions is already suspect, and it is very likely to become still more so in the future. For all the debate about whether affirmative action programs constitute just or unjust practices, whether quotas and goals are identical, and whether measurement should be based on equality of outcome or equality of opportunity, there remains a fundamental agreement on the principle that equal pay and equal rights are fair, that women should not suffer discrimination. Indeed, as compared to the blacks, women enjoy some considerable advantages. The abolition of sexual discrimination in the work force likely requires less social engineering and less intrusive policies than, for example, the desegregation of the schools. Sexism is probably less virulent than racism. A busing program inevitably generates more heat and controversy than an AT&T compliance order.

Thus, sooner rather than later women will enjoy equal pay and equal opportunity. Advances may well come first in the professions and filter down more slowly into blue-collar positions. But the gap between rhetoric and reality is bound to be closed, for the next generation of women if not for this one.

### Who Cares for the Child?

The concept of woman as person has also redirected the course of social policy toward the family. If women's career choices are to be enhanced, discrimination by sex is only one of the problems, and perhaps not even the thorniest one at that. Much more complicated and controversial is the potential redistribution of domestic responsibilities, particularly in the realm of child care. If women are going to enter the work force, who is going to be at home with the child? Here the broader sense of a conflict of interest within the family takes on an immediacy that is as troubling as it is unavoidable. The issue has divided groups in terms both of strategy and of goals. There is no agreement on whether child development will necessarily suffer if substitutes for full-time mothering, such as day care programs, are implemented. Nor is there consensus on which organizations should control the delivery of day care, or what the content of the program should be, or who should staff the centers. . . .

\*     \*     \*

The problem goes beyond the specifics of this issue. Day care is only a single instance of the confrontation between two conflicting social ideologies. To one group, traditional and established institutions will inevitably ignore a minority's best interests; day care, like welfare, will turn out to be a boon for the middle-class professionals, not for the poor. It will improve the lot of those who administer the program, not its clients. And if minority groups cannot capture and control the organizations and institutions that are ostensibly designed to serve them, how will they ever manage to increase their power in the larger society? To the other side, minority group advocates are attempting to change the rules of the game in midstream. The promise was that credentials would be rewarded in this society, that degrees and qualifications would count for most. Minority groups also seem to them to be violating every principle of social cohesion, trying to promote their own particular values and control their own particular institutions as though they were a nation apart. To make matters worse, the first victories in the 1960s went to the minorities, so that the opposition now believes that it must launch a vigorous counterattack to recapture lost ground. Its stance will be uncompromising, for fear that any further losses will cost it dearly in the job market and in the political arena.

So on the narrow front of day care, the prospects for immediate accomplishment are not very favorable. On the broader issue of comity in the political arena, there seems to be little bend, little trust, little room for maneuver. Perhaps the traditionally powerful forces in society will in the end dominate. Day care, for example, would not be the first instance of a group of professionals taking over a program that others designed. The precedents of Sheppard-Towner and birth control seem particularly relevant: a group of advocates enters an essentially empty field, calls for a novel program under its own direction, convinces the society of its value, and then witnesses a group of experts, using credentials that may not be at all relevant, taking it over. But there are now strong indications that such an outcome would not end the controversy. Activists are very much aware of conflict of interest and far more anti-professional in their orientation. To them, it is a question not of better service but of a different kind of service; it is a matter not of expertise but of values. So if vested groups capture the programs, they will probably find not only a continuing series of challenges to their authority, but also a bitterness and even an air of illegitimacy surrounding the victory.

## One More Round: Women and Their Doctors

The adversarial quality of politics emerges even more vividly in the third and final social policy concern of the new feminists, the field of health. It was inevitable that a definition of woman as person would open another round in the ongoing confrontation between women and physicians. Every generation, it seems, has to reformulate the relationship, and the post-1960s era proved no exception. In the past, collegiate education, Sheppard-Towner, and the birth control movement were the occasions for dispute and compromise; now feminists have set out to liberate themselves from inherited roles and traditional authorities. They have raised the most basic questions about women's right to control their bodies, or as the title of one book so aptly put it, *Our Bodies, Ourselves*. The issues were varied but all interrelated, ranging from the definition of disease (is pregnancy an illness?) to the nature of reproductive freedom (is there any limit to women's control over their bodies, whether pregnant or not?). In fact, the policy implications of a commitment to reproductive freedom have raised controversies that make the ERA and day care battles seem mild in comparison.

The first goal of the women's campaign has been to restrict the domain of the physician, to move away from the alliances that Sheppard-Towner and birth control advocates made. The prime targets were the obstetricians and gynecologists. *Our Bodies, Ourselves* labeled their care "condescending, paternalistic, judgmental and noninformative." These doctors not only treated women with an acute lack of sensitivity but even worse, exercised an "imperialism of knowledge." And medical imperialism subjugated women. "This kind of ignorance about our bodies, and particularly those parts related to reproduction and sexuality, is connected with the alienation and shame and fear that have been imposed upon us as women."

Accordingly, feminists started programs to educate women about their bodies: to demystify health care would liberate them from doctors' control. The efforts have taken many forms, from those that the press has sensationalized (such as teaching women to use a speculum) to those that were obvious and long overdue (instructing them in breast examination and the choice and use of contraceptives). Education in sexuality also assumed a new significance. Medical training no longer entitled a gynecologist to serve as a sexual counselor (a practice that Sanger had helped to create and to perpetuate). "Just because a doctor is certified ob-gyn," noted one tract, "doesn't mean that he is qualified or trained or prepared in any way to give advice or counsel or any other sort of help in any human relations area of a woman's life." The occasional courses in psychology or human behavior that he might take could bolster his confidence, "but these are simply not enough to qualify him for the delicate work of therapy or counseling about sexual adjustment." The goal of all these feminist efforts was not only to make women healthier but also to alter their self-image, to give them, in the way Vassar did in its time, new confidence and energy. "For us," declared *Our Bodies, Ourselves*, "body education is core education. . . . Picture a woman trying to do work and to enter into equal and satisfying relationships with other people—when she feels physically weak . . . when her internal bodily processes are a mystery to her . . . when she does not understand nor enjoy sex." Only by taking responsibility "for our physical selves" will women "start to use our untapped energies. . . . We can be better friends, and better lovers, better *people*, more self-confident, more autonomous, stronger, and more whole." In brief, bodily knowledge would promote, almost guarantee, the realization of the ideology of woman as person.

*   *   *

The movement for "reproductive freedom" has brought more accomplishments and generated deeper controversy. In the area of contraception, law finally did catch up to practice. By 1965, the number of Protestant families using some form of birth control had reached 87 percent, and the number of Catholic families was not far behind at 78 percent. That same year the Supreme Court ruled in the Griswold case that dispensing contraceptive "information, instruction and medical advice to *married persons*" was protected by "the zone of privacy created by several constitutional decrees." Its 1972 decision in *Eisenstadt v. Baird* dispelled whatever lingering doubts remained by expanding the Griswold precedent to include unmarried persons. "If the right of privacy means anything, it is the right of the *individual*, married or single to be free from unwarranted governmental intrusion into matters so fundamentally affecting a person as the decision whether to bear or beget a child." Indeed, by the time of the Eisenstadt decision, Congress had approved the Family Planning Act, providing birth control information without cost to anyone who wanted it and federal subsidies to underwrite the establishment of family planning clinics. There was so little opposition to the Act that one Senator felt compelled to remark that the committee holding hearings could not find any group to speak out against the concept of planned parenthood.

Predictably, the expanded view of women's rights came into conflict with state prohibitions on abortion. During the late 1960s a handful of states, including New York, broadened the grounds for which a woman could obtain an abortion. But the breakthrough came in January, 1973, when the Supreme Court decided that a woman in her first trimester of pregnancy, in consultation with her physician, had the right to obtain an abortion; state interference in that privilege was unconstitutional. In including the woman's right to terminate pregnancy under the right to privacy, the Court cited first the potential medical dangers to the woman. But it quickly left these traditional grounds, noting: "Maternity, or additional offspring, may force upon the woman a distressful life and future. Psychological harm may be imminent. Mental and physical health may be taxed by child-care. There is also the distress for all concerned, associated with the unwanted child." And hence the woman's right to an abortion.

The merits of the decision aside, the opinion itself was neither brilliant nor consistent. It did not persuasively demonstrate why states could not attempt to resolve so murky a question as when life begins. It did not establish abortion as a "right" in the sense that the poor had a claim on the government to pay for the procedure. But whatever its weaknesses, the decision had major consequences, both intended and unintended, for social policy.

The number and type of women who underwent abortions, and their experiences, effectively put to rest some long-standing objections. For once, it became immediately obvious that abortion was a very safe procedure. In New York State, from mid-1970 to mid-1972, about 402,000 abortions took place with only 16 deaths. In the country as a whole between 1972 and 1974, there were 3.4 deaths per 100,000 legal abortions, as compared to a maternal mortality rate of 14.8 per 100,000 live births. For another, abortion on an outpatient basis (relying upon the vacuum aspiration techniques instead of on surgery), proved to be a very practical and low-risk technique for women in their first trimester of pregnancy; it was also simple and inexpensive to administer. Moreover, the number of women who took advantage of the liberalization in the abortion law was staggering. In 1973, there were 747,000 abortions; in 1974, there were 900,000; in 1975, more than 1,000,000. And most women seemed to suffer none of the acute guilt that some psychiatrists had predicted; they were not filling hospital beds with post-abortion depression. Finally, public health officials noted not only a decrease in deaths from legal abortion as compared to illegal abortion, but also "lower out-of-wedlock birth rates and improved infant health."

The change in law prompted a change in public opinion. Before 1973, public opinion polls revealed that less than a majority of the population was in favor of abortion. After 1973, polls reported a majority in favor of the Supreme Court's liberalization of abortion (52 to 54 percent of the respondents to various Gallup polls). So, too, NBC polls indicated that a majority would keep abortion laws as they are now or further liberalize them. It was also evident that women used abortion for sound reasons. In most cases they were unmarried (in New York City in 1974, two-thirds of the women undergoing abortion were single) and very young (in New York, 51 percent were under twenty-five). Taken together, these findings pointed to a massive and safe reliance on abortion by women who seemed to be making sane and sensible decisions.

Yet the victories for the pro-abortion forces have been less than complete, and the controversies marking the policy have become more acute. Resistance to providing women with the option of abortion increases as one moves farther from urban centers. In nonmetropolitan areas, only 15 percent of private hospitals and 11 percent of public hospitals delivered abortion services in 1974 and 1975; indeed, in metropolitan areas, fewer than half the private hospitals (46 percent) and about one-third of the public hospitals carried out abortions. The low percentage of abortions in public facilities is all the more critical because they traditionally service the poor. In effect, an abortion could be obtained only in one or two urban centers of a state, and then not typically in public but in private hospitals and abortion clinics. Hence, for women who live at some distance from a city or who are poor, an abortion (even before the recently imposed Congressional restrictions) has not been available on demand.

A hospital's failure to deliver abortion services indicates not a lack of demand but an unwillingness to meet it. In New Jersey, for example, a Health Department survey in 1974 revealed that of the sixty-nine hospitals in the state, thirty-nine would perform an abortion only to save the mother's life—in clear disregard of the Supreme Court ruling. In a city like Milwaukee, doctors in one public hospital refused to perform abortions except where the life of the mother was in danger, and moreover, they refused to allow the hospital to hire doctors willing to perform abortions in compliance with the law. A suit finally did force the hospital to alter its policies, but the litigation process took two years.

The refusal of many hospitals to carry out abortions obviously reflects the pressure exerted by Catholic doctors and the Catholic church. (Milwaukee, for example, has a population that is 40 percent Catholic.) But the hospitals are responding to more than just Catholic sentiments. Religion quite apart, many doctors, for personal or professional reasons, remain ambivalent about or opposed to abortion. One hundred medical school professors in 1972 did urge their colleagues to recognize "that abortion has become a predominantly social as well as medical responsibility. For the first time, except perhaps for cosmetic surgery, doctors will be expected to do an operation simply because the patient asks that it be done." They accepted this change in order to serve "the new society in which they live." Many others, however, are reluctant to grant their patients this kind of authority.

Physicians' objections to abortion in the Milwaukee case revealed how much more than Catholic doctrine was at stake. (Indeed, since polls report that some 46 percent of Catholics favor legalized abortion, this is to be expected.) Some doctors argued that abortion was "a waste of valuable medical effort." As one of them put it, "Performance of an abortion is bad medicine. . . . If I were to do an act that I consider bad medicine it would be unethical on my part." Others frankly objected "to being ordered to perform any medical service." Still others insisted that "I cannot approve of the use of surgical approach for solution of a social problem." Given the fact that in the nation as a whole "only one-fourth of [all] hospitals, and fewer than one-fifth of public hospitals, provide any abortion services," clearly, doctors' social views are shaping institutional practices.

Opposition to abortion has come too from Right to Life groups where again, Catholic efforts have been prominent but not exclusive. The president of the National Right to Life Committee in 1976 was a black, Methodist woman surgeon. And for all the charges that she was a figurehead for an essentially Catholic movement, in fact, there was constituent support for her anti-abortion position in every one of her diverse identifications. Blacks have claimed that abortion constitutes genocide, the newest white man's technique to reduce their numbers in the population. Methodists have been joined by fundamentalist Protestant groups and Orthodox Jews in condemning abortion.

Traditional-minded women link the ERA with abortion because neither gives primacy to domestic and maternal obligations. And surgeons do object to being told to perform an operation.

The result of the staunch pro- and anti-abortion sentiments has been to make the controversy, in the political jargon, a "bullet" issue, that is, no matter how a representative or senator votes on all other matters, a "wrong" vote on abortion (be it yes or no) will cost constituent support. Congress may well have exaggerated the strength of the anti-abortion forces because they have been so active and energetic; and first evidence suggests that "congressmen who took a consistent, favorable position with regard to legalized abortion appeared to have a slight edge in the 1974 election over those with an anti-abortion record." In all events, the conflicts have been fierce and quintessentially adversarial. The 1977 stalemate in Congress on whether Medicaid funds could be used to cover the costs of abortion (the program had been funding 300,000 abortions a year at the cost of $50 million) was one indication of the volatility of the issue. And the resolution, taken months later, was objectionable to both sides: Medicaid funds would pay for an abortion when the mother would suffer "severe and long-lasting physical health damage" as certified to by two doctors, or for "medical procedures" in the case of rape or incest that was "promptly" reported. Anti-abortion forces found these provisions far too liberal. Pro-abortion forces were no less disturbed at being back in the all-too-familiar position of having to rely upon medical determinations. Once again, the doctor held the key, which meant that the poor would be subjected to inconsistent and varying decisions.

One final incident conveys the bitter quality of the confrontation. Secretary of Health, Education and Welfare Joseph Califano, in light of his own and President Carter's opposition to abortion, set up a special committee, chaired by a woman, to explore "alternatives to abortion." The committee's report concluded that "the literal alternatives to it are suicide, motherhood, and some would add, madness. Consequently, there is some confusion, discomfort, and cynicism greeting efforts to 'find' or 'emphasize' or 'identify' alternatives to abortion." Upon receiving the report, Califano disbanded the committee.

Thus in abortion, as in so many other cases, the attempt to implement a social policy reflecting the concept of woman as person has brought some benefits to the middle class but not to the lower class. As we have seen, at AT&T, the EEOC has helped educated women to rise in the ranks, but the less educated now find fewer jobs; the new legitimacy of day care affords greater options for the middle class, but does not provide the lower-class with services. So, too, middle-class women can rather easily obtain an abortion; lower-class women will be lucky to do so. This outcome may in part reflect the fact that American politics, especially when there are costs involved, is not responsive to the needs or the rights of the poor. But something deeper emerges too: women have not been able to unite in a movement that would allow the identity of sex to override the differences in class. Despite the reformers' belief that sisters would act together in an effective alliance, the results have not been satisfying. In the end, lower-class women receive little or nothing from WIN or day care or liberalized abortion. The women's movement has not managed to do much better for the lower classes than any of its predecessors.

There is, then, nothing altogether novel in the consequences of current social policies. However disappointing the present record of the EEOC or the WIN program, the performance of the Charity Organization Society or the child welfare reformers or the Sanger group was no more satisfying. The current conflicts over policy have a familiar ring. Not for the first time have the interests of women clashed with the interests of professionals. Day care and abortion do in some ways repeat the experiences of Sheppard-Towner and birth control.

Yet, something novel and encouraging does appear, if only faintly, in the present state of reform, and it emerges from this very recognition that interests and values are in conflict. Feminists and, not coincidentally, other advocates of minority rights share a new determination to advance their own interests as they, and not experts or surrogates, define them. They are acutely aware that a call to the common welfare, whether it be to the well-being of children, or to the future of the family, or to the stability of society, has all too often abridged women's freedom of action. If some women have been and remain eager to respond to this appeal, that is their prerogative. But others who may wish to reallocate the burden or avoid it altogether are asserting their right to choice. They now have a very clear, even raw, sense of what constitutes cooptation as opposed to real gains, where compromise becomes capitulation, and when trade-offs become surrender. One cannot be certain of the consequences of this orientation; an understanding of past and present developments does not chart future directions. Nevertheless, two observations and one small item of comfort are worth noting.

First, this new sense of the rules of the game may help to promote women's interests, at least middle-class women's interests. The willingness of activists to do battle in a second, a third, and a fourth round may well promote their ambitions. The women's movement is becoming another—and not altogether weak—vested interest group, and this transformation is likely to bear results in the American political system. Second, this approach to social policy is likely to exacerbate tensions, to make an appeal to the common welfare still more obsolete. Pressures will generate counterpressures, sharp disputes over "turf," and an unwillingness to make concessions. One need only look to the political activities of blacks, professionals, children's advocates, and labor unions to appreciate the strength of this dynamic. We are likely to live with lawsuits and challenges and an overheated political rhetoric for some time to come. Given the assumptions and the stakes, not only women but other groups as well are going to be ready for successive rounds.

The solace? As others have discovered before us, it is difficult to be king when the gods are changing.

Samuel P. Huntington

# The Disharmonic Polity

### "Our Practice of Your Principles"

As is His wont, God did not dare. Although it had showered the night before, the morning of the second Thursday in June 1969 dawned warm and sundrenched. Steamy vapors rose from the soaking grass and dripping chairs, carefully ordered in their rows in the Yard, promising a hot and humid day for Harvard's 318th commencement. But although the University authorities maintained their usual casual optimism about the cooperation of the Almighty, there was considerable concern that less godly creatures might dare to be less accommodating. Turmoil, protest, and violence were reaching new peaks on American campuses that spring. The previous year, Columbia University had erupted into chaos. In April 1969 had come Harvard's turn, with the seizure of University Hall, the police bust, the student strike, the disruption of classes, and the endless mass meetings and bullhorns, demonstrations and demands, caucuses and resolutions. The night before commencement, prolonged negotiations among university officials, student leaders, and SDS (Students for a Democratic Society) extremists had produced an agreement that the normal order of ceremony would be interrupted to permit one of the SDS revolutionaries to speak briefly to the throng of ten thousand. Before dawn a contingent of younger and presumably somewhat more robust faculty members had been quietly admitted through the locked gates of the Yard and had surrounded and occupied the platform—a preemptive measure to head off others with more disruptive intentions.

As it turned out, such precautions were unnecessary. Overt revolutionary challenges to civil and academic authority during the two-hour ceremony were minimal. The SDS speaker "blew it," as one student said, with a tedious, uncompromising monologue which elicited loud boos from the audience. The protest walkout from the ceremonies drew less than two hundred students. The revolutionary impulse was limited to a clenched-fist greeting to university president Nathan Pusey by the graduating seniors, serving along with the clenched fists stenciled on their academic gowns as a lingering reminder of the upheavals earlier in the spring.

The revolutionary challenge to established authority thus fizzled in Harvard Yard, as it has always fizzled in American society. But one major challenge to established authority was posed in the Yard that day, and in traditional American pattern it came not from the fringes but from the mainstream. In appropriate Harvard fashion, it was posed intellectually rather than physically. It was to be found in the English Oration delivered by Meldon E. Levine, a native of Beverly Hills, California, and a graduate student in law. "What is this protest all about?" Levine asked. Addressing himself to the alumni, faculty, and parents and presuming to speak for his fellow students, he answered this question briefly—and accurately. Our protest, he said, is not an effort "to subvert institutions or an attempt to challenge values which have been affirmed for centuries. We are *not*," he emphasized, ". . . conspiring to destroy America. We are attempting to do precisely the reverse: we are affirming the values which you have instilled in us and which you have taught us to respect. You have told us repeatedly that trust and courage were standards to emulate. You have convinced us that equality and justice were inviolable concepts. You have taught us that authority should be guided by reason and tempered by fairness. *And we have taken you seriously.*" We have tried to put into practice your principles, Levine told the older generation, and you have frustrated us and obstructed us. "You have given us our visions and then asked us to curb them." We want to do what you have taught us is right to do, but "you have made us idealists and then told us to go slowly." All we ask is that "you allow us to realize the very values which you have held forth."

Speaking on behalf of the younger generation, Levine did not contemptuously confront his elders with the claim that a youthful European Marxist or African nationalist might have made: We reject your reactionary, traditional, outworn beliefs and instead proclaim our own radical and revolutionary principles. Instead, his plea was a peculiarly American one: We of the younger generation simply want to put into practice those ideals in which you—and we—believe. It is, as he summed it up in the title of his talk, "a conflict of conscience: our practice of your principles." We question your war, your repression, your temporizing, your inaction in the name of your basic values. We do not proclaim a New Truth to challenge the old myths of earlier generations. We instead invoke the Old Truths and charge you, the older generations, with deserting those truths. You are the apostates, not we. You are, in effect, the subversives; we are the loyalists, who proudly reaffirm the principles that you ignore.

Levine's remarks were greeted with a loud, sustained, standing ovation from his classmates, while many parents and alumni, as one reporter put it, "sat stony-faced and silent." As a child of the 1960s (who had been president of the Berkeley student body during the 1964 uprising there), Levine had precisely caught the spirit of that decade. By and large, the struggles of the 1960s did not involve conflicts between partisans of different principles. What the 1960s did involve was a reaffirmation of traditional American ideals and values; they were a time of comparing practice to principle, of reality to ideal, of behavior to belief. Politically the 1960s began with sit-ins, bus boycotts, and civil rights marches, focused on that area of American life where the gap between ideal and reality was most obvious and blatant. Politically this period of idealistic reaffirmation came to a climax in the end of a Presidency in which the gap between practice and principle likewise became morally and politically intolerable. The years between were filled with protests, outraged moral protests, at the failure of political institutions and leaders to perform in the way expected of them, and with escalating exposures of the breadth of the gap between political ideal and political reality. The principal struggles were between those who wanted to reshape reality to conform with the ideal—immediately—and those who were willing to tolerate the gap for varying lengths of time. Many questioned, for instance, the means and the speed with which racial inequities should be remedied, but no one articulated a systematic defense of racial discrimination. Many were reluctant to see a President driven from office, but no one systematically defended dishonesty and dissimulation by public officials. What was at issue was not a matter of principle but the way in which those principles should and could be applied in practice.

This gap between political ideal and political reality is a continuing central phenomenon of American politics in a way that is not true of any other major state. The importance of the gap stems from three distinctive characteristics of American political ideals. First is the scope of the agreement on these ideals. In contrast to most European societies, a broad consensus exists and has existed in the United States on basic political values and beliefs. These values and beliefs, which constitute what is often referred to as "the American Creed," have historically served as a distinctive source of American national identity. Second is the *substance* of those ideals. In contrast to the values of most other societies, the values of this Creed are liberal, individualistic, democratic, egalitarian, and hence basically antigovernment and antiauthority in character. Whereas other ideologies legitimate established authority and institutions, the American Creed serves to delegitimate any hierarchical, coercive, authoritarian structures, including American ones. Third is the changing *intensity* with which Americans believe in these basic ideals, an intensity that varies from time to time and from group to group. Historically, American society seems to evolve through periods of creedal passion and of creedal passivity.

As a result of these three characteristics, an ever-present gap exists between American political ideals and American political institutions and practice. This gap has altered during the course of American history, at times narrowing and at other times broadening. These changes reflect both changes in "objective" reality—the distribution of power in American society—and also, of course, changes in the nature of American ideals and in the intensity of commitments that Americans have to those ideals. "Witness the intensity with which" we hold to our—and your—convictions, Levine implored his commencement audience. Other decades have lacked this intensity; the rhetoric of ceremonial addresses has been the same but the passion has been absent. The age of protest of the 1960s, however, was a period of moral reaffirmation, a period in which the best as well as the worst were filled with a passionate intensity focused on the need to realize in practice the central principles and values of the American Creed.

The 1960s thus had much in common with other periods of creedal passion, when the values of the American Creed had been invoked to challenge established institutions and existing practices—periods such as the Revolutionary era of the 1760s and 1770s, the Jacksonian age of the 1820s and 1830s, and the Populist-Progressive years of the 1890s and 1900s. In a sense, the gap between ideal and institution condemns Americans to coexist with a peculiarly American form of cognitive dissonance. At times, this dissonance is latent; at other times, when creedal passion runs high, it is brutally manifest, and at such times, the promise of American politics becomes its central agony.

## The One, the Two, and the Many: Structural Paradigms of American Politics

This central characteristic of American politics has received little notice in the traditional theories or paradigms of American politics. Over the years, the prevailing images of American politics have been shaped by three such paradigms.

What is often referred to as the "Progressive" theory emphasizes the continuing conflict between the few who are rich and the many who are poor. It is, indeed, better referred to as the "class-conflict" theory of American politics, since it has been espoused by many others in addition to early-twentieth-century Progressive historians. Federalist thinkers such as John Adams assumed that "there is no special providence for Americans, and their nature is the same with that of others." Consequently, they also assumed that the social divisions that existed elsewhere would be reproduced in America. "The people, in all nations," Adams said, "are naturally divided into two sorts, the gentlemen and the simplemen. . . . The great and perpetual distinction in civilized societies has been between the rich, who are few, and the poor, who are many." In similar terms, Alexander Hamilton agreed that "all communities divide themselves into the few and the many." In postulating this image, Hamilton's sympathies were with the rich, while Adams was deeply and equally suspicious of both rich and poor. At the end of the nineteenth century the Progressive historians attacked Federalist politics and identified themselves with the poor, while retaining the Federalist picture of American society. The essence of the Progressive paradigm was well summed up by Vernon Parrington in notes that he wrote for but did not use in *Main Currents of American Thought*:

*From the first we have been divided into two main parties. Names and battle cries and strategies have often changed repeatedly, but the broad party division has remained. On one side has been the party of the current aristocracy—of church, of gentry, of merchant, of slave holder, or manufacturer—and on the other the party of the commonality—of farmer, villager, small tradesman, mechanic, proletariat. The one has persistently sought to check and limit the popular power, to keep the control of the government in the hands of the few in order to serve special interests, whereas the other has sought to augment the popular power, to make government more responsive to the will of the majority, to further the democratic rather than the republican ideal—let one discover this and new light is shed on our cultural tendencies.*

The Progressive interpretation dominated American historical writing until after World War II, when it was displaced by the consensus theory. It was maintained, however, by Marxist analysts and radical sociologists, such as C. Wright Mills, and came back to the fore in the writings of New Left revisionist historians of the 1960s.

The key elements of the Progressive approach, as with that of the Federalists, were, first, a stress on the significance of economic interests, as distinguished from idealistic purposes, as the motive moving men in history, and, second, an emphasis on the extent to which American history (and, for the Federalists, history generally) could be interpreted in terms of the clash between two contenders for wealth and power: the popular party and the elite party. Over time, the particular groups in this conflict might change, but the struggle itself would continue. The Progressives clearly hoped that in due course the popular party would triumph, but there was nothing in their theory to specify why or when this should happen. Until that nebulous point in the distant future did arrive, American history would be an ongoing struggle between the good guys and the bad guys, and, as Louis Hartz pointed out, one of the comforting aspects of their theory was that it "always had an American hero available to match any American villain they found, a Jefferson for every Hamilton."

The consensus theory of American politics posits an image of American politics that is, in many respects, the polar opposite of the Federalist-Progressive approach. According to this theory, the key to understanding American history is not the conflict between two classes but rather the overwhelming predominance of the middle class. For a variety of reasons—the absence of feudalism, the abundance of free land, the shortage of labor, the resulting opportunities for vertical and horizontal mobility, the early introduction of universal manhood suffrage, and the prevalence of a "Lockean" ethos of liberty, equality, individualism—class consciousness and class conflict never developed in the United States as it did in Europe. Instead there was the "pleasing uniformity" that had struck Crèvecoeur and the social and political equality that had so impressed Tocqueville. As a result, class-based ideologies never developed in American politics as they did in European politics. A consensus on middle-class values prevailed, and the conflicts that have existed in American politics have been over relatively narrow issues of economics and personality within the framework of the all-pervading basic consensus.

The consensus theory received its classic statement in the works of Tocqueville. It was reformulated in more nationalistic terms by the "Patriotic" historians in the latter part of the nineteenth century and then reappeared in its most self-conscious and explicit form in the two decades after World War II in the writings of Richard Hofstadter, Daniel Boorstin, Talcott Parsons, David Potter, Daniel Bell, Seymour Martin Lipset, and, most notably, Louis Hartz. The popularity of the theory at this time reflected the success of the New Deal and the failure of social revolution in the 1930s, the general prosperity and abundance of American life, and the emergence of the Cold War as the central feature of American foreign relations.

In contrast to the Progressive theorists, the consensualists tended to place their argument about the United States in a comparative context. For Hartz in particular, comparison with Europe was a central theme. Viewed from a European vantage point, he argued, the dualism that had been the focus of the Progressives shrank almost to insignificance. Unlike Europe, America lacked both feudalism and socialism. The controversies of American history were all among different varieties of liberalism. Widespread liberalism, in turn, reflected the absence of an aristocracy and of a class-conscious proletariat and the dominance of a middle class. In so arguing, Hartz used Marxist categories to arrive at Tocquevillian conclusions. Unchallenged by competing ideologies, however, American liberalism in his view lost its ideological system and rigor; it became immobile, irrational, absolute, and unthinking, at times turning in on and shadowboxing against itself.

A third theory, the pluralist paradigm, holds that the central feature of American politics is the competition among interest groups. The process version of this approach sees politics as a struggle among large numbers of relatively small interest groups. The organization version emphasizes the dominant role of a small number of large, well-organized groups in shaping public policy. Proponents of the process theory tend to be favorably disposed toward that process, seeing a rough approximation of the public interest emerge out of open, competitive struggle in the political free market, where it can be assumed that constitutional and governmental structures do not significantly discriminate among groups in terms of their access to the political process. Proponents of the organization version, on the other hand, usually emphasize the extent to which the established groups control the political process and make meaningless many of the pretensions of the democratic system premised on individual equality. At the extreme, this version of the pluralist approach can have many resemblances to the class-conflict theory.

The pluralist paradigm received its classic statement by James Madison in *The Federalist* (particularly Number 10). It was reformulated by Arthur F. Bentley in the early twentieth century, and it reemerged as the dominant interpretation of American politics among political scientists after World War II. It is, in some measure, quite compatible with the consensus paradigm, since the conflicts among interest groups over particular issues can be conceived of as occurring within the framework of a broad agreement on basic political values. In fact, one paradigm almost implies the existence of the other: they differ in that one stresses the basic agreement and the other the specific issues that are fought over within the context of this agreement.

Each of these three theories has its strengths and its weaknesses. The class-conflict theory points accurately to the existence in America of significant inequalities in wealth and income. It argues inaccurately, however, that these differences have been a principal continuing basis for political cleavage in American society. While American politics has at times been polarized, it has seldom, if ever (the New Deal was the most notable exception), been polarized between rich and poor. More generally, in attempting to sandwich American political struggle into a simple, dualistic framework, the class-conflict theory does scant justice to the complexity and variability of the struggle. For many of the class-conflict theorists, class conflict more accurately describes what they think American politics should be like rather than what it actually has been like over the course of centuries. The consensus theory, on the other hand, rightly acknowledges the absence of European class-based ideologies and the widespread agreement in the United States on liberal, democratic, individualistic, Lockean political values. Particularly in its Hartzian formulation, however, it also tended to suggest that the existence of an ideological consensus meant the absence of any form of significant social conflict. In fact, the United States has had more sociopolitical conflict and violence than many European countries. "Americans," as Hofstadter neatly put it, "do not *need* ideological conflict to shed blood on a large scale." Why this should be the case is ignored by consensus theory. Finally, the pluralist paradigm—in both its process and organizational versions—clearly describes the way in which American politics functions a good part of the time. It does not, however, anymore than the consensus theory, provide for or explain the passion, upheaval, or moral intensity that at times envelopes the American political scene.

All three paradigms share one important characteristic: each explains politics in terms of social structure. The decisive influences on American politics are not the political values, institutions, and practices or the processes of change and development, but rather the nature of American society. The issue at stake among them is whether American society can best be understood in terms of one consensus, two classes, or many groups. From this structural approach flow two other implications.

First, the structural characteristics of society that shape its politics are held to be relatively permanent. Each theory, as we have seen, has had its own proponents over the years going back to the eighteenth century. The consensus theory acknowledges little or no change in the consensus. The class-conflict theory holds that the particular classes may change (that is, from landowners versus landless to capitalists versus workers), but the division of society between rich and poor—and the conflict between rich and poor—goes on. In similar fashion, the pluralist theory allows for the rise and fall of specific groups in the political process but not in the underlying pluralistic character of society or in the way groups interact in American politics. In its own way, each paradigm sets forth a picture of how American politics functions at any one point in time; none sets forth a picture of how American politics changes over time. Each is essentially static in its approach. How will American society and politics in the future differ from what they have been in the past? According to all three, the answer essentially is more of the same.

Second, all three paradigms posit the predominant role of economic and materialistic interests in politics. The upper and lower classes of the class-conflict theory are divided by their economic differences and they conflict with each other in politics over their respective efforts to maintain and enhance these differences or to reduce and perhaps even eliminate them. The interest groups of pluralist theory can include ethnic groups, but have been conceived primarily in economic terms as regional, occupational, and industrial groups. Lastly, the consensus theory does highlight the importance of political values and ideas, but argues that either the absence of such ideas or the broad agreement on them precludes serious political conflict. That agreement, in turn, rests on the overwhelming predominance of the middle class. Whereas the class-conflict and pluralist theories see American politics dominated by the scrambling of grubby materialistic interests, the consensus theory reduces it all to placid harmony and dullness.

## Ideals versus Institutions

The structural paradigms of American politics are not totally wrong, but they are limited. They omit almost entirely the role that political ideas and idealism, moral causes, and creedal passions have played in American politics. Almost everyone agrees that the United States was conceived in terms of certain political ideals and inspired by the promise or dream of liberty and equality. These political ideals are central to American national identity and have played a critical role in shaping American political evolution and development. Yet the pluralist theory of American politics ignores them entirely, the class-conflict theory sees them simply as the ideological weapons of opposing economic classes promoting their own materialistic interests, and the consensus theory suggests, in effect, that because they are universally accepted they are universally irrelevant. Rich fight poor for more of the economic pie, groups squabble over their allocations of the pie, or all relax in their enjoyment of it. That the political ideals and visions which define the existence of the nation might also be central to understanding its politics and might play a crucial role in shaping its political conflicts and political development seems to be an unrecognized possibility. The structural paradigms portray an American politics without purpose, without moral conflict, without passion, without promise, and, most importantly, without guilt. Can class conflict, group process, or consensus fully explain the passions and the intensity of the 1960s, the 1890s, the 1860s, the 1830s, and, most importantly, the 1770s? The structural picture of American politics is not so much Hamlet without the Prince of Denmark as it is Deuteronomy without the vision of the promised land.

When foreigners ask, "What is American politics all about?" it cannot be explained to them simply in terms of a Namier-like struggle of faction and group, or a Marxist-like confrontation of classes, or a complacent consensus. It is, in some measure, all of these things, but it is also much more. To see American politics purely as a reflection of social structure is to miss the teleological—as distinguished from the mechanistic—dimension of that politics. The ways in which individuals, groups, and classes act in politics are decisively shaped not only by their own perceptions of their immediate interests but also by the ideological climate and the common political values and purposes that they all recognize as legitimate. The United States has lacked European-style ideological conflict, yet its politics has been infused with more moral passion than that of any European country. "America," Santayana once observed, "is all one prairie, swept by a universal tornado." The consensus theory posits the uniformity of the prairie but not the fury of the tornado that the prairie's very flatness engenders. In the United States, ideological consensus is the source of political conflict, polarization occurs over moral issues rather than economic ones, and the politics of interest groups is supplemented and at times supplanted by the politics of moralistic reform. America has been spared class conflicts in order to have moral convulsions. It is precisely the central role of moral passion that distinguishes American politics from the politics of most other societies, and it is this characteristic that is most difficult for foreigners to understand.

The importance of political ideas and values in shaping the course of American development has not always been neglected in historical writing, and in part for this reason it tended to become discredited. The progressive realization of American ideals was a familiar theme among nineteenth-century "Patriotic" historians. "The unifying principle" of history for George Bancroft, as Hofstadter points out, "was progress ordained and planned by God —the advance of liberty, justice, and humanity, all of which were peculiarly exemplified in American history, where providential guidance had brought together a singularly fit people and fit institutions. . . . American history could be seen as a kind of consummation of all history." The same theme, viewed considerably more ambivalently, was also present in Tocqueville. Common to both was the concept of American history as a gradual but steady unfolding and realization of the ideals of liberty, equality, and democracy.

This interpretation accurately highlighted the extent to which the pursuit of these ideals was central to the American political experience. What it did not highlight, however, was the extent to which the failure to realize those ideals was equally central to that experience. The image of the triumphant realization of the American promise or ideal was an exercise in patriotic unreality at best and hypocrisy at worst. The history of American politics is the repetition of new beginnings and flawed outcomes, promise and disillusion, reform and reaction. American history is the history of the efforts of groups to promote their interests by realizing American ideals. What is important, however, is not that they succeed but that they fail, not that the dream is realized but that it is not and never can be realized completely or satisfactorily. In the American context there will always be those who say that the institutional glass is half-empty and who will spill much passion attempting to fill it to the brim from the spring of idealism. But in the nature of things, particularly in America, it can never be much more than half-full.

This gap between promise and performance creates an inherent disharmony, at times latent, at times manifest, in American society. In a harmonic society, as André Béteille has argued, the existential and normative orders are consistent with each other; in a disharmonic society they are in conflict. "In a harmonic system inequalities not only exist in fact but are also considered legitimate. In a disharmonic system inequalities are no longer invested with legitimacy although they continue to exist in fact." Traditional India with its caste system was a harmonic society because its social inequalities were considered legitimate. The United States, on the other hand, is a disharmonic society because its social and political inequalities "exist in a moral environment which is committed to equality."

Social, economic, and political inequalities may well be more limited and political liberties more extensive in the United States than they are in most other societies. Yet the commitment to equality and liberty and the opposition to hierarchy and authority are so widespread and deep that the incongruity between the normative and existential orders is far greater in the United States than elsewhere. Traditional India was clearly more unequal than modern America, but modern America is clearly more disharmonic than traditional India. The extent to which a society or a political system is harmonic or disharmonic depends as much upon the values of its people as upon the structure of its institutions. Any society, moreover, necessarily involves a certain irreducible minimum of inequality and hierarchy. The variations in attitudes toward inequality, hierarchy, and authority among the peoples of different societies are likely to be at least as great as the variations in actual inequality, hierarchy, and authority among those societies, particularly in the modern world. With its unique consensus on and commitment to liberal, democratic, and egalitarian political values, the United States is the modern disharmonic polity par excellence.

## SUGGESTIONS FOR FURTHER READING

Any list of books on the recent past where history and current events merge is in danger of quickly becoming obsolete. Eric Goldman, *The Crucial Decade and After* (New York, 1960), is a lively account of consensus and complacency during the years 1945–1960. Daniel Bell, *The End of Ideology: On the Exhaustion of Political Ideas in the Fifties* (New York, 1959); David Riesman et al., *The Lonely Crowd* (New York, 1959); William H. Whyte, Jr., *The Organization Man* (New York, 1956); and Samuel Lubell, *Revolt of the Moderates* (New York, 1956), are important for understanding the conformity of the fifties. Edward Quinn and Paul J. Dolan, eds., *The Sense of the 60's* (New York, 1968), is a start at understanding a complex decade. William L. O'Neill, *Coming Apart* (New York, 1971), is a lively account of our recent history. Morris Dickstein, *Gates of Eden: American Culture in the Sixties* (New York, 1977), concentrates on the literature, music, and journalism of the decade.

There is a vast and growing literature dealing with the new feminism and the women's liberation movement. An early but very influential book is Betty Friedan, *The Feminine Mystique* (New York, 1963). Robin Morgan, ed., *Sisterhood Is Powerful* (New York, 1970), is a good collection of articles and documents from the militant wings of the feminist movement. For a powerful opposing view see Midge Decter, *The New Chastity and Other Arguments Against Women's Liberation* (New York, 1974). Two books by William Henry Chafe, *The American Woman* (New York, 1972) and *Women and Equality* (New York, 1978), provide information for judging the progress of the women's movement in America. Mary Ryan, *Womanhood in America* (New York, 1983), is an excellent survey which places the contemporary movement in historical context.

There is a large and growing literature on the black revolution. A fine brief historical introduction is August Meier and Elliot Rudwick, *From Plantation to Ghetto* (New York, 1966). Works by participants themselves are invaluable in understanding the movement. See in particular Martin Luther King, Jr., *Stride Toward Freedom* (New York, 1958), and *Where Do We Go From Here: Chaos or Community?* (New York, 1967); Whitney M. Young, Jr., *To Be Equal* (New York, 1964); James Farmer, *Freedom–When?* (New York, 1965); Robert Williams, *Negroes with Guns* (New York, 1962); and *The Autobiography of Malcolm X* (New York, 1964). See also Charles E. Silberman, *Crisis in Black and White* (New York, 1964); C. Eric Lincoln, *The Black Muslims in America* (Boston, 1961); Howard Zinn, *SNCC: The New Abolitionists* (Boston, 1964). John H. Bracy, Jr., August Meier, and Elliot Rudwick, eds., *Black Nationalism in America* (Indianapolis, 1970), is a collection of documents with a good bibliography. In recent years some scholars have argued that class differences are far more significant than racial differences. See, for example, Thomas Sowell, *Race and Economics* (New York, 1975), and William J. Wilson, *The Declining Significance of Race: Blacks and Changing American Institutions* (New York, 1978).

The essays in Daniel Bell, ed., *The Radical Right* (New York, 1963), are interesting attempts to make sense of a baffling movement; see also the essays in

* Available in paperback edition.

Richard Hofstadter, *The Paranoid Style in American Politics* (New York, 1965). A sympathetic account of the Kennedy years is Arthur M. Schlesinger, Jr., *A Thousand Days* (Boston, 1965).

Richard M. Scammon and Ben J. Wattenberg, *The Real Majority* (New York, 1970), argues that the majority of voters in the country have moved to the right. Two books important for understanding contemporary political and social thought are Theodore Roszak, *The Making of a Counter Culture* (New York, 1970), and Charles A. Reich, *The Greening of America* (New York, 1971). The latter argues that there is already a radical consensus in America based mostly on a life style that he calls Consciousness III. There are many books dealing with the young, the New Left, and the crisis on the campus. Lewis Feuer, *Conflict of Generations* (New York, 1969), and Daniel J. Boorstin, *The Decline of Radicalism* (New York, 1969), are generally critical of today's youth, while Kenneth Kenniston, *Young Radicals: Notes on Committed Youth* (New York, 1968), and Paul Jacobs and Saul Landau, *The New Radicals: A Report with Documents* (New York, 1966), are generally sympathetic. A judicious general survey is John P. Diggins, *The American Left in the Twentieth Century* (New York, 1973). A nostalgic view of the old Left is Vivian Gornick, *The Romance of American Communism* (New York, 1977).

# 11

# *America Today and Tomorrow: The 1970s and 1980s*

On the night of June 17, 1972, five men were arrested in the act of breaking into the offices of the Democratic National Committee in the Watergate hotel-apartment-office complex in Washington, D.C. Few at the time could imagine the effects of that bungled burglary. In the presidential election five months later, Richard M. Nixon won a landslide victory, receiving over 60 percent of the popular vote. But within two years, scandals brought to light by the investigations of the Watergate break-in led to Nixon's resignation and to some of his chief aides' convictions on charges of criminal conspiracy, obstruction of justice, and other serious charges. In the wake of Watergate, the mid-term elections in 1974 increased the number of liberal Democrats in Congress.

Nevertheless, liberalism appeared to be on the wane, that is, at least the kind of liberalism that had been associated with the reforms of Franklin Roosevelt's New Deal and Lyndon Johnson's Great Society. A combination of factors—the Watergate scandals, the growing federal bureaucracy, high taxes, inflation, to name but a few—caused many to doubt the value of liberal reforms coming from Washington. In the 1976 presidential election, Jimmy Carter, a former Georgia governor with no Washington experience, defeated Gerald R. Ford, who had become President after Nixon's resignation. Carter's status as an "outsider" who promised to trim the Washington bureaucracy undoubtedly won him many votes.

As President, Carter found it difficult to make the changes he had promised. Many who had welcomed him as an outsider now attacked him as being inexperienced and inept. Continuing inflation, an energy crisis, and foreign policy problems, especially those stemming from the taking of American hostages in Iran, stimulated opposition in Congress and provided issues for presidential hopefuls eyeing the 1980 elections. At the same time, an enormous number of organized pressure groups, representing a wide array of interests, sought government support for their goals or demanded an end to certain government controls and regulations. Critics worried about one-issue politics and the distrust of government. If old-style liberalism had disappeared, it was not replaced by a new consensus.

In the 1980 elections, Ronald Reagan, an outsider like Carter, sought to mold a new conservative consensus by promising an end to inflation, tax cuts, and a decreased role for the federal government. Conservatives welcomed Reagan's victory in November, but many soon found themselves at odds with the new President when he did not give adequate support to their pet projects. Opposition to the President grew when an economic downturn brought massive unemployment. The elections of 1982 showed some discontent with the Republicans, but not enough to allow the Democrats to claim that the voters had repudiated Regan and his policies.

Many of those who study the history of the immediate past do so with one eye on the future. This is clearly evident in the selections that follow. Each author uses his evaluation of the immediate past to suggest what the future will bring.

In the first selection, Peter N. Carroll finds a new consensus arising in the aftermath of the conflicts of the 1960s. "Frustrated by the failure of government policy, critics . . . joined in denouncing the liberal vision." He describes how various groups of people, based in localities but often united in national organizations, have embarked on projects of self-help. Many of these groups call for local initiative and local control, and they favor limitations on federal government expenditures and interference. Yet, as he notes, within this new consensus are the seeds of renewed conflict because the community organizations "represented competing versions of the future."

Everett Carll Ladd, Jr., and Seymour Martin Lipset, in the second selection, interpret some of the same data used by Carroll to come to rather different conclusions. They note that throughout our history, "two values—those of equalitarianism and achievement—have influenced our national behavior." They suggest that although these two values often complement one another, they often lead to conflict. That conflict is not over fundamentals; Americans agree on the fundamentals. Americans share a set of common values and differ only on the degree of emphasis to be placed on one value versus another. Thus, they conclude, liberalism is far from dead even if the particular ways in which it has been expressed have changed since the time of the New Deal.

Richard Polenberg, in the third selection, disagrees with Carroll and Ladd and Lipset. He finds that the reforms of the 1960s sharpened economic and class divisions within the population and that these divisions have the potential for creating massive conflicts in the future.

In the final selection, economic historian Douglas F. Dowd tends to agree with Polenberg. He says that American society is in the midst of an economic and political crisis, the resolution of which will move the country either to the right (to a form of American fascism) or to the left (to a form of American socialism). Although Dowd's personal preference is for the latter and although he sees some reason to be optimistic, his optimism is cautious rather than buoyant.

In evaluating the different points of view presented here, readers will be doing far more than attempting to solve a complex historical problem. They will be attempting to understand the problems we face today. Their understanding will help to shape the world of tomorrow.

Peter N. Carroll

# The New Populists,
# the New Right,
# and the Search for
# the Lost America

On the thirteenth day of January 1978, a slowly spreading cancer clutched away the life of the last great symbol of American liberalism—former Vice President Hubert Horatio Humphrey. "For 30 years," eulogized President Carter, "his voice was heard from one end of the country to the other—most often in defense of the oppressed, the hungry, the victims of poverty and discrimination." Through the storms of controversy and personal defeat, the buoyant Minnesotan had preserved a fervent belief in the ability of government to alleviate social misery, and he had advocated, too, amid angry dissent, the importance of upholding the American way of life around the world. "I have no apologies for the federal government doing things," he told a reporter shortly before his death. "Who's going to take care of the environment, establish standards? . . . We've got to have federal government activity. The only question is not the size of the government, but does it work?" Four times Humphrey had tried—and failed—to occupy the White House. But, preached his protégé, Vice President Mondale, "he achieved something much more rare and valuable than the nation's highest office. He became his country's conscience."

The death of Hubert Humphrey (followed one year later by the demise of his liberal Republican counterpart, Nelson Rockefeller), portended the end of an era. Forty-five years after the inauguration of Franklin Delano Roosevelt, the nation no longer shared Humphrey's vision of a magnanimous federal government providing leadership for the hinterlands. "The moral test of government," said Humphrey in one of his last public appearances, "is how it treats those who are in the dawn of life, the children; those who are in the twilight of life, the aged; and those who are in the shadows of life, the sick, the needy and the handicapped." By such standards, liberal dreams often remained unfulfilled, despite heavy public expenditures for education, health, and welfare.

Frustrated by the failure of government policy, critics from the right and the left—for decidedly different reasons—joined in denouncing the liberal vision. "We've broken all the ground in all areas of human activity—the environment, outer space, human rights, civil rights, women's rights—right across the board," stated Richard Lesher, president of the conservative Chamber of Commerce. "We're just now waking up to the fact that government is ill-equipped to deal with many of these problems."

"In the crisis that's lying ahead," suggested Milton Kotler, director of the National Association of Neighborhoods, a coalition of community groups, "there's a new recognition that the country's not going to be saved by experts and bureaucrats. It's going to be saved by some moral vision and some moral hope coming from the grassroots and the neighborhoods." "We are not," announced antiwar veteran Gary Hart in running successfully for reelection to the Senate, "a bunch of little Hubert Humphreys."

Convinced of the inadequacies of federal programs, political activists turned increasingly to more manageable arenas—state, local, and neighborhood organizations. "The day of the state has come and gone," remarked Colorado Governor Richard Lamm, "—and come back again." By the late seventies, over 20 million Americans participated in some form of neighborhood improvement group, joining consumer advocates, labor organizers, independent farmer organizations, and proponents of alternative technology to form a massive grass-roots movement aimed at restoring the vitality of community democracy. "Most Americans . . . tend to think that political history is made only by great men—Kennedys or Kings, maybe, but not ordinary people," remarked Mike Ansara, organizer of the Massachusetts citizens group Fair Share. "A lot of what we are doing is challenging that notion and getting people over that tremendously debilitating sense of powerlessness and cynicism."

The contrast between liberal reformism sponsored by the federal government and the new community populism emerged dramatically in the revitalization of urban neighborhoods. While the nation's major cities continued to lose population to the suburbs and rural areas, communities throughout the country repudiated the traditional remedies of urban renewal—the razing of whole neighborhoods to be replaced by commercial structures or public housing projects—and instead chose to rebuild and restore existing dwellings. Reflecting the popular enthusiasm for cultural roots, such rehabilitation often began as a personal project—dictated partly by economics, partly by a preference for traditional architecture. But individual enterprise soon spread to larger community issues involving taxation, financing, zoning, and public services. "We came to restore old houses," stated the founder of St. Louis's Lafayette Square Restoration Committee, a pioneering program in urban homesteading, "but we wound up restoring the neighborhood."

These commitments often clashed with government and business policies that had contributed to urban decline and led many community builders to become political activists. The common practice by banks and insurance companies to "redline" deteriorating neighborhoods as bad investment risks, for example, blocked the funding necessary to rebuild old dwellings, reoccupy abandoned structures, and improve public spaces. But local pressure organizations, such as Chicago's Citizens Action Program, launched alternative "greenlining" campaigns which persuaded lending institutions in many cities to end such neighborhood-destroying activities. Another effective tactic was the formation of community credit unions, which expanded the equity base and so facilitated the acquisition of small loans for renovations. In Colorado, the state government initiated a program that distributed public deposits to encourage banks to underake "social lending." "We don't ask them to do business differently," explained a Philadelphia advocate, "only with an open and rational mind."

The attempt to protect communities from the intrusive power of the federal government and large corporations stimulated nationwide experimentation with alternative technologies, particularly in the area of energy resources. "If we're going to conserve energy as a nation," argued Dick Fiddler of Seattle's Office of Energy, "we've got to start at the local level." To maximize available resources, local governments and private organizations introduced innovative technologies, ranging from burning wood chips in Vermont, garbage in Milwaukee, and geothermal heat in Idaho, to limit energy dependence. At the frontiers of research, organizations such as the New Alchemy Institute at Cape Cod, the California Office of Alternative Technology, and the Shelter Institute in Maine repeatedly demonstrated the validity of small-scale technology in providing superior levels of food, shelter, and energy. Decentralized economies, partially freed from corporate control, promised to ensure local autonomy. "It's a question of getting the available technology into the proper hands," maintained Richard Kazis of the Institute for Self-Reliance. "Like the question of whether we can develop photovoltaic cells before the energy corporations get hold of the technology." But such enthusiasm could not prevent large businesses from gaining control of valuable patents in the race to develop solar technology.

The belief in community democracy encouraged the proliferation of grass-roots organizations that worked for social betterment. "We try to get people in touch with their own anger," stated Ernie Cortes, a community organizer who helped found effective mass coalitions in San Antonio, Texas, and in East Los Angeles. "What we mean by anger is being your brother's keeper. It means building a new community." In Massachusetts, a statewide citizens group, Fair Share, harnessed popular antagonism toward rising automobile insurance rates and forced the legislature to rebate extra premiums and to rescind probusiness legislation. "We tried to get back to real, everyday things, to a calm style," explained one organizer, formerly active in the anti-war movement. "We switched issues from Vietnam and Cambodia and just moved in with the community." In rural Minnesota, the construction of a high-voltage power line aroused bitter resistance in the conservative farm country, culminating in mass protests supported by the local Catholic churches.

"I hate to tell you my position during the Vietnam war," admitted Gloria Woida, a leader of the Minnesota movement. "I was totally against all that protesting, but now I see that war as the same as what . . . the Government is doing to us with that power line. I realize we're all at the mercy of government."

"I keep hearing that everything's dead and there's no big cause since civil rights and the Vietnam War," observed Gale Cincotta, head of National People's Action, a nationwide neighborhood coalition. "But that's a myth. There's a neighborhood movement that started in the sixties. It's not as dramatic with everybody out in the streets, but it's steadily gaining strength in every city and state. The base was there and people reached the point where they just had to do something."

"The media is selling us on this notion of apathy and paralysis in the country," objected former antiwar activist Sam Lovejoy. "Bullshit. The movement did not die. It did the most intelligent thing it could do: it went to find a home. It went into the community. It's working, unnoticed, in the neighborhood. They're starting to blossom and make alliances, connections."

Such passions usually focused on disparate local issues—a particular grievance, such as utility rates, that galvanized traditional liberals and conservatives to community action. But one issue had nationwide implications— the spread of nuclear reactors. On George Washington's birthday in 1974 ("I cannot tell a lie," he crowed, "I did knock down the cherry tree"), Lovejoy single-handedly toppled a five-hundred-foot tower designating the site of a planned nuclear power plant in Montague, Massachusetts. "Communities have the same rights as individuals," he announced upon surrendering to the police. "We must seize back control of our community." Amid considerable publicity, a local jury acquitted Lovejoy, boosting a grass-roots antinuclear protest that stretched from coast to coast. "This movement is built from the bottom up," commented a member of the antinuclear Clamshell Alliance. "Here the movement starts with the town. There is no other way."

Mustering public support, opponents of nuclear power attempted to restrict further proliferation through popular initiatives. In 1976, antinuclear measures appeared on ballots in California, Oregon, Washington, Colorado, Montana, Arizona, and Ohio. Attacked by lavishly funded advertisements from the nuclear power industry, the proposals failed everywhere. But public distrust of nuclear power, virtually unknown a decade earlier, had gained a self-perpetuating momentum. "We're feeling very disillusioned about the legal and legislative channels for stopping nuclear power," stated a member of San Francisco's People Against Nuclear Power. "Our new method is disciplined, nonviolent direct action."

The small beach community at Seabrook, New Hampshire, population 5,700, wanted no part of nuclear power, voting, despite promises of tax relief and new jobs, against a proposed plant in 1976. As ground-breaking ceremonies continued anyway, residents joined the Clamshell coalition in adopting passive resistance tactics perfected during the civil rights movement of the sixties. And, as in that earlier struggle, the uncompromising response of public authorities to nonviolent protest widened the appeal of the antinuclear crusade. In 1976, occupiers at the planned site, known as the Seabrook Ten, received six-month jail sentences for civil disobedience. "Ignorance of the law is no excuse," admitted one defendant, "but ignorance of the dangers of nuclear power is also no excuse." In 1977, as the sit-in tactics continued, national guardsmen arrested over fourteen hundred protesters and the costly incarceration further inflamed public opinion, inspiring even larger antinuclear rallies the next year. Such protests soon mushroomed around the country, and to the forefront came veterans of earlier populist crusades—Benjamin Spock, Daniel Ellsberg, Dennis Banks, Tom Hayden, Jane Fonda, and hordes of supporters.

This burgeoning dissent awakened public suspicions, reminiscent of the antiwar movement, about government credibility. The calamity at Three Mile Island in 1979 aroused new doubts about official assurances of nuclear safety. That spring, moreover, a jury verdict against a Kerr-McGee nuclear facility in Oklahoma vindicated the long-suppressed allegations of the deceased Karen Silkwood, confirming fears that nuclear plants were not only technologically deficient, but also poorly protected against theft and subversion. "The history of the nuclear power industry," Ralph Nader told a throng of over a hundred thousand gathered at Capitol Hill in May 1979 to protest nuclear energy, "is replete with cover-ups, deceptions, outright lies, error, negligence, arrogance, greed, innumerable unresolved safety questions and a cost-plus accounting that taxes our citizens as consumers and taxpayers. There has to be a better, safer way to heat water."

The opposition to nuclear power focused on practical matters of health, safety, and cost, but its philosophical underpinnings also evoked a distinct vision of the future of American society. Where nuclear energy involved the continued expansion of industrial capitalism along with elaborate government regulatory administration, the antagonists envisioned, in words of California Governor Jerry Brown, "a world with limits to its resources and a country with limits to its power and economy." This alternative view rejected the centralized authority inherent in nuclear energy, preferring inexpensive and ecologically sensitive technologies, such as solar power, to free individuals and communities from both big business and big government. Challenging what economist E. F Schumacher called "the forward stampede" of modern society, the antinuclear position assumed, more simply, that "small is beautiful."

The great popularity of Schumacher's ideas about the development of small-scale technology reflected not merely its ecological wisdom, but also a moral appeal based on traditional Christian principles, specifically the teachings of the Roman Catholic church to which Schumacher had recently converted. Where mainstream Catholicism of the sixties seemed to embrace the presidential summons toward New Frontiers and endless mobility, surveys of Catholic opinion in the seventies reported a preference for the more rooted values of family, neighborhood, and community and a casual style of interaction "rather than formal, bureaucratic, direct techniques." In the late seventies, church attendance among young adult Catholics suddenly increased by 10 percent, reversing a long downward trend. "To be Catholic," wrote Michael Novak, "is not so much to belong to an organization as to belong to a people. It is . . . to have a differentiated point of view and sensibility." Such values often clashed with the pressures of assimilation, individualism, and advancement. "One of the penalties of upward mobility," conceded Catholic novelist Mary Gordon, "is a sense of guilty indebtedness to the old neighborhood."

The ideal of small personal communities permeated the writings of numerous ecologically oriented commentators, such as Theodore Roszak and Ivan Illich—who, incidentally, shared Catholic antecedents—and closely paralleled the traditional values of an organic society. "The problem is to re-establish neighborhood and community responsibility," suggested Governor Brown, a former Catholic seminarian. "But it's difficult, given the fact that everybody's moving around, shifting jobs, driving 30 or 40 miles a day." "We need a politics of smallness," agreed Michael Novak. "Think small. It is a time for small states and quiet ways." Calling for "creative social disintegration," Roszak urged "a new sense of our organic reciprocity with the land" and appealed for a spirit of "conviviality . . . as a culminating relationship between free and unique persons." To the question "What can I actually do?" Schumacher offered the plain homily, that "each of us work to put our own inner house in order."

The repudiation of liberalism by community populists paralleled a reinvigorated attack on the same system by its traditional enemies—the conservative right. "For the average American, the message is clear," stated Ronald Reagan: "Liberalism is no longer the answer—it is the problem." Long hostile to bureaucracy and rising taxes, opponents of the liberal state successfully transformed public frustration at government inefficiency into a mass movement to slash property taxes and curb administrative waste. "You are the people," declared Howard Jarvis, a seventy-five-year-old curmudgeon who led the crusade for California's Proposition 13 in 1978, "and you will have to take control of the government again or else it is going to control you." Tax reforms of the sixties combined with runaway real-estate values in the seventies placed a mounting burden of taxation on California homeowners. Yet while assessments escalated rapidly, the state government held a $4 billion surplus. Propo-

sition 13, a ballot initiative supported by 1.5 million signatures, offered to reduce assessments, limit property taxes to one percent of full value, and
prevent the easy passage of new taxes. "Give the politicians a budget," suggested one pro-13 advertisement, "instead of a blank check."

Despite the opposition of state government and the generous contributions of big business, which feared the disruptive effects of a massive cut,
Californians voted to make bureaucracy accountable, approving the initiative
by a 2–1 margin. Overnight, homeowners gained tax relief worth hundreds,
sometimes thousands, of dollars, while the state's largest corporations saved
multi-million-dollar levies. "Let us hope that California's message will be
heard loud and clear . . . across the nation," exclaimed the exile of San
Clemente, who saved $27,500 on his $2 million home. "People everywhere
want to reduce government spending, the burden of taxes, and the spiral inflation which is the cruelest tax of all." After initial shock at the landslide
defeat, liberals announced that the state surplus would salvage the sunken
budgets. "We have our marching orders from the people," said Governor
Brown in belatedly endorsing the iniative. "This is the strongest expression
of the democratic process in a decade."

The ratification of Proposition 13 seemed to herald a conservative backlash against liberal programs. "Across the country," charged Senator McGovern in a farewell address as president of Americans for Democratic Action,
"politicians . . . are seeking a mandate to govern by running against government itself." "This isn't just a tax revolt," insisted President Carter's pollster,
Pat Caddell. "It's a revolution against government." Conservatives in other
states promptly introduced similar tax-cutting proposals, sometimes in language identical to Proposition 13. The measure, former Governor Reagan
told a Chicago audience, "triggered hope in the breasts of the people that
something could be done . . . a little bit like dumping those cases of tea
off the boat in Boston harbor."

Such pronouncements contradicted the drift of public opinion. While
Proposition 13 demonstrated widespread dissatisfaction with inefficiency,
waste, and unresponsiveness, taxpayers indicated little desire to reduce public
services. "The American people have not become more conservative in their
attitudes toward government," explained political scientist Everett Ladd after
analyzing a spate of opinion surveys. "The heart of the indictment is a call
not for *less* government but for *better* government." In Idaho and Nevada,
which like California had experienced soaring property taxes, voters did approve similar cutbacks. But elsewhere, in Oregon, Michigan, Colorado, Nebraska, the public rejected tax and spending limitations, and in other states,
such as New Jersey and Tennessee, voters accepted budgetary ceilings without attacking existing structures. Given an opportunity in 1980 to reduce
state income taxes in an initiative labeled Jarvis II (liberals called it "Jaws
II"), California voters chose to preserve the fiscal status quo. "The tax revolt
is not taking us on a conservative trip to the right," concluded Robert Teeter,
former pollster for President Ford. "This is a moderate country."

The populist rhetoric of reduced taxation nevertheless lent legitimacy to a conservative fiscal crusade led by big business to stop tax reform. Though President Carter promised to improve a tax system he considered a "disgrace to the human race," his plan to eliminate corporation loopholes encountered stiff resistance from a well-financed business lobby that demanded tax cuts to stimulate capital investment. "Proposition 13 gave us a lift," conceded one business adviser. "It helped give tax reduction a broader credibility." A proposal to reduce all taxes by one-third found little favor in the Democratic Congress. But mounting pressure from business to reduce capital gains taxes overcame liberal dissent. The resulting Revenue Act of 1978 gave three-quarters of all tax reductions to the wealthiest two percent of the nation's taxpayers. "It used to be that business would hire a tax counsel to get a special tax break," remarked Bob Brandon, director of Ralph Nader's Tax Reform Research Group. "Now they don't get special tax breaks; they change the whole system." It was, protested Senator Kennedy, "the worst tax legislation approved by Congress since the days of Calvin Coolidge and Andrew Mellon."

The ability of big business to engulf the taxpayers' revolt illuminated the growing power of a hitherto ignored force in American politics—the New Right. Four decades after the New Deal, orthodox conservatives, such as columnist William Buckley and the Republican party establishment, had made an uneasy peace with liberal programs. "The right wing in America," explained Garry Wills in *Confessions of a Conservative*, "is stuck with the paradox of holding a philosophy of 'conserving' and an actual order it does not want to conserve." The New Right, by contrast, dismissed these ideological contradictions. "We are radicals who want to change the existing power structure," said Paul Weyrich, who with the financial backing of brewer Joseph Coors founded the Committee for the Survival of a Free Congress in 1974. "We are not conservatives in the sense . . . [of] accepting the status quo."

The New Right ironically drew strength from social discontents similar in some ways to those that motivated community populists—a distrust of liberal economics and the expansion of government bureaucracy. But while opposing centralized power, the new conservatives paradoxically created tightly disciplined political organizations, often knit together not only by common goals, but also by interlocking leaderships and bureaucracies as well as the computerized operations of direct mail expert Richard Viguerie, so-called "godfather" of the New Right. Unlike the populists, moreover, the New Right condemned the liberalization of moral values. Appealing to single-issue voters opposed to gun control, abortion, homosexuality, pornography, and the ERA, this vocal minority promised to restore a world of simple virtues, an old America based on family, church, and the work ethic.

To revitalize the capitalistic spirit, conservatives embraced the panacea of laissez faire economics. "Instead of government serving to create a climate of opportunity," argued Representative Jack Kemp of New York, "govern-

ment has become the competition. . . . the other team—and it's winning!"
Adopting the theories of Arthur Laffer, a maverick economist at the University of Southern California, Kemp joined Senator William Roth in proposing
a drastic 30 percent cut in federal taxes designed to stimulate investment,
boost productivity, and simultaneously end inflation and unemployment. Conservative economics also attacked the proliferation of government regulations
—environmental rules, health and safety requirements, consumer protection
standards—as additional drags on capital investment. Conservative public interest law groups supported suits to prevent enforcement of administrative
rules that challenged business goals. In 1978, for example, the conservative
Mountain States Legal Foundation helped persuade the Supreme Court that
federal inspectors could not enter business facilities without a proper search
warrant. "If we could eliminate the unnecessary regulation of business," insisted Ronald Reagan, "we could cut the rate of inflation in half." Such prospects appealed to a public troubled by a world of limits. "No frontier need
be closed for long," promised Kemp. "The creative genius that has always
invigorated America is still there, submerged, waiting like a genie in a bottle
to be loosed."

The optimism of the New Right contrasted with the cranky tone of a
group of ex-liberal intellectuals who constituted the "neoconservatives"—Irving Kristol, Norman Podhoretz, Daniel Bell, Nathan Glazer, and Senator
Daniel Moynihan. Still committed to the principles of the welfare state and
the pursuit of the cold war, neoconservatives objected to specific government
policies initiated in the sixties. Glazer's *Affirmative Discrimination*, for example, emphasized that opportunity traditionally applied to individuals, not
to social groups, and that equality before the law mandated no equality of
result. "Unlike the New Right," explained Kristol, "we have no interest in,
and little sympathy for, methods of direct democracy like initiatives and referenda." "A society has vitality," argued Bell, "if it has a strong establishment."
In publications such as *The Public Interest* and *Commentary*, these writers
denounced affirmative action, feminism, and post-Vietnam isolationism. But
the very elitism that spawned their independent position starved the neoconservatives of their logical constituencies.

The democratization of conservative ideas hinged on more basic metaphors: the revival of an old American mythology about the self-made man.
Despite persistent inflation, unemployment, and the decline of real wages
in the seventies, public opinion surveys found that most poor Americans still
believed in the possibility of upward economic mobility and feared, most of
all, that government taxation would curtail opportunity. Two-thirds of the
public in 1978 consequently favored cuts in the capital gains tax, even though
the main beneficiaries would be business investors. These attitudes percolated
through the larger society, thanks to two dramatic success stories—one that
appealed to blacks, the other to working-class whites.

A black newspaper called him "a Patty Hearst in reverse," and a prominent leftist writer dismissed him as a "Bicentennial coon," but exiled Black

Panther polemicist Eldridge Cleaver, a fugitive on murder charges, returned to the United States in 1975 confident that he could win his freedom. "With all its faults," he declared, "the American political system is the freest and most democratic in the world." Cleaver promptly announced his conversion to evangelical Protestantism and made plans to manufacture expensive codpiece trousers. Released on bail, he emerged in public lectures to extol "the limitless possibilities of the American dream." "For 22 years I studied and practiced the communist ideology," he admitted. "Then I came face to face with a different kind of revolutionary. His name is Jesus Christ." Daniel Moynihan donated five hundred dollars to his cause, and Norman Podhoretz, in a conservative version of "radical chic," hosted a fund-raising party on his behalf. "People say I've changed," noted the former minister of information, "but they forget how America has changed." Plea-bargaining to assault charges dating from a 1968 shootout with Oakland, California, police, Cleaver threw himself at the mercy of the court. "I feel you have changed for the better," replied Judge Winton McKibben in sentencing the returned prodigal to probation and two thousand hours of community service. A gleeful Cleaver promised to "bring the gospel of Jesus Christ to bear on all activities."

"You're just a working stiff," scoffed Archie Bunker's boss on the loading dock. Someone was always yelling at him to move crates, and just to make ends meet he had to drive a cab at night. But, announced Archie in 1977, "I wanna raise myself up. I want my name on somethin' more than just a lunchpail." When the proprietor of the neighborhood tavern retired, Archie forged his wife's signature to obtain a bank mortgage. "He resented me because he never had a chance to better himself," explained his son-in-law in a rare moment of support. "Well, now he's got that chance. In Archie's mind it's a chance for him to be somebody. I don't think you can take that away from him." In the spirit of the delinquent Benjamin Franklin who ran away from home to build a fortune, "All in the Family" followed the hero of the television workingmen into a new setting, the fulfillment of one middle class dream, a saloon of his own: Archie's Place.

The celebration of the old American values coincided with an impassioned effort by the New Right to restore an old moral order. Threatened by the rapid spread of alternative social values—the decline of traditional marriage, the rise of sexual liberation movements, demands for equal opportunity and affirmative action—fundamentalist Christian sects vowed to extirpate a "secular humanism" that they claimed was destroying the country. "Moral decadence is a very serious problem today," stated Gary Jarmin of the lobby group Christian Voice, "and politics is a big reason for these problems." "Everywhere we turn," agreed the organization's director, Robert Grant, "Christian values are assaulted and are in retreat. As Christians, we are not going to take it anymore." "This country is fed up with radical causes," insisted Jerry Falwell, preacher-host of television's "Old-Time Gospel Hour," "fed up with the unisex movement, fed up with the departure from basics, from decency, from the philosophy of the monogamous home." Although public opinion polls demonstrated that a majority of Americans rejected the social values of these religious conservatives, special-interest minorities assumed inordinate importance, especially at a time when political participation in the larger population continued to decline. "I don't want everyone to vote," admitted Weyrich during the 1980 campaign. "Our leverage in the election quite candidly goes up as the voting population goes down. We have no responsibility, moral or otherwise, to turn out our opposition."

The defense of traditional morality began in the bosom of the family. "The Bible clearly states," announced Edward Hindson's *The Total Family*, a book endorsed by Falwell, "that the wife is to submit to her husband's leadership and help him fulfill God's will for his life. . . . She is to submit to him just as she would submit to Christ as her Lord." On such grounds, Protestant fundamentalists joined Phyllis Schlafly's Eagle Forum to lobby the state legislatures against passage of the ERA. "Homosexuality is a perversion, not an alternative life-style," maintained Falwell in a "Clean Up America" campaign that eagerly supported the preaching of Anita Bryant. "Abortion on demand is legalized murder," he said in backing the right-to-life movement. "You can stop the moral landslide," Falwell exhorted. "We can turn back the tide of situation ethics."

The protection of the family from outside interference required special vigilance against the favorite institutions of liberal infiltration—the mass media. "Pornography," argued Falwell, "particularly in television and literature, is brainwashing the American people into accepting as normal what is abnormal." According to the Reverend Don Wildmon, founder of the National Federation for Decency, television audiences witnessed over eleven thousand sexually suggestive comments each year (over eighteen thousand if "skin scenes" counted), a 45 percent increase in profanity between 1978 and 1979, and a preponderance of sexual activity outside marriage. Such findings bolstered a nationwide boycott of the sponsors of televised sexuality and succeeded in persuading Sears, Roebuck to drop "Charlie's Angels" and "Three's Company" and the Kentucky Fried Chicken chain to shift its support to blander programming.

The moral conservatives also challenged the attitudes of professional educators who tried to influence the thinking of their charges. "As long as we've got schools in this country," warned a West Virginia textbook protester in 1975, "we're going to have to realize that there are people who are trying to destroy our basic concepts." The introduction of school books that accepted premarital sex and abortion, for example, or that used language considered obscene, often violated community standards. Organizing protests, parent groups succeeded in censoring teaching materials, school publications, and library lists. The fear of cultural subversion also justified opposition to school busing and the employment of homosexual teachers. "The children in your neighborhood are in danger," cried the Christian Voice in describing a host of public school policies that constituted "just a fraction of a master plan to destroy everything that is good and moral here in America."

The revival of traditional morality extended beyond the doors of any single denomination or political group, increasingly influencing people opposed to liberal change, and it transformed public opinion about an old bone of moral contention—the practice of capital punishment. In the heyday of liberal reform, a 1966 Gallup poll found that more Americans opposed capital punishment than favored it (47 percent to 42 percent), an opinion that encouraged the Supreme Court to rule in 1973 that existing death penalty laws were imposed "wantonly and freakishly" and were consequently unconstitutional. By 1976, however, public opinion had changed and an overwhelming majority, according to a Gallup survey, now supported the death penalty (65 percent to 28 percent). "We hold," said the Supreme Court in a clarification of its thinking, "that the death penalty is not a form of punishment that may never be imposed." Though the Court disallowed state laws that demanded mandatory sentencing and insisted that "death is grossly disproportionate and excessive punishment" for the crime of rape, it encouraged "an individual decision . . . in capital cases."

The first victim of these changing postures ironically contributed to its public acceptance. Charged with two murders in Utah, defendant Gary Gilmore refused to appeal the death sentence. "Weak bad habits . . . have left me somewhat evil," he explained. "I don't like being evil and . . . desire to not be evil anymore." In January 1977, a state firing squad effectively ended a ten-year moratorium on capital punishment that itself represented a moral bulwark against legal executions. By 1977, public opinion polls found that the majority favoring capital punishment had increased. Such feelings, surveys found, remained constant even if people believed the practice had no deterrent effect. "The motives for the death penalty may indeed include vengeance," suggested sociologist Ernest van den Haag. "Legal vengeance solidifies social solidarity against lawbreakers and probably is the only alternative to the disruptive private revenge of those who feel harmed." In May 1979, the state of Florida reaffirmed those primal standards by electrocuting convicted murderer John Spenkelink in the first involuntary execution since 1967.

The resurgence of traditional values triggered the expansion of conservative churches dedicated to reversing the drift of modern society. Through television and radio pulpits, preachers such as Falwell, Pat Robertson, James Robison, and Jim Bakker reached an estimated 100 million Americans each week. This vast electronic church urged its members to support conservative causes, even as it undermined traditional religious institutions and the local church. The broadcast preachers also created an electronic feedback system of telephone lines and direct mail facilities that enabled them to garner, along with their converts, over $30 million a year to finance church activities. "We have enough votes to run the country," claimed Robertson. "And when the people say, 'We've had enough,' we are going to take over." Forming in 1979 what he called the "Moral Majority," Falwell launched a coalition of religious groups, primarily evangelical Protestants, as one of his supporters reported, "to mobilize at least two million Americans to work for pro-God, pro-family policies in government." "Get them saved, baptized, and registered," Falwell advised his ministerial colleagues.

The politicization of organized religion provided moral fervor in the rebirth of conservative politics. Following the Watergate scandals, Congress had limited the size of individual campaign contributions, forcing candidates to develop a mass base of support. Such revisions increased the importance of communications specialists, such as the conservative Viguerie, who solicited funds from likely contributors. "Direct mail has allowed conservatives to bypass the liberal media, and go directly into the homes of the conservatives in this country," Viguerie told the Conservative Political Action Conference in 1977. "There really is a silent majority in this country, and the New Right now has learned how to identify them and communicate with them and mobilize them." By targeting appeals to specific constituencies, such techniques allowed politicians to disregard the traditional party structures.

The attempt to minimize corporation interference in elections by limiting business contributions also caused powerful and unexpected reverberations when the Supreme Court ruled that political expenditures, as a form of public speech, could not be limited by Congress, and that corporations, as legal entities, shared these constitutional rights with private citizens. Business groups responded by organizing ever larger numbers of independent political action committees (PACs)—from 89 in 1974 to 821 in 1978 to more than 1,300 in 1979—to support favored candidates and causes. "They are multiplying like rabbits," warned Senator Kennedy, "and they are doing their best to buy every Senator, every Representative and every issue in sight." "It's just as much a civic responsibility," replied one executive, "as helping the Heart Fund." Permitted by the high court to participate in referenda campaigns, corporations often outspent citizens groups to protect vested interests. "If corporate interests can dominate both legislatures and referenda with their dollars," advised Mark Green, director of the Public Citizens Congress Watch, "then the golden rule of politics prevails—he who has the gold rules."

An invigorated alliance between corporate conservatives and the New Right produced unexpected results in the elections of 1978. With voters disdaining traditional party labels, conservative coalitions orchestrated elaborate campaigns against such liberal incumbents as Dick Clark of Iowa, Floyd Haskell of Colorado, and Thomas McIntyre of New Hampshire, toppled liberal governor Michael Dukakis of Massachusetts in the primaries, and danced on the grave of Humphrey's Democratic-Farmer-Labor organization by beating the entire ticket in Minnesota. In these contests, single-issue conservatives, such as antiabortion groups, often exerted a small but crucial margin of difference. "The people have had enough," stated Iowa's new senator, Roger Jepsen. "They are conservatives for change." Even moderates, such as Illinois Senator Charles Percy, slipped to the right to avoid defeat, and several Democratic candidates represented the conservative wing. Asked a glum White House aide after the final tally, "How would you like to be Frank Church or George McGovern in 1980?"

Sensing the changing winds, Democratic leaders quickly asserted their own brand of conservatism. At the party's mid-term convention in December 1978, President Carter unveiled a tight anti-inflationary budget which demanded "short-term sacrifices." In California, Governor Brown, victorious in a landslide after embracing Proposition 13, endorsed the summoning of a national constitutional convention to force a balanced budget, an unprecedented means of altering the Constitution that already had been approved by some thirty states. "It is time to get off the treadmill," declared Brown, "to challenge the assumption that more government spending automatically leads to better living." Such statements defied the tenets of traditional liberalism, opening deep rifts within the Democratic coalition. "The Administration's budget," retorted Senator Kennedy in staking out an alternative position, "asks the poor, the black, the sick, the young, the cities and the unemployed to bear a disproportionate share of the billions of dollars of reductions in Federal spending." "I did not become Speaker of the House," agreed Tip O'Neill, "to dismantle the programs I've worked all my life for."

The widening split within the Democratic party fired the imagination of the conservative opposition.

"We've changed the focus of politics in America from their ground to our ground," boasted Representative Kemp. "We've shifted from the defensive to the offensive. They're now arguing on our turf."

"We're the liveliest, most energetic political action force in America today," declared Representative Robert Bauman, chairman of the American Conservative Union. "Our time has come."

"We have moved the entire Democratic Party across the horizon, at least if you believe their rhetoric," said Ronald Reagan. "The people of America are demanding what we've always stood for."

"Perhaps we had to watch as the Democrats tried to prove that government could do everything," suggested Senate Minority Whip Ted Stevens, "—in order to show it could not."

About the only thing that might stand a chance getting through with this bunch," said a White House aide, "is higher defense spending."

Committed to restoring the old America, the new conservative leadership flatly rejected a foreign policy of limits—loathed détente, the Panama Canal treaties, and SALT II—and demanded implementation of the B-1 bomber, the neutron bomb, and a modernized navy. "Unless the international performance of the United States improves substantially over what has become the norm in recent years," advised Kemp, "we shall all bear the burden of failure directly." The most powerful nation on earth, argued the conservatives, could ill afford to appear timid. "Shouldn't we stop worrying whether someone likes us," suggested Reagan shortly before announcing his presidential candidacy in 1979, "and decide once again we're going to be respected in the world?"

The old Hollywood cowboy, dead of cancer in 1979, personified that lost respect. "John Wayne was bigger than life," eulogized President Carter. "In an age of few heroes, he was the genuine article." One month before his death, Congress had authorized a gold medal struck in his honor, a token that easily blurred the man and his numerous roles. "Celebrating the dead John Wayne," observed *Newsweek* critic Jack Kroll, "America was celebrating one of its gallant dead dreams—a dream of unflagging national virility, courage, moral righteousness and stone-fisted sincerity." In recent years, such virtues had won sparse applause. "That little clique back there in the East has taken great personal satisfaction reviewing my politics instead of my pictures," Wayne told fellow actor Ronald Reagan. "But one day those doctrinaire liberals will wake up to find the pendulum has swung the other way." Writing Wayne's obituary for *Reader's Digest*, Reagan found solace in that defiant prophecy. "Duke Wayne symbolized . . . the force of the American will to do what is right in the world," averred the presidential hopeful. "He could have left no greater legacy."

As the decade drew to a close, Americans stood at the crossroads of possibility. The revival of conservatism and the simultaneous proliferation of community organizations represented competing versions of the future. Each appealed to the frustrations of the age—the failure of government to assure economic stability, to provide social justice, to fulfill a sense of national purpose—and each insisted that the American people, left to their own devices, could better resolve these troublesome issues. But as conservatives forecast a world of endless opportunity and growth, the community populists predicted an era of roots and limits. To implement these rival visions, conservatives moved, naturally, to control the established institutions, while populists sought alternative bases of support at the grass roots. With such diverse tactics, both movements ironically could achieve success at the same time. The conflict between federal authority and community power, between the leadership groups and the citizenry, between advocates of social change and defenders of the old morality—this fundamental tension of values—would persist. Its resolution would constitute the nation's major dilemma in the eighties.

*Everett Carll Ladd, Jr.*
*Seymour Martin Lipset*

# Public Opinion
# and Public Policy

Any effort to anticipate the way in which the American public is likely to behave politically in the 1980s must involve an awareness of the country's enduring values and commitments. To a considerable extent, two values—those of equalitarianism and achievement—have influenced our national behavior. As noted by Alexis de Tocqueville and others in the early years of the republic, equalitarianism implies that all persons are deserving of respect; that people should not bend to others because of inequality of income, position, or power; and that differences in income reflect accidental and perhaps temporary variations in social relationships. The notion of achievement is a corollary to the belief in equality. For people to be equal, they must have equality of opportunity; then they should be judged on what they actually do. Success should be attainable to all who work hard and have ability, no matter what the accidents of birth, class, or race.

Although equality and achievement have reinforced each other over the course of American history, they have also led to conflict. Different policy implications have been derived from each. Equality has been associated with left or liberal forces, and implies breaking down sources of inequality and waging war on racism, sexism, and poverty. Achievement, on the other hand, has been identified with the philosophy of conservatism, as that word has been used in modern America, with a stress on individualistic or competitive values and opposition to increased state power. . . .

\*     \*     \*

Reprinted from The United States in the 1980's edited by Peter Duignan and Alvin Rabushka with the permission of the publishers, Hoover Institution Press. Copyright © 1980 by the Board of Trustees of the Leland Stanford Junior University.

Although both American historical and comparative international political experiences offer clues about the 1980s in America—whether more equalitarian or more achievement oriented, more liberal or more conservative—these clues are tentative and limited. To try to estimate where the United States is going, therefore, we turn to a more direct source of evidence: trends revealed by public opinion polls, as well as voting behavior and partisan choices. But even these more quantitative data are not without their contradictions.

## Public Opinion

It became something of an article of faith as the 1970s ended that Americans are moving away from liberal values and perspectives, toward commitments decidedly more conservative than those that prevailed in the past. The passage of California's Proposition 13 in June 1978 by a two-to-one margin, together with the strong campaigns in other states across the country to impose limits on taxing and spending, are the most frequently cited evidence for this presumed swing to the right. Buffeted by high taxes and inflation, people are turning away from the liberal, big-spending social programs first initiated in the United States under Franklin Roosevelt and greatly elaborated during the 1960s. Lewis Uhler, a political conservative who heads the National Tax Limitation Committee, argues that the new resistance to government spending has stimulated a general inclination to challenge the drift toward governmental, as opposed to private, market-centered solutions to social problems. And Walter Heller, a political liberal who chaired the Council of Economic Advisors under John F. Kennedy, laments Proposition 13 and its many counterparts as a "blind, self-interest-motivated lashing out at the government."

The sense of a swing toward conservatism does not rest simply on the evidence of a tax revolt. Polls inquiring about attitudes toward defense spending, an issue that generally separates liberals from conservatives, have found a steady increase since 1974 in the proportion favoring higher appropriations for the military. Americans have exhibited generally greater support for a firmer foreign policy.

The 1978 elections revealed some modest conservative victories. Some liberals went down to defeat within the primaries of both parties. Donald Fraser, the head of Americans for Democratic Action, lost to a conservative in his primary bid for the senatorial nomination of the Minnesota Democratic Farmer Labor party. In Massachusetts, liberal Democratic Governor Michael Dukakis was defeated for renomination by a tax-cutting conservative, Edward King. Clifford Case, one of the most liberal senators, was beaten in the New Jersey Republican primary by an arch-conservative, Jeffrey Bell. In the November elections, Republicans gained 3 seats in the Senate and 16 in the House, plus 310 legislative seats across the country.

Surveys of the ideological identification of samples of Americans, asking respondents to state whether they consider themselves liberals, conservatives, or moderates, find more self-identified conservatives than liberals. Thus, in a poll taken by Gallup in August 1978, 43 percent described their political position as "right of center," whereas 20 percent classified themselves as "left of center." Earlier in the year, a CBS News/New York Times poll reported that the ratio of self-described conservatives to liberals was 42 to 23 percent. A Roper survey in March 1979 found almost identical results, conservatives outnumbering liberals by 44 to 23 percent. Caution is needed in the interpretation of these data because people mean many different things when they employ the terms *liberal* and *conservative*. In the relatively conservative 1950s, polls occasionally found self-described liberals outnumbering self-proclaimed conservatives. In 1955, for example, a Gallup poll showed the United States public divided 53 percent liberals and 41 percent conservatives.

A shift toward greater conservatism is evident on the college campuses— the center of left-leaning protest during the 1960s and early 1970s. During the Vietnam years, American universities were awash in protest demonstrations; now the campuses are quiet, as career-oriented students concentrate on grades and securing jobs. Opinion polls of college students indicate a definite shift away from the left in political opinions in the 1970s. In 1970, 37 percent of first-year college students identified their political beliefs as liberal or far left; by 1978, that proportion had dropped to 26 percent. Interest in politics had also declined sharply, as only 37 percent reported in 1978 that it was essential or important to keep up-to-date with political affairs, compared to 53 percent in 1970.

Opinion surveys have documented broad popular concern with various consequences of the rapid social change of the last two decades (such as the perceived deterioration of the family) and some reassertion of support for traditional values. For example, a 1978 Yankelovich study found 84 percent of Americans indicating that they would welcome "more emphasis on religious beliefs." The public, concerned with the high incidence of crime, now takes a tougher stance toward punishment than it did ten years ago. Support has risen for the death penalty for persons convicted of murder. Only in 1966, in the period for which survey data are available, did a majority (53 percent) of Americans come out against the death penalty. By 1978, support had risen to a point near the post-1930s high: 70 percent endorsed use of the death penalty for convicted murderers, whereas just 30 percent were opposed.

It is not hard, then, to see why so many politicians and others who attend closely to election results and public opinion data see the United States as moving to the right. Yet other happenings in the political arena furnish contradictory signs. Although more people identify themselves as conservatives than as liberals, the Democrats have a considerable advantage over the Republicans in party registration figures and party identification distribution in opinion polls. In 1978, two areas that Republicans have long dominated in party registration—Orange County, California, and the state of Maine— shifted to the Democratic camp, the latter for the first time in its history. But according to the Louis Harris organization, the number claming to be

Democrats in opinion surveys has steadily declined since Jimmy Carter was elected, from 51 percent in 1976 to 38 percent in 1979. This result, however, does not offer solace to Republicans, for their proportion has remained constant at 24 percent over the three years, whereas independents have increased from 23 to 33 percent. These changes in party identification largely reflect a shift away from the Democrats by self-identified liberals, presumably because Jimmy Carter was viewed as having become conservative. In 1976, 74 percent of the liberals described their party affiliation as Democratic, but by 1979 only 41 percent did so. During this time, the percentage of independents among the liberals jumped from 15 to 39 percent.

Polls inquiring in 1979 about the presidential preferences of Americans invariably found that the most popular choice for 1980 was the most liberal one, Edward Kennedy. Kennedy is clearly a strong advocate of big government. He is the sponsor of the most extensive government medical care program ever advanced by a major American political figure. And he is an ideological opponent of big business, as reflected in his position on corporate taxes and his strong support for legislation restricting corporate mergers. Not surprisingly, a national survey conducted for the *Washington Post* in May 1979 found that a large proportion of Kennedy supporters had much more conservative views on various issues than he does. These supporters could turn against him, should they discover the contradiction between their political stance and his in the course of a campaign. Still, it should also be noted that the polls show that Kennedy was perceived by the electorate as more of a liberal than other contestants for the 1980 nominations of both parties. In trial heats among Democrats, Kennedy ran far ahead of both Carter and Jerry Brown. When Americans were asked in 1979 whether they would prefer each of the three leading Democrats against a variety of Republicans—including Ronald Reagan, Howard Baker, John Connally, and Gerald Ford —Kennedy invariably had a substantial lead over various Republicans. Carter and Brown did much more poorly, frequently running neck and neck with, or behind, prospective Republican rivals.

## Political Labels

Part of the problem in trying to determine the direction in which the country is moving lies in the ideological categories we employ: liberalism and conservatism. Students of American politics know that these categories have been recently used with so many different, and often conflicting, meanings that they have been robbed of much of their clarity and hence usefulness. Such labels have been so loosely employed that one cannot make easy, confident assertions about liberal or conservative trends in U.S. public opinion.

The problem of using the traditional terms is compounded by the fact that liberalism-conservatism has probably never been a single-dimension continuum. There is a series of distinct dimensions, and an individual can occupy quite different positions, relative to the entire public, on each of them—

liberal on domestic economic policies, centrist in foreign affairs, conservative on some cultural and life-style issues, and so on. Given the multidimensionality of liberalism-conservatism, it is possible for an individual to move in opposite directions at the same time—toward the liberal end of one continuum and the conservative end of another.

It should also be noted that terms like liberal and conservative are ideological categories; opinion analysts have shown that people simply do not hold views that are as coherently packaged or constrained as ideology implies. Individuals are not liberal just because they answer a given question in the liberal fashion. They may be appropriately described as liberal only if they employ some larger conceptual dimension—some variant of liberalism—to order their responses to a variety of issues. Put another way, there is a lot of opinion change in the United States and other countries that is not really ideological at all, but which is mistakenly described as evidence of ideological shifts.

Academic commentators on the ideological divisions in the United States since the 1930s have found it useful to differentiate between economic and noneconomic liberalism-conservatism. The first polarity basically refers to attitudes toward issues associated with New Deal reforms. Economic liberals have generally endorsed the extension of the welfare-planning state, and have backed government policies and expenditures to improve the lot of the less privileged, the poor, the unemployed, the elderly, and the sick. They have favored a progressive income tax, hitting harder at the wealthy and at corporations. They have supported trade unions and the regulation of business. Economic conservatives have generally opposed such policies. The noneconomic or social dimension, as it has come to be called in recent years, encompasses questions of civil liberties for unpopular groups and perspectives, the rights of criminals, the claims of minority groups and women, new social and cultural values, and, most recently, environmental issues. On this dimension those called conservatives, though not overt opponents of the rights of political and social minorities or of efforts to improve the environment, have tended to be less enthusiastic about involving the government actively. They have been more hard-line on issues of law and order and have been unhappy about changes in conventional morality.

The Great Depression, as implied earlier, brought about a fundamental change in the attitudes of Americans toward welfare state policies, government economic planning, progressive income taxes, and labor unions. In large measure, popular reactions to such issues were strongly correlated with social class. The less privileged overwhelmingly backed them. The higher a person's income, the less favorable his attitude toward economic liberalism. By electing and reelecting Franklin Roosevelt and Harry Truman, the majority of Americans voiced approval for such policies. By the time the Republicans returned to control of the White House in 1953 under Dwight Eisenhower, they had come to accept these policies as institutionalized, and only sought to modify their scope and administration. Still, these issues continue to separate economic liberals and conservatives and, to some extent, Democrats and Republicans.

Changes in attitudes involving noneconomic liberalism-conservatism, in general, occurred following World War II. Polls taken during the 1930s and during the war showed that large numbers of Americans had negative attitudes toward Jews and blacks, and that most people believed women should remain in their traditional roles, as nonemployed housewives and mothers. Prejudice against minority racial and religious groups, as reflected in opinion surveys, dropped strikingly in the years immediately following the end of the war. These shifts were reflected in changes in institutional policies toward Jews. Jews were admitted in large numbers to universities, which had had restrictive quotas both on student and faculty levels, as well as to various professions and businesses from which they had been barred. The improvement in popular feelings about blacks may have been reflected in the Supreme Court decisions in the 1950s outlawing segregation in schools as well as other public institutions. The populace moved in a more conservative direction, however, with respect to civil liberties for dissident political groups. Public unwillingness to allow equal political rights to communists and other unpopular ideological minorities, high during the 1930s, increased during the late 1940s and early 1950s. In addition, the cold war was developing, along with the hot war against North Korea and the People's Republic of China, events that encouraged repressive measures against groups identified with the enemy.

Attitudes toward civil liberties for unpopular, particularly leftist, groups, as well as civil rights for minority groups and women changed strikingly during the 1960s and 1970s. Public attitudes favoring equal rights increased sharply during this period. This change in the public's response spurred the passage of a variety of civil rights laws, beginning with voting rights and extending to the implementation of affirmative-action programs. During the 1960s, there was also a strong liberal shift regarding the death penalty, abortion, extramarital sex, the status of homosexuals, and the rights of political radicals.

Economic and social liberalism-conservatism are correlated. Some people, however, are economic conservatives and social liberals, others are conservative on social issues and liberal on economic ones. The first group has tended to be disproportionately composed of well-to-do, well-educated persons; the second has drawn strength from less affluent and poorly educated whites.

The politics of the 1960s—which emphasized noneconomic issues, including attitudes toward the Vietnam war and American foreign policy generally—identified many well-educated persons with left-of-center politics. This pressed them to favor as well a liberal orientation: support for government policies on behalf of underdog elements in society, including minorities, women, and the underprivileged. They also became hostile to establishment institutions generally, especially big business. As a result the liberal wing of the Democratic party gained greatly in ideological coherence and in support from well-to-do, well-educated people. Conversely, many less affluent whites, who belonged to or favored trade unions and supported welfare-planning state redistributionist policies, turned against liberalism. This they identified with support for minorities, for integration, busing, and affirmative-action policies giving special preference in employment and education to blacks and women; as well as with the coddling of criminals; with a rejection of traditional concepts of morality regarding sexual and family matters; and with the challenge to authority and patriotism reflected in campus and other protests of the 1960s and early 1970s.

The concerns of lower-status whites were particularly evident in the support given George Wallace in Democratic party presidential primaries from 1964 to 1976. The enthusiasm for him was expressed in the polls, in his high approval rating, in the 25 percent who indicated a preference for him for president as a third party candidate early in 1968, as well as in the 13 percent of the vote he received as the American Independent party candidate. These feelings were also apparent in the sizeable votes for law and order and anti-busing candidates in local elections in such cities as Boston (Louise Day Hicks), Philadelphia (Frank Rizzo), Los Angeles (Sam Yorty), and Minneapolis (Charles Stenvig).

The position of the Democratic party as the majority party was strengthened. Its ranks were reinforced by an infusion of support from well-educated middle- to upper-class elements for whom the social and foreign policy issues became salient. At the same time, poorer and less educated whites, who had identified with the Democrats as the party representing economic interests of persons like themselves, remained linked to the party, for they continued to see the Republican party as the instrument of big business, uninterested in the common man. Many, of course, were unhappy with the Democrats' association with the cause of minorities, campus protests, and cultural change, a fact reflected in the low votes received by Hubert Humphrey and George McGovern in 1968 and 1972, respectively. This group, however, generally continued Democratic in contests for congressional, state, and local offices, remained registered Democrats and in polls identified themselves as Democrats and conservatives. In 1976, many of them voted for Jimmy Carter, whom they regarded as a moderate or conservative Democrat. It is notable that he lost support during the campaign as some voters began to perceive that he was more liberal than they had earlier believed.

However, the backlash against the newer dimensions of social liberalism among less affluent whites did not involve an increase in the proportion expressing prejudice against minorities. Since World War II, there has been increasing acceptance of the equalitarian values of the American creed. Most Americans have come to recognize the rights of minorities and women to equal treatment. The social conservatives typically object not to the direction, but to the pace of the change. And they are generally less willing to support government policies that give the deprived special advantages. The majority of the population favors fair employment legislation, the legal right to equal treatment in securing employment, and the right of blacks to attend any school they desire or live where they want. But most oppose giving special preference to minorities or women; policies that require white children to attend schools they do not wish to attend; and government programs designed to move blacks into white neighborhoods. The upshot of these developments is an electorate that has become increasingly liberal on social issues, while remaining essentially committed to the New Deal welfare policies.

The picture became complicated in the last years of the 1970s by the emergence of sustained high inflation. By eating away at savings and retirement plans and reducing the real income of some, inflation has produced a sharp reaction. The public has come to see large-scale government spending as a major source of inflation and now supports policies that promise to bring inflation under control. Tax protests have been fueled by escalating taxes, produced by the inflationary increase in home prices, and by the movement of many into higher tax brackets as their dollar, but not their real, income increases. Hence, when people have the opportunity to vote for lower taxes in referenda, or when they are queried about taxes in the polls, they opt for lower taxes and reduced government spending.

This behavior has been interpreted as a conservative reaction. But the same citizens, when offered the chance to vote for rent control, a "liberal" measure, do so. And since the middle of 1978, most Americans have expressed support for wage, price, and profit controls. Particularly incensed by the sharp increase in the price of oil, they express much hostility to the oil companies and strong support for price control of petroleum products. In June 1979, a CBS News/New York Times poll reported a decisive majority (60 to 29 percent) in favor of rationing gasoline as an alternative to allowing prices to rise. Americans have also become increasingly angry toward both big business and trade unions, which they identify as powerful, self-seeking institutions that pursue unwarranted profits or higher wages at the expense of the public—and hence contribute to higher prices.

This analysis suggests that recent changes in public opinion do not reflect a consistent move to the right. Most Americans have remained or have become committed to liberal orientations in the economic and social spheres. But their reactions to specific electoral and policy alternatives will be determined by larger events in the domestic and economic spheres. Much as we could not have anticipated the political impact of Vietnam and Watergate at the start of the 1960s, it is impossible to know what major happenings will structure the way Americans will respond in the 1980s. Still, a detailed examination of American attitudes at the start of the new decade will give us some indication of the parameters of both opinion and action.

## The Growth of Social Liberalism

The increased support for social liberalism is evident in a variety of areas, including civil liberties, civil rights, and personal morality. Americans have become notably more supportive of pro-civil liberties positions. They are now more inclined to endorse the freedoms of speech, press, employment, and the like for unpopular minorities than at any time since the polls began inquiring into this area. This trend is particularly clear in a comparison of the replies to identical questions asked first in 1954 by Samuel A. Stouffer and his colleagues and then repeated in the 1970s in the General Social Surveys of the University of Chicago's National Opinion Research Center (NORC). Should someone who favors "government ownership of all railroads and all big industries be allowed to teach in a college or university?" Just 33 percent said yes in 1954. A quarter of a century later, a clear majority, 57 percent, agreed that this leftist teacher should have a right to a job. Similarly, the proportion who feel that a person who wants "to make a speech in your community against churches and religion" should be allowed to speak, moved up from 38 percent in 1954 to 62 percent in 1977.

Questions of civil rights—for blacks, other ethnic minorities, and women —show much the same sort of progression. The trends reported by Gallup on whether people would cast a presidential ballot for candidates of certain status or ethnic background are typical of such findings. The proportion who would vote for a woman rose from 32 percent in 1937 to 54 percent in 1955, to 69 percent in 1971, to 81 percent in July 1978. Those giving the same response for a Jewish candidate increased from 46 percent in 1937 to 62 percent in 1958 to 82 percent in 1978. For a black nominee, the favorable percentages shot up from 42 percent in 1958 to 57 percent in 1967 to 84 percent in 1978.

Voting for a black for president does not involve a major change in personal behavior. It is, therefore, important to note that the number of whites reporting that they have no objection to sending their children to schools in which half or more than half the students are black has also steadily increased. Among northern whites, individuals who object to children attending half-black schools have declined from 33 percent in 1963 to 23 in 1978. Over the same period, southern whites have also become much more liberal, moving from 78 percent opposed to their children going to half-black institutions in 1963, to just 28 percent in 1978.

One of the most severe attitudinal tests of white racial liberalism is racial intermarriage. As recently as 1965, more than half the American public endorsed legislation prohibiting marriages between blacks and whites. By 1977, however, nearly three-fourths of the population maintained that there should be no laws against racial intermarriage. Not surprisingly, these attitudes, like others in this area, correlated strikingly with education and age. The better educated and the younger the person interviewed, the more liberal he was.

Americans have become generally more supportive of equal rights for women. Just over half (51 percent) in 1970 stated that they favored "most of the efforts to strengthen and change women's status in society today." By 1979, with such efforts expanded, well over two-thirds of the populace (70 percent) indicated their approval. The propriety of a married woman not in financial need holding a job was supported by only 22 percent of the public in 1938, by 63 percent in 1970, and by 73 percent in 1978.

It must be noted, however, that the majority of Americans are not willing to approve of certain kinds of affirmative-action programs. These include programs that appear to give minorities or women special preference (for example, job or educational quotas) or that involve compulsory integration in schools (busing) or housing. Americans continue to favor equality in the context of equality of opportunity for individuals but oppose programs equalizing outcomes.

There are increasingly liberal reactions to a wide assortment of social, cultural, and life-style issues. There has been, for example a weakening of many of the old codes of personal comportment—meaning that there is now less opposition to premarital sex, abortion, the use of marijuana, and so on. In 1969, 13 percent of the public wanted the use of marijuana legalized; nine years later 31 percent held this view. Only 15 percent of the adult population in 1969 favored legalized abortions in the case of a woman who is married and simply does not want any more children; nine years later the proportion had risen appreciably to 40 percent.

The way surveyors phrase their questions in some ways gives the clearest sense of the amount of liberalizing that has occurred in views on personal comportment. In 1978, NORC interviewers asked, "If a man and a woman have sex relations before marriage, do you think it is always wrong, almost always wrong, wrong only sometimes, or not wrong at all?" Roper interviewers 39 years earlier had posed the same question quite differently: "Do you consider it all right, unfortunate, or wicked when young girls have sexual relations before marriage?"

## Military Spending and Foreign Policy

Attitudes toward foreign policy and military spending link in many ways with the social questions. In the post-World War II years, a hard-line foreign policy has implied opposition to Soviet policies and to the expansion of communism. Thus, it is not surprising that research on the factors correlated with support for increased U.S. military spending finds that such views are associated with a generally conservative political ideology. Polls taken by NORC during the 1970s show that self-identified conservatives and those who favor capital punishment for convicted murderers are disproportionately in favor of increased military expenditures.

Shifts in attitudes toward defense spending have closely paralleled international developments. In 1960, Gallup reported that 18 percent said we were spending "too much," as contrasted to 21 percent replying "too little." As opposition expanded to the Vietnam war and American entanglements abroad, the proportion who believed that American defense spending was excessive grew steadily until, by 1969, it comprised a majority, 52 percent; only 8 percent thought we were not spending enough. The Vietnam effect lasted through 1974, when the ratio of too much to too little was 44 to 12 percent. From then on, apparent concern with Soviet expansionist policies and the weakness of the American response brought about a change in public mood. Gallup surveys showed that, by 1977, more people replied too little (27 percent) than too much (23 percent), and by 1978, too little had a decisive lead (32 to 16 percent). Similar findings were reported by NORC in annual surveys taken from 1973 to 1978. Comparable shifts in opinion occurred between 1974 and 1978 with respect to support for sending American troops abroad. An analysis of factors related to these changes by the Chicago Council on Foreign Relations "suggested that the principal reason for increased support of both defense spending and willingness to commit troops in selected areas was the perceived growing influence of the Soviet Union."

Because attitudes toward foreign policy and defense spending are linked to liberal or conservative self-identifications, the growth of hard-line attitudes in these areas should strengthen conservatism in public opinion. This trend may be related to the small but steady increase in proportion of those who describe themselves ideologically as conservatives in the same 1973–1978 NORC polls that inquired into attitudes toward military expenditures. This change may parallel the shift to the left in public mood with the growth of anti-military attitudes during the Vienam war. It should be noted, however, that such attitudes do not correlate with party identification. Curiously, Republicans are no more likely to favor greater spending on armaments than Democrats. And according to a May 1979 CBS News/New York Times poll, party identification does not differentiate supporters from opponents of the SALT II treaty, although self-identified liberals are much more pro-SALT than conservatives.

## Economic Liberalism

At the time of this writing, support for economic or New Deal liberalism continues at a high level. In spite of the widespread speculation about a swing to the right, spurred by concerns about the level of government spending, there is as yet no indication of a widespread inclination to cut back substantially on the liberal, interventionist state. In some instances, the move is in the opposite direction. For example, 64 percent of those polled in a 1964 survey agreed that "the government in Washington ought to help people get doctors and hospital care at low cost." In 1968, the proportion was about the same—66 percent. But in 1978, 85 percent of those surveyed in another national study wanted the national government to assume this responsibility.

"In all industries where there is competition," the Opinion Research Corporation has asked, "do you think companies should be allowed to make all the profit they can or should the government put a limit on the profits companies can make?" In 1946, 31 percent wanted government to limit profits; 25 percent took this position in 1962. But in 1977 an all-time high of 55 percent endorsed this form of government intervention. Admittedly, this question touches on two separate opinions: views of business corporations and their profits, and judgments about the appropriate role of government. Still, the jump in support for a governmental role in this area is consistent with the generally expansive views of contemporary Americans on government responsibilities.

When asked whether the federal or state governments should cut back on spending for public services, the public today overwhelmingly favors sustaining or increasing current spending. (There are only isolated exceptions, such as welfare, which seems to connote a dole for people unwilling to work.) When questioned by the Survey Research Center of the University of Michigan in November 1978 as to whether they would trade off key government services for two major tax reductions, over three-fifths rejected the cut. Specifically, when asked whether "Federal income taxes should be cut by at least one-third even if it means reducing military spending and cutting down on government services such as health and education," 62 percent replied no, while 27 percent favored the proposal. People in all social classes, in all regions of the country, and of all political persuasions now consistenty endorse high levels of public expenditures for most social services, according to National Opinion Research Center polls. For example, 91 percent who refer to themselves as upper class maintain that we are either spending too little or the right amount "to improve educational systems." Ninety-four percent of professional and 95 percent of unskilled workers take these pro-spending positions on "improv[ing] the nation's health." Seventy-three percent of grade-school–trained Americans and 81 percent of college graduates want to maintain or increase expenditures "to improve the condition of blacks."

## Dissatisfaction with Government

This discussion is not intended to imply that every facet of contemporary American public opinion comes closer to sustaining the idea of economic liberalism than of conservatism. Americans are unhappy about welfare spending. Above all, they reject some features of the big government apparatus that has been established since the New Deal—even as they are profoundly supportive of a high level of public service. Government is now viewed as wasteful and inefficient.

The distrust of government is an attitude that has been building in America since the country became divided over the wisdom of the Vietnam war. It has been sustained through the various misfortunes that have occurred since: massive civil disobedience by students and minorities in the late 1960s, Watergate, recession, and inflation. One of the most widely noted shifts has been in the level of political trust expressed by the American public. The Survey Research Center (SRC) of the University of Michigan has asked four "political trust" questions in national surveys from 1958 to 1978.

Confidence changed little between 1958 and 1964; in that six-year period the average increase in "mistrust" as measured by the four questions was only 4 percent. In the subsequent six-year period, 1964–1970, mistrust increased by an average of 17 percent on the four items, and the increase exceeded 20 percent on three of the four. In that six-year period of intense political controversy and polarization, the percentage of Americans saying that "the government wastes a lot of money we pay in taxes" rose from 48 to 69 percent. The percentage maintaining that "the government is pretty much run by a few big interests looking out for themselves rather than for the benefit of all the people" climbed from 30 to 52 percent. And the percentage who felt that "you can trust the government in Washington to do what is right . . . only some of the time or none of the time" (rather than "always" or "most of the time") rose from 22 to 45 percent.

Political cynicism did not increase markedly during this period on one of the SRC's political trust questions. The percentage who felt that "quite a few of the people running the government are crooked" rose from 30 percent in 1964 to 33 percent in 1970—an increase hardly comparable to the enormous jump in cynicism measured by the other items. In 1972, the perception that most government officials are crooked again increased only modestly, to 38 percent. But as one might guess, the Watergate affair soon corrected the noticeable lag in this political trust item. By the end of 1973, the first year of the Watergate revelation, the proportion who agreed that most government officials are crooked rose to 57 percent. At the time of the 1974 election, a few months after President Richard Nixon's resignation, this figure fell below a majority, but remained high, at 45 percent. It was slightly lower, 42 percent, in 1976, and fell to 39 percent in 1978, back to its pre-Watergate level.

The earlier increases of the other "distrust attitudes," which mounted so markedly between 1964 and 1970, were sustained by the Watergate experience and have continued to move up since then. From 1970 to 1978, the percentage of Americans claiming that the government wastes a lot of money rose from 69 to 77. The percentage with the view that the government is run for a few big interests increased from 45 to 67 percent.

## Dissatisfaction with Institutions

Although the focus here is on attitudes toward government, it is important to note that the lowering of confidence after the mid-1960s has been general and is not limited to political institutions. As one major pollster, Daniel Yankelovich, noted in 1977:

*We have seen a steady rise of mistrust in our national institutions. . . . Trust in government declined dramatically from almost 80% in the late 1950s to about 33% in 1976. Confidence in other institutions, the universities, the unions, the press, the military, the professions—doctors and lawyers—sharply declined from* the mid-60s to the mid-70s. More than 61% of the electorate believe that there is something morally wrong in the country. More than 80% of voters say they do not trust those in positions of leadership as much as they used to. In the mid-60s a one-third minority reported feeling isolated and distant from the political process, by the mid-70s a two-thirds majority felt that what they think "really doesn't count." Approximately three out of five people feel the government suffers from a concentration of too much power in too few hands, and fewer than one out of five feel that congressional leaders can be believed. One could go on and on. The change is simply massive. Within a ten to fifteen year period, trust in institutions has plunged down and down, from an almost consensual majority, two-thirds or more, to minority segments of the American public.

The conclusion that there has been a drastic decline in confidence in almost all American institutions is sustained by the findings of many pollsters, among them Gallup, Harris, Yankelovich, Roper, NORC, and SRC. Louis Harris is probably the opinion analyst most widely cited on trends in public confidence because he has asked a continuing series of questions. In 1966, Harris for the first time posed this question: "As far as people in charge of running various institutions are concerned, would you say you have a great deal of confidence, only some confidence, or hardly any confidence at all in them?" In 1966, the average percentage voicing "a great deal of confidence" in the leadership of nine different institutions was 47 percent. Five years later, in 1971, the average percentage replying "a great deal" had fallen to 28 percent. The important point is that confidence fell in the leadership of every institution named by Harris.

It appears that Americans became increasingly distrustful of all the major institutions of society as the Vietnam war became a hopeless quagmire and as protest movements over the war and over minority rights disrupted national stability. Confidence in military leaders fell most precipitously between 1966 and 1971, from 67 percent expressing "a great deal of confidence" in the former year to a mere 27 percent in the latter. Confidence in the Congress declined from 42 to 19 percent, and confidence in the executive branch of the government fell from 41 to 23 percent. The schools, another institution at the focus of controversy during the late 1960s, suffered considerable loss of public support: from 61 percent expressing "a great deal of confidence" in the people in charge of the educational system in 1966 to 37 percent in 1971.

Private institutions were not immune to the prevailing trend of increasing distrust and cynicism. Harris asked Americans how much confidence they had in the leaders of major companies. Business leaders declined in public esteem from 55 to 27 percent from 1966 to 1971. Religious leaders also lost standing, falling from 41 to 27 percent. Confidence in the leaders of two institutions that were not highly regarded to begin with—the press and organized labor—deteriorated further, from 29 to 18 percent expressing high confidence in the press, and from 22 to 14 percent for labor. Two institutions well regarded in 1966 continued high, relatively speaking, in 1971: confidence in leaders of medicine fell only from 73 to 61 percent over the span, whereas confidence in the leaders of science dropped from 56 to 46 percent. Thus science and medicine, the two institutions most remote from the social turmoil of the late 1960s, showed the smallest decline in public confidence, although neither escaped the prevailing trend, and medicine caught up to the general decline pattern in the late 1970s.

During the 1970s, many polls analyzed confidence in institutions. The various surveys tend to concur that relatively little change has occurred since 1970, other than small-scale variations that probably reflect the effects of short-term events, sampling variations, or both. . . .

\*    \*    \*

The variations in reported absolute levels of confidence do not negate our interpretations, since what concerns us is trends. In this regard, the various surveys using different questions agree. We have reported Harris's findings in greater detail because he is the only pollster who has inquired about many institutions from 1966. It is clear from the Harris findings, as well as the more discrete results of other surveyors cited by Yankelovich, that a large drop in overall confidence in American institutions occurred during the second half of the 1960s and that there has been no recovery during the 1970s.

## The Problem of Government

The sources of public discontent with government performance have been thoroughly probed. As we have seen, they do not involve opposition to liberal policies—to those designed to aid the underprivileged, to control aspects of the economy, or to improve the leisure, home, and work environments. Rather, what seems to disturb many people is a sense of government incompetence and waste, as well as, in recent years, the inability of government to handle the number one problem, inflation. Virtually every major survey on the latter documents the exceptional emphasis voters place on government waste and inefficiency. Many people feel that tax dollars are not being efficiently used, and that property and income taxes could be sharply reduced without significant service reductions. Votes for tax-cutting measures do not reflect a desire for less government, but for less wasteful and more effective government.

This perception of a highly inefficient government is so strong that just after Proposition 13 mandated a 57-percent property tax cut in June 1978, two-thirds of Californians from public employee households said that it was not likely many of the state's public service workers would lose their jobs. There was, of course, the special California circumstance of a huge state surplus—the existence of which had led State Treasurer Jesse Unruh to describe Gov. Jerry Brown as the "father of Proposition 13." But it is also clear from extensive survey inquiries that California voters of all persuasions believed government was wasteful concerning their tax dollars. It cannot be ascertained how much people think waste can really be pared, and how much they are simply permitting themselves a symbolic slap at perceived malperformance. It is clear that most voters are not embracing tax limitations with the intent of reducing public services. In late June 1978, a CBS News/New York Times poll asked a special sample of Californians whether they were willing to see various services "cut back a lot, or only a little, or not at all" in the wake of passage of Proposition 13. At the same time, a cross-section of all Americans was asked a variant of this question. . . . The great preponderance of all voters, including heavy majorities among Proposition 13 proponents, rejected significant service cuts.

About the only service most people want to reduce is welfare. But detailed explorations of what people mean by the welfare programs they would like to reduce strongly suggest that they have "welfare chiselers" in mind. Many people believe that the welfare rolls are grossly inflated by the presence of able-bodied persons who should be required to take jobs. But the same polls that find that the public would like to reduce welfare also report that they oppose cuts for the elderly and for special education or services for blacks, the poor, the handicapped, or the needy. Seemingly, many of the same people who object to welfare (read "welfare chiselers") continue to back the welfare state.

The public, as noted earlier, has reacted to inflation in diverse ways. People want to cut taxes, but they give solid endorsement to controls over wages, prices, rents and profits. A clear majority say they would prefer a pay increase lower than the cost of living if there were assurances that inflation was in fact being brought under control. Taxes are felt to be too high and relief is desired, but the public is far more anxious about halting inflation than that taxes be cut. Surveys by CBS News/New York Times in 1978 showed that roughly two-thirds of Congress was in favor of some rollback of the social security tax increase mandated by the Ninety-fifth Congress—apparently an anticipatory response to voters' presumed anger—while two-thirds of voters wanted to keep the new taxes as they were. About 90 percent of the public maintained that "controlling inflation is more important than cutting taxes." Americans, in fact, in 1978–1979 came to see it as something of an either-or proposition, that is, they were convinced that governmental actions in the areas of taxing and spending are a major contributor to inflation.

Government is responsible for inflation, but people doubt government can take the necessary correctives. As of 1979, most people felt that no president and no unit of government outside the presidency could "keep prices from going up all the time." Two-thirds of Americans similarly believed in 1979 that a balanced federal budget within the next few years is unattainable, no matter who the players. During the 1974–1975 bout with double-digit inflation, about two-thirds of the populace did not agree that inflation was "one of the facts of life and here to stay," maintaining instead that it would be halted after a while. By summer 1978, however, high inflation was viewed as certain as the proverbial death and taxes. By an extraordinary 9–1 margin, Americans felt that high inflation would continue. Inflation is the prime reason for the public perception that big government, though essential, seriously lacks competence. Should either party be able to convince the American people that it can be counted upon for a competent, coherent response to inflation, it would reap large electoral dividends.

Still, many of these same people are willing to turn to the inefficient government to solve social ills. Government regulation to deal with air and water pollution, to assure product safety, and to protect the environment wins majority support in various polls. To fight inflation, most people endorse rent control, wage and price control, and gas rationing. Such a reponse may appear contradictory, but it may also reflect that the populace has become accustomed to the idea that the way to solve a problem is to have the government deal with it. And if many problems, such as those referred to here, result from the self-interested, income-enhancing motivations of people and institutions, as many believe they do, then the only force potentially available to control or regulate the problems produced by self-interest is the government—inefficient, incompetent, and wasteful as it appears to be.

### The Decline of New Deal Era Divisions

Today, the big economic issues—matters such as the appropriate role for government in economic life, business versus labor, taxation, and spending for social programs—no longer display any coherent class division. It was different 30 and 40 years ago, when lower socioeconomic groups espoused a liberal political economy while the preponderance of the middle class held to a conservative approach. All manner of groups—auto workers, public employees, farmers, blacks, and so on—still make economic demands, of course, and differ one with another. But there is nothing as all-encompassing and persistent as the great working class/middle-class split of the New Deal era. . . .

\*    \*    \*

. . . Although economic divisions remain, they are vastly more fragmented. Specific groups pursue policies designed to advance their interests. But the great class struggles of the New Deal era are gone.

The general acceptance of government responsibility to redress assorted perceived social problems—particularly to aid the underprivileged elements in the society—does not mean that the belief in individualism and achievement has disappeared from American society. The same public opinion surveys that report approval of specific proposals to aid the deprived also indicate a preference for individuals improving their own situation, rather than relying on the government for assistance. These surveys also reveal a strong suspicion of increased state power. But the same Americans who often reject a remedial role for government on the ideological level, when reacting to specific social and economic problems, support federal intervention. It seems evident that American egalitarianism—sympathy for the underdog—leads people to endorse proposals for government action designed to increase opportunity, while at the same time they continue to adhere to antigovernment, individualistic, and meritocratic values. Americans appear to want a society in which each individual is self-supporting and is able, through competition on an equal basis with others, to improve his situation without outside assistance. Because they are aware that such equal opportunity does not exist, they also endorse remedial programs by the state. As a result, in spite of their continued adherence on an ideological level to individualistic anti-state values, when asked to approve various proposed federal programs, their commitment to equal rights and opportunities leads them to support such proposals by sizeable majorities.

Many of the inconsistencies point up a deep contradiction between the two values that are at the core of the American creed—individualism and egalitarianism. Americans believe strongly in both values and, as the earlier discussion suggests, the history of social change in the country reflects a shifting back and forth between them. One consequence of this dualism in the American value system is that political debate often takes the form of one consensual value opposing the other. Liberals and conservatives do not typically take alternative positions on issues of equality and freedom. Instead, each side appeals to one or the other core value. Liberals stress the primacy of egalitarianism and the social injustice that flows from unfettered individualism, while conservatives enshrine individual freedom and the social need for mobility and achievement. Both sides treat the entire American public as their natural constituency. In this sense, liberals and conservatives are less opponents than they are competitors, like two department stores on the same block trying to draw the same customers by offering different versions of what everyone wants. . . .

*      *      *

Whatever the events that determine the outlook of the 1980s, Americans will probably continue their support for activist policies designed to implement the assumptions of equalitarianism—preferably perceived in the context of enhancing individual opportunity. Though Americans will continue to voice a preference for individuals improving their situation through their own efforts, they will readily turn to the state when it appears that individuals do not have a fair chance acting alone. . . .

*      *      *

What can be said about the larger state of opinion in domestic matters is that, since the 1930s, the large majority has been socialized by developments to look for government as a solution to both national and a variety of personal problems. Although events of the past decade and a half have resulted in considerable distrust of big institutions, including government, and most people would like to cut them back in size and power, there has not been an equivalent reduction in the propensity to turn to government. When this orientation is put in the context of the continuing desire of Americans to improve the situation of the underprivileged and minorities, it is likely that the political system will continue to seek to produce solutions to expressed social needs. A policy of "benign neglect" will not be popular, even when warranted.

Richard Polenberg

# *A Segmented Society*

Travelers crossing the United States by automobile in the late 1970s could hardly fail to be impressed by the evidence of regional homogeneity. Driving along highways commonly known by numbers rather than by names—Interstate 80, for example, stretched from New York City to San Francisco—they could stop to eat almost anywhere at a Kentucky Fried Chicken franchise or a McDonald's outlet and would discover, wherever they were, that one drumstick or hamburger tasted exactly like another. From Maine to Oregon a tourist could spend a night at a Holiday Inn, a Quality Court or a Howard Johnson's Motor Lodge, and, as historian Daniel Boorstin has remarked, in any one of them "he would know where to find the ice maker, the luggage rack, the TV set; he would recognize the cellophane wrapping on the drinking glass, the paper festoon on the toilet seat. . . . Wherever he travelled across the continent, he felt a new assurance that he would be at home, and somehow in the same place." To cross the Mississippi River on Interstate 20, one traveler commented, was to encounter "an almost imperceptible interruption." Behind the appearance of uniformity, however, differences along class, racial, and ethnic lines persisted. While they had changed dramatically over a forty-year period, these distinctions continued to shape the lives of most Americans.

## 1.

In the early morning hours of June 18, 1972, five agents of President Nixon's reelection committee were arrested while burglarizing Democratic National Committee headquarters in the Watergate Hotel. Although undertaken to

From One Nation Divisible by Richard Polenberg. Copyright © 1980 by Richard Polenberg. Reprinted by permission of Viking Penguin, Inc.

obtain political intelligence and to install wiretaps, the break-in was airily dismissed by the President as a "very bizarre incident." This disavowal of White House involvement was at first widely accepted, but in 1973, as a result of persistent inquiries by newspaper reporters and by Judge John J. Sirica, before whom the Watergate defendants were being tried, it became evident that the administration was telling anything but the whole truth. The Senate appointed a special investigating committee, headed by Sam Ervin of North Carolina, which held hearings from May to August 1973 and unearthed further evidence of wrongdoing. In February 1974 the House of Representatives authorized the Judiciary Committee to determine whether sufficient grounds existed for impeachment of the President. In July the committee voted three articles of impeachment, charging him with obstruction of justice, abuse of executive powers, and defiance of congressional subpoenas. In August, faced with the certainty of an impeachment vote in the Senate, Nixon resigned, relinquishing his office to Vice President Gerald Ford. Yet the political ramifications of Watergate were not at an end. In 1976 Jimmy Carter won the Democratic nomination and defeated Ford in the presidential election largely as "the candidate of the Watergate backlash." . . .

\*     \*     \*

Carter, receiving 40.8 million votes to Ford's 39.1 million, obtained a narrow 297–241 victory in the electoral college. The class, racial, and ethnic dimensions of the vote were notable. With the ending of the war in Vietnam and the declining importance of the social issue, class distinctions reasserted themselves in the polling booth. Whites earning under $5,000 a year were sixteen points more pro-Carter than whites earning over $15,000, a differential that, if not overwhelming, was substantial enough to permit one pollster to conclude: "The affluent, the well-educated, the suburbanites largely went for Ford; the socially and economically disadvantaged for Carter." Carter's appeal to blacks, however, provided the key to his triumph. Although Ford won more than 51 percent of the white vote, Carter garnered more than 90 percent of the black vote. It provided his margin of victory in Ohio, Pennsylvania, and seven of the ten states he carried in the Deep South. Ethnic voting patterns were more complex. Ford did better than expected among some groups, winning 55 percent of the Italian and 45 percent of the Jewish vote. On the other hand, Carter captured about 55 percent of the vote among Catholics of Irish and Eastern European origin.

The 1976 election did not witness a reincarnation of Franklin Roosevelt's New Deal coalition. Carter won support from the poor, but not to the same degree as Roosevelt had. He won support from blacks, but that support now enabled him to carry Texas, Louisiana, and Mississippi, states which had excluded blacks from the polls in the 1930s. Carter made a respectable showing among Jews and Catholics, but massive Democratic pluralities in ethnic wards were things of the past. Although sounding vaguely Rooseveltian when he attacked a ruling "political and economic elite," called for "an end to discrimination because of race or sex," and remarked that the Democrats had "welcomed generations of immigrants—the Jews, the Irish, the Italians, the Poles and all the others," Carter in the late 1970s faced a task of governing a nation that, in its class, racial, and ethnic composition, had changed markedly since the late 1930s.

**2.**

In December 1977 the Office of Federal Statistical Policy and Standards of the Department of Commerce published *Social Indicators, 1976*. Consisting of lavishly prepared graphs, charts, and maps, the 550-page work provided detailed information about population, the family, housing, Social Security and welfare, health and nutrition, public safety, education, work, income and expenditures, culture and leisure, and social mobility. The volume contained, as well, "indicators of well-being" which purportedly measured the degree of satisfaction Americans received from their jobs, their friendships, even their marriages. A poll on "Marital Happiness: 1973–1975," for example, divided people into three categories: "very happy," "pretty happy," and "not too happy." The statistics in *Social Indicators, 1976* were broken down—or, as social scientists prefer saying, "disaggregated"—by race, age, sex, and, to a lesser extent, income and occupation. While the editors, in their introduction, warned against "inferring the reasons for the differences which are apparent among those population groups," the differences were indeed striking. The government was, in part, depicting the American class structure, and the portrait was no less sharply defined for being painted in cool, statistical colors.

The picture that emerged showed levels of income rising dramatically since World War II but the degree of inequality remaining about the same. Real personal income, after being adjusted for a fourfold increase in consumer prices, doubled from the late 1930s to the late 1970s. By 1977 median family income had reached $15,000. Of the nation's 56.7 million families, 10 percent had incomes under $5,000, 20 percent had incomes between $5,000 and $10,000, 20 percent had incomes between $10,000 and $15,000, 32 percent had incomes between $15,000 and $25,000, and 18 percent had incomes over $25,000. The proportion of its weekly budget that the average family spent on food and clothing had declined sharply, while the amount it spent on transportation and medical care had risen appreciably. Yet personal income, while dwarfing the total of forty years before, was distributed only slightly less unequally: the wealthiest fifth of American families received about 40 percent of all income, while the poorest fifth received about 5 percent.

An income of $6,000, which would have enabled a family to live in moderate luxury in 1938, placed an urban family of four just below the poverty line in 1978. By this standard, nearly 26 million Americans, or 12 percent of the population, lived in poverty. One-third were children under the age of fourteen. Single men and women made up a disproportionate number of those in poverty. Poor families were, preponderantly, headed by the aged, nonwhites, and women. Poor people received wide-ranging forms of direct federal assistance. Fully one-third of their income came from Social Security payments, Aid to Families with Dependent Children, and other such programs. Without such assistance, more than twice as many people—about one-fourth of all Americans—would have been below the poverty line. In addition, the government spent $30 billion a year on "in-kind" transfers, such as food stamps, housing subsidies, and medical care premiums. The aggregate income deficit of those in poverty—that is, the amount of money required to lift every American to the line dividing the poor from the nonpoor— came to less than $15 billion, or 1 percent of the gross national product.

At the opposite extreme were the 1.1 million families, or 2 percent of the total, with annual incomes in excess of $50,000. Those families were usually headed by white males, in their prime earning years, who held executive or managerial positions. They still lived preponderantly in the Northeast, although, since 1970, per capita income had increased most rapidly in the South and regional differentials had narrowed sharply. Yet at a time when fully one-fourth of all workers were employed as professionals, managers, officials, and proprietors, only a small fraction scaled the upper reaches of the income ladder. Those who did found it possible to earn as much in forty-eight hours as an unskilled worker did in a year, as the title of one article ingeniously explained: "Another Day, Another $3,000." In 1976 the president of the Ford Motor Company earned $970,000 in salary and bonuses, and his counterpart at General Motors, at $950,000, did not trail far behind. Harold S. Geneen, the president of International Telephone and Telegraph, whose combined 1976 income amounted to a mere $846,000, still had miles to go, since he was on record as having said, "Maybe I'm worth $5 million a year." None of these figures included substantial payments under deferred compensation plans, profit-sharing arrangements, and stock purchase options.

Sociologists in the 1970s devised elaborate statistical techniques for measuring social mobility. One of them, the "OCG Scale," described occupational changes in a generation by cross-tabulating sons' jobs (or incomes, or educational attainment) with their fathers' (at appropriate points in the fathers' lives). Applied to a population sample in 1973, and reported in *Social Indicators, 1976*, the scale revealed "a marked tendency toward occupational status inheritance for the total male civilian labor force." Despite a general trend away from manual and toward white-collar work, "sons in a given occupational status category were more likely to have been recruited from their father's occupational category than from any other occupational category." Mobility, both upward and downward, occurred within that framework: 60 to 70 percent of the sons of white-collar workers had remained in that category, while 30 to 40 percent had become manual workers; 60 to 70 percent of the sons of manual workers had remained in that category, while 30 to 40 percent had become white-collar workers. A more intensive study of the inheritance of economic status among families in Cleveland confirmed these findings. A son whose parents' income ranked 10 percent from the top had a 51 percent chance of having a 1976 income of more than $25,000; a son whose parents' income ranked 10 percent from the bottom, however, had a 2 percent chance of earning that much. Since marriages almost always occurred along class lines, "parents' economic status was transferred to daughters almost to the same extent as it would have been if they had married their brothers." . . .

*    *    *

Most Americans lived longer and healthier lives in the 1970s than they had in the 1930s. In that period, average life expectancy increased from sixty-three to seventy-two years, the death rate (per 100,000) fell from 1,076 to 666, and the infant and neonatal mortality rates (per 1,000 live births) declined from 47 to 17. By 1975 per capita health expenditures amounted to $476, two-thirds of which was paid by public funds and private insurance plans. But prosperous people on the whole lived even longer and healthier lives than poor people, for mortality and illness were inversely related to income level. Poor people were bedridden twice as much as upper-income individuals and were eight times as likely to have limited mobility; their teenaged children, moreover, had four times as many decayed teeth as more privileged youngsters had. According to Social Indicators, 1976, a perfect correlation existed between perceptions of health and family income: of those earning under $5,000, 32 percent reported themselves in excellent health, compared with 45 percent of those earning $5,000–$10,000, 53 percent of those earning $10,000–$15,000, and 61 percent of those earning over $15,000. While the percentages declined perceptibly with advancing age, the class differential remained constant at all age levels.

Before World War II class distinctions in housing could be gauged by the presence of such fundamental necessities as indoor plumbing or central heating. But upgrading and modernization—resulting from the surge of new construction since the 1950s, steady migration from rural areas to cities and suburbs, and the advance in real income—meant that by the 1970s this was no longer true. In 1940, 45 percent of all homes were without some plumbing facilities, but in 1976 only 3 percent were; in 1940 one household in five had more than one person per room, but in 1976 that figure had declined to one in twenty. The persistence of class distinctions could, however, still be measured by the spaciousness of the home, the elegance of the furnishings, the desirability of the neighborhood, and the availability of certain conveniences. Social Indicators, 1976 provided information about the number of households at different income levels that owned television sets, washing machines, clothes dryers, refrigerators, freezers, dishwashers, and air conditioners. Of the households earning $3,000–$5,000, 55 percent owned washing machines, 25 percent clothes dryers, and 7 percent dishwashers; among house-holds earning $15,000–$25,000, the figures were 84 percent, 72 percent, and 42 percent. The one statistic that did not vary by income was ownership of a black-and-white television set. Sociologists noted that class distinctions re-volved not around the ownership of a television set but rather around its location in the home: poorer families placed it in their living rooms; well-to-do families, somewhere else.

Just as Americans had longer life expectancies and lived in more com-fortable dwellings, so they received more years of formal schooling. By 1974, among people aged twenty-five to thirty-four, fully 20 percent had completed four years of college while only 20 percent had not completed high school; by contrast, in the forty-five to fifty-four age-group, 12 percent held bachelor's degrees while 37 percent had not received high school diplomas. In 1976 colleges and universities awarded more than 900,000 bachelor's degrees, 300,000 master's degrees, 35,000 doctorates, and 60,000 professional degrees. Yet educational opportunity, while more widespread than in the past, re-mained in many respects a function of social position. More than intellectual capacity, more than academic motivation, class determined whether or not a young person would attend college. As *Social Indicators, 1976* made clear, the proportion of high school graduates who enrolled in four-year colleges varied directly with family income: in families earning more than $18,000, one in two; in families earning $13,500 to $18,000, one in three; in families earning $7,500 to $13,500, one in four or five; in families earning under $7,500, one in six.

In the 1970s, as in the 1930s, political controversies centered largely on such class-related issues of housing, health insurance, and education. More-over, most of the unresolved problems of the 1970s—how to restrain infla-tion while controlling unemployment, how to safeguard the environment while encouraging economic growth, how to obtain adequate supplies of energy while holding down the price of fuel—had equally clear class im-plications. This was also true of perhaps the paradigmatic issue of the 1970s: women's liberation and, more particularly, the Equal Rights Amendment. The amendment, stating that "equality of rights under the law shall not be denied or abridged by the United States or by any State on account of sex," empowered Congress to pass laws enforcing that provision. The House of Representatives passed the ERA by a vote of 354–23 in October 1971, the Senate by a vote of 84–8 in March 1972. Congress also stipulated that the amendment would have to be approved by the necessary thirty-eight states within seven years. The conflict over the ERA, like the women's rights move-ment itself, illustrated the importance of class divisions.

The women's liberation movement was instrumental in achieving vic-tories that aided virtually all working-women, regardless of their position in society. Title VII of the Civil Rights Act of 1964, which outlawed discrimi-nation in hiring and employment on account of sex as well as race and national origin, served as the cornerstone of the drive for economic equality.

In 1970, under heavy pressure from women's groups, the Office of Federal Contract Compliance issued guidelines banning sex discrimination by federal contractors. A triple breakthrough came in 1972, when Congress passed the Equal Pay Act, prohibited sexual discrimination in federally supported education programs, and expanded the jurisdiction of the Equal Employment Opportunity Commission to include local government agencies and educational institutions. By the mid-1970s affirmative-action programs were helping women even more than members of racial minorities. These federal efforts were associated with a dramatic increase in the number of women workers. From 1965 to 1975 about 10 million women entered the labor force, compared with 7 million men. By then nearly half of all American women held jobs.

As a movement, however, women's liberation drew its support largely from the upper middle class. Admittedly, some feminists argued that all women constituted an "oppressed class," maintaining that the relationship between a wife and husband was "a *class* relationship" and marital disputes "*political* conflicts which can only be solved collectively." But other feminists spoke frankly about "the reality of how class separates women." *Women: A Journal of Liberation*, for example, printed an article by several working women who asserted that "many of the values of Women's Liberation Movement are not the values of working class women but the values of upper middle class women" and proceeded to list thirteen ways in which privileged women betrayed their class bias (by "never remembering your waitress's face because you don't consider her on your own level" or by insisting that "a working class person speak in your own way without realizing that she has not had access to those speech patterns"). Jo Freeman's analysis of the "general social base of the women's liberation movement," based on a sample of the 200,000 subscribers to *Ms.* magazine in 1973, tended to support this interpretation of the movement's class composition: nine out of ten subscribers were college-educated, and two out of three who worked full time held professional, technical, managerial, or official positions.

From the start the debate over the ERA revealed a division along the lines of social class. That division was best exemplified by the dispute over existing laws that protected workingwomen by establishing minimum wages, limiting overtime, mandating special sanitary facilities, prescribing rest periods, and restricting the weights that had to be lifted. Conceding that the ERA would render such laws unconstitutional, advocates insisted that such forms of protection were unnecessary and discriminatory, for they prevented women from competing for certain desirable jobs. As Representative Shirley Chisholm of New York City put it: "Women need no protection that men do not need. What we need are laws to protect working people, to guarantee them fair pay, safe working conditions, protection against sickness and layoffs. Men and women need these things equally. That one sex needs protection more than the other is male supremacism." The opposing view, advanced by a spokeswoman for hotel and restaurant employees, held that women "working as maids, laundry workers, hospital cleaners, or dishwash-ers" benefited from protective legislation in a way professional women did not. But then, she added, "the feminists' movement in the main is middle class, professional women, college girl oriented."

The issue of protective labor legislation, while never becoming entirely moot, eventually lost some of its bite. By 1972 the courts had construed the 1964 Civil Rights Act so as to strike down many statutes which, although designed to protect women, effectively deprived them of equal job opportuni-ties. The feminist argument that useful forms of protection would, under the ERA, not be taken away from female employees but would be extended to males then become persuasive, so much so that the AFL-CIO, in October 1973, reversed its historic stand and supported the amendment. Yet the debate over ratification continued to strike sparks along class lines. In 1975, after voters in New York and New Jersey had rejected state equal rights amendments (although both states had ratified the federal amendment), Ms. magazine interviewed several women who had opposed the measure. One, who "resented what she perceives as the middle-class bias of the Women's Movement," exclaimed: "Like, why are they always putting down hard hats? I've gone out with guys in the construction trades. They're human too." By July 1978 the New York Times could note that waning support for the amendment "may also reflect a growing impression that the E.R.A. is some kind of elite measure designed mainly to improve the lives of highly edu-cated women who want full-time jobs outside the home. In this view, it seems to have little to offer poor women in routine jobs or women who in-tend to devote themselves fully to children and home."

Six years earlier the ratification of the ERA had seemed a certainty, not only because it had won lopsided majorities in the House and Senate but because it had drawn support from people who could agree on little else—Strom Thurmond and Jane Fonda, for example, or Richard Nixon and George McGovern. By mid-1973, a year after Congress passed the amendment, twenty-eight states had rushed to ratify it. Then groups opposing the measure, most of them of a strong conservative inclination, swung into action, their acronyms —such as HOME (Happiness of Women Eternal) or HOTDOG (Humani-tarians Opposed to Degrading Our Girls)—reflecting the grim attempts at humor that marked their efforts. By mid-1975 only six more states had ratified the ERA, and in January 1977 Indiana became the thirty-fifth state to do so. In the meanwhile, the amendment had gone down to defeat in a number of states, and several others had rescinded their approval (an unprecedented action, the constitutionality of which remained in doubt). As the March 1979 deadline approached, feminists obtained from Congress an extension of the ratification period to June 30, 1982. Opponents immediately challenged the legality of the extension and, in the winter of 1978–79, defeated the ERA in Oklahoma, North Carolina, and Illinois. The continuing battle reflected, above all, what one scholar termed "the class antagonisms that haunt the New Feminism as a political movement and women as a group."

3.

Most observers had expected that the Supreme Court would ultimately determine the constitutionality of affirmative-action programs. In 1974 the Court had barely avoided ruling in the case of Marco DeFunis, a white applicant who had been turned down by the University of Washington Law School in 1971, at a time when preferential admission was granted to blacks, Chicanos, Native Amercians, and Filipinos. Since DeFunis had then gained admission under a temporary restraining order and was, in fact, completing his studies, a majority of the justices concluded that the case was moot. The instance confronting the Court, therefore, involved Allan Bakke, who had been denied admission to the medical school of the University of California at Davis in 1973 and 1974. Since the school reserved 16 of the 100 places in its entering class for "disadvantaged students"—that is, for blacks, Chicanos, Native Americans, and Asian Americans—and since Bakke had a better academic record than some of the 16 minority students, he claimed that he had been denied the equal protection of the law. When the California Supreme Court ruled in his favor in 1976, the university appealed to the Supreme Court, which heard arguments in 1977 and handed down its decision on June 28, 1978.

By a 5–4 margin the Court ruled that the use of an "explicit racial classification," in situations where no former discriminatory behavior had been demonstrated, violated the equal protection clause of the Fourteenth Amendment. The University of California was therefore ordered to admit Bakke to the medical school. At the same time, also by a 5–4 margin, the Court found that affirmative-action programs that made race "simply one element" in the admissions process did not violate the equal protection clause, since universities had a legitimate interest in seeking diversity in their student populations. Although some criticized the ruling, most observers hailed it as "very civilized," as an "act of judicial statesmanship, a brilliant compromise that gives both sides what they want," and, in the most frequently applied phrase, as "a Solomonic decision." The justices, however, had faced a choice quite unlike that facing King Solomon, who, when he said "Divide the living child in two and give half to the one and half to the other," knew that the real mother would not permit the infant to be slain. The Supreme Court, attempting, at it were, to divide the equal protection clause in two, found that both advocates and opponents of affirmative action were only too eager to accept whatever part they were given.

Justice Lewis Powell, who wrote the Court's decision and provided the swing vote, accepted nearly every argument advanced by those who condemned affirmative action as reverse discrimination. Powell reasoned that it was impossible to determine which groups in society deserved special consideration. Since the white majority was itself made up of various minorities "most of which can lay claim to a history of prior discrimination," there could be "no principled basis for deciding which groups would merit 'heightened judicial solicitude' and which would not." Powell also believed that preferential admissions policies were not necessarily benign, for they might reinforce stereotypes "holding that certain groups are unable to achieve success without special protection based on a factor having no relationship to individual worth" and they might exacerbate "racial and ethnic antagonisms," since "there is a measure of inequity in forcing innocent persons . . . to bear the burdens of redressing grievances not of their making." In Powell's view, a "consistent application of the Constitution from one generation to the next" was possible only if rights were accorded to individuals rather than to racial groups. Nor were the stated goals of the Davis program—with the exception of seeking a diverse student body—acceptable. Davis wanted to increase the number of minority doctors in order to rectify, for its own sake, a historic deficit, but "preferring members of any one group for no other reason than race or ethnic origin is discrimination for its own sake." Davis wanted to counteract the general effects of societal discrimination, but, Powell concluded, doing so placed an unfair burden on white applicants "who bear no responsibility" for that discrimination. Davis wanted to improve health care in poverty-stricken communities but conceded it had no way of knowing whether minority students would later decide to practice in ghettos.

Four justices—William Brennan, Byron White, Thurgood Marshall, and Harry Blackmun—disagreed fundamentally with these premises. The Constitution, Brennan asserted, had not been color-blind in the past, and the nation could not afford to "let color blindness become myopia which masks the reality that many 'created equal' have been treated within our lifetimes as inferior both by the law and by their fellow citizens." Legitimate statutory purposes "could be found that would justify racial classifications," and Congress, in passing the 1964 Civil Rights Act, had not intended to bar "all race-conscious efforts to extend the benefits of federally financed programs to minorities who have been historically excluded from the full benefits of American life." Since the inability of many minority students to meet the usual admission standards at Davis "was due principally to the effects of past discrimination," it followed that "race-conscious programs" were permissible, and, indeed, indispensable. Brennan conceded that a white applicant who was thereby denied admission suffered an injury, but one that was "not distinguishable from disadvantages caused by a wide range of government programs." Since such an applicant was not branded as inferior, rejection would not "affect him throughout his life in the same way as the segregation of the Negro school children in *Brown I* would have affected them." Justice Marshall made the case forcefully: "It is unnecessary in 20th century America to have individual Negroes demonstrate that they have been victims of racial discrimination; the racism of our society has been so pervasive that none, regardless of wealth or position, has managed to escape its impact." Justice Blackmun put it more succinctly: "In order to get beyond racism, we must first take account of race."

Blackmun's argument, his very choice of words, closely followed an article by McGeorge Bundy, head of the Ford Foundation, in the November 1977 *Atlantic Monthly*. Insisting that no racially neutral admissions process would "produce more than a handful of minority students," Bundy wrote: "To get past racism, we must here take account of race." The question Bundy posed in his title was equally instructive: "Who Gets Ahead in America?" Alluding to the same point, Justice Marshall stated: "It is because of a legacy of unequal treatment that we now must permit the institutions of this society to give consideration to race in making decisions about who will hold the positions of influence, affluence and prestige in America." The debate over affirmative action—a debate that, given the disagreements on the Court, gave no indication of ending with *Bakke*—came down precisely to the question of the distribution of social rewards. Affirmative-action programs could be justified only on the grounds that blacks and other minorities continued to suffer from "a legacy of unequal treatment." If it could be shown they no longer did, racially preferential programs would, in Justice Blackmun's words, become "only a relic of the past." Consequently, evaluations of the social and economic status of blacks in the late 1970s assumed critical implications for the making of public policy.

Such evaluations, however, were rendered difficult by a number of developments—most importantly, the deepening of class divisions within the black community. Those divisions had always existed, but never to the same extent as in the 1970s, when the black middle class became larger, wealthier, and more dispersed geographically, while the black "underclass," also growing larger, became relatively poorer and more isolated residentially. Expanded opportunities for the one were more than matched by diminished opportunities for the other. Observing that the distribution of income among blacks was more unequal than among whites and that the disparity was widening, William Julius Wilson, a sociologist at the University of Chicago, pointed to the development of "a deepening economic schism . . . in the black community, with the black poor falling further and further behind middle- and upper-income blacks." Wilson concluded that "class has become more important than race in determining black life-chances."

Of the nation's 25 million black people, 7.5 million had incomes below the poverty line. That is, of every ten blacks, three lived in poverty, while of every ten whites, one did. Black workers found it harder to get jobs in the late 1970s than at any time since the Great Depression, as manufacturers abandoned northern cities for the Sun Belt and the suburbs, as automation eliminated many positions, as a rising federal minimum wage made employers reluctant to hire unskilled workers, and as young people proved "less willing to accept the kinds of low-paying and menial jobs that their grandfathers or fathers readily accepted." The unemployment rate among blacks, 13 to 14 percent, was twice that among whites; the rate among black teenagers, a staggering 40 percent, was two and one-half times that among white teenagers. Constituting 11 percent of the population, blacks received 27 percent of all welfare payments and made up 44 percent of the enrollees in the Aid to Families with Dependent Children program. One in every twenty-five white households purchased food stamps; one in every five black households did. "Nobody starved," a survey noted, "but many people are malnourished on a diet of hot dogs, Twinkies, Fritos, soda pop and, in rare cases whatever can be fished out of the garbage can." To an unemployed black worker in Kansas City things seemed no better in 1978 than they might have seemed in 1938: "The truth is that black people ain't no closer to catching up with whites than they were before."

Across town, the black dean of student affairs at a community college expressed a radically different view: "I think most of the racial barriers have fallen." For him, and many like him, they undoubtedly had. In 1976 a substantial number of black families had incomes that placed them solidly in the upper middle or middle class: 7 percent earned more than $25,000, 21 percent earned $15,000–25,000, and 11 percent earned $12,000–$15,000. Occupation was closely tied to income. By the late 1970s one-third of all black workers (twice the 1960 rate) held white-collar jobs as professionals, managers, officials, and clerical workers. As Wilson explained: "Talented and educated blacks are experiencing unprecedented job opportunities in the growing government and corporate sectors, opportunities that are at least comparable to those of whites with equivalent qualifications." Before World War II, the black middle class had consisted either of workers whose jobs and incomes most nearly resembled those of the white working class, or of salaried professionals—doctors, lawyers, teachers, ministers—who served a clientele predominantly or exclusively black. In the 1970s the occupational structure and earnings of the black middle class were comparable to those of the white middle class, and blacks made their way in the world of banks, corporations, government agencies, and universities. . . .

*      *      *

. . . The 1970s saw a reversal of a historic pattern of migration: for the first time, a substantial number of blacks began leaving the North for the South. In the past the stream of migrants from the South was comprised mainly of rural blacks seeking industrial jobs; in the 1970s the stream of migrants from the North was made up in some measure of college-educated blacks seeking white-collar positions. By 1978, when *Ebony* magazine listed the "ten best cities for Blacks" in the United States, five of them turned out to be Atlanta, Dallas, Houston, Baltimore, and Washington—all cities that had once been rigidly segregated. The magazine's comment on Atlanta was typical: "The fact that Blacks control Atlanta's government, its police and fire departments and the city's school system is a strong recommendation for Blacks who are planning to move to this clean, fast-growing and young city. In particular, professional advancement opportunities make the city attractive."

Blacks who moved South as well as those who never left faced radically changed conditions. "They can eat in any restaurant and sleep in any motel. They can register and vote. They can go to school with whites. They can sit in front of the bus." In many respects, the South had become the most truly integrated region of the country. About half the black children in the South, but only one-third of those in the North and West, attended integrated public schools. The civil rights movement had become enshrined as a part of southern tradition. In Birmingham the public library devoted a newly created archive to the movement, and in Selma a street was named after Martin Luther King. The media had once purveyed crudely bigoted stereotypes. Now, on a Jackson, Mississippi, television station "owned by whites who were once leaders of massive resistance, a black newscaster interviewed a white candidate for Governor who apologized for having belonged to a citizens' council that stood for white supremacy." There were signs that the ultimate taboo, that against interracial marriage, was weakening. Interracial couples in the South reported that they were generally accepted in their communities. The black mayor of Tuskegee and his white wife noted that they had "encountered no problems" in traveling through Alabama.

Perhaps nothing better exemplified the new order in the South than the black's role in politics. Gradually closing the registration gap, black voters began to flex their political muscles. In the 1976 election 46 percent of the southern blacks, compared to 57 percent of southern whites, went to the polls. (In the North and West the black turnout rate was 52 percent, and the white rate 63 percent). By 1978 more than 2,200 blacks held elective office in the South, a tenfold increase in a decade. Both Atlanta and New Orleans had black mayors. White politicians who had once favored segregation acted like repentant sinners. Senator Strom Thurmond of South Carolina decided to send his child to an integrated school, and James Eastland of Mississippi, who had fought civil rights legislation in the Senate ever since 1942, appealed to local NAACP officials for help in obtaining black support. . . .

*    *    *

The right to vote and the opportunity to hold office, equality before the law and free access to public facilities, the chance to live in the neighborhood of one's choice and send one's children to integrated schools—all represented major advances. Yet the limited nature of those advances was apparent. Although blacks constituted 20 percent of the population in the South, they accounted for only 3 percent of the elected officials. Of 100 counties with black majorities, two-thirds did not elect a single black to office. Atlanta and New Orleans were the exceptions; as a rule, black mayors were elected in small towns with dwindling populations and severely depressed local economies. The granting of political and legal rights hardly made a dent in certain chronic problems: rural poverty; unemployment; dilapidated housing; inadequate health care. Those problems were equally intractable under a black mayor and city council. An NAACP official in McComb, Mississippi, provided needed perspective: "There has been progress, certainly, but you have to measure that progress against how bad it was."

**4.**

By the late 1970s patterns of ethnicity were undergoing a transformation no less startling than patterns of class and race. The roots of the transformation could be traced to a legislative source: the Immigration Reform Act of 1965. Advocates of that measure had contended that Congress, by abolishing national origins quotas, could effect a major symbolic change in policy without changing very much. The act, its sponsors had claimed, would merely bring the law into harmony with existing practice. As oracles, however, they proved inferior even to Cassandra, who was at least blessed with the gift of prophecy even if it was ordained that her predictions would never be believed. The reform of 1965 promoted sweeping, if unforeseen, changes in the composition of the immigrant population. It produced, in addition, an influx of illegal aliens whose presence created a jarring discrepancy between the law and existing practice. Because illegal aliens constituted a "new urban poverty class," class divisions within the immigrant community, like those among blacks, intensified sharply.

The 1965 act had provided for the admission each year of 170,000 immigrants from Europe, Asia, and Africa (with a maximum of 20,000 from any one nation) and for the entry of 120,000 people from the Western Hemisphere (with no maximum assigned to any country). These numerical limitations, however, did not apply to relatives of American citizens, and with the reunion of families a stated priority of the law, about 100,000 such people were admitted each year. In the decade after 1965, therefore, 390,000 immigrants entered the United States, on the average, each year. In the late 1970s the figure was closer to 400,000. Although that represented less than one-quarter of 1 percent in a population of 218 million, as the national birthrate fell, immigration accounted for an ever-larger proportion of total population growth. In 1940 immigration had accounted for only 6 percent of that increase, but in 1976 it accounted for nearly 25 percent.

Not only were more people coming to the United States, but they were coming from different places and bringing with them different skills. The number of immigrants from Europe declined steadily until, by 1976, more than half of all immigrants came from seven Asian and Latin American nations: Mexico, the Philippines, Korea, Cuba, Taiwan, India, and the Dominican Republic. In 1969 three immigrants had arrived from Europe for every two from Asia; by 1976 two arrived from Asia for every one from Europe. By then the United States was receiving fewer immigrants from Italy and Greece combined than from India alone, fewer from Germany than from Thailand, fewer from Ireland than from Egypt, and fewer from Poland than from Trinidad and Tobago. This was accompanied by a shift in occupational patterns. In the 1930s perhaps one of every five immigrants had held a white-collar position. By 1976 one of every two had, and one of every four had acquired professional skills or technical expertise that qualified them, in most instances, for places at the top of the middle-class world.

The narrowing of the European stream of immigration and the widening of the Asian and Latin American streams modified the nature of ethnic culture in the United States. Before World War II that culture, European in linguistic origin, Catholic and Jewish in religion, flourished most fully in older cities of the North and West. In the 1970s all this changed. Although foreign languages were less widely used—the Census Bureau reported in 1975 that "as a Nation, few Americans are bilingual. Nine out of every ten persons reported that they had no second language"—more people whose usual language was not English spoke Spanish than all other foreign languages combined. There were more homes in which Chinese, Japanese, Korean, or Filipino was the usual language than homes in which people ordinarily used Italian, and nearly as many as homes in which people ordinarily used French, German, and Greek. Many immigrants, particularly from Mexico and the Philippines, were Roman Catholics, but Asian immigrants were usually Buddhists, Sikhs, or Hindus, and immigrants from Turkey, Egypt, and Pakistan were mostly Moslems. Settling, as always, near ports of debarkation, immigrants in the 1970s were more likely to be found in California, Texas, or Florida than in New York or Massachusetts. . . .

✳     ✳     ✳

If Asian Americans, on the whole, enjoyed better-than-average living standards, the reverse was true of the other major group of new immigrants; Spanish-speaking Americans. In 1979 the Census Bureau estimated that more than 12 million persons of Hispanic descent were living in the United States: 7.2 million from Mexico, 1.8 million from Puerto Rico, 700,000 from Cuba, 900,000 from Central and South America, and 1.4 million from other lands. The Spanish-origin population was overwhelmingly urban; one out of every two people resided in central cities, and one out of every three lived in the suburbs. It was, moreover, a youthful population: the median age was twenty-two years as compared with thirty years for Americans of other than Spanish ancestry. It was, finally, a relatively deprived population, with low levels of educational attainment, a high proportion of blue-collar as compared with white-collar workers, and a 1977 median family income ($10,300) about two-thirds that of other families. Nearly one out of four Spanish-speaking families subsisted below the poverty line, but some groups were distinctly worse off than others. While 17 percent of Cuban families lived in poverty, 22 percent of Mexican families and 39 percent of Puerto Rican families did.

The trouble with these statistics is that they did not take into account millions of recent immigrants, the vast majority from Mexico and Latin America, who had entered the United States illegally. . . .

✳     ✳     ✳

No one knew for sure just how many illegal aliens there were. Some estimates were based on the number of apprehensions made by the Immigration and Naturalization Service: 110,000 in 1965; 335,000 in 1970; 756,000 in 1975; and more than 1 million in 1977. It was, however, not at all certain whether the agency's rule of thumb—that it captured one in three or four illegal aliens—was accurate. As INS Commissioner Leonel J. Castillo admitted: "I know that we've apprehended some people 20 times. We apprehended one man five times in one day. . . . He came back five times in one day, and we picked him up five times. For all we know, he's here now." Other estimates were based on a common-sense attempt to strike an average. Figuring the number of illegal aliens to be 4 to 5 million in 1974, an official said: "It is just a midpoint between the two extremes. I had heard one or two million at one end of the scale and eight or 10 million at the other. So I am selecting a midpoint. . . . Just a guess, that is all. Nobody knows." By the late 1970s it was commonly assumed that at least 1 million illegal aliens succeeded in entering each year and that no fewer than 7 million were residing in the United States. . . .

*    *    *

By the late 1970s, then, the United States possessed a large and growing class of illegal aliens, most of whom lived at bare subsistence levels. As the *Wall Street Journal* observed: "The people who benefit the most from this situation are certainly the employers, who have access to an underground market of cheap productive labor, unencumbered by minimum wage laws, union restrictions or pension requirements." One such employer, who owned a chain of restaurants which hired illegal aliens as dishwashers and paid less than the minimum wage, was equally blunt: "It feels kind of good to see these boys come and work hard for you." The result was an enormous discrepancy in living standards—in levels of income, education, housing, and health—between the illegal arrivals and other immigrants, notably the Asian Americans. That discrepancy, however, rarely showed up in official statistics. In an age noted for its ability to collect data, the full extent of class differences among ethnic groups remained anybody's guess.

The controversy over the illegal alien issue, like those over the *Bakke* ruling and the Equal Rights Amendment, suggested that ethnicity, race, and class were no less important in the late 1970s than they had been in the late 1930s. Yet it is worth observing that these forty years were marked by change as well as by continuity. To measure that change, one need only imagine the reception that the women's rights movement, affirmative-action programs, or proposals to legalize the status of a vast number of illegal aliens might have received in 1938 or, better still, to speculate on the reception that, in 1978, would have been accorded arguments against establishing a 25-cent-an-hour minimum wage, passing an antilynching bill, or admitting 20,000 children fleeing totalitarian rule. The preacher's cry in Ecclesiastes—"There is no new thing under the sun"—should be taken not as witness to the immutability of class, racial, and ethnic patterns but as testament to their enduring influence.

Douglas F. Dowd

# The Future Lies Ahead

> These are transitional years and the dues will be heavy.
> Change is quick but revolution will take a while.
> America has not even begun as yet.
> This continent is seed.
>
> Diane di Prima, Revolutionary Letter # 10

Neither knowledge of history nor of social analysis can tell us what the future holds; taken together, they can tell us where we are, how we got there, what to look for in the unfolding present, and what questions to ask. Marx and Veblen, who most and best combined historical analysis with social theory, differed greatly on what the developments they studied augured for the future; yet they shared a healthy respect for the shaping importance of the past.

Both saw change as continuous, and marked always by conflict. Veblen saw social evolution as a race between the life-giving and life-destroying, cooperative and predatory, elements in human nature and society, but he feared that "force and fraud" were more likely than love and reason to take the lead in that race. His final hope was his ironic reservation that to foresee the future was itself hopeless; it was a matter of "opaque cause and effect," of "blind drift."

Marx was more hopeful, about both our ability to foresee the future, and what the future held. His theory of social change saw capitalism creating both a final crisis for itself and creating its own gravediggers—the organized working class—who would replace capitalism with socialism.

Like Veblen, Marx had a fundamental respect for how much the present and future are products of history, which both men saw as the great submerged bulk of an iceberg. In a famous passage, Marx said:

*Men make their own history, but they do not make it just as they please; they do not make it under circumstances chosen by themselves, but under circumstances directly encountered, given and transmitted from the past. The tradition of all the dead generations weighs like a nightmare on the brain of the living.*

The history of the United States is the history of a capitalist society. From its beginnings our political and social history took place in the stated terms of political democracy, human equality, and social mobility. But our economic history was shaped by capitalism's integral needs for economic and geographic expansion and only barely constrained human and resource exploitation.

Glorious though our political and social ideals may have been, our reality has been shaped predominantly by our economic development, which allowed white Americans to treat nonwhites as sub-humans or (along with women) as second-class citizens, to treat our natural environment as something to conquer, and, in this century, to view the rest of the world as our oyster.

Our long history of technological advance and economic expansion made us the primary world power in a world where economic power has been decisive. At home, quantitative economic achievement has encouraged and allowed the bulk of our population to be deflected from concern over the quality of their own and others' existence.

Will the future allow the continuation of these long-standing and deep-seated processes and relationships? It does not seem so. Although it is impossible to foresee what shape the American future will take, and whether we will shape it actively or passively, we may be reasonably sure that it will be substantially different from our distant and recent past. We are in a period of transition; for better or for worse, it is likely that the near future will see changes in basic political, economic, and social institutions. Why is this so? Can anything be said of likely directions?

## Troubles, Here and There

The past decade or so has been one of unprecedented searching and turbulence for the United States. Even though the 1970's began with a calming of the surface turbulence, uneasiness and searching continue; we may remember that the raucous sixties were preceded by the "silent fifties." In the perspective we have advanced, the explanation for this development should be looked for in the changing conditions of expansion and exploitation.

The developmental changes for the United States that have shaped the past generation were begun during World War II and took their current forms shortly thereafter: internationalization, militarization, and related and dependent patterns of domestic investment and "consumerism." The sustained economic growth since 1941 was made possible by these developments, guided by a growing State in close cooperation with the business community. But each of these developments has created conditions making it increasingly difficult for them to serve as continuing sources of sustained economic growth. Economic and geographic expansion and human and resource exploitation, which have for so long been sources of vitality for American capitalism, have now combined in their effects also to create a new time of troubles.

The nature of those troubles may be spelled out as a quick summary: 1) the expansion of American influence and investment in the rest of the industrial capitalist world has produced a growing source of effective competition for American products—in markets both at home and abroad—as well as increased demands and uncertainty in financial and resource terms; 2) the expansion of American power into the Third World has become excessive in its costs and has quite probably reached its limits, from which we are now drawing back, and which is a new and potentially unsettling experience for the United States; 3) the militarization of American production has created economic stability, jobs, and profits, but also corruption, an enlarged bureaucracy, and resistance; in addition, the slowed rate of increase in military expenditures (sharply declining as a *rate* of GNP) reduces their effectiveness in supporting the economy; 4) "consumerism" finds its limits in the distribution and levels of purchasing power and the ability of business to manipulate tastes and encourage indebtedness, a combination that does not hold out endless promise unless a new boom in economic growth ensues, a process difficult to anticipate; 5) domestic private investment depends upon actual and expected increases in demand and profits, here and abroad, which takes us back to expansive tendencies coming from points (1) through (4) and which closes the circle.

But more is involved: the economic buoyancy and the policies and processes making for buoyancy since World War II have produced other developments that have been and are likely to remain sources of trouble within the system. The stimulating role of the State for expansion has required a rise of all taxes to a level (over 30 percent) which constitutes an already substantial and increasing drag on purchasing power; it has also meant the proliferation of bureaucracy in both the public and the private sectors; it has meant a growing dependence of the principal beneficiaries of State policies and also a growing attention to the activities and non-activities of the State. In short, rightly or wrongly, the State is increasingly seen as the cause of what is both wanted and disliked in current society. The State becomes a target in ways new to our history, and it is likely that people at all levels and in all quarters of society will become increasingly political as a result. The turbulence of the sixties is likely to have been only the first round in that process of heightened politicization.

Much more could be said of the destabilizing consequences of American economic growth since World War II. Let us note only two developments of as yet unascertainable but clearly momentous implications: 1) all the talk of affluence for the past years has underscored the relative deprivation endured by tens of millions of Americans, while the great wealth and productivity of our economy makes the continuation of such deprivation difficult to smooth over; 2) continued reliance upon rapid industrial growth as a solvent for social problems must be set against the widespread conviction that such growth must somehow be controlled if we are not to poison ourselves out of existence.

The upshot is a developing crisis. Economic and political in its roots, the crisis is not only social, but moral in its tensions; its ultimate resolution will have to comprehend all these dimensions, for better or for worse. If the United States is approaching a crisis, that means some basic alteration in American institutions is in the offing. Just when, just what, just how, is presently unknowable; but the tensions characterizing the totality of American existence seem unlikely to persist for long without some means being found of subduing or eliminating them.

In general, this must mean a substantial move either to the Right or to the Left—toward an American version of fascism or toward an American version of socialism. For most Americans, either possibility sounds outlandish; still, one or the other is likely before this century ends. We can only look briefly at the conditions that might lead to either. First, American-style fascism.

## Waiting for Rightie

A movement to the Right has been underway for some years now in the United States, assuming such a movement is defined by increasing power in the hands of a few and increasing powerlessness for the many; by the resort to physical and judicial coercion to solve domestic and international problems; by a growing resort to secrecy and manipulation in both private and public affairs; by a steady erosion of civil liberties; by a decline in policies seeking, however weakly, to set a floor to deprivation and oppression; by a growth of venality and corruption; by the emergence of authoritarian leaders.

All these developments have become part of our daily news in recent years. Do they add up to fascism? Some would say they do; but by fascism it seems more appropriate to mean not merely the emergence of such tendencies but their coming together in a new combination requiring a decisive closure on the traditional forms of political existence. To put it this way is not to encourage a relaxed view of obvious and ominous tendencies; it is to say that fascism is considerably more terrible in its reality than are the tendencies toward it.

When fascism emerged in other nations, such as Italy and Germany, it came in on the heels of a deep socio-economic crisis, and in conjunction with a substantial threat from the Left. Other countries' histories are not likely to be repeated by the United States, nor to suggest the same preconditions for social change in the United States; our capitalist history has been significantly different from others' and our evolution toward either fascism or socialism is also likely to have its own qualities.

If and when the movement toward social crisis in America becomes more pronounced, and if it were to be joined by an actual or threatened economic collapse, it seems highly likely that American-style fascism would be attempted. It could be attempted in America even without economic collapse. Deepening racial fears and hostilities could threaten so much in the way of social chaos that only a strong authoritarian rule might promise any sort of stability; that, combined with increasing socio-cultural disintegration, with declining moral sensitivity, with yearning for simple, more "virtuous" and less challenging days, could be used as an excuse to seize power and lead the nation back to a past imbued with fantasy. There are right-wing leaders who will do what they can to encourage such a development, as Watergate makes "perfectly clear."

Whether or not such leaders can move far in such directions depends not only upon the existence of crisis, but upon the existence of alternatives. That means the Left. Is the Left now or will it be in the foreseeable future able to muster an effective opposition to such tendencies, which are already very real? Or, even more, will it be able eventually to win out and create an American socialism?

## Toward an American Revolution?

The emergence of fascism in the United States would require "only" a *political coup d'état*; there would be no need to alter basic economic institutions substantially, except to move more toward coordinated planning, more toward economic nationalism, more toward a regressive use of the State's taxing powers. But socialism would require a basic revolution of the whole range of institutions—economic, political, social, cultural—social ownership and control of the means of production, in turn enabling a structure of production and consumption suited to human needs and possibilities, a structure of power allowing and requiring democratic control of the society, and a social system (not least an educational system) that would contribute to equality and cooperation rather than to privilege and competition. To gain fascism is easy, by comparison: less is involved, and there is more power at hand to do the job. Harold Laski called fascism "capitalism with the gloves off," by which he meant capitalism without the political democracy that historically has accompanied it. Fascism is *counter*-revolutionary. Revolutionary change demands much, much more, especially if it is to be worthwhile.

For there to be a socialist society, there must be a socialist movement with the strength to cause and carry through a revolution. In turn, that requires an analysis that shows why socialism is necessary, and that convinces the largest percentage of the population of this need; a program that makes socialism attractive; a strategy that makes a socialist revolution possible.

If that is what is meant by a revolutionary movement, the United States has none. The United States does have large numbers of people of all ages, colors, sexes, and conditions whose lives seem to them increasingly intolerable and alienating; it will seem so until the country undergoes a social reconstruction of revolutionary proportions.

At present, although there is a good deal of revolutionary rhetoric and a recent past of semi-revolutionary tactics, the United States lacks a revolutionary political base both because and despite the ways in which the existing system horrifies, frightens, disaffects and oppresses growing numbers of people, while demeaning and crippling the potentialities of the large majority. In one degree or another, some or all of this has been so throughout American history. Why then has America polarized in attitudes now, but, except for a branch of the Populists, not before?

The key elements appear to have come together in the past decade or so. In that period, the interactions of domestic and international developments flowing from the victory against the fascist armies but not against our own or others' fascist tendencies, combined 1) with a rhetoric revolving around peace, democracy, and equality; 2) with an economy whose technology was widely hailed as making all things possible; and 3) with a determined drive against "communism" abroad and at home that had the unexpected consequence of illuminating the inadequacies of American society. It was of course the young, both black and white, who most quickly noted the gap between the rhetoric and the reality, and whose customary impatience with temporizing first led them to seek ways to close the gap by bringing reality closer to rhetoric.

None of that was entirely new, although the coming together of disparate developments in a white glare of attention perhaps was. The aims of the young were voiced pervasively by almost everyone else—politicians high and low, educators, businessmen, clerics, et al.—while at the same time the society became more bent on war, active racism intensified, poverty programs were abandoned and, among other things, the leadership of the nation became steadily more mediocre, to say the least. That was true at all levels; at the highest level, what seemed barely possible under Kennedy came to seem implausible under Johnson and impossible under Nixon. This tragic evolution was necessarily matched by an enhanced process of repression and further corruption of the judiciary, victimizing those who sought to realize the expressed ideals of America. And all the while America deteriorated even further: in the seventies, more poverty, more corruption, more economic troubles, more hypocrisy on racism—but somewhat less war.

It is vital to note and to understand that only a very small number of the young ever engaged in the political struggles of the sixties; it is equally vital to note how very great the attention and furor was that attended their efforts. In the United States that has always happened, whenever Left or radical movements seemed to be more than mere exercises in free speech. That this has been more true in the United States than elsewhere is a consequence of our uncompromising and uncontested capitalism. It is a matter of what Antonio Gramsci calls "hegemony," which is a concept worth exploring. Hegemony is:

*an order in which a certain way of life and thought is dominant, in which one concept of reality is diffused throughout society in all its institutional and private manifestations, informing with its spirit all taste, morality, customs, religious and political principles, and all social relations, particularly in their intellectual and moral connotations.*

Gramsci developed the idea of hegemony as a means of understanding both the power of capitalism and the needs of the working class if it were ever to gain power: "the working class, before it seizes State power, must establish its claim to be a ruling class in the political, cultural, and 'ethical' fields."

It would be difficult to find an industrial capitalist nation in which the "hegemony" of the ruling class is as thoroughgoing in its spread as in the United States; as we approach crisis, it is that hegemony which is breaking down. But we shall move through that crisis into fascism unless an alternative vision of society is created, and unless those who would bring socialism educate and organize around that vision. The hegemony of the ruling class is not simply economic, nor simply anything; it is the consenting acceptance of the main elements of social existence by the mass of the population. That hegemony will not be displaced by an economic crisis; quite the contrary, in the absence of a strong socialist movement working with a socialist program of coherence and comprehensiveness, an economic crisis would hasten fascism.

It is widely accepted that revolutionary periods are preceded by developments in which those who subsequently make the revolution see their hopes become raised within the system, but then without chance of realization within that same system. But revolutionaries alone do not make a revolution. The revolutions that have occurred in the past have occurred only during or after a *crisis*, which itself results from the system's own normal, interacting ("dialectical") processes and relationships. Revolutionaries have been able to seize the opportunities presented by the social crisis. An "historical" crisis of the system is thus a necessary condition for revolution. But it is not sufficient unto itself, as the American Depression of the thirties shows.

When a capitalist system's "natural" evolution leads through crisis to institutional discontinuity, the stage is set for revolution or counter-revolution, that is, fascism. It is not enough to believe, as I do, that fascism is deeply contrary to basic human needs, that reason and decency and well-being in our well-informed and productive world *should* vitiate the possibilities of fascism and enhance the possibilities of democratic socialism; that, in short, fascism "can't work," and would therefore mean the later emergence of a still larger crisis. Fascism has happened frequently in this century; it can still happen here. Should it, in an age of nuclear weapons, faith in the "ultimate" triumph of socialism becomes a cruel figure of speech, a dangerous delusion. Fascism must and can be prevented only by simultaneous efforts on two fronts: struggles *against* its lurking potential and *toward* democratic socialism.

Many who participated in the protest movements of the sixties will quarrel with what now will be said, but it must be said: despite the rhetoric, the furor, and the great heights of emotion and activity of that period, it was a period of revelation, not of revolution. The leading edge of that process was provided by young blacks, at least partially stimulated by minor institutional changes and a pleasing language of racial equality that began to be publicized—for the first time in our history, it is important to note—in the late fifties. The young blacks were joined by young whites who, unburdened by considerations of material striving, and later horrified or threatened by the Indochinese War, began to request and later to demand that this society live up to its fundamental promises. There was no excuse for not doing so, if their elders could be taken at their word. Both young blacks and young whites believed and acted, for a while, as though reason and the setting of virtuous examples would move society to fundamental change, almost as though they were priming a pump. Within a decade they had learned and others had been taught that the well is dry—or poisoned.

The process of revelation in the United States has been remarkable, not only in its swiftness—though its belated appearance is understandable—but also in the way in which the uncovering of one layer of oppression helped to reveal one after another layer of oppression, injustice, violence, material and spiritual deprivation, and repression. Now the United States can be compared to an onion, whose layers when peeled away finally reveal little worth preserving.

Still another remarkable feature of the last decade was that the impetus for change did not come from its expected sources, economic interest groups, but instead from those who, seeking to make America realize its promises, fought principally on grounds of morality rather than economic interest. The "Movement" thus lacked an adequate theoretical base, initially a perverse source of its strength. It is worth noting that the simultaneous existence of formal political democracy and economic autocracy, on the one hand, and widespread naïveté as to the manner in which the latter vitiates the former, on the other, raises interesting possibilities for the future, as it did in the sixties. A people that does not know it is *de facto* powerless can, by acting on mistaken assumptions, both improve its understanding and push further and more vigorously than it might otherwise do. At some point, in other words, the myth of American democracy could turn out to be a building block for a struggle to make the myth into a reality.

To become a Movement that is also a revolutionary movement, the moral and the analytical bases must be strengthened and combined, and these views will have to comprehend the numerous interests that are now and that remain to be articulated into both an analysis and a program. But morality and understanding only facilitate social change; they do not bring it about. That requires power.

Earlier it was noted that power arises from control over both intangibles and tangibles. The intangibles—morality, ideals, and understanding—are necessary if the nature of our developing crisis is to be grasped and in any sense dealt with. We may think of these as the normative sources of power. But unless the American crisis ushers in a complete breakdown of the existing power structure (as happened in Russia in 1917, but which is not yet to be expected in the United States), a socialist movement must have a non-normative source of power: it must have control over tangibles. In our society that means some control over the means of production.

Clearly, that in turn cannot refer to ownership, so it must mean control gained by the organization of the working class, defined in its contemporary and broadened sense. The working class has its sheer numbers to shut down production as its *potential* source of power; at the present time and in the foreseeable future, the potential has no counterpart in reality. Nor can it have until and unless the Left begins to operate in terms substantially different from its past.

This is another way of saying that the American Left must be both more and less American. Both the Old Left and New Left have adopted all too much of capitalist America's ways—individualist power drives, imagistic appeals, the search for simple or quick solutions, over-emphasis on narrow economic programs—and neither Old nor New have acted as though they understood the strength of American capitalism, or the degree to which the social system it has created has been accepted as natural and desirable by most Americans. Such shortcomings have been entirely understandable; but to continue with them is entirely too dangerous.

There are important, heart- and mind-warming signs that the defects of both Old and New Left are being overcome. There is much talk these days that "The Movement" has died out; that talk is based mostly on the dearth of media visibility for left-wing political activities—in part because the media have been intimidated and bored, in more important part because such activities are much less aimed at media coverage now than in the sixties, an entirely healthy sign. Hundreds and thousands of small community-oriented groups now function, centering on health care, new forms of education, improved housing and rent control efforts, "people's" presses and garages, and on personal liberation. In addition, virtually every profession now has its counterpart to URPE: there are radical caucuses and journals for (among other areas) sociology, political science, literature, the natural sciences and engineering, history, law, and medicine. And there are critical revolts in some trade unions. A recent and serious inquiry into the state of such matters yielded the following conclusions:

There are tens of thousands and perhaps millions of people who have come out of the Sixties with new ideas, new ways of looking at America, new perceptions of themselves, their families, and their communities, shorn of old loyalties and assumptions, no longer taking for granted the values and authority of things-as-they-are. These are the people, mostly but not exclusively young, who were truly "radicalized' in the last decade and haven't forgotten it in this one. . . . [T]he obituaries are, at the least, premature.

An American revolutionary socialist movement must comprehend both analytically and programmatically the diverse and common problems, needs, and aspirations of the many groups that have been raised to consciousness and anger and effort in recent years and serve to encourage many others; it must understand both the strengths and the weaknesses of the existing system; it must have an analysis of power that tells it where and how and when to move or to hold back (for "action" can be counter-productive, as recent years have shown); it must move toward the liberation, the well-being, and the power of wage-earners, of women, of the nonwhite, of the young—but also of those who in their different yet serious ways are unfree and crippled: the middle-aged, middle-class whites, men and women alike. The revolution we need is one that at least removes the fangs of America in the world and that seeks to make the United States liveable for its own people and a force for cooperative constructive change in the world.

All that is asking a lot. But it is no more, as a perspective, than is necessary if there is to be hope for an effective socialist movement in this society, or if such a movement is to deserve the effort and the sacrifices it will entail. A socialist movement will have to learn, and act upon its knowledge, of the inherent possibilities of all human beings; see itself as comprising not morally or intellectually superior creatures, but men and women privileged to understand the plight of society and to have the energy to spread that privilege until the plight is replaced by what society can make possible for people.

Those who are angry can build such a movement; those who hate cannot. Committed men and women are essential; zealots are a hindrance. Thought, analysis, and reflection are indispensable; dogmatism is poison.

"America," the midwestern poet Carl Sandburg wrote long ago, "was promises." Decency, sanity, and safety require that those promises be redeemed; with effort, patience and impatience, and love, they can be.

## SUGGESTIONS FOR FURTHER READING

George Gilder, *Wealth and Poverty (New York, 1981) and Stanley Lebergott, Wealth and Want (Princeton, N.J., 1975) question the value of liberal reforms in solving the problems of poverty. Both insist that the free market is more effective in improving general welfare than are attempts by the government to redistribute wealth. A broader statement in this vein is Milton Friedman, *Capitalism and Freedom (Chicago, 1962). Friedman argues that government interference in economic affairs is not merely inefficient and ineffective; it undermines American

---

* Available in paperback edition.

democracy. For a contrasting liberal view, see the works of John K. Galbraith, especially *The New Industrial State* (Boston, 1967). For a more radical view, similar to that of Dowd, see Paul Baran and Paul Sweezy, *Monopoly Capital* (New York, 1966). Varying perspectives on the future of the American economy may be found in Robert L. Heilbroner, *The Limits of American Capitalism* (New York, 1966); Fred Hirsch, *Social Limits to Growth* (Cambridge, Mass., 1966); and Daniel Bell, *The Coming of Post-Industrial Society: A Venture in Social Forcasting* (New York, 1973).

Betty Reid Mandell, ed., *Welfare in America: Controlling the "Dangerous Classes"* (Englewood Cliffs, N.J., 1975) is a collection of essays that see "the handout as a form of social control." The importance of direct political action in the streets rather than conventional politics is presented in Frances Fox Piven and Richard A. Cloward, *Poor People's Movements* (New York, 1979). A critical assessment of poverty programs may be found in a collection of essays edited by Pamela Roby, *The Poverty Establishment* (Englewood Cliffs, N.J., 1974).

A discussion of the effects of interest-group, one-issue politics is Kevin Phillips, "The Balkanization of America," *Harper's Magazine* (May 1978), 37–47. Different assessments may be found in Peter F. Drucker, *The Age of Discontinuity: Guidelines to Our Changing Society* (New York, 1979); Theodore Roszak, *Person-Planet: The Creative Disintegration of Industrial Society* (New York, 1978); and Alvin Toffler, *Future Shock* (New York, 1973).